The American Nation

STRAIT OF JUAN DE FUCA

LAKE WINNIP

LAKE MANITOBA

PUGET SOUND

Continental Divide

Columbia R.

Blue Mts.

Bitterroot Ra.

R O C

Yellowstone R.

LAKE OF THE WOODS

Red R. of the North

Cape Mendocino

Snake R.

Teton Ra.

Y

Wind River Ra.

Big Horn Mts.

Black Hills

Badlands

Sacramento R.

GREAT SALT LAKE

Wasatch Ra.

Wyoming Basin

Green R.

M

Medicine Bow Ra.

Laramie Ra.

Sand Hills

Missouri R.

SIERRA NEVADA

Great Salt Lake Desert

Uinta Mts.

O

Platte R.

San Francisco Bay

San Joaquin R.

U

Front Ra.

High Plains

Kansas

Monterey Bay

Sawatch Ra.

N

P A C I F I C

Mojave Desert

Colorado R.

Painted Desert

T

Sangre de Cristo Ra.

Continental Divide

A

Red R.

Canadian R.

Quachita M

O C E A N

Gila R.

I

Staked Plains

Pecos R.

Brazos R.

Trinity R.

N

S

Rio Grande

Baja California

Brooks Ra.

Seward Peninsula

Yukon R.

Alaska Ra.

Coast Ranges

Rio Grande

Nueces R.

BERING SEA

Aleutian Islands

Alaska Peninsula

Kodiak I.

ALASKA

0   200   400
MILES

PHYSICAL MAP
OF
THE UNITED STATES

Cape Breton I.

Prince
Edward I.

Nova Scotia

Bay of Fundy

St. Lawrence R.

White
Mts.

Green Mts.

Adirondack
Mts.

Cape Cod

Mohawk R.

Connecticut R.

Hudson R.

Long Island

LAKE ONTARIO

Georgian
Bay

LAKE SUPERIOR

LAKE HURON

LAKE MICHIGAN

LAKE ERIE

Delaware R.

DELAWARE
BAY

Susquehanna R.

Allegheny Mts.

Potomac
R.

Cape Charles

CHESAPEAKE
BAY

Mississippi R.

Till Prairies

Illinois R.

Drift Plains

Wabash R.

Ohio R.

Ohio R.

James R.

Appalachian Mts.

Cape Hatteras

Ozark Mts.

Cumberland R.

Cumberland Plateau

Great Smoky Mts.

Blue Ridge Mts.

PIEDMONT

Cape Lookout

Cape Fear

Arkansas R.

Mississippi R.

Tennessee R.

Savannah R.

A T L A N T I C   O C E A N

Red R.

Alabama R.

Mobile
Bay

Cape Canaveral

Mississippi
Delta

Tampa Bay

LAKE
OKEECHOBEE

The Everglades

GULF OF MEXICO

Florida Keys

0   100   200   300   400
MILES

PUERTO RICO
AND
VIRGIN ISLANDS

St. Thomas I.

St. John I.

St. Croix I.

0   40   80
MILES

Volume 2

The American Nation

A History of the United States Since 1865

THIRD EDITION

John A. Garraty

Columbia University

Harper & Row, Publishers
New York, Evanston, San Francisco, London

Sponsoring Editor: John G. Ryden
Special Projects Editor: Mary Lou Mosher
Project Editor: Alice M. Solomon
Designer: Rita Naughton
Picture Editor: Myra Schachne
Production Supervisor: Will C. Jomarrón

The author makes grateful acknowledgment to:

New Directions, New York; Faber & Faber, London; and A. V. Moore, Knebworth, Herts, England, for permission to quote from "Hugh Selwyn Mauberley" by Ezra Pound. From *Personae* by Ezra Pound. Copyright 1926, 1954 by Ezra Pound. Reprinted by permission of the publisher, New Directions Publishing Corp.

New Directions, New York, for permission to quote "The Great Figure" by William Carlos Williams, from *Collected Earlier Poems*. Copyright 1938 by William Carlos Williams. Reprinted by permission of New Directions Publishing Corp.

Harcourt Brace Jovanovich, Inc., New York, and MacGibbon & Kee Ltd., London, for permission to quote E.E. Cummings, "the first president to be loved by his." Copyright 1931, 1959 by E.E. Cummings. Reprinted from his volume *Poems 1923-1954* by permission of Harcourt Brace Jovanovich, Inc., and MacGibbon & Kee Ltd.

Alfred A. Knopf, Inc., New York, for permission to quote from "The Man with the Blue Guitar" by Wallace Stevens. Copyright 1935, 1936 by Wallace Stevens. From *The Collected Poems of Wallace Stevens*, Knopf, 1957.

Cover: Wide World

THE AMERICAN NATION   A History of the United States Since 1865
Third Edition

Library of Congress Cataloging in Publication Data

Garraty, John A
    The American nation.
    CONTENTS: v. 1. A history of the United States to
1877.—v. 2. A history of the United States since
1865.
    Includes index.
    1. United States—History.   I. Title.
E178.1.G24   1975   973   74-20509
ISBN 0-06-042262-9 (v. 2)

For Kathy, Jack, and Sarah

Contents

Maps and Graphs

Preface

This new edition of *The American Nation* has been constructed on the same principles as its predecessors. It assumes, to begin with, that American history is important for its own sake—an epic and indeed unique tale of human experience in a vast land, almost uninhabited at the start, now teeming with more than 200 million people. Beyond this, our history provides an object lesson in how the past affects the present, or rather, how a series of pasts have changed a series of presents in an unending pattern of development. Thus, while historians have never been any better at foretelling the future than politicians, economists, or soothsayers, good ones have always been able to illuminate their own times, adding depth and perspective to their readers' understanding of how they got to be where they were at any particular point. Put differently, as current events bring new issues to the front, we turn to history for help in deciding how to deal with them. President Nixon's Watergate problems, for example, compel us to study the impeachment of Andrew Johnson and the debates of the Founding Fathers at the Constitutional Convention; the women's liberation movement forces a re-examination of the whole history of women in America.

I have attempted to tell the story of the American past clearly and intelligibly, but also with adequate attention to the complexities and subtleties of this immense subject. Of course, it is not the final word—that will never be written. It is, however, up-to-date and as accurate and thoughtful and wide-ranging as I could make it. Aside from the picture portfolios, which provide a wealth of graphic material dealing with subjects that are difficult to explain with words alone, its special features are products of a personal point of view. Being a biographer, I am very interested in historical personalities. I reject the theory that a few great men, cut from larger cloth than the general run of human beings, have shaped the destiny of mankind; but I do think that history becomes more vivid and comprehensible when attention is paid to how the major figures on the historical stage have reacted to events and to one another. I have attempted to portray the leading actors in my account as distinct individuals and to explain how their personal qualities influenced the course of history. I also believe that generalizations require concrete illustration if they are to be grasped fully. Readers will find many anecdotes and quotations in the following pages along with the facts and dates and statistics that every good history must contain. I am confident that most of this illustrative material is interesting, but I think that it is instructive too. Above all I have sought to keep in mind the grandeur of my subject. One need not be an uncritical admirer of the American nation and its people to recognize that, as I have said, the history of the United States is a great epic. I have tried to treat this history with the dignity and respect that it deserves, believing, however, that a subject of such magnitude is not well served by foolish praise or by slighting or excusing its many dark and even discreditable aspects.

In preparing this edition I have again aimed at up-to-dateness, relevance, a personal point of view. My method has been to look at each chapter freshly in the light of the literature published since the last revision in 1970, of the new perspectives opened by this literature, and of the changes that have occurred in my own thinking in recent years. The most important of these changes relate to the role of women in American history. I have added a great deal of material both on what women have done and on how American conditions have affected their lives from colonial times to the present. I have also given further thought and devoted more space to the history of the Negro, to the experience of Mexican-Americans, and to social history generally. And of course I have tried to bring the story down as close to "yesterday" as the exigencies of printing schedules permit. This last task has involved an extensive reorganization of the last chapters, and the addition of a new final chapter.

John A. Garraty

Reconstruction and the South

On April 5, 1865, Abraham Lincoln visited the fallen capital of Richmond. The center of the city lay in ruins, sections of it blackened by fire, but the President was able to walk the streets unmolested and almost unattended; the townspeople seemed to have accepted defeat without resentment. A few days later, back in Washington, he delivered an important speech on reconstruction, urging that the subject be approached with compassion and open-mindedness. Then, on April 14, he held a Cabinet meeting at which postwar readjustment was considered at length. That evening, however, while he was watching a performance of the play *Our American Cousin* at Ford's Theater, a half-mad actor, John Wilkes Booth, slipped into his box and shot him in the back of the head with a small pistol. Early the next morning, without ever having regained consciousness, Lincoln died.

The murder was part of a complicated plot organized by die-hard pro-southerners. Seldom have fanatics displayed so little understanding of their own interests, for with Lincoln perished the South's best hope for a mild peace. After his body had been taken home to Illinois for burial, the national mood hardened. It was not a question of avenging the beloved Emancipator; rather a feeling took possession of the public mind that the years of pain and suffering were not yet over, that the awesome drama was still unfolding, that retribution and a final humbling of the South were inevitable.

Presidential Reconstruction

Despite its bloodiness, the Civil War had caused less intersectional hatred than might have been expected. Although civilian property was often seized or destroyed, the invading armies treated the southern population with remarkable forbearance, both during the war and after Appomattox. Not even the top leaders of the Confederacy were punished harshly. While he was ensconced in Richmond behind Lee's army, northerners boasted that they would "hang Jeff Davis to a sour apple tree," and when he was captured in Georgia in May 1865, he was at once taken to Fort Monroe and clapped into irons preparatory to being tried for treason and murder. But feeling against him subsided quickly. Soon he was given the run of the fort, and then, in 1867, the military turned him over to the civil courts, which released him on bail. He was never brought to trial. A few other Confederate officials spent short periods behind bars, but the only southerner executed for war crimes was Major Henry Wirz, the commandant of Andersonville military prison.

The legal questions related to bringing the defeated states back into the Union were extremely complex. Since they believed that secession was legal, logic should have compelled southerners to argue that they were out of the Union and would thus have to be formally readmitted. Northerners should have taken the contrary position, since they had fought to prove that secession was illegal. Yet the people of both sections did exactly the opposite. Senator Charles Sumner and Congressman Thaddeus Stevens, in 1861 uncompromising expounders of the theory that the Union was indissoluble, now declared that the Confederate states had "committed suicide" and should be treated like "conquered provinces." Erstwhile states'-rights southerners now argued that their states were still within the Union. Lincoln, believing the issue a "pernicious abstraction," wisely tried to ignore it.

The process of readmission began as early as 1862, when Lincoln appointed provisional governors for those parts of the South already occupied by federal troops. Then, on December 8, 1863, he issued a proclamation setting forth a general policy. He based his right to control reconstruction on the Presidential pardoning power. With the exception of high Confederate officials and a few other special groups, all southerners could reinstate themselves as United States citizens by taking a simple loyalty oath. When, in any state, a number equal to ten per cent of those voting in the 1860 election had taken this oath, they could set up a state government. Such governments had to be republican in form, must recognize the "permanent freedom" of Negroes, and provide for Negro education. The plan, however, did not require that Negroes be given the right to vote.

This "ten per cent plan" reflected Lincoln's moderation and lack of vindictiveness, and also his political wisdom. He realized that any government based on such a small minority of the population would be, as he put it, merely "a tangible nucleus which the remainder . . . may rally around as fast as it can," a sort of puppet regime, like the paper government established in those sections of Virginia under federal control.° The regimes established under this plan in Tennessee, Louisiana, and Arkansas bore, in the President's mind, the same relation to finally reconstructed states that an egg bears to a chicken. "We shall sooner have the fowl by hatching it than by smashing it," he shrewdly remarked. He knew that eventually representatives of the southern states would again be sitting in Congress, and he wished to lay the groundwork for a strong Republican party in the section, drawn mainly from former Whigs. Yet he did not see his creations as full-fledged state governments and he well realized that Congress had no intention of seating representatives from these "ten per cent" states at once.

However, the Radicals in Congress disliked the ten per cent plan, partly because of its moderation and partly because it enabled Lincoln to determine Union policy toward the recaptured regions. In July 1864 they passed the Wade–Davis bill, which provided for the calling of a constitutional convention only after a *majority* of the voters in a southern state had taken a loyalty oath and barred all Confederate officials and anyone who had "voluntarily borne arms against the United States" from voting in the election or serving at the convention. Besides prohibiting slavery, the new state constitutions would have to repudiate all Confederate debts. Lincoln disposed of the Wade–Davis bill with a pocket veto and thus managed to retain the initiative in reconstruction for the remainder of the war. There matters stood when Andrew Johnson became President after the assassination.†

Lincoln had picked Johnson for a running mate in 1864 because he was a border-state Unionist Democrat and something of a hero as a result of his courageous service as military

Andrew Johnson, as recorded by Mathew Brady's camera in 1865. Johnson, reported Charles Dickens, radiated purposefulness but no "genial sunlight." (Brady-Handy Collection, Library of Congress.)

nor of Tennessee. From origins even more lowly than Lincoln's, Johnson had risen before the war to be congressman, governor of Tennessee, and United States senator. He was able, efficient, and ambitious but fundamentally unsure of himself, as could be seen in his boastfulness and stubbornness. His political strength came from the poor whites and yeoman farmers in eastern Tennessee, and he was inordinately fond of extolling the common man and attacking "stuck-up aristocrats." Thaddeus Stevens called him a "rank demagogue" and a "damned scoundrel," and it is true that he was a masterful rabble-rouser, but few men of his generation labored so consistently to advance the interests of the small American farmer. Free homesteads, public education, abso-

°By approving the separation of the western counties which had refused to secede, this government provided a legal pretext for the creation of West Virginia.

†After the collapse of the Confederacy, Lincoln showed signs of moving toward an accommodation with the Radicals. He suggested, for example, that the vote be given to southern blacks who had fought in the Union army and to "very intelligent" freedmen.

lute social equality—such were his objectives throughout his career.

His accession posed political problems since officially he was a Democrat, yet that would have mattered very little had it not been for his personality. Because of his record and his reassuring penchant for excoriating southern aristocrats, the Republicans in Congress were ready to cooperate with him. "Johnson, we have faith in you," said Radical Senator Ben Wade, author of the Wade-Davis bill, the day after Lincoln's death. "By the gods, there will be no trouble now in running the government!"

Johnson's reply, "Treason must be made infamous," delighted the Radicals, but the President proved temperamentally unable to work with them. As Eric L. McKitrick has said in *Andrew Johnson and Reconstruction,* he was "never really a party man," an "outsider," a "lone wolf" in every way. "The only role whose attributes he fully understood was that of the maverick," McKitrick writes. "For the full nourishment and maximum functioning of his mind, matters had to be so arranged that all the organized forces of society could in some sense, real or symbolic, be leagued against him." Like Randolph of Roanoke, his very antithesis intellectually and socially, opposition was his specialty; he soon alienated every powerful Republican in Washington.

Radical Republicans, listening to Johnson's diatribes against secessionists and the great planters, had assumed that he was anti-southern. Nothing could have been further from the truth. He shared most of his poor white Tennessee constituents' prejudices against blacks. "Damn the negroes, I am fighting these traitorous aristocrats, their masters," he told a friend during the war. "I wish to God," he said on another occasion, "every head of a family in the United States had one slave to take the drudgery and menial service off his family."

Nor did the new President desire to injure or humiliate the entire South. On May 29, 1865, he issued an amnesty proclamation only slightly more rigorous than Lincoln's. It assumed, correctly enough, that with the war over most southern voters would freely take the loyalty oath and thus it contained no "ten per cent" clause. More classes of Confederates, including those who owned taxable property in excess of $20,000, were excluded from the general pardon. By the time Congress convened in December, all the southern states had organized governments, accepted the new Thirteenth Amendment abolishing slavery, and elected senators and representatives. Johnson promptly recommended these new governments to the attention of Congress.

Republican Radicals

Peace found the Republicans in Congress no more united than they had been during the war. A small group of "ultra"-Radicals insisted on immediate and absolute racial equality. Senator Sumner led this faction. A second group of Radicals, headed by Thaddeus Stevens in the House and Ben Wade in the Senate, agreed with the ultras' objectives° but were prepared to accept half a loaf if necessary to win the support of less radical colleagues. The moderate Republicans wanted to protect the freedmen against exploitation and guarantee their basic rights but were unprepared to push for full political and social equality for all blacks. A handful of Republicans sided with the Democrats in support of Johnson's approach, but all the rest insisted at least upon the minimum demands of the moderates. Thus Johnsonian reconstruction had no chance of winning congressional approval.

Johnson's proposal that Congress accept reconstruction as completed and admit the new southern representatives was also doomed for reasons having little to do with Negro rights. If Congress seated the southerners, the balance of power might swing to the Democrats. To expect

---

°When Stevens died, he was buried in a Negro cemetery. Here is his epitaph, written by himself: "I repose in this quiet and secluded spot, not from any natural preference for solitude, but finding other cemeteries limited as to race, by charter rules, I have chosen this that I might illustrate in my death the principles which I advocated through a long life, equality of man before his Creator."

Brady photographed two of the stalwart Radical Republicans, Thaddeus Stevens of Pennsylvania (left) and Benjamin Wade of Ohio (right). Stevens served in the House from 1859 until his death in 1868. During the Civil War, Senator "Bluff Ben" Wade had chaired the Joint Committee on the Conduct of the War. (Both: Brady-Handy Collection, Library of Congress.)

even the most high-minded Republicans to surrender power in such a fashion was unrealistic. Second, northern public opinion remained suspicious of the South and desirous of moving very cautiously toward granting full political rights to ex-Confederates. Former Copperheads gushing with extravagant praise of Johnson's work put Republicans instantly on their guard. Moreover, although most southerners had accepted the result of the war and were eager to re-enter the Union, they were not overflowing with good will toward their conquerors. Some of the new governments were less than straightforward even about accepting the most obvious results of the war. For example, instead of repudiating secession, South Carolina merely repealed its secession ordinance. A minority of southerners would have nothing to do with amnesties and pardons:

> Oh, I'm a good old rebel,
> Now that's just what I am;

> For the "fair land of freedom,"
> I do not care a dam.
> I'm glad I fit against it—
> I only wish we'd won
> And I don't want no pardon
> For anything I done.

Furthermore, southern voters had provoked northern resentment by their choice of congressmen. Georgia elected Alexander H. Stephens, Vice President of the Confederacy, to the Senate, although he was still in a federal prison awaiting trial for treason! Several dozen men who had served in the Confederate Congress had been elected to either the House or Senate, together with four generals and many other officials of the defunct Confederate administration. The southern people understandably selected locally respected and experienced leaders, but it was equally reasonable that these choices would sit poorly with many northerners.

Finally, the so-called Black Codes enacted by the new southern governments to control the freedmen alarmed the North. These varied from state to state in severity. When seen in historical perspective, even the strictest codes represented a considerable improvement over slavery. Most permitted Negroes to sue and to testify in court, at least in cases involving members of their own race. Blacks were allowed to own certain kinds of property; marriages were made legal; other rights were guaranteed. However, the codes also placed formidable limitations on their freedom. They could not bear arms, be employed in occupations other than farming and domestic service, or leave their jobs without forfeiting back pay. The Louisiana code required all Negroes to sign labor contracts for the year during the first ten days of January. In Mississippi any "vagrant" who could not pay the stiff fine assessed was to be "hired out . . . at public outcry" to the white person who would take him for the shortest period in return for paying his fine. Such laws, apparently designed to get around the Thirteenth Amendment, outraged even moderate northerners.

For all these reasons, the Republicans in Congress strongly opposed Johnsonian reconstruction. Quickly, the two houses established a joint committee on reconstruction, headed by Senator William P. Fessenden of Maine, a moderate Republican, to study the question of readmitting the southern states. This committee held extensive public hearings, which produced much evidence of the mistreatment of Negroes. Colonel George A. Custer, stationed in Texas, testified: "It is of weekly, if not of daily occurrence that Freedmen are murdered." The nurse Clara Barton told a gruesome tale about a pregnant woman who had been brutally whipped. Others described the intimidation of Negroes by poor whites. The hearings played into the hands of the Radicals, who had been claiming all along that the South was perpetuating slavery under another name.

President Johnson's attitude speeded the swing toward the Radical position. While the hearings were in progress, Congress passed a bill expanding and extending the Freedmen's Bureau, which had been established in March 1865 to care for refugees. The bureau, a branch of the War Department, was already exercising considerable coercive and supervisory influence in the South. Now Congress sought to add to its authority in order to protect the black population. The bill had wide support even among moderates. Nevertheless, Johnson vetoed it, arguing that it was an unconstitutional extension of military authority in peacetime. Congress then passed a Civil Rights Act, which, besides declaring that Negroes were citizens of the United States, denied the states the power to restrict their rights to testify in court and to hold property.

Once again the President refused to go along, although his veto was sure to drive more moderates into the arms of the Radicals. On April 9 Congress repassed the Civil Rights Act by a two-thirds majority, the first time in American history that a major piece of legislation became law over the veto of a President. This event marked a revolution in the history of reconstruction. Thereafter Congress, not President Johnson, had the upper hand, and progressively stricter controls were placed upon the South.

In the clash between the President and Congress, Johnson was his own worst enemy. His language was often intemperate, his handling of men inept, but above all his analysis of southern conditions was incorrect. He had assumed that the small southern farmers who made up the majority in all the states of the Confederacy shared his prejudices against the planter class. They did not, as their free choices in the postwar elections demonstrated. As a matter of fact, events seemed to indicate that his own hatred of the southern aristocracy might have been based more on jealousy than on principle. Under the reconstruction plan, persons excluded from the blanket amnesty could apply individually for the restoration of their rights. When men of wealth and status flocked to Washington, hat in hand, he found their flattery and humility exhilarating. He issued pardons wholesale, saying: "I did not expect to keep out all who were excluded from the amnesty. . . . I intended they should sue for pardon, and so realize the enormity of their crime."

The President also misread northern public feeling. He believed that Congress had no right to pass laws affecting the South before representatives of the southern states had been readmitted to Congress. In the light of the complete refusal of most southern whites to grant any real power or responsibility to the freedmen, an attitude that Johnson did not condemn, the public would not accept this point of view. Johnson placed his own judgment over that of the overwhelming majority of northern voters, and this was a great error, not merely morally but also tactically. By encouraging southerners to resist efforts to improve the lot of the freedmen it played into the hands of northern extremists.

However, the Radicals encountered grave problems in fighting for their program. Northerners might object to the Black Codes and to seating "rebels" in Congress, but few believed in granting Negroes true equality. Few northern states, it will be remembered, permitted blacks to vote. Between 1865 and 1868 Wisconsin, Minnesota, Connecticut, Nebraska, New Jersey, Ohio, Michigan, and Pennsylvania all rejected bills granting the suffrage to Negroes.

Like the abolitionists before the war, the Radicals lacked scientific arguments to prove that Negroes were equal to whites in intelligence and character. Moreover, they were, in effect, demanding not merely equal rights for freedmen but *extra* rights: not merely the right to vote but special protection of that right against the pressure that the dominant southern whites would surely apply to undermine it. This idea flew in the face of conventional American beliefs in equality before the law and individual self-reliance. Such protection would furthermore involve drastic interference by the federal government in local affairs, a concept totally at variance with previous American practice. Experience has repeatedly shown that the Radicals were correct—that what amounted to a political revolution in state-federal relations was essential if blacks were to achieve real equality. But in the climate of that day their proposals encountered bitter resistance, and not only from southerners.

Thus, while the Radicals sought partisan advantage in their battle with Johnson and sometimes tried to play upon war-bred passions in achieving their ends, they were also taking large political risks in defense of genuinely held principles. Many went down to defeat in local elections because of their support of Negro rights.

The Fourteenth Amendment

In June 1866 Congress passed and submitted to the states a new amendment to the Constitution. This Fourteenth Amendment was a milestone along the road to the centralization of political power in the nation, for it greatly reduced the power of *all* the states. In this sense it confirmed the great change wrought by the Civil War: the growth of a more complex, more closely integrated social and economic structure requiring closer national supervision. Few persons understood this aspect of the amendment at the time.

First of all, to cope with the possibility that the Supreme Court might find the Civil Rights Act unconstitutional, the amendment supplied a broad definition of American citizenship: "All persons born or naturalized in the United States, and subject to the jurisdiction thereof, are citizens of the United States and of the State wherein they reside." Obviously this included Negroes. Then it struck at discriminatory legislation like the Black Codes: "No State shall make or enforce any law which shall abridge the privileges or immunities of citizens of the United States; nor shall any State deprive any person of life, liberty, or property, without due process of law." The next section attempted to force the southern states to permit Negro voting. If a state denied the vote to any class of its adult male°

°Thus the amendment did nothing about the denial of the suffrage to women. The implication that black men were more fitted to vote than white women shocked and humiliated feminists. Elizabeth Cady Stanton warned prophetically that the amendment would create "an antagonism between black men and all women."

citizens, its representation was to be reduced proportionately. Under another clause, former federal officials who had served the Confederacy were barred from holding either state or federal office unless specifically pardoned by a two-thirds vote of Congress. Finally, the Confederate debt was repudiated.

These provisions were not as drastic as the Radicals had wished. The amendment did not specifically outlaw segregation or prevent a state from disfranchising Negroes if it was willing to see its representation in Congress reduced. Nevertheless, the South would have none of it. Except for Tennessee, all the former Confederate states refused to ratify. Without them, the necessary three-fourths majority of the states could not be obtained.

President Johnson vowed to make the choice between the Fourteenth Amendment and his own policy the main issue of the 1866 congressional elections. He embarked upon "a swing around the circle" to rally the public to his cause. He failed dismally, for by this time northern opinion had hardened; without changing their personal attitudes toward Negroes, a large majority was determined that blacks must have at least formal legal equality. The Republicans won better than two-thirds of the seats in both houses, together with control of all the northern state governments. Johnson emerged from the campaign discredited, the Radicals greatly increased in strength.

Since the South had refused to accept their terms voluntarily, the Radicals prepared to impose them by force. The southern states, said Congressman James A. Garfield of Ohio in February 1867, "with contempt and scorn [have] flung back into our teeth the magnanimous offer of a generous nation. It is now our turn to act."

The Reconstruction Acts

Framing effective reconstruction legislation was very difficult. No precedents existed to build upon, and differences of opinion among Republi-

can congressmen were wide. Moderate Republicans clung stubbornly to the hope that at least a semblance of local autonomy could be preserved in the South. Had the southern states been willing to reconsider their rejection of the Fourteenth Amendment, coercive measures might still have been avoided. Their recalcitrance and the continuing indications that local authorities were persecuting blacks finally led to the passage, on March 2, 1867, of the First Reconstruction Act.

This law divided the former Confederacy—exclusive of Tennessee, which had ratified the Fourteenth Amendment—into five military districts, each controlled by a major general. It gave these officers almost dictatorial power to protect the civil rights of "all persons," maintain order, and supervise the administration of justice. To rid themselves of military rule, the former states were required to frame and adopt new constitutions guaranteeing Negroes the right to vote and disfranchising the same broad classes of ex-Confederates excluded under the proposed amendment. If these new constitutions proved satisfactory to Congress, and if the new governments ratified the amendment, their representatives would be admitted to Congress and military rule ended. This stern measure passed the House of Representatives by 135 to 48 and the Senate by 38 to 10. Johnson's veto of the act was thus easily overridden.

Although drastic, the Reconstruction Act was so vague that it proved unworkable. Military control was easily established, for in practice federal bayonets were already exerting considerable authority all over the South. But in deference to moderate Republican views, the law had not spelled out the process by which the new constitutions were to be drawn up. Southerners preferred the status quo, even under army control, to enfranchising the Negro and retiring their own respected leaders. They made no effort to follow the steps laid down in the law. Congress, therefore, passed a second act, requiring the military authorities to register voters and supervise the election of delegates to constitutional conventions. A third act further clarified procedures.

Still, white southerners resisted. The laws provided that the new constitutions must be approved by a majority of the registered voters. Simply by staying away from the polls, the southerners defeated ratification in state after state. At last, in March 1868, a full year after the First Reconstruction Act was passed, Congress changed the rules again. The constitutions were to be ratified by a majority of the *voters*. In June 1868 Arkansas, having fulfilled the requirements, was readmitted to the Union. But it was not until July 1870 that the last southern state, Georgia, qualified to the satisfaction of Congress.

Congress v. the President

To carry out this program in the face of determined southern resistance required a degree of single-mindedness over a long period seldom demonstrated by American legislatures. This persistence resulted partly from the suffering and frustrations of the war years. The refusal of the South to accept the spirit of even the mild reconstruction designed by Johnson goaded the North to ever more overbearing efforts to bring the ex-Confederates to heel. President Johnson's stubbornness also influenced the mood of Congress; Republican leaders became obsessed with the desire to defeat him. The unsettled times and the large Republican majorities, always threatened by the possibility of a Democratic resurgence if "unreconstructed" southern congressmen were readmitted, sustained their determination.

Indeed, these considerations led the Republicans to attempt a kind of grand revision of the federal government, one that almost destroyed the balance between judicial, executive, and legislative power established in 1789. A series of measures passed between 1866 and 1868 increased the authority of Congress over the army, over the process of amending the Constitution, and over the Cabinet and lesser appointive officers. Even the Supreme Court felt the force of this congressional drive for power. Its size was reduced and also the range of its jurisdiction over

civil rights cases. Some Radicals talked of abolishing it altogether. The justices handed down some notably courageous decisions in the face of Radical pressure, but when their powers were reduced by legislation in a way that many lawyers considered unconstitutional, they meekly accepted the restriction. Generally speaking, the Court avoided taking a stand that might have challenged the constitutionality of the Reconstruction Acts, being disinclined, according to one judge, to "run a race with Congress."

Finally, in a showdown caused by emotional conflicts more than by practical considerations, the Republicans attempted to remove President Johnson from office. Johnson was a poor President and out of touch with public opinion, but he had done nothing to merit ejection from office under the Constitution. Although he had a low opinion of Negroes, his opinion was so widely shared by whites that it is unhistorical to condemn him as a reactionary on this ground. Johnson believed that he was fighting to preserve constitutional government. He was honest, devoted to his duty, and his record easily withstood the most searching examination of his enemies. When Congress passed laws taking away powers granted him by the Constitution, he refused to submit.

The chief issue was the Tenure of Office Act of 1867, which prohibited the President from removing officials who had been appointed with the consent of the Senate without first obtaining senatorial approval. In February 1868 Johnson "violated" this act by dismissing Secretary of War Edwin M. Stanton, who had been openly in sympathy with the Radicals for some time. The House, acting under the procedure set up in the Constitution for removing the President, promptly impeached him before the bar of the Senate, Chief Justice Salmon P. Chase presiding.

This "great act of ill-directed passion," as it has been characterized by one historian, would have been farcical had it not been conducted in so partisan and vindictive a manner. Johnson's lawyers easily established that he had removed Stanton only in an effort to prove the Tenure of Office Act unconstitutional. They also demonstrated that the act did not protect Stanton to begin with, since it gave Cabinet members tenure "during the term of the President by whom they may have been appointed," and Stanton had been appointed by Lincoln! Nevertheless, the Radicals pressed the charges (11 separate articles) relentlessly. To the argument that Johnson had committed no crime, the learned Senator Sumner retorted that the proceedings were "political in character" rather than judicial. Thaddeus Stevens, directing the attack on behalf of the House, warned the senators that although "no corrupt or wicked motive" could be attributed to Johnson, they would "be tortured on the gibbet of everlasting obloquy" if they did not convict him. Tremendous pressure was applied to the handful of Republican senators who were unwilling to disregard the evidence.

Seven of them resisted to the end, and the Senate failed by a single vote to convict Johnson. This was probably fortunate. Impeachment is a drastic remedy, not properly applied in a dubious case like Johnson's. Had he been forced from office on such flimsy grounds, the independence of the Executive might have been permanently weakened. Then the legislative branch would have become supreme.

The Fifteenth Amendment

The failure of the impeachment, however, had little effect on the course of reconstruction. The President was acquitted on May 16, 1868. A few days later the Republican National Convention nominated General Ulysses S. Grant for the Presidency. At the Democratic convention, Johnson received considerable support, but the delegates finally nominated Horatio Seymour, a former governor of New York. In November Grant won an easy victory in the Electoral College, 214 to 80, but the election was not actually a runaway for him. The popular vote was 3 million to 2.7 million. Although he would probably have carried the Electoral College in any case, it is an interesting fact that Grant's margin in the popular vote was supplied by southern Negroes enfranchised under the Reconstruction Acts. Of the estimated 500,000 Negro voters in 1868, about 450,000 supported Grant. In other words, a majority of the white voters probably preferred Seymour. Indeed, since many citizens undoubtedly voted Republican because of personal admiration for Grant, the election statistics suggest that a substantial majority of the white voters were opposed to the policies of the Radicals.

The ratification of the Fourteenth Amendment was finally completed in July 1868. Combined with the Reconstruction Acts it achieved the purpose of enabling southern Negroes to vote. The Radicals, however, were not satisfied; despite the unpopularity of the idea in the North, they wished to guarantee the right of Negroes to vote in every state. Amending the Constitution seemed the only way to accomplish this objective, but passage of such an amendment seemed on the surface utterly impossible. In 1867 and 1868 the voters of New York had rejected a proposal to remove the $250 property qualification for voting imposed on blacks in the state, and the voters of several middle western states had turned down new constitutional provisions authorizing Negro voting. The Republican platform in the 1868 Presidential election smugly distinguished between Negro voting in the South ("demanded by every consideration of public safety, of gratitude, and of justice") and in the North (where the question "properly belongs to the people").

However, the result of that election, which demonstrated how crucial Negro block voting could be, caused a sudden shift in Republican strategy. Grant had carried Indiana by less than 10,000 votes and lost New York by a similar number. If blacks in these and other closely divided states had voted, Republican strength would have been greatly enhanced. Suddenly both houses of Congress blossomed with suffrage amendments. After considerable bickering over details, the Fifteenth Amendment was passed and sent to the states for ratification in February 1869. It forbade *all* the states to deny the vote to anyone "on account of race, color, or previous condition of servitude." Once again, nothing was said about denial of the vote on the basis of sex.

Most of the southern states, still under federal pressure, ratified the amendment swiftly. The same was true in most of New England and in some of the western states. Bitter battles were waged in Connecticut, New York, Pennsylvania, and the states immediately north of the Ohio River, but by March 1870, most of these had ratified the amendment and it became part of the Constitution. The debates precipitated by these contests show that partisan advantage was not the only reason why the voters approved Negro suffrage at last. The unfairness of a double standard of voting, North and South, the contribution of black soldiers during the war, and a general hope that by passing the amendment the strife of reconstruction could be finally ended all played a part.

When the Fifteenth Amendment went into effect, President Grant called it "the greatest civil change and . . . the most important event that has occurred since the nation came to life." Negroes and former abolitionists rejoiced—the American Anti-Slavery Society formally dissolved itself, its work apparently completed. One prominent Radical Republican called this victory over northern prejudice "hardly explicable on any other theory than that God willed it." Of course many of the celebrants lived to see the amendment subverted in the South; indeed, that it could be evaded by literacy tests and other restrictions was apparent at the time and may even have influenced some persons in voting for it. But a stronger amendment, one, for instance, that positively granted the right to vote to all men and put the supervision of elections under national control, could not have been ratified.

"Black Republican" Reconstruction

For the moment, at least, the Radicals had succeeded in imposing their will upon the South. Throughout the region former slaves voted, held office, and, in general, exercised the "privileges"

and enjoyed the "immunities" guaranteed them by the Fourteenth Amendment. Almost to a man they voted Republican.

The spectacle of Negroes not five years removed from slavery in positions of power and responsibility attracted much attention at the time and has since been examined exhaustively by historians. The subject is controversial, but certain facts are beyond argument. For one thing, Negro officeholders were neither numerous nor inordinately influential. No black was ever elected governor of a state; fewer than a dozen and a half during the whole period served in Congress; only one (in South Carolina) rose to be a justice of a state supreme court. Negroes held many minor offices and were influential in southern legislatures, although except for a brief period in South Carolina, when they controlled the lower house, they never made up a majority. Certainly they did not share the spoils of office in proportion to their numbers. The real rulers of these "black Republican" governments were white: the "carpetbaggers"—northerners who went to the South as idealists eager to help the freedmen, as employees of the federal government, or more commonly merely as settlers hoping to improve their lot—and the "scalawags"—southerners willing to cooperate with the Negro out of principle or to advance their own interests. A few of the scalawags were well-to-do planters and merchants who had been Whigs until the great crises of the 1850's had destroyed that party in the South, but most were former Unionists from sections that had small slave populations before the war.

That the Negroes should fail to assert leadership is certainly understandable. They lacked experience in politics and were both poor and uneducated. They were also, even in the South, a minority. It would have been remarkable indeed if they had dominated the reconstruction governments. Those blacks who did hold office during reconstruction proved in the main able and conscientious public servants: able because the best tended to rise to the top in such a fluid situation and conscientious because most of those who achieved importance sought eagerly to demon-

South Carolina's House of Representatives in session during the reconstruction, from *Frank Leslie's Illustrated Newspaper*. Negroes were in the majority in South Carolina, and seven were elected to the federal Congress. (*Frank Leslie's Illustrated Newspaper*, January 6, 1877.)

strate the capacity of their race for self-government. Extensive studies of states such as Mississippi have shown that even at the local level, where the quality of officials was usually poor, there was little difference in the degree of competence displayed by white and black officeholders. In power, the Negroes displayed remarkably little vindictiveness; by and large, they did not seek to restrict the rights of ex-Confederates.

It is true that waste and corruption flourished in some of these governments. Legislators paid themselves large salaries and surrounded themselves with armies of useless, incompetent clerks. Half the budget of Louisiana in some years went for salaries and "mileage" for representatives and their staffs. In South Carolina the legislature ordered an expensive census in 1869, only one year before the regular federal census was to be taken. Large sums were appropriated for imposing state capitols and other less-than-essential buildings. As for corruption, in *The South During Reconstruction* Professor E. Merton Coulter has described dozens of defalcations of various sorts that occurred during these years. One Arkansas Negro took $9,000 from the state for repairing a bridge that had cost only $500 to build. A South Carolina legislator was voted an additional $1,000 in salary after he had lost that sum on a horse race.

However, this corruption must be seen in perspective. The big thieves were nearly always white men; blacks got merely the crumbs. Furthermore, graft and callous disregard of the public interest characterized government in every section and at every level during the decade after Appomattox. Big-city bosses in the North made off with sums that dwarfed the most brazen southern frauds. The defalcations of the New York City Tweed Ring probably amounted to a larger sum than all the southern thefts combined. The crimes of officials in Louisiana and South Carolina appear trivial when compared with the depravity in Washington during President Grant's administrations. While this evidence does not justify the southern corruption, it suggests that the unique features of reconstruction politics—Negro suffrage, military supervision, carpetbagger and scalawag influence—do not explain it.

The "black Republican" governments did display qualities that grew directly from the ignorance and political immaturity of the freedmen. There was a tragicomic aspect to the South Carolina legislature during these years, its many black members—some dressed in old frock coats, others in rude farm clothes—rising to points of order and personal privilege without reason, discoursing ponderously on subjects they did not understand. "A wonder and a shame to modern civilization," one northern observer called this spectacle.

The whole country might have been better served if the former slaves had been enfranchised only gradually, as Lincoln had suggested, and if a real effort had been made to educate them to the responsibilities of citizenship. Neither northerners nor southerners were willing to adopt such a solution to the problem. Two and a half centuries of slavery and the absence of the kind of psychological and sociological studies of Negro intelligence now available made it almost impossible for the best-intentioned southerners to see the Negro as a potential equal. Most simply guffawed and made crude jokes about the stupidity of "nigras." Even intelligent and well-meaning southern whites could not often view the freedman objectively. Robert E. Lee, no lover of slavery, testified that Negroes were an "amiable and social" people who loved "ease and comfort" and looked "more to their present than to their future condition." He did not realize that he was describing qualities found in human beings of all kinds, not merely in black ones. Northerners refused to recognize that a problem existed, shared the prejudices of their southern cousins, or cynically tried to manipulate the black vote for their own ends.

Southerners who complained about the ignorance and irresponsibility of Negro voters conveniently forgot that the whole tendency of 19th-century American democracy was away from educational, financial, or any other restrictions on

The Freedmen's Bureau established 4,329 schools, attended by some 250,000 ex-slaves, in the South in the postwar period. *Harper's Weekly* artist Alfred Waud did this sketch of a Freedmen's Bureau school in Vicksburg, Mississippi, in 1866. (Malcolm F. J. Burns Collection.)

the franchise. Thousands of white southerners were as illiterate and uncultured as the freedmen, yet no one suggested depriving them of the ballot. Some northern states allowed immigrants to vote before they became citizens.

Despite the corruption, confusion, and conflict, the Radical southern governments did accomplish many long-needed reforms. They spent money freely—the debt of the former Confederate states increased by more than $100 million—but not entirely wastefully. Tax rates zoomed, but the proceeds were used to finance the repair and expansion of the South's dilapidated railroad network, to rebuild crumbling levees, to care for the poor, and generally to expand social services. Before the Civil War, public education in the South had lagged far behind the rest of the country, and as for Negro education, it was not only nonexistent but illegal. During reconstruction an enormous gap had to be filled, and it took a great deal of money to fill it. The Freedmen's Bureau made a start at the task, and northern religious and philanthropic organizations also did important work. Eventually, however, the state governments established and supported systems of free public education that, while segregated, greatly benefited all the people, whites as well as Negroes.

Freedmen grasped eagerly at the opportunity to learn. Nearly all appreciated the immense importance of knowing how to read and write; the sight of elderly ex-slaves poring laboriously over elementary texts beside their grandchildren was common everywhere. Schools and other institutions were supported chiefly by property taxes, and these, of course, hit well-to-do white farmers hard. Hence much of the complaining about the "extravagance" of reconstruction governments concealed selfish objections to necessary public expenditures. Eventually, the benefits of expanded government services to the whole population became clear to all classes, and when the period finally ended and white supremacy was re-established, most of the new services, together with the corruption and inefficiency inherited from the carpetbagger governments, were retained.

Southern Economic Problems

The South's grave economic problems complicated the rebuilding of its political system. Taken as a whole, the section had never been as prosperous as the North and wartime destruction left it desperately poor by any standard. In addition to the physical damage, the South had suffered staggering financial losses. All Confederate bonds and currency became worthless. While freeing the slaves did not deprive the South of their labor, it cost slaveowners dearly, and these were the men accustomed by training and experience to develop and manage the resources of the region. Most of the 5 million bales of cotton on hand in the Confederacy when the war ended, an asset that might have gone a long way toward getting the area back on its feet, were seized and sold by agents of the federal government—much of the proceeds, indeed, being siphoned into their own pockets. The government also placed a heavy tax on cotton, which drained off another $68 million from the South in the immediate postwar years.

The war also disorganized the southern economy. In the long run, the abolition of slavery released immeasurable quantities of human energy previously stifled, but the immediate effect was to create confusion. Understandably enough, many former slaves tended to equate legal freedom with freedom from having to earn a living, a tendency reinforced for a time by the willingness of the Freedmen's Bureau to provide rations and other forms of relief in war-devastated areas.

Many Negroes expected that freedom would also mean free land, and the slogan "forty acres and a mule" achieved wide popularity in the South in 1865. This idea was most forcefully supported by the irascible, relentless Congressman Thaddeus Stevens, whose hatred of the planter class was pathological. "The property of the chief rebels should be seized," he stated. If the lands of the richest "70,000 proud, bloated and defiant rebels" were confiscated, the federal government would obtain 394 million acres. Every adult male Negro could easily be supplied with

40 acres. The beauty of his scheme, Stevens insisted, was that "nine-tenths of the [southern] people would remain untouched." Dispossessing the great planters would also make the South "a safe republic," its lands cultivated by "the free labor of intelligent citizens." If the plan drove the planters into exile, "all the better."

Although Stevens' figures were faulty and his logic shaky, many Radicals agreed with him. "We must see that the freedmen are established on the soil," Senator Sumner declared. "The great plantations, which have been so many nurseries of the rebellion, must be broken up, and the freedmen must have the pieces." Stevens, Sumner, and others who wanted to give land to the freedmen weakened their case by associating it with the idea of punishing the former rebels; the average American had too much respect for

property rights to tolerate a policy of confiscation. But aside from its vindictiveness, the extremists' view was too simplistic. Land without capital for tools, seed, and other necessities would have done the freedmen little good. Congress did throw open 46 million acres of poor-quality federal land in the South to blacks under the Homestead Act, but few settled upon it. Yet a scheme for establishing freedmen on small farms with adequate guidance and financial aid would have been of incalculable benefit to them and to the nation. The country, however, was no more ready for an economic revolution of this type than for the kind of political revolution that would have properly protected the Negroes' political rights.

The freedmen, therefore, had to work out their destiny within the already established

Among the few blacks to emigrate to the West and obtain land under the provisions of the Homestead Act was the Shores family. S. D. Butcher took this family portrait in Custer County, Nebraska, in the 1880's. Negro homesteaders received limited aid from the Freedmen's Relief Association and eastern philanthropists. (Nebraska State Historical Society.)

framework of southern agriculture. In the beginning, they usually labored for wages. Most southerners soon came to the conclusion that a free Negro produced no more than a third to a half as much as a slave and paid them far less than white workers could command. This was not entirely unjust. Freedmen often quit their jobs at harvest time when the work was hard, leaving the crops to rot in the fields, and went off with a few dollars, wandering aimlessly, reveling in their new right to travel without a pass. This explains in part why the Black Codes contained provisions forcing the Negroes to sign long-term labor contracts.

The payment of wages, however, did not work out well in the postwar South. Money was extremely scarce, and banking capital, never adequate even before the collapse of the Confederacy, accumulated very slowly. Interest rates were extremely high. This situation made it difficult for large landowners to meet their labor bills and also for freedmen and poor whites to obtain the funds necessary to buy land. In Georgia, for example, as late as 1880, Negroes owned fewer than 600,000 of the state's 37,700,000 acres. Planter and freedman attempted to solve their difficulties by developing the system known as sharecropping. Instead of cultivating his lands by gang labor as in antebellum times, the planter broke his estate up into small units and established on each a Negro family. He provided housing, agricultural implements, and other supplies, and the family provided labor. The crop was divided between them, usually on a 50–50 basis. If the laborer supplied tools or other equipment, he received a larger share. This system created incentive and also gave the sharecropper a chance to rise in the world. He became the independent manager of his own acres; if successful, he could save money and eventually buy land of his own. Of course the profit in personal dignity and self-confidence for the ex-slave was immense, but the economic benefit was also large.

All might have been well had the planters possessed enough capital to finance the system. They did not. Like their colonial ancestors and their fathers in the prewar era, they had to borrow against October's harvest to pay for April's seed. Thus the crop-lien system developed, and to protect his investment, the lender tended to insist that the grower concentrate on the readily marketable cash crops: tobacco, sugar, and especially cotton. Overproduction and soil exhaustion inevitably resulted. The system injured everyone. Diversified farming would have reduced the farmers' need for cash, preserved the fertility of the soil, and, by placing a premium on imagination and shrewdness, aided the best of them to rise in the world. Under the crop-lien system, both landowner and sharecropper depended upon credit supplied by local bankers, merchants, and storekeepers for everything from seed, tools, and fertilizer to blue jeans, coffee, and salt. Crossroads stores proliferated, and a new class of small merchants appeared. The prices of goods sold on credit were high, adding to the burden borne by the rural population. These small southern merchants were almost equally victimized by the system, for they also lacked capital, bought their goods on credit, and had to pay high interest rates.

Seen in broad perspective, the situation is not difficult to understand. The South, drained of every resource by the exhausting war, was now competing for funds with the North and West, both vigorous and expanding and therefore voracious consumers of capital. Reconstruction, in the literal sense of the word, was accomplished chiefly at the expense of the standard of living of the producing classes. The crop-lien system and the small storekeeper were only agents attending to the functioning of an economic process dictated by national, perhaps even worldwide, conditions.

This does not mean that the South's economy was paralyzed by the shortage of capital or that recovery and growth did not take place. But compared with the rest of the country, progress was slow. In the years just before the Civil War, cotton production averaged about 4 million bales. After the war, the former Confederate states did not enjoy a 4-million-bale year until 1870, and only after 1874 did the crop begin to

SOUTHERN AGRICULTURE, 1850-1900

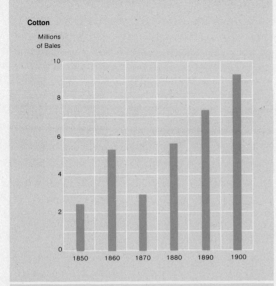

Cotton

Millions of Bales

Tobacco

Millions of Pounds

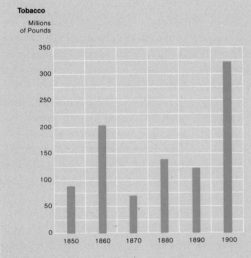

Sugar

Millions of Pounds

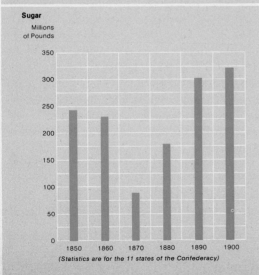

(Statistics are for the 11 states of the Confederacy)

top that figure consistently. The prewar production record of 5.3 million bales was not broken until 1879. In contrast, national wheat production in 1859 was 175 million bushels and in 1878, 449 million. About 7,000 miles of railroad were built in the South between 1865 and 1879, but in the rest of the nation, nearly 45,000 miles of track were laid.

In manufacturing the South made important gains. The tobacco industry, stimulated by the sudden popularity of the cigarette, expanded rapidly. The town of Durham, North Carolina, home of the famous Bull Durham pipe and cigarette tobacco, flourished. So did Virginia tobacco towns like Richmond, Lynchburg, and Petersburg. The exploitation of the coal and iron deposits of northeastern Alabama in the early 1870's made a boom town of Birmingham. The manufacture of cotton cloth also increased, productive capacity nearly doubling between 1865 and 1880. Yet the mills of Massachusetts alone had eight times the capacity of the entire South in 1880. Despite gains in many fields, the South's share of the national output of manufactured goods declined sharply during the reconstruction era.

The White Counterrevolution

Although economic conditions improved and federal troops supplied sporadic aid, the Radical governments of the southern states could sustain themselves only so long as they held the support of a significant proportion of the white population, for except in South Carolina and Louisiana, the blacks were neither numerous nor powerful enough to win elections alone. The key to Radical survival lay in the hands of the wealthy merchants and planters, mostly former Whigs, who had chosen to go along with the carpetbag governments in the interest of harmony and economic recovery. Men of this sort had nothing to fear from Negro economic competition. Taking a broad view, they could see that improving the lot of the former slave would benefit all classes.

These southerners exercised a restraining influence on the rest of the white population. Poor white farmers, the most "unreconstructed" of all southerners, bitterly resented the freedmen, whose every forward step seemed to weaken their own precarious economic and social position. When the Republicans began to organize and manipulate the new voters much the way big-city bosses were managing the masses of the North, these poorer whites seethed with resentment.

The southern Republicans used the Union League of America, a patriotic club founded during the war, to control the black vote. Employing secret rituals, exotic symbols, and other paraphernalia calculated to impress the Negroes' untutored imaginations, they enrolled the freedmen in droves, made them swear to support the League list of candidates at elections, and then marched them to the polls en masse. Powerless to check the League by open methods, dissident southerners established a number of secret terrorist societies, bearing such names as the Ku Klux Klan, the Knights of the White Camelia, and the Pale Faces.

The most notorious of these was the Klan, which originated in Tennessee in 1866. At first it was a purely social club, but by 1868 it had been taken over by vigilante types dedicated to driving the Negro out of politics and was spreading rapidly. All across the South, sheet-clad nightriders roamed the countryside, frightening the impressionable and chastising the defiant. Klansmen, using a weird mumbo jumbo and claiming even to be the ghosts of Confederate soldiers, spread horrendous rumors and published terrifying broadsides designed to persuade the freedmen that it was unhealthy for them to participate in politics:

Niggers and Leaguers, get out of the way,
We're born of the night and we vanish by day.
No rations have we, but the flesh of man—
And love niggers best—the Ku Klux Klan;
We catch 'em alive and roast 'em whole,
Then hand 'em around with a sharpened pole.
Whole Leagues have been eaten, not leaving a man,
And went away hungry—the Ku Klux Klan. . . .

A Prospective Scene in the "City of Oaks," 4th of March, 1869.

A graphic warning by the Alabama Klan to scalawags and carpetbaggers, "those great pests of Southern society"; from the Tuscaloosa *Independent Monitor.* (Alabama Department of Archives and History.)

When intimidation failed, the Klansmen employed more brutal tactics, beating their victims and in literally hundreds of cases murdering them, often in the most gruesome manner. Congress struck at the Klan by passing three Force Acts (1870-71) to protect Negro voters. These laws placed elections under federal jurisdiction and imposed fines and prison sentences on persons convicted of interfering with any citizen's exercise of the franchise. Troops were dispatched to areas where the Klan was strong, and finally, by 1872, the federal authorities had arrested enough Klansmen to break up the organization.

Nevertheless, the Klan contributed substantially to the destruction of Radical regimes in the South. Its depredations weakened the will of white Republicans (few of whom really believed in racial equality), and it intimidated many Negroes, who gave up trying to exercise their rights. More and more, even respectable white southerners came to the conclusion that terrorism was the most effective way both of controlling the black population and of escaping from northern domination.

Gradually it became respectable to intimidate Negro voters. Beginning in 1874 a number of movements, such as the "Mississippi plan," spread through the South. Instead of hiding behind masks and operating in the dark, these terrorists donned red shirts, organized into military companies, and paraded openly. The Mississippi red-shirts seized militant Negroes and whipped them publicly. Killings were frequent. When the blacks dared to fight back, the well-organized whites easily put them to rout. In other states similar organizations sprang up, and the same tragic results followed.

Terrorism fed on fear, fear on terrorism. White violence led to fear of black retaliation and therefore to even more brutal attacks. The slightest sign of resistance came to be seen as the beginning of race war, and when the blacks suffered indignities and persecutions in silence, the awareness of how much they must resent such mistreatment made them appear more dangerous still. Thus self-hatred was displaced, guilt suppressed, aggression justified as self-defense, individual conscience buried in the animality of the mob.

Before very long, the blacks learned to stay home on election day. Thereafter, one by one, "Conservative" parties—Democratic in national affairs—took over southern state governments. Angry northern Radicals attributed these Democratic victories entirely to the intimidation of Negro voters, but this was only a partial explanation. The increasing solidarity of the whites was equally significant.

No degree of southern white unity could have led to the overthrow of the Radical governments if northern public opinion had remained determined to defend the Negro's political rights. By the mid-seventies this was clearly not the case, and for a number of reasons. Many northerners had supported the Radical policy only out of irritation with President Johnson. After his retirement, their enthusiasm waned. The war was fading into the past and with it the worst of the bad feeling it had generated. Northern voters could still be stirred by references to the sacrifices Republicans had made to save the Union and by reminders that the Democratic party was the organization of rebels, Copperheads, and the Ku Klux Klan. Yet emotional appeals could not push legislation through Congress nor convince north-

erners that it was still necessary to maintain large armed forces in the South. Nationalism was reasserting itself. Men began to recall that Washington and Jefferson had been Virginians, that Andrew Jackson was Carolina-born. Since most northerners had little real love or respect for the Negro, their interest in his welfare flagged once they felt reasonably certain that he would not actually be re-enslaved if left to his own devices in the South.

Grant as President

Other matters increasingly occupied the attention of northern voters. The expansion of industry and the continued rapid development of the West, much stimulated by a new wave of railroad building, loomed more important to many than the fortunes of Negroes and "rebels." Growth did not mean universal prosperity; beginning in 1873, when a stock market panic struck at public confidence, economic difficulties plagued the country for nearly a decade. Heated controversies arose over the tariff, with western agricultural interests seeking to force reductions from the high levels established during the war, and over the handling of the wartime "greenback" paper money, with debtor groups and aggressive new manufacturers favoring expansion of the supply of dollars still further and conservative merchants and bankers arguing for retiring the greenbacks in order to get back to a "sound" currency. These controversies tended to divert the attention of Republicans from conditions in the South.

Still more damaging to the Republicans was the failure of Ulysses S. Grant to live up to expectations as President. Qualities that had made Grant a fine military leader for a democracy—his dislike of political maneuvering and his simple belief that the popular will could best be observed in the actions of Congress—made him a poor Chief Executive. When Congress failed to act upon his suggestion that the quality of the civil service needed improvement, he announced meekly that if Congress did nothing, he would assume the country did not want anything done, and dropped the subject. Grant remained independent-minded and honest, but his independence took such forms as appointing his Cabinet without consulting the politicians and thus saddling himself with men who added almost nothing to the political weight of his administration, and his honesty was of the naive type that made him the dupe of unscrupulous friends and schemers.

His most serious weakness as President was his failure to develop a coherent program to deal with economic and social problems, but the one that injured him and the Republicans most was his inability to cope with corruption in government. Grant, of course, did not cause the corruption, nor did he participate in the remotest way in the rush to "fatten at the public trough," as the reformers of the day might have put it. Corruption flourished in part because the times conspired to encourage materialism: people tended to consider the accumulation of wealth more important than the means used to acquire wealth. Furthermore, many persons were reacting against the idealism and self-sacrifice of the war years, which had cost the nation so dearly. Nevertheless, Grant did nothing to prevent the scandals that disgraced his administration and, out of a misplaced belief in the sanctity of friendship, he protected some of the worst culprits and allowed calculating tricksters to use his good name and the prestige of his office to advance their own interests at the country's expense.

The worst of the scandals—such as the Whiskey Ring affair, which implicated Grant's private secretary, Orville E. Babcock, and cost the government millions in tax revenue, and the defalcations of Secretary of War William W. Belknap in the management of Indian affairs—did not become public knowledge during Grant's first term. However, in 1872 a reform group in the Republican party, alarmed by rumors of corruption and disappointed by the failure of the President to achieve civil service reform, organized the Liberal Republican party and nominated Horace Greeley, the able but eccentric editor of the New York *Tribune,* for President. The Democrats also nominated Greeley, although he had devoted his whole political life to flailing

Thomas Nast was a staunch Grant man; in a *Harper's Weekly* cartoon, done during the 1872 campaign, Greeley (center) and Charles Sumner urge a Negro to "clasp hands" with a Klansman and a Tammany Hall instigator of Civil War draft riots. (*Harper's Weekly*, August 24, 1872.)

that party in the *Tribune,* and the obvious expediency of this, together with Greeley's temperamental unsuitability for the Presidency, made the campaign a fiasco for the reformers. Grant triumphed easily, with a popular majority of nearly 800,000.

Nevertheless, the defection of the Liberal Republicans hurt the Republican party in Congress. And when, no longer hampered as in the Presidential contest by Greeley's notoriety and Grant's fame, the Democrats carried the House of Representatives in the 1874 elections, it was clear that the days of military control in the South were ending. The trend toward white solidarity therefore speeded up, until by the end of 1875 only three southern states, South Carolina, Florida, and Louisiana, were still under Republican control. As a middle western newspaperman admitted to Carl Schurz, a prominent Liberal Republican, the Republican party in the South was "dead as a doornail." The reporter reflected the thinking of thousands when he added: "We ought to have a sound sensible republican . . . for the next President as a measure of safety; but only on the condition of absolute noninterference in Southern local affairs, for which there is no further need or excuse."

The Disputed Election of 1876

Against this background, the Presidential election of 1876 took place. Since corruption in government was the most widely discussed issue, in choosing their Presidential candidate the Republicans passed over their most attractive political personality, the dynamic James G. Blaine, Speaker of the House of Representatives, for Blaine had been connected with some chicanery involving railroad securities. Instead they nominated Governor Rutherford B. Hayes of Ohio, a former general with an unsmirched reputation. The Democrats picked Governor Samuel J. Tilden of New York, a prominent lawyer who had attracted national attention for his part in break-

ing up the Tweed Ring in New York City.

In November Tilden triumphed easily in all the southern states from which the carpetbagger regimes had been ejected. He also carried New York, New Jersey, Connecticut, and Indiana. In the three "unredeemed" southern states, Florida, South Carolina, and Louisiana, he also won apparent majorities. This seemed to give him 203 electoral votes to Hayes's 165, with a popular plurality in the neighborhood of 250,000 out of over 8 million votes cast.

However, Republican leaders had anticipated the possible loss of Florida, South Carolina, and Louisiana, and were prepared to use their control of the election machinery in these states to throw out sufficient Democratic ballots to alter the results if doing so would change the national outcome. Realizing that the 19 electoral votes of these states were exactly enough to elect their man, they telegraphed their henchmen on the scene to go into action. The board of canvassers in each of these states invalidated Democratic ballots in wholesale lots and filed returns showing Hayes the winner. Naturally enough, the local Democrats protested vigorously and filed their own returns.

The Constitution provides that Presidential electors must meet in their respective states to vote and forward the results to "the Seat of the Government." There, it adds, "the President of the Senate shall, in the Presence of the Senate and House of Representatives, open all the Certificates, *and the Votes shall then be counted.*" But who was to do the counting? The House was Democratic, the Senate Republican; neither would agree to allow the other to do the job. Finally, on January 29, 1877, scarcely a month before inauguration day, Congress created an Electoral Commission to decide the disputed cases. The commission consisted of five senators (three Republicans and two Democrats), five representatives (three Democrats and two Republicans), and five justices of the Supreme Court (two Democrats, two Republicans, and one "independent" judge, David Davis). Since it was a foregone conclusion that the others would vote for their party no matter what the evidence,

Davis would presumably swing the balance in the interest of fairness.

Unfortunately at this crucial moment, the Illinois legislature elected Davis senator! He had to resign from the commission. Since, in those partisan times, independents were rare even on the Supreme Court, no neutral was available to replace him. The vacancy went to Associate Justice Joseph P. Bradley of New Jersey, a Republican.

Evidence presented before the commission revealed a disgraceful picture of election shenanigans. On the one hand, in all three disputed states Democrats had clearly cast a majority of the votes; on the other, it was equally unquestionable that many Negroes had been forcibly prevented from voting.

The sordid truth was that both sides had been at fault in each of the states. Lew Wallace, a northern politician later famous as the author of the novel *Ben Hur,* visited Louisiana and Florida shortly after the election. "It is terrible to see the extent to which all classes go in their determination to win," he wrote his wife from Florida. "Money and intimidation can obtain the oath of white men as well as black to any required statement. . . . If we win, our methods are subject to impeachment for possible fraud. If the enemy win, it is the same thing." The governor of Louisiana was reported willing to sell his state's electoral votes for $200,000. The Florida election board was supposed to have offered itself to Tilden for the same price. "That seems to be the standard figure," Tilden remarked ruefully.

Most modern authorities take the view that in a fair election the Republicans would have carried South Carolina and Louisiana, but that Florida would have gone to Tilden, thus giving him the election by 188 electoral votes to 181. In the last analysis, this opinion has been arrived at simply by counting white and black heads: Negroes were in the majority in South Carolina and Louisiana. Amid the excitement and confusion of early 1877, however, even a Solomon would have been hard pressed to judge rightly amid the mass of rumors, lies, and contradictory statements, and the Electoral Commission was not composed of Solomons. Although shaken by the news of Da-

vis' election to the Senate, the Democrats had some hopes that Justice Bradley would be sympathetic to their case, for he was known to be opposed to harsh reconstruction policies. On the eve of the commission's decision in the Florida controversy, he was apparently ready to vote in favor of Tilden. But the Republicans subjected him to tremendous political pressure. When he read his opinion on February 8, it was for Hayes. Thus, by a vote of 8 to 7, the commission awarded Florida's electoral votes to the Republicans.

The rest of the proceedings were routine. Vote after vote, both upon details and in the final decisions in the other cases, went exactly according to party lines. The atmosphere of judicial inquiry and deliberation was a façade. With the spitefulness common to rejected suitors, the Democrats assailed Bradley until, as the New York *Times* put it, he seemed like "a middle-aged St. Sebastian, stuck full of Democratic darts." Unlike Sebastian, however, Bradley was protected against the arrows by the armor of his Republican faith. The commission completed its work, having assigned all the disputed electoral votes (including one in Oregon, where the Democratic governor had seized upon a technicality to replace a single Republican elector with a Democrat) to Hayes.

To such a level had the republic of Jefferson and John Adams descended. The American democratic tradition, shaken by the South's refusal to go along with the majority in 1860, and also by the suppression of civil rights during the rebellion, further weakened by both military intervention and the intimidation of Negroes in the South during reconstruction, seemed now completely destroyed, a mere farce. Democrats talked of not being bound by so obviously partisan a judgment. According to Tilden's campaign manager, the respected iron manufacturer Abram S. Hewitt, angry Democrats in 15 states, chiefly war veterans, were readying themselves to march on Washington to force the inauguration of Tilden. Tempers flared in Congress, where some spoke ominously of a filibuster that would prevent the recording of the electoral vote and leave the country, on March 4, with no President at all.

The Compromise of 1877

Fortunately, forces for compromise had been at work behind the scenes in Washington for some time. While northern Democrats threatened to fight to the last ditch, many southern Democrats were willing to accept Hayes if they could gain something in exchange. Nearly all the southern congressmen were more interested in ridding their section once and for all of federal interference than in electing a Democratic President. If Hayes would promise to remove the troops and allow the southern states to manage their internal affairs by themselves, these men would be sorely tempted to go along with his election. A more specialized but extremely important group consisted of the ex-Whig planters and merchants who had reluctantly abandoned the carpetbag governments and who were always uncomfortable when in alliance with the poor whites. If Hayes would agree to let the South alone and perhaps appoint a conservative southerner to his Cabinet, these men would support him willingly, eventually hoping to restore the two-party system that had been destroyed in the South during the 1850's.

Other southerners had economic interests congenial to Republican policies. The Texas and Pacific Railway Company, chartered to build a line from Marshall, Texas, to San Diego, had won wide support in the South, and friends of Hayes were quick to point out that a Republican administration would be more likely to help the Texas and Pacific than a retrenchment-minded Democratic one. Ohio Congressman James A. Garfield urged Hayes to find "some discreet way" of showing these southerners that he favored "internal improvements." Hayes replied: "Your views are so nearly the same as mine that I need not say a word."

Tradition has it that a great compromise between the sections was worked out during a dramatic, eleventh-hour meeting at the Wormley

Hotel in Washington on February 26. Actually, as C. Vann Woodward has demonstrated in his important book *Reunion and Reaction,* the negotiations were long-drawn-out and informal, and the Wormley conference was but one of many. At any rate, with the tacit support of many Democrats, the electoral vote was counted by the president of the Senate on March 2, and Hayes was declared elected, 185 votes to 184.

Like all compromises, this agreement was not entirely satisfactory, and like most, it was not honored in every detail. Hayes recalled the last troops from South Carolina and Louisiana in April. He appointed a former Confederate general, David M. Key of Tennessee, as his postmaster general and delegated to him the congenial task of finding southerners willing to serve their country as officials of a Republican administration. The new alliance of ex-Whigs and northern Republicans did not flourish, however, and the South remained solidly Democratic. The hoped-for federal aid for the Texas and Pacific did not materialize. The major significance of the compromise, one of the great intersectional political accommodations of American history, has been well summarized by Professor Woodward:

The Compromise of 1877 marked the abandonment of principles and force and a return to the traditional ways of expediency and concession. The compromise laid the political foundation for reunion. It established a new sectional truce that proved more enduring than any previous one and provided a settlement for an issue that had troubled American politics for more than a generation. It wrote an end to Reconstruction and recognized a new regime in the South. More profoundly than Constitutional amendments and wordy statutes it shaped the future of four million freedmen and their progeny for generations to come.

For most of the former slaves, this future was to be gloomy. Forgotten in the North, manipulated and then callously rejected by the South, rebuffed by the Supreme Court, voiceless in national affairs, they and their descendants were condemned in the interests of sectional harmony to lives of poverty, indignity, and little hope. Meanwhile, the rest of the United States continued its golden march toward wealth and power.

Supplementary Reading

J. G. Randall and David Donald, *The Civil War and Reconstruction* (1961), is as excellent a brief treatment of postwar readjustments as it is of the war years, but there are a number of longer studies that the student will find rewarding. Of recent works, K. M. Stampp, *The Era of Reconstruction*° (1964), and J. H. Franklin, *Reconstruction: After the Civil War*° (1961), are outstanding. E. M. Coulter, *The South During Reconstruction* (1947), presents a pro-southern point of view and is strong on economic developments. The older approach to the period, stressing the excesses of Negro-influenced governments and criticizing the Radicals, derives from the seminal work of W. A. Dunning, *Reconstruction, Political and Economic*° (1907). W. E. B. Du Bois, *Black Reconstruction in America*° (1935), militantly pro-Negro, was the pioneering counterattack against the Dunning view.

Lincoln's ideas about reconstruction are analyzed in W. B. Hesseltine, *Lincoln's Plan of Reconstruction*° (1960), and in many of the Lincoln volumes mentioned in earlier chapters. There is no satisfactory biography of Andrew Johnson: both G. F. Milton, *The Age of Hate: Andrew Johnson and the Radicals* (1930), and Milton Lomask, *Andrew Johnson: President on Trial* (1960), are far too sympathetic in approach. Of the special studies of Johnson's battle with the congressional Radicals, H. K. Beale, *The Critical Year* (1930), takes Johnson's side, but recent studies have been very critical of the President. See especially H. L. Trefousse, *The Radical Republicans: Lincoln's Vanguard for Racial Justice* (1969), E. L. McKitrick, *Andrew Johnson and Reconstruction*° (1960), LaWanda and J. H. Cox, *Politics, Principle, and Prejudice: 1865–1866* (1963), and W. R. Brock, *An American Crisis: Congress and Reconstruction*° (1963), the last a particularly thoughtful analysis of the whole era.

A number of biographies provide information helpful in understanding the Radicals. These include B. P. Thomas and H. M. Hyman, *Stanton* (1962), F. M. Brodie, *Thaddeus Stevens*° (1959), R. N. Current, *Old Thad Stevens* (1942), and H. L. Trefousse, *Benjamin Franklin Wade* (1963); J. M. McPherson, *The Struggle for Equality: Abolitionists and the Negro in the Civil War and Reconstruction*° (1964), is

°Available in paperback.

also valuable. On the Fourteenth Amendment, see Joseph James, *The Framing of the Fourteenth Amendment*° (1956); on the Fifteenth Amendment, see William Gillette, *The Right to Vote: Politics and the Passage of the Fifteenth Amendment* (1965).

Conditions in the South during reconstruction are discussed in all the works cited in the first paragraph. Of special studies, W. L. Fleming, *Civil War and Reconstruction in Alabama* (1905), and J. W. Garner, *Reconstruction in Mississippi*° (1901), represent the best of those adopting the Dunning approach. More recent "revisionist" state studies include V. L. Wharton, *The Negro in Mississippi*° (1947), C. E. Wynes, *Race Relations in Virginia* (1961), W. L. Rose, *Rehearsal for Reconstruction: The Port Royal Experiment*° (1964), and Joel Williamson, *After Slavery: The Negro in South Carolina During Reconstruction*° (1965). G. R. Bentley, *A History of the Freedmen's Bureau* (1955), discusses the work of that important organization, but see also W. S. McFeely, *Yankee Stepfather: General O. O. Howard and the Freedmen* (1968). On the Ku Klux Klan, see A. W. Trelease, *White Terror: The Ku Klux Klan Conspiracy and Southern Reconstruction* (1971).

F. A. Shannon, *The Farmer's Last Frontier*° (1945) is good on southern agriculture during reconstruction. For the growth of industry, see Broadus Mitchell, *The Rise of Cotton Mills in the South* (1921), and J. F. Stover, *The Railroads of the South* (1955).

The standard treatment of Grant's Presidency is W. B. Hesseltine, *Ulysses S. Grant: Politician* (1935), but Allan Nevins, *Hamilton Fish: The Inner History of the Grant Administration* (1936), and Matthew Josephson, *The Politicos*° (1938) contain much additional information. On the election of 1868, see C. H. Coleman, *The Election of 1868* (1933), and Stewart Mitchell, *Horatio Seymour* (1938); on the reform movement of the period within the Republican party, see E. D. Ross, *The Liberal Republican Movement* (1919), J. G. Sproat, *"The Best Men": Liberal Reformers in the Gilded Age* (1968), and M. B. Duberman, *Charles Francis Adams*° (1961). For the disputed election of 1876 and the compromise following it, consult C. V. Woodward, *Reunion and Reaction*° (1951), Harry Barnard, *Rutherford B. Hayes and His America* (1954), and Allan Nevins, *Abram S. Hewitt* (1935). P. H. Buck, *The Road to Reunion*° (1937) traces the gradual reconciliation of North and South after 1865.

Portfolio 4

The Plains Indians

The history of the plains Indians, those undying if often-killed favorites of American entertainment, is testimony that the truth is stranger and more interesting than the fiction. For about a century, from roughly 1780 to 1880, the plains tribes maintained a unique and colorful existence, living in the midst of an immense grassland, feeding upon the numberless buffalo, mobile and free on their fleet ponies. Much of the vitality of this culture, however, was a direct result of the Indians' adoption of such elements of the white man's civilization as horses, guns, and metal tools. And in the end the white man's lust for land, his diseases, and the deadly efficiency of his mechanical genius devastated the plains civilization.

Fortunately, at the height of this cultural flowering in the middle decades of the 19th century, artists such as George Catlin, Carl Bodmer, Paul Kane, Friedrich Kurz, and Alfred Jacob Miller, as well as the Indians themselves, created a vivid, accurate pictorial record of plains life. For example, Bodmer's 1832 portrait above of the Mandan chief Mato-Tope (Four Bears) is both a skillful work of art and a finely detailed reproduction of war paint patterns—even to the yellow hand painted over Mato-Tope's heart, which was meant to protect him during hand-to-hand combat.

HORSE INDIANS

In 1834 the western painter George Catlin wrote, "A Comanche on his feet is out of his element, . . . almost as awkward as a monkey on the ground, without a limb or a branch to cling to; but the moment he lays his hand upon his horse, his face even becomes handsome, and he gracefully flies away like a different being." Before the coming of the horse, the plains were populated by a few scattered tribes who found hunting buffalo on foot a risky business at best. For almost a century and a half after Coronado's trek from Mexico into the plains in the 1540's, the Spaniards were largely successful in keeping their horses out of Indian hands. But after a bloody revolt by the Pueblos in 1680 loosened Spain's grip on the Southwest, the horse spread northward rapidly. By 1780 the plains tribes were making full use of this highly efficient means of pursuing the buffalo, and the population of the region had tripled to an estimated figure of 150,000.

The elkskin painting above of a buffalo hunt is the work of a Crow artist and dates from about 1895. Three cowboys (upper left) suggest that by this time Indians no longer hunted alone.

George Catlin's painting at left, c. 1835, shows a Crow chieftain and his horse in full battle array. It is evident from Catlin's portrait why historian Walter Prescott Webb spoke of plains warriors as "The Red Knights of the Prairie."

At right is an 1862 sketch of a Cree saddle made of buffalo skin and stitched with buffalo sinew. Women's saddles had both a pommel and a cantle.

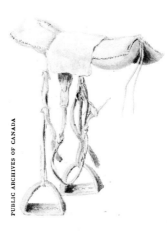

SIOUX CAMP

This remarkable photograph by J. H. C. Grabill shows a large Sioux encampment near the Pine Ridge Reservation in South Dakota. It was probably taken in March 1891 after the "battle" of Wounded Knee, in which some 150 Hunkpapa Sioux, including 44 women and 18 children, were massacred by the Seventh Cavalry. An encampment as extensive as this was rare until the plains tribes became wards of the government and were confined on

reservations. Except for special occasions—a tribal festival, a full-scale buffalo hunt, a war council—food was too scarce to permit an entire tribe to camp in one spot. The making, moving, and caring for the tepee was woman's work. In camp the men did little except feast, attend tribal councils and meetings of warrior societies, and decorate their tepees with figures and symbols based on highly valued dreams and visions and on past hunting and martial exploits.

THE NOMADIC LIFE

The plains Indian is best known as a wanderer who traveled by horse to follow the buffalo. He was indeed a nomad, but it should not be forgotten that the horse was a latecomer to the plains and that for thousands of years a few tribes had been farming the more fertile parts of the region as well as hunting buffalo. In the 18th and 19th centuries this pattern persisted. Along the upper Missouri in present-day North Dakota, for example, the Hidatsas and the Mandans continued to live in permanent earthen lodges, to farm, and to hunt buffalo only part-time, even after acquiring the horse.

But for most plains Indians farther west, such as the Arapahos, Crow, Comanches, Cheyenne, Apaches, Blackfeet, Sioux, and Kiowas, life was truly nomadic, spent ever on the move. They might pursue the roaming buffalo for hundreds of miles, taking food, clothing, and shelter with them packed on their travois. While traveling they subsisted on pemmican, an odoriferous but nourishing preserve concocted of dried meat, berries, bone marrow, and melted fat. The hunting grounds of the various tribes were only vaguely defined and intertribal contact was frequent, especially for trading purposes. On these occasions the nomads would barter their buffalo pelts and meat for corn and other agricultural products raised by the more sedentary peoples who made their homes on the fringes of the plains.

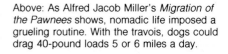

Above: As Alfred Jacob Miller's *Migration of the Pawnees* shows, nomadic life imposed a grueling routine. With the travois, dogs could drag 40-pound loads 5 or 6 miles a day.

Left: Friedrich Kurz drew these Hidatsas portaging their bullboats on the upper Missouri in 1851. The bullboat was made of buffalo hide stretched over a willow framework.

Right: A Mandan woman carrying a pack leads a loaded dog sled on which her child rides across the frozen Missouri in what is now North Dakota. A Bodmer watercolor, 1834.

SMITHSONIAN INSTITUTION

THE BUFFALO

"Again and again that morning rang out the same welcome cry of *buffalo, buffalo!* . . . At noon the plain before us was alive with thousands of buffalo—bulls, cows, and calves—all moving rapidly as we drew near. . . . In a moment I was in the midst of a cloud, half suffocated by the dust and stunned by the trampling of the flying herd; but I was drunk with the chase and cared for nothing but the buffalo." That was how historian Francis Parkman was affected by a buffalo hunt in 1846, the year before H. G. Hines painted the scene below. For Parkman the hunt was an exhilarating experience, but for the plains Indian it was the central act of his life, combining necessity, passion, and sport. Alfred Jacob Miller's *Yell of Triumph* (right) captures something of this feeling.

Once killed and butchered, there was little the buffalo did not provide. From the carcass came fresh meat for feasting and dried meat for lean times. The skin provided blankets, moccasins, mittens, shirts, leggings, dresses, and underclothes—and a "canvas" for the artist. Sinew was turned into thread and bowstrings; bones into farming tools; horns into cups, ladles, and spoons; the stomach into a water bottle. Even vanity was served. The rough side of a buffalo tongue was used as a hairbrush and the oily fat became a plains hair tonic.

ROYAL ONTARIO MUSEUM, UNIVERSITY OF TORONTO

RELIGION AND THE HUNT

In common with many primitive peoples, the plains Indians drew no clear distinction between the natural and the supernatural. They paid as much attention to the one as to the other, believing that all things had spirits and that these spirits controlled the natural world. No aspect of plains life reflects this harmonious fusion of natural and supernatural better than the buffalo hunt.

A hunt was as carefully organized and as skillfully managed as a modern military operation. In early spring the various bands of the tribe would gather at a predetermined place. There the chiefs and the elders convened a council and deliberated their strategy and tactics. To ensure that plans were followed precisely, one of the warrior societies policed the hunt while scouts kept tabs on the movements of the herd. Once the "battle" was joined, the animals were slaughtered until all needs were met. Little seemed left to chance.

Yet however effective and well organized the hunters were, they believed that without the assistance of the spirits the herds would not come within range, the hunters would lack courage and skill at the crucial moment, and ultimately the harmonious relationship between the shaggy "four-leggeds" and the "two-leggeds" would be destroyed. To insure the overall success of the hunt, the tribesmen therefore devoted as much attention to religious ceremonies and "medicine signs" as they did to planning, discipline, and the perfection of their hunting skills.

Devices for luring the buffalo varied from tribe to tribe. Carl Bodmer's watercolor of Assiniboin "magic" (lower left) was painted in 1834.

Of grimmer composition is the Mandan "medicine sign" for attracting the herds reproduced at the right.

For centuries before the plains Indians obtained the horse, a favorite method of buffalo hunting was impounding, as illustrated below by Canadian artist Paul Kane in 1845.

Bodmer's painting of a Mandan Bull Society dance, held periodically to draw the herds close to the village, reflects the plains Indians' intense feelings toward the buffalo.

AFTER THE HUNT

Plains life was not all buffalo hunting. There were days to be spent around the domestic hearth, children to be raised, ceremonies to be performed, games to be played. Work, other than hunting and making war, was generally for women. Education was in the school of experience—a boy learned his role by riding alongside his father, while a girl's mother was her tutor in the arts of the tepee. Elaborate rituals at the onset of puberty were rare, although in most tribes young men did go off on a lonely vigil in search of a vision to guide them. A young man could marry when he possessed the requisite number of horses to give to the girl's family as tokens of his esteem. Courtship largely consisted of the lover playing a flute to his sequestered sweetheart. There was no elaborate marriage ceremony in the modern sense, although custom demanded certain ceremonial observances. The bride, while very much the servant of her husband, was not considered an inferior being.

Hunting and war were in part sport, but they did not exhaust the plains Indians' delight in recreation. Horse racing and dice gave free rein to their love of chance; lacrosse and foot races provided tests of their athletic skills; storytelling presented the central myths of their culture; and clowning gave vent to a Rabelaisian wit.

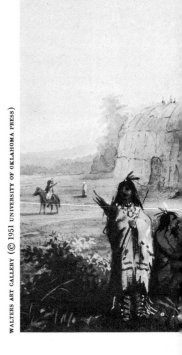

Not all horse-riding, buffalo-hunting plains Indians lived in tepees. The earthen lodges of the Mandans (at left, by Miller, and opposite, by Bodmer) each housed several families, a few favorite horses, a number of dogs, and a wide range of equipment for cooking, hunting, and ceremonial observances. The plains tribes enjoyed rough stick and ball games such as lacrosse (sketches on this page) and shinny, an early rugged form of field hockey favored by plains women. But naturally enough, as Paul Kane's painting below of a Blackfoot horse race suggests, equestrian games took the spotlight. Since Indians loved a sporting bet, games were carefully refereed to ensure fair play.

THE ROAD TO GLORY

War was the greatest game of all; it was also the plains Indian's career, hobby, and the touchstone of his honor and prestige. He was told from childhood, as a Blackfoot litany put it, that "It is bad to live to be old. Better to die young fighting bravely in battle." Young boys listened to the elaborate recountings of the valor of a successful war party or to the derisive mocking directed at a man unlucky enough to be accounted a coward as though they were hearing sermons on heaven and hell. They longed for the day when they could join a warrior society and embrace its Spartan discipline. In their teens they fasted alone in the hope of seeing a vision of the spirit of their adoptive father (usually an animal or an impressive natural phenomenon). This spirit would confirm the warrior's identity and give instructions for the "medicine bundle" that was to protect him in battle.

On occasion tribal war did have an economic motive, as in the defense of hunting grounds, but its usual objective was glory and all its trappings. Honor was quantified by the system of counting coups, which were won not just by mere slaughter, but also by such feats as stealing an enemy's favorite horse or touching an armed foe with the hand or with nothing more wounding than a decorated coup stick.

Above: About 1832 Carl Bodmer did a facsimile of an earlier Indian painting of a hand-to-hand fight with a trapper, a combat rating the highest coup.

Left: George Catlin's 1850 drawing shows the virtuoso horsemanship of a Comanche who, hanging only by his heel, unleashes a rapid-fire volley of arrows.

Opposite: Among the artifacts in Bodmer's print is a coup stick, complete with feathers for the number of coups, above the arrow at right. The edged weapon at right is a type of tomahawk, and at lower center is a war shield decorated with "medicine."

P4-XVII

This Apache skin painting shows a blending of plains and southwestern cultural elements. The ceremony in progress is a girls' puberty rite, rare in the northern plains but much observed in the Southwest. The rest of the tribe watches from in front of their tepees (a plains element) while the girls, paired with older women who are their guardians and accompanied by posturing medicine men (wearing southwestern-style headdresses), perform a dance around the purifying fire.

Alfred Jacob Miller's painting above, *Snake Indian Council* (c. 1840), pictures a tribal pow-wow as a dignified, ceremonious affair.

LOVERS OF CEREMONY

Few people have been as self-sufficient as the plains Indians while at the same time professing to be so dependent upon forces outside themselves. The plains resembled the ocean (a metaphor repeatedly appearing in the accounts of white explorers)—vast and mysterious, inspiring both humility and a feeling of what might be called "cosmic togetherness." Far from seeing himself as master of his environment, the Indian felt adrift on a great sea of whispering prairie grass, endlessly searching for the life-giving buffalo that symbolized for him and his people the miraculous world of nature.

Under such circumstances it is hardly surprising that the plains Indian believed himself to be dwelling within a web of supernatural powers. His survival depended upon maintaining contact with these powers; thus he became a seeker of visions and a practicer of rituals, devoted to ceremonies that would bring him into partnership with the cosmos. The primacy of this relationship helps explain the general lack of scientific curiosity in the plains cultures, but it also accounts for an estimable sense of humility and of awe.

MUSEUM OF THE AMERICAN INDIAN, HEYE FOUNDATION

A Shoshoni skin painting that dates from the 1880's portrays in careful detail a ritualistic sun dance as seen from above a tepee.

An Indian Horse Dance.

ART AND ARTIFACTS

The artifacts of the plains Indian, like so much else in his culture, combined art with utility. Textiles were poorly developed, pottery limited, and wood-carving and stone sculpture almost absent, all for good reasons—cotton was unknown, pottery easily broken in transit, trees few and far between, and stone too heavy to transport. But when it came to making clothes and utensils decorated with quills, beads, paint, feathers, and the fur from that all-purpose beast the buffalo, the plains artisan was in his element. The women dressed and prepared buffalo hides, and then, from beaded moccasin to feathered headdress, made the tribe's clothing, such as the girl's dress at the right. They also cut, fitted, and sewed buffalo hides to make the covering for the tepee, but it was the man's prerogative to decorate the tepee's exterior with his own paintings. The painting reproduced opposite, by Kills Two, an Oglala Sioux, is a striking demonstration of the skill and technical virtuosity of these plains artists.

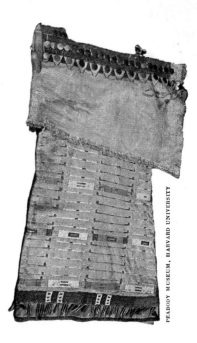

The examples below of porcupine quillwork include an Arapaho disk used as a tepee ornament, a Sioux knife sheath, a quill pouch made from an elk bladder, and a decorated tobacco pouch.

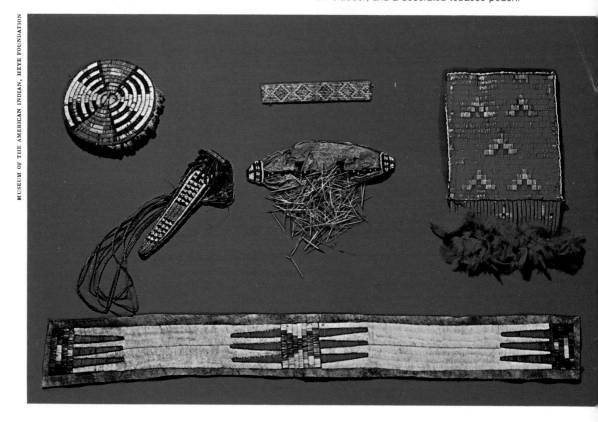

CHANGING WAYS

In just about 50 years, from 1840 to 1890, the plains civilization reached its apogee and then plunged to the verge of extinction. In his 1885 painting *Caught in the Act,* Charles Russell, the "cowboy artist," depicted a starving Indian family reduced to stealing ranchers' cattle. By this time the plains tribes had suffered the ravages of the white man's diseases, the debasing effects of his whiskey, the harassment of his army, and the grim hard-

ship resulting from his senseless slaughter of the buffalo. Having smashed the Indian's
way of life beyond repair, the government confined him to the reservation. Just before
committing suicide, Satanta, a Kiowa chief, spoke for all the plains tribes when he said, ''I
don't want to settle. I love to roam the prairie. . . . These soldiers cut down my timber,
they kill my buffalo, and when I see that, it feels as if my heart would burst with sorrow.''

Reproduced above, in a detail, is a heroic Sioux version of the Battle of the Little Big Horn, in which Crazy Horse (center) leads the slaughter of Custer's men. L.A. Huffman's portrait of the Cheyenne scout Red Panther (opposite) offers testimony to the true nobility of the "noble red man."

THE LEGACY

Although by the end of the 19th century the civilization of the plains tribesmen was "fast traveling to the shades of their fathers, towards the setting sun," the very conquerors who had been unable to live in peace with the Indians surrounded their memory with romance and myth. In defeat the Indian became the "noble savage"; Custer's Last Stand will be remembered as long as Gettysburg or Pearl Harbor. Yet the real importance of the plains Indian stems from his attitude toward life, not merely from his courage and his war skills.

In 1947 John Collier, former Commissioner of Indian Affairs, spoke out for another interpretation of Indian culture. "They had what the world has lost," Collier wrote, ". . . the ancient, lost reverence and passion for human personality, joined with the ancient, lost reverence and passion for the earth and its web of life. . . . They had . . . this power for living . . . as world-view and self-view, as tradition and institution, as practical philosophy dominating their societies, and as an art supreme. . . ."

17

An Age of Exploitation

As Americans turned from fighting and making weapons to more constructive occupations, a surge of activity transformed agriculture, trade, manufacturing, mining, and communication. Immigration increased rapidly. Cities grew in size and number, exerting upon every aspect of life an influence at least as pervasive as that exercised on earlier generations by the frontier. More and more Americans were abandoning the farm for the town and city, supporting themselves by laboring at machines or by scratching out accounts in ledgers, yet such was the expansive force of the time that agriculture did not actually decline. Farm production rose to new heights, and rural society was invigorated by new marketing methods and by the increased use of machinery. At the same time, railroad construction was stimulating and unifying the economy, helping to make possible still larger and more efficient industrial and agricultural enterprises. A continuing flow of gold and silver from western mines excited people's imaginations and their avarice too, while petroleum, the "black gold" discovered in Pennsylvania shortly before the war, gave rise to a new industry soon to become one of the most important in the nation. These developments amounted to more than a mere change of scale; they altered the structure of society.

"Root, Hog, or Die"

For nearly a decade after Appomattox, boom conditions existed everywhere outside the South. Americans seemed to have abandoned all restraint in a mad race for personal gain.

The immense resources of the United States, combined with certain aspects of the American character, such as the high value assigned to work and achievement, made the people strongly materialistic. From colonial times onward, they had assumed that prosperity was the natural state of things and shown an inordinate respect for wealth. "When he asked what a man was worth," Henry Steele Commager writes in describing the typical 19th-century American, "he meant material worth, and he was impatient of any but the normal yardstick."

Although the Civil War had many nonmaterialistic aspects—love of country, hatred of slavery, devotion to democratic principles—it greatly encouraged the glorification of material values by demonstrating the relationship between economic power and political and military success. The North's capacity to produce the tools of war had helped preserve the Union; the role of businessmen and manufacturers in winning the struggle was clear to every soldier from General Grant to the lowliest private.

During the emotional letdown that followed the war, Americans became even more enamored of material values. They were tired of sacrifice, eager to act for themselves. Except in their attitude toward the South, still psychologically "outside" the United States, they came to believe more strongly than ever before in a governmental policy of noninterference, or laissez faire. " 'Things regulate themselves' . . . means, of course, that God regulates them by his general laws," wrote Professor Francis Bowen of Harvard in his *American Political Economy* (1870). "The progress of the country," said another economist, "is independent of legislation."

Impressed by such logic, Americans, always imbued with the entrepreneurial spirit and never especially noted for their sophistication, taste, or interest in preserving the resources of the country, now tolerated the grossest kind of waste and seemed to care little about corruption in high places, so long as no one interfered with their own pursuit of profit. The writer Mark Twain, raised in an earlier era, called this a "Gilded Age," dazzling on the surface, base metal below. A later student, Vernon L. Parrington, named the period the "Great Barbecue," a time when everyone rushed to get his share of the national inheritance like hungry picnickers crowding around the savory roast at one of the big political outings common in those years. Twain, Parrington, and other critics took too dark a view of the era. Never, perhaps, did the American people display more vigor, more imagination, or greater confidence in themselves and the future of their country. Indeed, in his novel *The Gilded Age*, written with Charles Dudley Warner, Twain portrayed this aspect of the period along with its cheapness and corruption.

However, certain intellectual currents strengthened the exploitative drives of the people. Charles Darwin's *Origin of Species* was published in 1859, and by the seventies his theory of evolution was beginning to influence opinion in the United States. That nature had ordained a kind of inevitable progress, governed by the natural selection of those individual organisms best adapted to survive in a particular environment, seemed eminently reasonable to most Americans, for it fitted well with their own experiences. Some thinkers extended Darwin's strictly biological concept of the survival of the fittest to the activities of men in society, finding in this "Social Darwinism" further justification for aggressive and acquisitive activities. If left to themselves, unhampered by government regulations or other restrictions, the most efficient would "survive" in every field of human endeavor, be it farming, manufacturing, or even—according to one of the most enthusiastic exponents of the theory, William Graham Sumner—teaching Yale undergraduates.

"Professor," one student asked Sumner, "don't you believe in any government aid to industries?" "No!" Sumner replied, "it's root, hog, or die." The student persisted: "Suppose some professor of political science came along and took your job away from you. Wouldn't you be sore?" "Any other professor is welcome to try," Sumner answered promptly. "If he gets my job, it is my fault. My business is to teach the subject so well that no one can take the job away from me."

"Let the buyer beware; that covers the whole business," the sugar magnate Henry O. Havemeyer explained to an investigating committee. "You cannot wet-nurse people from the time they are born until the time they die. They have to wade in and get stuck, and that is the way men are educated."

Few men of practical affairs, and certainly not Havemeyer, went so far as Sumner. Few, indeed, were directly influenced by Darwin's ideas, which did not percolate down to the middle-class mass until late in the century. Most eagerly accepted any aid they could get from the government, many were active in philanthropy, some felt a deep sense of social responsibility. Nevertheless, most were sincere individualists. They believed in open competition, being convinced that the nation would best prosper if everyone were free to seek his personal fortune by his own methods. With such ideas ascendant, exploitation and complacency became the hallmarks of the postwar decades.

The Plains Indians

The force of this drive to possess, combined with monumental self-satisfaction, is well illustrated by the fate of the Indians after the Civil War. For 250 years they had been driven back steadily, yet on the eve of the Civil War they were still free to roam over roughly half of the area of the United States, a region much of which was then considered practically worthless—"the Great American Desert." By the time of Hayes's inauguration the Indians had been shattered as an independent people; in another decade the survivors were penned up on reservations, with the government committed to a policy of extinguishing their nomadic way of life. To have done otherwise, a Wyoming editor proclaimed, would have been "mawkish sentimentalism . . . unworthy of the age."

In 1860 the survivors of most of the eastern tribes were living docilely on reservations in what is now Oklahoma. Out in California the forty-niners had made short work of the local tribes. Elsewhere in the West—in the deserts of the Great Basin between the Sierras and the Rockies, in the mountains themselves, and on the semiarid, grass-covered plains between the Rockies and the edge of white civilization in eastern Kansas and Nebraska—nearly a quarter of a million Indians dominated the land. By far the most important lived on the High Plains. From the Blackfeet of southwestern Canada and the Sioux of Minnesota and the Dakotas to the Cheyenne of Colorado and Wyoming and the Comanche of northern Texas, these tribes possessed a generally uniform culture, although they differed considerably in temperament and language. All lived by hunting the hulking American bison, or buffalo, which ranged over the plains by the millions. The buffalo provided the Indians with food, clothing, even shelter, for the famous Indian tepee was covered with hides. On the treeless plains, dried buffalo dung was used for fuel. The buffalo was also an important symbol in Indian religion.

Although they seemed the very epitome of

freedom, pride, and self-reliance, they had already begun to fall under the sway of the white man. They eagerly adopted the products of the more technically advanced culture—cloth, metal tools, weapons, cheap decorations—but the most important thing the whites gave them was the horse. The geological record shows that the genus *Equus* was native to America, but it had become extinct in the Western Hemisphere long before Cortés brought the first modern horses to America in the 16th century. Multiplying rapidly thereafter, the animals soon roamed wild from Texas to the Argentine. By the 18th century the Indians of the plains had acquired them in large numbers and had made them a vital part of their culture. Horses thrived on the plains and so did their masters. Mounted Indians could run down the buffalo, their chief food supply, instead of stalking them on foot. They could roam more widely over the country and fight more effectively too. They could acquire and transport more possessions and increase the size of their tepees, for horses could drag heavy loads, heaped on A-shaped frames (called *travois* by the French), whereas earlier Indians had only dogs to depend on as pack animals. The frames of the travois, when disassembled, served as poles for tepees. The Indians also adopted modern weapons, both the cavalry sword, which they especially admired, and the rifle. Both added still more to their effectiveness as hunters and fighters. However, like the white man's liquor and diseases, to which they also quickly succumbed, horses and guns caused problems. The buffalo herds began to diminish, and warfare became bloodier and more frequent.

In a familiar, tragic pattern the majority of the western tribes greeted the first whites to enter their domains in a friendly fashion. As late as the 1820's and 1830's, white hunters and trappers ranged freely over most of the West, trading with the Indians and often taking Indian wives. Settlers pushing cross-country toward Oregon in the 1840's also met with relatively little trouble, although at times bands of braves on the warpath molested small groups or indulged in petty thievery that the migrants found annoying.

But after the start of the gold rush the whites began to undermine the Indian empire in the West. The need to link the East with California meant that the tribes would have to be pushed aside. Deliberately, the government in Washington prepared the way. In 1851 Thomas Fitzpatrick, an experienced mountain man, a founder of the Rocky Mountain Fur Company, scout for the first large group of settlers to Oregon in 1841 and for General Kearny's forces in their march to Santa Fe and California during the Mexican War, and now an Indian agent, summoned a great "council" of the tribes. About 10,000 Indians, representing nearly all the plains tribes, gathered that September at Horse Creek, 37 miles east of Fort Laramie, in what is now Wyoming. Fitzpatrick was an intelligent and sensible man whom the Indians respected. He had recently married a girl who was half Indian. At Horse Creek he persuaded each tribe to accept definite limits to its hunting grounds. For example, the Sioux nations were to keep north of the Platte, and the Cheyenne and Arapaho were to confine themselves to the Colorado foothills. In return, the Indians were promised gifts and various annual payments. This policy, known as "concentration," was designed to cut down on intertribal warfare and—far more important—to enable the government to negotiate separately with each tribe. It was the classic strategy of divide and conquer.

Although it made a mockery of diplomacy to treat with Indian tribes as though they were European powers, the United States maintained that each was a sovereign nation, to be dealt with as an equal in solemn treaties. Both sides knew that this was not the case. When Indians agreed to meet in council, they were tacitly admitting defeat. They seldom drove very hard bargains or broke off negotiations. Moreover, tribal chiefs had only limited power; young braves frequently refused to respect agreements made by their elders. On the other hand, the United States failed dismally to keep its own pledges.

In Indian relations even more than in most fields, 19th-century Americans displayed a grave lack of talent for administration. After 1849 the Department of the Interior supposedly had charge of tribal affairs. Most of its agents were corrupt placeholders who systematically cheated the Indians. To cite a single example, one agent, heavily involved in mining operations on the side, systematically diverted supplies intended for his charges to his private ventures. When an inspector looked into his records, he sold him shares in a mine. That worthy, in turn, protected himself by sharing some of the loot with the son of the commissioner of Indian Affairs. Also the army, influential in the West as long as the Indians were capable of fighting, continually made trouble for the civilian authorities. Officers squabbled frequently with Indian agents over policy. Congress aggravated the situation by its niggardliness in appropriating funds.

Indian Wars

Worst of all, the government and the people showed little interest in honoring treaties with Indians. No sooner had the Kansas–Nebraska Bill become law when tribes like the Kansa, Omaha, Pawnee, and Yankton Sioux began to feel pressure for further concessions of territory. By 1860 most of Kansas and Nebraska had been cleared; the Indians had lost all but 1.5 million of their 19-odd million acres. A gold rush into Colorado in 1859 sent thousands of greedy prospectors across the plains to drive the Cheyenne and Arapaho from land guaranteed them in 1851. Other trouble developed in the Sioux country. Thus it happened that in 1862, after federal troops had been pulled out of the West for service against the Confederacy, most of the plains Indians rose up against the whites. For the next five years, intermittent but bloody clashes kept the whole area in a state of alarm.

This was guerrilla warfare, with all its horrors and treachery. In 1864 a party of Colorado militia fell upon an unsuspecting Cheyenne community at Sand Creek and killed an estimated 450. "Kill and scalp all, big and little," Colonel J. M. Chivington, a minister in private life, told his men. "Nits make lice." As a white observer described the scene, "They were scalped, their brains knocked out; the men used their knives, ripped open women, clubbed little children, knocked them in the head with their guns, beat their brains out, mutilated their bodies in every sense of the word." General Nelson A. Miles called this "Chivington Massacre" the "foulest and most unjustifiable crime in the annals of America," but it was no worse than many incidents in earlier conflicts with Indians or than what was later to occur in guerrilla wars involving American troops in the Philippines and (more recently) in Vietnam.

In turn the Indians wiped out dozens of isolated white families, ambushed small parties, and fought many successful skirmishes against troops and militia. They achieved their most notable triumph in December 1866, when the Oglala Sioux, under their great chief Red Cloud, completely wiped out a party of 82 soldiers under Captain W. J. Fetterman. Red Cloud fought ruthlessly, but only when goaded by the construction of the Bozeman Trail, a road through the heart of the Sioux hunting grounds in southern Montana.

Finally, in 1867, the government evolved a new strategy. The "concentration" policy had evidently not gone far enough. All the plains Indians would be confined to two small reservations, one in the Black Hills of Dakota Territory, the other in Oklahoma, and forced to abandon their wild habits and become farmers. At two great conclaves held in 1867 and 1868 at Medicine Lodge Creek and Fort Laramie, the principal chiefs yielded to the government's demands.

However, many of the tribesmen refused to abide by these agreements. With their whole way of life at stake, they raged again across the plains, like a prairie fire and almost as destructive. General Philip Sheridan, Grant's great cavalry commander, explained the situation accurately: "We took away their country and their means of support, broke up their mode of living, their habits of life, introduced disease and decay among them, and it was for this and against this that they made war. Could anyone expect less?"

That a relative handful of "savages," without central leadership or plan, could hold off the cream of the army, battle-hardened in the Civil War, can be explained by the character of the vast, trackless country and the ineptness of most American military commanders. Indian leadership was also poor in that few of the chiefs were capable of organizing a campaign or following up an advantage, but the Indians made superb guerrillas. Every observer called them the best horse fighters in the world. Armed with stubby, powerful bows capable of driving an arrow clear through a bull buffalo, they were a fair match for troops equipped with carbines and Colt revolvers. Expertly they led pursuers into traps, swept down on unsuspecting supply details, stole up on small parties the way a mountain lion stalks a grazing lamb. They could sometimes be rounded up, as Sheridan herded the tribes of the Southwest into Indian Territory in 1869, but once the troops withdrew, braves began to melt away into the emptiness of the surrounding grasslands. The distinction between "treaty" Indians, who had agreed to live on the new reservations, and the "nontreaty" variety shifted almost from day to day. Trouble flared here one week, next week somewhere else, perhaps 500 miles away. No less an authority than General William Tecumseh Sherman testified that a mere 50 Indians could often "checkmate" 3,000 soldiers. The expense of military operations was enormous, considering the meager results. It cost $2 million a year to maintain a single regiment on the plains, and according to one estimate, the federal government spent a million dollars for each Indian actually killed in battle. Moreover, the continuing bloodshed angered both western settlers and eastern humanitarians.

If one concedes that no one could reverse the direction of history or stop the invasion of Indian lands, then some version of the "small reservation" policy would probably have been the best solution to the problem. If the Indians had been given a reasonable amount of land and adequate subsidies and had been allowed to maintain their way of life, they might have accepted the situation and ceased to harry the whites. But whatever chance the policy had was greatly weakened by the government's maladministration of

Indian affairs. Indian agents in the field were required to drive off trespassers, confiscate liquor found on the reservations, and keep the Indians in line, but they had no means of enforcement under their command. An "Indian Ring" in the Department of the Interior, much like the "Whiskey Ring" and the other rapacious gangs in Washington, systematically stole funds and supplies intended for the reservation Indians. "No branch of the national government is so spotted with fraud, so tainted with corruption, so utterly unworthy of a free and enlightened government, as this Indian Bureau," Republican Congressman James A. Garfield charged in 1869.

About this time a Yale paleontologist, Professor Othniel C. Marsh, who wished to dig for fossils on the Sioux reservation, asked Red Cloud for permission to enter his domain. The chief agreed on condition that Marsh, whom the Indians called "Big Bone Chief," take back with him samples of the moldy flour and beef that government agents were supplying to his people. Appalled by what he saw on the reservation, Marsh took the rotten supplies directly to President Grant and prepared a list of charges against the agents. General Sherman, in overall command of the Indian country, claimed in 1875: "We could settle Indian troubles in an hour, but Congress wants the patronage of the Indian bureau, and the bureau wants the appropriations without any of the trouble of the Indians themselves."

Grant, well-intentioned as usual, wanted to place the reservations under army control, but even the Indians opposed this. In areas around army camps Indians fared no better than on the reservations. A quartermaster in the Apache country in New Mexico sequestered 12,000 pounds of corn from the meager supplies set aside for Indian relief. Some soldiers gave liquor to the Indians, and according to one late-19th-century historian, "officers at those camps where the Indians were fed habitually used their official position to break the chastity of Indian women." In 1869 Congress created a distinguished nonpolitical Board of Indian Commissioners to oversee Indian affairs, but the bureaucrats in Washington stymied the commissioners at every turn. "Their recommendations were ignored . . . gross breaking of the law was winked at, and . . . many matters were not submitted to them at all," the biographer of one commissioner has written. "They decided that their task was as useless as it was irritating."

Nevertheless, the majority of the Indians might have eventually submitted had they been allowed to hold even the lands granted them under the "small reservation" policy, for they knew they could never really eject the whites from their country. This was not to be. Gold was discovered in the Black Hills in 1874. By the next winter thousands of miners had invaded the reserved area. Already alarmed by the approach of crews building the Northern Pacific Railroad, the Sioux once again went on the warpath. Joining with nontreaty tribes to the west, they concentrated in the region of the Bighorn River, in southern Montana Territory. The summer of 1876 saw three columns of troops in the field against them. The commander of one of these, General Alfred H. Terry, sent a small detachment of the Seventh Cavalry under Colonel George A. Custer ahead with orders to locate the Indians' camp and then block their escape route into the inaccessible Bighorn Mountains.

Custer was a vain and rash commander, and vanity and rashness were especially grave handicaps in Indian fighting. Grossly underestimating the number of the Indians, he decided to attack directly with his tiny force of 264 men. At the Little Bighorn he found himself surrounded by 2,500 Sioux under Rain-in-the-Face, Crazy Horse, and Sitting Bull. He and his men fought bravely, but every one of them died on the field. Because it was so one-sided, "Custer's Last Stand" (June 26, 1876) was not a typical battle, although it may be taken as symbolic of all the Indian warfare of the period in the sense that it was characterized by bravery, foolhardiness, and a tragic waste of life. The battle greatly heartened the Indians; however, it did not gain them their cause, for that autumn, short of rations and hard pressed by overwhelming numbers of soldiers, they surrendered and returned to the reservation.

Destruction of Tribal Life

Thereafter, the plains fighting slackened. For this the destruction of the buffalo rather than the effectiveness of the army was chiefly responsible. An estimated 13 to 15 million head had roamed the plains in the mid-sixties. Then the slaughter began. Thousands were butchered to feed the gangs of laborers engaged in building the Union Pacific Railroad, and thousands more fell before the guns of sportsmen. Buffalo hunting became a fad, and a brisk demand developed for mounted buffalo heads and for buffalo rugs. Railroads ran excursion trains for hunters; even the shameful practice of gunning down the beasts directly from the cars was allowed. In 1871–72 the Grand Duke Alexis of Russia engaged in a gigantic hunt, supported by "Buffalo Bill" Cody, most famous of the professional buffalo killers, the Seventh United States Cavalry under General Sheridan, and hundreds of Indians.

The discovery in 1871 of a way to make commercial use of buffalo hides completed the tragedy. In the next three years about 9 million were killed; after another decade the animals were almost extinct. No more efficient way could have been found for destroying the plains Indians. The disappearance of the bison left them starving, homeless, purposeless.

In 1887 Congress passed the Dawes Severalty Act, designed to put an end to tribal life and

Buffalo robes for carriages and sleighs were enormously popular in the eastern states, as were buffalo overcoats that sold for less than $20. Hides were also widely used as belts on power-driven machinery. (Bella C. Landauer Collection, New-York Historical Society.)

After his surrender in 1886, the celebrated Chiricahua Apache Geronimo posed with a fellow chief, Naiche (left), at an army post in Arizona Territory. Geronimo and the Chiricahuas were eventually settled in Oklahoma. (Museum of the American Indian, Heye Foundation.)

convert the Indians to the white way of living. Tribal lands were split up into small units, each head of a family being given a quarter section (160 acres). In order to keep speculators from wresting it from the Indians during the period of adjustment, this land could not be disposed of for 25 years. Indians who accepted allotments, took up residence "separate and apart from any tribe," and "adopted the habits of civilized life" were granted United States citizenship. The government also set aside funds for educating and training the Indians. Now that their spirit had been broken, many persons became interested in helping them, stimulated by books like Helen Hunt Jackson's aptly titled *A Century of Dishonor* (1881), a somewhat romantic but essentially just denunciation of past policy.

Although intended as a humane reform, the Dawes Act had disastrous results. Devised in an age that knew almost nothing about anthropology or social structure, it assumed that Indi-ans could be transformed into small agricultural capitalists by an act of Congress. It shattered what was left of the Indians' culture without enabling them to adapt to white ways. Moreover, unscrupulous white men systematically tricked the tribesmen into leasing their allotments for a pittance, while local authorities often taxed Indian lands at excessive rates. In 1934, after about 86 million of the 138 million acres assigned under the Dawes Act had passed into white hands, the government went back to a policy of encouraging tribal ownership of Indian lands, but by that time irreparable damage had been done.

By 1887 the tribes of the mountains and deserts beyond the plains had also given up the fight. Typical of the heartlessness of the government's treatment of these peoples was that afforded the Nez Percé of Oregon and Idaho who were led by the remarkable Chief Joseph. After outwitting federal troops in a campaign that ranged across more than a thousand miles of rough country,

Joseph finally surrendered in October 1877. He and his people were then uprooted from their lands and settled on "the malarial bottoms of the Indian Territory" in far-off Oklahoma. The last Indians to abandon the unequal battle were the bitter, relentless Apaches of the Southwest, who carried on the fight until the capture of their fanatical chief, Geronimo, in 1886.

The Plight of Minorities

Americans shunted the Indians aside merely because they stood in their way. Other minorities were treated with equal callousness and contempt in the postwar decades. That the South would deal harshly with the former slaves once federal control was relaxed probably should have been expected, although men like Governor Wade Hampton of South Carolina had piously promised to respect Negro civil rights. "We . . . will secure to every citizen, the lowest as well as the highest, black as well as white, full and equal protection in the enjoyment of all his rights under the Constitution," Hampton said in 1877. Hampton's pledge, repeated by supposedly honorable southerners in other states, was not kept. President Hayes had urged Negroes to trust the southern whites. A new "Era of Good Feelings" had dawned, he announced after making a goodwill tour of the South shortly after his inauguration. By December 1877 he had been sadly disillusioned. "By state legislation, by frauds, by intimidation, and by violence of the most atrocious character, colored citizens have been deprived of the right of suffrage," he wrote in his diary. However, although he had written earlier, "My task was to wipe out the color line," he did nothing to remedy the situation except, as his biographer Harry Barnard says, "to scold the South and threaten action." Frederick Douglass called Hayes's policy "sickly conciliation."

Hayes's successors in the 1880's did no better. "Time is the only cure" for the Negro problem, President Garfield said, thus confessing that he had no policy at all. President Arthur gave federal patronage to extreme anti-Negro groups in an effort to split the Democratic South. In President Cleveland's day the Negro had scarcely a friend in high places, North or South. In 1887 Cleveland explained to a correspondent why he opposed "mixed schools." Expert opinion, the President said, believed "that separate schools were of much more benefit for the colored people."

Hayes, Garfield, and Arthur were Republicans, Cleveland a Democrat; party made little difference as far as the Negro was concerned. Both parties subscribed to hypocritical statements about equality and constitutional rights, but neither did anything to implement them. For a time blacks were not totally disfranchised in the South. Rival white factions tried to manipulate Negro votes in their struggle for power, and corruption flourished as widely in the South as in the machine-dominated wards of the northern cities.

In the nineties, however, the southern states, led by Mississippi, began to deprive blacks of the vote systematically. Poll taxes, often cumulative, raised a formidable economic barrier, one that also disfranchised many poor white men. Literacy tests completed the work; a number of states provided a loophole for illiterate whites by including an "understanding" clause whereby an illiterate person could qualify by demonstrating an ability to explain the meaning of a section of the state constitution when an election official read it to him. Of course Negroes who attempted to take this subjective test were uniformly declared to have failed it. With unctuous hypocrisy, white southerners insisted that they loved "their" blacks dearly and wished only to protect them from "the machinations of those who would use them only to further their own base ends." "We take away the Negroes' votes," a Louisiana politician explained, "to protect them just as we would protect a little child and prevent it from injuring itself with sharp-edged tools."

Practically every Supreme Court decision after 1877 that affected blacks somehow "nullified or curtailed" their rights, Professor Rayford W.

Logan writes. In *Hall v. De Cuir* (1878) the Court even threw out a state law *forbidding* segregation on river boats, arguing that it was an unjustifiable interference with interstate commerce. The *Civil Rights Cases* (1883) declared unconstitutional the Civil Rights Act of 1875 barring segregation in public facilities. Negroes who were refused equal accommodations or privileges by hotels, theaters, and other privately owned facilities had no recourse at law, the Court announced. The Fourteenth Amendment guaranteed their civil rights against invasion by the states, not by individuals.

Finally, in *Plessy v. Ferguson* (1896), the Court decided that even in places of public accommodation, such as railroads and, by implication, schools, segregation was legal so long as "separate but equal" facilities were provided. "If one race be inferior to the other socially, the Constitution of the United States cannot put them upon the same plane." In a noble dissent Justice John Marshall Harlan protested against this line of argument. "Our Constitution is colorblind," he said. "The arbitrary separation of citizens, on the basis of race . . . is a badge of servitude wholly inconsistent with civil freedom and the equality before the law established by the Constitution." Alas, more than half a century was to pass before the Court came around to Harlan's reasoning and reversed the Plessy decision. Meanwhile, total segregation was imposed throughout the South. Separate schools, prisons, hospitals, recreational facilities, and even cemeteries were provided for blacks, and these were almost never equal to those available to whites.

Most northerners supported the government and the Court in their attitude toward Negroes. Nearly all the newspapers commented favorably on the decision in the *Civil Rights Cases.* In news stories, papers presented a stereotyped, derogatory picture of blacks, no matter what the actual circumstances. Northern magazines, even high-quality ones such as *Harper's, Scribner's,* and the *Century,* repeatedly made Negroes the butt of crude jokes. Since nearly all contemporary biologists, physicians, and other supposed experts on race were convinced that blacks were inferior

beings, well-educated northerners could hardly avoid accepting black inferiority as fact. "They are gregarious and emotional, rather than intelligent," Richard Watson Gilder, editor of the *Century,* wrote in 1883, "and are easily led in any direction by white men of energy and determination." James Bryce, the brilliant Englishman whose study of the United States at this time, *The American Commonwealth,* has become a classic, saw much of Americans of this type and often absorbed their point of view. Negroes, Bryce wrote, were docile, pliable, submissive, lustful, childish, impressionable, emotional, heedless, "unthrifty," with "no capacity for abstract thinking, for scientific inquiry, or for any kind of invention." Being "unspeakably inferior," they were "unfit to cope with a superior race." Like Bryce, most Americans did not especially wish the Negroes ill; they simply refused to consider them quite human and consigned them complacently to oblivion, along with the Indians. A vicious circle was established. By denying blacks decent educational opportunities and good jobs, the dominant race could use their resultant ignorance and poverty to justify the inferior facilities offered them.

Southern Negroes reacted to this deplorable situation in a variety of ways. Some sought redress in racial pride and what would later be called black nationalism. Such persons founded a number of all-black communities in Oklahoma Territory and led the great "exodus" of 1879, when, to the consternation of southern whites, thousands of Negroes suddenly migrated to Kansas.° A few became so disaffected with American life that they tried to revive the African colonization movement. "Africa is our home," Bishop Henry M. Turner, a huge, plain-spoken man who had served as an army chaplain during the war and as a member of the Georgia legislature during reconstruction, insisted. "Every man that has

°When a congressman asked Henry Adams, a leader of the exodus, why he and his followers had left the South, Adams replied: "We seed there was no way on earth . . . that we could better our condition there. . . . The white people . . . treat our people so bad in many respects that it is impossible for them to stand it."

the sense of an animal must see there is no future in this country for the Negro." Another militant, T. Thomas Fortune, editor of the New York *Age* and founder of the Afro-American League (1887), called upon Negroes to demand full civil rights, better schools, and fair wages, and to fight against discrimination of every sort. "Let us stand up like men in our own organization," he urged. "If others use . . . violence to combat our peaceful arguments, it is not for us to run away from violence."

Militancy and black separatism, however, won few adherents among southern blacks. The forces of repression were too strong. The late 19th century saw more lynchings in the South than in any other period of American history. This helps explain the tactics of Booker T. Washington, one of the most extraordinary Americans of that generation.

Washington had been born a slave in Virginia in 1856. Laboriously, he obtained an education, supporting himself while a student by working as a janitor. In 1881, with the financial help of northern philanthropists, he founded Tuskegee Institute in Alabama, which specialized in vocational training. His experiences in the South convinced Washington that the Negroes must lift themselves by their own bootstraps, but that they must also accommodate themselves to white prejudices. A persuasive speaker and a brilliant fund raiser, he soon developed a national reputation as a "reasonable" champion of his race. (As early as 1891, Harvard awarded him an honorary degree.) But his greatest fame and influence followed his speech to a mixed white and black audience in Atlanta in 1895. To the blacks he said: "Cast down your bucket where you are," that is, stop fighting segregation and second-class citizenship and concentrate upon learning useful skills. "Dignify and glorify common labor," he urged. "Agitation of questions of racial equality is the extremest folly." Progress up the social and economic ladder for Negroes would come not from "artificial forcing" but from self-improvement. "There is as much dignity in tilling a field as in writing a poem."

Washington asked the whites of what he

Booker T. Washington about 1901, when his autobiography, *Up From Slavery*, was published. He wrote his memoirs in the hope of gaining aid for Tuskegee. (Brown Brothers.)

called "our beloved South" to lend the Negroes a hand in their efforts to advance themselves. If you will do so, he promised, you will be "surrounded by the most patient, faithful, law-abiding, and unresentful people that the world has seen."

This "Atlanta Compromise" delighted white southerners and won Washington still more influence and financial support in every section of the country. He became one of the most powerful men in the United States, consulted by Presidents, in close touch with business and philanthropic leaders, and capable of influencing in countless unobtrusive ways the fate of millions of Negroes.

Blacks responded to the Compromise with mixed feelings. Accepting Washington's approach would relieve them of many burdens and dangers and bring them considerable material assistance. But the cost was high in surrendered personal dignity and lost hopes of obtaining real justice.

Washington's career illustrates the terrible dilemma that American Negroes have always faced: the choice between confrontation and accommodation. This choice was particularly difficult in the late 19th century.

Washington chose accommodation. It is easy to condemn him as a toady, but difficult to see how, at that time, a more aggressive policy could have succeeded. One can even interpret the Atlanta Compromise as a subtle form of black nationalism; in a way, Washington was urging his fellows not to *accept* inferiority and racial slurs but to *ignore* them. His own behavior lends force to this view, for his method of operating was indeed subtle, even devious. In his public speeches, he minimized the importance of civil and political rights, accepted separate but equal facilities—if they were truly equal. Behind the scenes he lobbied against restrictive measures, marshaled large sums of money to fight test cases in the courts, and worked hard in northern states to organize the Negro vote and make sure that black political leaders got a share of the spoils of office. As one black militant put it, Washington knew the virtue of "sagacious silence." He was perhaps not personally an admirable man, but he was a useful one. His defects point up more the unlovely aspects of the age than of his own character.

Other minority groups also suffered from the contempt and disdain of the majority. Beginning in the mid-fifties a steady flow of Chinese had migrated to the United States, most of them finding work in the California gold fields. The annual influx had averaged only about four or five thousand however, until the negotiation of the Burlingame Treaty of 1868, the purpose of which was to provide cheap labor to fill out the construction crews building the Central Pacific Railroad. Thereafter, the number of annual immigrants from China more than doubled, although before 1882 it exceeded 20,000 only twice. Yet when the railroads were completed and the Chinese began to compete with native workers, a great

cry of resentment went up on the West Coast. Riots broke out in San Francisco as early as 1877. Chinese workers were called "groveling worms," "more slavish and brutish than the beasts that roam the fields." When the migration suddenly increased in 1882 to nearly 40,000,° the protests reached such a peak that Congress passed a law prohibiting all Chinese immigration for ten years. Later, legislation extended the ban indefinitely.

The Chinese in the West created genuine social problems. Most did not intend to remain in the United States and therefore made little effort to accommodate themselves to American ways. Their attachment to gambling, opium, and prostitutes—over 90 per cent of the Chinese in America at this time were males—alarmed respectable citizens. But the attitudes of westerners toward Chinese differed only in degree from their attitude toward the Mexicans who flocked into the Southwest to work as farm laborers and to help build the railroads of the region, or from that of the rest of the country toward the European immigrants who were flooding into the country in the 1880's. While industrialists wished to keep the gates wide open in order to obtain plentiful supplies of cheap labor, organized workers and many middle-class Americans were beginning to display antiforeign attitudes reminiscent of the 1850's, when Know-Nothingism was at its height. Especially during economic depressions and in periods of social unrest, the underlying intolerance of the majority burst forth. For example, the Chicago Haymarket bombing of 1886, supposedly the work of foreign anarchists, produced a wave of denunciations of "long-haired, wild-eyed, bad-smelling, atheistic, reckless foreign wretches."

Black, red, or white; aboriginal inhabitant or recent arrival; savage, husbandman, or city worker—anyone who blocked the ambitions or offended the sensibilities of his more powerful fellows received short shrift in post-Civil War America.

°This was still only about five per cent of the immigration of that year. From Germany alone, in 1882, over 250,000 people came to the United States.

Exploiting Mineral Wealth in the West

The inanimate resources of the nation were exploited in these decades as ruthlessly and thoughtlessly as its human resources. Americans had long regarded the West as a limitless treasure to be gobbled up as rapidly as possible, but after 1865 they engrossed its riches still faster and in a wider variety of ways. Miners had invaded the western mountains even before the Civil War. For 20 years from the mid-fifties to the mid-seventies thousands of gold-crazed prospectors fanned out through the Rockies, panning every stream and hacking furiously at every likely outcropping from the Fraser River country of British Columbia to Tucson in southern Arizona, and from the eastern slopes of the Sierras to the Great Plains.

Gold and silver were scattered throughout the area, although usually too thinly to make mining profitable. Whenever anyone made a "strike," prospectors flocked to the site, drawn by rumors of stream beds gleaming with auriferous gravel and of nuggets the size of men's fists. For a few brief months the area teemed with activity. Towns of 5,000 or more sprang up overnight; improvised roads were crowded with men and supply wagons. Claims were staked out along every stream and gully. Then, usually, expectations faded in the light of reality: high prices, low yields, hardship, violence, and deception. The boom collapsed and the towns died as quickly as they had risen. A few would have found real wealth, the rest only backbreaking labor and disappointment, until tales of another strike sent them scurrying feverishly across the land on another golden chase.

In the spring of 1858 it was upon the Fraser River in Canada that the horde descended, 30,000 Californians in the van. The following spring, Pike's Peak in Colorado attracted the pack, experienced California prospectors ("yonder siders") mixing with "greenhorns" from every corner of the globe. In June 1859 came the finds in Nevada, where the famous Comstock

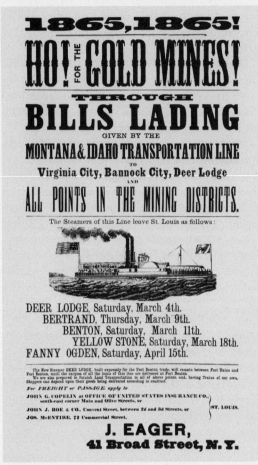

A broadside offering transportation to the Montana gold strikes. It took a steamboat as long as two months to reach Fort Benton on the upper Missouri. (New-York Historical Society.)

Lode yielded ores worth nearly $4,000 a ton. In 1861, while men in the settled areas were laying down their tools to take up arms, the miners were racing to the Idaho panhandle, hoping to become millionaires overnight. The next year the rush was to Snake River valley, then in 1863 and 1864 to Montana. In 1870 Leadville, Colorado, had a brief boom, and in 1874–76 the Black Hills in the heart of the Sioux lands were inundated.

In a sense, the Denvers, Aurarias, Virginia Cities, Orofinos, and Gold Creeks of the West during the war years were harbingers of the point of view that flourished in the East in the age of President Grant and his immediate successors. The miners enthusiastically adopted the get-rich-quick philosophy, willingly enduring privations and laboring hard, but always with the object of striking it rich. Anything that stood in the way of their ambitions, they smashed. The idea of reserving any part of the West for future generations never entered their heads. The sudden prosperity of the mining towns attracted every kind of shady character, all bent on extracting wealth from the pockets of the miners rather than from the unyielding earth. Gambling houses, dance halls, saloons, and brothels mushroomed wherever precious metal was found. Around these tawdry palaces of pleasure and forgetfulness gathered thieves, confidence men, degenerates, and desperadoes. Crime and violence were commonplace, law enforcement a constant problem.

The lawless could be controlled when their depredations became too annoying; sooner or later the "better element" in every mining community formed a "vigilance committee" and by a few summary hangings drove the outlaws out of town. Fundamentally, much of the difficulty lay in the antisocial attitudes of the miners themselves. "They were hardened individualists who paid little attention to community affairs unless their own interests were threatened," Ray Allen Billington, historian of the frontier, has written.

Western mining was at its gaudy height during the era of President Grant. Gold and silver dominated everyone's thoughts and dreams, and few paid much attention to the means employed in accumulating this wealth. Storekeepers charged outrageous prices, claim holders "salted" worthless properties with nuggets in order to swindle gullible investors. Ostentation characterized the successful, braggadocio those who failed, while all reveled in liquor and every vulgar pleasure. Virginia City, Nevada, was at the peak of its prosperity, producing an average of $12 million a year in ore. Built upon the richness of the Comstock Lode ($306 million in gold and silver were extracted from the Comstock in 20 years), it had 25 saloons before it had 4,000 people. By the seventies its mountainside site was disfigured by huge, ornate houses in the worst possible taste, where successful mine operators ate from fine china and swilled champagne as though it were water.

In 1873, after the discovery of the Big Bonanza, a rich seam more than 50 feet thick, the future of Virginia City seemed boundless. Other new discoveries shortly thereafter indicated to optimists that the mining boom in the West would continue indefinitely. The finds in the Black Hills district in 1875 and 1876, heralding deposits yielding eventually $100 million, led to the mushroom growth of Deadwood, home of Wild Bill Hickok, Deadwood Dick, Calamity Jane, and such lesser-known characters as California Jack and Poker Alice. In Deadwood, according to Professor Billington, "the faro games were wilder, the hurdy-gurdy dance halls noisier, the street brawls more common, than in any other western town." New strikes in Leadville, Colorado, in 1876 and 1877 caused that ghost town to boom again. This, however, was the last important flurry to ruffle the mining frontier. The West continued to yield much gold and silver, especially the latter, but big corporations produced nearly all of it. The mines around Deadwood, for example, were soon controlled by one large company, Homestake Mining.

This was the culminating irony of the history of the mining frontier. The shoestring prospectors, independent and enterprising, made the key discoveries, established local institutions, and supplied the West with much of its color and folklore. But almost none of them was really successful. Stockholders of large corporations, many of whom had never seen a mine, made off with the lion's share of the mineral wealth. The men whose worship of gold was so direct and incessant, the actual prospectors who peopled the mining towns and gave the frontier its character, mostly died poor, still seeking a prize as elusive if not as illusory as the pot of gold at the end of the rainbow.

For the mining of gold and silver is essentially like that of coal and iron. To operate profitably, large capital investments, heavy machinery, railroads, and hundreds of hired hands are required.

Henry Comstock, the prospector who gave his name to the Comstock Lode, was luckier than most, but he sold his claims to the lode for a pittance, disposing of what became one valuable mine for $40 and receiving only $10,000 for his share of the fabulous Ophir, the richest concentration of gold and silver ever found. His greatest financial gain from the Comstock came some years later when the owners of the Ophir paid him well to testify in their corporation's behalf in an important lawsuit. More typical of the successful mine owner was George Hearst, senator from California and father of the newspaper tycoon William Randolph Hearst, who, by shrewd speculations, obtained large blocks of stock in mining properties scattered from Montana to Mexico.

Though marked by violence, fraud, greed, impermanence, and lost hopes, the gold rushes had certain valuable results. The most obvious was the new metal itself, which bolstered the financial position of the United States during and after the Civil War. Quantities of European goods needed for the war effort and for postwar economic development were paid for with the yield of the new mines. Gold and silver also caused a great increase of interest in the West. A valuable literature appeared, part imaginative, part straightforwardly reportorial, describing the mining camps and the life of the prospectors. These works fascinated contemporaries as they have continued to fascinate succeeding generations when adapted to the motion picture and to television. Mark Twain's *Roughing It* (1872), based in part on his experiences in the Nevada mining country, is the most famous example of this literature.

Furthermore, each new strike and rush, no matter how ephemeral, brought permanent settlers along with the prospectors: farmers, cattlemen, storekeepers, teamsters, lawyers, ministers, and so on. Some saw from the start that a better living could be made supplying the needs of the gold seekers than looking for the elusive metal. Others, abandoning hope of finding mineral wealth, simply took up whatever occupation they could rather than starve or return home empty-handed. In every mining town—along with the saloons and brothels—schools, churches, and newspaper offices sprang up.

The mines also speeded the political organization of the West. Colorado and Nevada became territories in 1861, Arizona and Idaho in 1863, Montana in 1864. Although Nevada was admitted prematurely in 1864 to ratify the Thirteenth Amendment and help re-elect Lincoln, most of these territories did not become states for decades, but because of the miners, the framework for future development was early established.

The Land Bonanza

While the miners were engrossing the mineral wealth of the West, other interests were snapping up the region's choice farmland. Presumably the Homestead Act, passed in 1862 after years of agitation, had ended the reign of the speculator and the large landholder. The West, land reformers had assumed, would soon be dotted with 160-acre family farms. An early amendment to the Homestead Act even prevented husbands and wives from filing separate claims. The system did not work out as planned. Most landless Americans were too poor to become independent farmers, even when they could obtain land without cost. The expense of moving a family to the ever-receding frontier exceeded the means of many, and the subsequent costs, from simple hoes and scythes to harvesting machines, fencing, and housing, presented an even more formidable barrier. Nor did the industrial workers for whom the free land was supposed to provide a "safety valve" have either the skills or the inclination to become farmers. Most homesteaders were already farmers, usually from districts not far removed from frontier conditions. And despite the intent of the law, wealthy speculators often used it to obtain large tracts. They hired men to stake out claims, falsely swear that they had fulfilled the conditions laid down in the law for obtaining legal title, and then deed the land over to their employers.

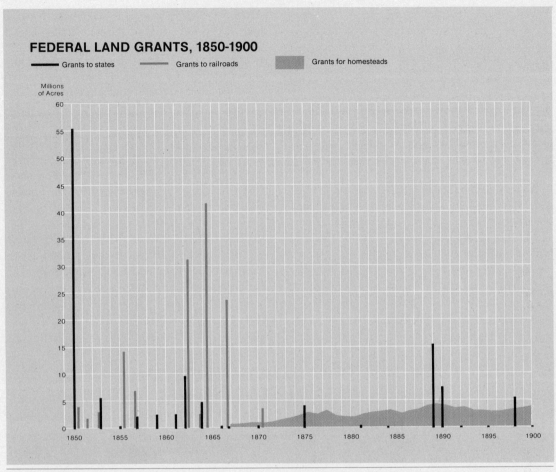

FEDERAL LAND GRANTS, 1850-1900

— Grants to states   — Grants to railroads   Grants for homesteads

Millions of Acres

Between 1850 and 1871, grants of federal land to railroads totaled some 130 million acres. The homestead acreage shown indicates land to which homesteaders took title after fulfilling the necessary conditions.

Furthermore, 160 acres was not enough for raising livestock or for the kind of commercial agriculture that was developing west of the Mississippi. Congress made a feeble attempt to make larger holdings available to homesteaders by passing the Timber Culture Act of 1873, which permitted individuals to claim an additional 160 acres if they would agree to plant a quarter of it in trees within ten years. This law proved helpful to farmers in the tier of states running from North Dakota to Kansas. Nevertheless, fewer than 25 per cent of the 245,000 who took up land under it obtained final title to the property. Rais-

ing large numbers of seedling trees on the plains was a difficult task.

While futilely attempting to make a forest of parts of the treeless plains, the government permitted private interests to gobble up and destroy many of the great forests that clothed the slopes of the Rockies and the Sierras. The Timber and Stone Act of 1878 allowed anyone to claim a quarter section of forest land for $2.50 an acre if it was "unfit for civilization." This laxly drawn measure enabled lumber companies to obtain thousands of acres by hiring dummy entrymen, whom they marched in gangs to the land offices, paying them a few dollars for their time after they had signed over their claims. "In many instances whole townships have been entered under this law in the interest of one person or firm, to whom the lands have been conveyed as soon as receipts for the purchase price were issued," the commissioner of the General Land Office complained in 1901. "Congress was very remiss in the phraseology," a recent historian has written. "An acre cost less than the value of one log from one tree where it stood as yet unfelled."

Even if the land laws had been better drafted and more honestly enforced, it is unlikely that the policy of granting free land to small homesteaders would have succeeded. Aside from the built-in difficulties faced by small-scale agriculturalists in the West, too many people in every section were eager to exploit the nation's land for their own profit, without regard for the general interest. Immediately after the war, for example, Congress reserved 47.7 million acres of public land in the South for homesteaders, stopping all cash sales in the region. But in 1876 this policy was reversed, the land thrown open. Speculators flocked to the feast in such numbers that the Illinois Central Railroad began running special trains from Chicago to Mississippi and Louisiana. Between 1877 and 1888 over 5.6 million acres were sold, much of them covered with valuable pine and cypress.

However they attained their acres, frontier farmers of the 1870's and 1880's grappled with a variety of novel problems as they pushed across the grasslands of Kansas, Nebraska, and the Da-

The crews of five combines stopped harvesting wheat on a bonanza farm in eastern Washington in 1890 to have their picture taken. Such combines as these reaped, threshed, cleaned, and bagged grain in a single operation. (Library of Congress.)

kotas with their wives and children. The first settlers took up land along the rivers and creeks, where they found enough timber for home-building, fuel, and fencing. Later arrivals had to build houses of the tough prairie sod and depend upon hay, dried sunflower stalks, even buffalo dung for fuel. The soil was rich, but the climate, especially in the semiarid regions beyond the 98th meridian of longitude, made agriculture frequently difficult and often impossible. Blizzards, floods, grasshopper plagues, and prairie fires caused repeated heartaches, but periodic drought and searing summer heat were the worst hazards, destroying the hopes and fortunes of thousands.

At the same time, the flat immensity of the land, combined with newly available farm machinery and the development of rail connections with the East—to be discussed below—encouraged the growth of gigantic, corporation-controlled "bonanza" farms running sometimes into the tens of thousands of acres. One such organization was the railroad-owned empire managed by Oliver Dalrymple in Dakota Territory, which harvested 25,000 acres of wheat in 1880. Dalrymple employed 200 pairs of harrows to prepare his soil, 125 seeders to sow his seed, and 155 binders to harvest his crop. Such farmers could buy supplies wholesale and obtain concessions from railroads and processors, which added to their profits.

Even the biggest organizations could not cope with prolonged drought, however, and most of the bonanza outfits failed in the dry years of the late eighties. Those wise farmers who diversified their crops and cultivated their land intensively fared better in the long run, though even they could not hope to earn a profit in really dry years.

Despite the hazards of plains agriculture, the region became the breadbasket of America in the decades after the Civil War. By 1889 Minnesota topped the nation in wheat production, and ten years later four of the five leading wheat states lay west of the Mississippi. The plains also accounted for heavy percentages of the nation's other cereal crops, together with immense quantities of beef, pork, and mutton.

Like other exploiters of the nation's resources, farmers took whatever they could from the soil with little heed for preserving its fertility and preventing erosion. The resultant national loss was less obvious since it was diffuse and slow to assume drastic proportions, but it was very real.

Western Railroad Building

Further exploitation of the land resources of the nation by private interests resulted from the government's policy of subsidizing western railroads. Here was a clear illustration of the conflict between the idea of the West as a national heritage to be disposed of to deserving citizens and the concept of the region as a boundless prize to be gobbled up in giant chunks by interests powerful and determined enough to take it. When it came to a choice between giving a particular tract to railroads or to homesteaders, the homesteaders nearly always lost out. To serve a necessary national purpose, the linking of the sections by rail, the land of the West was dispensed wholesale as a substitute for cash subsidies.

Federal land grants to railroads began in 1850 with those allotted the Illinois Central. Over the next two decades about 49 million acres were given to various lines indirectly in the form of grants to the states, but the most lavish gifts of the public domain were those made directly to builders of intersectional trunk lines. These roads received over 155 million acres in this fashion, although about 25 million acres eventually reverted to the government when certain companies failed to construct the required miles of track. About 75 per cent of this went to aid the construction of four transcontinental railroads: the Union Pacific-Central Pacific line, running from Nebraska to San Francisco, completed in 1869; the Atchison, Topeka and Santa Fe, running from Kansas City to Los Angeles by way of Santa Fe and Albuquerque, completed in 1883; the Southern Pacific line, running from San Francisco to New Orleans by way of Yuma and El

Paso, completed in 1883; and the Northern Pacific, running from Duluth, Minnesota, to Portland, Oregon, completed in 1883.

Unless the government had been willing to build the transcontinental lines itself, and this was unthinkable in an age so dominated by the spirit of individual exploitation and laissez faire, some system of subsidy was essential; private investors would not hazard the huge sums needed to lay tracks across hundreds of miles of rugged, empty country when traffic over the road could not possibly produce profits for many years. Grants of land seemed a sensible way of financing construction. The method avoided direct outlays of public funds, for the companies could pledge the land as security for bond issues or sell it directly for cash. Moreover, land and railroad values were intimately linked in contemporary thinking. "The occupation of new land and the building of new mileage go hand in hand," the *Commercial and Financial Chronicle* explained in 1886. "There could be no great or continuous opening up of new territory without the necessary facilities in the way of railroads. On the other hand, most new mileage on the borders of our Western territory is prosecuted with the idea and expectation that it is to pave the way for an accession of new settlers and an extension of the area of land devoted to their uses." It even seemed possible that in many cases the value of the land granted might be recovered by the government when it sold other lands in the vicinity, for such properties would certainly be worth more after transportation facilities to eastern markets had been constructed. "Why," asked the governor of one eastern state in 1867, "should private individuals be called upon to make a useless sacrifice of their means, when railroads can be constructed by the unity of public and private interests, and made profitable to all?"

The Pacific Railway Act of 1862 established the pattern for these grants. This law gave the builders of the Union Pacific and Central Pacific railroads five square miles of public land on each side of their right of way for each mile of track laid. The land was allotted in alternate sections, forming a pattern like a checkerboard, the squares of one color representing railroad property, the other government property. Presumably this arrangement benefited the government, since half the land close to the railroad remained in its hands.

However, whenever grants were made to railroads, the adjacent government lands were not opened to homesteaders, the theory being that free land in the immediate vicinity of a line would prevent the road from disposing of its properties at good prices. Since, in addition to the land actually granted, a wide zone of "indemnity" lands was reserved to allow the roads to choose alternative sites to make up for lands that settlers had already taken up within the checkerboard, homesteading was in fact prohibited near land-grant railroads. Grants per mile of track ranged from five alternate sections on each side of the track to the Union and Central Pacific to 40 sections to the Northern Pacific, authorized in 1864. In the latter case, when the indemnity zone was included, homesteaders were barred from an area 100 miles wide, running all the way from Lake Superior to the Pacific. Over 20 years after receiving its immense grant, the Northern Pacific was still attempting to keep homesteaders from filing in the indemnity zone. President Cleveland finally put a stop to this in 1887, saying that he could find "no evidence" that "this vast tract is necessary for the fulfillment of the grant."

Historians have argued at length about the fairness of the land-grant system. No railroad corporation waxed fat directly from the sale of its lands, which were sold at prices averaging between $2 and $5 an acre. Collectively the roads have taken in between $400 and $500 million from this source, but only over the course of a century. Land-grant lines did a great deal to encourage the growth of the West, advertising their property widely and providing both cheap transportation for prospective settlers and efficient shipping services for farmers. They were also required by law to carry troops and handle government business free or at reduced rates, which has saved the government many millions over the years. At the same time, the system imposed no

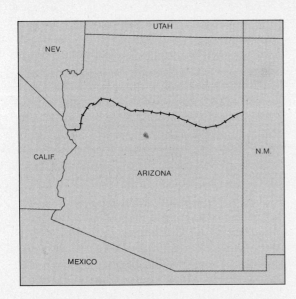

The Atlantic and Pacific's land grant in Arizona on the contemporary map below appears as shaded squares on the checkerboard. The grant cut a 100-mile-wide swath across the entire territory (above). (Below: National Archives.)

effective restraints on the railroads in their use of the funds raised with federal aid. Building their lines largely with money obtained from land grants, the operators tended to be extravagant and often downright corrupt.

The Union Pacific, for example, was built by a construction company, the Crédit Mobilier, which was owned by the promoters. These men awarded themselves large contracts at prices that assured the Crédit Mobilier exorbitant profits. When Congress threatened to investigate the Union Pacific in 1868, Oakes Ames, a stockholder in both companies who was also a member of Congress, sold key congressmen and government officials over 300 shares of Crédit Mobilier stock at a price far below its real value. These shares were placed "where they will do the most good," Ames said. "I have found," he also said, "there is no difficulty in inducing men to look after their own property." When these transactions were later exposed, the House of Representatives censured Ames, but such was the temper of the times that neither he nor most of his associates believed he had done anything immoral.

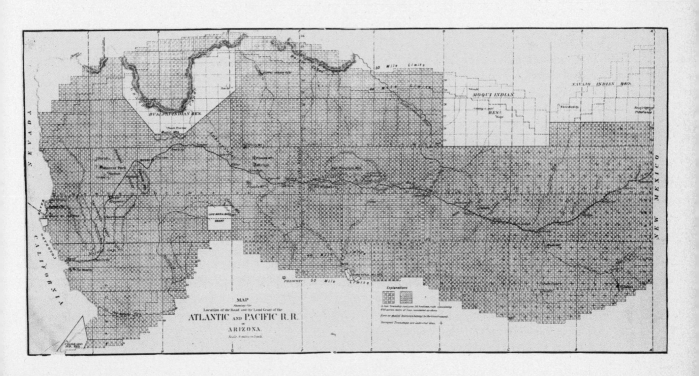

According to the president of one western railroad, congressmen frequently tried to use their influence to get railroad land at bargain prices. "Isn't there a discount?" they would ask. "Surely you can give the land cheaper to a friend. . . ." The railroads seldom resisted this type of pressure.

The construction of the Central Pacific in the 1860's illustrates how the system encouraged extravagance. In addition to their land grants, the Central Pacific and the Union Pacific were given loans in the form of government bonds, ranging in value from $16,000 to $48,000 for each mile of track laid, depending upon the difficulty of the terrain. The two competed with each other for these subsidies, the Central Pacific building eastward from Sacramento, the Union Pacific westward from Nebraska. They put huge crews to work grading and laying track, bringing up supplies over the already completed road. The Union Pacific depended upon Civil War veterans and Irish immigrants, the Central upon Chinese immigrants.

This plan, typical of the dog-eat-dog philosophy of the times, favored the Union Pacific—while the Central Pacific was inching upward through the gorges and granite of the mighty Sierras, the Union Pacific was racing across the level plains. Once the Sierras were surmounted, the Central Pacific would have easy going across the Nevada-Utah plateau country, but by then it might be too late. To prevent the Union Pacific from making off with most of the government aid, the Central Pacific construction crews, headed by Charles Crocker, a hulking, relentless driver of men, who had come to California during the gold rush and made a small fortune as a merchant in Sacramento, wasted huge sums by working right through the winter in the High Sierras. Often the men labored in tunnels dug through 40-foot snowdrifts to get at the frozen ground. To speed construction of the Summit Tunnel, Crocker had a shaft cut down from above so that crews could work out from the middle as well as in from each end. In 1866, over the most difficult terrain, he laid 28 miles of track, but at a cost of over $280,000 a mile. Experts later estimated that 70 per cent of this sum could have been saved had speed not been such a factor. Such prodigality made economic sense to the "Big Four" (Collis P. Huntington, Leland Stanford, Mark Hopkins, and Crocker) who controlled the Central Pacific because of the fat profits they were making through its construction company and because of the gains they could count upon once they reached the flat country beyond the Sierras, where construction costs amounted to only half the federal aid.

Crocker's truly herculean efforts paid off. The mountains were conquered, and then the crews raced across the Great Basin to Salt Lake City and beyond. The final meeting of the rails—the occasion of a national celebration—took place at Promontory, north of Ogden, Utah, on May 10, 1869, Leland Stanford driving the final ceremonial golden spike with a silver hammer.° The Union Pacific had built 1,086 miles of track, the Central 689.

However, in the long run the wasteful way in which the Central Pacific was built hurt the road severely. It was ill-constructed, over too-steep grades and too-sharp curves, and burdened with too-heavy debts. Such was the fate of nearly all the railroads constructed with government subsidies. The only transcontinental built without land grants was the Great Northern, running from St. Paul, Minnesota, to the Pacific. Spending private capital, its guiding genius, James J. Hill, was compelled to build economically and to plan carefully. As a result, his was the only transcontinental line to weather the great depression of the 1890's without going into bankruptcy.

The Cattle Kingdom

While the miners were digging out the mineral wealth of the West and the railroads were taking

---

°A mysterious "San Francisco jeweler" passed among the onlookers, taking orders for souvenir watch chains which he proposed to make from the spike at $5 each. Of course he was an impostor.

The meeting of the rails at Promontory, Utah, May 10, 1869. Andrew J. Russell took this picture from atop the Central Pacific's Jupiter as it moved slowly toward the Union Pacific's No. 119. Dignitaries are gathered for the ceremony of the driving of the golden spike by rail magnate Leland Stanford. Stanford swung and missed. (Oakland Museum.)

possession of much of its land, another group was avidly acquiring its endless acres of grass. For 20 years after the Civil War, cattlemen and sheep raisers dominated huge areas of the High Plains, making millions of dollars by grazing their herds on lands they did not own.

Columbus brought the first cattle to the New World in 1493, on his second voyage, and later *conquistadores* took them to every corner of Spain's American empire. Mexico proved to be particularly well-suited to cattle raising. Over the years many Mexican cattle were allowed to roam loose, and they multiplied rapidly. By the late

18th century what is now southern Texas contained enormous herds. These beasts interbred with nondescript "English" cattle, brought into the area by American settlers, to produce the Texas longhorn. Hardy, wiry, ill-tempered, and fleet, with horns often attaining a spread of six feet, these animals were far from ideal as beef cattle and almost as hard to capture as wild horses, but they existed in southern Texas by the millions, most of them unowned.

The lack of markets and transportation explains why Texas cattle were so lightly regarded. But conditions were changing. Industrial growth in the East was causing an increase in the urban population and a consequent rise in the demand for food. At the same time, the expansion of the railroad network made it possible to move cattle cheaply over long distances. As the iron rails inched across the plains, astute cattlemen began to do some elementary figuring. Longhorns could be had locally for $3 or $4 a head. In the northern cities they would bring ten times that much, perhaps even more. Why not round them up and herd them northward to the railroads, allowing them to feed along the way on the abundant grasses of the plains?

In 1866 a number of Texans drove large herds northward toward Sedalia, Missouri, railhead of the Missouri Pacific. This route, however, took the herds through wooded and settled country and across Indian reservations, which provoked many difficulties. The next year the drovers, inspired by a clever young Illinois cattle dealer named Joseph G. McCoy, led their herds north by a more westerly route, across unsettled grasslands, to Abilene, Kansas, on the Kansas Pacific line.

They earned excellent profits, and during the next five years about 1.5 million head made the "Long Drive" over the Chisholm Trail to Abilene. Other shipping points sprang up as the railroads pushed westward. Altogether, before the era ended, about 4 million longhorns were driven from Texas to the central plains across the public lands.

The technique of the Long Drive, which involved guiding herds of two or three thousand cattle slowly across as much as a thousand miles of trackless country, produced the American cowboy, renowned in song, story, and on film. Half a dozen of these men could control several thousand steers. Mounted on wiry ponies, they would range alongside the herd, keeping the animals on the move but preventing stampedes, allowing them time to rest yet steadily pressing them toward the yards of Abilene.

Although the cowboy's life was far more prosaic than it appears in modern legend, consisting mainly of endless hours on the trail surrounded by thousands of bellowing beasts, he was indeed an interesting type, perfectly adapted to his environment. Cowboys virtually lived on horseback, for their work kept them far from human habitation for months on end. Most, accustomed to solitude, were indeed "strong, silent men." They were courageous, and expert marksmen, too, for they lived amid many dangers and had to know how to protect themselves. Few grew rich, yet like the miners they were true representatives of their time—determinedly individualistic, contemptuous of authority, crude of manner, devoted to coarse pleasures.

"Cow towns" like Abilene, Ellsworth, and Dodge City were as riotous and as venal as any mining camp. A local merchant characterized Abilene as a "seething, roaring, flaming hell"; its saloons, bearing names like Alamo, Applejack, Longhorn, and Old Fruit, were packed during the season with crowds of rambunctious, guntoting pleasure seekers. Gambling houses and brothels abounded. When Ellsworth, Kansas, had a population of only a thousand, it had 75 resident professional gamblers. At dance halls like Rowdy Joe's, the customers were expected to buy drinks for themselves and their partners after each dance. Little wonder that McCoy wrote in his *Historic Sketches of the Cattle Trade* (1874): "Few more wild, reckless scenes of abandoned debauchery can be seen on the civilized earth than a dance hall in full blast in one of these frontier towns."

Open-Range Ranching

Soon cattlemen discovered that the hardy Texas stock could survive the winters of the northern plains. Attracted by the apparently limitless forage, they began to bring up herds to stock the vast regions where the buffalo had so recently roamed. By introducing pedigreed Hereford bulls, they improved the stock without weakening its resistance to harsh conditions. By 1869 a million longhorns grazed in Colorado Territory alone, and by 1880 some 4.5 million head had

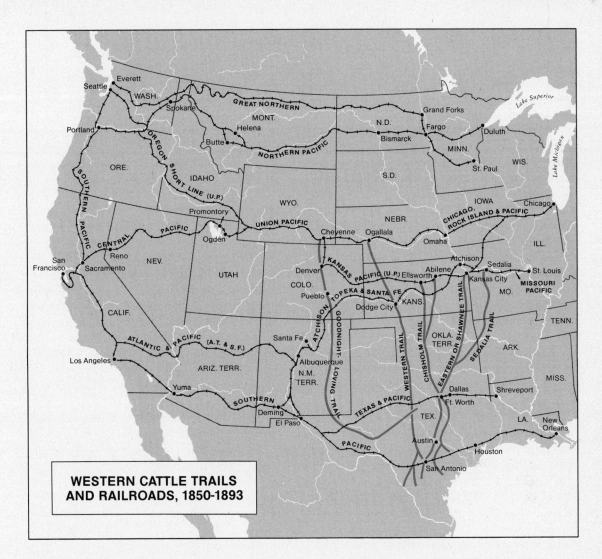

WESTERN CATTLE TRAILS AND RAILROADS, 1850-1893

spread across the great sea of grass that ran from Kansas to Montana and west to the Rockies.

The prairie grasses offered cattlemen a bonanza almost as valuable as the gold mines. Open-range ranching required actual ownership of no more than a few acres along some watercourse. In this semiarid region, control of water enabled a rancher to dominate all the surrounding area back to the divide separating his range from the next stream without investing a cent in the purchase of land. His cattle, wandering freely on the public domain, fattened on grass owned by all the people, to be turned into beefsteak and leather for the profit of the rancher. Theoretically, anyone could pasture stock upon the open range, but without access to water it was impossible to do so. "I have two miles of running water," a cattleman said in testifying before the Public Land Commission. "That accounts for my ranch being where it is. The next water from me in one direction is 23 miles; now no man can have a ranch between these two places. I have control of the grass, the same as though I owned it." By having his cowhands take out homestead claims along watercourses in his region, a rancher could greatly expand the area he dominated. In the late 1870's one Colorado cattle baron controlled an area roughly the size of Connecticut and Rhode Island, although he owned only 105 small parcels that totaled about 15,500 acres.

Generally, a group of ranchers acted together, obtaining legal title to the lands along the bank of a stream and grazing their cattle over the whole area drained by it. The herds became thoroughly intermixed, each owner's being identified by his individual brand mark. Every spring and fall the ranchers staged a great roundup, driving in all the cattle to a central place, separating them by brand marks, culling steers for shipment to market, and branding new calves.

With the demand for meat rising and transportation relatively cheap; a princely fortune could be made in a few years with a relatively small investment. Capitalists from the East and from Europe began to pour funds into the business. Attracted by what one writer called the "Beef Bonanza"—in a book subtitled *How to Get Rich on the Plains*—Eastern "dudes" like Theodore Roosevelt, a young New York assemblyman who sank over $50,000 in his Elkhorn Ranch in Dakota Territory in 1883, bought up cattle as a sort of profitable hobby, and large outfits like the Prairie Cattle Company and the Nebraska Land and Cattle Company, controlled by British investors, and the Union Cattle Company of Wyoming, a $3 million corporation, were beginning to dominate the business, just as large companies had taken over most of the important gold and silver mines.

Unlike other exploiters of the West's resources, the ranchers did not at first injure or reduce any public resource. Grass eaten by their stock annually renewed itself, the soil enriched by the droppings of the animals. Furthermore, ranchers poached on the public domain because there was no reasonable way for them to obtain legal possession of the large areas necessary to raise cattle on the plains. Federal land laws made no allowances for the needs of stockmen and the special conditions of the semiarid West. "Title to the public lands [of the West] cannot be honestly acquired under the homestead laws," S. E. Burdett, commissioner of the General Land Office, wrote in an 1875 report. "That cultivation and improvement which are required . . . in the place of price, are impossible. . . . A system of sale should be authorized in accordance with the necessities of the situation."

Such a system was soon devised by Major John Wesley Powell, later the director of the United States Geological Survey. His *Report on the Lands of the Arid Region of the United States* (1879) suggested that western lands be divided into three classes: irrigable lands, timber lands, and "pasturage" lands. On the pasturage lands the "farm unit" ought to be at least 2,560 acres (four sections), Powell urged. Groups of these units should be organized into "pasturage districts" in which the ranchers "should have the right to make their own regulations for the division of lands, the use of the water . . . and for the pasturage of lands in common or in severalty."

However, Congress refused to change the land laws in any basic way, and this had two harmful effects. First, it encouraged fraud: men who could not get title to enough land honestly soon turned to subterfuges. The Desert Land Act (1877) provided well-to-do ranchers with a relatively simple way to do this. It allowed anyone to obtain 640 acres in the arid states for $1.25 an acre provided he irrigated part of it within three years. Since the original claimant could transfer his holding, the ranchers set their cowboys and other hands to filing claims, which were then signed over to them. Over 2.6 million acres were taken up under the act, and according to the best estimate, about 95 per cent of the claims were fraudulent—no sincere effort was made to irrigate the land.

Secondly, overcrowding became a problem, leading in turn to serious conflicts, even to shooting, because no one had an uncontestable title to the land. The leading ranchers banded together in cattlemen's associations to deal with overcrowding and with such problems as quarantine regulations, water rights, and thievery. In most cases these associations devised remarkably effective and sensible rules, but their functions

In 1885 masked Nebraskans seeking access to water posed for photographer S. D. Butcher, who captioned the picture, "Settlers taking the law in their own hands: cutting 15 miles of the Brighton Ranch fence." (Nebraska State Historical Society.)

would better have been performed by the government, as such matters usually are.

To keep other ranchers' cattle from those sections of the public domain they considered their own, these associations, and many individuals, began to fence huge areas. This was possible only because of the invention in 1874 of barbed wire by Joseph F. Glidden, an Illinois farmer. By the 1880's thousands of miles of the new fencing had been strung across the plains, often across roads, and in a few cases around entire communities. "Barbed-wire wars" resulted, fought by rancher against rancher, cattleman against sheepman, herder against farmer. The associations tried to police their fences and to punish anyone who cut their wire. Signs posted along lonely stretches

gave dire warnings to trespassers. "The Son of a Bitch who opens this fence had better look out for his scalp," one such sign announced, a perfect statement of the philosophy of the age.

By installing these fences the cattlemen were unwittingly destroying their own way of doing business. On a truly open range, cattle could fend for themselves in any weather, instinctively finding water during droughts, drifting safely downwind before the wildest blizzards. Barbed wire prevented their free movement. During winter storms these slender strands became as lethal as high-tension wires: the drifting cattle piled up against them and died by the thousands. "The advent of barbed wire," wrote Walter Prescott Webb in his classic study *The Great*

Plains (1931), "brought about the disappearance of the open, free range and converted the range country into the big-pasture country."

The boom times were ending. Overproduction was driving down the price of beef; expenses were on the rise; many sections of the range were becoming badly overgrazed. The dry summer of 1886 left the stock in poor condition as winter approached, and experienced cattlemen were badly worried. The *Rocky Mountain Husbandman* urged its readers to sell their cattle despite the prevailing low prices rather than "endanger the whole herd by having the range overstocked."

Some ranchers took this advice; those who did not made a fatal error. Winter that year arrived early and with unparalleled fury. Blizzards raged and temperatures plummeted far below zero. Cattle crowded into low places only to be engulfed in giant snowdrifts; barbed wire took a fearful toll. When spring finally came, the streams were choked with rotting carcasses. Between 80 and 90 per cent of all the cattle on the range were dead. "We have had a perfect smash-up all through the cattle country," Theodore Roosevelt wrote sadly in April 1887 from Elkhorn Ranch.

After that cruel winter, open-range cattle-raising quickly disappeared. The large companies were bankrupted, many independent operators, such as Roosevelt, became discouraged and sold out. When the industry revived, it was on a smaller, although more efficiently organized scale. The fencing movement continued, but now each stockman confined himself to enclosing land he actually owned. It then became possible to bring in blooded bulls to improve the breed scientifically. Cattle-raising, like mining before it, ceased to be an adventure in rollicking individualism and reckless greed and became a business.

Thus, by the late eighties, the bonanza days of the West were over. No previous frontier had caught the imagination of Americans so completely as the Great West, with its wealth, its heroic size, its awesome emptiness, its massive, sculptured beauty. Now the frontier was no more. Most of what Professor Webb called the "primary windfalls" of the region—the furs, the precious metals, the forests, the cattle, and the grass—had been snatched up by first-comers and by men already wealthy. Big companies were taking over all the West's resources. The nation was becoming more powerful, richer, larger, and its economic structure more complex and diversified as the West yielded its treasures; but the East, and especially eastern industrialists and financiers, were increasingly dominating the economy of the whole nation.

Supplementary Reading

The psychology and the political ideas current in this period are covered in Sidney Fine, *Laissez Faire and the General Welfare State*° (1956), Richard Hofstadter, *Social Darwinism in American Thought*° (1945), and J. W. Hurst, *Law and the Conditions of Freedom in the Nineteenth-Century United States*° (1956). C. D. Warner and Mark Twain, *The Gilded Age*° (1873), is a useful and entertaining contemporary impression. On the views of businessmen, see E. C. Kirkland, *Dream and Thought in the Business Community*° (1956), Kirkland's edition of Andrew Carnegie's writings, *The Gospel of Wealth* (1962), R. G. McCloskey, *American Conservatism in the Age of Enterprise*° (1951), T. C. Cochran, *Railroad Leaders* (1953), and J. D. Rockefeller, *Random Reminiscences of Men and Events* (1909).

R. A. Billington, *Westward Expansion* (1967), is the best introduction to the history of the exploitation of the West. On the Indians, general works include Paul Radin, *The Story of the American Indian* (1944), John Collier, *Indians of the Americas*° (1947), and W. T. Hagan, *American Indians*° (1961). Of more specialized works, the following are useful: F. G. Roe, *The Indian and the Horse* (1955), L. B. Priest, *Uncle Sam's Stepchildren: The Reformation of United States Indian Policy* (1942), H. E. Fritz, *The Movement for Indian Assimilation* (1963), D. A. Brown, *The Galvanized Yankees* (1963), S. L. A. Marshall, *Crimsoned Prairie: The War Between the United States and the Plains Indians* (1972), L. R. Hafen and W. J. Ghent, *Broken Hand: The Life Story of Thomas Fitzpatrick* (1931), and R. G. At-

°Available in paperback.

hearn, *William Tecumseh Sherman and the Settlement of the West* (1956). The destruction of the buffalo is described in vivid if highly imaginative terms
in Mari Sandoz, *The Buffalo Hunters* (1954). H. H.
Jackson, *A Century of Dishonor°* (1881), is a powerful contemporary indictment of United States Indian
policy.

For the fate of other minority groups, see J. H.
Franklin, *From Slavery to Freedom* (1956), R. W.
Logan, *The Negro in American Life and Thought:
The Nadir°* (1954), L. R. Harlan, *Booker T. Wash-
ington* (1972), S. P. Hirshson, *Farewell to the Bloody
Shirt* (1962), V. P. De Santis, *Republicans Face the
Southern Question* (1959), C. V. Woodward, *The
Strange Career of Jim Crow°* (1966), J. A. Garraty
(ed.), *Quarrels That Have Shaped the Constitution°*
(1964), Gunther Barth, *Bitter Strength: A History of
the Chinese in the United States* (1964), R. A. Bil-
lington, *The Protestant Crusade°* (1938), and John
Higham, *Strangers in the Land°* (1955).

For the mining frontier, consult R. W. Paul, *Mining Frontiers of the Far West°* (1963), W. T. Jackson, *Treasure Hill: Portrait of a Silver Mining Camp°*
(1963), D. A. Smith, *Rocky Mountain Mining Camps:
The Urban Frontier* (1967), and W. J. Trimble, *The
Mining Advance into the Inland Empire* (1914).
Mark Twain, *Roughing It°* (1872), is a classic contemporary account, and W. H. Goetzmann, *Exploration and Empire* (1966) throws much light on all aspects of western development. For federal land
policy, see R. M. Robbins, *Our Landed Heritage°*
(1942), P. W. Gates, *Fifty Million Acres°* (1954), and
F. A. Shannon, *The Farmer's Last Frontier°* (1945),
which is excellent on all questions relating to post-
Civil War agriculture. Everett Dick, *The Sod-House
Frontier* (1937), presents a graphic picture of farm
life on the treeless plains. Bonanza farming is described in H. M. Drache, *The Day of the Bonanza*
(1964).

The development of transcontinental railroads is
discussed in R. E. Riegel, *The Story of the Western
Railroads°* (1926), Julius Grodinsky, *Transcontinental
Railway Strategy* (1962), O. O. Winther, *The Transportation Frontier* (1964), and G. R. Taylor and I. D.
Neu, *The American Railroad Network* (1956). For a
sampling of the literature on specific roads, see
James McCague, *Moguls and Iron Men* (1964), Oscar
Lewis, *The Big Four* (1938), J. B. Hedges, *Henry Villard and the Railroads of the Northwest* (1930), and
L. L. Waters, *Steel Rails to Santa Fe* (1950). Matthew Josephson, *The Robber Barons°* (1934), discusses the chicanery connected with railroad construction at length.

On cattle ranching on the plains, a good account
is Lewis Atherton, *The Cattle Kings* (1961), but see
also E. S. Osgood, *The Day of the Cattleman°*
(1929), and Louis Pelzer, *The Cattlemen's Frontier*
(1936). For the cowboy and his life, see E. E. Dale,
Cow Country (1942), Andy Adams, *The Log of a
Cowboy°* (1902), and J. B. Frantz and J. E. Choate,
The American Cowboy: The Myth and Reality
(1955). W. P. Webb, *The Great Plains°* (1931), is a
fascinating analysis of the development of a unique
civilization on the plains.

18

An Industrial Giant

When the Civil War began, the United States was still a primarily agricultural country; its industrial output, while important and increasing, did not approach that of major European powers. By the end of the century the nation had become far and away the colossus among the world's manufacturers, dwarfing the production of such countries as Great Britain and Germany. The value of manufactured products rose from $1.8 billion in 1859 to $3.3 billion in 1869, $5.3 billion in 1879, $9.3 billion in 1889, and to over $13 billion in 1899. Modern economists estimate that the output of goods and services in the country (the gross national product, or GNP) increased by 44 per cent between 1874 and 1883 and continued to expand in succeeding years. According to the historian Carter Goodrich, the United States in the 19th century was "the world's greatest example of economic development."

Industrial Growth: An Overview

No radical change explains why industrialization proceeded at such a pace. American manufacturing merely continued to gather momentum. New natural resources were always being discovered and exploited, thus increasing opportunities, attracting the brightest and most energetic of a large, vigorous, and expanding population. The growth of the country added constantly to the size of the national market, while protective tariffs guarded it against foreign competition. However, foreign capital entered the market freely, perhaps in part because tariffs kept out many foreign goods. By 1893 foreigners had poured $3 billion into the United States, although, of course, not all of this was invested in industry. The dominant spirit of the time encouraged businessmen to maximum effort by emphasizing progress, glorifying material wealth, and justifying aggressiveness. European immigrants provided the manpower needed by expanding industry. Two-and-a-half million arrived in the seventies, twice that number in the eighties.

New inventions played a particularly important role in this growth. It was a period of rapid advance in basic science, and technicians created a bountiful harvest of new machines, processes, and power sources. These stimulated every branch of the economy. In agriculture, to take but one field, there were James Oliver's chilled iron plow, perfected by 1877, what one contemporary expert called "an endless variety of cultivators," better harvesters, binding machines, and great combines capable of threshing and bagging 450 pounds of grain a minute. An 1886 report of

the Illinois Bureau of Labor Statistics claimed that "new machinery has displaced fully 50 per cent of the muscular labor formerly required to do a given amount of work in the manufacture of agricultural implements." Packaged cereals appeared on the American breakfast table at this time, and the commercial canning of food, spurred by improved machinery which cut costs, expanded so rapidly that by 1887 a writer in *Good Housekeeping* magazine could say: "Housekeeping is getting to be ready made, as well as clothing." This profusion of ingenuity in the field of raising and processing food was typical. Statistics of the United States Patent Office show that whereas in the 1850's about 1,000 inventions a year were patented, in the 1870's the average was over 12,000. In 1890 alone 25,322 patents were issued.

The Railroad Network

In 1866, returning from his honeymoon in Europe, 30-year-old Charles Francis Adams, Jr., grandson and great-grandson of Presidents, full of ambition and ready, as he put it, to confront the world "face to face," looked about in search of a career. "Surveying the whole field," he later explained, "I fixed on the railroad system as the most developing force and the largest field of the day, and determined to attach myself to it." Adams' judgment was acute: for the next 25 years the railroads were probably the most significant element in American economic development, railroad executives the most powerful people in the country.

Some historians claim that the railroads were not indispensable to 19th-century economic growth, arguing that the canal and river network could have sustained the post-Civil War expansion and that the motorcar and truck would have been developed sooner if railroads had not existed. In *Railroads and American Economic Growth,* Robert W. Fogel insists that "no single innovation was vital" and that the railroads did not make "an overwhelming contribution." In the sense that it warns us against oversimplified explanations, Fogel's work is valuable. It does not, however, suggest that railroads were anything but a major influence.

Railroads were important first of all as an industry in themselves. Less than 35,000 miles of track existed when Lee laid down his sword at Appomattox. In 1870 railroad mileage exceeded 52,000, by 1875 it was over 74,000. In 1880 mileage passed the 93,000 mark, and then, after so much growth, came the real boom: 73,000 miles were laid during the next decade. In 1890 some 166,700 miles of track spanned the United States. Railroads took in over $1 billion in passenger and freight revenues in that year. (The federal government's income in 1890 was only $403 million.) The value of railroad properties and equipment was over $8.7 billion. The national *railroad* debt of $5.1 billion was almost five times as large as the national debt itself, $1.1 billion!

The emphasis in railroad construction after 1865 was on organizing integrated systems. This resulted from sheer necessity. The lines had high fixed costs: taxes, interest on their bonds, maintenance of track and rolling stock, salaries of office personnel. A short train with half-empty cars required almost as many men and as much fuel to operate as a long one jammed with freight or passengers. In order to earn profits the railroads had to carry as much traffic as possible. They therefore spread out feeder lines to draw business to their main lines the way the root network of a tree draws water into its trunk.

Before the Civil War, as we have seen, passengers and freight could travel by rail from beyond Chicago and St. Louis to the Atlantic Coast, but only after the war did true trunk lines appear. In 1861, for example, the New York Central ran from Albany to Buffalo. One could proceed from Buffalo to Chicago, but on a different

Links in the nation's increasingly interdependent transportation network can be glimpsed in this 1878 painting by a primitive artist, Herman Decker. The scene is the bustling Lonsdale Wharf in Providence, Rhode Island. (Museum of Art, Rhode Island School of Design.)

company's trains. In 1867 the Central passed into the hands of "Commodore" Cornelius Vanderbilt, who had made a large fortune in the shipping business. Vanderbilt already controlled lines running from Albany to New York City; now he merged these properties with the Central. In 1873 he integrated the Lake Shore and Michigan Southern into his empire and two years later the Michigan Central. The Commodore spent large sums improving his properties and buying strategic feeder lines. At his death in 1877 the Central operated a network of over 4,500 miles of track between New York City and most of the principal cities of the Middle West.

While Vanderbilt was putting together the New York Central complex, Thomas A. Scott was making the Pennsylvania Company into a second important trunk line, fusing roads to Cincinnati, Indianapolis, St. Louis, and Chicago to his Pennsylvania Railroad, which linked Pittsburgh and Philadelphia. In 1871 the Pennsylvania also obtained access to New York and soon reached Baltimore and Washington. By 1869 another important system, the Erie, controlled by a triumvirate of railroad freebooters, Daniel Drew, Jay Gould, and Jim Fisk, had extended itself from New York to Cleveland, Cincinnati, and St. Louis. Soon thereafter it, too, tapped the markets of Chicago and other principal cities. In 1874 the Baltimore and Ohio also obtained access to Chicago.

The transcontinental lines, of course, were trunk lines from the start; the emptiness of the western country would have made short lines unprofitable, and builders quickly grasped the need for direct connections to eastern markets and thorough integration of feeder lines. The dominant systematizer of the Southwest was Jay Gould. A soft-spoken, delicate, unostentatious man who looked, according to one newspaperman, "like an insignificant pigmy," Gould was actually ruthless, cynical, and aggressive. His mere appearance in Wall Street, one Texas newspaper reported in 1890, made "millionaires tremble like innocent sparrows . . . when a hungry hawk swoops down upon them." (A railroad president used a better image when he called

Gould a "perfect eel.") With millions acquired in shady railroad and stock market ventures, Gould invaded the West in the 1870's, buying 370,000 shares of Union Pacific stock. He also took over the Kansas Pacific, running from Denver to Kansas City, which he consolidated with the Union Pacific; and the Missouri Pacific, a line from Kansas City to St. Louis, which he expanded through mergers and purchases into a 5,300-mile system. Often Gould put together such properties merely to unload them on other railroads at a profit, but his grasp of the importance of integration was sound. In the Northwest, Henry Villard, a German-born ex-newspaperman, constructed another great railroad complex, based on his control of the Northern Pacific and various properties in Oregon and California. James J. Hill's expansion of the St. Paul and Pacific Railroad into the Great Northern system, absorbing a number of other lines in addition to laying track all the way to Seattle, produced still another western network.

The Civil War had demonstrated the lack of through railroad connections in the South. Shortly after the conflict, this situation began to be corrected as northern capital flowed into southern railroad construction. The Chesapeake and Ohio, organized in 1868, soon opened a direct line from Norfolk, Virginia, to Cincinnati. The Richmond and Danville absorbed some 26 lines after the war, forming a system that ran from Washington to the Mississippi. It in turn became part of the Richmond and West Point Terminal Company, which by the late eighties controlled an 8,558-mile network, largest in the region. Like other southern trunk lines, such as the Louisville and Nashville and the Atlantic Coast Line, this great system was largely controlled by northern capitalists. Gradually over the years the trunk lines had adopted a standard gauge (4 feet 8½ inches) for their tracks. After the southern lines accepted standard gauge in 1886, cars could move freely from system to system all over the country.

The railroads also stimulated the economy indirectly, acting as had foreign commerce and then the textile industry in earlier times as a multiplier speeding development. In 1869 they bought $41.6 million worth of railroad cars and locomotives, in 1889 $90.8 million. Such purchases created thousands of jobs, consumed raw materials, and led to countless technological advances. The roads in 1881 consumed about 94 per cent of all the rolled steel manufactured in the United States.

Because of their voracious appetite for traffic, railroads in sparsely settled regions and in areas with undeveloped resources devoted much money and effort to stimulating local economic growth. The Louisville and Nashville, for instance, was a prime mover in the expansion of the iron industry in Alabama in the 1880's. The state's output of iron increased tenfold between 1880 and 1889, in considerable part because of the railroad's activities in building spur lines to mines and furnaces and attracting capital into the industry.

The land-grant railroads sought incessantly to speed the settlement of new regions. They sold land cheaply and on easy terms, since sales meant future business as well as quick income. Roads like the Northern Pacific offered special reduced rates to travelers interested in buying farms, and entertained potential customers with a free hand. Land-grant lines also set up "bureaus of immigration," which distributed elaborate brochures describing the wonders of the new country. Their agents greeted immigrants at the great eastern ports and tried to steer them to railroad property. Overseas branches advertised the virtues of American farmland. They sent agents who were usually themselves immigrants—often ministers—all over Europe to drum up prospective settlers, many of whom could be expected to buy railroad land. Occasionally, whole colonies migrated to America under railroad auspices, such as the 1,900 Mennonites who came to Kansas from Russia in 1874 to settle on the land of the Atchison, Topeka and Santa Fe.

Technological advances in railroading also accelerated economic development in complex ways. In 1869 George Westinghouse invented the air brake. By enabling an engineer to apply

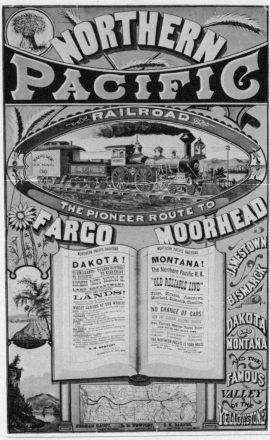

A Northern Pacific poster touts its land offerings as the "best and cheapest" available. By 1917 the railroad had realized $136 million on its land grants. (Chicago Historical Society.)

the brakes simultaneously to all his cars, whereas formerly each car had to be braked separately by its own conductor or brakeman, this invention made possible revolutionary increases in the size of trains and the speed at which they could safely operate. The sleeping car, invented in 1864 by George Pullman, now came into its own.

To pull these heavier trains, more powerful locomotives were needed. These in turn produced a call for stronger and more durable rails to bear the additional weight. Steel, itself reduced in cost because of technological developments, supplied the answer, for steel rails outlasted iron many times despite the use of much heavier equipment. "Steel rails," one expert said in the eighties, "form the very 'cornerstone' of the great improvements which have taken place in railroad efficiency." In 1880 only 50 per cent of the nation's rails were of steel; by 1890 less than 1 per cent were not.

A close tie developed at this time between the railroads and the nation's telegraph network, dominated by the Western Union Company. Commonly, the roads allowed Western Union to string wires along their rights of way, and they transported telegraphers and their equipment without charge. In return they received free telegraphic service, important for efficiency and safety. It is no mere coincidence that the early 1880's, a period of booming railroad construction, also saw a fantastic expansion of Western Union. By 1883 the company was transmitting 40 million messages a year over 400,000 miles of wire. The two industries, as Jay Gould put it, went "hand in hand, . . . integral parts" of American civilization.

Iron, Oil, and Electricity

The transformation of iron manufacturing affected the nation almost as much as railroad development. America was blessed with rich deposits of iron ore and with fuels—first wood and then coal—for smelting and refining it. As we have seen, considerable iron was produced in colonial times. After independence, growth was rapid: 22,000 tons in 1820; 321,000 in 1840; 920,000 in 1860. In the postwar era, however, iron production increased still more spectacularly. In 1870 output reached 1.86 million tons. In 1880 it was 4.29 million; in 1890, 10.3 million; in 1900, 15.4 million.

Steel production expanded even more rapidly. Steel is a very special form of iron. In its pure form (wrought iron) the metal is tough but relatively soft. On the other hand, ordinary cast iron, which contains large amounts of carbon and other impurities, is hard but brittle. Steel, which

contains one or two per cent carbon, combines the hardness of cast iron with the toughness of wrought iron. For nearly every purpose—structural girders for bridges and buildings, railroad track, machine tools, boiler plate, barbed wire—steel is immensely superior to other kinds of iron. But steel was so expensive to manufacture that it could not be used for bulky products until the invention in the 1850's of the Bessemer process, perfected independently by Henry Bessemer, an Englishman, and William Kelly of Kentucky. Bessemer and Kelly discovered that a stream of air directed into a mass of molten iron caused the carbon and other impurities to combine with oxygen and burn off. When measured amounts of carbon, silicon, and manganese were then added, the whole brew became steel. What had been a rare metal now could be produced by the hundreds and thousands of tons. The Bessemer process and the open-hearth method, a slower but more precise technique that enabled producers to sample the molten mass and thus control quality closely, were introduced commercially in the United States in the sixties. In 1870, 77,000 tons of steel were manufactured, less than four per cent of the volume of pig iron. By 1880, however, 1.39 million tons were pouring annually from the converters. In 1890 production reached 4.79 million tons, by 1900 nearly 11.4 million.

Such growth would have been impossible but for the huge supplies of iron ore in the United States and the coal necessary to fire the furnaces that refined it. In the 1870's the great iron fields rimming Lake Superior started to yield their treasures. The Menominee range in Michigan began production in 1877, followed in 1884 by the Gogebic range, on the Michigan-Wisconsin border. In each case the completion of rail connections to the fields had been necessary before large-scale mining could take place, another illustration of the importance of railroads in the economic history of the era. The Vermilion range, in the northeast corner of Minnesota, was opened up at about the same time, and somewhat later the magnificent Mesabi region, where the enormous iron concentrations made a compass needle spin like a top. Mesabi ores could literally be

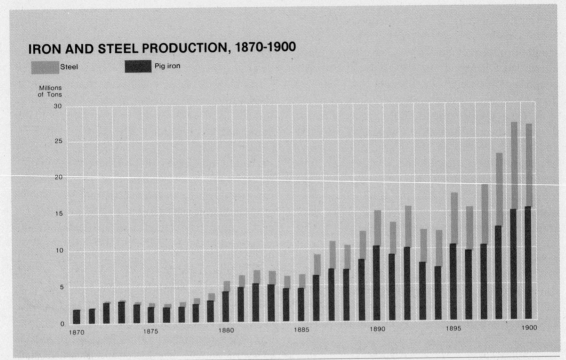

IRON AND STEEL PRODUCTION, 1870-1900

Minnesota's Mesabi Range (right, shown in 1899) was developed largely with Rockefeller money. It shipped 4,000 tons of iron ore in 1892, and within a decade tripled that amount—an increase reflected in the graph above. (Photo: Minnesota Historical Society.)

mined with steam shovels, almost like gravel. Pittsburgh, surrounded by vast coal deposits, became the iron and steel capital of the country, the Minnesota ores reaching it by way of steamers on the Great Lakes and rail lines from Cleveland. Other cities in Pennsylvania and Ohio were also important producers, and a separate complex, centering around Birmingham, Alabama, developed to exploit local iron and coal fields.

By 1880 the leading iron and steel producer was Andrew Carnegie. His company—atypical in that it was a partnership rather than a corporation—turned out about a quarter of the nation's steel ingots and a larger percentage of certain basic forms, such as rails and armor plate. In 1875 he had opened his J. Edgar Thomson Steel Works, one of the finest and most efficient in the industry, named in honor of a former president of the Pennsylvania Railroad, his best customer. As late as 1880 many hundreds of small produc-

ers still existed, but the number declined steadily, Carnegie's share of the market increasing proportionately. Like mining, the iron and steel business was ill-suited to small-scale operation. It required much heavy and expensive equipment, a large labor force, and financial reserves to withstand the buffeting of bad times. By the last years of the century, really small forges had practically disappeared and a few giants controlled the field.

The petroleum industry expanded even more spectacularly than iron and steel. The business had not even existed in pre-Civil War days; Edwin L. Drake drilled the first successful well in Pennsylvania in 1859. During the Civil War, production ranged between 2 and 3 million barrels a year. In 1873 almost 10 million barrels were produced, and in the early eighties annual output averaged over 20 million barrels. A decade later this figure had leaped to about 50 million.

Before the invention of the gasoline engine

and the automobile, the most important petroleum product was kerosene. This fuel, burned in lamps, accounted for well over two-thirds of all oil production in the early 1870's. In the early years in Pennsylvania hundreds of tiny refineries, often reminiscent of the ramshackle stills of nearby moonshiners, were engaged in the business. They heated crude oil in large kettles and after the volatile elements had escaped, condensed the kerosene in coils cooled by water. The heavier petroleum tars were simply discarded.

Technological advances came rapidly. By the early 1870's, refiners had learned how to "crack" petroleum by applying high temperatures to the crude in order to break up and rearrange its mo-

lecular structure, thus increasing the percentage of kerosene yielded. By-products such as naphtha, gasoline (used in vaporized form as an illuminating gas), rhigolene (a local anesthetic), cymogene (a coolant for refrigerating machines), and many lubricants and waxes began to appear on the market. At the same time a great increase in the supply of crude oil—especially after the chemist Herman Frosch perfected a method for removing sulfur from low-quality petroleum—drove prices down. Naturally, these circumstances put a premium on refining efficiency. Larger plants utilizing expensive machinery and employing skilled technicians became more important. In the mid-sixties only three refineries in the country could process 2,000 barrels of crude

A scene on the Oil Creek Railroad in western Pennsylvania in the early 1860's. Initially, crude oil was shipped to refineries in barrels by barge or on railroad flatcars, as shown here. The familiar "boiler-shaped" tank car was invented in 1869, and by the 1870's a network of pipelines was laid to handle the growing oil output. (Drake Museum.)

a week; ten years later plants capable of handling 1,000 barrels a day were common.

By this time the chief oil-refining centers were Cleveland, Pittsburgh, Baltimore, and the New York City area. Of these Cleveland was the fastest growing, chiefly because it enjoyed very low freight rates. The New York Central and Erie railroads competed fiercely for its oil trade, and the Erie Canal offered an alternative route. Pittsburgh, on the other hand, depended entirely upon the Pennsylvania Railroad, while New York and Baltimore suffered from being far removed from the oil fields. During the 1870's the Standard Oil Company of Cleveland, whose president was a successful merchant named John D. Rockefeller, emerged as the giant among the refiners, exploiting every possible new technical advance and employing fair means and foul to persuade competitors first in the Cleveland area and then elsewhere either to sell out or join forces. By 1873 Rockefeller controlled between 30 and 40 per cent of the nation's oil-refining capacity; by 1879 more than 90 per cent was in his hands. He soon owned a network of oil pipelines and added huge reserves of petroleum in the ground to his empire. The existence of this monopoly, together with the remarkable expansion of the entire industry, caused Standard Oil to attract far more attention than its importance warranted in the late 19th century. The period of its greatest growth and economic influence did not come until later. The first 100-million-barrel year was 1903. Thereafter, production really spurted, passing the *billion*-barrel mark in 1929.

Two other important new industries were the telephone and electric light businesses. Both were typical of the period, being entirely dependent upon technical advances and intimately related to the growth of a high-speed, urban civilization that put great stress on communication. The telephone was invented in 1876 by Alexander Graham Bell, who had been led to the study of acoustics through his interest in the education of the deaf. His work with a device for transcribing tone vibrations electrically to aid deaf-mutes in learning to speak encouraged him to experiment with a "speaking telegraph" that used electrified metal disks, acting like the drum of the human ear, to convert sound waves into electrical impulses and electrical impulses back into sound waves. Although considered little more than a clever gadget at first—the Western Union Company passed up an opportunity to buy the invention for $100,000, its president calling the telephone an "electrical toy"—Bell's invention soon proved its practical value. By 1880, 85 towns and cities had local telephone networks. In 1895 there were over 300,000 phones in the country, in 1900 almost 800,000, twice the total for all Europe. By that date the American Telephone and Telegraph Company, a consolidation of over 100 local systems, dominated the business.

When Western Union realized the importance of the telephone, it tried for a time to compete with Bell by developing a machine of its own. The man it commissioned to devise this machine was Thomas A. Edison. Eventually, Bell's patents proved unassailable, and Western Union abandoned the effort to maintain a competing system, but not until Edison had vastly improved telephonic transmission. Not yet 30 when he turned to the telephone problem, Edison had already made a number of contributions toward solving what he called the "mysteries of electri-

Edison patented the phonograph in 1878, budgeting $18 for its invention. He was photographed in his laboratory in 1888 working on a wax-cylinder model. (Edison Laboratory National Monument.)

cal force," including a multiplex telegraph capable of sending four messages over a single wire at the same time. At Menlo Park, New Jersey, he built the prototype of the modern research laboratory, where specific problems could be attacked on a mass scale by a team of trained specialists. During his lifetime he took out over 1,000 patents, dealing with machines as varied as the phonograph, the motion-picture projector, the storage battery, and the mimeograph. He also contributed substantially to the development of the electric dynamo, ore-separating machinery, and railroad signal equipment.

But Edison's most significant achievement was unquestionably his perfection of the incandescent lamp, or electric light bulb. Others before Edison had experimented with the idea of producing light by passing electricity through a thin filament in a vacuum. Always, however, the filaments quickly broke. Edison tried hundreds of fibers before producing, late in 1879, a carbonized filament that would glow brightly in a vacuum tube for as long as 170 hours without crumbling. At Christmastime he decorated the grounds about his laboratory with a few dozen of the new lights. People flocked by the thousands to see this miracle of the "Wizard of Menlo Park." To these admirers of his "bright, beautiful light, like the mellow sunset of an Italian autumn," the inventor boasted that soon he would be able to illuminate whole towns, even great cities like New York.

He was true to his promise. In 1882 his Edison Illuminating Company opened a power station in New York and began to supply current for lighting to 85 consumers, including the New York *Times* and the banking house of J. P. Morgan and Company. Soon central stations were springing up everywhere until, by 1898, there were about 3,000 in the country. Edison's manufacturing subsidiaries flourished equally: in 1885 they turned out 139,000 incandescent lamps, by the end of the decade nearly a million a year.

The Edison system employed direct current at low voltages, which limited the distance that power could be transmitted to about two miles. Technicians soon demonstrated that by using alternating current, stepped up to high voltages by transformers, power could be transported over great distances economically and then reduced to safe levels for use by consumers. This encouraged George Westinghouse, inventor of the air brake, to found the Westinghouse Electric Company in 1886. Edison stubbornly refused to accept the superiority of high-voltage alternating current. "Just as certain as death Westinghouse will kill a customer within 6 months," he predicted, and indeed, for a time, the language was graced with the verb "to Westinghouse," meaning to electrocute. But the Westinghouse system quickly proved itself safe as well as efficient, and alternating current became standard. The industry expanded rapidly until by the early years of the 20th century almost 6 billion kilowatt-hours of electricity were being produced annually. Yet this, of course, was only the beginning.

Competition and Monopoly: The Railroads

In all these industries and in many others during the post-Civil War era expansion went hand in hand with concentration; with each passing decade, fewer, larger firms captured an increasing share of the business. The principal cause of this trend, aside from the obvious economies resulting from large-scale production and the growing importance of expensive machinery, was the downward trend of world prices after 1873. This deflation affected agricultural goods as well as manufactures, and it lasted until 1896 or 1897.

Contemporaries believed they were living through a "great depression," but the name is misleading, since output expanded almost continuously, and at a rapid rate, until 1893, when a "true" depression struck the country. Falling prices, however, kept a steady pressure on profit margins, and this led to increased production and thus to intense competition for markets. Rival concerns battled for business, the strongest, most efficient, and most unscrupulous destroying or absorbing their foes. If no clear victor emerged, the exhausted contenders frequently ended the warfare by combining voluntarily. At least for a time, the government did little about laying down rules for the fighting or preventing the consolidations that seemed to result from it.

According to the theory of laissez faire, competition supposedly advanced the public interest by keeping prices low and assuring the most efficient producer the largest profit. Up to a point it accomplished these purposes in the years after 1865, but it also fathered side effects that injured both the economy and society as a whole.

In railroading, for instance, there were no firmly fixed rates for carrying passengers or freight. Besides charging more for transporting valuable manufactured goods than for bulky products like coal or wheat, the lines often made special concessions to shippers to avoid hauling empty cars. In other words, they charged whatever the traffic would bear. Generally speaking, rates became progressively lower as time passed,

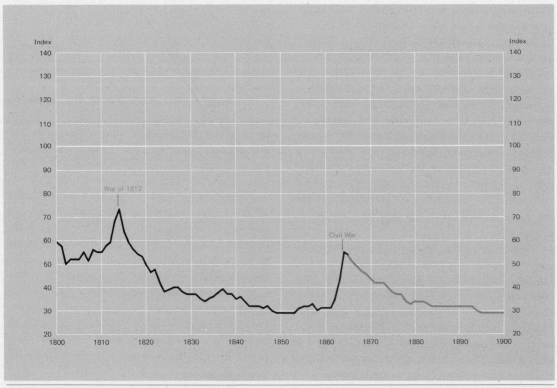

See page 129 for explanation of purpose of this chart. If you have only Volume 2 of this book, the chart is based on a rough series of price indexes provided by the Bureau of Labor Statistics. 100 is the base line, and is the consumer price index, averaged, for the years 1957-1959.

for as the railroad network expanded, competition naturally intensified. In 1865 it cost from 96 cents to $2.15 per hundred pounds, depending on the class of freight, to ship goods from New York to Chicago. In 1888 rates ranged from 35 cents to 75 cents. In the three decades after the Civil War, the cost of shipping 100 pounds of wheat from Chicago to New York dropped from 65 cents to 20 cents.

Competition cut deeply into railroad profits, causing the lines to seek desperately to increase volume. Paradoxically, they did so chiefly by reducing rates still more, on a selective basis. They gave rebates (secret, unofficial reductions below the published rates) to large shippers in order to capture their business. The granting of some discount to those who shipped in volume made economic sense: it was easier to handle freight in carload lots than in smaller units. Because of the volume of its shipments, Standard Oil received a 10 per cent discount from all the Cleveland carriers merely on the promise that it would divide its business equitably among them. So intense was the battle for business, however, that the roads made concessions to big customers far beyond what the economies of bulk shipment justified. In the 1870's the New York Central regularly reduced the rates charged important shippers by 50 to 80 per cent. One large Utica dry-goods merchant received a rate of 9 cents while others paid 33 cents. Two big New York City grain merchants paid so little that they soon controlled the grain business of the entire city. Between 1877 and 1879, a critical period in the oil business, the major trunk lines carried Standard's petroleum products to the Atlantic seaboard for 80 cents a barrel while charging the independent refiners of Cleveland $1.44½.

Railroad officials disliked rebating but found no way to avoid the practice. "Notwithstanding my horror of rebates," the president of a New England trunk line told one of his executives in discussing the case of a prominent brick manufacturer, "bill at the usual rate, and rebate Mr. Cole 25 cents a thousand." In extreme cases the railroads even gave large shippers drawbacks, which were rebates on the business of the shippers' competitors. For many years Standard Oil collected 20 cents from the Cleveland carriers for each barrel of "independent" oil they transported.

Besides rebating, railroads granted other favors to certain shippers. They issued passes to officials, built sidings at the plants of important companies without charge, and gave freely of their landholdings to attract businesses to their territory. Railroads also battled directly with one another in ways damaging to themselves and to the public. Unscrupulous operators often threw together roundabout, inefficient trunk lines merely to blackmail already established roads, forcing them to buy up the competing properties at inflated prices. Others tried to win control of competing lines in the stock market. Between 1866 and 1868 Vanderbilt of the New York Central fought a futile campaign to win control of the Erie. The raffish Erie directors struck back by issuing themselves thousands of shares of new stock without paying for them, thus gravely overinflating the capitalization of the line. Both roads stooped to bribery in an effort to obtain favorable action in the New York legislature, and there were even pitched battles between the hirelings of each side.

"The force of competition," a railroad man explained, "is one that no carrying corporation can withstand and before which the managing officers of a corporation are helpless." James F. Joy of the Chicago, Burlington, and Quincy made the same point more bluntly: "Unless you prepare to defend yourselves," he advised the president of the Michigan Central, "you will be boarded by pirates in all quarters." Railroad ex-

ecutives are "hardly better than a race of horse-jockeys," Charles Francis Adams, Jr., wrote in *Railroads: Their Origin and Problems* (1879). A person trying to run a railroad honestly, Adams also said, would be like Don Quixote tilting at a windmill.

To make up for losses forced upon them by competitive pressures, railroads charged higher rates at way points along their tracks where no competition existed. As a result, it sometimes cost more to ship a given product a short distance than a longer one. Rochester, New York, was served only by the New York Central. In the 1870's it cost 30 cents to transport a barrel of flour from Rochester to New York City, a distance of 350 miles. At the same time flour could be shipped from Minneapolis to New York, a distance of well over 1,000 miles for only 20 cents.° One Rochester businessman told a state investigating committee that he could save 18 cents a hundredweight by sending goods to St. Louis by way of New York, where several carriers competed for the traffic, even though, in fact, the goods might come back through Rochester over the same tracks on the way to St. Louis! Local farmers 165 miles from New York paid 70 cents a tub to ship their butter to the metropolis, while producers as far away as Illinois could ship butter there for only 30 cents.

Although cheap transportation stimulated the economy, few persons really benefited from cutthroat competition. Small shippers, and all businessmen in cities and towns with limited rail outlets, suffered heavily; railroad discrimination against such customers unquestionably speeded the concentration of industry in large corporations located in major centers. The instability of rates troubled even interests like the middle-western flour millers who benefited from the competitive situation, for it hampered planning. Nor could manufacturers who received rebates be entirely happy, since few could be sure that some other producer was not getting a still larger reduction.

°During one period of intense competition, the rate on flour from Minneapolis to New York fell to 10 cents a barrel.

Edward Steichen's memorable photographic study of J. Pierpont Morgan, taken in 1903. Looking the formidable Morgan in the eye, Steichen said, was akin to facing the headlights of an onrushing express train. (Museum of Modern Art.)

Probably the worst sufferers were the roads themselves. The loss of revenue resulting from rate-cutting, combined with inflated debts, put most of them in grave difficulty when faced with a downturn in the business cycle. In 1876 two-fifths of all railroad bonds were in default; three years later 65 lines were bankrupt. Since the public would not countenance bankrupt railroads going out of business, these companies were placed in the hands of court-appointed receivers. The receivers, however, seldom provided efficient management and had no funds at their disposal for new equipment.

A new, strong leadership that would enforce belt-tightening all along the line and bring an end to the chaotic rate wars was sorely needed. This leadership was supplied—at a price—by a handful of important financiers, most notably J. Pierpont Morgan, head of a powerful firm of New York private bankers. Morgan became prominent in railroad affairs in the 1880's when he negotiated "peace settlements" first between the New York Central and the Pennsylvania and then among all the eastern trunk lines. His main contribution came in the mid-nineties, after the depression of those years had brought lines controlling 67,000 miles of track to the wall. The House of Morgan and other private bankers, such as Kuhn, Loeb of New York and Lee, Higginson of Boston reorganized—critics said they "Morganized"—most of these shattered corporations. The economic historian A. D. Noyes described this method accurately in 1904:

Bondholders were requested to scale down interest charges, receiving new stock in compensation, while the shareholders were invited to pay a cash assessment, thus providing a working fund. [The bankers] combined to guarantee that the requisite money should be raised. They too were paid in new stock. . . . Though the total capital issues were increased, fixed charges were diminished and a sufficient fund for road improvement and new equipment was provided.

These reorganizations put such great trunk lines as the Erie, the Baltimore and Ohio, the Union Pacific, and the Northern Pacific back on their feet. They were kept there by the termination of practices that had toppled them to begin with. Representatives of the bankers sat on the board of every line they saved. Although they generally took no part in handling the everyday affairs of the roads, their influence was predominant, and they consistently opposed rate wars, rebating, and other competitive practices. In effect, control of the railroad network became centralized, even though the companies maintained their separate existences and operated in a seemingly independent manner. When Morgan died in 1913, "Morgan men" dominated the boards of the New York Central, the Erie, the New York, New Haven and Hartford, the Southern, the Pere Marquette, the Atchison, Topeka and Santa Fe, and many other lines.

The Steel Industry: Carnegie

The iron and steel industry was also intensely competitive. Despite the general trend toward higher production, demand varied erratically from year to year, even from month to month. The price of iron products fluctuated wildly. Throughout the mid-seventies, demand was relatively slack. Prices fell, until by 1878 they had reached the lowest levels since colonial times. Then came a revival, but within a three-month period in 1880 the price of pig iron fell from $41 a ton to $25. However, 1881 was again a banner year, the price of pig iron touching $60 a ton. Twelve months later, iron had fallen to $39 a ton.

Such conditions played havoc with many firms. In good times producers tended to build new facilities, only to suffer heavy losses when demand declined and much of their capacity lay idle. The forward rush of technology put a tremendous emphasis on efficiency; expensive plants quickly became obsolete. Improved transportation facilities allowed manufacturers in widely scattered regions to compete with one another; despite the importance of the Pittsburgh region, in the early nineties multimillion-dollar mills existed in Alabama, Colorado, Illinois, and elsewhere.

The kingpin of the industry was Andrew Carnegie. Born in Dunfermline, Scotland, Carnegie came to the United States in 1848 at the age of 12. His first job as a bobbin boy in a cotton mill brought him $1.20 a week, but his talents perfectly fitted the times, and he rose rapidly: Western Union messenger boy, to telegrapher, to private secretary, to a railroad executive. He saved his money, made some shrewd investments, and by 1868 had an income of $50,000 a year. At about this time he decided to specialize in the iron business, saying, in an oft-quoted remark, that he believed in putting all his eggs in one basket and then watching the basket. Carnegie possessed great talent as a salesman, boundless faith in the future of the country, an uncanny knack of choosing topflight subordinates, and

enough ruthlessness to survive in the iron and steel jungle. Whereas other steelmen built new plants in good times, he preferred to expand in bad times, when it cost far less to do so. During the 1870's, he later recalled, "many of my friends needed money. . . . I . . . bought out five or six of them. That is what gave me my leading interest in this steel business."

Carnegie grasped the importance of technological improvements in his industry. Slightly skeptical of the Bessemer process at first, once he became convinced of its practicality he adopted it enthusiastically. He employed chemists and other specialists freely and was soon making steel from iron oxides that other manufacturers had discarded as waste. He was also a driver of men and a merciless competitor. When a plant manager announced: "We broke all records for making steel last week," Carnegie replied: "Congratulations! *Why not do it every week?*" When another informed him of an especially outstanding record compiled by the crew of one furnace, he answered coldly: "What are the other ten furnaces doing?" Carnegie sold rails by paying "commissions" to railroad purchasing agents, and he was not above reneging on a contract if he thought it profitable and safe to do so.

By 1890 the Carnegie Steel Company dominated the industry and its output increased nearly tenfold over the next decade. Profits mounted from $3 million in 1893 to $6 million in 1896 and soared to $40 million in 1900. Alarmed by his increasing control of the industry, the makers of finished steel products such as barbed wire and tubing began to combine and to consider entering the primary field. Carnegie, his competitive temper aroused, then threatened to turn to finished products himself. A colossal steel war seemed imminent.

However, Carnegie longed to retire in order to devote himself to philanthropic work. He had for years professed the belief that great wealth entailed social responsibilities and that it was a disgrace to die rich. When J. P. Morgan approached him through an intermediary with an offer to buy him out, he assented readily. In 1901 Morgan put together United States Steel, the "world's first billion-dollar corporation." This huge combination included all the Carnegie properties, the Federal Steel Company (Carnegie's largest competitor), and such important fabricators of finished products as the American Steel and Wire Company, the American Tin Plate Company, and the National Tube Company. Vast reserves of Minnesota iron ore and a fleet of Great Lakes ore steamers were also included. U. S. Steel was capitalized at $1.4 billion, about twice the value of its separate properties but not necessarily an overestimation of its profit-earning capacity. The owners of Carnegie Steel received $492 million, of which $250 million went to Carnegie himself.

The Standard Oil Trust

The pattern of fierce competition leading to combination and monopoly is well illustrated by the history of the petroleum industry. Irresistible pressures pushed the refiners into a brutal struggle to dominate the business. Production of crude oil, subject to the uncertainties of prospecting and drilling, fluctuated constantly and without regard for need. In general, output surged ahead in huge bounds, far in excess of demand. Refining capacity also grew beyond the requirements of the day, for it took little capital to erect a new plant and low crude prices encouraged even incompetent manufacturers. As John D. Rockefeller later explained, "all sorts of people . . . the butcher, the baker, and the candlestick-maker began to refine oil."

Rockefeller's Standard Oil Company emerged victorious in the resulting competitive wars because Rockefeller and his associates were the toughest and most imaginative fighters as well as the most efficient refiners in the business. In addition to obtaining rebates from the railroads, Standard Oil cut prices locally to force small independents to sell out or face ruin. One Massachusetts refiner testified that Standard drove down the price of kerosene in his district

John D. Rockefeller carried his passion for perfection onto the golf course, hiring a boy to do nothing but intone "keep your head down" on each shot. (Brown Brothers.)

from $9\frac{1}{4}$ cents to $5\frac{1}{4}$ simply to destroy his business. Since kerosene was largely sold through grocery stores, Standard supplied its own outlets with meat, sugar, and other products at artificially low prices to help crush the stores that handled other brands of kerosene. The company employed spies to track down the customers of independents and offer them oil at bargain prices. Bribery was also a Standard practice, as is illustrated in the quip of the reformer Henry Demarest Lloyd, who said that the company had done everything to the Pennsylvania legislature except refine it. Rockefeller's most sympathetic biographer, Allan Nevins, admits that Standard Oil "committed acts against competitors which could not be defended."

Although a bold planner and a daring taker of necessary risks, Rockefeller was far too orderly and astute to enjoy the free-swinging battles that plagued his industry. Born in an upstate New York village in 1839, he settled in Cleveland in 1855 and became a successful produce merchant. During the Civil War he invested in a local refinery and by 1865 was engaged full time in the oil business.

Like Carnegie, Rockefeller was an organizer; he knew little about the technology of petroleum. He sought efficiency, order, and stability. His forte was meticulous attention to detail: stories are told of his ordering the number of drops of solder used to seal oil cans reduced from 40 to 39, and of his insisting that the manager of one of his refineries account for 750 missing barrel bungs. Not miserliness but a profound grasp of the economies of large-scale production explain this behavior; by reducing the cost of refining a gallon of crude oil by a mere .082 cents, Standard Oil increased its annual profit about $600,000. Rockefeller competed ruthlessly not primarily to crush other refiners but to persuade them to join with him, to share the business peaceably and rationally so that all could profit. Competition was obsolescent, he argued, although no more effective competitor than he ever lived. In truth most of the independent refiners that Standard Oil destroyed by unfair competition had previously turned down offers to merge or sell out on terms that modern students consider generous.

Rockefeller achieved his monopoly by convincing other refiners that resistance would be unprofitable, if not suicidal. As we have seen, by 1879 most of them had given up the fight, and Standard Oil controlled more than 90 per cent of the nation's oil business. He stabilized and structured his monopoly by creating a new type of business organization, the trust. Standard Oil was an Ohio corporation, prohibited by local law from owning plants in other states or holding stock in out-of-state corporations. As Rockefeller and his associates took over dozens of companies with facilities scattered across the country, serious legal and managerial difficulties arose. How could these many organizations be integrated with Standard Oil of Ohio? A rotund, genial little Pennsylvania lawyer named Samuel C. T. Dodd

came up with an answer to this question in 1879.° The stock of Standard of Ohio and of all the other companies that the Rockefeller interests had swallowed up was turned over to nine trustees, who were empowered to "exercise general supervision" over all these properties. Stockholders received in exchange trust certificates, on which dividends were paid. Thus order came to the petroleum business. Competition almost disappeared; prices steadied; profits skyrocketed. By 1892 John D. Rockefeller was worth over $800 million.

The Standard Oil Trust was not a corporation. Indeed, it had no charter, no legal existence at all. For many years few people outside the organization knew that it existed. The form chosen persuaded Rockefeller and other Standard Oil officials that without violating their consciences, they could deny under oath that Standard Oil of Ohio owned or controlled other corporations "directly or indirectly through its officers or agents." The *trustees* controlled these organizations—and Standard of Ohio too!

After Standard Oil's secret was finally revealed during a New York investigation in 1888, the word *trust,* formerly signifying a fiduciary arrangement for the protection of the interests of individuals incompetent or unwilling to guard them themselves, immediately became a synonym for monopoly, and Standard Oil became the most hated and feared company in the United States. However, from the company's point of view, monopoly was not the purpose of the trust—that had been achieved before the device was invented. Centralization of the management of diverse and far-flung operations was its chief function. Standard Oil headquarters in New York became the brain of a complex network where information from the field was collected and digested, where decisions were made, and whence orders went out to drillers, refiners, scientists, and salesmen. The resulting advantages explain why the trust device was soon adopted by many other industries.

°The trust formula was not "perfected" until 1882.

Public Utilities

That public utilities like the telephone and electric lighting industries tended to form monopolies is not difficult to explain, for in such fields competition involved costly duplication of equipment and, especially in the case of the telephone, loss of service efficiency. However, competitive pressures were very strong in the early stages of their development. Since these industries depended upon patents, Bell and Edison had to fight mighty battles in the courts against rivals seeking to infringe upon their rights. Few quibbled over means when so much money hung in the balance. After having turned down a chance to buy Bell's invention for a pittance, Western Union organized the American Speaking Telephone Company, capitalized at $300,000, and employed Edison to invent a device that would enable it to circumvent Bell's rights. In return, the Bell interests challenged Edison's improved telephone transmitter, claiming that it infringed upon patents issued to one Emile Berliner, which they had bought up. Western Union was the victor in this particular battle, but in the end the telegraph company became convinced that the courts would uphold Bell's claims and abandoned the field.

As for Edison himself, much of his time was taken up with legal battles to protect his rights under his many patents. When he first announced his electric light, capitalists, engineers, and inventors flocked to Menlo Park. Edison proudly revealed to them the secrets of his marvelous lamp. Many of them hurried away to turn this information to their own advantage, thinking the "Wizard" a naive fool. When they invaded the field, the law provided Edison with far less protection than he had expected. He had to fight a "Seven Years' War" with Westinghouse over the carbon-filament incandescent lamp. Although he won, his costs were over $2 million, and when the courts finally decided in his favor, only two years remained before the patent expired. "My electric light inventions have brought me no profits, only forty years of litigation," Edison later complained. A patent, he said bitterly, was "simply an invitation to a lawsuit."

The attitude of businessmen toward the rights of inventors and industrial pioneers is illustrated by this early advertisement of the Westinghouse Company:

We regard it as fortunate that we have deferred entering the electrical field until the present moment. Having thus profited by the public experience of others, we enter ourselves for competition, hampered by a minimum of expense for experimental outlay. . . . In short, our organization is free, in large measure, of the load with which [other] electrical enterprises seem to be encumbered. The fruit of this . . . we propose to share with the customer.

Competition in the electric-lighting business raged for some years between Edison, Westinghouse, and still another corporation, the Thomson-Houston Electric Company, which was operating 870 central lighting stations by 1890. Finally, in 1892, the Edison and Thomson-Houston companies merged, forming General Electric, a $35 million corporation. Thereafter, General Electric and Westinghouse maintained their domination in the manufacture of bulbs and much other electrical equipment as well as in the distribution of electrical power.

The pattern of competition leading to dominance by a few great companies was repeated in many other businesses. In life insurance, for example, an immense expansion took place after the Civil War, triggered by the perfection of a new type of group policy, the "tontine," by Henry B. Hyde of the Equitable Life Company.° High-pressure salesmanship prevailed; agents gave rebates to customers by shading their own commissions; companies stole crack agents from their rivals and raided new territories. They sometimes invested as much as 96 per cent of the

---

°A tontine policy paid no dividends for a stated period of years. If a policyholder died, his heirs received the face value but no dividends. At the end of the tontine period, survivors collected not only their own dividends but those of the unfortunates who had died or permitted their policies to lapse. This was psychologically appealing, since it stressed living rather than dying and added an element of gambling to insurance.

first year's premiums in obtaining new business. By 1900, after three decades of fierce competition, three giants dominated the industry, Equitable, New York Life, and Mutual Life, each with approximately $1 billion of insurance in force.

Americans React to Big Business

The expansion of industry and its concentration in fewer and fewer hands caused a major shift in the thinking of the people about the role of government in economic and social affairs. The fact that Americans, strongly individualistic, disliked powerful government in general and strict regulation of the economy in particular had never meant that they objected to *all* government activity in the economic sphere. Banking laws, tariffs, internal-improvement legislation, and the granting of public land to railroads are only the most obvious of the economic regulations enforced in the 19th century by both the federal government and the states. Americans saw no contradiction between government activities of this type and the free-enterprise philosophy, because such laws were intended to release human energy and thus *increase* the area in which freedom could operate. Tariffs stimulated industry and created new jobs, railroad grants opened up new regions for development, and so on. As J. W. Hurst has put it in a thought-provoking study, *Law and the Conditions of Freedom in the Nineteenth-Century United States,* the people "resort[ed] to law to enlarge the options open to private individual and group energy."

After about 1870 the public attitude began to

The Verdict, a cartoon weekly that flourished briefly at the turn of the century, devoted its pages to unremitting attacks on the Republicans, big business, and monopolists. George Luks, one of the "ashcan" artists, did this cartoon. (New-York Historical Society.)

change. The growth of huge industrial and financial organizations and the increasing complexity of economic relations frightened people yet made them at the same time greedy for more of the goods and services the new society was turning out. To many, the great new corporations and trusts resembled Frankenstein's monster—marvelous and powerful, but a grave threat to society. The astute James Bryce described the changes clearly in *The American Commonwealth:*

New causes are at work. . . . Modern civilization . . . has become more exacting. It discerns more benefits which the organized power of government can secure, and grows more anxious to attain them. Men live fast, and are impatient of the slow working of natural laws. . . . There are benefits which the law of supply and demand do not procure. Unlimited competition seems to press too hard on the weak. The power of groups of men organized by incorporation as joint-stock companies, or of small knots of rich men acting in combination, has developed with unexpected strength in unexpected ways, overshadowing individuals and even communities, and showing that the very freedom of association which men sought to secure by law . . . may, under the shelter of the law, ripen into a new form of tyranny.

To some extent public fear of the new industrial giants reflected concern about monopoly. If Standard Oil completely dominated oil refining, it might raise prices inordinately at vast cost to consumers. Charles Francis Adams, Jr., expressed this feeling when he wrote in the 1870's: "In the minds of the great majority, and not without reason, the idea of any industrial combination is closely connected with that of monopoly, and monopoly with extortion."

Although in isolated cases monopolists did raise prices unreasonably, generally they did not; indeed, prices tended to fall, until by the 1890's a veritable "consumer's millennium" had arrived. Far more important in causing resentment against the new corporate giants was the fear that they were destroying economic opportunity, and threatening democratic institutions. It was not the *wealth* of the new tycoons like Carnegie and Rockefeller and Morgan so much as their *influence* that worried people. In the face of the growing disparity between rich and poor, could republican institutions survive? Was the avalanche of cheap new products made available by the new corporations worth the sacrifice of the American way of life? "We must place . . . ethics above economics," one foe of monopoly insisted at a great turn-of-the-century conference on trusts at Chicago, and his audience gave him an ovation.

Some observers believed either autocracy or a form of revolutionary socialism to be almost inevitable. In 1890 former President Rutherford B. Hayes pondered over "the wrong and evils of the money-piling tendency of our country, which is changing laws, government, and morals and giving all power to the rich," and decided that he was going to become a "nihilist." Campaigning for the governorship of Texas in 1890, James S. Hogg, a staunch conservative, said: "Within a few years, unless something is done, most of the wealth and talent of our country will be on one side, while arrayed on the other will be the great mass of the people, composing the bone and sinew of this government. . . . The commune threatens us, but it is the legitimate child and offspring of the cormorant." John Boyle O'Reilly, a liberal Catholic journalist, wrote in 1886: "There is something worse than Anarchy, bad as that is; and it is irresponsible power in the hands of mere wealth." William Cook, a New York lawyer, warned in *The Corporation Problem* (1891) that "colossal aggregations of capital" were "dangerous to the republic."

These are typical examples of the reactions of responsible citizens to the rise of industrial combinations. Less thoughtful Americans sometimes went much further in their hatred of entrenched wealth. In 1900 Eddie Cudahy, son of a prominent member of the Beef Trust, was kidnaped. His captor, Pat Crowe, received $25,000 ransom but was apprehended. Crowe's guilt was clear: "I want to start right by confessing in plain English that I was guilty of the kidnapping," he wrote. But a jury acquitted him, presumably on the theory that it was all right to rob a member of the Beef Trust if you could get away with it.

As the volume of criticism mounted, the leaders of the trusts rose to their own defense. Rockefeller described in graphic terms the chaotic conditions that plagued the oil industry before the rise of Standard Oil: "It seemed absolutely necessary to extend the market for oil . . . and also greatly improve the process of refining so that oil could be made and sold cheaply, yet with a profit. We proceeded to buy the largest and best refining concerns and centralized the administration of them with a view to securing greater economy and efficiency." Carnegie, in an essay published in 1889, insisted that the concentration of wealth was necessary if humanity was to progress, softening this "Gospel of Wealth" by insisting that the rich must use their money "in the manner which . . . is best calculated to produce the most beneficial results for the community." The rich man was merely a trustee for his "poorer brethren," Carnegie said, "bringing to their service his superior wisdom, experience, and ability to administer." Lesser tycoons echoed these arguments.

The voices of the critics were louder if not necessarily more influential. Many clergymen rejected the Social Darwinist view of progress and competition, which they considered unethical and un-Christian. The new class of professional economists (the American Economic Association was founded in 1885) tended to repudiate laissez faire. State aid, wrote Richard T. Ely of Johns Hopkins University, "is an indispensable condition of human progress."

The Radical Reformers

More revealing of the dissatisfaction in the country was the popularity of a number of radical theorists. In 1879 Henry George, a California newspaperman, published *Progress and Poverty,* a forthright attack on the maldistribution of wealth in the United States. George argued that labor was the true and only source of capital. Observing the speculative fever of the West,

which enabled landowners to reap profits merely by holding on to property while population increased, George proposed a "Single Tax" that would confiscate all this "unearned increment" of the owner. The value of land depended upon society and should belong to society; allowing individuals to keep this wealth was the major cause of the growing disparity between rich and poor, George believed. The Single Tax would bring in so much money that no other taxes would be necessary, and the government would have plenty of funds to establish new schools, museums, theaters, and other badly needed social and cultural services. Although the Single Tax was never adopted, George's ideas attracted enthusiastic attention. Single Tax clubs sprang up all over the nation, and more than 2 million copies of *Progress and Poverty* were sold in the next 25 years.

Even more spectacular was the reception afforded *Looking Backward, 2000–1887,* a utopian novel written in 1888 by Edward Bellamy. This book, which sold over a million copies in its first few years, described a future America that was completely socialized, all economic activity carefully planned. Bellamy compared 19th-century society to a great, lumbering stagecoach upon which the favored few rode in comfort while the great mass of the people toiled to haul them along life's route. Occasionally, one of the toilers managed to fight his way onto the coach; whenever a rider fell from it, he had to join the multitude dragging it along. Such, Bellamy wrote, was the working of the vaunted American competitive system. He suggested that the ideal socialist state, in which all men shared equally, would arrive without revolution or violence. The trend toward consolidation would continue, he predicted, until one monstrous trust controlled *all* economic activity. At this point everyone would realize that nationalization was essential.

A third influential attack on the trend toward monopoly was that of Henry Demarest Lloyd, whose *Wealth Against Commonwealth* appeared in 1894. Lloyd, a journalist of independent means, devoted years to preparing a denunciation of the Standard Oil Company. Marshaling masses of fact, presenting his material with patent sincerity, packing his pages with vivid examples, he assaulted the trust at every point. Although in his zeal Lloyd sometimes distorted and exaggerated the evidence to make his indictment more effective—"Every important man in the oil, coal and many other trusts ought to-day to be in some one of our penitentiaries," he wrote in a typical overstatement—as a polemic his book was peerless. His forceful, uncomplicated arguments and his copious references to official documents made *Wealth Against Commonwealth* utterly convincing to thousands. The book was more than an attack on Standard Oil. Lloyd denounced the application of Darwin's concept of survival of the fittest to economic and social affairs, and he condemned the laissez-faire philosophy as leading directly to monopoly.

The popularity of these books indicates that the trend toward monopoly in the United States was worrying many people, but despite the drastic changes suggested in their pages, none of them really questioned the underlying values of the middle-class majority. The popular reformers rejected Marxian ideas, abjured the use of force to achieve their goals, assumed that men were basically altruistic and reasonable and that reform could be accomplished without serious inconvenience to any individual or class. In *Looking Backward* Bellamy pictured the socialists of the future gathered around a radiolike gadget in a well-furnished parlor listening to a minister delivering an inspiring sermon.

Nor did most of their millions of readers seriously consider trying to apply the reformers' ideas. Henry George ran for mayor of New York City in 1886 and lost only narrowly to Abram S. Hewitt, a wealthy iron manufacturer, but even if he had won, he would have been powerless to apply the Single Tax to metropolitan property. Bellamyites founded over 150 "Nationalist Clubs" but steered clear of politics in nearly every case. The national discontent was apparently not very profound. If John D. Rockefeller became the bogeyman of American industry because of Lloyd's attack, no one prevented him from also becoming the richest man in the United States. The writings of these reformers focused American thinking on the monopoly problem and prepared the way for the rejection of laissez faire, but when the government finally took action, the new laws only slightly altered the *status quo.*

Railroad Regulation

Political action came first on the state level and dealt chiefly with the regulation of railroads. Even before the Civil War a number of New England states established railroad commissions to supervise lines within their borders; by the end of the century, 28 states had such boards. The New England type held mere advisory powers, but those set up in the Middle West around 1870 were true regulatory bodies with authority to fix rates and control other railroad activities.

Strict systems of regulation were largely the result of agitation by western farm groups, principally the National Grange of the Patrons of Husbandry. The Grange, founded in 1867 by Oliver H. Kelley, was created in order to provide social and cultural benefits for isolated rural communities, but as it spread and grew in influence—14 states had Granges by 1872 and membership reached 800,000 in 1874—the movement became political too. "Granger" political leaders, often not themselves farmers (for many local businessmen resented such railroad practices as rebating), won control of a number of state legislatures in the West and South. Railroad regulation invariably followed, for while farmers were eager boosters of every internal improvement, they tended to become disillusioned when the lines were completed. Intense competition might reduce rates between major centers like Chicago and the East, but most western farm districts were served by only one line. In 1877, for example, the freight charges of the Burlington road were almost four times as high west of the Missouri as they were east of the river. It cost less to ship wheat all the way from Chicago to Liverpool, England, than from some parts of the Dakotas to Minneapolis.

Granger-controlled legislatures tried to eliminate this kind of discrimination. The Illinois Granger laws were typical. The revised state constitution of 1870 declared railroads to be public highways and authorized the legislature to "pass laws establishing reasonable maximum rates" and to "prevent unjust discrimination." The legislature did so and also set up a commission to enforce the laws and punish violators. The railroads protested, insisting that they were being deprived of property without due process of law, but in *Munn v. Illinois* (1877),° one of the most important decisions in its long history, the Supreme Court upheld the constitutionality of this kind of act in very broad terms. Any business that served a public interest, such as a railroad or a grain warehouse, was subject to state control, the justices ruled. Legislatures might fix maximum charges, and if the charges seemed unreasonable to the parties concerned, they should direct their complaints to the legislatures or to the people, not to the courts.

Regulation of the railroad network by the separate states was inefficient, however, and in some cases the commissions were incompetent and even corrupt. When the Supreme Court, in the Wabash case (1886), declared unconstitutional an Illinois regulation outlawing the long-and-short-haul evil, federal action became necessary. The Wabash, St. Louis and Pacific Railroad had charged 25 cents a hundred pounds for shipping goods from Gilman, Illinois, to New York City and only 15 cents from Peoria, which was 86 miles farther from New York. Illinois judges had held this to be illegal, but the Supreme Court decided that Illinois could not regulate interstate shipments.

Congress had been considering federal railroad regulation for years, so the legislators were

°The Munn case actually involved a grain elevator whose owner had refused to comply with a state warehouse act. It was heard along with seven railroad cases dealing with violations of Illinois regulatory legislation.

prepared to fill the gap created by the Wabash decision. In February 1887 the Interstate Commerce Act was passed. All charges made by railroads "shall be reasonable and just," the act stated. Rebates, drawbacks, the long-and-short-haul evil, and other competitive practices were declared unlawful, and so were their monopolistic counterparts—pools and traffic agreements. Railroads were required to publish schedules of rates and forbidden to change them without due public notice. Most important, the law established an Interstate Commerce Commission, the first federal regulatory board, to supervise the affairs of railroads, investigate complaints, and issue "cease and desist" orders when the roads acted illegally.

The Interstate Commerce Act broke new ground, but it was neither a radical nor a particularly effective measure. Its terms contradicted one another, some being designed to stimulate, others to penalize competition. The chairman of the commission soon characterized the law as an "anomaly." It sought, he said, to "enforce competition" at the same time that it outlawed "the acts and inducements by which competition is ordinarily effected." The commission, furthermore, had less power than the law seemed to give it. It could not fix rates, only bring the roads into court when it considered rates unreasonably high. Such cases could be extremely complicated; applying the law "was like cutting a path through a jungle." With the truth so hard to determine and the burden of proof on the commission, the courts, in nearly every instance, decided in favor of the railroads.

State regulatory commissions also fared poorly in the Supreme Court in the last years of the century. Overruling part of their decision in *Munn v. Illinois*, the justices declared in *Chicago, Milwaukee and St. Paul Railroad Company v. Minnesota* (1890) that the reasonableness of rates was "eminently a question for *judicial* investigation." In a Texas case, *Reagan v. Farmers' Loan and Trust Company* (1894), the Court held that it had the "power and duty" to decide if rates were "unjust and unreasonable" even when the state legislature itself had established them. Nev-

Thomas Nast's "The Senatorial Round-House," drawn for *Harper's Weekly* in 1886, predicted that any federal legislation passed to regulate railroads would be toothless.

ertheless, by stating so clearly the right of Congress to regulate private corporations engaged in interstate commerce, the Interstate Commerce Act seriously challenged the philosophy of laissez faire. Later legislation made the commission more effective. The commission also served as the prototype of a host of similar federal administrative authorities, such as the Federal Communications Commission (1934).

Sherman Antitrust Act

As with railroad legislation, the first antitrust laws originated in the states, but these were southern and western states with relatively little industry and most of the statutes were vaguely worded and ill-enforced. Federal action came in 1890 with the passage of the Sherman Antitrust Act. Any combination "in the form of trust or otherwise" that was "in restraint of trade or commerce among the several states, or with foreign nations," was declared to be illegal. Persons forming such combinations were made subject to fines of $5,000 and a year in jail. Individuals and businesses suffering losses because of actions performed in violation of the law were authorized to sue in the federal courts for triple damages.

Whereas the Interstate Commerce Act sought to outlaw the excesses of competition, the idea behind the Sherman Act was to restore competition. If men formed together to "restrain" (monopolize) trade in a particular field, they should be punished and their work undone. Monopoly was already illegal under the common law, but as Senator George Frisbie Hoar of Massachusetts pointed out during the antitrust debates, no *federal* common law existed.

"The great thing this bill does," Hoar explained, "is to extend the common-law principle . . . to international and interstate commerce." This was important because the states ran into legal difficulties when they tried to use the common law to restrict corporations engaged in interstate activities. The Sherman Act was rather loosely worded—Thurman Arnold, a modern authority, once said that it made it "a crime to violate a vaguely stated economic policy"—and critics have argued that the congressmen were more interested in quieting the public clamor for action against the trusts than in actually breaking up any of the new combinations. This seems unlikely, for the bill passed with only one dissenting vote. *All* the legislators could not have been party to a plot to deceive the people. Congress was trying to solve a new problem and was not sure how to proceed. Most Americans assumed that the courts would deal with the details, as they always had in common-law matters.

Actually, the Supreme Court quickly emasculated the Sherman Act. In *U. S. v. E. C. Knight Company* (1895) it held that the American Sugar Refining Company had not violated the law by taking over a number of important competitors. Although the Sugar Trust now controlled about 98 per cent of all sugar refining in the United States, it was not restraining *trade*. "Doubtless the power to control the manufacture of a given thing involves in a certain sense the control of its disposition," the Court said in one of the greatest feats of judicial understatement of all time. "Although the exercise of that power may result in bringing the operation of commerce into play, it does not control it, and affects it only incidentally and indirectly."

If the creation of the Sugar Trust did not violate the Sherman Act, it seemed unlikely that any other combination of manufacturers could be convicted under the law. In *The History of the Last Quarter-Century in the United States* (1896), E. Benjamin Andrews, president of Brown University, presented a strong indictment of the trusts. "The crimes to which some of them resorted to crush out competition were unworthy of civilization," he wrote. Yet he referred only obliquely to the Sherman Act, dismissing it as "obviously ineffectual" and "of little avail."

Little wonder that the years around the turn of the century saw a new surge of mergers and combinations. Excluding railroads, in 1896 less than a dozen American corporations possessed assets of over $10 million. In 1903 over 300 such giants existed. The enormous United States Steel Corporation was put together by J. P. Morgan without a word of protest from the government. When, some years after his retirement, Andrew Carnegie was asked by a committee of the House of Representatives to explain how he had dared participate in the formation of the great Steel Trust, he replied: "Nobody ever mentioned the Sherman Act to me, that I remember."

American industry was flourishing, but each year a larger portion of it seemed to fall under the control of a handful of rich men. As with the railroads, other industries were coming to be strongly influenced, if not completely dominated by investment bankers—the Money Trust seemed fated to become the ultimate monopoly. The firm of J. P. Morgan and Company controlled many railroads, the largest steel, electrical, agricultural machinery, rubber, and shipping companies, two giant life insurance companies, and a number of banks. By 1913 Morgan and the Rockefeller-National City Bank group between them could name 341 directors to 112 corporations worth over $22.2 billion. The public benefited immensely from the productive efficiency and the rapid growth of the new industrial empires. Living standards rose. But despite decades of protest and great masses of state and federal legislation, the trend toward giantism was continuing unchecked. With ownership falling into fewer and fewer hands, what would be the ultimate effect of big business on American democracy?

Supplementary Reading

Of general works dealing with industrial growth, E. C. Kirkland, *Industry Comes of Age*° (1961) is the most up-to-date and thoughtful, but see also V. S. Clark's detailed *History of Manufactures in the United States* (1929), Allan Nevins, *The Emergence of Modern America* (1927), I. M. Tarbell, *Nationalizing Big Business* (1936), and T. C. Cochran and William Miller, *The Age of Enterprise*° (1942). Matthew Josephson, *The Robber Barons*° (1934), is highly critical but provocative. Rendigs Fels, *American Business Cycles* (1959), is technical but valuable. On technological developments, in addition to many of the volumes on specific industries cited below, see H. J. Habakkuk, *American and British Technology in the Nineteenth Century*° (1962), W. P. Strassmann, *Risk and Technological Innovation: American Manufacturing Methods During the Nineteenth Century* (1959), and Lewis Mumford, *Technics and Civilization*° (1934).

For the railroad industry, consult G. R. Taylor and I. D. Neu, *The American Railroad Network* (1956), J. F. Stover, *American Railroads*° (1961), T. C. Cochran, *Railroad Leaders* (1953), Julius Grodinsky, *Transcontinental Railway Strategy* (1962) and *Jay Gould* (1957). R. W. Fogel, *Railroads and American Economic Growth* (1964), deals mainly with pre-Civil War events but is also important for this period. C. F. Adams, Jr., *Railroads: Their Origin and Problems* (1879), is a valuable contemporary analysis.

The iron and steel business is discussed in great detail in J. F. Wall, *Andrew Carnegie* (1970), Peter Temin, *Iron and Steel in Nineteenth-Century America* (1964), an economic analysis, J. H. Bridge, *The Inside History of the Carnegie Steel Company* (1903), and in Carnegie's *Autobiography* (1920); there is no solid scholarly history of the industry. For

the oil industry, however, a number of excellent volumes exist. See H. F. Williamson and A. R. Daum, *The American Petroleum Industry: Age of Illumination* (1959), Allan Nevins, *Study in Power: John D. Rockefeller* (1953), and R. W. and M. E. Hidy, *Pioneering in Big Business* (1955), the first volume of their *History of Standard Oil Company (New Jersey)* (1955–56). The electrical industry is discussed in an excellent study, H. C. Passer, *The Electrical Manufacturers* (1953), and in an equally good biography, Matthew Josephson, *Edison*° (1959). H. G. Prout, *A Life of George Westinghouse* (1921), is also useful.

Many of these volumes deal with the problems of competition and monopoly. See also, however, E. G. Campbell, *The Reorganization of the American Railroad System* (1938), Gabriel Kolko, *Railroads and Regulation* (1965), which is critical of both railroad leaders and of government policy, J. D. Rockefeller, *Random Reminiscences of Men and Events* (1909), H. D. Lloyd, *Wealth Against Commonwealth*° (1894), Lewis Corey, *The House of Morgan* (1930), H. W. Laidler, *Concentration of Control in American Industry* (1931), and J. W. Jenks, *The Trust Problem* (1905).

For contemporary discussions of the monopoly problem, see Lloyd's *Wealth Against Commonwealth*, Henry George, *Progress and Poverty* (1879), and Edward Bellamy, *Looking Backward*° (1888). The background of government regulation of industry is treated in Sidney Fine, *Laissez Faire and the General-Welfare State*° (1956), J. W. Hurst, *Law and the Conditions of Freedom in the Nineteenth-Century United States*° (1956), J. A. Garraty, *The New Commonwealth*° (1968), and Lee Benson, *Merchants, Farmers, and Railroads* (1955). Other useful volumes include W. Z. Ripley, *Trusts, Pools, and Corporations* (1905), H. B. Thorelli, *The Federal Antitrust Policy* (1954), S. J. Buck, *The Granger Movement*° (1913), and G. W. Miller, *Railroads and the Granger Laws* (1971).

°Available in paperback.

19

The Response to Industrialism

The industrialization that followed the Civil War profoundly affected American life. New machines, improvements in transportation and communication, the appearance of the great corporation with its uncertain implications for the future—all made deep impressions not only on the economy but also on the social and cultural development of the nation. Indeed, the history of the period may be treated, historian Samuel P. Hays suggests, as a "response to industrialism," the "story of the impact of industrialism on every phase of human life."

The American Worker

Of course the wage earner felt the full force of the tide, being affected in countless ways—some beneficial, others unfortunate. As industry became more important in the United States, the number of industrial workers multiplied rapidly: from 885,000 in 1860 to over 3.2 million in 1890. Although these workers lacked much sense of solidarity, they exerted a far larger influence on society at the turn of the century than they had in the years before the Civil War. Furthermore, more efficient methods of production enabled them to increase their output, making possible a rise in their standard of living. But an unskilled worker could still not maintain a family decently by his own efforts. The weight of the evidence also indicates that industrial workers did not receive a fair share of the fruits of economic growth. Nevertheless, it is incontestable that materially most workers were improving their position.

On the other hand, industrialization created grave problems for those who toiled in the mines, mills, and shops. When machines took the place of handicrafts, jobs became monotonous. Mechanization undermined both the craftsman's pride and his bargaining power vis-à-vis his employer. As expensive machinery became more important, the workingman seemed of necessity less important. As businesses grew larger, personal contact between employer and hired hand tended to disappear. Relations between them became less human, more businesslike and ruthless. The trend toward bigness also seemed to make it more difficult for workers to rise from the ranks of labor to become themselves manufacturers, as Andrew Carnegie, for example, had done during the Civil War era.

It is difficult to generalize about the actual conditions of laborers in the late 19th century. In good times something approaching full employment existed; in periods of depression unemployment caused much hardship. Workers in some industries fared better than others. By and large, skilled workers, always better off than the un-skilled, improved their positions relatively, despite the increased use of machinery. Women and children continued to supply a significant percentage of the industrial working force, always receiving lower wages than adult male workers.

Furthermore, a great deal depended upon the education, intelligence, and motivation of workers. Early social workers who visited the homes of industrial laborers in this period reported enormous differences in the standard of living of men engaged in the same line of work, differences related to such variables as the wife's ability as a homemaker and the degree of the family's commitment to middle-class values. Some families spent most of their income on food, others saved substantial sums even when earning no more than $400 or $500 a year. Family incomes also varied greatly among workers who received similar hourly wages, depending on the steadiness of employment and on the number of family members holding down jobs.

For most laborers, the working day still tended to approximate the hours of daylight, but it was shortening perceptibly by the 1880's. In 1860 the average was 11 hours; by 1880 only one worker in four labored more than 10, and radicals were beginning to talk about 8 hours as a fair day's work. To some extent the exhausting pace of the new factories made longer hours uneconomical, but employers realized this only slowly, and until they did, many workers suffered.

Despite the improvement in living standards, there was a great deal of dissatisfaction among industrial workers. Writing in 1885, the labor leader Terence V. Powderly said it was undeniable "that a deep-rooted feeling of discontent pervades the masses," and a few years later a Connecticut official conducted an informal survey of labor opinion in the state and found a "feeling of bitterness" and "distrust of employers" endemic. This discontent rose from many causes. For some, poverty was still the chief problem, but for others, rising aspirations triggered discontent.

Workers everywhere were becoming confused about their destiny; the tradition that no one of ability need remain a hired hand died hard. They wanted to believe their bosses and they wanted to believe the politicians when those worthies voiced the old slogans about a classless society and the community of interest of capital and labor.

"Our men," said William Vanderbilt of the New York Central in 1877, "feel that, although I . . . may have my millions and they the rewards of their daily toil, still we are about equal in the end. If they suffer, I suffer, and if I suffer, they cannot escape." "The poor," said another conservative spokesman a decade later, "are not poor because the rich are rich." Instead "the service of capital" softened their lot and gave them many benefits.

Statements like these, although self-serving, were essentially correct. The rich were growing richer and more people were growing rich, but ordinary workers were also better off. However, the gap between the very rich and the ordinary citizen was widening. "The tendency . . . is toward centralization and aggregation," the Illinois Bureau of Labor Statistics reported in 1886. "This involves a separation of the people into classes, and the permanently subordinate status of large numbers of them." Thus even a worker whose personal standard of living was rising might find his relative position in society declining.

To study social and economic mobility in a large industrial country is extraordinarily difficult. Late-19th-century Americans believed their society offered great opportunities for individual advancement, and to prove it they could point to men like Andrew Carnegie and dozens of other poor boys who accumulated large fortunes over a short span of time. How general was the rise from rags to riches, or even to modest comfort, is another question.

Fascinating studies of census records, the most important being those of Stephan Thernstrom, show first of all that there was a very considerable geographical mobility in urban areas all through the last half of the 19th century and beyond. Most investigations reveal that only about half the people recorded in one census were still in the same place ten years later; as Thernstrom puts it, "transiency was part of the American way of life. . . . The country had an enormous reservoir of footloose men, who could be lured to new destinations when opportunity beckoned." In most of the cities studied, this mobility was accompanied by substantial economic and social improvement. On the average, about a quarter of the manual laborers traced rose to middle-class status during their lifetimes and the sons of manual laborers were still more likely to improve their place in society. Even in Newburyport, Massachusetts, a town that was something of an economic backwater, most laborers made some progress, although far fewer rose to skilled or white-collar positions than in more prosperous cities.

The exception to this evidence that America was truly a land of opportunity was the Negro population. Blacks showed little upward mobility either in large cities or small, in the North or in the South—another tragic illustration of the evil results of race prejudice. And none of the evidence indicates that progress from rags to real riches was common. Contemporaries were overly influenced by spectacular examples such as Carnegie in concluding that American society was highly mobile. The Carnegies, clearly, were the exception.

The dissatisfaction of labor probably resulted more from the dashing of unrealistic hopes inspired by such cases than from the absence of real opportunity, which was surely greater than in any other industrial nation at the time. Any conclusion must be tentative, but this one offers a plausible explanation for the coexistence of discontent and rising living standards. In any case, it remains probable that most workers, even when expressing dissatisfaction with their present lot, continued to subscribe to middle-class values like hard work and thrift—that is, they continued to hope. Thernstrom notes that hundreds of poor families in Newburyport, by practicing what he calls "ruthless underconsumption," gradually accumulated enough money to buy their own homes and provide for themselves in their old age.

Growth of Labor Organizations

Discontent and class consciousness led some workers to join unions, but only a small percentage of the work force was organized and most of this consisted of craftsmen, such as cigarmakers, printers, and carpenters, rather than semiskilled factory hands. Aside from skilled ironworkers, railroad workers, and miners, few industrial laborers belonged to unions. Nevertheless, in a sense, the union was the worker's response to the big corporation: a combination designed to eliminate competition for jobs and provide efficient organization for labor. As one labor leader said: "Modern industry evolves these union organizations out of existing conditions."

After 1865 the growth of national craft unions like the iron molders, the printers, and the cigarmakers, which had been organized in the fifties, quickened perceptibly. By the early 1870's about 300,000 workers belonged to such organizations, and many new trades, most notably in railroading, had been unionized. A federation of such unions, the National Labor Union, was created in 1866, but it remained chiefly a paper organization. Most of its leaders were visionaries out of touch with the practical needs and aspirations of the workers. They opposed the wage system, strikes, and anything that increased the laborers' sense of being members of the working class. A major objective was the formation of worker-owned cooperatives. Because the union desired social reforms that had little to do with bargaining between workers and employers, it eventually became a political organization, the National Labor Reform party. When the election of 1872 proved this venture a fiasco, the organization disappeared.

Far more remarkable was the Knights of Labor, a curious organization with one foot in the past, the other in the future. Founded in 1869 by a group of Philadelphia garment workers headed by Uriah S. Stephens, the Knights flourished in the 1880's. Like so many labor organizers of the period, Stephens was a reformer of wide interests rather than a man dedicated to the specific

A Negro delegate introduces Terence V. Powderly at a Knights of Labor Convention held in Richmond. At one point, the union had some 60,000 Negro members.

problems of industrial workers. He, his successor Terence V. Powderly, and many of its other leaders would have been thoroughly at home in any of the labor organizations of the Jacksonian era. Like the Jacksonians, they supported political objectives that had no direct connection with working conditions, such as currency reform and the curbing of land speculation. They rejected the idea that workers must resign themselves to remaining wage earners. By pooling their resources, workingmen could advance up the economic ladder and enter the capitalist class. "There is no good reason," Powderly wrote in his autobiography, *The Path I Trod,* "why labor cannot, through cooperation, own and operate mines, factories, and railroads." The leading Knights saw no contradiction between their denunciation of "soulless" monopolies and of "drones" like bankers and lawyers, and their talk of "combining all branches of trade in one common brotherhood." Such muddled thinking led the Knights to attack the wage system and also to frown on strikes as "acts of private warfare."

At the same time the Knights supported some startlingly advanced ideas about labor organization. They rejected the traditional grouping of workers by crafts, developing a concept closely resembling modern industrial unionism. They welcomed Negroes (chiefly in segregated locals), women, and immigrants and accepted unskilled workers as well as craftsmen. The eight-hour day was one of their basic demands, their argument being that increased leisure would give workers time to develop more cultivated tastes and thus higher aspirations. Higher pay would inevitably follow.

The growth of the union, however, had little to do with ideology. Stephens had made the Knights a secret organization with an elaborate ritual. Under his leadership, as late as 1879 it had fewer than 10,000 members. Under Powderly, secrecy was discarded. Between 1882 and 1886 a series of successful strikes by local "assemblies" against western railroads, including one against the hated Jay Gould's Missouri Pacific, brought recruits by the thousands. The membership passed 42,000 in 1882, 110,000 in 1885, and then, in 1886, soared beyond the 700,000 mark. Alas, sudden prosperity was too much for the Knights. Its national leadership was ineffective and unable to control local groups. A series of poorly planned strikes failed dismally; public opinion was alienated by sporadic acts of violence and intimidation. Disillusioned recruits began to drift away.

However, circumstances largely fortuitous caused the collapse of the organization. By 1886 the movement for the eight-hour day had gained wide support among workers. Several hundred thousand (estimates vary) were on strike in various parts of the country by May of that year. In Chicago, an important center of the eight-hour movement, about 80,000 workers were involved, and a small group of anarchists was taking advantage of the excitement to stir up radical feeling. When a striker was killed in a fracas at the McCormick Harvesting Machine Company, the anarchists called a protest meeting on May 4, at Haymarket Square. Police intervened to break up the meeting, and someone—his identity was never established—hurled a bomb into their ranks. Seven policemen were killed and many others injured. While the anarchists were the direct victims of the resulting public indignation and hysteria—seven were condemned to death and four eventually executed—organized labor, and especially the Knights, suffered heavily. No tie between the Knights and the bombing could be established, but the union had been closely connected with the eight-hour movement, and the public tended to associate it with violence and radicalism. Its membership declined as suddenly as it had risen, and soon it ceased to exist as an important force in the labor movement.

The Knights' place was taken by the American Federation of Labor, an organization of national craft unions established in 1886. In a sense

An anarchist group printed and distributed 20,000 of these bilingual handbills on the day of the Haymarket Square bombing incident in Chicago in 1886. (*Century Magazine*, April, 1893.)

the AFL was a reactionary organization. Its principal leaders, Adolph Strasser and Samuel Gompers of the Cigarmakers Union, were, like the founders of the Knights of Labor, originally interested in utopian social reforms; they even toyed with the idea of forming a workingmen's political party. Experience, however, soon led them to abandon such ambitions and concentrate on organizing skilled workers and fighting for specific "bread-and-butter" issues such as higher wages and shorter hours. "Our organization does not consist of idealists," Strasser explained to a congressional committee. "We do not control the production of the world. That is controlled by the employers. . . . I look first to cigars." Yet the AFL was modern in view of industrial trends; it accepted the fact that most workers would remain wage earners all their lives, and tried to develop in them a sense of common purpose and pride in their skills and station. Strasser and Gompers paid great attention to building a strong organization based on regular dues-paying members committed to unionism as a way of improving their lot.

The chief weapon of the federation was the strike, which it used both to win concessions from employers and to attract recruits to the member unions. Gompers, president of the AFL almost continuously from 1886 to his death in 1924, encouraged workers to make "an intelligent use of the ballot" in order to advance their own interests, and the federation adopted a "legislative platform" which demanded such things as eight-hour, employers'-liability, and mine-safety laws, but it avoided direct involvement in politics. "I have my own philosophy and my own dreams," Gompers once told a left-wing French politician, "but first and foremost I want to increase the workingman's welfare year by year. . . . The French workers waste their economic force by their political divisions." Gompers' approach to labor problems produced solid, if unspectacular, growth for the AFL. Unions with a total of about 150,000 members formed the federation in 1886. By 1892 the membership had reached 250,000, and in 1901 it passed the million mark.

Labor Unrest

The stress of the AFL on the strike weapon reflected rather than caused the increasing militancy of labor. Workers felt themselves threatened from all sides: the growing size and power of their corporate employers, the substitution of machines for human skills, the invasion of foreign workers willing to accept substandard wages. At the same time they had tasted some of the material benefits of industrialization and had learned the advantages of concerted action.

The average employer, on the other hand, behaved like a tyrant when dealing with his workers. He discharged them arbitrarily when they tried to organize unions; he hired scabs to break strikes; he frequently failed to provide the most rudimentary protections against injury on the job. Some employers professed to approve of unions, but almost none of them was really willing to bargain with labor collectively. To do so, they argued, would be to deprive the individual worker of his sacred freedom to contract for his own labor in any way he saw fit.

Of course the industrialists of the period were not all ogres; they were as alarmed by the rapid changes of the times as their workers, and since they had more at stake materially, they were probably more frightened by the uncertainties. The pressures produced by deflation, technological change, and intense competition kept even the most successful under constant strain. The thinking of most employers was remarkably confused. They considered workers who joined unions "disloyal," but at the same time treated labor as a commodity to be purchased as cheaply as possible. "If I wanted boiler iron," Henry B. Stone, a railroad official, explained, "I would go out on the market and buy it where I could get it cheapest, and if I wanted to employ men, I would do the same." Yet Stone was furious when the men he had "bought" on such terms joined a union. When labor was scarce, employers resisted demands for higher wages by arguing that the price of labor was controlled by its productivity, but when it was plentiful, they justified reducing wages by referring to the law of supply and demand.

Thus both capital and labor were often spoiling for a fight—frequently without fully understanding why. When labor troubles developed, they tended to be bitter, even violent. As early as 1877 a great railroad strike convulsed much of the nation. It began on the Baltimore and Ohio system in response to a wage cut and spread first to other eastern lines and then throughout the West, until about two-thirds of the railroad mileage of the country had been shut down. Violence broke out, rail yards were put to the torch, dismayed and frightened businessmen formed militia companies to patrol the streets of Chicago and other cities. Eventually President Hayes, responding to the request of the governors of four states, sent federal troops to the trouble spots to restore order, and the strike collapsed. There had been no real danger of revolution, but the violence and destruction of the strike had been without precedent in America.

The disturbances of 1877 were a response to a business slump, those of the next decade a response to good times. Twice as many strikes occurred in 1886 as in any previous year. Even before the Haymarket bombing centered the country's attention on labor problems, the situation had become so disturbing that President Cleveland, in the first Presidential message devoted to labor problems, had urged Congress to create a voluntary arbitration board to aid in settling labor disputes—a remarkable suggestion for a man of Cleveland's conservative, laissez-faire approach to economic issues.

In 1892 a violent strike broke out among the silver miners at Coeur d'Alene, Idaho, and a far more important clash shook Andrew Carnegie's Homestead steel plant near Pittsburgh when strikers attacked 300 private guards brought in to protect strikebreakers, killing seven of them and forcing the rest to "surrender" and march off ignominiously. The Homestead affair was part of a bitter struggle between capital and labor in the steel industry. The steel men believed that the workers were holding back progress by resisting

After the collapse of his American Railway Union in 1897, Eugene V. Debs (shown here addressing a Socialist party gathering) devoted himself to politics. (UPI.)

technological changes, while the workers argued that the company was refusing to share the fruits of more efficient operation fairly. The strike was precipitated by the decision of company officials to crush the union at all costs. The final defeat, after a five-month walkout, of the 24,000-member Amalgamated Association of Iron and Steel Workers, one of the most important elements in the AFL, destroyed unionism as an effective force in the steel industry and set back the progress of organized labor all over the country.

As in the case of the Haymarket bombing, the activities of radicals on the fringe of the dispute turned the public against the steelworkers. The boss of Homestead was Henry Clay Frick, a tough-minded foe of unions who was determined to "teach our employees a lesson." Frick had made the decision to bring in strikebreakers and employ Pinkerton detectives to protect them. During the course of the strike, Alexander Berkman, an anarchist, burst into Frick's office and attempted to assassinate him. Frick was only slightly wounded, but the attack brought him much sympathy and redounded quite unjustly to the discredit of the strikers.

The most important strike of the period took place in 1894, when the workers at George Pullman's Palace Car factory outside Chicago walked out in protest against a series of wage cuts. (While reducing wages, Pullman insisted on holding the line on rents in the company town of Pullman; when a delegation called upon him to remonstrate, he refused to give in and had three of the leaders fired.) Some Pullman workers belonged to the American Railway Union, an independent union of 150,000 members headed by Eugene V. Debs. After the strike had dragged along for weeks, this group voted to refuse to handle trains with Pullman cars. The resulting railroad strike tied up trunk lines running in and out of Chicago.

The railroad owners were "determined to crush the strike." By-passing Governor Altgeld of Illinois because of his known prolabor views, they appealed to President Cleveland to send troops to preserve order. On the pretext that the soldiers were needed to ensure the movement of the mails,° Cleveland agreed. Thus the strike was broken, and when Debs defied a federal court's injunction, he was jailed for contempt.

The crushing of the Pullman strike demonstrated the power of the courts to break strikes by issuing injunctions. Even more ominous for organized labor, perhaps, was the fact that the government based its request for the injunction on the Sherman Antitrust Act, arguing that the American Railway Union was a combination in restraint of trade. Another result of the strike was to make Eugene V. Debs a national figure. While serving out his sentence for contempt, he was visited by a number of prominent socialists, who sought to convert him to their cause. One gave him a copy of Karl Marx's *Capital*, which he found too dull to finish, but he did read works like *Looking Backward* and *Wealth Against Commonwealth*, and in 1897 he became an active socialist. Thereafter, he ran for President five times on the Socialist party ticket.

The "New" Immigration

Industrial expansion increased the need for labor, and this in turn powerfully stimulated immigration; between 1866 and 1915 about 25 million foreigners entered the United States. Industrial growth alone does not explain this influx. The Atlantic crossing, once so hazardous and uncomfortable, became safe and speedy with the perfection of the steamship. Competition between the great packet lines such as Cunard, North German Lloyd, and Holland-America drove down the cost of the passage, and advertising by the lines further stimulated traffic. Improved transportation also wrought changes in the economies of many European countries that caused an increase in the flow of people to America. Cheap wheat from the United States, Russia, and

---

°Actually the union was perfectly willing to handle mail trains. The owners, however, refused to run trains unless they were made up of a full complement of cars. When Pullman cars were added to mail trains, the workers refused to move them.

other parts of the world could now be imported into western Europe, bringing disaster to farmers in England, Germany, and the Scandinavian countries. The spreading industrial revolution led to the collapse of the peasant economy of central and southern Europe. For rural inhabitants this meant the loss of self-sufficiency, the fragmentation of landholdings, poverty, and, for many, the decision to make a new start in the New World. Political and religious persecutions pushed still others into the migrating stream. However, the main reason for immigration remained the desire for economic betterment. "In America," as a British immigrant put it, "you get pies and puddings."

While immigrants continued to people the farms of America, industry absorbed an ever-increasing number. As early as 1870 one industrial worker in three was foreign-born. In 1890, 48 per cent of all British immigrants were employed in industry. When congressional investigators examined 21 major industries early in the new century, they discovered that 57.9 per cent of the labor force was foreign-born.

Most of these new millions came into the United States by way of New York City. A Serbian immigrant, Michael Pupin, later a distinguished physicist at Columbia University, has left a moving description of what it was like to enter. He arrived in 1874 on the Hamburg-American liner *Westphalia* amid a great horde of peasants and craftsmen. After disembarking at Hoboken, he was brought by tug to the immigration reception center at Castle Garden on the southern tip of Manhattan. He confessed to the authorities that he had only five cents to his name and knew no Americans except—by reputation—Franklin, Lincoln, and Harriet Beecher Stowe. But he explained in eloquent phrases why he wanted to live in the land of liberty rather than in the aristocratic Austro-Hungarian empire. The officials conferred briefly, then admitted him. After a good breakfast, supplied by the immigration authorities, the Castle Garden Labor Bureau offered him a job as a farm hand in Delaware. Within 24 hours of his arrival he had reached his destination, ready to work.

Before 1882 when—in addition to the Chinese—criminals, idiots, lunatics, and persons liable to become public charges were excluded, entry into the United States was almost unrestricted. A host of private agencies, philanthropic and commercial, served as a link between the new arrivals and employers looking for labor. Until the Foran Act of 1885 outlawed the practice, a few companies brought in skilled craftsmen under contract, advancing them passage money and collecting it in installments from their pay checks. However, ordinary unskilled immigrants were not handled in this way. Various nationality groups assisted, and sometimes exploited, their compatriots by organizing "immigrant banks" which recruited labor in the old country, arranged the necessary transportation, and then housed the newcomers in boarding houses in the United States while finding them jobs. The *padrone* system of the Italians and Greeks was typical. The *padrone,* a sort of contractor who agreed to supply gangs of unskilled workers to companies for a lump sum, usually signed on immigrants unfamiliar with American wage levels at rates that assured him a fat profit.

Beginning in the 1880's, the spreading effects of industrialization in Europe caused a massive shift in the sources of American immigration from northern and western to southern and eastern sections of the Continent. In 1882, when 789,000 immigrants entered the United States, over 350,000 of them came from Great Britain and Germany, only 32,000 from Italy, and less than 17,000 from Russia. In 1907—the all-time peak year, with 1,285,000 immigrants—Great Britain and Germany supplied only 116,000, whereas 285,000 Italians and 258,000 Russians entered.° These "new" immigrants were culturally far different from both "native" stock and the run of earlier immigrants. Poor, isolated, uneducated, more than ordinarily clannish in their strange surroundings, they seemed to contemporaries much harder to assimilate than earlier arrivals. In fact, most of the older immigrant

°Throughout history up to 1880, only about 200,000 southern and eastern Europeans had migrated to America. Between 1880 and 1910, approximately 8.4 million arrived.

groups had been equally ill-prepared for local conditions when they arrived in the United States; what made the new breed appear to dissolve so slowly in the American "melting pot" was their large number, not their resistance to acculturation. Failing to appreciate this fact, many Americans concluded, wrongly but understandably, that the new immigrants were incapable of becoming good citizens and should be kept out.

The first to show concern about the new trend were reformers, who were worried by the social problems that arose when so many poor immigrants flocked into cities already bursting at the seams because of the flow of population to urban areas. As early as 1883 Henry George, author of *Progress and Poverty,* expressed alarm about the "human garbage" descending upon the nation from foreign parts. During the 1880's large numbers of social workers, economists, and church leaders basically sympathetic to immigrants began to feel that some kind of restriction should be placed on the incoming human tide. The directors of charitable organizations, who bore the burden of aiding the most unfortunate of the immigrants, were soon complaining that their resources were being exhausted by the needs of the new flood.

Organized labor, fearing the competition of workers with low living standards and no bargaining power, became increasingly vocal against the "enticing of penniless and unapprised immigrants . . . to undermine our wages and social welfare." Some corporations, especially in fields like mining, which employed large numbers of unskilled workers, made use of immigrants as strikebreakers, and this particularly angered union men. "The Poles, Slavs, Huns and Italians," a labor paper editorialized in 1909, "come over without any ambition to live as Americans live and . . . accept work at any wages at all, thereby lowering the tone of American labor as a whole." David Brody, historian of the steelworkers, describes an "unbridgeable gulf" in the steel industry between native and foreign laborers.

Naturally, employers were not disturbed by the continuing influx of people with strong backs willing to work hard for low wages. Nevertheless, by the late 1880's many of them were becoming alarmed about the supposed radicalism of the immigrants. The Haymarket bombing focused attention on the handful of foreign-born extremists in the country and loosed a flood of unjustified charges that "anarchists and communists" were dominating the labor movement. Nativism, which had waxed in the 1850's under the Know-Nothing banner and waned during the Civil War, now flourished again as a wave of nationalist hysteria swept across the land. Denunciations of "long-haired, wild-eyed, bad-smelling, atheistic, reckless foreign wretches," of "Europe's human and inhuman rubbish," of the "cutthroats of Beelzebub from the Rhine, the Danube, the Vistula and the Elbe" crowded the pages of the nation's press. The Grand Army of the Republic, an organization of Civil War veterans, commenced grumbling about foreign-born radicals.

This new nativism struck more at Catholics and other minority groups than at immigrants as such; it was primarily a middle-class movement inspired by the social tensions of the time, a "response to industrialism" in the broadest sense. Neither labor leaders nor important industrialists, despite their misgivings about immigration, took a broad antiforeign position. The most powerful nativist organization of the period, the American Protective Association, a secret society founded in 1887, existed primarily to resist what its members called "the Catholic menace."

Despite so much thunder, however, very little was done to slow down the pace of immigration. After the Exclusion Act of 1882 and the almost meaningless 1885 ban on importing contract labor, no further laws were passed until the 20th century. Strong support for a literacy test for admission developed in the 1890's, pushed by a new organization, the Immigration Restriction League. Since there was much more illiteracy in the southeastern quarter of Europe than in the northwestern, such a test offered a convenient method of discrimination without seeming to do so on national or racial grounds. A literacy-test bill passed both houses of Congress in 1897, but

President Cleveland vetoed it. Such a "radical departure" from the "generous and free-handed policy" of the past, Cleveland said, was unjustified. He added, perhaps with tongue in cheek, that a literacy requirement would not keep out "unruly agitators," who were only too adept at reading and writing.

The Expanding City and Its Problems

Americans who favored restricting immigration made much of the fact that so many of the newcomers crowded into the cities, aggravating problems of housing, public health, crime and immorality, and a host of other social evils. Immigrants concentrated in the cities because the new jobs created by expanding industry were located there. So, of course, did native Americans; the proportion of urban dwellers had been steadily increasing since about 1820.

It is important to keep in mind that national population density is not necessarily related to the existence of large cities. In the late 19th century there were areas in Asia as large as the United States that were as densely populated as Belgium and England but still overwhelmingly rural. The United States, on the other hand, was by any standard sparsely populated, but well before the Civil War it had become one of the most urban nations in the world. Industrialization does not entirely explain the growth of 19th-century cities, in the United States or elsewhere. All the

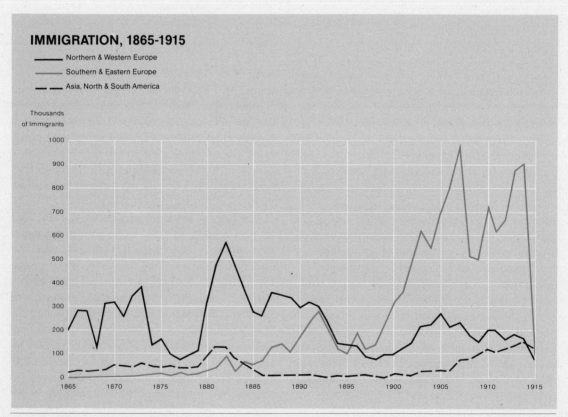

IMMIGRATION, 1865-1915

——— Northern & Western Europe
——— Southern & Eastern Europe
— — — Asia, North & South America

Note the great tide of "new" immigration in the early 1900's.

large American cities got their start as commercial centers, and the development of huge metropolises like New York and Chicago would have been impossible without the national transportation network. But by the latter decades of the century, the enormous expansion of industry had become the chief cause of city growth. Thus the urban concentration continued; by 1890 one person in three lived in a city, by 1910 nearly one in every two.

Throughout this period a steadily increasing proportion of the urban population was made up of immigrants. In 1890 the foreign-born population of Chicago almost equaled the *total* population of Chicago in 1880, a third of all Bostonians and a quarter of all Philadelphians were immigrants, and four out of every five residents of New York City were either foreign-born or the children of immigrants.

After 1890 the immigrant concentration became even more dense. Like the Irish newcomers of the 1840's and 1850's, these "new" migrants from eastern and southern Europe were desperately poor; they lacked even the resources to travel to the agriculturally developing regions, to say nothing of the sums necessary to acquire land and farm equipment. As the process of concentration progressed it fed upon itself, for all the eastern cities developed many ethnic neighborhoods, in each of which immigrants of one particular nationality congregated. Lonely, confused, often unable to speak English, the Italians, the Greeks, the Polish and Russian Jews, and other ethnic groups tended to settle where their predecessors had settled. Each great American city became a Europe in microcosm, where it sometimes seemed that every language in the world but English could be heard. New York, the great entrepôt, had a "Little Italy," a Polish, a Greek, a Jewish, and a Bohemian quarter—even a Chinatown.

However, the rapidity of urban expansion explains the troubles associated with city life far better than the high percentage of foreigners. The cities were suffering from growing pains. Sewer and water facilities frequently could not keep pace with skyrocketing needs. By the nine-

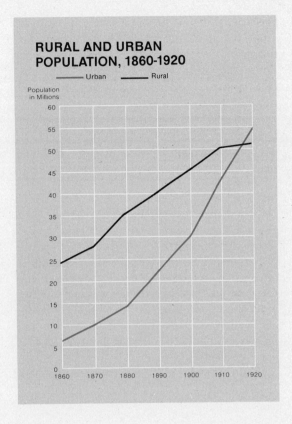

RURAL AND URBAN POPULATION, 1860-1920

—— Urban   —— Rural

ties the tremendous growth of Chicago had put such a strain on its sanitation system that the Chicago River had become practically an open sewer, and the city's drinking water contained so many germ-killing chemicals that it tasted like creosote. In the eighties all the sewers of Baltimore emptied into the sluggish Back Basin, and, according to the journalist H. L. Mencken, every summer the city smelled "like a billion polecats."

Fire protection became increasingly inadequate, garbage piled up in streets faster than it could be carted away, and the streets themselves crumbled beneath the pounding of heavy traffic. Urban growth proceeded with such speed that new streets were laid out more rapidly than they could be paved. Chicago, for example, had more than 1,400 miles of dirt streets in 1890.

Housing posed by far the most serious urban problem, for substandard living quarters aggravated other evils, such as disease, the danger of fire, and the disintegration of family life with its attendant mental anguish, crime, and juvenile delinquency. People poured into the great cities faster than apartments could be built to accommodate them. This terrible crowding of areas already densely packed in the 1840's became literally unbearable as rising property values and the absence of zoning laws conspired to make builders utilize every possible foot of space, jamming their structures together, squeezing out light and air ruthlessly in order to wedge in a few additional family units. The bloody New York riots of 1863, although sparked by dislike of the Civil War draft and of Negroes, also reflected the bitterness and frustration of thousands jammed together amid filth and threatened by disease. A citizens' committee seeking to discover the causes of the riots expressed its amazement after visiting the slums "that so much misery, disease, and wretchedness can be huddled together and hidden . . . unvisited and unthought of, so near our own abodes."

The city fathers at last created a Metropolitan Health Board in 1866, and a tenement house law the next year made a feeble beginning at regulating city housing. A new tenement house law in 1879 finally placed a limit on the percentage of lot space that could be covered by *new* construction and established minimal standards of plumbing and ventilation. The magazine *Plumber and Sanitary Engineer* sponsored a contest to pick the best design for a tenement that met these specifications. The winner of the competition was James E. Ware, whose plan for a "dumbbell" apartment house managed to crowd from 24 to 32 four-room apartments on a plot of ground only 25 by 100 feet.

The feat was accomplished [writes Oscar Handlin in *The Uprooted*] by narrowing the building at its middle so that it took on the shape of a dumbbell. The indentation was only two-and-a-half feet wide and varied in length from five to fifty feet; but, added to the similar indentations on the adjoining houses, it created on each side an air-shaft five feet wide. . . . The stairs, halls, and common water closets were cramped into the narrow center of the building so that almost the whole of its surface was available for living quarters.

Despite such reforms, in 1890 over 1.4 million persons were living on Manhattan Island, and in some sections the population density exceeded 900 persons per acre. Jacob Riis, a New York reporter, captured the horror of these crowded warrens in his classic study of life in the slums, *How the Other Half Lives* (1890):

Be a little careful, please! The hall is dark and you might stumble. . . . Here where the hall turns and dives into utter darkness is . . . a flight of stairs. You can feel your way, if you cannot see it. Close? Yes! What would you have? All the fresh air that enters these stairs comes from the hall-door that is forever slamming. . . . The sinks are in the hallway, that all the tenants may have access—and all be poisoned alike by their summer stenches. . . . Here is a door. Listen! That short, hacking cough, that tiny, helpless wail—what do they mean? . . . The child is dying of measles. With half a chance it might have lived; but it had none. That dark bedroom killed it.

The unhealthiness of the tenements was notorious; one noxious corner of New York became known as the "lung block" because of the prevalence of tuberculosis among its inhabitants. In 1900 three out of every five babies born in one poor district of Chicago died before their first birthday. Equally frightening was the impact of such overcrowding on the morals of the tenement dweller. Crime flourished. The number of prison inmates in the United States increased by 50 per cent in the eighties and the homicide rate nearly tripled, most of the rise occurring in cities. Driven into the streets by the squalor of their homes, poor, ignorant, and hopeless, the youth of the slum districts formed gangs bearing names like Alley Gang, Rock Gang, and Hell's Kitchen Gang. From petty thievery and shoplifting they graduated to housebreaking, bank robbery, and murder. According to Jacob Riis, when the leader of the infamous Whyo Gang, convicted of murder, finally confessed his sins to a prison chaplain, "his father confessor turned pale . . . though many years of labor as chaplain of the Tombs had hardened him to such rehearsals."

Slums bred criminals—the wonder being that they bred so few. They also drove the well-to-do element to exclusive sections and to the suburbs.

From Boston's Beacon Hill and Back Bay to San Francisco's Nob Hill, the rich retired into great cluttered mansions and ignored conditions in the poorer parts of town.

The big-city political bosses, with their corrupt yet useful "machines," filled the vacuum created by upper-class abdication of responsibility. The immigrant masses, largely of peasant stock, had no experience with representative government. The aforementioned tendency of poor workers to move frequently lessened the likelihood that they would develop political influence independently. Furthermore, the difficulties of life in the slums bewildered and often overwhelmed them. Hopeful, passive, naive, they could not be expected to take a broad view of social problems when so harassed by personal ones. Shrewd urban politicians, most of them of Irish origin—the Irish being the first-comers among the migrants and less likely to move about, according to the mobility studies—quickly took command of these immigrants. They shepherded them through the complexities of taking out citizenship papers and then marched them in obedient phalanxes to the polls.

Most city machines were not tightly geared hierarchical bureaucracies ruled by a single leader, but loose-knit neighborhood organizations, each headed by a ward boss. Men like "Big Tim" Sullivan of New York's Lower East Side and "Hinky Dink" Kenna of Chicago were typical of the breed. Such men found jobs for new arrivals and distributed food and other help to all in bad times. Anyone in trouble with the law could obtain at least a hearing from the ward boss, and often, if the crime was venial or due to ignorance, the difficulty was quietly "fixed" and the culprit sent off with a word of caution. Sullivan provided turkey dinners for 5,000 or more derelicts each Christmas, distributed new shoes to all the poor children of his district on his birthday, arranged summer boat rides and picnics for young and old alike. At any time of year the victim of some sudden disaster could turn to the local clubhouse for help. Informally, probably without consciously intending to do so, the bosses educated the immigrants in the complex-

ities of American civilization, helping them to leap across the gulf between the almost medieval society of their origins and the modern industrial world.

The price of such aid—for the bosses were no altruists—was unquestioning political support, which the bosses converted into cash. In New York Sullivan levied tribute on gambling, had a hand in the liquor business, controlled the issuance of peddlers' licenses. When he died in 1913, he was reputedly worth a million dollars. Yet he and others like him were immensely popular; 25,000 grieving constituents followed Big Tim's coffin to the grave.

The more visible and better-known "city" bosses played less socially justifiable roles than the ward bosses. Their principal technique for extracting money from the public till was the "kickback." In order to get city contracts, suppliers were made to pad their bills and turn over the excess to the politicians. Similarly, operators of streetcar lines, gas and electricity companies, and other public utilities were compelled to pay huge bribes to obtain favorable franchises.

The most notorious—and probably the most despicable—of the major 19th-century city bosses was William Marcy Tweed, whose "Ring" extracted tens of millions of dollars from New York City during the brief period 1869–71. Tweed, quite properly and relatively swiftly, was lodged in jail. More typical of the city bosses was Richard Croker, who ruled New York's Tammany Hall organization from the mid-1880's to the end of the century. Croker held a number of local offices, but his power rested upon his position as chairman of the Tammany Hall finance committee. Although more concerned than Tweed with the social and economic services that machines provided for the city masses, Croker was primarily a corrupt political manipulator; he accumulated a large fortune, owned a $200,000 mansion and a stable of racehorses, one of which was good enough to win the English Derby in 1907.

Despite their welfare work and their admitted popularity with the masses, most bosses were essentially thieves. Efforts to romanticize them as

An alley known as "Bandit's Roost," on New York's Lower East Side, photographed for the New York *Sun* in 1887 or 1888 by police reporter Jacob Riis, himself an immigrant. "What sort of an answer, think you, would come from these tenements to the question 'Is life worth living?' " Riis asked in his *How the Other Half Lives*. (Jacob A. Riis Collection, Museum of the City of New York.)

the Robin Hoods of industrial society grossly distort the facts. However, the system developed and survived because too many middle-class city dwellers were indifferent to the fate of the poor. Except spasmodically, during "reform waves," few tried to check the rapaciousness of the politicos. Many substantial citizens shared at least indirectly in the corruption. The owners of tenements, interested only in crowding as many rent payers as possible into their buildings, and utility companies seeking franchises preferred a system that enabled them to buy favors. Honest men who had no selfish stake in the system and who were repelled by the sordidness of city govern-

ment were seldom sufficiently concerned to do anything about it. When young Theodore Roosevelt decided to seek a political career in 1880, his New York socialite friends laughed in his face. "[They] told me," Roosevelt wrote in his autobiography, "that politics were 'low'; that the organizations were not controlled by 'gentlemen'; that I would find them run by saloon-keepers, horse-car conductors, and the like."

Indeed, many so-called urban reformers resented the boss system mainly because it gave political power to those who were not "gentlemen," or as one reformer put it, to a "proletarian mob" of "illiterate peasants, freshly raked from

Irish bogs, or Bohemian mines, or Italian robber nests." A British visitor in Chicago struck at the root of the urban problem of the era. "Everybody is fighting to be rich," he said, "and nobody can attend to making the city fit to live in."

Urban Improvement

Nevertheless, as American cities grew larger and more crowded, thus aggravating a host of social problems, various practical forces operated to bring about improvements. Once the relationship between polluted water and disease was fully understood, everyone saw the need for decent water and sewage systems. Although some businessmen profited from corrupt dealings with the city machines, more of them wanted efficient and honest government in order to reduce their tax bills. City dwellers of all classes resented dirt, noise, and ugliness, and in many communities public-spirited groups formed societies to plant trees, clean up littered areas, and develop recreational facilities. When one city undertook im-

Thomas Nast's devastating assaults on the Tweed Ring, printed in *Harper's Weekly,* helped bring about its demise. Tweed and his fellow vultures cower under the storm raised against them. Tweed offered Nast a $500,000 bribe to stop the cartoons. (Picture Collection, New York Public Library.)

provements, others tended to follow suit, spurred on by local pride and the booster spirit.

Gradually, in the eighties and nineties, the basic facilities of urban living were improved. Streets were paved, first with cobblestones and wood blocks and then with smoother, quieter asphalt. Gaslight, then electric arc lights, and finally Edison's incandescent lamps brightened the cities after dark, making law enforcement easier, stimulating night life, and permitting factories and shops to operate after sunset.

Urban transportation advanced phenomenally during the period. Elevated steam railways helped reduce the congestion, New York leading the way in the 1870's. However, the cheaper, quieter, and less unsightly electric trolley car soon became the principal means of municipal transportation. A retired naval officer, Frank J. Sprague, pioneered in this field, installing his first practical line in Richmond, Virginia, during the winter of 1887–88. At once other cities seized upon the trolley; by 1895 some 850 lines were busily hauling city dwellers over 10,000 miles of track, and mileage more than doubled in the next decade. As with other new enterprises, control of street railways quickly became centralized until a few big operators—Charles T. Yerkes in Chicago, P. A. B. Widener and William L. Elkins in Philadelphia, William C. Whitney and Thomas Fortune Ryan in New York—controlled the trolleys of over 100 eastern cities and towns. Their various companies were capitalized at about $1 billion.

Streetcars changed the whole character of big-city life. Before their introduction urban communities were limited by the distances people could conveniently walk to work. This "walking city" could not easily extend more than two-and-a-half miles from its center. Streetcars increased this radius to six miles or more, which meant that the *area* of the city expanded enormously. Dramatic population shifts resulted. Rich and poor previously lived close together; now the better-off moved out from the center in search of air and space, abandoning the crumbling, jam-packed older neighborhoods to the immigrant poor and the Negroes. Thus economic

segregation speeded the growth of ghettos. Older peripheral towns that had maintained some of the self-contained qualities of village life were swallowed up, becoming part of a vast urban sprawl. As time passed, each new area, originally peopled by rising economic groups, tended to become crowded and then to deteriorate. The middle class pushed steadily outward, which helps to explain why this group abandoned its interest in city government so easily. On the other hand, by extending their tracks *beyond* the city limits, the streetcars enabled city dwellers to escape into the countryside on holidays.

Advances in bridge design, most notably the perfection of the steel-cable suspension bridge by John A. Roebling, also aided the ebb and flow of metropolitan populations. The Brooklyn Bridge—"a weird metallic Apparition under a metallic sky, out of proportion with the winged lightness of its arch, traced for the conjunction of worlds . . . the cables, like divine messages from above . . . cutting and dividing into innumerable musical spaces the nude immensity of the sky"— was Roebling's triumph. Completed by Roebling's son in 1883 at a cost of $15 million, it was soon carrying more than 33 million passengers a year over the East River between Manhattan and Brooklyn.

Even the extremely high cost of urban real estate, which fathered the tenement, produced some beneficial results for the cities in the long run. Instead of crowding squat structures cheek by jowl on 25-foot lots, some imaginative architects began to build upward. The introduction of the iron-skeleton type of construction, which freed the walls from bearing the immense weight of a tall building, was the work of a group of Chicago architects who had been attracted to the metropolis of the Midwest by opportunities to be found amid the ashes of the great fire of 1871. The group included William Le Baron Jenney, John A. Holabird, Martin Roche, John W. Root, and Louis H. Sullivan. Jenney's Home Insurance Building, completed in 1885, was the first metal-frame edifice, employing cast-iron columns and wrought-iron crossbeams. Mere height, however, did not satisfy these innovators; they were determined to create a truly new style. Instead of erecting grotesque enlargements of Romanesque and Gothic structures, they sought a new form that would reflect the structure and purpose of their buildings. Their leader was Louis Sullivan. Builders must discard "books, rules, precedents, or any such educational impedimenta" and design functional buildings, he argued. A tall building "must be every inch a proud and soaring thing, rising in sheer exultation . . . from bottom to top . . . a unit without a single dissenting line."

Sullivan's Wainwright Building in St. Louis and Prudential Building in Buffalo, both completed in the early nineties, combined beauty, low construction costs, and efficient use of scarce space in pathbreaking ways. Soon a "race to the skies" was on in all the great cities of America, and the words *skyscraper* and *skyline* entered the language.

Efforts to redesign American cities, much stimulated by the remarkable "White City" built for the Chicago World's Fair of 1893 by Daniel H. Burnham, with its broad vistas and acres of open space, resulted in a "City Beautiful" move-

ment of considerable scope. Burnham and the landscape architect Frederick Law Olmsted, designer of New York's Central Park, gave direction to the movement. Ambitious civic centers were all the rage around the turn of the century, as impressive projects were undertaken in Washington, Cleveland, and other cities. But these never became more than expensive showplaces, broad plazas fringed by pretentious public buildings in the classic style made popular by White City, but surrounded by close-packed, dingy ugliness.

The City Beautiful movement also gave birth to many public parks, and these, of course, brought immense benefits to the people. However, few could be located where they were most needed. Similarly, efforts to relieve the congestion in the slum districts made little headway. In Brooklyn Alfred T. White established Home Buildings, a 40-family model tenement, in 1877; eventually, he expanded the experiment to include 267 apartments. Each unit had plenty of light and air and contained its own sink and toilet. Ellen Collins developed a smaller project in

Looking south on Dearborn Street in Chicago around 1910, it is easy to see how the streetcar changed big-city life in many ways, not the least being some of the densest traffic jams ever. (Chicago Historical Society.)

THE RESPONSE TO INDUSTRIALISM

Manhattan's Fourth Ward in the nineties. These model tenements were self-sustaining, but of necessity they yielded only modest returns. The landlords were essentially philanthropists; their work had no significant impact upon urban housing in the 19th century.

Religion Responds to Industrialism

The modernization of the great cities, in short, was not solving most of the social problems of the slums. As this fact became clear in the late 19th century, a number of urban religious leaders began to take a hard look at the situation. Traditionally, American churchmen had insisted that where sin was concerned there were no such things as extenuating circumstances. To the well-to-do they preached the virtues of thrift and hard work, to the poor they extended the possibility of a better existence in the next world, but to all they stressed the individual's responsibility for his own behavior, and thus for his salvation.

Such a point of view brought meager comfort to residents of slums. As a result, the churches lost influence in the poorer sections of the big cities. Furthermore, as better-off citizens followed the streetcar lines out from the city centers, their church leaders followed them. In New York, 17 Protestant congregations abandoned the depressed areas of Lower Manhattan between 1868 and 1888. Catering almost entirely to middle- and upper-class worshipers, they tended to become even more conservative and individualistic in their approach. No more strident defender of reactionary ideas existed than Henry Ward Beecher, pastor of Brooklyn's fashionable Plymouth Congregational Church. Beecher attributed most of the poverty of the slums to the improvidence of laborers, who, he claimed, squandered their wages on liquor and tobacco. "No man in this land suffers from poverty," he said, "unless it be more than his fault—unless it be his *sin.*" The best check on labor unrest was a plentiful supply of cheap immigrant labor, he told President Hayes. Unions were "the worst form of despo-

tism and tyranny in the history of Christendom."

Although an increasing proportion of the residents of the blighted districts were Catholics, the Roman Church confined its assistance to distributing alms and maintaining homes for orphans, wayward girls, and old people; church leaders were deeply committed to the idea that sin and vice were personal, poverty an act of God. The release of Pope Pius IX's encyclical *Syllabus of Errors* (1864), which declared every form of liberalism and reform anathema, did nothing to encourage parish priests and Catholic laymen to try to change the *status quo.* As Arthur Mann has pointed out in his study of late-19th-century Boston reformers, despite the heavy concentration of Catholics in that city, "the Archdiocese of Boston failed to send a single priest into the army of social reform . . . during the period 1880–1900." Catholic leaders deplored the rising trend of crime, disease, and destitution among their co-religionists but failed to see the connection between these evils and the squalor of the slums. "Intemperance is the great evil we have to overcome," wrote the president of the leading Catholic charitable organization, the Society of St. Vincent de Paul. "It is the source of the misery for at least three-fourths of the families we are called upon to visit and relieve." The Church, according to a Catholic historian, Aaron I. Abell, "seemed oblivious to the bearing of civil legislation on the course of moral and social reform." Instead it invested much money and energy in chimerical attempts to colonize poor city dwellers in the West. In the early 1880's, for example, the Irish Catholic Colonization Association of America settled some 35,000 acres in Nebraska and Minnesota. Of course this effort to reverse the national trend from farm to city had little effect on urban conditions.

Like conservative Protestant clergymen, the Catholic hierarchy opposed, or was at best neutral toward, organized labor. Although Terence V. Powderly was a Catholic, a number of priests and bishops looked askance at his Knights of Labor. The situation changed somewhat after Pope Leo XIII issued his great encyclical *Rerum novarum* (1891), which criticized the excesses of capitalism, defended the right of labor to form unions, and even gave qualified approval to certain aspects of socialism. The workingman was entitled to a wage that would guarantee him a reasonable and frugal comfort, Leo declared, and he committed no sin by seeking government aid to get it. Concrete action by American Catholic leaders, however, was slow in coming.

The conservative attitudes of most religious leaders, both Protestant and Catholic, did not prevent some earnest preachers from working directly to improve the lot of the city poor. Some followed the path blazed by Dwight L. Moody, who became famous all over America and Great Britain as a lay evangelist. A gargantuan figure weighing nearly 300 pounds, Moody conducted a vigorous campaign to persuade the denizens of the slums to cast aside their sinful ways. He went among them full of enthusiasm and God's love and made an impact no less powerful than that of George Whitefield during the Great Awakening of the 18th century. Moody and other evangelists founded mission schools in the worst parts of the slums and tried to provide spiritual and recreational facilities for the unfortunate. Men of this type were prominent in the establishment in the United States of the Young Men's Christian Association (1851) and the Salvation Army (1880).

However, the evangelists paid little heed to the causes of urban poverty and vice. In effect, they depended upon old-fashioned faith in God to enable the poor to transcend the material difficulties of life. For a number of Protestant clergymen who had become familiar with the terrible problems of the slums, a different approach seemed called for. Slum conditions produced the sins and crimes of the cities; the wretched humans who actually committed them could not be blamed, these men argued. They began to preach a "Social Gospel," which focused on trying to improve living conditions rather than on merely saving souls. If people were to lead pure lives, they must have enough to eat, decent homes, and opportunities to develop their talents.

Social Gospelers rejected the theory of laissez faire. They advocated civil service reform to break the power of the machines, child labor legislation, the regulation of the trusts, and heavy taxes on incomes and inheritances. The most influential preacher of the Social Gospel was probably Washington Gladden. At first, Gladden, who was raised on a Massachusetts farm, had opposed unions and all governmental interference in social and economic affairs, but his experiences as a minister in Springfield, Massachusetts, and Columbus, Ohio, exposed him to some of the harshness of life in industrial cities, and his views changed. In *Applied Christianity* (1886) and in other works, he defended labor's right to organize and strike and denounced the idea that supply and demand should control wage rates. He favored factory inspection laws, strict regulation of public utilities, and other reforms.

Gladden was a mild-mannered man who never questioned the basic values of capitalism. By the nineties a number of ministers had gone all the way to socialism. The Reverend William D. P. Bliss of Boston, for example, believed in the kind of welfare state envisioned by Edward Bellamy in *Looking Backward.* He founded the Society of Christian Socialists (1889) and edited a radical journal, *The Dawn.* In addition to nationalizing industry, Bliss and other Christian Socialists advocated government unemployment-relief programs, public housing and slum-clearance projects, and other measures designed to aid the city poor.

Nothing so well reveals the receptivity of the public to the Social Gospel as the popularity of Charles M. Sheldon's novel *In His Steps* (1896), one of America's all-time best-sellers. Sheldon, a minister in Topeka, Kansas, described what happened in the mythical city of Raymond when a group of leading citizens decided to live truly Christian lives, asking themselves "What would Jesus do?" before adopting any course of action. Naturally, the tone of Raymond's society was immensely improved, but basic social reforms also followed quickly. The "Rectangle," a terrible slum area, "too dirty, too coarse, too sinful, too awful for close contact," became the center of a great reform effort. One of Raymond's "leading society heiresses" undertook a slum-clearance project, and a concerted attack was made on drunkenness and immorality. The moral regeneration of the whole community was soon accomplished.

The Settlement Houses

Although millions read *In His Steps,* its effect, and that of other Social Gospel literature, was merely inspirational. On the practical level, a number of earnest souls began to grapple with slum problems directly by organizing what were known as "settlement houses." These were community centers located in poor districts which provided guidance and services to all who would use them. The settlement workers, most of them idealistic, well-to-do young people, lived in the houses and took active parts in neighborhood affairs. A large percentage of them were women fresh from college—the first generation of young women to experience the trauma of having developed their capacities only to find that society offered them few opportunities to use them.

The prototype of the settlement house was London's Toynbee Hall, founded in the early eighties; the first American example was the Neighborhood Guild, opened on the Lower East Side of New York in 1886 by Dr. Stanton Coit. By the turn of the century a hundred had been established, the most famous being Jane Addams' Hull House in Chicago (1889), Robert A. Woods's South End House in Boston (1892), and Lillian Wald's Henry Street Settlement in New York (1893).

The settlement workers tried to interpret American ways to the new immigrants and to create a community spirit among the rootless and the deprived. But unlike most charity workers, who acted out of a sense of upper-class responsibility toward the unfortunate, they expected to benefit morally and intellectually themselves by experiencing a way of life far different from their own. Lillian Wald, a nurse by training, explained the concept succinctly in *The House on Henry Street* (1915): "We were to live in the neighborhood . . . identify ourselves with it socially, and, in brief, contribute to it our citizenship."

Miss Wald and other leaders soon discovered that practical problems occupied most of their energies. They agitated for tenement house laws, the regulation of the labor of women and children, and better schools, and they employed private resources to establish playgrounds in the slums, along with libraries, classes in arts and crafts, social clubs, and day nurseries. In Boston Robert A. Woods organized clubs to get the youngsters of the South End off the streets, helped establish a restaurant where a meal could be had for five cents, acted as an arbitrator in labor disputes, and lobbied for laws tightening up on the franchises of public utility companies. In Chicago Jane Addams developed an outstanding cultural program that included classes in music and art and an excellent "little theater" group. Hull House soon boasted a gymnasium, a day nursery, and several social clubs. Miss Addams also worked tirelessly and effectively at the state and local levels for improved public services and social legislation of all kinds. She even got herself appointed garbage inspector in her ward and hounded local landlords and the garbage contractor until something approaching decent service was established.

A few critics considered the settlement houses mere devices to socialize the unruly poor by teaching them the "punctilios of upper-class propriety," but almost everyone appreciated their virtues. By the end of the century even the Catholics, so laggard in entering the arena of practical social reform, were joining the movement, partly because they were losing many communicants to socially minded Protestant churches. The first Catholic-run settlement house was founded in 1898 in an Italian district of New York. Two years later Brownson House in Los Angeles, catering chiefly to Mexican immigrants, threw open its doors. Yet with all their accomplishments, the settlement houses seemed to be fighting a losing battle. "Private beneficence," wrote Jane Addams, of Hull House, "is totally inadequate to deal with the vast numbers of the city's disinherited." As a tropical forest grows faster than a handful of men armed with machetes can cut it down, so the slums, fed by an annual influx of hundreds of thousands, blighted additional areas more rapidly than the intrepid settlement-house workers could clean up old ones. It became increasingly apparent that the wealth and authority of the state must be brought to bear in order to keep abreast of the problem.

Social Legislation

State laws aimed at the social problems resulting from industrialism and urbanization date from before the Civil War, but the earlier ones were either so imprecise as to be unenforceable or—like the Georgia law "limiting" textile workers to 11 hours a day and the New York Housing Act of 1867, which set a standard to which the city's dreadful tenements easily conformed—so weak as to be ineffective. As time passed, however, a scattering of workable laws was enacted. In 1874 a Massachusetts law restricted the working hours of women and children to ten per day, and by the 1890's many other states, mostly in the East and Middle West, had followed suit. Illinois even passed an eight-hour law for women workers in 1893. A New York law of 1882 struck at the sweatshops of the slums by prohibiting the manufacture of cigars on premises "occupied as a house or residence." Many states passed fire and sanitary inspection laws that improved conditions in the cities.

As part of this trend, some states established special rules for workers in hazardous industries. In the 1890's Ohio and several other states began to regulate the hours of railroad workers on the ground that fatigue sometimes caused railroad accidents. New York set a ten-hour-per-day limit for brickyard workers (1893) and bakers (1897). Utah restricted the hours of work in mining to eight in 1896; Montana, Colorado, and several other states did the same. California, in 1881,

even made it illegal for women to work as waitresses in saloons. In 1901 New York finally enacted an effective tenement house law, greatly increasing the area of open space on building lots and requiring separate toilets for each apartment, better ventilation systems, safer fire escapes, and more adequate fireproofing. New Jersey, Connecticut, Wisconsin, and many other states soon passed laws modeled after New York's.

The collective impact of these laws was not very impressive. Powerful vested interests, such as manufacturers and landlords, threw their weight against many kinds of social legislation, and since the laws ran counter to the American traditions of individualism and laissez faire, they often succeeded in either defeating them or rendering them innocuous. Many of the early laws limiting hours, for example, were made to apply only "in the absence of agreements" to work longer hours.

The federal system itself further complicated the task of obtaining effective legislation. Throughout the 19th century few authorities contested the right of government to protect society and individuals against anything that threatened the general welfare, but these authorities assumed that such problems would be dealt with by the states, not the national government.° As a rule, this "police power" of the states was broadly interpreted; the courts even upheld laws prohibiting the manufacture and sale of liquor on the ground that drunkenness was a social as well as an individual problem, affecting nonimbibers as well as the drinkers themselves.

However, the development of a truly national economy after the Civil War greatly complicated the problem of coping with social and industrial problems at the state level. Obviously, until *all* the states outlawed child labor, that evil could not be completely eradicated, yet once producers all over the country could compete effectively with one another, it became very hard to persuade legislators in one state to prohibit child

°Congress enacted an eight-hour law for government workers in 1892.

labor so long as others refused to do so. If they did, they would injure their own manufacturers by giving firms in other states an unfair advantage. Yet a federal child labor law seemed out of the question on constitutional grounds.

Furthermore, the enemies of state social legislation soon discovered still another weapon—the Fourteenth Amendment to the Constitution. Although enacted to protect the civil rights of Negroes against southern Black Codes, this amendment imposed a revolutionary restriction on state power, for it forbade the states to "deprive any person of life, liberty, or property without due process of law." This restriction did not abolish the police power of the states, but tenement-house laws, child-labor laws, and other social legislation represented extensions of police power that conservative judges considered dangerous and unwise, and the Fourteenth Amendment gave them an excuse to overturn them. Both state and federal courts began to draw a line beyond which the states could not go in this area. Some measures seemed unexceptionable; the courts did not, for example, interfere with laws requiring fire escapes on tall buildings, although these certainly deprived builders of property by increasing their costs and of the liberty to erect any kind of structure they pleased. Laws regulating the hours and conditions of labor, however, met mixed fates, depending upon the wording of the acts and the prejudices of particular judges.

Laws affecting women and children, and those regulating conditions in dangerous and unhealthy occupations like mining, fared better than those attempting to deal with the population as a whole, but it is very difficult to generalize. The pioneering Massachusetts ten-hour law of 1874, restricting the working day of women and children, was upheld as a valid exercise of the police power by the Massachusetts courts. On the other hand, the Illinois law of 1893 limiting the hours of women employed in manufacturing to eight per day was declared unconstitutional. "The mere fact of sex will not justify the legislature in putting forth the police power," the Illinois court declared in *Ritchie v. People.*

"There is no reasonable ground . . . for fixing upon eight hours in one day as the limit within which woman can work without injury to her physique." The New York Court of Appeals threw out the sweatshop law of 1882 on similar grounds. "It cannot be perceived," Justice Earl wrote in a decision so unrealistic that it appears preposterous to anyone who knows a little about slum conditions in the 1880's, "how the cigar maker is·to be improved in his health or his morals by forcing him from his home with its hallowed associations and beneficient influences, to ply his trade elsewhere." The United States Supreme Court upheld the Utah mining law of 1896 (*Holden v. Hardy,* 1898), but the nearly identical Colorado act was declared by the state courts to have violated the Fourteenth Amendment by depriving workers of the liberty to work as long as they wished.

As stricter and more far-reaching laws were enacted, conservative judges, sensing what they took to be a trend toward socialism and regimentation, adopted an increasingly narrow interpretation of state police power. The severest blow came in 1905, when for the first time the Supreme Court of the United States declared a piece of state social legislation unconstitutional. New York's ten-hour act for bakers, the Court decided in *Lochner v. New York,* deprived bakers of the liberty of working as long as they wished, and thus violated the Fourteenth Amendment. Justice Oliver Wendell Holmes, Jr., wrote a brilliant dissenting opinion in this case, arguing that if a majority of the people of New York believed that the public health was endangered by bakers working long hours, it was not the Court's business to overrule them. "A constitution is not intended to embody a particular economic theory, whether of paternalism . . . or of *laissez faire,*" Holmes said. "The word 'liberty,' in the Fourteenth Amendment, is perverted when it is held to prevent the natural outcome of a dominant opinion." Of course Holmes's sensible doctrine did not alter the decision, which was deplored by all those who hoped to limit the hours of labor through legislation.

Civilization and Its Discontents

As the 19th century died, the majority of the American people, especially those comfortably well off, the residents of small towns, the shopkeepers, many farmers, some skilled workingmen, remained confirmed optimists and uncritical admirers of their own civilization. However, Negroes, immigrants, and others who failed to share in the good things of life, along with a growing number of humanitarian reformers, found few reasons to cheer and many to lament the state of affairs in their increasingly industrialized society. Giant monopolies flourished despite federal restrictions. The gap between rich and poor was widening, while the slum spread its poison and the materially successful made a god of their success. Human values seemed in grave danger of being crushed by impersonal materialistic forces, typified by the great corporations.

As early as 1871 Walt Whitman, usually so full of extravagant praise for the American way of life, called his fellow countrymen the "most materialistic and money-making people ever known":

I say we had best look our times and lands searchingly in the face, like a physician diagnosing some deep disease. Never was there, perhaps, more hollowness of heart than at present, and here in the United States.

By the late eighties a well-known journalist could write to a friend: "The wheel of progress is to be run over the whole human race and smash us all." Others noted an alarming jump in the national divorce rate and an increasing taste for all kinds of luxury. "People are made slaves by a desperate struggle to keep up appearances," a Massachusetts commentator declared, and the economist David A. Wells expressed concern over statistics showing that heart disease and mental illness were on the rise. These "diseases of civilization," Wells explained, were "one result of the continuous mental and nervous activity which modern high-tension methods of business have necessitated."

Wells was a prominent liberal, but pessimism was no monopoly of men of his stripe. A little later, Senator Henry Cabot Lodge of Massachusetts, himself a millionaire, complained of the "lawlessness" of "the modern and recent plutocrat" and his "disregard of the rights of others." Lodge also spoke of "the enormous contrast between the sanguine mental attitude prevalent in my youth and that, perhaps wiser, but certainly darker view, so general today."

Of course intellectuals often tend to be critical of the world they live in, whatever its nature. Thoreau, for example, had denounced materialism and the worship of progress in the 1840's as vigorously as any late-19th-century prophet of gloom. But the voices of the dissatisfied were rising. Despite the many benefits that industrialization had made possible, it was by no means clear around 1900 that the American people were really better off under the new dispensation.

Supplementary Reading

The idea of interpreting social and economic history in the post-Civil War decades as a broad reaction to the growth of industry is presented in S. P. Hays, *The Response to Industrialism°* (1957). Other general treatments of the period include R. H. Wiebe, *The Search for Order°* (1968), and Ray Ginger, *The Age of Excess°* (1965). J. A. Garraty, *The New Commonwealth°* (1968) treats all the subjects covered in this chapter; A. M. Schlesinger, *The Rise of the City* (1933), stresses the importance of urban developments but also provides a wealth of information about social trends. Both H. U. Faulkner, *Politics, Reform, and Expansion°* (1959), and Blake McKelvey, *The Urbanization of America* (1962), also contain useful information. An excellent collection of source materials dealing with many aspects of social and economic history in these years may be found in Sigmund Diamond (ed.), *The Nation Transformed°* (1963). Henry Adams, *The Education of Henry Adams°* (1918), is a fascinating if highly personal view of the period. James Bryce, *The American Commonwealth°* (1888), while primarily a political analysis, contains a great deal of information about social con-

°Available in paperback.

ditions, as does D. A. Wells, *Recent Economic Changes* (1889).

The standard history of American labor is J. R. Commons *et al.*, *History of Labour in the United States* (1918-35), but see also Philip Taft, *Organized Labor in America* (1964), N. J. Ware, *The Labor Movement in the United States*° (1929), and the appropriate chapters of E. C. Kirkland, *Industry Comes of Age*° (1961). J. A. Garraty (ed.), *Labor and Capital in the Gilded Age*° (1968), provides a convenient selection of testimony from the great 1883 Senate investigation of that subject, while David Brody, *Steelworkers in America*° (1960), and Stephan Thernstrom, *Poverty and Progress: Social Mobility in a Nineteenth-Century City*° (1964), throw much light on the lives of workingmen. Thernstrom's *The Other Bostonians: Poverty and Progress in the American Metropolis* (1973), is both a brilliant analysis of social and geographical mobility and an excellent summary of work on these important topics. Businessmen's attitudes are covered in T. C. Cochran, *Railroad Leaders*° (1953), and E. C. Kirkland, *Dream and Thought in the Business Community*° (1956). On the growth of unions, see J. P. Grossman, *William Sylvis* (1945), Philip Taft, *The A.F. of L. in the Time of Gompers* (1957), G. N. Grob, *Workers and Utopia*° (1961), Samuel Gompers, *Seventy Years of Life and Labor* (1925), and T. V. Powderly, *Thirty Years of Labor* (1889). The important strikes and labor violence of the period are described in R. V. Bruce, *1877: Year of Violence* (1959), Henry David, *History of the Haymarket Affair*° (1936), Leon Wolff, *Lockout* (1965), Almont Lindsey, *The Pullman Strike*° (1942), and W. G. Broehl, Jr., *The Molly Maguires*° (1964).

On immigration, see M. A. Jones, *American Immigration*° (1960), M. L. Hansen, *The Immigrant in American History*° (1940), and I. S. Hourwich, *Immigration and Labor* (1923). Oscar Handlin, *The Uprooted*° (1951), describes the life of the new immigrants with imagination and sensitivity, while John Higham, *Strangers in the Land*° (1955), and B. M. Solomon, *Ancestors and Immigrants*° (1956), stress the reactions of native Americans to successive waves of immigration. Moses Rischin, *The Promised City: New York's Jews*° (1962), T. N. Brown, *Irish-American Nationalism*° (1966), Charlotte Erickson, *American Industry and the European Immigrant* (1957), and R. T. Berthoff, *British Immigrants in In-*

dustrial America: 1790-1950 (1953), are important monographs.

A brief interpretive history of urban development is C. N. Glaab and A. T. Brown, *A History of Urban America*° (1967). For the growing pains of American cities, consult the volumes by Schlesinger and McKelvey mentioned above, and also R. H. Bremner, *From the Depths*° (1956), Jacob Riis, *How the Other Half Lives*° (1890), Gordon Atkins, *Health, Housing, and Poverty in New York City* (1947), and R. M. Lubove, *The Progressives and the Slums: Tenement House Reform in New York City* (1962). For urban government, see the classic criticisms in Bryce's *American Commonwealth,* and also F. W. Patton, *The Battle for Municipal Reform: Mobilization and Attack* (1940). Urban architecture is discussed in O. W. Larkin, *Art and Life in America* (1949), Lewis Mumford, *The Brown Decades*° (1931), and J. E. Burchard and Albert Bush-Brown, *The Architecture of America*° (1961). S. B. Warner, Jr., *Streetcar Suburbs*° (1962) is an interesting study of Boston's development that is full of suggestive ideas about late-19th-century growth.

The response of religion to industrialism is discussed in H. F. May, *Protestant Churches and Industrial America*° (1949), in two books by A. I. Abell, *The Urban Impact on American Protestantism* (1943) and *American Catholicism and Social Action*° (1960), Arthur Mann, *Yankee Reformers in the Urban Age*° (1954), and C. H. Hopkins, *The Rise of the Social Gospel in American Protestantism*° (1940). See also Washington Gladden, *Applied Christianity* (1886), and R. T. Ely, *Social Aspects of Christianity* (1889). For the settlement-house movement, see A. F. Davis, *Spearheads for Reform* (1967), Davis' life of Jane Addams, *American Heroine* (1973) and two classic personal accounts, Jane Addams, *Twenty Years at Hull House*° (1910), and Lillian Wald, *The House on Henry Street*° (1915).

Sidney Fine, *Laissez Faire and the General-Welfare State*° (1956), deals with both social and economic thought and with state and federal social legislation, but see also C. G. Groat, *Attitude of American Courts in Labor Cases* (1911), A. M. Paul, *Conservative Crisis and the Rule of Law: Attitudes of Bar and Bench*° (1960), and R. G. McCloskey, *American Conservatism in the Age of Enterprise*° (1951).

Portfolio 5

A Nation Industrialized

As the nation turned toward peace in 1865, Senator John Sherman of Ohio wrote: "The truth is, the close of the war with our resources unimpaired gives an elevation, a scope to the ideas of leading capitalists. . . . They talk of millions as confidently as formerly of thousands." A decade later a homespun commentator remarked that the new technology was enough "to run anybody's idees up into majestic heights and run 'em round and round into lofty circles and spears of thought they hadn't never thought of runnin' into before." In 1876, when the United States celebrated its 100th birthday, the great majority of middle-class Americans still considered the industrialization process as an unmixed blessing.

As the decades passed, however, a gradual sense of unease began to erode this happy mood. The graphic representations of the period, as the following pages demonstrate, reflected this change. Where Henry Clay Frick's coke operations were guilelessly portrayed in an 1870's print, the spectacle of young boys laboring as coal breakers shocked the reformer-photographer Lewis Hine in 1910; where once four-color advertising represented real artistic merit, as in the locomotive builder's lithograph above, by 1914 it disfigured nearly every city in the land. With the coming of the new century, a nation industrialized was also a nation troubled.

THE NEW LANDSCAPE

Travelers passing through the Monongahela Valley in the 1880's glimpsed a new America in the making. The checkerboard landscape of field and farm was giving way to the age of iron and steel. Nor was this phenomenon limited to western Pennsylvania; indeed, it was transforming much of the nation. At a bend in the Monongahela, several miles upstream from Pittsburgh, lay the Homestead steel mill. In 1883 Andrew Carnegie absorbed the mill into his empire, soon add-

ing Bessemer converters and installing one of the revolutionary new open-hearth furnaces. William C. Wall painted Homestead a year after Carnegie took it over. In rendering the mill, the toylike trains, and the company town (right) as integral parts of a pastoral setting, Wall was reflecting the widespread belief—or at least the hope—that this new American landscape would blend painlessly into the old.

MIRACLES OF INDUSTRY

"The people have a wonderful appetite for science just now," trumpeted the New York *Tribune* in 1872, reporting that an enthusiastic crowd had braved the worst blizzard to hit the city in years to hear a lecture on light by British physicist John Tyndall. His audience thrilled to the prediction that their everyday lives would soon reflect the latest scientific advances, and within a matter of months Americans bought over 100,000 copies of his lectures. Tyndall returned to England proclaiming, "mechanical ingenuity engages a greater number of minds in the United States than in any other nation. . . ."

There seemed no end to the miracles being wrought by this American ingenuity. Technology surely heralded a golden age; manifest destiny was bound up in each new ore strike, each new mile of railroad track laid, each new bridge raised. Americans boasted of the great Brooklyn Bridge, the four-mile Sutro tunnel in Nevada's silver region, the canal at Sault Ste. Marie that by the mid-1880's was carrying three times the tonnage of the Suez Canal. Thousands flocked to little Wabash, Indiana, in 1880 to celebrate the city's new system of electric arc lamps. When the lights were turned on for the first time, "men fell on their knees . . . and many were dumb with amazement." Walt Whitman, singing of America's "sacred industry," was simply echoing the national mood.

Not surprisingly, Machinery Hall was the central attraction at the Centennial Exposition in Philadelphia in 1876. An *Atlantic Monthly* writer declared that "nowhere else are the triumphs of ingenuity, the marvels of skill and invention so displayed. . . . Surely here, and not in literature, science or art, is the true evidence of man's creative powers. Here is Prometheus unbound."

Steelmaster Andrew Carnegie summarized the growing miracle of production: "Two pounds of ironstone mined upon Lake Superior, and transported nine hundred miles to Pittsburgh; one pound and one-half of coal, mined and manufactured into coke, and transported to Pittsburgh; one-half pound of lime, mined and transported to Pittsburgh; a small amount of manganese ore mined in Virginia and brought to Pittsburgh—and these four pounds of materials manufactured into one pound of steel, for which the consumer pays one cent."

After the Civil War, Americans collected views of the latest industrial miracles with the enthusiasm that an earlier age showed for patriotic prints. Some of these views were given away for advertising purposes, others were sold outright. The Frick coke works, which supplied fuel for Pittsburgh's steel plants, distributed the print at right. Above is a testimonial to the design of James Eads's railroad bridge across the Mississippi at St. Louis.

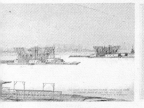

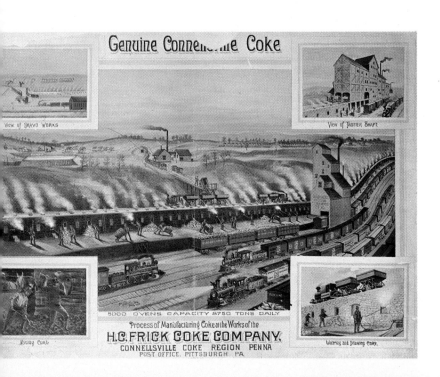

MOVING THE GOODS

Subscribers to the *North American Review* might well have wondered if the civilized world was coming to an end when they received their copies for September 1893. Missing for the fourth time in as many issues was the familiar cover typography; in its place were quarter-page displays for Royal baking powder, W. & J. Sloane carpets, Baker's breakfast cocoa, and Waterbury watches. Inside the magazine, no less than 42 pages were given over to various consumer products, ranging from cement and Londonderry Lithia Spring Water to a remedy for the "Morphine Habit" and a painless cure offered by the Baltimore Hernia Institute. Following the lead already taken by such upstarts as *Harper's,* the *Atlantic Monthly,* and the *Ladies' Home Journal,* the *North American Review,* a veritable national bastion of refinement and culture since 1815, had finally succumbed to the advertising mania.

The rising output of America's factories posed some new and unexpected problems. How were the barons of industry to keep their machines from outracing consumer demand? Or, more specifically, how was a New York sewing machine manufacturer to capture a sizable share of the market in Boston and Chicago? Massive doses of advertising, combined with new marketing techniques, provided the answers. By the eighties advertising was big business. Like the industries that supported it, advertising owed much to new technology, particularly advances in color lithography, stereotyping, and printing that made magazine advertising practicable.

A Russian visitor complained in 1895 that most American newspapers contained "almost nothing but advertisements." Moreover, he said, "the mails are choked with circulars, throwaways, and brochures." Another foreign observer complained that in every part of the country he visited he was confronted by "huge white-paint notices of favorite articles of manufacture." The American people, however, seemed to be taking the onslaught in stride, accepting the logic of the slogan, "If your business isn't worth advertising, advertise it for sale."

Above is the cover of a 1901 Singer sales brochure, while the Ford ad is an example of magazine displays in the early 1900's. The Duluth flour poster made imaginative use of the ballooning craze around the turn of the century. Endorsements appeared early and revealed a relaxed attitude toward the notion of "fair use"; witness the checkers contest at the right between Presidents Cleveland and Harrison.

Harper's Weekly, FEBRUARY 13, 1904

The FORD
MOTOR CAR

In the eyes of the Chauffeur

is the most satisfactory Automobile made for every-day service. The two cylinder (opposed) motor gives 8 actual horse-power, and eliminates the vibration so noticeable in other machines. The body is luxurious and comfortable and can be removed from the chassis by loosening six bolts.

Price with Tonneau, $900.00
As a Runabout, $800.00
Standard equipment includes 3-inch heavy double tube tires

We agree to assume all responsibility in any action the TRUST may take regarding alleged infringement of the Selden Patent to prevent you from buying the Ford—"*The Car of Satisfaction.*"

We Hold the World's Record
The Ford "999" (the fastest machine in the world), driven by Mr. Ford, made a mile in 39⅖ seconds—equal to 92 miles an hour.
Write for illustrated catalogue and name of our nearest agent.

Ford Motor Co., Detroit, Mich.

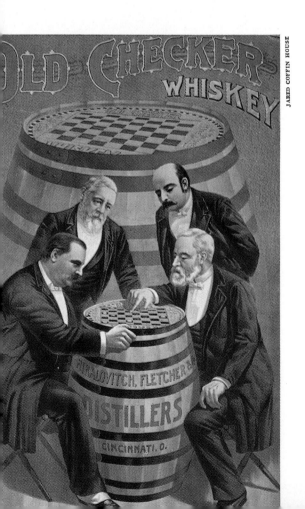

MAN AND MACHINE

At a hearing of a Senate committee investigating working conditions in New York City in 1883, Conrad Carl, a tailor, testified that before the Civil War his had been "a very still business, very quiet." Then the sewing machine appeared. "It stitched very nicely, nicer than the tailor could do; and the bosses said: 'We want you to use the sewing machine. . . .'" Asked how this innovation affected the tailors, Carl replied: "We work now in excitement—in a hurry. It is hunting; it is not work at all; it is a hunt."

In Chicago in 1900 an industrial commission heard a Russian immigrant named Abraham Bisno describe the job of a fellow worker, a buzz saw operator. "I asked him how long he had worked there," Bisno related. "He said 10 years. He gets $1.50 a day. He had worked at that buzz saw for 3 years. He has a big stack of rubber plates he must feed into that buzz saw every day, that is, 10 hours." As the operator talked to him he unconsciously repeated the motions of his work, Bisno said, and he added: "It is not hard work. He has not developed his muscles and has not become hardy enough to apply himself to common labor anywhere. . . . He has become a part of that machine he operates."

Mechanization and what one contemporary observer called the "minute subdivision of labor" was to reach near-perfection on Henry Ford's assembly lines by 1914, but the trends had been visible in other industries for decades. As the products of industry grew increasingly complex, the steps in their manufacture were simplified and standardized. This increased output and lowered costs, but it also spawned boredom, unrest, and carelessness among workmen. Frederick W. Taylor, whose time-and-motion studies ("Taylorism") had gained considerable popularity with employers by the turn of the century, pointed out that worker morale was very much a dollar-and-cents matter. Writing in 1895, he listed as one advantage of a new piecework system he was proposing the fact that it "promotes a most friendly feeling between the men and their employers, and so renders labor unions and strikes unnecessary."

J.I. CASE COMPANY

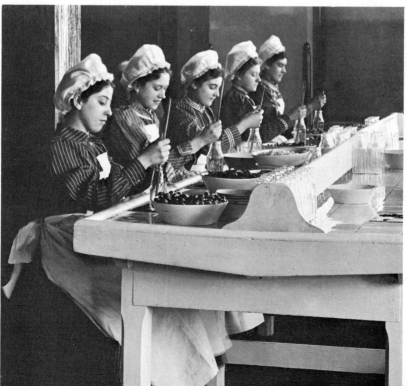

Above, workers at the Case steam tractor factory, photographed in 1902. At lower left is a Cincinnati slaughterhouse gang, depicted in an 1872 lithograph, on an early form of assembly line. At right, spruce Heinz girls bottle olives in about 1907. Specialization posed perplexing problems of status for workingmen. Shoe-making, for example, was divided into 64 steps; hence, asked an economist, was a shoemaker but a 64th as skilled as he once was?

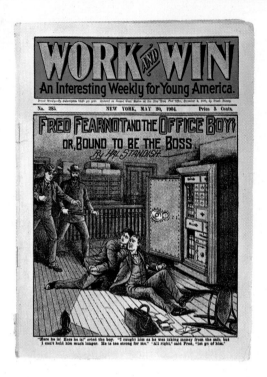

A GOSPEL OF WEALTH

Only fools and sluggards, according to the popular American tradition, failed to make their way in the world. Materialism was the common denominator; Americans were constantly reminded that they could and, indeed, they should make every effort to amass a fortune. "Godliness is in league with . . . riches," as Bishop Lawrence of Massachusetts explained it to his congregation.

There was no shortage of success stories on which to set one's sights. Had not Andrew Carnegie arrived from Scotland in steerage and by dint of hard work and virtuous living gained an annual income of $25 million? Examples of other self-made men were easy to find: Vanderbilt and Rockefeller, Swift and Armour, Edison, Marshall Field, the Guggenheims. It was this gospel of success that the tireless Horatio Alger served up to three generations of American youth. With but slight alterations Alger wrote the same tale at least 115 times; between the Civil War and World War I some 200 million copies of his works were sold.

Success bred imitation, and by the end of the century dime novel publishers were churning out a new brand of thriller, the Wall Street success story—or, as *Fame and Fortune Weekly* candidly put it, "Stories of Boys who Make Money." Beneath the lurid covers of dime novels (which competition drove down to a nickel) were oceans of small type that added up to a liberal borrowing on the Alger formula. The surest way to success was still the time-honored ritual of rescuing a tycoon's offspring from certain death, but quick wits paid off in other ways as well. Take, for example, Hal Morton, *Fame and Fortune Weekly*'s "Young Wonder of Wall Street" (above right). Hal, a messenger boy for a brokerage house, developed eavesdropping into a fine art (while still managing to look impressively busy) in order to catch stock tips. Thus forearmed, a few forays into the market brought him a cool $250,000. Only then did the Young Wonder quit his messenger's job and go into business for himself—at the age of 16.

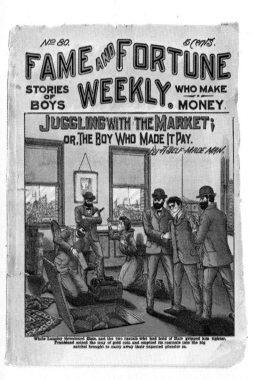

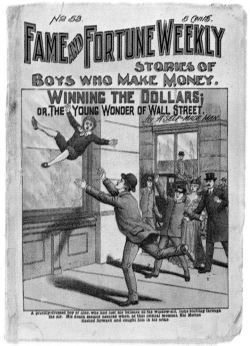

UNDERWOOD & UNDERWOOD

Andrew Carnegie's "The Gospel of Wealth" made provision for generous philanthropy. "Thirty-three and an income of $50,000 per annum!" he wrote in 1868, pleased by his early success. "Beyond this never earn. . . ." The dime novel genre (examples above) is credited to one Erastus Beadle, who began his publishing career labeling grain bags.

The wrecks of ruined railroads and bankrupt investors littered the paths of Jay Gould (above) and Jim Fisk (below). Observing their portraits on one of Fisk's Fall River Line steamboats, a stockbroker muttered, "There are the two thieves, but where's Christ?" W. H. Vanderbilt was exposed by *Puck* in 1879 (left) as a "Colossus of Roads" monopolizing the routes to New York. Assisting him are two lesser industrial demigods, Cyrus Field, of the city's transit system, and the unsavory Gould.

THE PUBLIC BE DAMNED

Flush times in the postwar era produced a new kind of business titan. Freebooters such as Daniel Drew, Jay Gould, and Jim Fisk swindled each other as well as the public and boasted of the legislatures they bought; not even the Crédit Mobilier nor the worst political corruptionists were more brazen in their pillaging. In their scorn for the public welfare they shared the attitudes of their political ally Boss Tweed ("Well, what are you going to do about it?") and W. H. Vanderbilt, son of "Commodore" Cornelius Vanderbilt ("The public be damned!").

The battle to control the Erie Railroad in 1868, pitting Drew, Gould, and Fisk against the elder Vanderbilt, was the archetype of financial piracy: judges and legislatures in two states corrupted, 50,000 shares of stock illegally printed and sold, a railroad looted of millions. Victorious, Gould and Fisk next embarked on a scheme notable for its audacity—a corner on the nation's gold supply. Possessing enough cash to control the open market, they sought to neutralize the Treasury's stock of gold through the influence of President Grant's brother-in-law. The price of gold shot up at their bidding until September 24, 1869 ("Black Friday"), when Grant belatedly released the government reserves. Gould and Fisk slipped out from under their collapsing scheme, but hundreds of investors were ruined. "Nothing is lost save honor," said the carefree Fisk. "Let everyone carry out his own corpse."

Such depredations, although denounced from the pulpit and cursed in the press, met with only half-hearted government censure. Fisk's flamboyant career was cut short in 1872, not by the law but by two bullets from the gun of a rival suitor. He was accorded a funeral befitting a statesman, and a jaded public sang the sentimental ballad, "Jim Fisk, or He Never Went Back on the Poor." In later years Gould transferred his attentions to such western railroads as the Union Pacific and the Central Pacific; Western Union; and the New York *World,* which he found useful for improving his public image. He left a fortune estimated at $75 million.

TITANS OF WALL STREET

Financial panic, like a plague, made periodic visits to the nation after Appomattox. Barely recovered from Black Friday, Wall Street plunged once more in 1873, then in 1882, in 1893, again in 1907. In each instance, reckless speculation overinflated values. Confidence collapsed, heralding long, cyclical depressions with their attendant business failures and unemployment. Not a few of the victims joined in cursing the titans of Wall Street.

Labor and agrarian interests saw themselves being sacrificed to speculation and manipulation. To them, as to Henry Adams, hard times were the work of a "dark, mysterious, crafty, rapacious, and tyrannical power . . . to rob and oppress and enslave the people." One solution was to banish the thieves from the temple, a course that suggested to one cartoonist this intriguing scene: "When We All Get Wise."

THE TRUSTS

Mr. Dooley, Finley Peter Dunne's irreverent philosopher, offered a solution to the trust problem based on his assessment of the trust-busting techniques of Theodore Roosevelt. "Lave us be merry about it an' jovial an' affectionate," he proposed. "Lave us laugh an' sing th' octopus out iv existence." Mr. Dooley's line of attack was not exactly new. For three decades monopolistic combinations, "in the form of trusts or otherwise," as the Sherman Antitrust Act described them, had felt the sting of some of the most savage barbs in the history of American caricature.

Public response to the trusts took a variety of forms, but for sheer ingenuity, the campaigns waged by the cartoonists of *Harper's Weekly, Frank Leslie's Illustrated, Puck,* and other pictorial weeklies were unsurpassed. *Puck,* the most outspoken and flamboyant of the critics, was founded in New York in 1876 by Joseph Keppler, who made the large colored cartoon his hallmark, printing three of them in each issue. Keppler drew and published his first attack on the evils of monopoly in 1881, and as an avowed Democrat he delighted in regularly jabbing at a group of Republican senators headed by Nelson Aldrich of Rhode Island and Donald Cameron of Pennsylvania, whom he considered the mouthpieces of big business.

The effects of this prolonged, uninhibited barrage by Keppler and his fellow artists is difficult to assess precisely, but it seems likely that they were no less effective in bringing the trusts to bay than the revelations of such reform writers as Ida Tarbell, Upton Sinclair, and Henry Demarest Lloyd. For one thing, the combined circulation of the picture weeklies was enormous; for another, this was an era when cartoonists had greater influence—and maintained higher artistic standards—than at any time before or since. Boss Tweed, who blamed his downfall on Thomas Nast's exposures in *Harper's Weekly,* testified feelingly on the power of the cartoons. He cared little about what reformers wrote, Tweed said, since few of his constituents could read, but they could "look at the damned pictures."

Joseph Keppler's "The Bosses of the Senate" (right) appeared in *Puck* in 1889, not long before debate began on the Sherman Antitrust bill. No less devastating was the work of Thomas Nast (below) and W.A. Rogers (below right) of *Harper's Weekly.* Rogers' inspired creation, "the trustworthy beast," was a fixture in his antimonopoly cartoons. In this example Uncle Sam remarks, "I guess this new breed of cattle has got to go next."

WORKINGMEN ORGANIZE

Something more than real and imagined threats by big business and monopoly caused the embattled common people to close ranks in the last decades of the 19th century. In an age when commerce and the machine were exalted above all else, American workers, whether farmers or factory hands, felt a grievous loss of status. To revive the Jeffersonian image of the yeoman husbandman, to restore the artisan's once-proud position in society, became important although elusive goals.

Agitation alone could not salve injured pride. Thus Uriah Stephens and Terence Powderly committed the Knights of Labor—on principle at least—to education rather than to direct economic action, and even the militant Samuel Gompers hastened to include compulsory public education among the demands of the American Federation of Labor. Self-respect and the dignity of honest toil became the Knights' watchwords. "Respect industry in the person of every intelligent worker," Stephens exhorted his followers. "Unmake the shams of life by deference to the humble but useful craftsman." The secrecy and elaborate ritual of the Knights not only protected the identity of the workers but offered them a sense of solidarity and self-importance.

The agrarian orders, in addition to working to improve the economic position of farmers, went to considerable lengths to improve the outlook of their members. The Grange and the Farmers' Alliance, the chief nationwide organizations, successfully established local study groups, circulating libraries, and newspapers. One prominent Alliance leader looked fondly to that day in the future when a "general system of home culture, somewhat on the plan of Chautauqua" could be established on a broad scale. Even if the wider vision remained unfulfilled, such schemes had a profound and widespread influence. "People commenced to think who had never thought before, and people talked who had seldom spoken," reported a contemporary observer. "Everyone was talking and everyone was thinking. . . ."

"The Purposes of the Grange" (opposite), a lithograph published in Cincinnati in 1873, and the United Mine Workers membership certificate reproduced above, dating from about 1900, celebrate the virtues of the yeoman farmer ("I pay for all," says the central figure in the Granger print) and the inherent dignity of "daily toil in the recesses of the earth."

GIFT FOR THE GRANGERS.

"I PAY FOR ALL."

FAITH. HOPE. CHARITY. FIDELITY.

THE PUBLIC INTEREST

The Pullman strike was in its seventh week when in the early morning hours of July 4, 1894, a special train carrying cavalry, artillery, and infantry regulars rolled into Chicago. The troops were there by order of President Cleveland to enforce an injunction, issued two days earlier, enjoining Eugene Debs and the American Railway Union from continuing a rail boycott. The injunction and the troops clearly dashed whatever hopes the Pullman strikers had for success, but in a real sense the strike was doomed the moment the ARU entered the struggle.

Considerable public sympathy had greeted the walkout of 3,000 Pullman workers in mid-May, but when Debs's union voted to support the strikers by means of a boycott, the full hostility of the press was aroused. The boycott, *Harper's Weekly* reported, was an attempt ''to subjugate the people of the United States, to extort from the nation the control and management of its highways, intercourse and commerce. . . .'' Newspapers and magazines, paying little heed to facts, depicted Chicago in the hands of a crazed mob bent on destroying private property. The government based its intervention on ''uncontrolled violence'' and the interruption of the mails. Yet no mail had accumulated in Chicago, and before the arrival of the troops damage to railroad property had not exceeded $6,000.

Serious rioting, however, broke out less than 18 hours after the troops encamped in the city. The press became hysterical: REGULARS POWERLESS BEFORE CHICAGO'S RIOTOUS ARMY; GUNS AWE THEM NOT; MOB WILL IS LAW. Most of the destruction was in the railroad yards, but now the citizenry was thoroughly frightened. ''Men must be killed,'' a clergyman demanded. ''The soldiers must use their guns.''

At storm center were Debs and Governor John Peter Altgeld, who denounced the federal government's intervention. The mild-mannered Debs was described as ''a reckless, ranting, contumacious, impudent braggadocio,'' while the New York *Times* suggested that ''his present conduct is due . . . to the disordered condition of his mind and body, brought out by the liquor habit. . . .''

On July 10 Debs was arrested for conspiracy. The same day the 14,000-man antistrike force began moving the trains out of Chicago. The strike was crushed, ''anarchy'' put to rout.

For four consecutive weeks in 1894 *Harper's Weekly* devoted most of its editorial columns and picture spreads to the Pullman strike. The magazine made little effort to conceal its bias. Debs and the American Railway Union were the targets of three full-page cartoons by W. A. Rogers; in "The Vanguard of Anarchy" (left), dictator Debs is borne by clownish prolabor politicians led by Governor Altgeld of Illinois. The *Harper's* correspondent on the scene was Frederic Remington, who sent back a steady stream of dispatches and sketches depicting the "rape of government" in Chicago. In "Giving the Butt" (below), Remington demonstrated how infantry regulars dealt with what he described as a "malodorous crowd of anarchistic foreign trash." When the federal troops began moving trains (lower left), *Harper's* hailed the action as a triumph of public opinion.

THE EXPLOITED

Even if government was slow to respond to the plight of the exploited worker and the slum dweller, reform-minded citizens were not. Some, such as social workers Jane Addams and Lillian Wald, set a course of direct action and example with their settlement houses. Others, such as Henry George and Edward Bellamy, proposed major revisions of the capitalistic system. Still others, most notably Jacob Riis and Lewis Hine, sought by documentary photography to make Americans *see* the social ills in their midst.

Riis, a Danish immigrant, was a pioneer in the use of the camera to document reporting. His book, *How the Other Half Lives* (1890), and the dozens of newspaper and magazine articles he wrote were instrumental in arousing New Yorkers to conditions within their city. Hine lacked Riis's skill as a writer, but he had few equals as a photographer. Also, printing advances allowed his pictures to reproduce accurately in halftone rather than in the inferior woodblock engraving of Riis's day.

Hine taught himself to use a camera in 1903, and he soon earned a reputation for his studies of immigrants. In 1910 he joined the National Child Labor Committee. According to his biographer, Robert Doty, Hine managed ''to smuggle his camera into mills and factories despite threatening foremen. Often he had to pose as an insurance salesman or fire inspector. Winning the confidence of the children, he would interview them while scribbling notes on a pad inside his pocket. These would be rewritten later, in a legible form.'' He photographed young girls in southern textile mills, boys breaking coal in Pennsylvania mines, women laboring in New York's garment district, and his pictures provided illustration for booklets, articles, and posters, as well as factual documentation for crusading playwrights. He made it possible for the evils of child and sweatshop labor to be ''emotionally recognized,'' said the chairman of the committee. ''The work Hine did for this reform was more responsible than all other efforts in bringing the need to public attention.''

THE OUTLOOK

In 1901 Yale's eminent sociologist William Graham Sumner tried to project America's future by examining the legacy of the past century. "The competition of life is so mild," Sumner decided, "that men are hardly conscious of it. So far as we can see ahead there is every reason for even rash optimism in regard to the material or economic welfare of mankind." Sumner's sunny outlook had substantial basis in fact. Many were certainly reaping the material benefits of invention and industrialization. By 1901, for example, Americans could enjoy "opera at home" through the magic of Thomas Edison's Victrola or make a pictorial record of the good life with George Eastman's Kodak or, if they were particularly adventuresome, take a drive in Ransom Olds's runabout.

Other observers found small comfort in the legacy of the 19th century. They were made apprehensive by evidence of continuing poverty (fewer than 10 per cent of America's families earned more than $380 a year in 1890); by the chaotic growth of cities (New York had grown 460 per cent in 50 years, Chicago 5,500 per cent); by mounting labor discontent (there were some 24,000 strikes and lockouts between 1880 and 1900). "What will be the fate of personal individuality?" asked another sociologist in 1904. Would that "cockleshell, the individual soul" enjoy greater freedom in the future, or would it, "too frail to navigate the vaster expanses, become more and more the sport of irresistible waves and currents?"

Six O'Clock Winter, by the "ashcan" painter John Sloan, is dominated by the thundering presence of New York's Third Avenue el. Sloan's canvas evokes an image of the early 20th-century metropolis that displayed to a contemporary observer "all the signs of the heaped industrial battle-field, all the sounds and silences, grim, pushing, intruding. . . ."

20

Intellectual and Cultural Trends

The great forces that governed American economic and social development after the Civil War also shaped American thinking and American culture; industrialization altered ways of looking at life at the same time that it transformed ways of making a living. Technological advances revolutionized the communication of ideas more drastically than the transportation of goods or the manufacture of steel. The growth of cities provided a favorable environment for intellectual and artistic expression. The materialism that permeated American attitudes toward business also affected contemporary education and literature, while Charles Darwin's theory of evolution influenced American philosophers, lawyers, and historians profoundly. At the same time, older ideologies like romantic individualism and faith in democracy continued to affect American thinking deeply. No really dominant pattern emerged; the American mind, like the people themselves, was too diverse—one might say confused, even incoherent—to be neatly delimited.

Public Education

The history of American education after about 1870 reflects the impact of many social and economic forces. While men like Horace Mann and Henry Barnard had laid the foundations for state-supported school systems back in the Age of Jackson, these systems did not become compulsory until after the Civil War. Only then did the growth of cities provide the concentrated populations necessary for economical mass education; only then did the upward spurt of human productivity resulting from industrialization produce the huge sums that universal education required. In the 1860's about half the children in the country received some formal education, but this did not mean that half the children were attending school at any one time. Sessions were short, and many children dropped out after only two or three years of classes; as late as 1870 the average American had received only four years of schooling.

Thereafter, steady growth and improvement took place. Attendance in the public schools increased from 6.8 million in 1870 to 15.5 million in 1900, a remarkable expansion even when allowance is made for the growth of the population. Public expenditures for education rose from $63 million in 1870 to $145 million in 1890 and $234 million in 1902. The national rate of illiteracy declined from 20 per cent in 1870 to 10.7 per cent in 1900.° Nearly all the states outside the South had compulsory education laws by

°At present, the rate is about 2 per cent.

1900, and over the years these were gradually extended to cover broader age groups and longer school sessions. Most notable was the increase in secondary education: the number of high schools jumped from perhaps 100 in 1860 to 6,000 at the end of the century. At the other extreme, the kindergarten, developed in Germany in the 1830's by Friedrich Froebel, caught on rapidly. The first public kindergarten was opened in St. Louis in 1873, and by the 1890's most systems of any size had adopted the idea.

Southern schools lagged far behind the rest of the nation, partly because the section was poor and still predominantly rural. The restoration of white rule in the 1870's brought an abrupt halt to the progress in Negro public education that the reconstruction governments had made. Church groups, and private foundations such as the Peabody Fund and the Slater Fund, financed chiefly by northern philanthropists, did support Negro schools after 1877, including two important experiments in vocational training, Hampton Institute (1868) and Booker T. Washington's Tuskegee Institute (1881).

These schools, however, had to overcome considerable resistance and suspicion in the white community; they survived only because they taught a docile, essentially subservient philosophy, preparing students to accept second-class citizenship and become farmers and craftsmen. Since proficiency in academic subjects might have given the lie to the southern belief that blacks were intellectually inferior to whites, such subjects were avoided. The southern insistence upon segregating the public schools, buttressed by the "separate-but-equal" decision of the Supreme Court in *Plessy v. Ferguson,* imposed a crushing financial burden on sparsely settled communities, while the dominant opinion that Negroes were not really educable did not encourage communities to make special efforts in their behalf.

An industrial society created demands for vocational and technical training. Science courses appeared in the new high schools. In 1880 Calvin M. Woodward opened a Manual Training School in St. Louis, and soon a number of institutions

Tuskegee, said Booker T. Washington, began as "a broken down shanty and an old hen house." As shown here, students built many of the school's buildings, learning a trade and earning their board. A 1903 photograph. (Library of Congress.)

were offering courses in carpentry, metalwork, sewing, and other manual arts. By 1890, 36 American cities had public vocational high schools. Woodward, who was inspired by the work of Victor Della Vos, director of the Russian Imperial Technical School, thought of vocational training as part of a broad general education rather than as preparation for a specific occupation, but manual training also attracted the backing of prominent industrialists with more practical objectives. Their support, in turn, made organized labor suspicious of the new trend. One union leader called the trade schools "breeding schools for scabs and rats." Fortunately, the usefulness of such training soon became evident to the unions; by 1910 the AFL was lobbying side by side with the National Association of Manufacturers for more trade schools.

Foreign influences also triggered a revolution in teaching methods. Traditionally, American teachers had emphasized the three R's and de-

pended upon strict discipline and rote memory to enforce learning. Typical of the pedagogues of the period was the Chicago teacher, described by a reformer in the 1890's, who told her students firmly: "Don't stop to think, tell me what you know!" But the ideas of early-19th-century German educators, most notably Johann Friedrich Herbart, were beginning to attract attention in the United States. According to Herbart, the teacher should arouse the interest of the child by relating new information to what he already knew; good teaching called for skilled professional training, psychological insight, enthusiasm, and imagination, not merely for factual information and a birch rod. At the same time, evolutionists were also pressing for a kind of education that would help children to "survive" by adapting to the demands of their environment.

Forward-looking American educators seized upon these ideas avidly because dynamic social changes were making the old system increasingly inadequate. Settlement-house workers, for example, discovered that slum children needed training in handicrafts, good citizenship, and personal hygiene as much as in reading and writing. They were appalled by the local schools, which suffered from the same diseases—filth, overcrowding, rickety construction—that plagued the surrounding tenements, and by the school systems, most of which were controlled by corrupt machine politicians who doled out teaching positions to party hacks and other untrained persons. They also recognized the great value of school playgrounds, kindergartens, adult education programs, and extracurricular clubs. Gradually, they came to regard educational reform as central to the whole problem of improving society. Soon they were advocating the broader kind of schooling that the theoreticians had been long describing. "We are impatient with the schools which lay all stress on reading and writing," Jane Addams declared. This type of education, she added, "fails to give the child any clew to the life about him."

The philosopher who summarized and gave direction to these forces in the educational world was John Dewey, a professor at the University of Chicago. Dewey was concerned with the implications of evolution and indeed of all science for education. Essentially his approach was ethical. Was the nation's youth being properly prepared for the tasks it faced in the modern world? He became interested in Francis W. Parker's remarkable experimental school in Chicago, which was organized as "a model home, a complete community and embryonic democracy." In 1896, together with his wife, Dewey founded the Laboratory School to put his educational ideas to the test. Three years later he published *The School and Society,* describing and defending his theories.

The schools must engage in new activities, Dewey argued, because in an industrial society the family no longer performed many of the educational functions it had carried out in an agrarian society. Farm children learn about nature, about work, about human character in countless ways denied to children in cities. The school can fill the gap by becoming "an embryonic community . . . with types of occupations that reflect the life of the larger society." At the same time, education should center on the child, and new information should be related to what he already knows. The child's imagination, energy, and curiosity are tools for broadening his outlook and increasing his store of information. Finally, the school should become an instrument for social reform, "saturating [the child] with the spirit of service" and helping to produce a "society which is worthy, lovely, and harmonious." Education, in other words, ought to build character and teach good citizenship as well as transmit knowledge.

The School and Society created a great stir, and Dewey immediately assumed leadership of the movement which, in the next generation, was called "progressive education." Although the gains made in public education before 1900 were more quantitative than qualitative and the philosophy dominant in most schools not very different at the end of the century from that prevailing in Horace Mann's day, change was in the air. The best educators of the period were full of optimism, convinced that the future was theirs.

Keeping the People Informed

The inadequacy of so much of their schooling left many Americans with a hunger for knowledge. As in early times, lecturers toured the country constantly, attracting large audiences. Nothing so well illustrates the mass desire for information as the rise of the Chautauqua movement, founded by John H. Vincent, a Methodist minister, and Lewis Miller, an Ohio manufacturer of farm machinery. Vincent had charge of Sunday schools for the Methodist Church. In 1874 he and Miller organized a two-week summer course for Sunday-school teachers on the shores of Lake Chautauqua in New York. Besides instruction, they offered good food, evening song fests around the campfire, and a relaxing atmosphere—all for $6 for the two weeks. The 40 young teachers who attended were delighted with the program, and the idea caught on swiftly.

Soon the leafy shore of Lake Chautauqua became a city of tents each summer as thousands poured into the region from all over the country. The founders expanded their offerings to include instruction in literature, science, government, and economics. Famous authorities, including, over the years, six Presidents of the United States, came to lecture to open-air audiences on every subject imaginable. Eventually Chautauqua even offered correspondence courses leading over a four-year period to a diploma, the program being designed, in Vincent's words, to give "the college outlook" to persons who had not had the opportunity to obtain a higher education. Books were written specifically for the program and a monthly magazine, the *Chautauquan,* was published.

Such success naturally provoked imitation, until, by 1900, there were about 200 Chautauqua-type organizations in existence. Intellectual standards in these programs varied greatly; in general they were very low. By and large, entertainment was as important an objective as enlightenment. Musicians (good and bad), homespun humorists, inspirational lecturers, and assorted quacks shared the platform with prominent divines and scholars. Moneymaking undoubtedly motivated many of the entrepreneurs who operated these centers, all of which, including the original Chautauqua, reflected the prevailing tastes of the American people—diverse, enthusiastic, uncritical, and shallow. Nevertheless, the movement provided opportunities for thousands seeking stimulation and intellectual improvement.

Still larger numbers profited from the proliferation of public libraries after the Civil War. By the end of the century nearly all the states were supporting libraries, and private donors, led by the ironmaster Andrew Carnegie, contributed many millions to the cause. In 1900 over 1,700 libraries in the United States had collections of more than 5,000 volumes.

Newspapers and magazines, of course, were also important means for disseminating information and educating the masses. Here the new technology supplied the major incentive for change. The development by Richard Hoe and Stephen Tucker of the web press (1871), which printed simultaneously on both sides of paper fed into it from large rolls, and Ottmar Mergenthaler's linotype machine (1886), which cast rows of type as needed directly from molten metal, cheapened the cost of printing and speeded the production of newspapers. Machines for making paper out of wood pulp reduced the cost of newsprint to a quarter of what it had been in the 1860's. By 1895 there were machines capable of printing, cutting, and folding 24,000 32-page newspapers an hour. The spread of the telegraph network and the laying of transoceanic cables wrought a similar transformation in the gathering of news. Press associations, led by the New York Associated Press, flourished, the syndicated article appeared, and a few publishers—Edward W. Scripps was the first—began to acquire chains of newspapers.

Population growth and educational improvements created an ever larger demand for printed matter. At the same time, the integration of the economy enabled manufacturers to sell their goods all over the country. Advertising became important, and sellers soon learned that newspapers and magazines were excellent means of placing their products before millions of eyes. Advertising revenues soared just at the time when new machines and general expansion were making publishing a very expensive business. The day of the journeyman printer-editor ended. Magazine publishing and especially newspaper publishing were becoming big business. Rich men such as railroad magnates Jay Gould, Henry Villard, and Tom Scott, and mining tycoon George Hearst invested heavily in important newspapers in the postwar decades, and such publishers tended to be conservative, a tendency increased by the prejudices of their businessmen-advertisers. On the other hand, reaching the masses meant lowering intellectual and cultural standards, appealing to the emotions, and adopting popular, sometimes radical, causes.

Cheap, mass-circulation papers had first appeared in the 1830's and 1840's, the most successful being the *Sun,* the *Herald,* and the *Tribune* in New York, the Philadelphia *Public Ledger,* and the Baltimore *Sun.* None of these, however, much exceeded a circulation of 50,000 before the Civil War. The first publisher to reach a truly massive audience was Joseph Pulitzer, a Hungarian-born immigrant who had learned his trade in St. Louis, where he made a first-rate paper of the St. Louis *Post-Dispatch.* In 1883 Pulitzer bought the New York *World,* a sheet with a circulation of perhaps 20,000. Within a year he was selling 100,000 copies daily, and by the late nineties the *World's* circulation regularly exceeded 1 million.

Pulitzer achieved this brilliant success by casting a wide net among New York's teeming, variegated population. For the educated and affluent, he provided better political and financial coverage than the most respectable New York journals. To the masses he offered bold black headlines devoted to crime (ANOTHER MURDERER TO HANG), scandal (VICE ADMIRAL'S SON IN JAIL), catastrophe (TWENTY-FOUR MINERS KILLED), society and the theater (LILY LANGTRY'S NEW ADMIRER), together with feature stories, political cartoons, comics, and pictures. Pulitzer also made the *World* a crusader for civic improvement, attacking political corruption, monopoly, and slum problems. His energetic reporters literally made news, masquerading as criminals and poor workers in order to write graphic accounts of conditions in New York's jails and sweatshops.

"The *World* is the people's newspaper," Pulitzer boasted, and in the sense that it interested

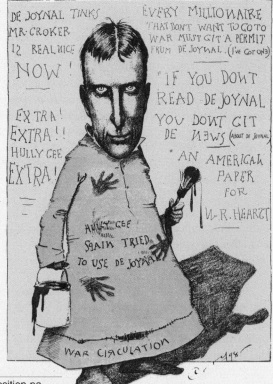

Left, J. S. Sargent's portrait of Joseph Pulitzer. Right, an opposition paper's caricature of Hearst as the Yellow Kid, a sleazy comic strip character and inspiration for the phrase "yellow journalism." (Respectively: Joseph Pulitzer, Jr., Collection; *The Bee,* 1898.)

men and women of every sort, he was correct. Pulitzer's methods were quickly copied by competitors, especially by William Randolph Hearst, who purchased the New York *Journal* in 1895 and soon outdid the *World* in sensationalism. But no other newspaperman of the era approached Pulitzer in originality, boldness, and the knack of reaching the masses without abandoning seriousness of purpose and basic integrity.

Growth and ferment also characterized the magazine world. In 1865 there were about 700 magazines in the country, 20 years later about 3,300, by the turn of the century over 5,000. Until the mid-eighties, few of the new magazines were in any way unusual. A handful of serious periodicals, such as the *Atlantic Monthly, Harper's,* and the *Century* among the monthlies and the *Nation* among the weeklies, dominated the field. They were staid in tone and conservative in political caste. Articles on current topics, a good deal of fiction and poetry, historical and biographical studies, and similar material filled their pages, and many of them justly prided themselves on the quality of their illustrations. Although they had great influence, none even approached a mass circulation because of the limited size of the upper-middle-class audience they aimed at. The *Century* touched a peak in the eighties of about 250,000 when it published a series of articles on Civil War battles by famous commanders, but could not sustain that level. A circulation of 100,000 was considered good for such magazines, and the *Nation,* although extremely influential, seldom sold more than 8,000 copies.

Magazines directed at the average citizen also existed in the immediate post-Civil War era, but all were of very low quality. The leading publisher of this type of magazine in the sixties and seventies was Frank Leslie, who controlled such periodicals as *Frank Leslie's Popular Monthly, Frank Leslie's Chimney Corner, Frank Leslie's Illustrated Newspaper,* and *Frank Leslie's Jolly Joker.* Leslie specialized in illustrations of current events (he put as many as 34 engravers to work on a single picture in order to bring it out quickly) and on providing what he frankly admit-

ted was "mental pabulum"—a combination of cheap romantic fiction, old-fashioned poetry, jokes, and advice columns. Some of his periodicals sold as many as 300,000 copies per issue.

After about 1885, however, vast changes began to take place. New magazines such as the *Forum* (1886) and the *Arena* (1889) emphasized hard-hitting articles on controversial subjects by leading experts. The weekly *Literary Digest* (1890) offered summaries of press opinion on current events, and the *Review of Reviews* (1891) provided monthly commentary on the news. Even more startling changes revolutionized the mass-circulation field. Between 1883 and 1893 the *Ladies' Home Journal, Cosmopolitan, Munsey's,* and *McClure's* appeared on the scene. Although superficially similar to the Frank Leslie type, these magazines maintained a far higher intellectual level. In 1889 Edward W. Bok became editor of the *Ladies' Home Journal.* Besides advice columns ("Ruth Ashmore's Side Talks with Girls"), he offered articles on child care, gardening, and interior decorating, published fine contemporary novelists, including Rudyard Kipling, William Dean Howells, and Mark Twain, and employed public figures, such as Presidents Grover Cleveland and Benjamin Harrison, to discuss important questions. He printed colored reproductions of art masterpieces—the invention of cheap photoengraving was of enormous significance in the success of mass-circulation magazines—and crusaded for women's suffrage, conservation, and other reforms. Bok did not merely cater to public tastes, he created new tastes. He even refused to accept patent medicine advertising, a major source of revenue for many popular magazines.

Samuel S. McClure and Frank A. Munsey were also masters of popular journalism. *McClure's* specialized in first-class fiction, serious historical studies, and exciting articles attacking political corruption, monopoly, and other social evils. *Munsey's* adopted the same formula but pitched its appeal somewhat lower.

Bok, McClure, Munsey, and a number of their competitors reached millions of readers. Like Pulitzer in the newspaper field, they found ways of interesting every type: rich and poor, cultivated and ignorant. Utilizing the new printing technology to cut costs and drawing heavily on advertising revenues, they sold their magazines for 10 or 15 cents a copy and still made fortunes. Under Bok, the *Journal* eventually reached a circulation of 2 million. Between 1894 and 1907, Munsey cleared over $7.8 million from his numerous publications. All had an acute sensitivity to the shifting interests of the masses. "I want to know if you enjoy a story," McClure once told his star reporter, Lincoln Steffens. "If you do, then I know that, say, ten thousand readers will like it. . . . But I go most by myself. For if I like a thing, then I know that millions will like it. My mind and my taste are so common that I'm the best editor."°

Colleges and Universities

Improvements in public education and the needs of an increasingly complex society for every type of intellectual skill led to advances in higher education and professional training during the last quarter of the century. The number of colleges rose from about 350 to 500 between 1878 and 1898, and the student body roughly tripled. Although as yet only a mere fraction of the population even contemplated college, the aspirations of the nation's youth were rising, and more and more parents had the financial means necessary for fulfilling them.

More significant than the expansion of the colleges were the alterations that took place in their curricula and in the atmosphere permeating the average campus. In 1870 most colleges were much as they had been in the 1830's: small, impoverished, limited in their offerings, intellectually stagnant. The ill-paid professors were seldom scholars of any stature. Thereafter, change came like a flood tide. State universities flourished; the

°McClure added ruefully: "There's only one better editor than I am, and that's Frank Munsey. If *he* likes a thing, then *everybody* will like it."

federal government's "land-grant" program in support of training in "agriculture and the mechanic arts," established under the Morrill Act of 1862, came into its own; wealthy philanthropists poured fortunes into old institutions and founded new ones; a number of educators began to introduce new courses and adopt new teaching methods; professional schools of law, medicine, education, business, journalism, and other specialties increased in number.

In the forefront of reform was Harvard, the oldest and most prestigious college in the country. In the 1860's it possessed an excellent faculty, including James Russell Lowell in literature, Benjamin Peirce in mathematics, Wolcott Gibbs in chemistry, and the naturalists Asa Gray and Louis Agassiz. But teaching methods were antiquated, and the curriculum had remained almost unchanged since the colonial period. In 1869, however, a dynamic new president, the chemist Charles W. Eliot, undertook a great transformation of the college. Eliot introduced the elective system, gradually eliminating required courses and expanding offerings in such areas as modern languages, economics, and the laboratory sciences. He did away with the "scale of merit," under which students had received a daily grade in each course based on routine recitals in class, and encouraged his faculty to experiment with new teaching methods. He brought in men with original minds and new ideas like Henry Adams, grandson of John Quincy Adams, who made the study of medieval history a true intellectual experience. "Mr. Adams roused the spirit of inquiry and controversy in me," one student later wrote; another, the historian Edward Channing, called Adams "the greatest teacher that I ever encountered."

Under Eliot's guidance the standards of the medical school were raised, and the case method was introduced in the law school. For the first time, students were allowed to borrow books from the library! In some respects he went too far—the elective system eventually led to the fragmentation of the curriculum and encouraged superficiality and laxness in many students—but on balance he transformed Harvard from a college, "a place to which a young man *is sent*," to a university, a place "to which he *goes*."

An even more important development in higher education was the founding of Johns Hopkins in 1876. This university was one of many established in the period by wealthy industrialists; its benefactor, the Baltimore merchant Johns Hopkins, had made his fortune in the Baltimore and Ohio Railroad. Its distinctiveness, however, was due to the vision of Daniel Coit Gilman, its first president. Gilman modeled Johns Hopkins on the great German universities, where meticulous research and absolute freedom of inquiry were the guiding principles. In staffing the institution, he aimed in every field of knowledge for scholars of the highest reputation, scouring Europe as well as America in his search for talent and offering outstanding men high salaries for that time—up to $5,000 for a professor. On the other hand, he also employed a number of relatively unknown but brilliant younger scholars, such as the physicist Henry A. Rowland and Herbert Baxter Adams, whom he made an associate in history on the strength of his excellent doctoral dissertation at the University of Heidelberg. Gilman promised his teachers good students and ample opportunity to pursue their own research, which explains why Hopkins professors repeatedly turned down attractive offers from other universities.

Johns Hopkins specialized in graduate education. In the generation after its founding, it turned out a remarkable percentage of the most important scholars in the nation, including Woodrow Wilson in political science, John Dewey in philosophy, Frederick Jackson Turner in history, and John R. Commons in economics. The seminar conducted by Herbert Baxter Adams was particularly productive: the Adams-edited *Johns Hopkins Studies in Historical and Political Science,* consisting of the doctoral dissertations of his many students, was both voluminous and influential—"the mother of similar studies in every part of the United States." The success of Johns Hopkins did not stop the migration of American scholars to Europe—over 2,000 matriculated at German universities during the 1880's—but as Hopkins graduates took up professorships at other institutions and as men trained elsewhere adopted the Hopkins methods, true graduate education became possible in most sections of the country.

The immediate success of Johns Hopkins encouraged other rich men to endow universities offering advanced work. Clark University in Worcester, Massachusetts, founded by Jonas Clark, a merchant and real-estate speculator, opened its doors in 1889. Its president, G. Stanley Hall, had been a professor of psychology at Hopkins, and he built the new university in that institution's image. More important was John D. Rockefeller's creation, the University of Chicago (1892). The president of Chicago, William Rainey Harper, was a brilliant Biblical scholar—he received his Ph.D. from Yale at the age of 18— and an energetic and imaginative administrator. The new university, he told Rockefeller, should be designed "with the example of Johns Hopkins before our eyes." Like Daniel Coit Gilman, Harper sought the best men possible for his faculty. He offered such high salaries that he was besieged with over a thousand applications. Armed with Rockefeller dollars, he "raided" all the best institutions in the nation. He decimated the faculty of the new Clark University—"an act of wreckage," the indignant President Hall complained, "comparable to anything that the worst trust ever attempted against its competitors." From the start, Chicago offered first-class graduate and undergraduate education. During its first year there were 120 instructors for fewer than 600 students, and despite fears that the mighty tycoon Rockefeller would enforce his social and economic views on the institution, complete academic freedom was the rule.

Also noteworthy during these years was the rapid expansion of state and federal aid to higher education. The Morrill Act granting land to each state at a rate of 30,000 acres for each senator and representative provided princely endowments, especially for the populous states. In this way many important modern universities, such as Illinois, Michigan State, and Ohio State, got their start. While the federal assistance was earmarked for specific subjects, the land-grant colleges offered a full range of courses and all received additional state funds. Other state institutions also benefited, for the public was displaying an increasing willingness to support their activities.

In general the land-grant universities adopted new ideas quickly. They were co-educational from the start, and most developed professional schools and experimented with extension work and summer programs. Typical of the better state institutions was the University of Michigan, which reached the top rank among the nation's universities during the presidency of James B. Angell (1871-1909). Like Eliot at Harvard, Angell expanded the undergraduate curriculum and strengthened the law and medical schools. He also encouraged graduate studies, seeking to make Michigan "part of the great world of scholars," and sought to find ways in which the university could serve the general community.

While, on balance, higher education made great strides between 1870 and 1900, not all the results were beneficial. On the one hand, the elective system led to superficiality; students gained a smattering of knowledge of many subjects but mastered none. On the other hand, intensive graduate work often produced narrowness of outlook and dry-as-dust research monographs on trivial subjects. Attempts to apply the scientific method in fields such as history and economics often enticed students into making smug claims to objectivity and definitiveness which from the nature of the subjects they could not even approach in their actual work.

The gifts of rich industrialists sometimes came with strings attached, and college boards of trustees tended to be dominated by businessmen, who sometimes attempted to impose their own social and economic beliefs on faculty members. Although few professors lost their positions because their views offended conservative trustees, at many institutions trustees exerted constant nagging pressures that limited academic freedom and scholarly objectivity. At state colleges politicians often interfered in academic affairs, even treating professorships as part of the patronage system.

Thorstein Veblen pointed out in his caustic study of *The Higher Learning in America* (1918) that "the intrusion of businesslike ideals, aims and methods" harmed the universities in countless subtle ways. Mere size—the verbose Veblen called it "an executive weakness for spectacular magnitude"—became an end in itself, and the practical values of education were exalted over the humanistic. When universities grew bigger, administration became more complicated, and the prestige of administrators rose inordinately. At many institutions professors came to be regarded as mere employees of the governing boards. In 1893, for example, the members of the faculty of Stanford University were officially classified as personal servants of Mrs. Leland Stanford, widow of the founder. This was done in a good cause—the Stanford estate was tied up in probate court and this ruling made it possible to pay the professors out of Mrs. Stanford's generous allowance for household expenses—but that such a procedure was even conceivable must have appalled the scholarly world.

As the number of college graduates increased and as colleges ceased being primarily training institutions for clergymen, the influence of alumni on educational policies began to make itself felt, not always happily. Social activities became more important on most campuses. Fraternities proliferated. Interest in organized sports first appeared as a laudable outgrowth of the general expansion of the curriculum, but soon athletic contests were playing a role all out of proportion to their real significance. Football evolved as the leading intercollegiate sport, especially after Walter Camp, coach of the Yale team, began selecting "All America" squads in 1889. By the early nineties important games were attracting huge crowds (over 50,000 attended the Yale-Princeton game in 1893), and thus the sport became a source of revenue that many colleges dared not neglect. Since students, alumni, and the general public demanded winning teams, college administrators stooped to subsidizing student athletes, in extreme cases even employing players who were not students at all. One exasperated college president quipped that the B.A.

degree was coming to mean Bachelor of Athletics.

In short, higher education reflected American values, with all their strengths and weaknesses. A complex society required a more professional and specialized education for its youth. Naturally, the coarseness and the rampant materialism and competitiveness of the era also found expression in the colleges and universities.

Scientific Advances

Much has rightly been made of the crassness of late-19th-century American life, yet the period also produced intellectual achievements of the highest quality. If the business mentality dominated society, and if the great barons of industry, exalting practicality over theory, tended to look down upon the life of the mind, nonetheless men of intellect, quietly pondering the problems of their generation, created works that eventually affected the country as profoundly as the achievements of industrial organizers like Rockefeller and Carnegie and technicians like Edison and Bell.

In pure science America produced a number of outstanding figures in these years. The giant among these, one whose contributions some experts rank with those of Newton, Darwin, and Einstein, was Josiah Willard Gibbs, professor of mathematical physics at Yale from 1871 to 1903. Gibbs created an entirely new science, physical chemistry, and made possible the study of how complex substances respond to changes in temperature and pressure. Purely theoretical at the time, Gibbs's ideas led eventually to vital advances in metallurgy and in the manufacture of plastics, drugs, and other products. Gibbs is often used to illustrate the supposed indifference of the age to its great minds, but this is hardly fair. He was a shy, self-effacing man who cared little for the spotlight or for collecting disciples. He published his major papers in the obscure *Transactions of the Connecticut Academy of Arts and Sciences*. Furthermore, he was so far ahead of his

times that only a handful of specialists had the faintest glimmering of the importance of his work. The editors of the *Transactions* frankly admitted that they did not understand his papers.

Of lesser but still major significance was the work of Henry A. Rowland, the first professor of physics at Johns Hopkins University. President Gilman, with characteristic insight, had plucked the youthful Rowland from the faculty of Rensselaer Polytechnic Institute, where his brilliance was not fully appreciated.° Rowland conducted valuable research in spectrum analysis and contributed to the development of electron theory. His work, too, was purely theoretical, but it led to the improvement of transformers and dynamos and laid the basis for the modern electric-power industry.

Still another important American physicist was Albert A. Michelson of the University of Chicago, who made the first accurate measurements of the speed of light. Michelson's researches in the 1870's and 1880's helped prepare the way for Einstein's theory of relativity; in 1907 he became the first American scientist to win a Nobel prize.

Many other scientists of the period deserve mention: the astronomer Edward C. Pickering, director of the Harvard Observatory, a pioneer in the field of astrophysics; Samuel P. Langley of the Smithsonian Institution, an expert on solar radiation who also contributed to the development of the airplane; the paleontologist Othniel C. Marsh, whose study of fossil horses provided one of the most convincing demonstrations of the truth of evolution ever made; John Wesley Powell, director of the U. S. Geological Survey, noted for his studies of the Grand Canyon as well as for his already mentioned work on the uses of water in arid regions; Benjamin Peirce, the Harvard mathematician and physicist. These men and many others of only slightly lesser stature give the lie to the myth that late-19th-century Americans were only interested in applied science.

°One of Rowland's path-breaking scientific papers had been rejected by a leading American journal on the ground that he was "too young to publish such."

The New Social Sciences

In the social sciences, of course, a close connection existed between the practical issues of the age and the achievements of the leading thinkers. The application of the theory of evolution to every aspect of human relations, the impact of industrialization on society—such topics were of intense concern to American economists, sociologists, and historians. An understanding of Darwin increased the already strong interest in studying the *development* of institutions and their interactions one with another, while controversies over trusts, slum conditions, and other contemporary problems drew scholars out of their towers into practical affairs. Furthermore, social scientists were deeply impressed by the progress being made all about them in the physical and biological sciences. They applied the scientific method to their own specialties eagerly, hoping thereby to arrive at objective truths in fields which were by their very nature essentially subjective.

Among the economists something approaching a revolution took place in the 1880's. The old classical school, which maintained that immutable natural laws governed all human behavior, and used the insights of Darwin only to justify unrestrained competition and laissez faire, was challenged by a group of young economists who argued that as times changed, economic theories and laws must be modified in order to remain relevant. Richard T. Ely, another of the scholars who made Johns Hopkins a font of new ideas in the eighties, summarized the thinking of this group in 1885. "The state [is] an educational and ethical agency whose positive aid is an indispensable condition of human progress," Ely proclaimed. Laissez faire was both outmoded and dangerous. Economic problems were basically moral problems; their solution required "the united efforts of Church, state and science." The proper way to study these problems was by analyzing actual conditions, not by applying abstract laws or principles.

This approach led Henry Carter Adams (Ph.D., Johns Hopkins, 1878) to analyze the circumstances under which the government might regulate competition and even, in certain industries, establish monopolies under strict public control. Simon Patten of the University of Pennsylvania offered a theory justifying state economic planning and vast public works programs. Such ideas gave birth to the so-called institutionalist school of economics, whose members made detailed on-the-spot investigations of sweatshops, factories, and mines, studied the history of the labor movement, and conducted similar research activities of a concrete nature. The study of institutions would lead both to theoretical understanding and to practical social reform, they believed. John R. Commons, one of Ely's students at Johns Hopkins and later professor of economics at the University of Wisconsin, was perhaps the outstanding member of this school. His ten-volume *Documentary History of American Industrial Society* (1910–11) reveals the institutionalist approach at its best.

A similar revolution struck sociology in the mid-eighties. Once again prevailing opinion up to that time utterly rejected the idea of government interference with the organization of society. The influence of the Englishman Herbert Spencer, who objected even to public schools and the postal system, was immense. Spencer and his American disciples, such as William Graham Sumner of Yale, who "elevated laissez faire into a social and economic law and assigned to it the same standing as the law of gravity," and Edward L. Youmans, editor of *Popular Science Monthly,* twisted the ideas of Darwin to mean that society could be changed only by the force of evolution, which moved, of course, with cosmic slowness. "You and I can do nothing at all," Youmans told the reformer Henry George. "It's all a matter of evolution. Perhaps in four or five thousand years evolution may have carried men beyond this state of things."

Such a point of view had little relevance in America, where society was changing rapidly and the range of government social and economic activity was expanding. The first important challenger of the Spencerians was an obscure scholar employed by the U. S. Geological Survey, Lester

Frank Ward, whose *Dynamic Sociology* was published in 1883. Ward's style was turgid, but his mind was penetrating. He assailed the Spencerians for ignoring the possibility of "the improvement of society by cold calculation." In *The Psychic Factors of Civilization* (1893) he blasted the "law of competition." Human progress, he argued, consisted of "triumphing little by little over this law," as, for example, by interfering with biological processes through the use of medicines to kill harmful bacteria. Government regulation of the economy offered another illustration of man's ability to control his environment. "Nothing is more obvious today," Ward wrote in the *Forum* in 1895, "than the signal inability of capital and private enterprise to take care of themselves unaided by the state." Society must indeed evolve, but it would evolve through careful social planning. Man should not abandon his responsibilities by handing over his future to the forces of nature, which, Ward demonstrated, were enormously wasteful and inefficient.

Like the new economists, Ward emphasized the practical and ethical sides of his subject. Sociologists should seek "the betterment of society," he said. "Dynamic Sociology aims at the organization of happiness." He had little direct influence because his writings were highly technical. In six years, only 500-odd copies of *Dynamic Sociology* were sold. However, a handful of specialists, including the economist Ely, president Andrew D. White of Cornell, the Social Gospel preacher Washington Gladden, and the sociologists Albion W. Small and Edward A. Ross—two more products of Johns Hopkins—carried his ideas to a wider audience. The new sociologists' arguments yielded few concrete results before 1900, but they effectively demolished the Spencerians and laid the theoretical basis for the modern welfare state.

Similar currents of thought influenced other social sciences. In his *Systems of Consanguinity* (1871) the pioneer anthropologist Lewis Henry Morgan developed a theory of social evolution and showed how kinship relationships reflected and affected tribal institutions. Morgan's *Ancient Society* (1877-78) stressed the mutability of so-cial and cultural patterns and the need to adjust these patterns to meet altered conditions. Applying his knowledge of primitive societies to modern life, he warned against the current overemphasis of property values. "Since the advent of civilization, the outgrowth of property has been so immense . . . that it has become, on the part of the people, an unmanageable power," he wrote. "The time will come, nevertheless, when human intelligence will rise to the mastery over property, and define the relations of the state to the property it protects."

The new political scientists were also evolutionists and institutionalists. The Founding Fathers, living in a world dominated by Newton's concept of the universe as an immense, orderly machine governed by fixed natural laws, had conceived of the political system as an impersonal set of institutions and principles—a government of laws rather than of men. Nineteenth-century thinkers (John C. Calhoun is the best example) concerned themselves with abstractions, such as states' rights, and ignored the extra-legal aspects of politics, such as parties and pressure groups. In the 1880's, however, political scientists began to employ a different approach. In his doctoral dissertation at Johns Hopkins, *Congressional Government* (1885), Woodrow Wilson analyzed the American political system, concluding that the real locus of authority lay in the committees of Congress, which had no constitutional basis at all. Wilson was by no means a radical—he idolized the great English conservative Edmund Burke. Nevertheless, he viewed politics as a dynamic process and offered no theoretical objection to the expansion of state power. In *The State* (1889) he distinguished between essential functions of government, such as the protection of property and the punishment of crime, and "ministrant" functions, such as education, the regulation of corporations, and social welfare legislation. The desirability of any particular state action of the latter type was simply a matter of expediency. "Every means," he wrote, "by which society may be perfected through the instrumentality of government . . . ought certainly to be diligently sought."

Law and History

Even jurisprudence, by its nature conservative and rooted in tradition, felt the pressure of evolutionary thought and the new emphasis on studying institutions as they actually were. In 1881 Oliver Wendell Holmes, Jr., son of the "Autocrat of the Breakfast-Table," published *The Common Law*. Rejecting the idea that judges should limit themselves to the mechanical explication of statutes, and that law consisted merely of what was written in lawbooks, Holmes argued that "the felt necessities of the time" rather than precedent should determine the rules by which people are governed. "The life of the law has not been logic; it has been experience," he wrote. "It is revolting," he added on another occasion, "to have no better reason for a rule of law than that so it was laid down in the time of Henry IV."

Holmes went on to a long and brilliant career on the bench, during which he repeatedly stressed the right of the people, through their elected representatives, to deal with contemporary problems in any reasonable way, unfettered by outmoded ideas of the proper limits of governmental authority. Like the societies they regulated, laws should evolve as times and conditions changed, he said. This way of reasoning caused no sudden reversal of judicial practice. Holmes's most notable opinions as a judge tended, as in the Lochner bakeshop case, to be dissenting opinions. But his philosophy reflected the advanced thinking of the late 19th century, and his influence grew with every decade of the 20th.

The new approach to knowledge did not always advance the cause of liberal reform, however. Historians in the new graduate schools became intensely interested in studying the origins and evolution of political institutions. They concluded, after much "scientific" study of old charters and law codes, that the roots of democracy were to be found in the customs of the ancient tribes of northern Europe. This theory of the "Teutonic origins" of democracy, which has since been thoroughly discredited, fitted well with the prejudices of men of British stock, and it provided ammunition for those who favored restricting immigration from other parts of the world as well as for those who argued that Negroes were inferior beings.

Out of this work, however, came the frontier thesis of Frederick Jackson Turner, still another scholar who was trained at Johns Hopkins. Turner's essay, "The Significance of the Frontier in American History" (1893), showed how the frontier experience, through which every section of the country had passed, had affected the thinking of the people and the shape of American institutions. The isolation of the frontier, the need during each successive westward advance to create civilization anew, account, he said, for the individualism of Americans and for the democratic character of their society. Indeed, nearly everything unique in our culture, Turner argued, could be traced to the existence of the frontier.

Turner, and still more his many disciples, made too much of his basic insights. Life on the frontier was not as democratic as Turner believed, and certainly does not "explain" American development as completely as he claimed. Nevertheless, Turner's work showed how important it was to investigate the evolution of institutions and encouraged historians to study social and economic, as well as purely political, subjects. And if the claims of the new historians to objectivity and definitiveness were absurdly overstated, their emphasis on thoroughness, exactitude, and impartiality did much to raise standards in the profession. Perhaps the finest product of the new scientific school, a happy combination of meticulous scholarship and literary artistry, was Henry Adams' nine-volume *History of the United States During the Administrations of Jefferson and Madison*.

Realism in Literature

When what Mark Twain called "The Gilded Age" began, American literature was dominated by the romantic mood. All the important writers of the 1840's and 1850's except Hawthorne, Thoreau, and Poe were still living. Longfellow stood at the height of his fame, and the lachrymose Susan Warner—"tears on almost every page"—continued to turn out stories in the style of her popular *The Wide, Wide World.* Romanticism, however, had lost its creative force; most writing in the decade after 1865 was sentimental trash pandering to the emotions and preconceptions of middle-class readers. Magazines like the *Atlantic Monthly* overflowed with stories about fair ladies worshiped from afar by stainless heroes, women coping selflessly with drunken husbands, perfidious adventurers, and poor but honest youths rising through a combination of virtue and assiduity to positions of wealth and influence. Most writers of fiction in this period tended to ignore both the eternal problems inherent in human nature and the particular social problems of the age; polite entertainment and pious moralizing appeared to be their only objectives.

The patent unreality, even dishonesty of contemporary fiction eventually caused a reaction. As early as the mid-sixties, Thomas Wentworth Higginson, essayist, historian, Garrisonian abolitionist, Civil War commander of a Negro regiment, was attacking the sentimentality of American literature and urging writers to concern themselves with "real human life." New antiromantic foreign influences—Emile Zola's first novels appeared in the sixties—also began to affect American interests and tastes. But the most important forces giving rise to the Age of Realism were those that were transforming every other aspect of American life: industrialism, with its associated complexities and social problems; the theory of evolution, which made people more aware of the force of the environment and the basic conflicts of existence; the new science, which challenged traditional values and taught dispassionate, empirical observation.

The decade of the 1870's saw a gradual shift in styles; by the 1880's realism was beginning to flower. Novelists undertook the examination of current social problems such as slum life, the conflict between capital and labor, and political corruption. They created multidimensional characters, depicted persons of every social class, used dialect and slang to capture the flavor of particular local types, fashioned painstaking descriptions of the surroundings into which they placed their subjects.°

One early sign of the new realism can be seen in the rise of the "local color" school, for writers seeking to describe real situations quite naturally turned to the regions they knew best for material. Beginning in 1880, Joel Chandler Harris wrote his "Uncle Remus" stories, faithfully reproducing the dialect of Georgia Negroes and incidentally creating a remarkably realistic literary character. The novels of Edward Eggleston, from *The Hoosier Schoolmaster* (1871) to *The Graysons* (1888), drew vivid pictures of middle-western life. Sarah Orne Jewett's carefully constructed tales of life in Maine, first published in the *Atlantic Monthly* in the mid-seventies, caught the spirit of that region. Most local colorists could not rise above the conventional sentimentality of the era. By concentrating, as most did, on depicting rural life, they were retreating from current reality. But their concern for exact description and their fascination with local types reflected a growing interest in realism.

Mark Twain

Although it was easy to romanticize the West, that region also lent itself to the realistic approach. Almost of necessity, western writers employed dialect, described coarse characters from the lower levels of society, and dealt with crime and violence. It would have been difficult indeed to write a genteel romance about a mining camp.

°It must be emphasized, however, that the romantic novel did not disappear. Books like General Lew Wallace's *Ben Hur* (1880) and Frances Hodgson Burnett's *Little Lord Fauntleroy* (1886) were best-sellers. Francis Marion Crawford's shamelessly romantic tales, published in wholesale lots between 1883 and his death in 1909, were very popular. In the nineties a spate of historical romances made the realists fume.

The outstanding figure of western literature, the first great American realist, was Mark Twain. Born Samuel L. Clemens in 1835, he grew up in Hannibal, Missouri, on the banks of the Mississippi. After having mastered the printer's trade and worked as a river-boat pilot, he went west to Nevada in 1861. The wild, rough life of Virginia City fascinated him, but prospecting got him nowhere, and he became a reporter for the *Territorial Enterprise*. Soon he was publishing humorous stories about the local life under the *nom de plume* Mark Twain. In 1865, while working in California, he wrote "The Celebrated Jumping Frog of Calaveras County," a story that brought him national recognition. A tour of Europe and the Holy Land in 1867-68 led to the writing of *The Innocents Abroad* (1869), which made him famous.

Twain's greatness stemmed from his acute reportorial eye and ear, his eagerness to live life to the full, his marvelous sense of humor, his ability to be at once "in" society and outside it, to love mankind yet be repelled by human vanity and perversity. He epitomized all the zest and adaptability of his age, and also its materialism. No contemporary pursued the almighty dollar more assiduously. An inveterate speculator, he made a fortune with his pen and lost it in foolish business ventures. He wrote tirelessly and endlessly about America and Europe, his own times and the feudal past, about tourists, slaves, tycoons, cracker-barrel philosophers—and human destiny. He was equally at home and equally successful on the Great River of his childhood, in the mining camps, and in the eastern bourgeois society of his mature years.

But every prize slipped through his fingers and he died a black pessimist, surrounded by adulation yet alone, an alien and a stranger in the land he loved and knew so well.

Twain excelled every contemporary in the portrayal of character. In his biting satire *The Gilded Age* (1873), he created that magnificent mountebank Colonel Beriah Sellers, purveyor of eyewash ("the Infallible Imperial Oriental Optic Liniment") and false hopes, ridiculous, unscrupulous, but lovable. In *Huckleberry Finn* (1884), his masterpiece, his portrait of the slave Jim, loyal, patient, naive, yet withal a man, is unforgettable. When Huck takes advantage of Jim's credulity merely for his own amusement, the slave turns from him coldly and says: "Dat truck dah is *trash;* en trash is what people is dat puts dirt on de head er dey fren's en makes 'em ashamed." And, of course, there is Huck Finn himself, one of the great figures of all literature, full of deviltry, romantic, amoral—up to a point—but at bottom the complete realist. When Miss Watson tells him he can get anything he wants by praying for it, he makes the effort, is disillusioned, and then concludes: "If a body can get anything they pray for, why don't Deacon Winn get back the money he lost on pork? . . . Why can't Miss Watson fat up? No, I says to myself, there ain't nothing in it."

Whether directly, as in *The Innocents Abroad* and in his fascinating account of the world of the river pilot, *Life on the Mississippi* (1883), or when transformed by his imagination in works of fiction such as *Tom Sawyer* (1876) and *A Connecticut Yankee in King Arthur's Court* (1889), Mark Twain always put much of his own experience and feeling into his work. "The truth is," he wrote in 1886, "my books are mainly autobiographies." A story, he once told a fellow author, "must be written with the blood out of a man's heart." His very inner confusions, the clash between his recognition of the pretentiousness and meanness of human beings and his wish to be accepted by society, added depths and overtones to his writing that together with his comic genius give it lasting appeal. He could not rise above the sentimentality and prudery of his generation entirely, for these qualities were part of his nature. He never dealt effectively with sexual love, for example, and often—even in *Huckleberry Finn*—he contrived to end his tales on absurdly optimistic notes that ring false after so many brilliant pages portraying men and the world as they are. On balance, however, Twain's achievement was magnificent. Rough and uneven like the man himself, his works catch more of the spirit of the age he named than those of any other writer.

William Dean Howells

Mark Twain's realism was far less self-conscious than that of his long-time friend William Dean Howells. Like Twain, Howells, who was born in Ohio in 1837, had little formal education. He learned the printer's trade from his father and became a reporter for the *Ohio State Journal*. In 1860 he wrote a campaign biography of Lincoln and was rewarded with an appointment as consul in Venice. His sketches in *Venetian Life* (1866) were a product of this experience. After the Civil War he worked briefly for the *Nation* in New York and then moved to Boston, where he became editor of the *Atlantic Monthly*. In 1886 he returned to New York as editor of *Harper's*.

A long series of novels and much literary criticism poured from his pen over the next 34 years. Although he insisted upon treating his material honestly, at first he was not a critic of society, voting the straight Republican ticket and being content to write about what he called "the smiling aspects" of life. Howells held the sentimental novelists of the sixties and seventies in contempt because they offered readers saccharine falsehoods and catered to their "gross appetite for the marvellous." By realism, he meant concern for the complexities of individual personalities and faithful description of the genteel, middle-class world he knew best. Nevertheless, he did not hesitate to discuss what prudish critics called "sordid" and "revolting" subjects, such as the unhappy marriage of respectable people, which he treated sensitively in *A Modern Instance* (1882).

However, besides a sharp eye and an open mind, Howells had a real social conscience. Gradually he became aware of the problems that industrialization was creating. As early as 1885, in *The Rise of Silas Lapham*, he dealt with some of the ethical conflicts faced by businessmen in a competitive society. The harsh public reaction to the Haymarket bombing in 1886 stirred him deeply, and he threw himself into a futile campaign to prevent the execution of the anarchist suspects. Thereafter, he moved rapidly toward the left; soon he was calling himself a socialist. "After fifty years of optimistic content with 'civilization' . . . I now abhor it, and feel that it is coming out all wrong in the end, unless it bases itself anew on a real equality," he wrote.° His great novel *A Hazard of New Fortunes* (1890), in which Howells put his own ideas in the mouth of a magazine editor, Basil March, contained a broad criticism of industrial America—of the slums, of the callous treatment of workers, of the false values of the promoter and the new-rich tycoon.

But Howells was more than a reformer, more than an inventor of utopias like Edward Bellamy, although he admired Bellamy and wrote a utopian novel of his own, *A Traveller from Altruria* (1894). *A Hazard of New Fortunes* attempted to portray the whole range of metropolitan life, its plot weaving the destinies of a dozen interesting and fully realized personalities from diverse sections and social classes. The book represents a triumph of realism, not only in its careful descriptions of various sections of New York and of the ways of life of rich and poor, and in the intricacy of its characters, but also in its rejection of sentimentality and even of romantic love. "A man knows that he can love and wholly cease to love, not once merely, but several times," the narrator says, "but in regard to women he cherishes the superstition of the romances that love is once for all, and forever." And Basil March, himself happily married, tells his wife: "Why shouldn't we rejoice as much at a nonmarriage as a marriage? . . . In reality, marriage is dog cheap, and anyone can have it for the asking—if he keeps asking enough people."

Aside from his own works, which were widely read, Howells had an immense impact on American literature. He was the most influential critic of his times. He helped bring the best contemporary foreign writers, including Tolstoy, Dostoevsky, Ibsen, and Zola, to the attention of

---

°With remarkable self-insight he added immediately: "Meanwhile I wear a fur-lined overcoat, and live in all the luxury my money can buy." Like nearly all American reformers of the era, he was not really very radical.

An 1897 drawing from the comic weekly *Life,* titled ''Our Popular but Over-advertised Authors,'' features (from left) William Dean Howells, George W. Cable, John K. Bangs, James Whitcomb Riley, Mark Twain, Mary Freeman, Richard Harding Davis, F. Marion Crawford, Frances Burnett, and Joel Chandler Harris. (*Life.*)

readers in the United States, and he encouraged many important young American novelists, such as Stephen Crane, Theodore Dreiser, Frank Norris, and Hamlin Garland. Some of these Americans went far beyond Howells' realism, to what they called naturalism. Many of them, like Twain and Howells, began as newspaper reporters, which provided excellent training for any realist. Working for a big-city daily in the 1890's taught these naturalists much about the dark side of life. They believed that man was essentially an animal, a helpless creature, whose fate was determined by his environment. Their world was Darwin's world—mindless, without either mercy or justice. They wrote chiefly about the most primitive emotions—lust, hate, greed. In *Maggie, A Girl of the Streets* (1893) Stephen Crane described the seduction, degradation, and eventual suicide of a young girl, all set against the background of a sordid slum; in *The Red Badge of Courage* (1895) he captured the pain and horror of war. In *McTeague* (1899) Frank Norris told the story of a brutal, dull-witted dentist who murdered his greed-crazed wife with his bare fists.

Such stuff was too strong for Howells, but he recognized its importance and befriended these younger writers in many ways. He found a publisher for *Maggie* after it had been rejected many times, and wrote appreciative reviews of the work of Garland and Norris. Even Theodore Dreiser, who was contemptuous of Howells' writings and considered him hopelessly middle-class in point of view, appreciated his aid and praised his influence on American literature. Dreiser's first novel, *Sister Carrie* (1900), treated sex so forthrightly that it was withdrawn after publication.

Henry James

Howells also knew and admired the other great novelist of the time, Henry James. Like Howells, James was very different in spirit and background from the tempestuous naturalists. Born to wealth, reared in a cosmopolitan atmosphere, twisted in some strange way while still a child and thus unable to achieve satisfactory relationships with women, James spent most of his mature life in Europe, writing novels, short stories, plays, and volumes of criticism. Although far-removed from the world of practical affairs, he was pre-eminently a realist, determined, as he once said to Robert Louis Stevenson, "to leave a multitude of pictures of my time" for the future to contemplate. He admired the European realists and denounced the "floods of tepid soap and water which under the name of novels are being vomited forth" by the romancers. "All life belongs to you," he told his fellow novelists. "There is no impression of life, no manner of seeing it and feeling it, to which the plan of the novelist may not offer a place."

Although he rejected the New World in favor of the Old and lived in the narrow, cultivated surroundings of London high society, James yearned for the recognition of his countrymen almost as avidly as Mark Twain. However, he was incapable of modifying his rarefied, overly subtle manner of writing. Most of the serious writers of the time admired his books and he received many honors, but he never achieved widespread popularity. His major theme was the clash of American and European cultures, his primary interest the close-up examination of wealthy, sensitive, yet often corrupt persons in a cultivated but far from polite society. He dealt with social issues, such as feminism and the difficulties faced by artists in the modern world, but always subordinated these to his interest in his subjects as individuals. *The American* (1877) told the story of the love of a wealthy American in Paris for a French noblewoman who rejected him because her family disapproved of his "commercial" background. *The Portrait of a Lady* (1881) described the disillusionment of an intelligent girl married to a charming but morally bankrupt man and her eventual decision to remain with him nonetheless. *The Bostonians* (1886) was a complicated and psychologically sensitive study of the varieties of female behavior in a seemingly uniform social situation.

James's reputation, far greater today than in his own lifetime, rests more on his highly refined accounts of the interactions of individuals and their environment and his masterful commentaries on the novel as a literary form than on his ability as a storyteller. Few major writers have been more long-winded, more prone to circumlocution. Yet few have been so dedicated to their art, possessed of such psychological penetration, or so uniformly successful in producing a large body of serious work.

Realism in Art

American painters responded to the times much the way writers did, but with this difference: despite the new concern for realism, the romantic tradition retained its vitality. Pre-eminent among the realists was Thomas Eakins, who was born in Philadelphia in 1844. Eakins studied in Europe in the late sixties and was much influenced by the great realists of the 17th century, Velásquez and Rembrandt. Returning to America in 1870, he passed the remainder of his life teaching and painting in Philadelphia.

The scientific spirit of the age suited Eakins perfectly. He mastered human anatomy; some of his finest paintings, such as *The Gross Clinic* (1875), are graphic illustrations of surgical operations. He was also an early experimenter with motion pictures, seeking to capture exactly the attitudes of human beings and animals in action. Like his friend Walt Whitman, whose portrait is one of his greatest achievements, Eakins gloried in the ordinary, but he had none of Whitman's weakness for sham and self-delusion. His portraits are monuments to his integrity as well as to his craftsmanship: never would he touch up or

Thomas Eakins' interest in science nearly equaled his interest in art. In the early 1880's he collaborated with the photographer Eadweard Muybridge in serial-action photographic experiments and later devised a special camera for his anatomical studies; one of his pictures is reproduced above. The impact of these studies can be seen in *The Swimming Hole* (right), painted by Eakins in 1883. He was then director of the Pennsylvania Academy's art school. (Philadelphia Museum of Art and Fort Worth Art Association.)

soften a likeness to please his sitter. When the Union League of Philadelphia commissioned a canvas of Rutherford B. Hayes, Eakins showed the President working in his shirt sleeves, which scandalized the club fathers. His work was no mere mirror reflecting surface values. His study of six men bathing *(The Swimming Hole)* is a stark portrayal of nakedness, his surgical scenes catch the tenseness of the situation without descending into sensationalism.

Realism was also characteristic of the work of Eakins' contemporary Winslow Homer, a Boston-born painter best known for his brilliant watercolors. Homer was trained as a lithographer and was one of the world's great masters of the watercolor medium, but he had almost no formal training. Indeed, he had contempt for academicians and refused to go abroad to study. Aesthetics did not seem to concern him at all; he liked to shock people by referring to his profession as "the picture line." His concern for accuracy was so intense that as preparation for painting *The Life Line* (1884) he made a trip to Atlantic City to observe the handling of a breeches buoy. "When I have selected [a subject]," he said, "I paint it exactly as it appears."

During the Civil War, Homer worked as an artist-reporter for *Harper's Weekly,* and he continued to do magazine illustrations for some years thereafter. He roamed across America, painting scenes of southern farm life, Adirondack campers, and after about 1880, magnificent seascapes and studies of fishermen and sailors. For years he made his home in a cottage at Prout's Neck, in Maine, although he also traveled extensively in the Caribbean region, where some of his best watercolors were executed.

In some ways Homer resembled the local colorists of American literature, and like many of the members of that group there are romantic elements in his work. His *Gulf Stream* (1899), showing a Negro sailor on a small broken boat menaced by an approaching waterspout and a school of sharks, and his *Fox Hunt* (1893), in which huge, ominous crows hover over a fox at bay, express his interest in the violence and dra-

ma of raw nature, a distinctly romantic theme. However, his approach, even in these works, was utterly prosaic. When some silly women complained about the fate of the poor sailor in *Gulf Stream*, Homer wrote his dealer sarcastically: "Tell these ladies that the unfortunate Negro . . . will be rescued and returned to his friends and home, and live happily ever after."

The outstanding romantic painter of the period was Albert Pinkham Ryder, a strange, neurotic genius haunted by the mystery and poetry of the sea. Ryder was born in New Bedford, Massachusetts, in 1847, during that city's heyday as a whaling port, but spent most of his mature years in New York City, living and working in a dirty, cluttered attic studio. He typified the solitary romantic—brooding, eccentric, otherworldly, mystical. His heavily glazed paintings of dark seas

Between the Civil War and the 1880's, when he turned to the sea for artistic inspiration, much of Winslow Homer's work dealt with the New England scene. He painted *The Berry Pickers* in 1873. (Harold T. Pulsifer Collection, Colby College.)

and small boats "bathed in an atmosphere of golden luminosity" beneath a pale moon, and weird canvases like *The Race Track (Death on a Pale Horse)*, which shows a specter carrying a scythe riding on an empty track under an ominous sky, radiate a strange magic. Yet they are also masterpieces of design.

The careers of Eakins, Homer, and Ryder show that the late-19th-century American environment was not uncongenial to first-rate artists. Nevertheless, at least two major American painters abandoned native shores for Europe. One was James A. McNeill Whistler, whose portrait of his mother, which he called *Arrangement in Grey and Black,* is probably the most famous canvas ever painted by an American. Whistler

left the United States in 1855 when he was 21 and spent most of his life in Paris and London. "I shall come to America," he announced grandly, "when the duty on works of art is abolished!" Whistler made a profession of eccentricity, but he was also a remarkably talented and versatile artist. Some of his portraits are triumphs of realism, while his misty studies of the London waterfront, which the critic John Ruskin characterized as pots of paint flung in the face of the beholder, but which Whistler conceived of as visual expressions of poetry, are thoroughly romantic in conception. Paintings like "Whistler's Mother" represent still another expression of his talent. Such pictures, spare and muted in tone, are more interesting as precise arrangements of color and space than as images of particular objects; they had a tremendous influence on the course of modern art.

The second important expatriate artist was Mary Cassatt, daughter of a wealthy Pittsburgh banker, and sister of Alexander J. Cassatt, president of the Pennsylvania Railroad around the turn of the century. She went to Paris originally as a tourist and dabbled in art like many conventional young socialites, but she was caught up in the impressionist movement and decided to become a serious painter. Her work is more French than American and was little appreciated in the United States before the First World War. Once, when she came back to America for a visit, the Philadelphia *Public Ledger* reported: "Mary Cassatt, sister of Mr. Cassatt, president of the Pennsylvania Railroad, returned from Europe yesterday. She has been studying painting in Paris, and owns the smallest Pekinese dog in the world."

If Mary Cassatt was unappreciated and if Whistler had some reasons for considering his fellow countrymen uncultured, it remains true that interest in art was considerable in America. Museums and art schools flourished; settlement-house workers put on exhibitions that attracted enthusiastic crowds; wealthy patrons gave countless commissions to portrait painters, the most fashionable of whom, a fine craftsman if not a great artist, was John Singer Sargent. Many men of wealth poured fortunes into collecting, and if some were interested only in vain display and others had execrable taste, some were discriminating collectors. Martin A. Ryerson, with a fortune made in lumber, bought the works of the French impressionists when few Americans understood their importance. Charles L. Freer of the American Car and Foundry Company was a friend and admirer of Whistler and a specialist in oriental art. John G. Johnson, a successful corporation lawyer, covered the walls of his Philadelphia mansion with a carefully chosen collection of Italian primitives, accumulated before anyone appreciated them.

Other rich men, most notably the great J. P. Morgan, employed experts to help them put together their collections. Nor were the advanced painters of the day rejected by all wealthy patrons. It is true that only a handful of his contemporaries recognized the talent of the weird, avant-garde Ryder. But while Eakins' work was undervalued, he received many important commissions. Some of Homer's canvases commanded thousands of dollars, and so did those of the radical Whistler.

The Pragmatic Approach

It would have been remarkable indeed if the intellectual ferment of the late 19th century had not affected contemporary ideas about the meaning of life, the truth of revealed religion, moral values, and similar fundamental problems. In particular, the theory of evolution, so important in altering contemporary views of science, history, and social relations, produced significant changes in American thinking about religious and philosophical questions.

Evolution posed an immediate challenge to religion: if Darwin was correct, the Biblical account of the creation was obviously untrue, and the idea that man had been formed in God's image was highly unlikely at best. A bitter controversy erupted, described by president Andrew D. White of Cornell in *The Warfare of Science with Theology in Christendom* (1896). Although millions continued to believe in the literal truth of the Bible, among intellectuals, lay and clerical, victory went to the evolutionists because in addition to the arguments of the geologists and the biologists, scholars were throwing light on the historical origins of the Bible, showing it to be of human rather than divine inspiration. However, evolution did not permanently undermine the faith of any large percentage of the population. If the account of the creation in Genesis could not be taken literally, the Bible remained a great depository of wisdom and inspiration. Soon such books as John Fiske's *The Outlines of Cosmic Philosophy* (1874) were providing religious persons with the comforting thesis that evolution, while true, was merely God's way of ordering the universe. As the liberal preacher Washington Gladden explained in 1889, evolution was "a most impressive demonstration of the presence of God in the world."

The effects of Darwinism on philosophy were less dramatic but in the end far more significant. Fixed systems and eternal verities were difficult to justify in a world that was constantly evolving. By the early 1870's a few philosophers had begun to reason that ideas and theories mattered little except when applied to specifics. "Nothing justifies the development of abstract principles but their utility in enlarging our concrete knowledge of nature," wrote Chauncey Wright, secretary of the American Academy of Arts and Sciences. In "How to Make Our Ideas Clear" (1878), Wright's friend Charles S. Peirce, an amazingly versatile and talented albeit obscure thinker, argued that concepts could be fairly understood only in terms of their practical effects. Once the mind accepted the truth of evolution, Peirce also believed, logic required that it accept the impermanence even of scientific laws. There was, he wrote, "an element of indeterminacy, spontaneity, or absolute chance in nature."

This startling philosophy, which Peirce called pragmatism, was presented in language understandable to the intelligent layman by William James, brother of the novelist. James was one of the most remarkable men of his generation. Educated in London, Paris, Bonn, and Geneva as well as at Harvard, he studied painting, participated in a zoological expedition to South America, took a medical degree, and was a professor at Harvard successively of comparative anatomy, psychology, and finally philosophy. His *Principles of Psychology* (1890) may be said to have established that discipline as a modern science; an abridged version was for years the leading college textbook in the field. His *Varieties of Religious Experience* (1902), which treated the subject from both psychological and philosophical points of view, helped thousands of readers to reconcile their religious faith with their increasing knowledge of psychology and the physical universe.

Psychologist and philosopher William James explored the Amazon with zoologist Louis Agassiz before embarking on his notable 35-year career at Harvard. (Brown Brothers.)

Although less rigorous a logician than Peirce, who was his friend, James's wide range and his verve and imagination as a writer made him by far the most influential philosopher of his times. He rejected wholly the deterministic interpretation of Darwinism and all other one-idea explanations of existence. Belief in free will was one of his axioms; environment might influence survival, but so did the *desire* to survive, which existed independently of surrounding circumstances. Truth was relative; it did not exist in the abstract; it *happened* under particular circumstances. What a man thought helped make what he thought occur, or come true. The mind, James wrote in a typically vivid phrase, has "a vote" in determining truth. Religion was true, for example, because men were religious.

The pragmatic approach inspired much of the reform spirit of the late 19th century and even more of that of the early 20th. James's hammer blows shattered the Social Darwinism of Spencer and Sumner. In "Great Men and Their Environment" (1880) he argued that social changes were brought about by the actions of geniuses whom society had selected and raised to positions of power, rather than by the impersonal force of the environment. Such reasoning fitted the preconceptions of rugged individualists but also encouraged those dissatisfied with society to work for change. Educational reformers like John Dewey, the institutionalist school of economists, settlement-house workers, and other reformers accepted pragmatism eagerly. Thus, James's philosophy did much to revive the buoyant optimism that had characterized the pre-Civil War reform movement.

Yet pragmatism also brought Americans face to face with many somber problems. While relativism made them optimistic, it also bred insecurity, for there could be no certainty, no comforting reliance on any eternal value in the absence of absolute truth. Pragmatism also seemed to suggest that the end justified the means, that what worked was more important than what ought to be. At the time of James's death in 1910, the *Commercial and Financial Chronicle* pointed out that the pragmatic philosophy was very helpful to businessmen in making decisions. By emphasizing practice at the expense of theory, the new philosophy also encouraged materialism, anti-intellectualism, and other unlovely aspects of the American character. And what place had conventional morality in such a system? Perhaps pragmatism placed too much reliance on the free will of human beings, ignoring their capacity for selfishness and self-delusion.

In any case, the people of the new century found pragmatism a heady wine. They would quaff it freely and enthusiastically—down to the bitter dregs.

Supplementary Reading

All the surveys of American intellectual history deal extensively with this period. See, for example, Merle Curti, *The Growth of American Thought* (1943),

Louis Hartz, *The Liberal Tradition in America*° (1955), and Clinton Rossiter, *Conservatism in America: The Thankless Persuasion*° (1962). P. A. Carter, *The Spiritual Crisis of the Gilded Age* (1971), H. S. Commager, *The American Mind*° (1950), and A. M. Schlesinger, *The Rise of the City* (1933), contain much interesting information, and there are useful essays on some aspects of the subject in H. W. Morgan (ed.), *The Gilded Age: A Reappraisal*° (1970). Ray Ginger, *The Age of Excess*° (1965), is also stimulating.

L. A. Cremin, *The Transformation of the School: Progressivism in American Education* (1961) is an excellent introduction to the subject. On education in the South, see C. W. Dabney, *Universal Education in the South* (1936). For the work of Dewey, consult Sidney Hook, *John Dewey* (1939). The best treatment of the Chautauqua movement is Victoria and R. O. Case, *We Called It Culture* (1948). Trends in the history of journalism are discussed in J. M. Lee, *History of American Journalism* (1923), B. A. Weisberger, *The American Newspaperman* (1961), and F. L. Mott, *A History of American Magazines* (1938–57). George Juergens, *Joseph Pulitzer and the New York World* (1966), W. A. Swanberg, *Citizen Hearst*° (1961), and Peter Lyon, *Success Story: The Life and Times of S. S. McClure* (1963), are useful biographies.

On higher education, see L. R. Veysey, *The Emergence of the American University* (1965), and Richard Hofstadter and W. P. Metzger, *The Development of Academic Freedom in the United States*° (1955). Of the many histories of particular universities, S. E. Morison, *Three Centuries of Harvard* (1936), and Hugh Hawkins, *Pioneer: A History of the Johns Hopkins University* (1960), are particularly important for this period. E. D. Ross, *Democracy's College* (1942), deals with the land-grant institutions. Hugh Hawkins, *Between Harvard and America: The Educational Leadership of Charles W. Eliot* (1972), and Allan Nevins, *John D. Rockefeller: The Heroic Age of American Enterprise* (1940), also contain valuable information. Thorstein Veblen, *The Higher Learning in America*° (1918), is full of stimulating opinions.

For developments in American science, see the excellent essay by P. F. Boller, Jr., in H. W. Morgan (ed.), *The Gilded Age*° (1970), and also Bernard Jaffe, *Men of Science in America* (1944). Muriel Ru-

°Available in paperback.

keyser, *Willard Gibbs°* (1942), is a good biography. A good general introduction to the work of the social scientists is Sidney Fine, *Laissez Faire and the General-Welfare State°* (1957), but H. S. Commager's above-mentioned *American Mind* is also useful, as are Richard Hofstadter, *Social Darwinism in American Thought°* (1944), and Jurgen Herbst, *The German Historical School in American Scholarship* (1965). Biographies of prominent figures include P. G. Rader, *The Academic Mind and Reform: The Influence of Richard T. Ely in American Life* (1967), H. W. Bragdon, *Woodrow Wilson: The Academic Years* (1967), Samuel Chugerman, *Lester F. Ward: The American Aristotle* (1939), Carl Resek, *Lewis Henry Morgan* (1960), M. DeW. Howe, *Justice Oliver Wendell Holmes: The Proving Years* (1963), and W. H. Jordy, *Henry Adams: Scientific Historian°* (1952).

The great literary figures of the age are discussed in Everett Carter, *Howells and the Age of Realism* (1954), Alfred Kazin, *On Native Grounds°* (1942), Larzer Ziff, *The American 1890s°* (1966), and Van Wyck Brooks, *New England: Indian Summer, 1865-1915°* (1940) and *The Confident Years: 1885-1915* (1952). See also, on Twain, Bernard De Voto, *Mark Twain's America°* (1932), and Justin Kaplan, *Mr. Clemens and Mark Twain°* (1966); on Howells, E. H. Cady, *The Realist at War* (1958); on James, Leon Edel, *Henry James°* (1953-62).

American painting is discussed in O. W. Larkin, *Art and Life in America* (1949). Biographies of leading artists include Lloyd Goodrich, *Thomas Eakins* (1933) and *Winslow Homer* (1944), F. N. Price, *Ryder* (1932), and E. R. and Joseph Pennell, *The Life of James McNeill Whistler* (1911).

On pragmatism, see Hofstadter's *Social Darwinism,* Commager's *American Mind,* and R. B. Perry, *The Thought and Character of William James°* (1935).

21

National Politics: 1877–1896

Modern students generally conclude that the
political history of the United States in the last
quarter of the 19th century was singularly
divorced from what now seem the meaningful
issues of that day. On the rare occasions when
important, supposedly controversial measures
such as the Sherman Antitrust Act, the Interstate
Commerce Act, the Pendleton Civil Service Act,
and the Dawes Severalty Act were debated, they
excited far less argument than they merited.

A graduated income tax, the greatest
instrument for orderly economic and social

change that a democratic society has devised, was enacted during the Civil War, repealed after that conflict, re-enacted in 1894 as part of the maneuvering over tariff reform, and then declared unconstitutional in 1895 without, in most instances, causing more than a ripple in the world of partisan politics. Proponents of the tax argued only that it offered a fairer way of distributing the costs of government, its foes that it penalized efficiency and encouraged governmental extravagance. Almost no one saw it as a means of redistributing wealth. This was typical. As the English observer James Bryce noted in the late eighties, the politicians were "clinging too long to outworn issues" and "neglecting to discover and work out new principles capable of solving the problems which now perplex the country." Congress, wrote another critic, "does not solve the problems, the solution of which is demanded by the life of the nation."

Yet the public remained intensely interested in politics. Huge crowds turned out to hear vapid orators mouth hackneyed slogans and meaningless generalities. Most elections were closely contested and millions of voters turned out enthusiastically to choose, essentially, between Tweedledum and Tweedledee.

The American Commonwealth

A succession of weak Presidents presided over the White House. Although the impeachment proceedings against Andrew Johnson had failed, Congress dominated the government. "There has not been a single presidential candidate since Abraham Lincoln," Bryce wrote in 1888, "of whom his friends could say that he had done anything to command the gratitude of the nation."

Within Congress, the Senate generally overshadowed the House of Representatives. Indeed, in his novel *Democracy* (1880), the cynical Henry Adams wrote that the United States had a "government of the people, by the people, for the benefit of Senators." Critics called the Senate a "rich man's club," and it did contain many mil-

lionaires, such as Leland Stanford, founder of the Central Pacific Railroad, James G. "Bonanza" Fair of Nevada, who extracted a fortune of $30 million from the Comstock Lode, Philetus Sawyer, a self-made Wisconsin lumberman, and Nelson Aldrich of Rhode Island, whose wealth derived from banking and a host of corporate connections. However, the true sources of the Senate's influence lay in the long tenure of many of its members, which enabled them to master the craft of politics, in the fact that it was small enough to encourage real debate, and in its long-established reputation for wisdom, intelligence, and statesmanship.

The House of Representatives, on the other hand, was one of the most disorderly and inefficient legislative bodies in the world. "As I make my notes," a reporter wrote in 1882 while sitting in the House gallery, "I see a dozen men reading newspapers with their feet on their desks. . . . 'Pig-Iron' Kelley of Pennsylvania has dropped his newspaper and is paring his fingernails. . . . The vile odor of . . . tobacco . . . rises from the two-for-five-cents cigars in the mouths of the so-called gentlemen below. . . . They chew, too! Every desk has a spittoon of pink and gold china beside it to catch the filth from the statesman's mouth."

More serious was the infernal din that rose from the crowded chamber. Desks slammed, members held private conversations, hailed pages, shuffled from place to place, clamored for the attention of the Speaker, and all the while some poor orator tried to discuss the question of the moment. Speaking in the House, one writer said, was like trying to address the crowd on a passing Broadway bus from the curb in front of the Astor House in New York. On one occasion, in 1878, the adjournment of the House was held up for more than 12 hours because most of the members of an important committee were too drunk to prepare a vital appropriations bill for final passage. President Hayes was furious. *"It should be investigated,"* he wrote in his diary.

The great political parties professed undying enmity to each other, but seldom took clearly opposing positions on the questions of the day.

Joseph Keppler's 1890 *Puck* cartoon, "None but millionaires need apply: the coming style of Presidential election," comments acidly on the low status of the Presidency. The tag on the Chief Executive's chair refers to the Cabinet. As the examples in this chapter indicate, the late 19th century was a heyday for political cartoonists. (New-York Historical Society.)

Democrats were separated from Republicans more by accidents of geography, religious affiliation, ethnic background, and emotion than by economic issues. Questions of state and local importance, unrelated to national politics, often determined congressional elections, and thus who controlled the federal government. The fundamental division between Democrats and Republicans was sectional, resulting from the Civil War. The South, after the political rights of Negroes had been drastically circumscribed, became heavily Democratic. Most of New England was solidly Republican. Elsewhere the two parties stood in fair balance, although the Republicans tended to have the advantage. A preponderance of the well-to-do, cultured northerners was Republican. Perhaps in reaction to this concentration, immigrants, Catholics, and—except for

the Negroes—other minority groups tended to vote Democratic. But there were so many exceptions that these generalizations are of little practical importance. German and Scandinavian immigrants usually voted Republican. Many powerful business leaders supported the Democrats.

The personalities of political leaders often dictated the voting patterns of individuals and groups. In 1884 J. P. Morgan voted Democratic because he admired Grover Cleveland, while Irish-Americans, traditionally Democrats, cast thousands of ballots for Republican James G. Blaine. In 1892, when Cleveland defeated Benjamin Harrison, a prominent steel manufacturer wrote to Andrew Carnegie: "I am very sorry for President Harrison, but I cannot see that our interests are going to be affected one way or the other." And Carnegie replied: "We have nothing to fear. . . . Cleveland is [a] pretty good fellow. Off for Venice tomorrow." The bulk of the people—farmers, laboring men, shopkeepers, white-collar workers—distributed their ballots fairly evenly between the two parties in most elections; the balance of political power after 1876 was almost perfect—"the most spectacular degree of equilibrium in American history." Between 1856 and 1912 the Democrats elected a President only twice (1884 and 1892), but most of the contests were extremely close. Majorities in both the Senate and the House fluctuated continually. Between 1876 and 1896, the "dominant" Republican party controlled both houses of Congress and the Presidency at the same time for only one two-year period.

Issues of the "Gilded Age"

Four questions obsessed the politicians in these years. One was the "bloody shirt." The term, which became part of the language after a Massachusetts congressman had dramatically displayed to his colleagues in the House the blood-stained shirt of an Ohio carpetbagger who had been flogged by terrorists in Mississippi, referred to the tactic of reminding the electorate of the northern states that the men who had taken the South out of the Union and precipitated the Civil War had been Democrats, and that they and their descendants were still Democrats. Should their party regain power, former rebels would run the government and undo all the work accomplished at such sacrifice during the war. "Every man that endeavored to tear down the old flag," a Republican orator proclaimed in 1876, "was a Democrat. Every man that tried to destroy this nation was a Democrat. . . . The man that assassinated Abraham Lincoln was a Democrat. . . . Soldiers, every scar you have on your heroic bodies was given you by a Democrat." Naturally, every scoundrel or incompetent who sought office under the Republican banner

waved the bloody shirt in order to divert the attention of northern voters from his own shortcomings, but the technique worked so well that many decent candidates could not resist the temptation to employ it in close races. Nothing, of course, so effectively obscured the real issues of the day.

Waving the bloody shirt was related intimately to the issue of Negro rights. Throughout this period, the Republicans vacillated between trying to build up their organization in the South by appealing to black voters—which incidentally required them to make sure that blacks in the South could vote—and trying to win conservative white support by stressing economic issues, such as the tariff. When the former strategy seemed wise, they waved the bloody shirt with vigor; in the latter case they piously announced that the Negro's future was "as safe in the hands of one party as it is in the other."

The question of veterans' pensions also bore a close relationship to the bloody shirt. After the Civil War, Union soldiers formed the Grand Army of the Republic, and by 1890 the organization had a membership of 409,000. Beginning in the 1880's, the GAR put immense pressure on Congress, first for aid to veterans with service-connected disabilities, then for those with *any* disability, and eventually for all former Union soldiers. Republican politicians played upon the emotions of the ex-soldiers by waving the bloody shirt, but the tough-minded leaders of the GAR demanded they prove their sincerity by treating in openhanded fashion the warriors whose blood had stained the shirt.

The tariff was another perennial issue in post-Civil War politics. Despite much loose talk about free trade, almost no one in the United States except for a handful of professional economists, most of them college professors, actually believed in eliminating duties on imports. Manufacturers naturally desired protective tariffs, and a majority of their workers were convinced that wage levels would fall sharply if goods produced by cheap foreign labor entered the United States untaxed. Even many farmers supported protection. Congressman William McKinley of Ohio, who reputedly could make a tariff schedule sound like poetry, stated the majority opinion in the clearest terms: high tariffs foster the growth of industry and thus create jobs. "Reduce the tariff and labor is the first to suffer," he said. Whatever college professors may say about the virtues of free trade and international competition, "the school of experience" teaches that protection is necessary if America is to prosper.

Voters found such logic irrefutable. Duties had been raised during the Civil War to an average of about 50 per cent ad valorem. Some slight reductions were made in the seventies and eighties, but in 1890 the McKinley tariff restored these cuts. This law even granted protection to a nonexistent industry, the manufacture of tin plate, and to such agricultural products as eggs and potatoes, which would not have been imported even under free trade. When the legislators decided to remove the duty on raw sugar in order to get rid of an embarrassing revenue surplus, they compensated domestic sugar raisers by awarding them a bounty of two cents a pound on their product.

The tariff could have been a real political issue despite the general belief in protection, for American technology was advancing so rapidly that many industries no longer required protection against foreign competitors. A powerful argument could have been made also for scientific rate-making that would adjust duties to actual conditions and avoid overprotection. The Democrats professed to believe in moderation, but whenever party leaders tried to revise the tariff downward, Democratic congressmen from industrial states like Pennsylvania and New York deserted them and sided with the Republicans. Many Republicans also endorsed tariff reform in principle, but when particular schedules came up for discussion, most of them demanded the highest possible rates for industries in their own districts and traded votes shamelessly with colleagues representing other interests in order to get what they wanted. Every new tariff bill became an occasion for logrolling, lobbying, and outrageous politicking rather than for sane discussion and careful evaluation of the true public interest.

A third political question in this period was currency reform. During the Civil War, it will be recalled, the government, faced with obligations it could not meet by taxing or borrowing, suspended specie payments and issued about $450 million in paper money. These "greenbacks" did not command the full confidence of a people accustomed to money readily convertible into gold or silver. Greenbacks seemed to threaten inflation, for how could one trust the government not to issue them in wholesale lots to avoid passing unpopular tax laws? Thus, when the war ended, a strong sentiment developed for withdrawing the greenbacks from circulation and getting back to a bullion standard. "By a law resting on the concurring judgment . . . of mankind in all ages and countries, the precious metals have been the measure of value," one politician wrote in 1878. "That law can no more be repealed by act of Congress than the law of gravitation."

On the other hand, the nation's burgeoning population and the rapid expansion of every kind of economic activity increased the need for currency. In actual fact, prices declined sharply after Appomattox. This deflation increased the real income of bondholders and other creditors but injured debtors. Farmers were particularly hard hit, for many of them had borrowed heavily during the wartime boom to finance expansion.

Here was a question of real significance. Many groups supported some kind of currency inflation. A National Greenback party nominated Peter Cooper, an iron manufacturer, for President in 1876. Although Cooper received only 81,000 votes, a new Greenback Labor party polled over a million in 1878, electing 14 congressmen. However, the major parties refused to confront each other over the currency question. While Republicans professed to be the party of sound money, most western Republicans favored expansion of the currency. And while one wing of the Democrats flirted with the Greenbackers, the conservative, or "Bourbon," Democrats favored deflation as much as any Republicans.

In 1874 a bill to increase the supply of greenbacks was defeated in a Republican-dominated

Congress only by the veto of President Grant. The next year Congress voted to resume specie payments, but in order to avoid a party split on the question, the Republicans agreed to allow $300 million in greenbacks to remain in circulation and to postpone actual resumption of specie payments until 1879. Spurred on by the silver miners as well as by those advocating any measure that would increase the volume of money in circulation, various congressmen introduced proposals to coin large amounts of silver. Neither party took a clear-cut stand on silver, however. Although under various administrations steps were taken to increase or decrease the amount of money in circulation, the net effect on the economy was not significant. Few politicians before 1890 considered treating fiscal policy as a device for influencing economic development. The effect of all the controversy was thus, in the words of economist Joseph Schumpeter, "so light as to justify exclusion from the general analysis of the determining factors of the economic process."

The final major political issue of these years was civil service reform. That the federal bureaucracy needed overhauling nearly everyone agreed. As American society grew larger and more complex in an industrial age, the government necessarily took on more functions. The need for professional administration increased. The number of federal employees rose from 53,000 in 1871 to 256,000 at the end of the century. Corruption flourished; waste and inefficiency were the normal state of affairs. The collection of tariff duties offered perhaps the greatest opportunity for venality. The New York Custom House, one observer wrote in 1872, teemed with "corrupting merchants and their clerks and runners, who think that all men can be bought, and . . . corrupt swarms [of clerks], who shamelessly seek their price."

With a succession of relatively weak Presidents and a Congress that squandered its energies on private bills, pork-barrel projects, and other trivia, the whole administration of the government was monumentally ineffective. "The federal system from Grant through McKinley was generally undistinguished," the historian Leonard D. White concluded after an exhaustive study of the period. "Nobody, whether in Congress or in the executive departments, seemed able to rise much above the handicraft office methods that were cumbersome even in the simpler days of the Jacksonians."

Every honest observer could see the need for reform, but the politicians refused to surrender the power of dispensing government jobs to their henchmen without regard for their qualifications. They argued that patronage was the lifeblood of politics, that parties could not function without armies of loyal political workers, and that these workers expected and deserved the rewards of office when their efforts were crowned with victory at the polls. Typical was the attitude of the New York assemblyman who, according to Theodore Roosevelt, had "the same idea about Public Life and the Civil Service that a vulture has of a dead sheep." When reformers suggested establishing even the most modest kind of professional, nonpartisan civil service, politicians of both parties subjected them to every kind of insult and ridicule, although both the Democratic and Republican parties regularly wrote civil service reform planks into their platforms.

Political Strategy and Tactics

The major American parties have nearly always avoided clear-cut stands on controversial questions in order to appeal to as wide a segment of the electorate as possible, but in the last quarter of the 19th century their equivocations assumed abnormal proportions. This was due in part to the precarious balance of power between them: neither dared declare itself too clearly on any question lest by so doing it drive away more voters than it attracted. But the rapid pace of social and economic change in those years also militated against political decisiveness. No one in or out of politics had as yet devised effective solutions for many current problems. When the party leaders tried to deal with the money question, they discovered that the bankers and the professional economists were as confused as the public at large. "We dabble in theories of our own and clutch convulsively at the doctrines of others," a Philadelphia banker confessed. "From the vast tract of mire by which the subject is surrounded, overlaid, and besmeared, it is almost impossible to arrive at anything like a fair estimate of its real nature." How could mere politicians act rationally or consistently under such circumstances?

The parties stumbled so badly when they confronted the tariff problem because tariffs in a complex industrial economy are not susceptible to solution by counting noses. As modern experience has shown, they are better determined by the executive branch, once broad policies have been laid down by Congress. But in the 19th century specialists had not yet arrived at this conclusion. Reformers could thunder self-righteously against the spoils system, but how could political parties exist without it? They could denounce laissez faire, but who had devised instruments for social and economic control that could be centrally administered with intelligence and efficiency? The embryonic social sciences had not devised the techniques, or even collected the statistical information necessary for efficient social management.

If the politicians steered clear of the "real" issues, they did so as much out of a healthy respect for their own ignorance as out of any desire to avoid controversy. Unable to provide answers to the meaningful questions, they had to turn to other, simpler issues that they and their constituents could understand, merely in order to provide the political system with a semblance of purposefulness, while society blindly but steadily accumulated the experience and skills required for dealing with the results of the industrial revolution.

With the Democrats invincible in the South and the Republicans predominant in New England and most of the states beyond the Mississippi, the outcome of Presidential elections was usually determined in a handful of populous states: New York (together with its satellites,

New Jersey and Connecticut), Ohio, Indiana, and Illinois. The fact that opinion in these states on important questions like the tariff and monetary policy was sharply divided goes far to explain why the parties hesitated to commit themselves on issues. In every Presidential election, Democrats and Republicans concentrated their heaviest guns on these states.

Campaigns were conducted in a carnival atmosphere, entertainment being substituted for serious debate. Large sums were spent on brass bands, barbecues, uniforms, and banners. Men of national reputation were imported to attract crowds, and spellbinders noted for their leather lungs—this was before the day of the loudspeaker—and their ability to rouse popular emotions were brought in by the dozens to address mass meetings. With so much depending upon so few, the level of political morality was abysmal. Mudslinging, character assassination, and plain lying were standard practice, bribery routine. Drifters and other dissolute citizens were paid in cash—or more often in free drinks—to vote the party ticket. The names of persons long dead were solemnly inscribed in voting registers, their suffrages exercised by impostors. Since both parties indulged in these tactics, their efforts were often self-canceling, but in some instances Presidents were made and unmade in this sordid fashion.

The Men in the White House

The leading statesmen of the period showed as little interest in truly important contemporary questions as the party hacks who made up the rank and file of their organizations. Let us consider first the Presidents.

Rutherford B. Hayes, President from 1877 to 1881, came to office with a distinguished record. Born in Delaware, Ohio, in 1822, he attended Kenyon College and the Harvard Law School before settling down to practice in Cincinnati.

Although he had a wife and family to support, he volunteered for service within weeks after the first shell fell on Fort Sumter. "This [is] a just and necessary war," he wrote in his diary. "I would prefer to go into it if I knew I was to die . . . than to live through and after it without taking any part."

Hayes fought bravely, even recklessly, through nearly four years of war. He was wounded at South Mountain, on the eve of Antietam, and later served under Sheridan in the Shenandoah Valley campaign of 1864. Entering the army as a major, he emerged a major general. In 1864 he was elected to Congress; four years later he became governor of Ohio, serving three terms altogether. The Republicans nominated him for President in 1876 because of his reputation for honesty and moderation, and his election, made possible by the Compromise of 1877, seemed to presage an era of sectional harmony and political probity.

Hayes was a long-faced man with deep-set blue eyes, a large nose, a broad, smooth forehead, and a full beard. Outwardly he had a sunny disposition, inwardly, in his own words, he was sometimes "nervous to the point of disaster." Despite his geniality, he was utterly without political glamour. Politically temperate and cautious, he had never been a vigorous waver of the bloody shirt, although in the heat of a hard campaign he was not above urging others to stress the dangers of "rebel rule" should the Democrats win. He tended to play down the tariff issue whenever possible, favoring protection in principle but refusing to become a mere spokesman for local interests. On the money question he was conservative. He cheerfully approved the resumption of gold payments in 1879 and vetoed bills to expand the currency by coining silver. He accounted himself a civil service reformer, appointing Carl Schurz, a leader of the movement, to his Cabinet. He opposed the collection of political contributions from federal officeholders and issued an order forbidding them "to take part in the management of political organizations, caucuses, conventions, or election campaigns."

As President, Hayes adopted the Whig approach; he saw himself more as a caretaker than a leader and felt that Congress should assume the main responsibility for settling national problems. According to a recent biographer, "he had no intention of . . . trying to be a President in the heroic mold," and another historian writes that he showed "no capacity for such large-minded leadership as might have tamed the political hordes and aroused the enthusiasm, or at least the interest, of the public." He hated having constantly to make decisions on controversial questions. He complained about the South's failure to treat the Negro decently after the withdrawal of federal troops, but took no action. He fought harder for civil service reform but failed to achieve the "thorough, rapid and complete" change he had promised. In this, as in most other matters, he was content to "let the record show that he had made the requests."

In the eyes of his contemporaries his administration was a failure. Neither he nor they seriously considered him for a second term. "I am not liked as President," he confessed to his diary, and the Republican minority leader of the House admitted that the President was "almost without a friend" in Congress.

Hayes's successor, James A. Garfield, was cut down by an assassin's bullet only four months after his inauguration. Even in that short time, however, his ineffectiveness had been clearly demonstrated. Garfield grew up in poverty on an Ohio farm. He was only 29 when the Civil War broke out, but he helped organize a volunteer regiment and soon proved himself both a fine disciplinarian and an excellent battlefield commander. He fought at Shiloh and later at Chickamauga, where he was General Rosecrans' chief of staff. He rose in two years from lieutenant colonel to major general. Then, in 1863, he won a seat in Congress, where his oratorical and managerial skills soon brought him to prominence in the affairs of the Republican party.

Garfield was a big, broad-shouldered man, balding, with sharp eyes, an aquiline nose, and a thick, full beard. Studious, industrious, with a wide-ranging, well-stocked mind, he was called by one friend "the ideal self-made man." His one great weakness was indecisiveness—what another of his admirers described as a "want of certainty" and a "deference for other men's opinions." As President Hayes put it, Garfield "could not face a frowning world. . . . His course at various times when trouble came betrayed weakness."

Like many other ex-soldiers, including Hayes and even General Grant, Garfield did not really enjoy waving the bloody shirt, but when hard-pressed politically, as when his name was linked with the Crédit Mobilier railroad scandal, he would lash out hard at the South in an effort to distract the voters. Intellectually he was inclined toward low tariffs. "The scholarship of modern times," he said in 1870, "is . . . leading in the direction of what is called free trade." Nevertheless, he would not sacrifice the interests of Ohio manufacturers for a mere principle. "I shall not admit to a considerable reduction of a few leading articles in which my constituents are deeply interested when many others of a similar character are left untouched," he declared. Similarly, though eager to improve the efficiency of the government and resentful of the "intellectual dissipation" resulting from time wasted listening to the countless appeals of office seekers, he often wilted under pressure from the spoilsmen. Only on fiscal policy did he take a firm stand: he opposed categorically all inflationary schemes.

Political patronage proved to be Garfield's undoing. The Republican party in 1880 was split into two factions, the "Stalwarts" and the "Half-Breeds." The Stalwarts, led by the New York politico Senator Roscoe Conkling, believed in the blatant pursuit of the spoils of office. The Half-Breeds did not really disagree but behaved more circumspectly, hoping to attract the support of independents. Actually, competition for office was the main reason for their rivalry.

Garfield had been a compromise choice at the 1880 Republican convention; his election precipitated a great battle over patronage, the new President standing in a sort of no man's land between the factions. "I am considering all day whether A or B shall be appointed to this or that office," he moaned. "Once or twice I felt like crying out in the agony of my soul against the greed for office and its consumption of my time." Soon he was complaining to his secretary of state: "My God! What is there in this place that a man should ever want to get into it?"

Garfield did stand up against the most grasping of the politicians, resisting particularly the demands of Senator Conkling. By backing the investigation of a post office scandal, and by appointing a Half-Breed collector of the Port of New York, he infuriated the Stalwarts. In July 1881 an unbalanced Stalwart lawyer named Charles J. Guiteau, who had been fruitlessly haunting Washington offices in search of a consulship or some other minor post, shot Garfield in the Washington railroad station. After lingering for weeks, the President died on September 19.

The assassination of Garfield elevated Chester A. Arthur to the Presidency. Arthur was born in Vermont in 1829. After graduating from Union College, he studied law and settled in New York City. An abolitionist, he became an early convert to the Republican party and rose rapidly in its local councils. In 1871 Grant gave him the juiciest political plum in the country, the collectorship of the Port of New York, which he held until removed by Hayes in 1878 for refusing to keep his hands out of party politics. The only elective position he ever held was the Vice Presidency. Before Garfield's death he had paid little attention to questions like the tariff and monetary policy, being content to collect annual fees ranging upward of $50,000 and oversee the operations of the New York customs office, with its hordes of clerks and laborers. (During Arthur's tenure, the novelist Herman Melville was employed as an "outdoor inspector" by the Custom House.) Of course Arthur was an unblushing defender of the spoils system, although it must be said in fairness that he was personally honest and an excellent administrator.

The tragic circumstances of his elevation to the Presidency sobered Arthur considerably. Although a genial, convivial man, perhaps overly fond of good food and flashy clothes, he comported himself with great dignity as President.

In one of Keppler's more original—and outrageous—*Puck* cartoons, done for the 1890 campaign, "bride" Garfield is reminded of a shady past. "But it was such a little one!" the bride murmurs (Garfield's alleged link with Crédit Mobilier netted him but $329). GOP worthies Carl Schurz and Whitelaw Reid are the bridesmaids. (*Puck,* August 25, 1880.)

He did not cut his ties with the Stalwart faction, but he handled patronage matters with restraint, continuing the investigation of the post office scandals over the objections of important Republican politicians who were involved in them, and he gave at least nominal support to the movement for civil service reform, which had been greatly strengthened by public indignation following the assassination of Garfield. In 1883 Congress passed the Pendleton Act, "classifying" about ten per cent of all government jobs and creating a bipartisan Civil Service Commission to prepare and administer competitive examinations for these positions. The law also made it illegal to force officeholders to make political contributions and empowered the President to expand the list of classified positions at his discretion.

Although many politicians resented the new system bitterly—one senator denounced it as "unAmerican"—the Pendleton Act opened a new era in government administration. The results have been summed up by historian Ari Hoogenboom: "An unprofessional civil service became more professionalized. Better educated civil servants were recruited and society accorded them a higher place. . . . Local political considerations gave way in civil servants' minds to the national concerns of a federal office. Business influence and ideals replaced those of the politician."

Arthur also took an intelligent and moderate position on the tariff. He urged the appointment of a nonpartisan commission to study existing rates and suggest rational reductions, and after such a commission was created, he urged Congress to adopt its recommendations. He came out for federal regulation of railroads several years before the passage of the Interstate Commerce

Act. "Congress should protect the people . . . against acts of injustice which the State governments are powerless to prevent," he said. He vetoed pork-barrel legislation and pushed for much-needed construction of a modern navy. As an administrator he was systematic, thoughtful, businesslike, and at the same time cheerful and considerate. Just the same, he, too, was a political failure. He made no real attempt to push his program through Congress, instead devoting most of his energies to a futile effort to build up his personal following in the Republican party by distributing favors. But the Stalwarts would not forgive his "desertion," and the reform element could not forget his past. At the 1884 convention the politicos shunted him aside.

The election of 1884 brought the Democrat Grover Cleveland to the White House. Born in New Jersey in 1837, Cleveland grew up in western New York. After studying law, he settled in Buffalo. Although somewhat lacking in the social graces and in intellectual pretensions, he had a basic integrity that everyone recognized; when a group of civic reformers sought a candidate for mayor in 1881, he was a natural choice. His success in Buffalo led to his election as governor of New York in 1882. In the governor's chair his nononsense attitude toward public administration endeared him to civil service reformers at the same time that his basic conservatism pleased businessmen. When he vetoed a popular bill to force a reduction of the fares charged by the New York City elevated railway on the ground that it was an unconstitutional violation of the company's franchise, his stock soared. Here was a man who cared more for principle than the adulation of the multitude, a man of courage, honest, hard-working, and eminently sound. As a result, the Democrats nominated him for President in 1884.

Parodying a popular painting of the day of a beautiful Greek courtesan being unveiled before Athenian statesmen, *Puck's* Bernhard Gillam drew James G. Blaine revealed to Republican leaders in 1884. The "Mulligan letters" receive prominent display among the tattoos, and Blaine's renowned personal magnetism is labeled as a fraud. (Culver Pictures.)

The election revolved around personal issues, for the platforms of the parties were almost identical. The Republican candidate, the dynamic James G. Blaine, had an immense following, but his reputation had been soiled by the publication of the "Mulligan letters," which connected him with the corrupt granting of congressional favors to the Little Rock and Fort Smith Railroad. On the other hand, it came out during the campaign that Cleveland, a bachelor, had fathered an illegitimate child. Instead of debating public issues, the Republicans chanted the ditty

> Ma! Ma! Where's my pa?
> Gone to the White House,
> *Ha! Ha! Ha!*

to which the Democrats countered

> Blaine, Blaine, James G. Blaine,
> The continental liar from the State of Maine,

Blaine lost more heavily in this mudslinging than Cleveland. The latter's quiet courage in saying "Tell the truth" when his past was brought to light contrasted favorably with Blaine's glib but unconvincing denials. A significant group of distinguished eastern Republicans, who were known as "Mugwumps,"* campaigned for the Democrats. However, Blaine was enormously popular and ran a very strong race against a general pro-Democratic trend; Cleveland won the election by fewer than 25,000 votes. The change of a mere 600 ballots in New York would have given that state, and the Presidency, to his opponent.

Cleveland was a sound-money man and a moderate tariff reformer. As a Democrat, he had no stomach for refighting the Civil War in every campaign, yet he did not overly favor the South when in office, thus quieting Republican fears that a Democratic administration would fill Washington with unreconstructed rebels. Civil service reformers overestimated his commitment

*The Mugwumps considered themselves reformers, but on social and economic questions nearly all of them were very conservative. They were sound-money men and advocates of laissez faire. Reform to them consisted almost entirely of doing away with corruption and making the government more efficient.

to their cause, for he believed in rotation in office, being as convinced as Andrew Jackson that anyone of "reasonable intelligence" could handle most government jobs. He would not summarily dismiss Republicans, but he thought that when they had served four years, they "should as a rule give way to good men of our party." He did, however, insist upon honesty and efficiency regardless of party and scrutinized all applications for patronage. As a result, he made few poor appointments.

Probably no President could have handled patronage problems much better, considering the times. The Democrats, having been out of the White House since before the Civil War, clamored for the spoils of victory. The Mugwumps, who had contributed considerably to Cleveland's election, were dead set against politicking with government jobs. Steering a middle course, Cleveland failed to satisfy either group.

Cleveland had little imagination and too narrow a conception of his powers and duties to be a successful President. His appearance perfectly reflected his character: a squat, burly man weighing well over 200 pounds, he could defend a position against heavy odds, but his mind lacked flexibility and he provided little effective leadership. He took a fairly broad view of the powers of the federal government—he supported the Interstate Commerce Act, agricultural research, and even came out for federal arbitration of labor disputes—but he thought it unseemly to put pressure on Congress, believing in "the entire independence of the executive and legislative branches."

As a mayor and governor, Cleveland had been best known for his vetoes. Little wonder that he found being President a burdensome duty. Scarcely a year after his inauguration he was complaining of the "cursed constant grind." Later he grumbled about "the want of rest" and "the terrible nagging" he had to submit to. One of his biographers says that he "approached the presidency as though he were a martyr."

Toward the end of his term, Cleveland bestirred himself and tried to provide constructive leadership on the tariff question. The govern-

Republican cartoonists found a friendly welcome in the weekly *Judge.* In this comment on the Democrats' return to power, ungainly Miss Democracy makes her debut, introduced to society by President Cleveland. (Chicago Historical Society.)

ment was embarrassed by a large surplus revenue, which Cleveland hoped to reduce by cutting the duties on necessities and on the raw materials of manufacturing. He devoted his entire annual message of December 1887 to the tariff, thus focusing public attention on the subject. When worried Democrats reminded him that an election was coming up and that the tariff might cause a rift in the organization, he replied simply: "What is the use of being elected or reelected, unless you stand for something?"

The House of Representatives, dominated by southern Democrats, passed a bill reducing many duties, but the measure, known as the Mills bill, was flagrantly partisan: it slashed the rates on iron products, glass, wool, and other items made in the North, but left those on southern goods almost untouched. The Republican-controlled Senate rejected the Mills bill and the issue was left to be settled by the voters at the 1888 election. However, in a fashion typical of the period, it did not work out this way. The Democrats hedged by nominating a protectionist, 75-year-old Allen G. Thurman, for Vice President and putting another high-tariff man at the head of the Democratic National Committee. Cleveland toned down his attacks on the important protected industries. Other issues also attracted much attention, such as the "Murchison letter," in which Sir Lionel Sackville-West, the British minister at Washington, was tricked into expressing the opinion that the re-election of Cleveland would best advance the interests of Great Britain. This undoubtedly cost the Democrats the votes of many Irish-Americans, who were rabidly anti-British. Corruption was perhaps more flagrant than in any other Presidential election. Cleveland obtained a plurality of the popular vote, but his opponent, Benjamin Harrison, grandson of President William Henry Harrison, carried most of the key northeastern industrial states by narrow margins, thus obtaining a comfortable majority in the Electoral College, 233 to 168.

The new President was a short, rather rotund but erect man with a full, graying beard, narrow blue eyes, and a broad forehead. Intelligent and able, he was too reserved to make a good politician. He did not suffer fools gladly and kept even his most important advisers at arm's length. One observer called him a "human iceberg." Nevertheless, his career, like his ancestry, had been distinguished. After graduating from Miami University in 1852 at the age of 18, he studied law. He settled in Indiana, where for a number of years he was Indiana Supreme Court reporter, editing five volumes of *Reports* with considerable skill. During the Civil War he rose to command a brigade. He fought under Sherman at Atlanta and won a reputation as a stern, effective disciplinarian. In 1876 he ran unsuccessfully for governor of Indiana, but in 1881 he was elected to the Senate.

Harrison believed ardently in the principle of protection, stating firmly if somewhat illogically that he was against "cheaper coats" because cheaper coats seemed "necessarily to involve a cheaper man and woman under the coat." His approach to fiscal policy was conservative, although he was extremely freehanded in the matter of veterans' pensions. He would not use "an apothecary's scale," he said, "to weigh the rewards of men who saved the country." No more

Cartoonist Keppler finds Harrison not measuring up to the Presidential hat of his grandfather, William Henry Harrison. Raven Blaine croaks, "Nevermore."

flamboyant waver of the bloody shirt existed. "I would a thousand times rather march under the bloody shirt, stained with the lifeblood of a Union soldier," he said in 1883, "than to march under the black flag of treason or the white flag of cowardly compromise." Harrison professed to favor civil service reform, but his biographer, Father Harry J. Sievers, admits that he fashioned a "singularly unimpressive" record on the question. He objected to the law forbidding the solicitation of campaign funds from officeholders. He appointed the vigorous young reformer Theodore Roosevelt to the Civil Service Commission but then proceeded to undercut him systematically. Before long the frustrated Roosevelt was calling the President a "cold blooded, narrow minded, prejudiced, obstinate, timid old psalm singing Indianapolis politician."

Under Harrison, Congress distinguished itself by expending, for the first time in a period of peace, more than $1 billion in a single session. It also raised the tariff to an all-time high. The Sherman Antitrust Act was passed and so was a Silver Purchase Act authorizing the government to coin large amounts of that metal, a measure much desired by mining interests and those favoring inflation. A Federal Elections, or "Force" bill, providing for federal control of elections as a means of protecting the right of southern Negroes to vote, a right increasingly under attack, passed the House, only to be filibustered to death in the Senate. Harrison had little to do with the fate of any of these measures. By and large, he failed, as one historian has said, to give the people "magnetic and responsive leadership." The Republicans lost control of Congress in 1890, and two years later Grover Cleveland swept back into power, defeating Harrison by over 350,000 votes.

Congressional Leaders

As for the lesser politicians of the period, the most outstanding figure was unquestionably James G. Blaine of Maine, who served in Congress from 1863 to 1881, first in the House and then in the Senate. Blaine had many of the qualities that mark a great leader: personal dynamism, imagination, political intuition, oratorical ability, and a broad view of the national interest. President Lincoln spotted him when he was a freshman congressman, calling him "one of the brightest men in the House" and "one of the coming men of the country." Blaine was essentially a reasonable man, favoring sound money without opposing inflexibly every suggestion for increasing the volume of the currency, supporting the protective system but advocating reciprocity agree-

ments to increase trade, adopting a moderate and tolerant attitude toward the South. Almost alone among the men of his generation, he was deeply interested in foreign affairs. His personal warmth captivated thousands. He never forgot a name. His handshake—he would grasp a visitor's hand firmly at a reception and often hold it throughout a brief conversation with unaffected, manly friendliness—won him hundreds of adherents. This was perhaps calculated, yet he was capable of impulsive acts of generosity and kindness too.

That Blaine, although perennially an aspirant, never became President was partly a reflection of his very abilities and his active participation in so many controversial affairs over the years. Naturally, he aroused jealousies and made many enemies. But some inexplicable flaw marred his character. He had a streak of recklessness entirely out of keeping with his reasonable position on most issues. He waved the bloody shirt with cynical vigor, heedless of the effect on the nation as a whole. He showered contempt on civil service reformers, characterizing them as "noisy but not numerous . . . ambitious but not wise, pretentious but not powerful." The scandal of the Mulligan letters made a dark blot on his record, but there is also reason to doubt his general honesty, for, as one historian has pointed out, he "became wealthy without visible means of support." Sometimes he seemed almost deliberately to injure himself by needlessly antagonizing powerful colleagues. Blaine moved through history amid cheers and won a host of spectacular if petty triumphs, yet his career was barren, essentially tragic.

Roscoe Conkling's was another remarkable but empty career. Handsome, colorful, companionable, and dignified, Conkling served in Congress almost continually from 1859 to 1881 and was a great power, dominating the complex politics of New York for many years. Such was his prestige that two Presidents offered him a seat on the Supreme Court. Yet no measure of importance was attached to his name. He squandered his energies in acrimonious personal quarrels, caring only for partisan advantage. Although he wanted very much to be President, he had no conception of what a President must be, and in the end, even his own hack followers deserted him.

Dozens of other figures of the period merit brief mention; the following are representative types. Congressman William McKinley of Ohio was perhaps the most personally attractive. He was a man of simple honesty, nobility of character, and quiet warmth—and a politician to the core. The tariff was McKinley's special competence, the principle of protection his guiding star. The peak of his career still lay in the future in the early 1890's. Another Ohioan, John Sherman, brother of the famous Civil War general, accomplished the remarkable feat of holding national office continuously for nearly half a century, from 1855 to 1898. Three times a prominent candidate for the Republican Presidential nomination, he had a deserved reputation for expertness in financial matters. However, he was colorless, stiff—he was called "the Ohio Icicle"—and while personally honest, altogether too willing to compromise his beliefs for political advantage. He admired Andrew Johnson and sympathized with his attitude toward reconstructing the South, yet he voted to convict him at the impeachment trial. Repeatedly he made concessions to the inflationists, despite his personal belief in sound money. Sherman gave his name (and not much else) to the Antitrust Act of 1890 and to other important legislation, but in retrospect left little mark on the history of his country, despite his long service.

Another prominent figure of the age was Thomas B. Reed, Republican congressman from Maine, a witty, widely read man of immense latent energy but ultraconservative and cursed with a sharp tongue that he could never curb. Reed coined the famous definition of a statesman—"a politician who is dead." When one pompous politico said in his presence that he would rather be right than President, Reed advised him not to worry, since he would never be either. In 1890 Reed was elected Speaker of the House and quickly won the nickname "Czar" because of his autocratic way of expediting business. Since the Republicans had only a paper-

thin majority, the Democrats attempted to block action on partisan measures by refusing to answer to their names on quorum calls. Reed coolly ordered the clerk to record them as present and proceeded to carry on the business of the House. His control soon became so absolute that Washington jokesters began to say that representatives dared not even breathe without his permission. Reed had large ambitions and the courage of his convictions, but his vindictiveness kept him from exercising a constructive influence on his times.

One of the most attractive Democratic politicians of the era was Richard P. "Silver Dick" Bland of Missouri, congressman from 1873 until the late nineties. As a young man, Bland had spent ten years as a prospector and miner, and he devoted most of his energies in politics to fighting for the free coinage of silver. Although almost fanatical on this question, he was no mere mouthpiece for special interests, fighting against monopolies and consistently opposing the protective tariff. He lived simply and was immune to the temptations that led so many of his colleagues to use their political influence to line their own pockets. Yet he never emerged as a truly national leader.

More colorful, yet utterly sterile, was the career of Benjamin F. Butler of Massachusetts. Butler was a political chameleon. A states'-rights Democrat before the Civil War, he supported Jefferson Davis for the Democratic Presidential nomination in 1860. During the conflict he served as a Union general, during reconstruction as a Radical Republican congressman. In 1878 he came out for currency inflation and won a seat in Congress as a Greenbacker. In 1882 he was elected governor of Massachusetts, this time as a Democrat! Butler had a sharp wit, a vivid imagination, a real feeling for the interests of industrial workers. He detested all kinds of sham and pretense. But he was also a brutal, corrupt demagogue, almost universally hated by persons of culture and public spirit. Although by no means a typical politician, Butler typified many aspects of the age—its shaky morality, its extremism, its intense interest in meaningless political controversy.

Agricultural Discontent

The vacuity of American politics may well have stemmed from the complacency of the middle-class majority. The country was growing; no foreign enemy threatened it; the poor were mostly recent immigrants, blacks, and others with little influence, easily ignored by those in comfortable circumstances. However, one important group in society was suffering increasingly as the years rolled by—the farmers. Out of their travail came the force that finally, in the 1890's, brought American politics face to face with the real problems of the age.

Long the backbone of American society, the farmer was rapidly being left behind in the race for wealth and status. The number of farmers and the volume of agricultural production continued to rise, but agriculture's relative place in the national economy was declining steadily. Between 1860 and 1890 the number of farms rose from 2 million to 4.5 million, wheat output leaped from 173 million bushels to 449 million, cotton from 5.3 million bales to 8.5 million. The rural population increased from 25 million to 40.8 million. But industry was expanding far faster, and the urban population, quadrupling in the period, was soon destined to overtake and pass that of the countryside. Immediately after the Civil War, wheat sold at nearly $1.50 a bushel, and even in the early 1870's it was still worth well over a dollar. By the mid-nineties the average price stood in the neighborhood of 60 cents. Cotton, the great southern staple, which was selling for over 30 cents a pound in 1866 and 15 cents in the early 1870's, at times in the nineties fell below 6 cents. The tariff on manufactured goods appeared to aggravate the farmers' predicament, and so did the domestic marketing system, which enabled a multitude of middlemen to gobble up a large share of the profits of agriculture. Furthermore, the improvements in transportation that made it practicable for farmers in Australia, Canada, Russia, and Argentina to sell their produce in western European markets increased the competition faced by Americans seeking to dispose of surplus produce abroad.

Along with declining income, farmers suffered a decline in status. Compared to city dwellers, farmers seemed increasingly provincial and behind the times. Rural educational standards did not keep pace, modern concepts like evolution were either ignored or rejected, and religious fundamentalism, cast aside by eastern sophisticates, maintained its hold in the countryside. Soon people in the cities began to refer to farmers as "rubes," "hicks," or "hayseeds" and to view them with amused tolerance or even contempt.

This combination of circumstances angered and frustrated the farmers. Repeated waves of radicalism swept the agricultural regions, giving rise to demands for social and economic experiments that played a major role in breaking down rural laissez-faire prejudices. Much of this reform spirit was both illiberal and illogical. Some farmers talked almost paranoiacally about dark conspiracies organized by bloated tycoons to milk them of their hard-earned dollars. Of course no such conspiracies existed. Others claimed to desire a return to the self-sufficient agriculture of frontier days, when every tiller of the soil was an "independent yeoman," whereas, in fact, nearly all of them eagerly adopted the values of a commercial society.

However, many of the farmers' complaints had a firm basis in reality, and whatever their motives and self-delusions, they advanced many practical proposals that would aid nonagricultural elements as well as themselves. As we have seen, in the 1870's, pressure from the Patrons of Husbandry produced legislation regulating railroads and warehouses. This Granger movement also led to many cooperative experiments in the marketing of farm products and in the purchase of machinery, fertilizers, and other goods.

Actually, farmers did not react to economic developments as a unit. Because of the steady decline of the price level, those in newer settled regions were usually worse off than those in older areas, since they had to borrow money to get started and were therefore burdened with fixed interest charges that became harder to meet with each passing year. In the 1870's farmers in states like Illinois and Iowa suffered most, which accounts for the popularity of the Granger movement in that region. Except as a purely social organization, the Grange had little importance in eastern states where farmers were relatively prosperous. However, by the late eighties farmers in the old Middle West had become better established. When prices dipped sharply and a general depression gripped the country, they were able to weather the bad times nicely, as Allan G. Bogue has shown. Illinois farmers took advantage of the new technology to increase output, shifting from wheat to the production of corn, oats, hogs, and cattle, which did not decline so drastically in price.

On the new agricultural frontier in Kansas, Nebraska, and the Dakotas, farmers were less fortunate. All the hardships of frontier life existed in exaggerated form on the Great Plains—the backbreaking labor, the natural hazards of storm, drought, and insect plagues, and especially the isolation and loneliness, the effects of which were probably heightened by the flat, treeless terrain extending in every direction to the horizon, and by the farmers' awareness that elsewhere in the country citizens were increasingly enjoying comforts and diversions made possible by industrialization. Hamlin Garland, a writer of the naturalist school who grew up in the region, described this side of frontier life in graphic and moving terms in his autobiography, *A Son of the Middle Border* (1890) and in *Main-Travelled Roads* (1891). Conditions were particularly hard for farm women, who in addition to endless heavy chores were forced to endure drab, cheerless surroundings without the companionship of neighbors or the respites and stimulations of social life. After Garland's mother read the grim discussions of women's lot in *Main-Travelled Roads,* she wrote him: "You might have said more, but I'm glad you didn't. Farmers' wives have enough to bear as it is."

However, throughout the middle eighties this region had experienced boom conditions. Adequate rainfall produced bountiful harvests, credit was available, and property values rose rapidly.

In the decade of the 1880's the population of Kansas increased by 43 per cent, that of Nebraska by 134 per cent, of the Dakotas by 278 per cent. Such booms occurred periodically in every frontier district, and like all others, this one collapsed when settlers and investors took a more realistic look at the prospects of the region. However, in this case special circumstances turned the slump into a major catastrophe. The bitter winter of 1886-87 dealt a smashing blow to the open-range cattle industry. Then a succession of dry years shattered the hopes of the farmers. The downward swing of the business cycle in the early 1890's completed the devastation. Settlers who had paid more for their lands than they were worth and borrowed money at high interest rates to do so found themselves squeezed relentlessly. Thousands lost their farms and returned eastward, penniless and dispirited. The population of Nebraska increased by fewer than 4,000 persons in the entire decade of the nineties.

The Populist Movement

This profound agricultural depression triggered a new outburst of farm radicalism, the Alliance movement. The alliances were organizations of farmers' clubs, most of which had sprung up during the bad times of the late seventies. Improved conditions in the early eighties held back the growth of these groups, but after about 1885 they expanded rapidly. In the perennially depressed South the Agricultural Wheel and the Southern Alliance recruited thousands of new members. In the northern regions, the Northwestern Alliance experienced a similar revival. These organizations adopted somewhat differing policies, but all agreed that agricultural prices were too low, that transportation costs were too high, and that something was radically wrong with the nation's financial system. "There are three great crops raised in Nebraska," an angry rural editor proclaimed in 1890. "One is a crop of corn, one is a crop of freight rates, and one a

The western land boom reached a climax on April 22, 1889, when parts of Oklahoma were opened to settlers. Within a few hours nearly 2 million acres were claimed by hordes of "boomers." This photograph by Harman T. Swearingen was taken a few weeks later in the boom town of Guthrie, whose sign painter was working overtime. (Western History Collection, University of Oklahoma Library.)

crop of interest. One is produced by farmers who by sweat and toil farm the land. The other two are produced by men who sit in their offices and behind their bank counters and farm the farmers." All agreed, too, on the need for political action of some kind if the lot of the agriculturalist was to be improved.

Although the state alliances of the Dakotas and Kansas joined the Southern Alliance in 1889, for a time local prejudices and conflicting interests prevented the formation of a single national organization. Northern farmers mostly voted Republican, southerners Democratic, and resentments created during the Civil War lingered in all sections. Cotton-producing southerners opposed the protective tariff, whereas most northerners, fearing the competition of foreign grain producers, favored it. The Southern Alliance was

a secret society, a fact offensive to many in the other groups. Railroad regulation and federal land policy seemed the vital questions to northerners, financial reform loomed most important in southern eyes. Northerners were receptive to the idea of forming a third party, while southerners, wedded to the one-party system, preferred working to capture local Democratic machines.

Although unable to unite, the farm groups entered local politics actively in the 1890 elections. Utterly convinced of the righteousness of their cause, they campaigned with tremendous fervor. The results were most encouraging. In the South, Alliance-sponsored gubernatorial candidates won in Georgia, Tennessee, South Carolina, and Texas; 8 southern legislatures fell under Alliance control; 44 congressmen and 3 senators committed to Alliance objectives were sent to Washing-

Mary Elizabeth Lease, whose signature under this picture includes "Famous spellbinder," was a prominent Populist noted for her rallying cry to "raise less corn and more hell." (Culver Pictures.)

ton. In the West, Alliance men swept the Kansas elections, captured a majority in the Nebraska legislature, and enough seats in Minnesota and South Dakota to hold the balance of power between the major parties.

Such success, coupled with the reluctance of the Republicans and Democrats to make concessions to their demands, encouraged Alliance men to create a new national party. If they could also recruit industrial workers, perhaps a real political revolution could be accomplished. In February 1892 farm leaders, representatives of the Knights of Labor, and various professional reformers, some 800 in all, met at St. Louis, organized the People's, or Populist party, and issued a call for a national convention to meet at Omaha in July.

That convention nominated General James B. Weaver of Iowa for President (with a one-legged Confederate veteran as his running mate) and drafted a platform that called for a graduated income tax and national ownership of railroads and the telegraph and telephone systems. A "subtreasury" plan that would permit farmers to hold nonperishable crops off the market when prices were low was also advocated. Under this proposal the government would make loans to farmers secured by crops held in storage. When prices rose, the farmers could sell their crops and repay the loans. To combat deflation, the platform demanded the unlimited coinage of silver and an increase in the money supply "to no less than $50 per capita." To make the government more responsive to public opinion, it urged the adoption of the initiative and referendum procedures and the election of U. S. senators by popular vote. To win the support of industrial workers the platform denounced the use of Pinkerton detectives in labor disputes and backed the eight-hour day and the restriction of "undesirable" immigration.

The Populists were not, however, revolutionaries. They saw themselves as a victimized majority, not as a persecuted minority. They were at most ambivalent about the free enterprise system, and tended to attribute the social and economic injustices of the times not to built-in inequities in the system but to nefarious conspiracies that had been organized by selfish interests in order to subvert the system.

Nevertheless, the appearance of the new party was by far the most exciting and significant aspect of the Presidential campaign of 1892, which saw Harrison and Cleveland refighting the election of 1888. The Populists put forth a host of colorful spellbinders: Tom Watson, a Georgia congressman, whose temper was such that on one occasion he administered a beating to a local planter with the man's own riding crop; William A. Peffer, senator from Kansas, whose long beard and grave mien gave him the look of a Hebrew prophet; "Sockless Jerry" Simpson of Kansas, unlettered but full of grassroots shrewdness and wit, a former Greenbacker and an admirer of the Single Tax doctrine of Henry George; Ignatius Donnelly, "the Minnesota Sage," who claimed to be an authority on science, Shakespeare—he believed that Francis Bacon wrote the plays—and economics, and who had just published a widely read novel, *Caesar's Column* (1891), which pictured an America of the future wherein a handful of plutocrats tyrannized over masses of downtrodden workers and serfs.

In the one-party South, Populist strategists sought to wean Negro farmers away from the ruling Democratic organization. Their competition forced the "subsidies" paid for black votes up to as much as a dollar—two days' wages. Southern Negro farmers had their own Colored Alliance, and even before 1892 their leaders had worked closely with the white alliances. Nearly 100 black delegates had attended the Populist convention at St. Louis. Of course the Negroes would be useless if they could not vote; therefore white Populist leaders opposed the southern trend toward disfranchising blacks and called for full civil rights for all. In the Northwest the Populists assailed the "bankers' conspiracy" in unbridled terms. Ignatius Donnelly, running for governor of Minnesota, wrote another novel of political prognostication, *The Golden Bottle,* made 150 speeches, talked personally with 10,000 voters, vowing to make the campaign "the liveliest ever seen" in the state.

The results, however, proved disappointing. Tom Watson, for example, lost his seat in Congress, and Donnelly ran a poor third in the Minnesota gubernatorial race. The Populists did manage to sweep Kansas. They also carried numbers of local offices in other western states and cast over a million popular votes for Weaver. But the effort to unite white and Negro farmers in the South failed miserably. Conservative Democrats, while continuing with considerable success to attract black voters, played on racial fears cruelly, insisting that the Populists sought to destroy white supremacy. Since most white Populists saw the alliance with Negroes as at most a marriage of convenience—they did not really believe in racial equality, or propose to do anything for black sharecroppers—this argument had a deadly effect. Elsewhere, even in the old centers of the Granger movement, the party made no

significant impression. Urban workers remained aloof. By standing firmly for conservative financial policies, Cleveland attracted much Republican support and won a solid victory over Harrison in the Electoral College, 277 to 145. Weaver's electoral vote was 22.

Showdown on Silver

One obvious conclusion that the politicians reached after analyzing the 1892 returns was that the money question, especially the controversy over the coinage of silver, was of paramount interest to the voters. Despite the wide-ranging appeal of the Populist platform, most of Weaver's strength came from the silver-mining states. On the other hand, Cleveland's strong stand for gold proved very popular in the Northeast. In truth, the issue of gold versus silver was superficial; the real question was what, if anything, should be done to check the continuing deflationary spiral. Undoubtedly, the declining price level benefited bondholders and others with fixed incomes, and injured debtors. Industrial workers profited from deflation except during periods of depression when unemployment rose, which helps explain why the Populists made little headway among them. Southern farmers, prisoners of the crop-lien system, and farmers in the plains states were hit hard by the downward trend.

By the early 1890's, discussion of federal monetary policy revolved around the coinage of silver. Traditionally, the United States had been on a bimetallic standard. Both gold and silver were coined, the numbers of grains of each in the dollar being periodically adjusted to reflect the commercial value of the two metals. An act of 1792 established a 15:1 ratio—371.25 grains of silver and 24.75 grains of gold were each worth one dollar at the Mint. In 1834 the ratio was changed to 16:1, and in 1853 to 14.8:1, the latter reduction in the value of gold reflecting the new discoveries in California. This ratio slightly undervalued silver. In 1861, for example, the amount of silver bullion in a dollar was worth $1.03 in the open market, so no one brought silver to the Mint for coinage. However, an avalanche of silver from the mines of Nevada and Colorado gradually depressed the price, until, around 1874, it again became profitable for miners to coin their bullion. Alas, when they tried to do so, they discovered that the new Coinage Act of 1873, taking account of the fact that no silver had been presented to the Mint in years, had demonetized the metal.

The silver miners denounced this "Crime of 1873" and inflationists, who desired more money regardless of its base, joined them in demanding a return to bimetallism. Conservatives, then still fighting the battle against greenback paper money, resisted strongly. The result was a series of compromises. In 1878 the Bland-Allison Act authorized the purchase of $2-4 million of silver a month at the market price, but this had little inflationary effect, since the government consistently purchased only the minimum amount. The commercial price of silver continued to fall, until in 1890 its ratio to gold was 20:1. In that year the Sherman Silver Purchase Act required the government to buy 4.5 million *ounces* of silver monthly, but in the face of increasing supplies the price of silver fell still further—the ratio reaching 26:1 in 1893 and 32:1 in 1894.

These compromises satisfied no one. The silver miners grumbled because their bullion brought in only half of what it had in the early seventies. Debtors noted angrily that because of the general decline of prices, the dollars they used to meet their obligations were worth more than twice as much as in 1865. Advocates of the gold standard feared that unlimited coinage would be authorized, "destroying the value of the dollar." When a financial panic brought on by the collapse of the great London banking house of Baring Brothers ushered in a severe industrial depression, the confidence of both silverites and "gold bugs" was further eroded.

President Cleveland believed that the agitation over silver had caused the depression by shaking the confidence of the business community and that all would be well if the country returned to a single gold standard. He summoned a special session of Congress, and by exerting immense political pressure, forced the repeal of the Sherman Silver Purchase Act in October 1893. All that this accomplished was to split the Democratic party, its southern and western wings deserting him almost to a man.

During 1894 and 1895, while the nation floundered in the worst depression it had ever experienced, a series of events further undermined public confidence. In the spring of 1894 an "army" of unemployed led by Jacob S. Coxey, an eccentric Ohio businessman, marched on Washington to demand relief. Coxey wanted the government to undertake a program of federal public works and to authorize local communities to exchange noninterest-bearing bonds with the Treasury for $500 million in paper money, the funds to be used to hire unemployed workers to build roads. The scheme, Coxey claimed, would pump money into the economy, provide work for the jobless, and benefit the whole nation by improving transportation facilities. But when Coxey's little group of demonstrators, perhaps 500 in all, reached the Capitol grounds, he and two other leaders were arrested, their followers dispersed by club-wielding policemen. This callous treatment convinced many Americans that the government had little interest in the suffering of the people, an opinion much strengthened when Cleveland, in July 1894, used federal troops to crush the Pullman strike.

The next year the Supreme Court handed down a series of reactionary decisions. First, in *U. S. v. E. C. Knight Company,* it refused to employ the Sherman Antitrust Act to break up the Sugar Trust. Next, in *Pollock v. Farmers' Loan and Trust Company,* it invalidated a federal income tax law, despite the fact that a similar measure levied during the Civil War had been upheld by the Court in *Springer v. U. S.* (1881). Finally the Court denied a writ of habeas corpus to Eugene V. Debs of the American Railway Union, who had been imprisoned for disobeying a federal injunction during the Pullman strike.

On top of these indications of official conser-

Mutiny aboard the good ship *Democracy,* as seen by W. A. Rogers of *Harper's Weekly,* 1894. Civil Service and tariff reform (along with one of its advocates) are about to get the deep six, the Tammany tiger gorges himself, and, at the stern, Captain Cleveland determinedly vetoes mutineers promoting a silver-purchase bill. (*Harper's Weekly,* April 14, 1894.)

vatism came a desperate financial crisis. Throughout 1894 the Treasury's gold reserve had dwindled fast as alarmed citizens exchanged greenbacks (now convertible into specie) for hard money and foreign investors cashed in large amounts of American securities. The government tried to float new gold-bond issues to bolster the reserve, but since investors mostly purchased the bonds with gold-backed paper money, in effect withdrawing gold from the Treasury and then returning it for the bonds, the reserve continued to melt away. Early in 1895 it touched a low point of $41 million. At this juncture a syndicate of bankers headed by J. P. Morgan turned the tide by underwriting a new $62 million bond issue, guaranteeing that half the bullion would come from Europe. But this caused a great pub-

lic outcry; the spectacle of the nation being saved from bankruptcy by a private banker infuriated millions. Morgan's profit was estimated as high as $16 million—it was actually about $250,000—and the silverites even went so far as to accuse Cleveland of profiting personally from the transaction.

All these events, together with the continuing depression, discredited the Cleveland administration. "I haven't got words to say what I think of that old bag of beef," Governor "Pitchfork Ben" Tillman of South Carolina, who had resolutely resisted the Populists in 1892, told a local audience two years later. "If you send me to the Senate, I promise I won't be bulldozed by him."

Increasingly, the silver issue was coming to dominate politics. As the Presidential election of

1896 approached, with the Populists demanding unlimited coinage of silver at a ratio of 16:1, the major parties found it impossible to continue straddling the money question. The Populist vote had increased by 42 per cent in the 1894 congressional elections. Southern and western Democratic leaders feared that they would lose their entire following unless Cleveland was repudiated. Western Republicans, led by Senator Henry M. Teller of Colorado, were threatening to bolt to the Populists unless their party came out for silver coinage. After a generation of political equivocation, the major parties had to face a real issue squarely.

The Republicans, meeting to choose a candidate at St. Louis in June 1896, announced for the gold standard. "We are unalterably opposed to every measure calculated to debase our currency or impair the credit of our country," the platform declared. "We are therefore opposed to the free coinage of silver. . . . The existing gold standard must be maintained." The party then nominated Ohio's William McKinley for President. McKinley, best known for his staunch advocacy of the protective tariff but also highly regarded by labor, was expected to run strongly in the Middle West and East.

The Democratic convention met in July at Chicago. Although the pro-gold Cleveland element made a hard fight, the silverites swept them aside. The high point came when a youthful Nebraskan named William Jennings Bryan spoke for silver against gold, for western farmers against the industrial East, his every sentence provoking ear-shattering applause.

We have petitioned [he said] and our petitions have been scorned; we have entreated, and our entreaties have been disregarded; we have begged, and they have mocked when our calamity came. We beg no longer; we entreat no more; we petition no more. *We defy them!*

The crowd responded like a great choir to Bryan's every gesture. "Burn down your cities and leave our farms," he said, "and your cities will spring up again as if by magic; but destroy our farms and the grass will grow in the streets of every city in the country." And he ended with a marvelous figure of speech that set the tone for the coming campaign. "You shall not press down upon the brow of labor this crown of thorns," he warned, bringing his hands down suggestively to his temples. "You shall not crucify mankind upon a cross of gold!" Dramatically, he extended his arms to the side, the very figure of the crucified Christ.

The convention promptly adopted a platform calling for "the free and unlimited coinage of both silver and gold at the present legal ratio of 16 to 1" and went on to nominate Bryan, who was barely 36, for President. This action put tremendous pressure on the Populists. By supporting Bryan they risked losing their party identity, but if they nominated another man, they would insure McKinley's election. Some preferred the latter choice, figuring that in the long run their major goals could best be achieved in this way. "The Democratic idea of fusion," Tom Watson complained, is "that we play Jonah while they play whale." But most Populists, trusting in Bryan's liberal sentiments, were ready to follow the Democratic lead. "We must join with [the Democrats] or be destroyed," one of them explained. Their convention nominated the Nebraskan late in July, seeking to preserve the party identity by substituting Watson for the Democratic Vice Presidential nominee, Arthur Sewall of Maine.

Election of 1896

Never did a Presidential campaign raise such intense emotions or produce such drastic political realignments. The Republicans from the silver-mining states swung solidly behind Bryan. The gold Democrats refused to accept the decision of the Chicago convention. Cleveland professed to be "so dazed by the political situation that I am in no condition for speech or thought on the subject," and many others adopted the policy of Governor David B. Hill of New York, who said: "I am a Democrat still—very still." The extreme gold bugs, calling themselves National Democrats, nominated a candidate of their own, 79-year-old Senator John M. Palmer of Illinois. Palmer ran only to injure Bryan. "Fellow Democrats," he announced, "I will not consider it any great fault if you decide to cast your vote for William McKinley."

At the start the Republicans seemed to have everything in their favor. Bryan's youth and his relative lack of political experience—two terms in the House—contrasted unfavorably with McKinley's distinguished war record, his long service in Congress and as governor of Ohio, and his reputation for honesty and good judgment. The severe depression also operated in favor of the party out of power, although by repudiating Cleveland, the Democrats escaped much of the burden of explaining away his errors. Furthermore, the newspapers came out almost unanimously for the Republicans. Important Democratic papers such as the New York *World*, the Boston *Herald*, the Baltimore *Sun*, the Chicago *Chronicle*, and the Richmond *Times* not only supported McKinley editorially, but also slanted their news stories against the Democrats. The New York *Times* even accused Bryan of being insane, his affliction being variously classified as "paranoia querulenta," "graphomania," and "oratorical monomania." The Democrats had almost no money and few well-known speakers to fight the campaign.

Bryan, however, quickly proved himself a formidable opponent. Casting aside tradition, he took to the stump personally, traveling 18,000 miles and making over 600 speeches. Unquestionably, he was one of the very greatest of orators. A big, handsome man with a voice capable of carrying without strain to the far corners of a great hall, yet equally effective before a cluster of auditors at a rural crossroads, he projected an image of absolute sincerity without appearing fanatical or argumentative. At every major stop on his tour, huge crowds assembled. In Minnesota, for example, he packed the 10,000-seat St. Paul Auditorium, while thousands more milled in the streets outside. His energy was amazing, his charm and good humor unfailing. At one whistle stop, while he was shaving in his compartment, a small group outside the train began clamoring for a glimpse of him. Flinging open the window and beaming through the lather, he shook hands cheerfully with each of these admirers. Everywhere he hammered away at the money question, but he did not totally neglect other issues, speaking, he said, for "all the people who suffer from the operations of trusts, syndicates, and combines."

McKinley's campaign was managed by a new type of politician, Marcus Alonzo Hanna, an Ohio businessman. Politics fascinated Hanna, and despite his wealth and wide interests, he was willing to labor endlessly at the routine work of political organization. He aspired to be a king-maker and early fastened upon McKinley, whose honesty and charm he found irresistible, as the vehicle for satisfying his ambition. He spent about $100,000 of his own money on the preconvention campaign. His attitude toward the candidate, one mutual friend observed, was "that of a big, bashful boy toward the girl he loves."

Before most Republicans realized how effective Bryan was on the stump, Hanna perceived the danger and sprang into action. Since the late 1880's the character of political organization had been changing. The Civil Service Act was cutting down on the number of jobs available to reward campaign workers and thus on the sums of money the parties could raise by assessing these workers. At the same time, the new mass-circulation newspapers and the nationwide press associations were increasing the pressure on candidates to speak openly and often on national issues. This trend put a premium on party organization and consistency—the old political trick of speaking out of one side of the mouth to one audience, out the other to another, no longer worked very well. Moreover, as the federal government became more involved in economic issues, business interests found more reason to be concerned about national elections and willing to spend money freely in behalf of candidates whose views they approved. As early as the campaign of 1888 the Republicans had set up a businessmen's "advisory board" to raise money and stir up enthusiasm for Benjamin Harrison.

William Jennings Bryan (center) strides to the speaker's platform at a Democratic rally in California in 1896. Delivering as many as 30 speeches a day, Bryan spoke directly to some 5 million people during the campaign. (Bancroft Library, University of California.)

Hanna clearly understood what was happening to politics. Certain that money was the key to political power, he began amassing an enormous campaign fund. When businessmen hesitated to contribute, he pried open their purses by a combination of persuasiveness and intimidation. Banks and insurance companies were "assessed" a percentage of their assets, big corporations a share of their receipts, until some $3.5 million had been collected. Hanna disbursed these funds with efficiency and imagination. He sent 1,500 speakers into the doubtful districts and blanketed the land with no less than 250 million pieces of campaign literature, printed in a dozen languages. "He has advertised McKinley as if he were a patent medicine," Theodore Roosevelt exclaimed.

Incapable of competing with Bryan as a swayer of mass audiences, McKinley conducted what was known as a "front-porch campaign." This technique also dated from the first Harrison-Cleveland election, when Harrison had regularly delivered off-the-cuff speeches to groups of visitors representing special interests or regions in his home town of Indianapolis. This system conserved the candidate's energies and enabled him to avoid the appearance of seeking the Presidency too openly—which was still considered bad form—and at the same time allowed him to make headlines all over the country. McKinley,

McKinley speaks to the faithful from the front porch of his Canton, Ohio home. He flattered visitors with his full attention, listening to their prepared speeches, said an observer, "like a child looking at Santa Claus." (Ohio Historical Society.)

guided by the masterful Hanna, now brought the front-porch method to perfection. Superficially the proceedings were delightfully informal. From every corner of the land, groups representing various regions, occupations, and interests descended upon McKinley's unpretentious frame house in Canton, Ohio. Gathering on the lawn—the grass was soon reduced to mud, the fence stripped of pickets by souvenir hunters—the visitors paid their compliments to the candidate and heard him deliver a brief speech, while beside him on the porch his aged mother and adoring

invalid wife listened with rapt attention. Then there was a small reception, during which the delegates were given an opportunity to shake their host's hand.

Despite their air of informality, these performances were carefully staged. The delegations arrived on a tightly coordinated schedule worked out by McKinley's staff and the railroads, which operated cut-rate excursion trains to Canton from all over the nation. McKinley was fully briefed on the special interests and attitudes of each group, and the speeches of delegation leaders were submitted in advance. Often his secretary amended these remarks, and upon occasion McKinley even wrote the visitors' speeches himself. Naturally, his own talks were also prepared in advance, each calculated to make a particular point. All were reported fully in the newspapers. Thus, without moving from his doorstep, McKinley met thousands of people from every section.

These tactics worked admirably. On election day McKinley carried the East, the Middle West, including even Iowa, Minnesota, and North Dakota, and the Pacific Coast states of Oregon and California, while Bryan won in the South, the plains states, and the Rocky Mountain region. McKinley collected 271 electoral votes to Bryan's 176, the popular vote being 7,036,000 to 6,468,000.

The sharp sectional division indicated that the industrial part of the country had triumphed over the agricultural; it did not, however, represent a division of the nation along economic or social lines. The business and financial interests, it is true, voted solidly for the Republicans, fearing that a Democratic victory would bring economic chaos. When a Nebraska landowner tried to float a mortgage during the campaign, a loan-company official wrote him: "If McKinley is elected, we think we will be in the market, but we do not care to make any investments while there is an uncertainty as to what kind of money a person will be paid back in." Other groups were far from united, however. Many thousands of farmers voted for McKinley, as his success in states such as North Dakota, Iowa, and Minnesota proved. In the East and in the states bordering the Great Lakes, the agricultural depression was not very severe, and farm radicalism practically nonexistent.

A preponderance of the labor vote also went to the Republicans. In part this resulted from the tremendous pressures that many industrialists applied to their workers. "Men," one manufacturer announced, "vote as you please, but if Bryan is elected . . . the whistle will not blow Wednesday morning." A number of companies placed orders for materials subject to cancellation if the Democrats won. But coercion was not a major factor, for McKinley was highly regarded in labor circles. While governor of Ohio, he had advocated the arbitration of industrial disputes and backed a law fining employers who refused to permit workers to join unions. During the Pullman strike he had sent his brother to try to persuade George Pullman to deal fairly with the strikers. He had invariably based his advocacy of high tariffs on the argument that American wage levels would be depressed if foreign goods could enter the country untaxed. Mark Hanna, too, had the reputation of always giving his employees a square deal. The Republicans ran strongly in all the large cities, and in critical states like Illinois and Ohio this made the difference between victory and defeat.

During the campaign, some frightened Republicans had laid plans for fleeing the country if Bryan were elected, and belligerent ones, such as Theodore Roosevelt, then police commissioner of New York City, readied themselves to meet the "social revolutionaries" on the battlefield. Victory sent such men into transports of joy. Most conservatives concluded happily that the way of life they so fervently admired had been saved for all time.

However heartfelt, such sentiments were not founded upon fact. With workers standing beside capitalists, with the farmers divided, it cannot be said that the election divided the nation class against class or that McKinley's victory saved the country from revolution.

Far from representing a triumph for the status quo, the election marked the coming of age of modern America. The battle between gold and silver, which everyone had considered so vital, had little real significance. The inflationists seemed to have been beaten, but new gold discoveries in Alaska and South Africa and improved methods of extracting gold from low-grade ores soon led to a great expansion of the money supply. In any case, within two decades the whole system of basing the volume of currency on bullion had been abandoned. Bryan and the Populists, supposedly the advance agents of revolution, were oriented more toward the past than the future. Their ideal was the rural Amer-

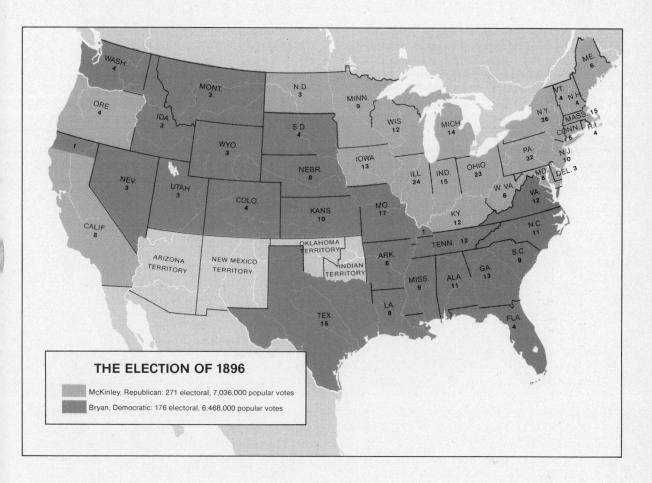

THE ELECTION OF 1896

McKinley, Republican: 271 electoral, 7,036,000 popular votes

Bryan, Democratic: 176 electoral, 6,468,000 popular votes

ica of Jefferson and Jackson. McKinley, on the other hand, for all his innate conservatism was essentially a man of his own times, one even capable of looking ahead toward the new century. His approach was national where Bryan's was basically parochial. While never daring and seldom imaginative, he was capable of dealing pragmatically with current problems. Before long, as America became increasingly an exporter of manufactures, he would even modify his position on the tariff. And no one better reflected the spirit of the age than Mark Hanna, the outstanding political realist of his generation. Far from preventing change, the outcome of the election of 1896 made possible still greater changes as the United States moved into the 20th century.

Supplementary Reading

The political history of this period is covered in lively and controversial fashion by Matthew Josephson, *The Politicos°* (1938), in briefer but equally controversial style by Ray Ginger, *Age of Excess°* (1965), and more solidly and sympathetically in H. W. Morgan, *From Hayes to McKinley* (1969). Both H. U. Faulkner, *Politics, Reform, and Expansion°* (1959), and J. R. Hollingsworth, *The Whirligig of Politics* (1963), treat the politics of the nineties in some detail, while H. S. Merrill, *Bourbon Democracy of the Middle West* (1953), and C. V. Woodward, *Origins of the New South°* (1951), are impor-

°Available in paperback.

tant regional studies. J. A. Garraty, *The New Commonwealth*° (1968), attempts to trace the changing character of the political system after 1877. See also R. D. Marcus, *Grand Old Party: Political Structure in the Gilded Age* (1971).

There are three superb analyses of the political system of the period written by men who studied it firsthand: James Bryce, *The American Commonwealth*° (1888), Woodrow Wilson, *Congressional Government*° (1886), and Moisei Ostrogorski, *Democracy and the Organization of Political Parties*° (1902). L. D. White, *The Republican Era*° (1958), is an excellent study of the government in that period by a modern scholar. D. J. Rothman, *Politics and Power: The United States Senate, 1869-1901* (1966), analyzes the shifting structure of the Upper House. R. J. Jensen, *The Winning of the Midwest* (1971), and Paul Kleppner, *The Cross of Culture: A Social Analysis of Midwestern Politics* (1970), are important studies based on modern computer techniques. Frances Carpenter (ed.), *Carp's Washington* (1960), is a useful collection of the writings of a perceptive Washington reporter of the 1880's.

The issues of postreconstruction politics are discussed in P. H. Buck, *The Road to Reunion*° (1937), S. P. Hirshson, *Farewell to the Bloody Shirt*° (1962), J. W. Oliver, *History of the Civil War Military Pensions* (1917), F. W. Taussig, *The Tariff History of the United States*° (1914), D. R. Dewey, *Financial History of the United States* (1918), A. D. Noyes, *Forty Years of American Finance* (1909), Irwin Unger, *The Greenback Era*° (1964), Milton Friedman and A. J. Schwartz, *A Monetary History of the United States* (1963), W. T. K. Nugent, *Money and American Society* (1968), Geoffrey Blodgett, *The Gentle Reformers: Massachusetts Democracy in the Cleveland Era* (1966), J. G. Sproat, *"The Best Men": Liberal Reformers in the Gilded Age* (1968), Ari Hoogenboom, *Fighting the Spoilsmen*° (1961), and in several essays in H. W. Morgan (ed.), *The Gilded Age*° (1970).

Among biographies of political leaders, the following are especially worth consulting: Harry Barnard, *Rutherford B. Hayes and His America* (1954), R. G. Caldwell, *James A. Garfield* (1931), G. F. Howe, *Chester A. Arthur* (1934), Allan Nevins, *Grover Cleveland* (1932), H. S. Merrill, *Bourbon Leader: Grover Cleveland and the Democratic Party*° (1957), H. J. Sievers, *Benjamin Harrison* (1952-68), D. S. Muzzey, *James G. Blaine* (1934), and D. M. Jordan, *Roscoe Conkling* (1971).

For the farmers' problems, see F. A. Shannon, *The Farmer's Last Frontier*° (1945), S. J. Buck, *The Granger Movement*° (1913), J. D. Hicks, *The Populist Revolt*° (1931), and Theodore Saloutos, *Farmer Movements in the South*° (1960). Populism has been the subject in recent years of intensive re-examination. Richard Hofstadter, *The Age of Reform*° (1955), takes a dim view of Populism as a reform movement, while Norman Pollack, *The Populist Response to Industrial America*° (1962), pictures it as a truly radical one. W. T. K. Nugent, *The Tolerant Populists* (1963), leans in Pollack's direction but is more restrained. Sheldon Hackney's *Populism to Progressivism in Alabama* (1969) is more than a merely local study. C. V. Woodward, *Tom Watson: Agrarian Rebel*° (1938), and Martin Ridge, *Ignatius Donnelly: Portrait of a Politician* (1962), are excellent biographies of Populist leaders. F. E. Haynes, *James Baird Weaver* (1919), is also useful.

On the depression of the 1890's, consult Rendigs Fels, *American Business Cycles* (1959). The political and social disturbances connected with the depression are discussed in G. H. Knoles, *The Presidential Campaign and Election of 1892* (1942), Allan Nevins, *Grover Cleveland*, D. L. McMurry, *Coxey's Army* (1929), Almont Lindsey, *The Pullman Strike*° (1942), Ray Ginger, *The Bending Cross: Eugene V. Debs*° (1949) and *Altgeld's America*° (1958), and F. L. Allen, *The Great Pierpont Morgan*° (1949).

For the election of 1896, see S. L. Jones, *The Presidential Election of 1896* (1964), R. F. Durden, *The Climax of Populism: The Election of 1896*° (1965), and P. W. Glad, *McKinley, Bryan, and the People*° (1964). On Bryan, consult Glad's *The Trumpet Soundeth*° (1960), and P. E. Coletta, *William Jennings Bryan* (1964); on McKinley, consult Margaret Leech, *In the Days of McKinley* (1959), and H. W. Morgan, *William McKinley and His America* (1963). Herbert Croly, *Marcus Alonzo Hanna* (1912), is the best life of Hanna.

22

From Isolation to Empire

Americans have always been somewhat confused and ambivalent in their attitudes toward other nations, but at no point in their history has this been more clearly the case than in the decades following the Civil War. Fully occupied with the task of exploiting the West and building their great industrial machine, they gave little thought to foreign affairs. Benjamin Harrison reflected a widely held belief when he said during the 1888 Presidential campaign that the United States was "an apart nation" and thus it should remain. James Bryce made the same point in *The American Commonwealth*. "Happy America," he wrote, stood "apart in a world of her own . . . safe even from menace."

One recent historian, David W. Pletcher, has called the period "the awkward age" of American diplomacy, a time when the foreign service was "amateurish" and "spoils-ridden," when policy was either nonexistent or poorly planned, when treaties were clumsily drafted and state secrets ill kept. More than ever before or since, foreign affairs were the playthings of politics. "The general idea of the diplomatic service," one reporter commented at this time, "is that it is a soft berth for wealthy young men who enjoy court society." An important New York newspaper, the *Sun,* suggested in the 1880's that the State Department had "outgrown its usefulness" and ought to be abolished.

America's Divided View of the World

Of course late-19th-century Americans never ignored world affairs entirely. They had little direct concern for what went on in Europe, but their interest in Latin America was great and growing, in the Far East only somewhat less so. And economic developments, especially certain shifts in foreign commerce resulting from industrialization, were strengthening this interest with every passing year. Whether one sees isolation or expansion as the hallmark of American foreign policy after 1865 depends upon what part of the world one looks at.

The disdain of the people of the United States for Europe rested upon a number of historical foundations. Faith in the unique character of American civilization and the converse of that belief—suspicion of Europe's supposedly aristocratic and decadent society—formed the basis of this isolation. Bitter memories of indignities suffered during the Revolution and the Napoleonic Wars and anger at the hostile attitude of the great powers toward the United States during the Civil War strengthened it, as did the dislike

of Americans for the traditional pomp and punctilio of European diplomacy. More important still was the undeniable truth that the United States was both practically invulnerable to European attack and incapable of mounting an offensive against any European power. In turning their backs on Europe, Americans were taking no risks and passing up few opportunities—hence their indifference.

When occasional conflicts with one or another of the great powers erupted, the United States pressed its claims hard. It insisted, for example, that Great Britain should pay for the loss of some 100,000 tons of American shipping sunk by Confederate cruisers that had been built in British yards during the rebellion, and some politicians even demanded that the British pay for the entire cost of the war after the Battle of Gettysburg—some $2 billion—on the ground that without British backing the Confederacy would have collapsed at about that point. However, the controversy never became critical, and in 1871 the two nations signed the Treaty of Washington, agreeing to arbitrate these so-called *Alabama* claims. The next year the judges awarded the United States $15.5 million for the ships and cargoes that had been destroyed.

In the 1880's a squabble developed with Germany, France, and a number of other countries over their banning of American pork products, ostensibly because some uninspected American pork was discovered to be diseased. This affair produced a great deal of windy oratory denouncing European autocracy and led to threats of economic retaliation. But Congress eventually provided for the inspection of meat destined for export, and in 1891 the European nations lifted the ban. Similarly, there were repeated alarms and outbursts of anti-British feeling in the United States in connection with Great Britain's treatment of Ireland, all, however, motivated chiefly by the efforts of politicians to appeal to Irish-American voters. None of these incidents amounted to very much.

On the other hand, the nation's interest in other parts of the world gradually increased after 1865. During the Civil War France had established a protectorate over Mexico, setting up the Archduke Maximilian of Austria as emperor. In 1866 Secretary of State William H. Seward demanded that the French withdraw, and the government moved 50,000 soldiers to the Rio Grande. Although fear of American intervention was only one of many reasons for their action, the French did pull their troops out of Mexico during the winter of 1866–67. Nationalist rebels promptly seized and executed Maximilian. In 1867, at the instigation of Seward, the United States purchased Alaska from Russia for $7.2 million, thus ridding the continent of another foreign power.

The aggressive Seward also acquired the Midway Islands in the western Pacific in 1867, and he made overtures toward annexing the Hawaiian Islands and looked longingly at Cuba. But at this date the nation was unready for such grandiose schemes; Seward soon had to admit that there was no significant support in the country for his expansionist plans.

The issue came to a head in 1870, when President Grant submitted a treaty to the Senate annexing the Dominican Republic. He applied tremendous pressure in an effort to obtain ratification, thus forcing a "great debate" on extracontinental expansion. He stressed the wealth and resources of the country, the markets it would provide, even its "salubrious climate." But the arguments of the opposition proved more persuasive. The distance of the Dominican Republic from the continent, its crowded, dark-skinned population of what one congressman called "semi-civilized, semi-barbarous men who cannot speak our language," made annexation appear unattractive. The treaty was rejected. Prevailing opinion was well summarized by a Philadelphia newspaper: "The true interests of the American people will be better served . . . by a thorough and complete development of the immense resources of our existing territory than by any rash attempts to increase it."

However, the very internal growth that distracted Americans from foreign ventures eventually led them to look outward again. By the late 1880's the country was producing enormous amounts of agricultural and industrial goods and exporting a steadily increasing share of this production. Exports rose in value from $450 million in 1870 to $853 million in 1880 and passed the billion-dollar mark early in the 1890's. Imports increased at an only slightly less spectacular rate.

The character of foreign trade was also changing: manufactures loomed ever more important among exports, until in 1898 the country shipped abroad more manufactured goods than it imported. By this time American steelmakers could compete with British producers for business anywhere in the world. In 1900 one company received a large order for steel plates from a Glasgow shipbuilder, and an American firm won contracts for structural steel used in constructing bridges for the Uganda Railroad in British East Africa. When a member of Parliament questioned the colonial secretary about the latter deal, the secretary replied: "Tenders [bids] were invited in the United Kingdom . . . [but] one of the American tenders was found to be considerably the lowest in every respect and was therefore accepted." As American industrialists became conscious of their ability to compete with Europeans in far-off markets, they began to take a new interest in world affairs, especially in periods of depression, when domestic consumption fell off.

The shifting intellectual currents of the times further altered the attitudes of Americans toward foreign affairs. Darwin's theories, applicable by analogy to international relations, gave the concept of manifest destiny a new plausibility. Darwinists like the historian John Fiske argued that the American democratic system of government was clearly the world's "fittest" and must spread inevitably over "every land on the earth's surface." In *Our Country,* Josiah Strong found racist and religious justifications for American expansionism, also based upon the theory of evolution. The Anglo-Saxon race, centered now in the United States, possessed "an instinct or genius for colonization," Strong claimed. "God, with infinite wisdom and skill is training the Anglo-Saxon race for . . . *the final competition of races.*" Christianity, he added, had developed "aggres-

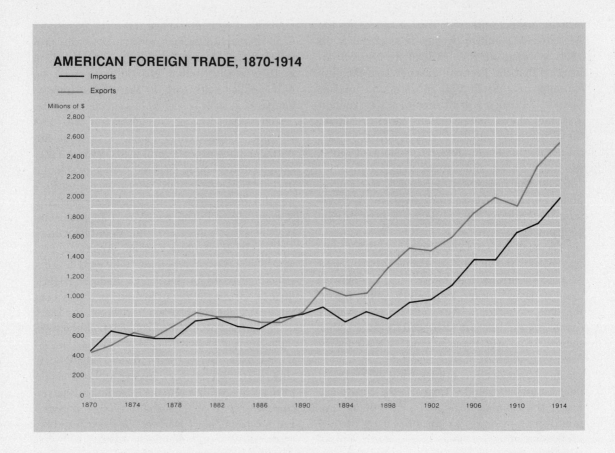

sive traits calculated to impress its institutions upon mankind." Soon American civilization would "move down upon" Mexico and all Latin America, and "out upon the islands of the sea, over upon Africa and beyond." "Can anyone doubt," Strong asked, "that the result of this . . . will be 'the survival of the fittest'?"

The completion of the conquest of the American West also encouraged Americans to consider expansion beyond the seas as a means of preserving the vitality of the nation. "For nearly 300 years the dominant fact in American life has been expansion," declared Frederick Jackson Turner, propounder of the frontier thesis. "That these energies of expansion will no longer operate would be a rash prediction." Turner and writers who advanced other expansionist arguments were much influenced by foreign thinking. European liberals had tended to disapprove of

colonial ventures, but in the 1870's and 1880's many of them were modifying their positions. English liberals in particular began to talk and write about the "superiority" of English culture, to describe the virtues of the "Anglo-Saxon race" in Darwinist terms, to stress a "duty" to spread Christianity among the heathen, and to advance various economic arguments for overseas expansion.

European ideas were reinforced for Americans by their observations of the imperialist activities of the European powers in what would today be called underdeveloped areas. By swallowing up most of Africa and systematically destroying the independence of the crumbling empire of China, the French, British, Germans, and other colonizers inspired some patriots in the United States to advocate joining the feast before all the choice morsels had been digested. "While the great powers of Europe are steadily enlarging their colonial domination in Asia and Africa," said James G. Blaine in 1884, "it is the especial province of this country to improve and expand its trade with the nations of America." While Blaine emphasized commerce, the excitement and adventure of overseas enterprises appealed to many perhaps more than their economic possibilities or any sense of obligation to fulfill a supposed national or racial destiny.

Finally, military and strategic arguments were advanced to justify adopting a "large" policy. The powerful Union army had been demobilized rapidly after Appomattox; in the 1880's only about 25,000 men were under arms, their chief occupation fighting Indians in the West. Half the navy had been scrapped after the war, and the remaining ships had soon become obsolete. While other nations were building steam-powered iron warships, the United States depended upon a handful of wooden sailing vessels. As early as 1867 a British naval publication accurately described the American fleet as "hapless, brokendown, tattered [and] forlorn."

Although no foreign power menaced the country, the decrepit state of the navy vexed many of its officers, and led one of them, Captain Alfred Thayer Mahan, to develop a startling theory about the importance of sea power, which he explained to the public in two important books, *The Influence of Sea Power upon History* (1890) and *The Influence of Sea Power upon the French Revolution and Empire* (1892). History proved, according to Mahan, that a nation with a powerful navy and the overseas bases necessary to maintain it would be invulnerable in war and prosperous in time of peace. Applied to the current American situation, Mahan explained in a series of magazine articles, this meant that in addition to building a modern fleet, the United States should obtain a string of coaling stations and bases in the Caribbean, annex the Hawaiian Islands, and cut a canal across Central America. Eventually, a more extensive colonial empire might follow, but these defensive bases and the canal they would protect were essential first steps to insure America's future as a great power.

Writing at a time when the imperialist-minded European nations were showing signs of extending their influence in South America and the Pacific islands, Mahan attracted many influential disciples. One of these was Congressman Henry Cabot Lodge of Massachusetts, a prominent member of the Naval Affairs Committee. Lodge had married into a navy family and was intimate with the head of the new Naval War College, Commodore Stephen B. Luce, whose son had married his wife's sister. Lodge soon became a good friend of Mahan. He helped push an act through Congress in 1883 authorizing the building of three steel warships and consistently advocated expanding and modernizing the fleet. Elevated to the Senate in 1893, he continually pressed for expansionist policies, basing his arguments on the strategic concepts of Mahan. "Sea power," he proclaimed, "is essential to the greatness of every splendid people." Another important follower of Mahan was Benjamin F. Tracy, Harrison's secretary of the navy, who greatly improved the administration of his department and helped persuade Congress to increase naval appropriations. Lodge's close friend Theodore Roosevelt was still another ardent supporter of the "large" policy, but he had little influence until he became assistant secretary of the navy in 1897.

The Course of Empire

The interest of the United States in the Pacific and the Far East dated back to the late 18th century, when the first American merchant ship dropped anchor in Canton harbor. After the Treaty of Wanghia (1844), American merchants in China enjoyed many privileges and trade expanded rapidly. Missionaries began to flock into the country in increasing numbers too—in the late eighties, over 500 were established there.

The Hawaiian Islands were an important way station on the route to China, and by 1820 merchants and missionaries were making contacts there. As early as 1854 a movement to annex the

This double-spread engraving from *Harper's Weekly,* portraying major units of the United States fleet, appeared in January 1892, at the height of the Chilean "crisis." The cruiser *Baltimore,* whose seamen were attacked by a mob in Valparaiso, triggering the incident, is at right center (number 12). The *Baltimore* later fought under Admiral Dewey in the Battle of Manila Bay in 1898. At center foreground is the ill-fated battleship *Maine.* (*Harper's Weekly,* January 30, 1892.)

islands existed, although this foundered because of Hawaii's insistence on being admitted to the Union as a state. Commodore Perry's expedition to Japan led to the signing of a commercial treaty (1858), which opened several Japanese ports to American traders. In general the United States pursued a policy of cooperating with the European powers in expanding commercial opportunities in the Far East. In Hawaii the tendency was to claim a special position for America but to accept the fact that the Europeans also had interests in the islands.

This state of affairs did not change radically after the Civil War. Despite Chinese protests over the exclusion of their nationals from the United States after 1882, American commercial privileges in China were not disturbed. American influence in Hawaii increased, the descendants of missionary families, most of them engaged in raising sugar, dominating the native monarchy. In 1875 a reciprocity treaty admitted Hawaiian sugar to the United States free of duty in return for a promise not to yield any territory to a foreign power. When this treaty was renewed in 1887, the United States obtained the right to establish a naval base at Pearl Harbor. In addition to occupying Midway, America also obtained a foothold in the Samoan Islands in the South Pacific.

During the 1890's American interest in the Pacific area steadily intensified. Conditions in

Hawaii had much to do with this. The McKinley Tariff Act of 1890, discontinuing the duty on raw sugar and compensating American producers of cane and beet sugar by granting them a bounty of two cents a pound, struck Hawaiian sugar growers hard, for it destroyed the advantage they had gained in the reciprocity treaty. The next year the death of the complaisant King Kalakaua brought Queen Liliuokalani, a determined nationalist, to the throne. Placing herself at the head of a "Hawaii for the Hawaiians" movement, she abolished the existing constitution under which the white minority had pretty much controlled the islands and attempted to rule as an absolute monarch. The local Americans then decided to stage a coup. In January 1893, with the connivance of the United States minister, John L. Stevens, who ordered 150 marines from the cruiser *Boston* into Honolulu, they deposed Queen Liliuokalani and set up a provisional government. Stevens recognized their regime at once, and the new government promptly sent a delegation to Washington to seek a treaty of annexation.

In the closing days of the Harrison administration, such a treaty was negotiated and sent to the Senate, but when Cleveland took office in March, he withdrew it. The new President disapproved of the way American troops had been used to overthrow the native government. He sent a special commissioner, James H. Blount, to Hawaii to investigate. When Blount reported that the Hawaiians opposed annexation, the President dismissed Stevens and attempted to restore Queen Liliuokalani. Since the provisional government was by that time firmly entrenched, this could not be accomplished peacefully, and Cleveland was unwilling to use force against the Americans in the islands, however much he objected to their actions. Thus he found himself unable to do anything at all. The revolutionary government of Hawaii remained in power, independent but still eager to be annexed.

The Hawaiian debate continued sporadically over the next four years, providing a thorough airing of the question of overseas expansion. Fears that another power—Great Britain or perhaps Japan—might step into the void created by Cleveland's refusal to act greatly alarmed those who favored annexation. When the Republicans came back to power in 1897, a new annexation treaty was negotiated, but domestic sugar producers now threw their weight against it, and the McKinley administration could not obtain the necessary two-thirds majority in the Senate. Finally, in July 1898, after the outbreak of the Spanish-American War, Congress annexed the islands by joint resolution, a procedure requiring only a simple majority vote.

Most of the arguments for extending American influence in the Pacific applied even more strongly to Central and South America, where the United States had much larger economic interests and where the strategic importance of the region was clearly defined. Furthermore, the Monroe Doctrine had long conditioned the American people to the idea of acting to protect national interests in the Western Hemisphere.

As early as 1869 President Grant had come out for an American-owned canal across the Isthmus of Panama, in spite of the fact that the United States had agreed in the Clayton-Bulwer Treaty with Great Britain (1850) that neither nation would "obtain or maintain for itself any exclusive control" over an interoceanic canal. In 1880, when the French engineer Ferdinand de Lesseps organized a company to build a canal across the isthmus, President Hayes announced that the United States would not permit any European power to control such a waterway. "The policy of the country is a canal under American control," he announced, another blithe disregard of the Clayton-Bulwer agreement.

In 1888 Congress authorized the convening of a Pan-American Conference in Washington to discuss hemispheric problems. Secretary of State James G. Blaine, who had planned such a conference as early as 1881, hoped to use this meeting to obtain a general reciprocity agreement with the Latin-American countries, for the United States was importing about three times as much from them as they were purchasing in America. Blaine even persuaded the influential protectionist congressman William McKinley to advocate placing hides on the free list in order to get the South Americans to make similar concessions. When they gathered in Washington in 1889, however, the delegates accomplished nothing beyond the establishment of an International Bureau—later known as the Pan-American Union—to promote commercial and cultural exchange. The conference was nevertheless significant, for it marked the first effort by the United States to assume the leadership of the nations of the hemisphere.

At the Washington meeting the United States posed as a friend of peace; Blaine's proposals included a general arbitration treaty to settle hemispheric disputes. However, a minor disagreement with the Republic of Chile in 1891 soon demonstrated that the country could quickly be brought to the verge of war with one of its southern neighbors. Anti-*Yanqui* feeling was high at that time in Chile, chiefly because the United States had refused to sell arms to the current government during the revolution that had brought it to power. In October a group of sailors from the U.S.S. *Baltimore* on shore leave in Valparaiso were set upon by a mob. Two of the sailors were killed and more than a dozen others injured. President Harrison, furious at what he called an "insult . . . to the uniform of the United States sailors," demanded "prompt and full reparation." When the Chilean authorities delayed in supplying an appropriate apology and went so far as to issue a statement that "imputed untruth and insincerity" on Harrison's part, the President sent a special message to Congress virtually inviting it to declare war. Faced with this threat, Chile backed down, offering the required apology and agreeing to pay damages to the sailors. Of course Chile's humiliation destroyed much of the goodwill engendered by the Pan-American Conference.

When Cleveland returned to power in 1893, the possibility of trouble in Latin America seemed remote, for he had always opposed imperialistic ventures. The Latin-American diplomatic colony in Washington greeted him with real warmth after its experience with Harrison. Yet scarcely two years later the United States was again on the verge of war in South America as a result of a crisis in Venezuela, and before this issue was settled Cleveland had proclaimed the most powerful statement of American hegemony in the hemisphere ever uttered.

The tangled borderland between Venezuela and British Guiana had long been in dispute, with Venezuela demanding more of the region than it was entitled to and Great Britain also submitting exaggerated claims and imperiously refusing to submit the question to arbitration. What now made a crisis of this controversy was chiefly the political situation in the United States. A recent minor incident in Nicaragua, where the British had temporarily occupied the port of Corinto to force compensation for injuries done British subjects in that country, had alarmed American supporters of the Monroe Doctrine. Cleveland had wisely avoided involvement, but along with his refusal to take Hawaii, the incident had angered expansionists. With his party rapidly deserting him because of his stand on the silver question, and with the election of 1896 approaching, the President desperately needed a popular issue.

There was much latent anti-British feeling in the United States. A disagreement over fishing rights off Canada in 1885 had caused a nasty flurry. A clash over seal-hunting in the Bering Sea, during which American revenue cutters had seized Canadian vessels beyond the three-mile limit, had exacerbated Anglo-American relations between 1886 and 1892 and cost the United States nearly $500,000 in damages when it was finally arbitrated. By taking the Venezuelan side in the boundary dispute, Cleveland would be defending a weak neighbor against a great power, a position sure to evoke a popular response. "Turn this Venezuela question up or down, North, South, East or West, and it is a 'winner,'" one Democrat advised the President.

Convinced that Venezuela's cause was just, Cleveland could not resist the temptation to intervene. In July 1895 he ordered his secretary of state, Richard Olney, to send a near-ultimatum to the British. By occupying the disputed territory, Olney insisted, Great Britain was invading Venezuela and thus violating the Monroe Doctrine. Quite gratuitously, he went on to boast: "To-day the United States is practically sovereign on this continent, and its fiat is law upon the subjects to which it confines its interposition." Unless Great Britain responded promptly by agreeing to arbitration, the President would call the question to the attention of Congress.

The note threatened war, but the British ignored it for months. They did not take the United States seriously as a world power, and with much reason, since the American navy, although now expanding, could not hope to stand up against the British, which had no less than 50 battleships and 25 armored cruisers, together with many smaller vessels. When Lord Salisbury, the prime minister and foreign secretary, finally replied, he rejected outright the argument that the Monroe Doctrine had any status under international law and refused to arbitrate what he called the "exaggerated pretentions" of the Venezuelans.

If Olney's note had been belligerent, this reply was supercilious and sharp to the point of asperity. Cleveland was furious. On December 17, 1895, he asked Congress for authority to appoint an American commission to determine the correct line between British Guiana and Venezuela. When that had been done, he added, the United States should "resist by every means in its power" the appropriation by Great Britain of any territory "we have determined of right belongs to Venezuela." Congress responded at once, and unanimously, appropriating $100,000 for the boundary commission. Popular enthusiasm was almost equally universal. In Great Britain, on the other hand, government and people suddenly awoke to the seriousness of the situation. No one wanted a war with the United States, certainly not over a remote patch of tropical real estate. Britain's position in Europe was being threatened by a rising Germany; trouble was developing in British South Africa; the Royal Navy was mighty but widely scattered; Canada would be terribly vulnerable in the event of war. Most important of all, the British faced up at last to the immense *potential* strength of the United States. Could

they afford to make an enemy of a nation of 70 million, already the richest industrial power in the world? Obviously they could not. To fight with America, the British colonial secretary said, "would be an absurdity as well as a crime."

And so Great Britain backed down and agreed to arbitrate the boundary. At once the war scare subsided; soon Olney was talking about "our inborn and instinctive English sympathies" and offering "to stand side by side and shoulder to shoulder with England in . . . the defence of human rights." When the boundary tribunal awarded nearly all the disputed region to Great Britain, whatever ill-feeling the surrender may have occasioned in that country faded away. Instead of leading to war, the affair marked the beginning of an era of Anglo-American friendship. It had the unfortunate effect, however, of adding to the long-held American conviction that the nation could get what it wanted in international affairs by threats and bluster—a dangerous illusion.

Cuba and the War with Spain

On February 10, 1896, scarcely a week after Venezuela and Great Britain had signed the arbitration treaty ending their dispute, Spanish General Valeriano Weyler arrived in Havana from Madrid to take up his duties as governor of Cuba. His assignment to this post was occasioned by the guerrilla warfare that Cuban nationalist rebels had been waging on the island for almost a year. Weyler, a tough and ruthless man, set out to administer Cuba with "a salutary rigor." He began herding the rural population into "reconcentration" camps in order to deprive the rebels of food and recruits. Conditions in these camps were wretched. Resistance in Cuba hardened and the conflict, already bitter, became a cruel, bloody struggle that could not help affecting the American people.

The United States had been interested in Cuba since the time of John Quincy Adams, and except for northern opposition to adding more slave territory might well have taken the island at one time or another before the Civil War. When the Cubans revolted against Spain in 1868, considerable support for intervening on their behalf developed, although the firmness of Hamilton Fish, Grant's secretary of state, held this sentiment in check. Spain managed to pacify the rebels in 1878 by promising reforms, but these were slow in coming—slavery was not abolished until 1886. The worldwide depression of the 1890's hit the Cuban economy hard, and when an American tariff act in 1894 jacked up the rate on Cuban sugar by 40 per cent, the resulting distress precipitated another revolt.

The new uprising caused immediate concern in the United States. Public sympathy went out to the Cubans, who seemed to be fighting for liberty and democracy against an autocratic Old World power, and this sympathy was played upon cleverly by a junta of Cuban propagandists resident in the United States. Most American newspapers supported the Cubans; labor unions, veterans' organizations, many Protestant clergymen, and important politicians in both major parties demanded that the United States aid the rebel cause. Furthermore, rapidly increasing American investments in Cuban sugar plantations, now approaching $50 million, were endangered by the fighting and the social chaos sweeping across the island. When reports, often exaggerated, of the cruelty of "Butcher" Weyler and the horrors of his reconcentration camps began to filter into America, the cry for action intensified. In April 1896 Congress adopted a resolution suggesting that the revolutionaries be granted the rights of belligerents. Cleveland would not take this unneutral step, but he did exert diplomatic pressure on Spain to remove the causes of the rebels' complaints, and in addition he offered the services of his government as mediator. The Spanish rejected this suggestion.

For a time, however, the issue subsided. The election of 1896 deflected American attention from Cuba, and then McKinley, recoiling from the thought of war, refused to take any action that might disturb Spanish–American relations.

Business interests—except those with holdings in Cuba—backed McKinley, for they feared that a crisis would upset the economy, which was just beginning to pick up after the long depression. In Cuba General Weyler made some progress toward stifling rebel resistance. American expansionists continued to demand intervention, and the press, especially Joseph Pulitzer's New York *World* and William Randolph Hearst's New York *Journal,* competing fiercely to increase circulation, kept resentments alive with tales of Spanish atrocities. But McKinley remained adamant. Although he warned Spain that Cuba must be pacified, and soon, his tone was friendly and he issued no ultimatum. A change in government in Spain in the fall of 1897 further relieved the situation, for the new regime recalled Weyler and promised partial self-government to the Cubans. In a message to Congress in December 1897, McKinley urged that Spain be given "a reasonable chance to realize her expectations" in the island. McKinley was not insensible to Cuba's plight—although far from being a rich man, he made an anonymous contribution of $5,000 to the Red Cross Cuban relief fund—but he genuinely desired to avoid intervention.

His hopes were doomed, primarily because Spain failed to "realize her expectations." The war continued. Riots broke out in Havana in January 1898. To protect American citizens, McKinley ordered the battleship *Maine* to Havana harbor. Then, early in February, Hearst's New York *Journal* printed a letter written to a friend in Cuba by the Spanish minister in Washington, Depuy de Lôme. The letter had been stolen by a spy. De Lôme, an experienced but arrogant and reactionary diplomat, failed to appreciate McKinley's efforts to avoid intervening in Cuba. In this letter he characterized the President as a *politicastro,* or "would-be politician," which was a gross error, and a "bidder for the admiration of the crowd," which was equally insulting, although somewhat closer to the truth. Americans were outraged, and De Lôme's hasty resignation did little to soothe their feelings.

Before the furor over this incident could subside, the *Maine* was blown up in Havana harbor,

This cartoon appeared in *The Bee* after Dewey's Manila Bay victory, but before the destruction of Spain's Caribbean squadron (the *New York* was one of the vessels blockading Santiago); thus its label, a "prophescopic-scoopograph," is appropriate if improbable. The rowboat is a swipe at editor Hearst's reporting from Cuba. (*The Bee*, May 16, 1898.)

260 of her crew perishing in the explosion. Interventionists in the United States immediately accused Spain of having destroyed the ship and clamored for war. The willingness of Americans to blame Spain indicates the extent of anti-Spanish opinion in the United States by 1898; actually, no one has ever discovered what really happened. A naval court of inquiry decided that the vessel had indeed been sunk by a submarine mine, but it was absurd to think that the Spanish government would have been foolish enough to commit an act so likely to bring American troops into Cuba. Probably some fanatical rebel group was responsible.

With admirable courage, McKinley refused to panic, but he could not resist the wishes of millions of citizens that something be done to stop the carnage and allow the Cubans to determine their own fate. In the last analysis, Spanish pride and Cuban intransigence had taken the issue of peace or war out of his hands. The Spanish government could not suppress the rebellion, but it would not yield to the nationalists' increasingly extreme demands. To have granted independence to Cuba might have caused the Madrid government to fall, might even have led to the collapse of the monarchy, because the Spanish public was in no mood for abject surrender. The Cubans, sensing that the continuing bloodshed aided their cause, refused to give the Spanish regime any room to maneuver. After the *Maine* disaster, Spain might have agreed to an armistice if the rebels had asked for one and in the result-ing negotiations might well have given up the island. The rebels refused to make the first move. The fighting went on, bringing the United States every day closer to intervention.

The President faced a fearful dilemma. Most of the business interests of the country, to which he was particularly sensitive, still opposed intervention. His personal feelings were equally firm. "I have been through one war," he told a friend. "I have seen the dead piled up, and I do not want to see another." Congress however, seemed determined to act. When he submitted a restrained report on the sinking of the *Maine,* congressional hotheads exploded with wrath. The Democrats, even most of those who had supported Cleveland's policies, now gleefully accused McKinley of timidity. Vice President Hobart warned him that the Senate could not be held in check for long; should Congress decide to declare war on its own, the administration would be discredited. McKinley spent a succes-

sion of sleepless nights; even sedatives brought him no repose. Finally, early in April, the President drafted a message asking for authority to use the armed forces "to secure a full and final termination of hostilities" in Cuba.

At the last moment, however, the Spanish government seemed to yield; it ordered its troops in Cuba to cease hostilities. McKinley passed this information on to Congress along with his war message, but he gave it no emphasis and did not try to check the march toward war. It would have been more courageous to seek further delay at this point but not necessarily wiser. Merely to stop fighting was not enough. The Cuban nationalists now insisted upon full independence, and the Spanish politicians were still unprepared to abandon the last remnant of their once-great American empire. If the United States took Cuba, they might save their political skins; if they surrendered the island, they were done for.

On April 20 Congress, by joint resolution, recognized the independence of Cuba and au-

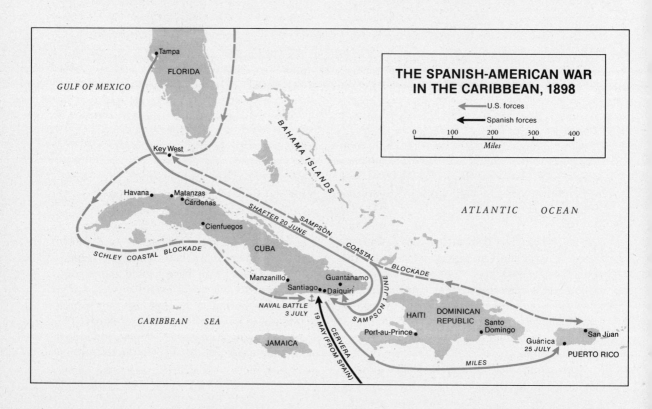

THE SPANISH-AMERICAN WAR IN THE CARIBBEAN, 1898

U.S. forces
Spanish forces

0   100   200   300   400
Miles

thorized the use of the armed forces to drive out the Spanish. An amendment proposed by Senator Henry M. Teller disclaiming any intention of adding Cuban territory to the United States passed without opposition. Four days later Spain declared war on the United States.

The Spanish–American War was fought to free Cuba, but the first action took place on the other side of the globe, in the Philippine Islands. Weeks earlier, Theodore Roosevelt, whom McKinley had appointed assistant secretary of the navy, had alerted the United States Asiatic Squadron under Commodore George Dewey to move against the Spanish base at Manila if war came. Dewey had reacted promptly and efficiently, drilling his gun crews, taking on supplies, giving his gleaming white ships a coat of battle-gray paint, and establishing secret contacts with Filipino nationalist forces under Emilio Aguinaldo. When word of the declaration of war

reached him, he steamed from Hong Kong across the South China Sea with four cruisers and two gunboats. On the night of April 30 he entered Manila Bay, and at daybreak opened fire on the Spanish fleet at 5,000 yards. His squadron made five passes, each time slightly reducing the range, and when the smoke had cleared, all ten of Admiral Montojo's ships had been destroyed. Not a single American was killed in the engagement.

The American people received the news of Dewey's victory joyfully, although many had never heard of the Philippines before the bold headlines announced his triumph. The commodore asked for troops to take and hold Manila, for now that war had been declared, he could not return to Hong Kong or put in at any neutral port. McKinley promptly dispatched some 11,000 soldiers and additional naval support. On August 13 these forces, assisted by Filipino irregulars under Aguinaldo, captured Manila.

Spanish admiral Cervera evaded the American naval blockade to reach Santiago (map at left). At the right is the grim aftermath of the storming of San Juan Hill, recorded by William Glackens, a painter later famous as a pioneer of American realism. (Wadsworth Atheneum, Hartford.)

Meanwhile, in the main theater of operations, the United States had won a quick and complete victory, more, however, because of the feebleness of the Spanish than because of the power or efficiency of the Americans. When the war began, the regular army consisted of about 28,000 men. This tiny force was bolstered by 200,000 ill-trained and poorly supplied volunteers. In May an expeditionary force began to gather at Tampa, Florida. That semitropical hamlet was soon inundated by the masses of men and supplies that descended upon it. Whole regiments sat without uniforms or weapons while hundreds of freight cars lay forgotten on sidings, jammed with equipment. Army staff work was abominable, rivalry between commanders a serious problem. Aggressive units like the regiment of "Rough Riders" that Theodore Roosevelt, now a lieutenant colonel of volunteers, had raised, scrambled for space and supplies, shouldering aside other units to get what they needed. "No words could describe . . . the confusion and lack of system and the general mismanagement of affairs here," the angry Roosevelt complained.

Since a Spanish fleet under Admiral Pascual Cervera was known to be in Caribbean waters, no invading army could safely embark until it could be located. Finally, on May 29, the American fleet found Cervera at Santiago harbor, on the eastern end of Cuba, and established a blockade. In June a 17,000-man expeditionary force commanded by General William Shafter landed at Daiquiri, east of Santiago, and pressed quickly toward the city, handicapped more by its own inadequate equipment than by the enemy, although the Spanish troops resisted bravely. The Americans sweated through Cuba's torrid summer in heavy wool winter uniforms, ate "embalmed beef" out of cans, and fought mostly with old-fashioned rifles using black powder cartridges that marked the position of each soldier with a puff of smoke whenever he fired his weapon. On July 1 they broke through undermanned Spanish defenses and stormed San Juan Hill, the intrepid Colonel Roosevelt in the van. ("Are you afraid to stand up while I am on horseback?" Roosevelt demanded of one soldier.)

With Santiago harbor now in range of American artillery, Admiral Cervera had to run the blockade. On July 3 his black-hulled ships, flags proudly flying, steamed forth from the harbor and fled westward along the coast. Like hounds after rabbits, five American battleships and two cruisers, commanded by Rear Admiral William T. Sampson and Commodore Winfield Scott Schley, quickly ran them down. In four hours the entire Spanish force was destroyed by a hail of 8- and 13-inch projectiles. Damage to the American ships was superficial; only one seaman lost his life in the engagement.

The end then came abruptly. Santiago surrendered on July 17. A few days later, other United States troops completed the occupation of Puerto Rico. On August 12, one day before the fall of Manila, Spain agreed to get out of Cuba and to cede Puerto Rico and an island in the Marianas (Guam) to the United States. The future of the Philippines was to be settled at a formal peace conference, convening in Paris on October 1.

Developing a Colonial Policy

Although the Spanish resisted surrendering the Philippines at Paris, they had been so thoroughly defeated that they had no choice. The decision hung rather upon the outcome of a conflict over policy within the United States. The war, won at so little cost militarily,° produced problems far larger than those it solved. The nation had become a great power in the world's eyes. As a French diplomat wrote a few years later: "[The United States] is seated at the table where the great game is played, and it cannot leave it." European leaders had been impressed by the forcefulness of Cleveland's diplomacy in the Venezuela boundary dispute as well as by the efficiency displayed by the new navy in the war.

°Over 5,000 Americans died as a result of the conflict, but less than 400 fell in combat. The others were mostly victims of diseases like yellow fever and typhoid.

The annexation of Hawaii and other overseas bases intensified their conviction that the United States was determined to become a major force in international affairs.

The debate over taking the Philippine Islands throws much light on the state of American opinion at this time. The imagination of Americans had been captured by the *trappings* of empire, not by its essence. It was titillating to think of a world map liberally sprinkled with American flags and of the economic benefits that colonies might bring, but few citizens were ready to join in a worldwide struggle for power and influence. They entered blithely upon adventures in far-off regions without realistically facing the implications of their decision.

The expansionists, of course, were eager to annex the entire Philippine archipelago. Even before he had learned to spell the name, Senator Lodge was saying that "the Phillipines mean a vast future trade and wealth and power," offering the nation a greater opportunity "than anything that has happened . . . since the annexation of Louisiana." President McKinley adopted a more cautious stance, but he, too, favored "the general principle of holding on to what we can get." A speaking tour of the Middle West in October 1898, during which he experimented with varying degrees of commitment to expansionism, soon convinced him that the public wanted the islands. Business opinion, to which he was especially responsive, had shifted dramatically during the war, and saw the Philippines as the gateway to the markets of the Far East.

On the other hand, an important minority objected strongly to the United States acquiring colonies. Persons as varied in interest and philosophy as the tycoon Andrew Carnegie and the labor leader Samuel Gompers, as the Social Darwinist William Graham Sumner and the pragmatist William James, as the venerable Republican Senator George Frisbie Hoar of Massachusetts and "Pitchfork Ben" Tillman, the southern Democratic firebrand, together with writers like Mark Twain and William Dean Howells, reformers like Lincoln Steffens and Jane Addams, and educators like presidents Charles W. Eliot of Harvard and David Starr Jordan of Stanford united in opposing the annexation of the Philippines. These anti-imperialists insisted that it was unconstitutional to own colonies and a violation of the spirit of the Declaration of Independence to govern a foreign territory without the consent of its inhabitants. Senator Hoar argued that by taking over "vassal states" in "barbarous archipelagoes" the United States was "trampling . . . on our own great Charter, which recognizes alike the liberty and the dignity of individual manhood."

McKinley was not insensitive to this appeal to idealism and tradition, but he rejected it for several reasons. Many anti-imperialists opposed Philippine annexation for selfish and unworthy motives. Pure partisanship led many of the Democrats to object. Most southern anti-imperialists were governed more by race prejudice than by democratic principles. Labor leaders feared the possible competition of "the Chinese, the Negritos, and the Malays" who presumably would flood into the United States if the islands were taken over.

Even more compelling to McKinley was the absence of any practical alternative to annexation. Public opinion would not sanction restoring Spanish authority in the Philippines or allowing some other power to have them. That the Filipinos were sufficiently advanced and united socially to form a stable government if granted independence seemed highly unlikely. Senator Hoar believed that "for years and for generations, and perhaps for centuries, there would have been turbulence, disorder and revolution" in the islands if they were left to their own devices. Strangely—for he was a kind and gentle man—Hoar faced this possibility with equanimity. McKinley was unable to do so. The President searched the depths of his soul but could find no alternative to annexation. Of course the state of public feeling made the decision easier, and he must have found the idea of presiding over an empire appealing. The commercial possibilities did not escape him either. But in the end it was with a heavy sense of responsibility that he ordered the American peace commissioners to insist upon acquiring the Philippines. To salve the feelings of the Spanish, the United States agreed to pay $20 million for the archipelago, but it was a forced sale, accepted by Spain with bitter resignation.

The peace treaty still faced a hard battle in the United States Senate, where a combination of partisan politics and anticolonialism made it difficult to amass the two-thirds majority necessary for ratification. McKinley had shrewdly appointed three senators, including one Democrat, to the five-man commission, and this predisposed many members of the Upper House to approve the treaty, but the vote was very close. William Jennings Bryan, titular head of the Democratic party, could probably have prevented ratification if he had urged his supporters to vote *nay*. Although he was personally opposed to taking the Philippines, he would not do so. To reject the treaty would leave the United States technically at war with Spain and the fate of the Philippines undecided. Better to accept the islands and then grant them independence. The question should be decided, he said, "not by a *minority* of the Senate but by a *majority* of the people" at the forthcoming Presidential election. Perplexed by Bryan's stand, a number of Democrats allowed themselves to be persuaded by the expansionists' arguments and by McKinley's judicious use of patronage; the treaty was ratified in February 1899 by a vote of 57 to 27.

The national referendum that Bryan had hoped for never materialized. Bryan himself confused the issue in 1900 by making free silver a major plank in his platform, thus driving conservative anti-imperialists into McKinley's arms. Moreover, early in 1899, the Filipino nationalists under Aguinaldo, furious because the United States would not withdraw, rose in rebellion. A savage guerrilla war resulted. Like all such conflicts, waged in tangled country, chiefly by small, isolated units surrounded by a hostile civilian population that had little regard for the "rules" of war, this one produced many atrocities. Goaded by sneak attacks and isolated instances of cruelty to captives, American soldiers, many of whom had little respect for Filipinos to begin

with, responded in kind. Horrible tales of rape, arson, and murder by United States troops began to filter into the country, providing much ammunition for the anti-imperialists. "You seem to have about finished your work of civilizing the Filipinos," Andrew Carnegie wrote angrily to one of the American peace commissioners. "About 8,000 of them have been completely civilized and sent to Heaven. I hope you like it." However, so long as the fighting continued it was politically impossible for the United States to withdraw from the islands. A commission appointed by McKinley in 1899 attributed the revolt to the ambitions of the nationalist leaders but recommended that the Philippines be granted independence at some indefinite future date. This seems to have been the wish of most Americans.

In any case, the re-election of McKinley in 1900 settled the Philippine question, although it took the efforts of 70,000 American soldiers and three years of brutal guerrilla warfare before peace was restored. Meanwhile, McKinley sent a second commission headed by William Howard Taft, an Ohio judge, to establish civil government in the islands. Taft, a warm-hearted, affable man, took an instant liking to the Filipinos and soon won from them a large measure of confidence; his policy of encouraging natives to participate in the new territorial government attracted many converts. In July 1901 he became the first civilian governor of the Philippines.

Anti-imperialists claimed that it was unconstitutional to take over territories without the consent of the local population, but their reasoning, while certainly not specious, was unhistorical. No American government had seriously considered the wishes of the American Indians or of the French and Spanish settlers in Louisiana or of the natives of Alaska when it had seemed in the national interest to annex new lands.

Nevertheless, grave new constitutional questions did arise as a result of the acquisitions that followed the Spanish–American War. McKinley had acted with remarkable independence in handling the problems involved in expansion, setting up military governments, for example, in Cuba,

A photograph taken in 1899 shows guerrilla troops captured during the Philippine Insurrection. Although the guerrilla leader, Emilio Aguinaldo, was seized in March 1901, fighting in the islands did not end until mid-1902. (Library of Congress.)

Puerto Rico, and the Philippines without specific congressional authority. But eventually both Congress and the Supreme Court took a hand in working out the colonial policy of the country. In 1900 Congress passed the Foraker Act, establishing a civil government for Puerto Rico but granting the Puerto Ricans neither American citizenship nor full local self-government. The law also placed a tariff on Puerto Rican products imported into the United States. The tariff provision was promptly challenged in the courts on the ground that Puerto Rico was part of the United States, but in *Downes v. Bidwell* (1901) the Supreme Court upheld the legality of the duties.

In this and other "insular cases" the reasoning of the judges was more than ordinarily difficult to follow. ("We suggest, without intending to decide, that there may be a distinction between certain natural rights enforced in the Constitution . . . and what may be termed artificial or remedial rights," the Downes opinion ran.) The effect, however, was clear: the Constitution did not follow the flag; Congress could act toward the colonies almost as it pleased; a colony, as one dissenter put it, could be kept "like a disembodied shade, in an indeterminate state of ambiguous existence for an indefinite period."

Although the most heated arguments raged over Philippine policy, the most difficult colonial problems concerned the relationship between the United States and Cuba, for there idealism and self-interest clashed painfully. Despite the desire of most Americans to see Cuba establish a free and independent government, such a regime could not easily be created. Order and prosperity did not automatically appear when the red-and-gold ensigns of Spain were hauled down from the flagstaffs of Havana and Santiago. The insurgent government was feeble, corrupt, and oligarchic, the Cuban economy in a state of collapse, the social order chaotic. The first Americans entering Havana found the city a shambles, the streets littered with garbage and the corpses of horses and dogs, all public services at a standstill. It was essential for the United States, as McKinley said, to give "aid and direction" until "tranquillity" could be restored.

Yet as soon as Americans landed in Cuba, trouble broke out between them and the local populace. Most American soldiers viewed the ragged, half-starved insurgents as "thieving dagoes," and displayed an unfortunate race prejudice against their dark-skinned allies. As the novelist Stephen Crane, who covered the war for Pulitzer's *World*, reported: "Both officers and privates have the most lively contempt for the Cubans. They despise them." General Shafter did not help matters. He believed the Cubans "no more fit for self-government than gun-powder is for hell" and employed the insurgent forces chiefly as labor troops. After the fall of Santiago, he even refused to let rebel leaders participate in the formal surrender of the city. This infuriated the proud and idealistic Cuban commander, General Calixto García. When McKinley established a military government for Cuba late in 1898, it was soon embroiled with local leaders. Then an eager horde of American promoters descended upon Cuba in search of profitable franchises and concessions. Congress put a stop to this exploitation, however, by forbidding all such grants so long as the occupation continued.

The problems were indeed knotty, for no strong local leader capable of uniting Cuba appeared. Even Senator Teller, father of the Teller Amendment, expressed concern lest "unstable and unsafe" elements get control of the country. European leaders confidently expected that the United States would eventually annex Cuba, and many Americans, including General Leonard Wood, who became military governor in December 1899, considered this the best solution. The

desperate state of the people, the heavy economic stake of Americans in the region, and its strategic importance militated against withdrawal.

Yet, in the end, the United States did withdraw, after doing a great deal to modernize sugar production, improve sanitary conditions, establish schools, and restore orderly administration. In November 1900 a Cuban constitutional convention met at Havana and proceeded without substantial American interference or direction to draft a frame of government. The chief restrictions imposed by this document on Cuba's freedom concerned foreign relations; at the insistence of the United States, it authorized American intervention whenever necessary "for the preservation of Cuban independence" and "the maintenance of a government adequate for the protection of life, property, and individual liberty." Cuba also had to promise not to make any treaty with a foreign power compromising its independence and to grant naval bases on its soil to the United States. This arrangement, known as the Platt Amendment, was accepted, after some grumbling, by the Cubans. It also had the support of most American opponents of imperialism. The amendment was a true compromise; as David F. Healy, a student of Cuban-American relations, has said, "it promised to give the Cubans real internal self government . . . and at the same time to safeguard American interests." Finally, in May 1902, the United States officially turned over the reins of government to the new republic. The next year the two countries signed a reciprocity treaty tightening the economic bonds between them.

True friendship did not result. Repeatedly the United States used the threat of intervention to coerce the Cuban government, although American troops occupied Cuba only once, in 1906, and then at the specific request of Cuban authorities. American economic penetration proceeded rapidly but without regard for the well-being of the Cuban peasants, many of whom lived in a state of peonage on great sugar plantations. Furthermore, their good intentions did not make up for the distressing tendency of Americans to consider themselves innately superior to the Cubans and to overlook the fact that Cubans did not always wish to adopt American customs and culture. The admirable reform program instituted during the occupation was marred by attempts to apply American standards at every step. In the new schools American textbooks were translated into Spanish without trying to adapt the material to the experience of Cuban children. General Wood considered the Cubans "inert" because they showed little interest in his plans to grant a large measure of self-government to municipal authorities, failing to understand that the people were accustomed to a highly centralized system with decision-making concentrated in Havana. Wood complained that the Cubans were mired in "old ruts," yet exactly the same charge might well have been leveled at him, although he was an efficient and energetic administrator.

If the purpose of the Spanish–American War had been to bring peace and order to Cuba, the Platt Amendment was a logical step. The same purpose soon necessitated a further extension of the principle, for once the United States accepted the role of protector and stabilizer in part of Latin America it seemed desirable, for the same economic, strategic, and humanitarian reasons, to supervise the entire region.

The Caribbean countries were economically underdeveloped, socially backward, politically unstable, and desperately poor. Everywhere a few families owned most of the land and dominated social and political life. The mass of the people were uneducated peasants, many of them little better off than slaves. Rival cliques among the wealthy minority struggled for power, force being the normal method of effecting a change in government. Most of the meager income of the average Caribbean state was swallowed up by the military or diverted into the pockets of the currently ruling party.

Cynicism and fraud poisoned the relations of most of these nations with the great powers. European merchants and bankers systematically cheated their Latin American customers, who, in turn, frequently refused to honor their obliga-

tions. Foreign bankers floated Caribbean bond issues on outrageous terms, while revolutionary Caribbean governments annulled concessions and repudiated debts with equal disdain for honest business dealing. Because these countries were so weak, the powers tended to intervene whenever their nationals were cheated or when chaotic conditions endangered the lives and property of foreigners. In one notorious instance, Germany sent two warships to Port-au-Prince, Haiti, and by threatening to bombard the town compelled the Haitian government to pay $30,000 in damages to a German citizen who had been arrested and fined for allegedly assaulting a local policeman. Such actions as this always aroused the concern of the United States government.

In 1902, shortly after the United States pulled out of Cuba, trouble erupted in Venezuela, where the local dictator, Cipriano Castro, was refusing to honor debts owed the citizens of European nations. To force him to pay up, Germany and Great Britain established a blockade of Venezuelan ports and destroyed a number of Venezuelan gunboats and harbor defenses. Under American pressure, the Europeans agreed to arbitrate the dispute. At last the great powers were coming to accept the broad implications of the Monroe Doctrine. The British prime minister Arthur Balfour went so far as to state publicly that "it would be a great gain to civilization if the United States were more actively to interest themselves in making arrangements by which these constantly recurring difficulties . . . could be avoided."

By this time Theodore Roosevelt had become President of the United States, and he quickly capitalized on the new European attitude. In 1903 the Dominican Republic defaulted on bonds totaling some $40 million. When European investors urged their governments to intervene, Roosevelt decided to make a general statement of policy. Under the Monroe Doctrine, the United States could not permit foreign nations to intervene in Latin America. But Latin American nations should not be allowed to escape their obligations. "If we intend to say 'Hands off' . . .

As the Monroe Doctrine became increasingly significant around the turn of the century, chauvinistic cartoonists used it to taunt European powers. In this example, from a 1901 issue of *Puck*, Europe complains, "You're not the only rooster in South America!" to which Uncle Sam retorts, "I was aware of that when I cooped you up!" (Culver Pictures.)

sooner or later we must keep order ourselves," he told Secretary of War Elihu Root. The President did not want to make a colony of the Dominican Republic. "I have about the same desire to annex it as a gorged boa constrictor might have to swallow a porcupine wrong-end-to," he said. He therefore arranged for the United States to take charge of the Dominican customs service—the one reliable source of revenue in that poverty-stricken country. Fifty-five per cent of the customs duties would be devoted to debt payment, the remainder turned over to the Dominican government to care for its internal needs.

Roosevelt defined his policy, known as the Roosevelt Corollary to the Monroe Doctrine, in a message to Congress in December 1904. "Chronic wrongdoing" in Latin America, he

stated with his typical disregard for the subtleties of complex affairs, might require outside intervention. Since, under the Monroe Doctrine, no other nation could step in, the United States must "exercise . . . an international police power." In the short run, this policy worked admirably. Dominican customs were honestly collected for the first time and the country's finances put in order. The presence of American warships in the area discouraged revolutionary elements, most of whom were cynical spoilsmen rather than social reformers, providing a much needed measure of political stability. In the long run, however, the Roosevelt Corollary caused a great deal of resentment in Latin America, for it added to nationalist fears that the United States wished to exploit the region for its own benefit.

The Open Door Policy

The insular cases, the Platt Amendment, and the Roosevelt Corollary established the framework for American colonial policy. Within this framework, a considerable expansion of activity took place, both in Latin America and in the Far East. Coincidental with the Cuban rebellion of the nineties, a far greater upheaval had convulsed the ancient empire of China. In 1894–95 Japan had easily defeated China in a war over Korea. Alarmed by Japan's new aggressiveness, the European powers hastened to check it by rushing to carve out for themselves new concessions, or spheres of influence, along China's coast. After the annexation of the Philippines, McKinley's secretary of state, John Hay, urged on by businessmen fearful of losing out in the scramble to exploit the Chinese market, tried to prevent the further absorption of China by the great powers. For the United States to join in the dismemberment of China was politically impossible because of anti-imperialist feeling, so Hay sought to protect American interests by clever diplomacy. In a series of "Open Door" notes (1899), he asked the powers to agree to respect the trading rights of all countries and to impose no discriminatory duties within their spheres of influence. Chinese tariffs should continue to be collected in these areas and by Chinese officials.

Although the replies to these notes were at best noncommittal, Hay blandly announced in March 1900 that the powers had "accepted" his suggestions! Thus he could claim to have prevented the breakup of the empire and protected the right of Americans to do business freely in its territories. In reality nothing had been accomplished; the imperialist nations did not extend their political control of China only because they feared that by doing so they might precipitate a major war among themselves. Nevertheless, Hay's action marked a revolutionary departure from the traditional American policy of isolation, a bold step into the complicated and dangerous world of international power politics.

Within a few months of Hay's announcement, the Open Door policy was put to the test. Chinese nationalists, angered by the spreading influence of foreign governments, launched the so-called Boxer Rebellion, overrunning Peking and driving foreigners within the walls of their legations, which were placed under siege. For weeks, until an international rescue expedition, which included 2,500 American soldiers, broke through to free them, their fate was unknown. Fearing that the Europeans would use the rebellion as a pretext for further expropriations, Hay sent off another round of Open Door notes announcing that the United States believed in the preservation of "Chinese territorial and administrative entity" and in "the principle of equal and impartial trade with all parts of the Chinese Empire."

Collier's magazine devoted a cover story to the Boxer Rebellion in 1900. The international expeditionary force sent to relieve Peking included American, British, French, German, Russian, and Japanese contingents. (*Collier's*, September 22, 1900.)

This broadened the Open Door policy to include all China, not merely the European spheres of influence.

Hay's diplomacy was superficially successful. Although the United States maintained no important military force in the Far East, American business and commercial interests there were free to develop and to compete with Europeans. But once again European jealousies and fears rather than American cleverness were responsible. When the Japanese, mistrusting Russian intentions in Manchuria, asked Hay how he intended to implement his policy, he replied meekly that the United States was "not prepared . . . to enforce these views on the east by any demonstration which could present a character of hostility to any other power." Willy-nilly, the United States was being caught up in the power struggle in the Far East without having faced the implications of its actions.

Eventually, the country would pay a heavy price for this unrealistic attitude, but in the decade following 1900 its policy of diplomatic meddling unbacked by bayonets worked fairly well. Japan attacked Russia in a quarrel over Manchuria, smashing the Russian fleet in 1905 and winning a series of battles on the mainland. Japan was unprepared for a long war, however, and told President Roosevelt that an American offer to mediate would be favorably received.

Eager to preserve the nice balance in the Far East, which enabled the United States to exert influence without any significant commitment of force, Roosevelt accepted the hint. In June 1905 he invited the belligerents to a conference at Portsmouth, New Hampshire. At the conference the Japanese won title to Russia's sphere around Port Arthur and a free hand in Korea, but when they asked for all of Sakhalin Island and a large money indemnity, the Russians balked. Unwilling to resume the war, the Japanese then settled for half of Sakhalin and no money.

This arrangement was unpopular in Japan, and the government managed to place the blame on Roosevelt, who had supported the compromise. Ill-feeling against Americans increased in 1906, when the San Francisco school board, responding to local opposition to the influx of cheap labor from Japan, instituted a policy of segregating oriental children in a special school. Japan protested, and President Roosevelt persuaded the San Franciscans to abandon segregation in exchange for his pledge to cut off further Japanese immigration. He accomplished this through a "Gentlemen's Agreement" (1907) in which the Japanese promised not to issue passports to laborers seeking to come to America. Discriminatory legislation based specifically on race was thus avoided.

The next year, in the Root-Takahira Agreement, the United States and Japan outlined their "common aim" in the Far East to develop commerce, maintain the status quo in China, and respect each other's interests. However, the atmosphere between the two countries remained charged. Japanese resentment at American race prejudice was great. Many Americans talked fearfully of the "yellow peril."

In most instances Roosevelt was pre-eminently a realist in foreign relations. "Don't bluster," he once said. "Don't flourish a revolver, and never draw unless you intend to shoot." In the Far East, however, he failed to follow his own advice. He considered the situation in that part of the world fraught with peril. The Philippines, he said, were "our heel of Achilles," indefensible in case of a Japanese attack. He suggested privately that the United States ought therefore "be prepared for giving the islands independence . . . much sooner than I think advisable from their own standpoint." He did not, however, either try to increase American naval and military strength in the Orient appreciably or cease to attempt to influence the course of events in the area, and he took no step toward withdrawing from the Philippines. He sent the fleet on a world cruise to demonstrate its might to Japan but well realized that this was mere bluff. "The 'Open Door' policy," he warned his successor, "completely disappears as soon as a powerful nation determines to disregard it." Nevertheless, he allowed the belief to persist in the United States that the nation could influence the course of Far Eastern history without risk or real involvement.

Theodore Roosevelt's high-powered pursuit of personal diplomacy captured wide attention. A Copenhagen paper comments on his mediation of the Russo-Japanese War, which won him the Nobel peace prize.

Caribbean Diplomacy

In the Caribbean region American policy centered on the building of an interoceanic canal across Central America. Expanding interests in both Latin America and the Far East made a canal vitally necessary, a truth pointed up dramatically at the time of the war with Spain by the two-month voyage of the U.S.S. *Oregon* around South America from California waters to participate in the action against Admiral Cervera's fleet at Santiago. The first step was to get rid of the old Clayton–Bulwer Treaty with Great Britain, which barred the United States from building a canal on its own. Great Britain realized after the Spanish–American War that the United States would go ahead with the canal in any case and therefore posed no serious objections. In 1901 Lord Pauncefote, the British ambassador, and Secretary of State John Hay negotiated an agreement abrogating the Clayton–Bulwer pact and giving America the right to build, and by implication fortify, a trans-

isthmian waterway. The United States agreed in turn to maintain any such canal "free and open to the vessels of commerce and of war of all nations."

Next, the location of the canal had to be determined. One possible route lay across the Colombian province of Panama, where the French-controlled New Panama Canal Company had taken over the franchise of the old De Lesseps company. Only 50 miles separated the oceans in Panama. The terrain, however, was rugged and unhealthy—although the French company had sunk much money into the project, it had little to show for its efforts aside from some rough excavations. A second possible route ran across Nicaragua. This route was about 200 miles long but relatively easy, since much of it traversed Lake Nicaragua and other natural waterways.

At first American opinion favored the Nicaraguan route. But the French company in Panama, eager to unload its assets on the United States, employed a New York lawyer, William Nelson Cromwell, as a lobbyist and succeeded in stirring up considerable support. President McKinley appointed a commission to study the alternatives. It reported that the Panamanian route was technically superior but recommended building in Nicaragua because the French company was asking $109 million for its assets, which the commission valued at a mere $40 million. Lacking another possible purchaser, the French company quickly lowered its price to $40 million, and after a great deal of clever propagandizing by Cromwell and Philippe Bunau-Varilla, a French engineer with heavy investments in the company, President Roosevelt settled upon the Panamanian route. Early in January 1903 Secretary of State Hay negotiated a treaty with Tomás Herrán, the Colombian chargé in Washington. In return for a 99-year lease on a zone across Panama six miles wide, the United States agreed to pay Colombia $10 million and an annual rent of $250,000. The Colombian senate, however, unanimously rejected this treaty, partly because it did not adequately protect Colombian sovereignty over Panama and partly for purely materialistic reasons. The Colombians thought it hardly fair that the New Panama Canal Company should receive $40 million for its frozen assets and they only $10 million. They demanded $15 million directly from the United States, plus $10 million of the company's share.

A little more patience might have produced a mutually satisfactory settlement, but Roosevelt looked upon the Colombians as highwaymen who were "mad to get hold of the $40,000,000 of the Frenchmen." "You could no more make an agreement with the Colombian rulers," he later remarked, "than you could nail currant jelly to a wall." Therefore, when local Panamanians, egged on by the French company, staged a revolution in November 1903, he ordered the cruiser *Nashville* to Panama to cow the Colombian forces. The revolution succeeded, and in a matter of hours Roosevelt recognized the new Republic of Panama. Hay and the new Panamanian minister, Bunau-Varilla, quickly negotiated a treaty granting the United States a zone *ten* miles wide *in perpetuity,* on the same terms as those rejected by Colombia. Within the Canal Zone the United States could act as "the sovereign of the territory . . . to the entire exclusion of . . . the Republic of Panama." The United States also undertook to guarantee the independence of the republic. Of course the New Panama Canal Company then received its $40 million.

Historians have condemned Roosevelt for his actions in this shabby affair, and with good reason. It was not that he fomented the revolution, for he did not. Separated from the government at Bogotá by an impenetrable jungle, the people of Panama province had long wanted to be free of Colombian rule. Furthermore, knowing that an American-built canal would bring a flood of dollars and job opportunities to the area, they were prepared to take any necessary steps to avoid having the United States shift to the Nicaraguan route. Nor was it that Roosevelt prevented Colombia from suppressing the revolution, although his excuse for doing so—an 1846 treaty authorizing the United States to protect the freedom of transit across the isthmus—was extremely flimsy. He sinned, rather, in his disregard of Latin American sensibilities. He referred to the Colom-bians as "dagoes" and insisted smugly that he was defending "the interests of collective civilization" when he overrode their opposition to his plans. "They cut their own throats," he said. "They tried to hold us up; and too late they have discovered their criminal error." If somewhat uncharitable, this analysis was not entirely inaccurate, but it did not justify Roosevelt's haste in taking Panama under his wing. "Have I defended myself?" Roosevelt asked Secretary of War Elihu Root. "You certainly have, Mr. President," Root retorted. "You were accused of seduction and you have conclusively proved that you were guilty of rape." All over Latin America, especially as nationalist sentiments grew stronger, Roosevelt's intolerance and aggressiveness in the canal incident bred resentment and fear.

Eventually, in 1921, the United States made amends for Roosevelt's actions by giving Colombia $25 million. Colombia, in turn, recognized the independence of the Republic of Panama.

Meanwhile, the canal had been built—the first vessels passed through its locks in 1914—and American hegemony in the Caribbean further expanded. Yet even in that strategically vital area, there was more show than substance to American strength. The navy ruled Caribbean waters largely by default, for it lacked adequate bases in the region. In 1903, as authorized by the Cuban constitution, the United States obtained an excellent site for a base at Guantanamo Bay, but before 1914 Congress appropriated only $89,000 to develop it.

The tendency was to try to influence outlying areas without actually controlling them. Roosevelt's successor, William Howard Taft, gave the policy its clearest expression when he called it "dollar diplomacy," his theory being that American economic penetration would bring stability to underdeveloped areas and power and profit to the United States without making it necessary to commit American troops or spend public funds.

Under Taft, the State Department won a place for American bankers in an international syndicate engaged in financing railroads in Manchuria. When Nicaragua defaulted on its foreign debt in 1911, the department arranged informally for a group of bankers to reorganize Nicaraguan finances and take over the operation of the customs service. Although the government truthfully insisted that it did not "covet an inch of territory south of the Rio Grande," dollar diplomacy provoked further apprehension in Latin America. Efforts to establish similar arrangements in Honduras, Costa Rica, and Guatemala all failed. Even in Nicaragua, orderly administration of the finances did not bring internal peace. In 1912, 2,500 American marines and sailors had to be landed to put down a revolution.

On the other hand, economic penetration in the Caribbean area proceeded briskly. American investments in Cuba reached $200 million by 1910 and $500 million by 1920, and smaller but

Two views of Roosevelt's handling of the Panamanian affair. At left, a drawing from the Republican *Judge,* captioned "A crown he is entitled to wear." (*Judge,* June 4, 1904.) A New York *Times* cartoonist saw the matter very differently, charging a conspiracy (above). When Bunau-Varilla asked the President to send a warship to Panama "to protect American lives and interests," he got no answer. "But his look was enough for me," Bunau-Varilla recalled. (New York *Times,* 1903.)

significant investments were also made in the Dominican Republic and in Haiti. In Central America the United Fruit Company accumulated large holdings in banana plantations, railroads, and other ventures. Other firms plunged heavily in Mexico's rich mineral resources.

"Noncolonial Imperial Expansion"

Generally speaking, the United States deserves fair marks for effort in its post-Spanish–American War foreign relations, barely passable marks for performance, and failing ones for results. If one defines imperialism narrowly as a policy of occupying and governing foreign lands, American imperialism lasted for an extremely short time. With trivial exceptions, all the American colonies—Hawaii, the Philippines, Guam, Puerto Rico, the Guantanamo base, and the Canal Zone—were obtained between 1898 and 1903. In retrospect it seems clear that the urge to own colonies was only fleeting; sober second thoughts and the headaches connected with overseas possessions caused a swift change of policy. The objections of protectionists to the lowering of tariff barriers, the shock of the Philippine Insurrection, the worldwide unfavorable reaction of liberals to the costly British war against the Boers of South Africa, and a growing conviction that the costs of colonial administration outweighed the profits all affected American thinking. Hay's Open Door notes (which, incidentally, anti-imperialists praised highly) marked the beginning of the retreat from imperialism thus defined, while the Roosevelt Corollary and dollar diplomacy signaled the consolidation of a new policy. Elihu Root summarized this policy as it applied to the Caribbean (and by implication to the rest of the underdeveloped world) in 1905: "We do not want to take them for ourselves. We do not want any foreign nations to take them for themselves. We want to help them."

Yet imperialism can be given a broader definition than this one. The historian William Appleman Williams, a sharp critic, has described 20th-century American foreign policy as one of "non-colonial imperial expansion." Its object was to obtain profitable American economic penetration of underdeveloped areas without the trouble of owning and controlling them. Its subsidiary aim was to encourage these countries to "modernize," modernize meaning to remake themselves in the image of the United States. The Open Door policy, in Williams' view, was not unrealistic, and by no means a failure—indeed, it was *too* successful. He criticizes American policy not because it did not work or because it led to trouble with the powers, but because of its harmful effects on underdeveloped countries.

Examined from this perspective, the Open Door policy, the Roosevelt Corollary, and dollar diplomacy make a single pattern of exploitation, "tragic" according to Williams rather than evil, because its creators were not evil but only of limited vision. They did not recognize the contradictions in their ideas and values. They saw American expansion as mutually beneficial to all concerned—and not exclusively in materialistic terms. They genuinely believed that they were exporting democracy along with capitalism and industrialization.

Williams probably goes too far in arguing that American statesmen consciously planned their foreign policy in these terms. American economic interests in foreign nations expanded enormously in the 20th century, but diplomacy had relatively little to do with this. Western industrial society (not merely American) was engulfing the rest of the world, as it continues to engulf it. Yet he is correct in pointing out that western economic penetration has had many unfortunate results for the nonindustrial nations, and that Americans were particularly, although not uniquely, unimpressed by the different social and cultural patterns of people in far-off lands and insensitive to the wish of such people to develop in their own way.

Both the United States government and American businessmen showed little interest in finding out what the people of Cuba wanted out of life. They assumed that it was what *everybody* (read, "Americans") wanted, and if by some strange chance this was not the case, that the best thing to do was to give it to them anyway. Dollar diplomacy had as its primary objectives the avoidance of violence and the economic development of Latin America; it paid small heed to how peace was maintained and how the fruits of development were distributed. The policy, therefore, was self-defeating, for in the long run stability depended upon the support of the masses, which was seldom forthcoming.

By the eve of World War I the United States had become a major world power, and had assumed what it saw as a duty to guide the development of many countries with traditions far different from its own. The American people, however, did not really understand what these changes involved. Although they stood ready to extend their influence into distant lands, they did so blithely, with little awareness of the implications of their behavior for themselves or for other peoples. The national psychology, if such a term has any meaning, remained fundamentally isolationist. Americans fully understood that their wealth and numbers made their nation strong, and that geography made it practically invulnerable. They proceeded, therefore, to do what they wanted to do in foreign affairs, limited more by their humanly flexible consciences than by any rational analysis of the probable consequences. This seemed safe enough—in 1914.

Supplementary Reading

Among the many general diplomatic histories, Alexander De Conde, *A History of American Foreign Policy* (1963), is the most detailed, and R. W. Leopold, *The Growth of American Foreign Policy* (1962), is the most thoughtful and interpretative. Milton Plesur, *America's Outward Thrust* (1971), offers fuller detail, while J. A. S. Grenville and G. B. Young, *Politics, Strategy, and American Diplomacy: Studies in Foreign Policy* (1966), throws new light on many aspects of the period. Post-Civil War expan-

°Available in paperback.

sionism is treated in Dexter Perkins, *The Monroe Doctrine: 1867–1907* (1937), and Allan Nevins, *Hamilton Fish* (1936). Walter LaFeber, *The New Empire* (1963), presents a forceful but somewhat overstated argument on the extent of expansionist sentiment, especially on the part of American businessmen.

The new expansionism is also discussed in A. K. Weinberg, *Manifest Destiny*° (1935), J. W. Pratt, *Expansionists of 1898*° (1936), and Harold and Margaret Sprout, *The Rise of American Naval Power*° (1939). Contemporary attitudes are reflected in Josiah Strong, *Our Country* (1885), while A. T. Mahan, *The Influence of Sea Power upon History: 1660–1783*° (1890), provides the clearest presentation of Mahan's thesis. W. D. Puleston, *Mahan* (1939), is a good biography.

D. W. Pletcher, *The Awkward Years: American Foreign Relations Under Garfield and Arthur* (1962), is definitive. Other useful studies include A. F. Tyler, *The Foreign Policy of James G. Blaine* (1927), S. K. Stevens, *American Expansion in Hawaii* (1945), Allan Nevins, *Grover Cleveland* (1932) and *Henry White* (1930), L. M. Gelber, *The Rise of Anglo-American Friendship* (1938), and Henry James, *Richard Olney* (1923).

On the Spanish-American War, a good brief summary is H. W. Morgan, *America's Road to Empire*° (1965). For greater detail, consult E. R. May, *Imperial Democracy* (1961), Walter Millis, *The Martial Spirit* (1931), Margaret Leech, *In the Days of McKinley* (1959), and Orestes Ferrara, *The Last Spanish War* (1937). H. W. Morgan, *William McKinley and His America* (1963), is a good modern biography.

On imperialism, see David Healy, *U. S. Expansionism: The Imperialist Urge in the 1890's* (1970), E. R. May, *American Imperialism: A Speculative Essay* (1968), and W. A. Williams, *The Tragedy of American Diplomacy*° (1962), the last extremely critical of what the author calls "non-colonial imperial expansion." R. L. Beisner, *Twelve Against Empire: The Anti-Imperialists* (1968), contains lively and thoughtful sketches of leading foes of expansion. For colonial problems, see Leon Wolff, *Little Brown Brother* (1961), on the Philippines, D. F. Healy, *The United States in Cuba: 1898–1902* (1963), and D. G. Munro, *Intervention and Dollar Diplomacy in the Caribbean: 1900–1921* (1964). S. F. Bemis, *The Latin American Policy of the United States*° (1943), is an excellent general account of the subject. Other useful volumes include D. C. Miner, *The Fight for the Panama Route* (1940), H. K. Beale, *Theodore Roose-*

velt and the Rise of America to World Power°
(1956), A. W. Griswold, *The Far Eastern Policy of
the United States°* (1938), Tyler Dennett, *John Hay*
(1938), C. S. Campbell, Jr., *Special Business Interests
and the Open Door Policy* (1951), Thomas McCormick, *China Market* (1967), and H. C. Hill, *Roosevelt and the Caribbean* (1927). R. E. Osgood, *Ideals
and Self-Interest in America's Foreign Relations°*
(1953), and G. F. Kennan, *American Diplomacy:
1900–1950°* (1951), are important interpretations of
early-20th-century United States policy, more general
in scope than May's *American Imperialism* and Williams' *Tragedy of American Diplomacy*, mentioned
above.

23

The Progressive Era

The period of the history of the United States marked roughly by the end of the Spanish-American War and American entry into World War I is usually called the Progressive Era. Like all such generalizations about complex subjects, this title involves a great oversimplification. Whether *progressive* is taken to mean "tending toward change," or "improvement," or is merely used to suggest an attitude of mind, it was not a universal characteristic of the early years of the 20th century. Furthermore, progressive elements existed in earlier periods and did not disappear when the first doughboys took ship for France. In many important ways the progressivism of the time was only a continuation of the response to industrialism that began after the Civil War, a response which, of course, has not ended. Historians have scoured the sources trying to define and explain the Progressive Era without devising an interpretation of the period satisfactory to all. Indeed, as their investigations go on, it seems at times that the meaning of the word *progressive* is becoming progressively less clear. Surveying the literature in his study *Businessmen and Reform*, Robert H. Wiebe remarks: "Over the years historians have gradually closed the door to the progressive club," by which he means that under close examination, most progressives appear far less radical than at first glance. Another writer has called his work on the period *The Triumph of Conservatism*! Nevertheless, the term *progressive* provides a useful description of this exciting and significant period of American history.

Roots of Progressivism

The progressives were never a unified group seeking a single objective. The movement sprang from many sources. One of these was the fight against corruption and inefficiency in government, dating back at least to the Grant era. The struggle for civil service reform was only the first skirmish in this contest; the continuing power of corrupt big-city political machines and the growing influence of large corporations and their lobbyists on municipal and state governments outraged thousands of citizens and led them to seek ways of purifying politics and making the machinery of government responsive to the majority rather than to special-interest groups.

Progressivism also had roots in the effort to regulate and control big business, which characterized the Granger and Populist agitation of the 1870's and 1890's. The failure of the Interstate Commerce Act to end railroad abuses and of the Sherman Antitrust Act to check the growth of monopolies became ever more apparent after 1900. The return of prosperity after the great depression of the nineties aggravated these problems by strengthening the big corporations. It also encouraged the opposition by removing the inhibiting fear, so influential in the 1896 Presidential campaign, that an assault on the industrial giants might lead to the collapse of the whole economy. Between 1897 and 1904 the trend toward concentration in industry suddenly accelerated. Such new giants as Amalgamated Copper (1899), U. S. Steel (1901), and International Harvester (1902) attracted most of the attention, but even more alarming were the overall statistics. In a single year (1899) over 1,200 firms were absorbed in mergers, the resulting combinations being capitalized at $2.2 billion. By 1904 there were 318 industrial combinations with an aggregate capital of some $7.5 billion in the country. Persons who considered bigness inherently evil demanded that these huge new "trusts" be broken up or at least strictly controlled.

Settlement-house workers and other reformers concerned about the welfare of the urban poor made up a third battalion in the progressive army. The working and living conditions of slum dwellers remained abominable. The child labor problem was particularly acute. In 1900 about 1.7 million children under the age of 16 were working full time—more than the membership of the American Federation of Labor. Laws regulating the hours and conditions of women in industry were also far from adequate, and almost nothing had been done, despite the increased use of dangerous machinery in the factories, to enforce safety rules or provide some kind of compensation or insurance for workers injured on the job. As the number of professionally competent social workers grew larger, the movement for social-welfare legislation gained momentum.

The return of prosperity after the election of McKinley strengthened the political reformers, the antimonopolists, and the social workers, and by attracting additional thousands of sympathizers to the general cause of reform, it produced the progressive movement. Good times made people tolerant and generous, willing to help others, not merely to advance their own interests. So long as his own profits were on the rise, the aver-

The impact of *The Silent War*, a 1906 novel by J. Ames Mitchell which dealt with the growing class struggle in America, was enhanced by William Balfour Ker's graphic illustration, "From the Depths."

age businessman did not object if labor improved its position too. Many middle-class Americans who had been prepared to man the barricades in the event of a Bryan victory in 1896 now became conscience-stricken when they compared their own comfortable circumstances with those of the "huddled masses" of immigrants and native poor. Nonmaterialistic, humanitarian motives governed their behavior; they were reformers more "of the heart and the head than of the stomach."

The new industrial and commercial giants threatened not so much the economic well-being as the ambitions and sense of importance of the middle class. What owner of a small mill or shop could now hope to rise to the heights attained by Carnegie, or by great merchants like John Wanamaker or Marshall Field? The growth of large labor organizations also worried such men. Union membership tripled between 1896 and 1910; bargaining became a clash of massive economic interests; individual relationships between employer and worker no longer counted for much in the industrial world. In general, human character and moral values seemed less influential; organizations—cold, impersonal, heartless— were coming to control business, politics, and too many other aspects of life.

The historian Richard Hofstadter suggested still another explanation of the movement. Numbers of established, moderately prosperous businessmen, together with members of the professions and other educated persons, felt themselves threatened and discomfited by the increasing power and status of the new tycoons, many of them coarse, assertive men fond of vulgar display, and by machine politicians, who made a mockery of the traditions of duty, service, and patriotism associated with statesmanship. The comfortably off, middle-level businessman lived in what seemed like genteel poverty compared to a Rockefeller or a Morgan and often found that the influence in the community which he considered his birthright had been usurped by a cynical local boss.

Protestant pastors accustomed to the respect and deference of their flocks found their moral leadership challenged by materialistic vestrymen who did not even pay them decent salaries. College professors watched their institutions fall increasingly under the sway of wealthy trustees who had little interest in or respect for learning. The law, once the most powerful and independent of professions, was also being affected by the business world. Attracted by fat fees, many lawyers could not resist the blandishments of great corporations, but they resented the loss of freedom involved nonetheless. "The profession is commercialized," one lawyer complained in 1904. "The lawyer today does not enjoy the position and influence that belonged to the lawyer of seventy-five or a hundred years ago." Members of other professions echoed this complaint.

Such people could support reform measures without feeling that they were being very radical because the intellectual currents of their time harmonized with the ideas of social improvement and the welfare state. The new doctrines of the social scientists, the Social Gospel religious leaders, and the philosophers of pragmatism provided a salubrious climate for progressivism. Many of the thinkers who formulated these doctrines in the eighties and nineties turned to the task of putting them into practice in the new century: for example, the economist Richard T. Ely, the sociologist E. A. Ross, the philosopher John Dewey, the Baptist clergyman Walter Rauschenbusch, who, in addition to his many books extolling the Social Gospel, was active in civic reform movements in Rochester, New York.

The Muckrakers

As the diffuse and unorganized progressive army gradually formed its battalions, a new journalistic fad suddenly brought the movement into focus. For many years magazines like *Forum, Arena, McClure's,* and even the staid *Atlantic Monthly* had been publishing articles describing political, social, and economic evils. Henry Demarest Lloyd's first blast at the Standard Oil monopoly appeared in the *Atlantic Monthly* as far back as 1881; radicals such as Henry George and Eugene V. Debs had discussed a variety of problems in the pages of *Arena* in the early 1890's; Josiah Flynt had exposed the corrupt relationship between criminals and the New York police for *McClure's* in 1900.

Over the years the tempo and forcefulness of this type of literature steadily increased. Then, in the fall of 1902, *McClure's* began publishing two particularly hard-hitting series of articles, one on

Standard Oil by Ida Tarbell, the other on urban political machines by Lincoln Steffens. These evoked much comment. When S. S. McClure decided to include in the January 1903 issue an attack on labor gangsterism in the coal fields along with the next installments of the Tarbell and Steffens series, he called attention to the coincidence in a striking editorial. Something was radically wrong with the "American character," he wrote. These articles showed that large numbers of American employers, workers, and politicians were fundamentally immoral. Furthermore, lawyers were becoming the tools of big business, judges were permitting evildoers to escape justice, the churches were materialistic, the colleges incapable even of understanding what was happening. "There is no one left; none but

"The smile that won't come off": a caricature of muckraker Ida M. Tarbell, the nemesis of Standard Oil, reproduced in the New York *Telegram* in 1906. (New York *Telegram,* May 5, 1906.)

all of us," McClure concluded. "We have to pay in the end."

McClure's editorial, one of the most influential ever published in an American magazine, loosed a chain reaction. The January issue sold out quickly. Other editors jumped to adopt the McClure formula. Thousands of readers found their own vague apprehensions brought into focus, some becoming active in progressive movements, more lending passive support.

A small army of professional writers was soon flooding the periodical press with denunciations of the insurance business, the drug business, college athletics, prostitution, sweatshop labor, political corruption, and dozens of other subjects. The intellectual level and the essential honesty of their work varied greatly; much of it was lurid, distorted, designed to titillate and scandalize rather than to inform.

The latter type of article inspired Theodore Roosevelt, with his gift for vivid phraseology, to compare these journalists to "the Man with the Muck-Rake" in Bunyan's *Pilgrim's Progress,* whose attention was so fixed on the filth at his feet that he could not notice the "celestial crown" that was offered him in exchange. This characterization grossly misrepresented the more worthy literature of exposure, but the label *muckraking* was thereafter permanently affixed to the type, and despite the connotations, *muckraker* became a term of honor.

The Progressive Mind

Progressives were essentially middle-class moralists seeking to arouse the conscience of "the people" in order to purify American life. Local, state, and national government must be made more responsive to the will of the unorganized mass of decent citizens who stood for all the traditional virtues. Next, the government (once purified) must *act.* Whatever its virtues, laissez faire was obsolete. Businessmen, especially big businessmen, must be compelled to behave fairly, their acquisitive drives curbed in the interests of

universal justice and equal opportunity for all. Finally, the weaker elements in society—women, children, the poor, the infirm—must be protected against unscrupulous power. The people, by which the progressives usually meant the comfortable middle class, must assume new responsibilities toward the unfortunate.

Despite its fervor and democratic rhetoric, progressivism was paternalistic, moderate, and somewhat soft-headed. The typical reformer of the period oversimplified complicated issues and treated his own highly personal values as absolute standards of truth and morality. Thus progressives often acted at cross-purposes; at times some were even at war with themselves. This accounts for the diffuseness of the movement. Cutthroat business practices were criticized by great tycoons seeking to preserve their own positions and by small operators trying to protect themselves against the tycoons. But the former wanted federal regulation of big business and the latter strict enforcement of the antitrust laws. Political reforms like the direct primary election appealed especially to rural progressives but found few adherents among progressive businessmen.

Many persons who genuinely desired to improve the living standards of industrial workers rejected the proposition that these workers could best help themselves by organizing powerful national unions. Union leaders favored government action to outlaw child labor and restrict immigration but adopted a laissez-faire attitude toward wages-and-hours legislation; they preferred to win these objectives through collective bargaining, thus justifying their own existence. Many who favored "municipal socialism," meaning public ownership of streetcars, waterworks, and other local utilities, adamantly opposed the national ownership of railroads. Progressives stressed individual freedom, yet gave strong backing to the drive to deprive the public of its right to drink alcoholic beverages. Few progressives worked more assiduously than Congressman George W. Norris of rural Nebraska for reforms that would increase the power of the ordinary voter, such as the direct primary and popular election of senators, yet Norris characterized the mass of urban voters as "the mob." Theodore Roosevelt fulminated against the "malefactors of great wealth" while also speaking of "the immense good effected by corporate agencies [and] . . . their officers and directors."

Finally, it must be emphasized that the progressives never challenged the fundamental principles of capitalism, nor did they attempt any basic reorganization of society. The Socialist party developed considerable strength during the period, capturing control of a dozen or more city administrations, sending a few representatives to state legislatures, and polling nearly 900,000 votes in the 1912 Presidential election. But the progressives would have little to do with the socialist brand of reform. Wisconsin was the most progressive of states, but its leaders never cooperated with the Social Democrats of Milwaukee. When socialists threatened to win control of Los Angeles in 1911, California progressives made common cause with their reactionary foes in order to defeat them. Many progressives were also anti-immigrant and only a handful had anything to offer the Negroes, surely the most exploited class in American society.

A good example of the relatively limited radicalism of progressives is offered by the experiences of progressive artists. Early in the century a number of painters, including Robert Henri, John Sloan, and George Luks, tried to develop a distinctively American style, one that would probe the very heart of the world they lived in. These "ashcan" artists were individualists, yet in sympathy with social reform. They turned to city streets and the people of the slums for their models, depended more upon inspiration and inner conviction than careful craftsmanship to achieve their effects. They were caught up in the progressive movement. Their idols were socially conscious painters like Hogarth, Goya, and Daumier; they thought of themselves as rebels.

In 1912 they formed the Association of American Painters and Sculptors, determined to press their "radical" ideas on the art world. The next year, in New York's 69th Regiment Armory, they organized a big showing of their work. Almost incidentally, they decided to include a sampling of recent and current European art to add another dimension to the exhibition.

But artistically the ashcan painters were not really very advanced, being uninfluenced by, if not ignorant of, the outburst of post-impressionist activity taking place at the time in Europe. These Europeans almost literally stole the show. For the first time Americans—well over 250,000 of them—were offered a comprehensive view of "modern" art, from Manet and Cézanne through Van Gogh and Seurat to Rouault, Matisse, and Picasso.° Most found the dazzling color and weird distortions of the European "madmen" shocking but fascinating. A relatively unimportant cubist painting, Marcel Duchamp's *Nude Descending a Staircase,* became the focal point of the exhibition, attracting the scorn of conservative critics and the snickers of unschooled observers. One critic proposed renaming it "Explosion in a Shingle Factory"; another wit suggested "Rush Hour at the Subway"; Theodore Roosevelt, reviewing the exhibition for the *Outlook,* compared it unfavorably with a Navaho rug in his bathroom.

Amid the furor the work of the Americans was almost ignored. As a means of demonstrating their daring and originality, the show was an almost total failure. Even Roosevelt, who praised the ashcan painters highly while laughing off the cubist "Knights of the Isosceles Triangle" and other members of the "lunatic fringe," believed that the association had arranged the Armory Show "primarily . . . to give the public a chance to see what has recently been going on abroad." Most of the ashcan painters were confused and disheartened by their show; their hopes for creating a new American style died.

Neither the confusions nor the limitations of the progressives should, however, obscure their accomplishments. They elevated the tone of politics, raised the aspirations of the American people, and fashioned many valuable practical reforms.

°Before this exhibition, one art historian has said, "a painting truly modern was only a rumor" in the United States.

Reforming the Political System

To most progressives, political corruption and in-efficiency lay at the root of all the other evils plaguing American society. As the cities grew, their antiquated and boss-ridden administrations became more and more disgraceful. San Francisco may serve as a typical example. After 1901, a clever lawyer named Abe Ruef ruled over one of the most powerful and dissolute organizations in the nation. Only one kind of paving material was used on San Francisco's streets—Ruef was the lawyer for the company that supplied it. When the local gas company asked for a rate increase of ten cents per 100 cubic feet, Ruef, who was already collecting $1,000 a month from the company as a "retainer," demanded and got an outright bribe of $20,000 in return. A street-car company needed city authorization to install overhead trolley wires. Ruef's approval cost the company $85,000. Prostitution flourished, with Ruef and his henchmen sharing in the profits; there was a brisk illegal trade in liquor licenses and other favors. Similar conditions existed in dozens of communities. For his famous muckrak-ing series for *McClure's* Lincoln Steffens visited St. Louis, Minneapolis, Pittsburgh, New York, Chicago, and Philadelphia and found them all riddled with corruption.

Beginning in the late nineties, progressives mounted a massive assault upon dishonest and inefficient urban governments. In San Francisco a group headed by the newspaperman Fremont Older and Rudolph Spreckels, a wealthy sugar manufacturer, broke the machine and eventually lodged Ruef in jail. In Toledo, Ohio, Samuel M. "Golden Rule" Jones won election as mayor in 1897 and succeeded in arousing the local citi-zenry against the corruptionists. The signs that Jones placed on the lawns of Toledo's parks ad-mirably reflected the spirit of his administration. Instead of "Keep Off the Grass," they read: "Citizens, Protect Your Property." Other impor-tant progressive mayors included Tom L. John-son of Cleveland, whose administration Lincoln

Steffens called the best in the United States, Seth Low and later John P. Mitchell of New York, and Hazen S. Pingree of Detroit. In St. Louis, pros-ecutor Joseph W. Folk led a major reform drive.

In nearly every case, however, city reformers could not permanently destroy the machines without changing urban political institutions. Some cities obtained "home rule" charters, which gave them greater freedom from state control in dealing with their problems. Many cre-ated research bureaus, which investigated gov-ernmental problems in a scientific and nonparti-san manner. A number of middle-sized communities (Galveston, Texas, provided the prototype) experimented with a system that inte-grated executive and legislative powers in the hands of a small elected commission, thus con-centrating responsibility and making it easier to coordinate complex activities. Out of this experi-ment came the city-manager system, wherein still further centralization was achieved by having the commissioners appoint a single professional manager to administer city affairs on a nonparti-san basis. Dayton, Ohio, which adopted the city-manager plan after the town had been devas-tated by a great flood in 1913, offers the best illustration of the city-manager system in the Pro-gressive Era.

To carry out this kind of change required the support of state legislatures, since all municipal government depends upon the authority of a sov-ereign state. Such approval was often difficult to obtain, partly because local bosses were usually entrenched in powerful state machines and partly because most legislatures were controlled by rural majorities insensitive to urban needs. The progressives, therefore, had to strike at in-efficiency and corruption at the state level too.

Wisconsin provides by far the most successful example of state progressivism. During the first decade of the new century, that state was trans-formed by Robert M. La Follette, one of the most remarkable figures of the age. La Follette was a reformer in the agrarian tradition, although he had never been a Populist. Born in Primrose, Wisconsin, in 1855, he had served three terms as a Republican congressman (1885-91) and devel-

Robert M. La Follette speaking to Wisconsin farmers in 1897. After six years as governor of the state, he won election to the Senate, serving four terms. (State Historical Society of Wisconsin.)

for nominating candidates, a corrupt practices act, and laws limiting campaign expenditures and lobbying activities. In power he became something of a boss himself. He made ruthless use of patronage, demanded absolute loyalty of his subordinates, often stretched, or at least oversimplified, the truth in presenting complex issues to the voters. La Follette was also a consummate showman, and he never rose entirely above rural prejudices, being prone to scent a nefarious "conspiracy" organized by what he called "the interests" behind even the mildest opposition to his proposals. But he was devoted to the cause of honest government. Realizing that some state functions called for highly technical expert knowledge, he and his supporters pushed for the creation of special commissions and agencies to handle such matters as railroad regulation, tax assessment, conservation, and highway construction. They established a legislative reference library to assist lawmakers in drafting bills. In work of this kind, La Follette made effective use of the faculty of the University of Wisconsin, enticing men like the economist Balthasar H. Meyer and the political scientist Thomas S. Adams into the public service and drawing freely upon the advice of such outstanding social scientists as Richard T. Ely, John R. Commons, and E. A. Ross.

The success of what became known as the "Wisconsin Idea" led other states to adopt similar programs. Reform administrations swept into power in Iowa and Arkansas (1901), Oregon (1902), Minnesota, Kansas, and Mississippi (1904), New York and Georgia (1906), Nebraska (1909), New Jersey and Colorado (1910). In some cases the reformers were Republicans, in others Democrats, but in all these states and in many others, the example of Wisconsin was very influential. From every section of the country, requests for information and advice flooded in upon Wisconsin administrators. As early as 1910, 15 states had established legislative reference services, most of them staffed by men trained in Wisconsin. The direct primary system soon became almost universal; some states even went beyond Wisconsin in striving to make their gov-

oped a reputation as an uncompromising foe of corruption and business control of politics before being elected governor in 1900. That the people would do the right thing in any situation if properly informed and inspired was the fundamental article of his political faith. "Machine control is based upon misrepresentation and ignorance," he said. "Democracy is based upon knowledge. . . . The only way to beat the boss and ring rule [is] to keep the people thoroughly informed." His own career seemed to prove his point, for in his repeated clashes with the conservative Wisconsin Republican machine, he won battle after battle by vigorous grassroots campaigning.

As governor, La Follette overhauled the political structure of the state. Over the opposition of conservative Republicans subservient to Wisconsin railroad and lumbering interests, he and his followers obtained a direct primary system ernments responsive to the popular will. In 1902 Oregon began to experiment with the initiative, a system by which a bill could be forced upon the attention of the legislature by popular petition, and the referendum, a method for allowing the electorate to approve measures rejected by their representatives and to repeal measures that the legislature had passed. Eleven states, most of them in the West, had legalized these devices by 1914.

On the national level, the Progressive Era also saw the culmination of the struggle for women's suffrage. The shock occasioned by the failure of the Thirteenth and Fourteenth Amendments to give women the vote resulted in a split among feminists. One group, the American Women's Suffrage Association, focused on the vote question alone. The more radical National Women's Suffrage Association, led by Elizabeth Cady Stanton and Susan B. Anthony, adopted a broader approach, concerning itself with many other issues of importance to women as well as the suffrage. At the same time this group took an exceedingly partisan stance, placing the immediate interests of women ahead of everything else. Thus it was deeply involved in efforts to unionize women workers, but did not hesitate to urge women to be strikebreakers if they could get better jobs by doing so.

Aside from the weaknesses resulting from their lack of unity, the feminists were handicapped in the late 19th century by Victorian sexual inhibitions, which most of their leaders shared. Dislike of male-dominated society was hard enough to separate from dislike of men under the best of circumstances, but at a time when sex was an unmentionable topic in polite society and sexual feelings often deeply repressed, some of the most militant advocates of women's rights probably did not understand their own feelings. Most feminists, for example, opposed contraception, insisting that birth control by any other means than continence would only encourage what they called masculine lust. The Victorian idealization of female "purity" and the popular image of women as the revered guardians of home and family further confused many reform-

ers. In addition, the trend of 19th-century scientific thinking, influenced by the Darwinian concept of biological adaptation, led to the conclusion that the female personality was fundamentally different from the male, and that the differences were inherent, not culturally determined.

These ideas and prejudices enticed feminists into a logical trap. If women were morally superior to men—a tempting conclusion—they could advance a practical argument for giving women the suffrage: it would improve the character of the electorate. Society would benefit in dozens of ways—politics would become less corrupt, war would become a thing of the past, and so on. The trouble with this argument (aside from the fact that opponents could easily demonstrate that in states where women did vote, governments were no better or worse than elsewhere) was that it surrendered the principle of equality. In the long run this was to have serious consequences for the women's movement, although the immediate effect probably was to advance the suffragists' cause.

By the early 20th century signs of progress were appearing. In 1890 the two major women's groups combined as the National American Women's Suffrage Association. Although Mrs. Stanton and Miss Anthony were the first two presidents of the association, new leaders were emerging, the most notable being Carrie Chapman Catt, a person who combined superb organizing abilities and political skills with a genuine commitment to broad social reform. The NAWSA made winning the right to vote its main objective, and concentrated on a state-by-state approach. In the 1890's it won some minor victories; by 1896 Wyoming, Utah, Colorado, and Idaho had been conquered. Although it suffered some discouraging setbacks the burgeoning of the progressive movement helped the association, as large numbers of middle-class recruits of both sexes adopted the cause. California voted for women's suffrage in 1911 after having defeated the proposal some years earlier, then several other states fell in line. The suffragists then shifted the campaign back to the national level,

The suffragists used all the trappings of early 20th century political campaigning to bring their cause to the public's eye: parades, signs, slogans, and as the banner held up in this wagon announces, a ''Giant Suffrage Day, Aug. 30'' at the Greater New York Fair at Empire City Park in Yonkers. (Culver Pictures.)

the lead taken by a new organization, the Congressional Union, headed by Alice Paul. After some hesitation the NAWSA, ably led by Mrs. Catt, also began to campaign for a Constitutional amendment, which finally won congressional approval in 1918. By 1920 the necessary three-quarters of the states had approved this Nineteenth Amendment; the long fight was over.

The progressive drive for political democracy also found expression in the Seventeenth Amendment to the Constitution, ratified in 1913, which required the popular election of senators. A group of ''insurgent'' congressmen also managed to reform the House of Representatives by limiting the power of the Speaker. During the early years of the century, operating under the system

established in the 1890's by ''Czar'' Thomas B. Reed, Speaker Joseph G. Cannon exercised tyrannical authority, appointing the members of all committees and controlling the course of legislation. A representative could seldom even obtain the floor without first explaining his purpose to Cannon and obtaining the Speaker's consent. In 1910, however, the insurgents, led by George W. Norris of Nebraska, stripped Cannon of his control over the House Rules Committee. Thereafter, appointments to committees were determined by the whole membership, acting through party caucuses. The spirit of this change was thoroughly progressive. "We want the House to be representative of the people and each individual member to have his ideas presented and passed on," Norris explained.

No other important alterations of the national political system were made during the Progressive Era. Although some 20 states passed Presidential primary laws, no change in the cumbersome and undemocratic method of electing Presidents was accomplished. An attempt to improve the efficiency of the federal bureaucracy led Congress to create a Commission on Efficiency and Economy in 1911, but it did not act on the commission's recommendations. Congress did, however, pass a law in 1911 requiring representatives to file statements of their campaign expenses.

Social and Economic Reform

Most progressives saw political reform only as a means to an end; once the system had been made responsive to the desires of the people, they hoped to use it to improve society itself. Many cities began to experiment with "gas and water socialism," taking over public-utility companies and operating them as departments of the municipal government. Progressive mayors achieved a wide range of social and economic improvements as well. Toledo's "Golden Rule" Jones established a minimum wage for city employees, built playgrounds and golf courses, and moderated the city's harsh penal code. Seth Low improved New York's public transportation system and obtained the passage of the tenement house law of 1901. Tom Johnson forced a fare cut to three cents on the Cleveland street railways.

At the state level, progressives continued to battle for legislation based on the police power, despite restrictions imposed by the courts under the Fourteenth Amendment. In general, industrial workers improved their position during the period but mainly because good times kept unemployment down. Real wages rose only slightly in spite of the rapid increase in labor productivity, and the length of the work week declined very slowly. Government action did force a significant decline in the employment of children, however. Sparked by the National Child Labor

Committee, organized in 1904 to coordinate the drive, reformers over the next ten years obtained laws in nearly every state banning the employment of young children (the minimum age varied from 12 to 16) and limiting the hours of older children to eight or ten per day. Many states also outlawed night work and labor in dangerous occupations by minors. These laws fixed no uniform standards and many were poorly enforced, yet when Congress passed a federal child labor law in 1916, the Supreme Court, in *Hammer v. Dagenhart* (1918), declared it unconstitutional.°

The states also extended increasing protection to female workers. By 1917 nearly all had placed limitations on the hours of women employed in industry, and about ten states also had set minimum wage standards for women. Once again, however, federal action that would have extended such regulations to the entire country did not materialize. Even a ten-hour law for women workers in the District of Columbia was thrown out by the Court in *Adkins v. Children's Hospital* (1923).

Legislation protecting workers against on-the-job accidents was also enacted by many states. Disasters like the 1911 Triangle fire in New York City, in which nearly 150 women perished because the Triangle shirtwaist factory had no fire escapes, led to the passage of stricter municipal building codes and to many state factory inspection acts. By 1910 most states had modified the old common-law principle that a worker accepted the risk of accident as one of the conditions of employment and was not entitled to compensation if injured unless it could be proved that the employer had been negligent, a costly, uncertain, and time-consuming procedure. Gradually, they adopted accident insurance systems, and some also began to grant pensions to widows with small children.

The passage of so much state social legislation sent conservatives scurrying to the Supreme

°A second child labor law, passed in 1919, was also thrown out by the Court, and a child labor amendment, submitted in 1924, failed to achieve ratification by the necessary three-quarters of the states.

Court for redress. Such persons believed, quite sincerely in most instances, that *no* government had the power to deprive either workers or employers of the right to negotiate any kind of labor contract they wished. The decision of the Supreme Court in the Lochner bakeshop case (1905) seemed to indicate that the justices would adopt this point of view. But when an Oregon law limiting women laundry workers to ten hours a day was challenged in the case of *Muller v. Oregon* (1908), Florence Kelley and Josephine Goldmark of the Consumers' League, one of the most effective women's organizations of the period, persuaded Louis D. Brandeis to defend the statute before the Court. With the aid of League researchers Brandeis prepared a remarkable brief stuffed with economic and sociological evidence indicating that *in fact* long hours damaged both the health of individual women and the health of society. This nonlegal evidence greatly impressed the judges. "It may not be amiss," they declared, "to notice . . . expressions of opinion from other than judicial sources" in determining the constitutionality of such laws. "Woman's physical structure, and the functions she performs in consequence thereof, justify special legislation," they concluded. "The limitations which this statute places upon her contractual powers . . . are not imposed solely for her benefit, but also largely for the benefit of all."

The fact that the Oregon law applied only to women reduced the importance of the Muller case somewhat. In some later cases it threw out labor laws based on the police power. Nevertheless, after 1908 the right of states to protect the weaker members of society by special legislation was widely accepted. The use of the "Brandeis brief" technique to demonstrate the need for such action became standard practice.

Progressives also launched a massive if ill-coordinated attack on the economic problems of the times, particularly those related to monopoly and business influence on government. The variety of regulatory legislation passed by the states between 1900 and 1917 was almost endless. In Wisconsin the progressives created a powerful railroad commission staffed with nonpartisan ex-

perts; they enacted a graduated income tax and strengthened the state tax commission, which then proceeded to force corporations to bear their proper share of the cost of government; they overhauled the laws regulating insurance companies, passing some two dozen acts in a single year (1907) and setting up a small state-owned life insurance company to serve as a yardstick for evaluating the rates of private companies. In 1911, besides creating an industrial commission to enforce the state's labor and factory legislation, they established a conservation commission, headed by Charles R. Van Hise, president of the University of Wisconsin.

A similar spate of legislation characterized the brief reign of Woodrow Wilson as governor of New Jersey (1911–13). Urged on by the relentless Wilson, the New Jersey legislature created a strong public-utility commission with authority to evaluate the properties of railroad, gas, electric, telephone, and express companies, and to fix rates and set standards for these corporations. The legislature also passed storage and food inspection laws, and in 1913, after Wilson had moved on to the Presidency, it enacted seven bills (the "Seven Sisters" laws) tightening the state's notoriously loose controls over corporations, which had won New Jersey the unenviable reputation of being "the mother of trusts."

Economic reform movements in other states were less spectacular but impressive in the mass. In New York an investigation of the big life insurance companies led to comprehensive changes in the insurance laws and put Charles Evans Hughes, who had conducted the investigation, in the governor's chair, where he achieved other progressive reforms. In Iowa stiff new laws regulating railroads were passed in 1906. In Nebraska the legislature created a system of bank deposit insurance in 1909. Minnesota levied an inheritance tax and built a state harvesting machine factory to combat the harvester trust at about this time. Georgia raised the taxes on corporations. These are but typical examples, plucked almost at random from among hundreds of laws passed by states in every part of the nation. However, as in the area of social legislation, piecemeal state regulation failed to solve the problems of an economy growing yearly more integrated and complex. It was on the national level that the most significant battles for economic reform were fought.

Theodore Roosevelt

On September 6, 1901, an anarchist named Leon Czolgosz shot President McKinley during a public reception at the Pan-American Exposition at Buffalo, New York. Eight days later McKinley died and Theodore Roosevelt became President of the United States. The new President hastened to assure the country that he intended to carry on in his predecessor's footsteps, but his ascension to the Presidency marked the beginning of a new era in national politics.

Although only 42, by far the youngest President in the nation's history up to that time, Roosevelt brought solid qualifications to his high office. Son of a well-to-do New York merchant of Dutch ancestry, he had graduated from Harvard in 1880 and had studied law briefly at Columbia, although he did not complete his degree. In addition to political experience that included a term in the New York assembly, six years on the United States Civil Service Commission, two years as police commissioner of New York City, another as assistant secretary of the navy, and a term as governor of New York, he had been a rancher in Dakota Territory and a soldier in the Spanish War. He was also a well-known author: his *Naval War of 1812* (1882), begun during his undergraduate days at Harvard, and his four-volume *Winning of the West* (1889–96) were valuable works of scholarship, and he had written two popular biographies and other books as well. Politically, he had always been a loyal Republican. He rejected the Mugwump heresy in 1884, despite his distaste for Blaine, and he vigorously denounced Populism, Bryanism, and "labor agitators" during the tempestuous nineties.

Nevertheless, his elevation to the Presidency alarmed many conservatives, and not without reason. To begin with, he did not fit their conception, based on a composite image of the Chief Executives from Hayes to McKinley, of what a President should be like. He seemed too undignified, too energetic, too outspoken, colorful, unconventional. It was one thing to have operated a cattle ranch, another to have captured a gang of rustlers at gunpoint; one thing to have run a metropolitan police force, another to have roamed New York slums in the small hours in order to catch patrolmen fraternizing with thieves and prostitutes; one thing to have commanded a regiment, another to have killed a Spaniard personally.

Roosevelt had been a weak and sickly child, plagued by asthma and poor eyesight, and he seems to have spent much of his adult life compensating for the sense of inadequacy that these troubles bred in him. Mark Twain called him "the Tom Sawyer of the political world . . . always hunting for a chance to show off." He repeatedly carried his displays of physical stamina and personal courage, and his interest in athletics and big-game-hunting, to preternatural lengths. Once, while fox-hunting, he fell from his horse, cutting his face severely and breaking his left arm. Instead of waiting for help to come or struggling to some nearby house to summon a doctor, Roosevelt clambered back on his horse and resumed the chase. "I was in at the death," he wrote next day. "I looked pretty gay, with one arm dangling, and my face and clothes like the walls of a slaughter house." That evening, after his arm had been set and put in splints, he attended a dinner party.

Roosevelt also worshiped aggressiveness and was extremely sensitive to any threat to his honor as a gentleman. When another young man showed some slight interest in Roosevelt's fiancée, he sent off for a set of French dueling pistols. His teachers found him an interesting student, for he was intelligent and imaginative, but rather annoyingly argumentative. "Now look here, Roosevelt," one Harvard professor finally said to him, "let me talk. I'm running this course."

Few individuals have rationalized or sublimated their feelings of inferiority as effectively as Roosevelt and to such good purpose. And few have been more genuinely warm-hearted, more full of spontaneity, more committed to the ideals of public service and national greatness. As a political leader he was energetic and hard-driving but seldom lacking in good judgment: responsibility usually tempered his aggressiveness. But conservatives and timid souls, sensing his aggressiveness even when he held it in check, distrusted Roosevelt's judgment, fearing he might go off half-cocked in some crisis.

Above all, Roosevelt believed in action. When he was first mentioned as a possible running mate for McKinley in 1900, he wrote: "The Vice Presidency is a most honorable office, but for a young man there is not much to do." It would have been unthinkable for him to preside over a mere caretaker administration devoted to maintaining the *status quo*. However, the reigning Republican politicos, basking in the sunshine of the prosperity that had contributed so much to their victory in 1900, distrusted anything suggestive of change. Mark Hanna reflected the mood of most of his fellow senators when he urged the country to "stand pat and continue Republican prosperity," and the same sentiment pervaded the House, where Speaker Cannon said that his philosophy could be summed up in the phrase: "Stand by the status."

If Roosevelt had been the impetuous hothead that conservatives feared, he would have plunged ahead without regard for their feelings and influence. Instead he moved slowly and won his major victories by using his executive power rather than by persuading Congress to pass new laws. His domestic program, ill-defined at first, included some measure of control of big corporations, more power for the Interstate Commerce Commission (ICC), and the conservation of natural resources. By consulting fully with congressional leaders and following their advice not to bring up controversial matters like the tariff and currency reform, with which he was not deeply concerned in any case, he obtained a modest budget of new laws. The Newlands Act (1902) funneled the proceeds from land sales in the West into federal irrigation projects. The Expedition Act (1903) speeded the handling of antitrust suits in the courts. Another 1903 law created a Department of Commerce and Labor, which was to include a Bureau of Corporations, with authority to investigate industrial combines and issue reports. The Elkins Railroad Act of 1903 strengthened the Interstate Commerce Commission's hand against the railroads by making the receiving as well as the granting of rebates illegal and by forbidding the roads to deviate in any way from their published rates.

Roosevelt and Big Business

Roosevelt soon became known as a "trustbuster," and in the sense that he considered the monopoly problem the most pressing issue of the times, the title has some meaning. But he did not believe in breaking up big corporations indiscriminately. "Much of the legislation . . . enacted against trusts," he said in 1900 while governor of New York, "is not one whit more intelligent than the mediaeval bull against the comet, and has not been one particle more effective." Industrial giantism, he believed, "could not be eliminated unless we were willing to turn back the wheels of modern progress." Regulation, rather than disruption, seemed the best way to deal with the big corporations.

However, with Congress unwilling to pass a stiff regulatory law—even the bill creating the relatively innocuous Bureau of Corporations ran into much opposition—Roosevelt resorted to the Sherman Act to get at the problem. Although the Supreme Court decision in the Sugar Trust case seemed to have emasculated that law, in 1902 he ordered the Justice Department to bring suit against the Northern Securities Company.

He chose his target wisely. The Northern Securities Company controlled the Great Northern, the Northern Pacific, and the Chicago, Burlington and Quincy railroads. It had been created in 1901, after a titanic battle on the New York Stock Exchange between the forces of J. P. Morgan and James J. Hill and those of E. H. Harriman, who was associated with the Rockefeller interests. In their efforts to obtain control of the Northern Pacific, the rivals had forced its stock up to $1,000 a share, ruining many speculators and threatening to cause a major panic. Neither side could win a clear-cut victory, so they decided to put the stock of all three railroads in a holding company owned by the two groups. Since Harriman also controlled the Union Pacific and the Southern Pacific, a virtual monopoly of western railroads was thus effected. The public had been greatly alarmed, for the merger seemed to typify the rapaciousness of the great tycoons. Few big corporations had more enemies; thus Roosevelt's attack won wide support. He would not surrender, he said, even if it were necessary to "cripple industry, stagnate business or tie up the commerce of the world."

The announcement of the suit caused consternation in the business world. Morgan rushed to the White House. "If we have done anything wrong," he said to the President, "send your man to my man and they can fix it up." Roosevelt was not fundamentally opposed to exactly this sort of agreement, but it was too late to compromise in this particular instance. Attorney General Philander C. Knox pressed the case vigorously, and in 1904 the Court ordered the dissolution of the Northern Securities Company. Although ownership of the three railroads was not affected, this decision had extremely important results. It made further prosecutions possible—Roosevelt soon ordered suits against the meat packers, the Standard Oil Trust, and the American Tobacco Company—and served notice on all the great corporations that they could no longer ignore the Sherman Act. Roosevelt's stock among progressives rose, yet he had not embarrassed the conservatives in Congress by demanding new antitrust legislation.

Furthermore, he went out of his way to assure *cooperative* corporation magnates that he had no intention of attacking them. He saw no basic conflict between capital and labor and was not against size per se. "In our industrial and social system," Roosevelt said, "the interests of all men are so closely intertwined that in the immense majority of cases a straight-dealing man who by his efficiency, by his ingenuity and industry, benefits himself must also benefit others." His Bureau of Corporations followed a policy of "obtaining hearty co-operation rather than arousing [the] antagonism of business and industrial interests." At an informal White House conference in 1905, Roosevelt and Elbert H. Gary, chairman of the board of U. S. Steel, reached a "gentlemen's agreement" whereby Gary promised "to co-operate with the Government in every possible way." The Bureau of Corporations would conduct an investigation of U. S. Steel, Gary providing it with full access to company records. Roosevelt, in turn, promised that if the investigation revealed any malpractices on the part of the corporation, he would allow Gary to set matters right voluntarily, thus avoiding an antitrust suit. He reached a similar agreement with the International Harvester Company two years later.

There were limits to the effectiveness of such arrangements; Standard Oil, for example, first agreed to a similar détente and then reneged, refusing to turn over vital records to the bureau. The Justice Department then brought suit against the company under the Sherman Act, and eventually it was broken up at the order of the Supreme Court. Roosevelt would have preferred a more binding kind of regulation, but when he asked for laws giving the government supervisory authority over big combinations, Congress refused to act. Given this situation, his gentlemen's agreements seemed the best alternative. Trusts that conformed to his somewhat subjective standards could remain as they were; others must take their chances with the Supreme Court.

Roosevelt also made remarkable use of his executive power during the anthracite coal strike of 1902. In June of that year the United Mine Workers, led by John Mitchell, laid down their picks and demanded higher wages, an eight-hour day, and recognition of the union. Most of the anthracite mines were owned by railroads. Two years earlier the miners had won a ten per cent wage increase in a similar strike, chiefly because

The comic weekly *Life* ran a series called "The Teddyssey" in 1907. In this episode Columbia steers T. R. safely past the monopolistic Sirens— Rockefeller, harpist J. P. Morgan, and Carnegie, a Scotch-plaid mermaid. (*Life*, May 16, 1907.)

the owners feared that labor unrest might endanger the election of McKinley. Now the mine operators were dead set against further concessions; when the men walked out, they shut down their properties and prepared to starve the strikers into submission.

Throughout the summer and early fall the miners held firm. They conducted themselves with great restraint, avoiding violence and offering to submit their claims to arbitration. As the price of anthracite soared with the approach of winter, sentiment in their behalf mounted. The fact that great railroad corporations closely allied with Wall Street controlled most of the mines and that the owners refused even to discuss terms with the union also predisposed the public in the workers' favor. The operators' spokesman, George F. Baer of the Reading Railroad, proved particularly inept at handling public relations. Baer stated categorically that God was on the side of the owners, but when someone suggested asking an important Roman Catholic prelate to arbitrate the dispute, he replied icily: "Anthracite mining is a business and not a religious, sentimental or academic proposition."

Roosevelt shared the public's sympathy for the miners, and the threat of a coal famine naturally alarmed him. But for months he could think of no legal way to intervene. Finally, early in October, he summoned both sides to a conference in Washington, asking them as patriotic Americans to sacrifice "personal consideration[s]" for the "general good." His action enraged the operators, for they believed he was trying to force them to recognize the union. They refused even to speak to the UMW representatives at the conference and demanded that Roosevelt end the strike by force and bring suit against the union under the Sherman Act. Mitchell, on the other hand, aware of the immense prestige that Roosevelt had conferred upon the union by calling the conference, cooperated fully with the President.

The refusal of the operators to bargain infuriated Roosevelt and strengthened public support of the miners. Even former President Grover Cleveland, who had used federal troops to break the Pullman strike, said that he was "disturbed and vexed by the tone and substance of the operators' deliverances." Encouraged by this state of affairs, Roosevelt took a bold step—he announced that unless a settlement was reached promptly, he would order federal troops into the anthracite regions, not to break the strike but to seize and operate the mines.

This threat of government intervention brought the owners to terms. Secretary of War Root worked out the details with J. P. Morgan, whose firm had great interests in the Reading and other railroads, while cruising up and down the Hudson River on Morgan's yacht. The miners would go back to the pits, and all issues between them and the operators would be submitted for settlement to a commission appointed by Roosevelt. After a last-minute crisis over the inclusion of a union man on the commission—solved by Roosevelt's appointing the president of one of the Railroad Brotherhoods but classifying him as an "eminent sociologist" to save the faces of the operators—both sides accepted this arrangement and the men went back to work. In March 1903 the commission granted the miners a ten per cent wage increase and a nine-hour day. The owners, however, were not required to recognize the United Mine Workers.

To the public, the incident seemed a perfect illustration of the progressive spirit—in Roosevelt's words, everyone had received a "square deal." Actually, the results were by no means so clear-cut. The miners gained relatively little and the operators lost still less, for the commission recommended a ten per cent increase in the price of coal, ample compensation for their increased wage costs. Eventually, George F. Baer came to believe that Roosevelt's appointment of the commission was the best thing he ever did. The President was the main winner. The public acclaimed him as a fearless, imaginative, and public-spirited executive. Construing the powers of his office broadly, he had interjected the federal government into a labor dispute, forced both sides to accept his leadership, and established an extralegal committee of neutrals representing the national interest to arbitrate the questions at issue. Without calling upon Congress for support, he had expanded his own authority and hence that of the federal government in order to protect the public interest. His action marked a major forward step in the evolution of the modern Presidency.

Roosevelt's Second Term

By reviving the Sherman Act, settling the coal strike, and pushing a number of moderate reforms through Congress, Roosevelt insured that he would be elected President in 1904 in his own right. Progressives were pleased by his performance if not yet captivated. Conservative Republicans, impressed by his deference to men like Senator Nelson Aldrich and Speaker Cannon, offered no serious objection to his renomination and supported him during the campaign. Sensing that Roosevelt had won over the liberals, the Democrats nominated a conservative candidate, Judge Alton B. Parker of New York, and bid for the support of eastern industrialists. This strategy failed, for businessmen continued to eye the party of Bryan with intense suspicion. Despite his resentment at Roosevelt's handling of the Northern Securities incident, J. P. Morgan contributed $150,000 to the Republican campaign. Other tycoons gave with equal generosity. As the New York Sun put it, most businessmen preferred "the impulsive candidate of the party of conservatism to the conservative candidate of the party which the business interests regard as permanently and dangerously impulsive." Roosevelt swept the country, piling up a majority of more than 2.5 million votes. Even border states like Maryland and Missouri gave him their electoral votes. According to one wit: "Parker ran for the presidency against Theodore Roosevelt and was defeated by acclamation."

Encouraged by this landslide and by the increasing militancy of progressives in the separate states, Roosevelt began to press Congress for reform legislation. His most imaginative proposal was a plan to make the District of Columbia a model progressive community. He suggested a variety of reforms, including a child labor law, a factory inspection law, and a slum-clearance program, but Congress refused to act. Likewise, his request for a minimum wage for railroad workers was rejected.

He had greater success, however, when he urged Congress to increase the power of the Interstate Commerce Commission again. The El-kins Railroad Act had proved a bitter disappoint-ment, for the courts continued to favor the railroads in most cases. Rebating remained a seri-ous problem. With progressive state governors urging him to act and with farmers and manufac-turers, especially in the Middle West, clamoring for relief against discriminatory rates, Roosevelt was ready by 1905 to make railroad legislation his major objective. The ICC should be empow-ered to fix rates, not merely to challenge unrea-sonable ones. It should also have the right to in-spect the private records of the railroads, since fair rates could not be determined unless the true financial condition of the roads was known.

Since these proposals struck at rights that businessmen considered sacrosanct, many con-gressmen balked at them. Roosevelt cleverly threatened to call a special session of Congress to revise the tariff unless they agreed, and this pro-posal so alarmed conservative Republicans that most of them fell into line. The conservatives did manage to obtain amendments preserving the right of the roads to challenge ICC rate decisions in the courts. Much to the chagrin of some of his progressive supporters, Roosevelt meekly ac-cepted this compromise, for he remained eager to conciliate his party's right wing. In June 1906 the Hepburn bill became law. It gave the com-mission the power to inspect the books of rail-road companies, to fix rates (subject to judicial review), and to control sleeping car companies, owners of oil pipelines, and other firms engaged in transportation. The roads could no longer issue passes freely, an important check on their politi-cal influence. All in all, the Hepburn Act was a major achievement. Although the right of the federal government to regulate interstate carriers had been long recognized, this law made that regulation reasonably effective for the first time.

Roosevelt also obtained passage of meat in-spection and pure food and drug legislation in 1906. The question of federal regulation of slaughterhouses was an old one, dating back to the "pork controversy" with the European pow-ers in the 1880's. Feelings about meat inspection in the business world were mixed. The major packers tended to favor it because of their inter-est in the export market, while most local pack-ers objected. Other businessmen were also di-vided, some objecting on grounds of principle to any extension of government regulation. In 1906, for example, the president of the National Asso-ciation of Manufacturers opposed regulating the packers, but the NAM's board of directors voted not to campaign against inspection.

The issue was precipitated by the publication in 1906 of Upton Sinclair's novel *The Jungle,* a devastating exposé of the filthy conditions in the Chicago slaughterhouses. Sinclair was more in-terested in writing a socialist tract than in meat inspection, but his book, which became a best-seller, raised a storm against the packers. When Roosevelt read *The Jungle,* he sent two officials to Chicago to investigate. Their report was so shocking, he said, that its publication would "be well-nigh ruinous to our export trade in meat." He threatened to release the report, however, unless Congress acted. After a hot fight, the meat inspection bill passed. A Pure Food and Drug Act, forbidding the manufacture and sale of adul-terated and fraudulently labeled products, rode through Congress on the coattails of this measure.

Roosevelt has probably received more credit than he deserves for these laws. He had never been deeply interested in pure food legislation and considered Dr. Harvey W. Wiley, chief chemist of the Department of Agriculture and the leader of the fight for this reform, something of a crank. In the case of the meat inspection law, as with the Hepburn Act, he placed accom-modating the conservatives above total victory, accepting a halfway measure cheerfully, despite his loud denunciations of the evils under attack. "As now carried on the [meat-packing] business is both a menace to health and an outrage on decency," he said. "No legislation that is not drastic and thoroughgoing will be of avail." Yet he went along with the packers' demand that the government pay the costs of inspection, although he believed that "the only way to secure effi-ciency is by the imposition upon the packers of a fee." Nevertheless, the end results were positive and generally in line with his conception of the public good.

To advanced liberals, Roosevelt's achievements seemed limited when placed beside his professed objectives and his smug evaluations of what he had done. They did not see how he could be a reformer and a defender of established interests at the same time. Roosevelt, however, found no difficulty in holding such a position. As one historian has said, "he stood close to the center and bared his teeth at the conservatives of the right and the liberals of the extreme left." He also changed with the times; as the progressive movement advanced, he advanced with it, never accepting all the ideas of what he called its "lunatic fringe," but taking steadily more liberal positions. For example, he always insisted that he was not hostile to business interests, but when these interests sought to exploit the national domain, they had no more implacable foe. He placed some 150 million acres of forest lands in federal reserves, and he enforced the laws governing grazing, mining, and lumbering strictly. When his opponents managed to attach a rider to an essential appropriation bill prohibiting the creation of further reserves without the approval of Congress, Roosevelt, in a typical example of his broad use of executive power, hurriedly transferred an additional 17 million acres to the reserve before signing the bill. In 1908 he organized a National Conservation Conference, attended by 44 governors and 500 other persons, to discuss conservation matters. As a result of this meeting, most of the states created conservation commissions.

As Roosevelt became more liberal, conservative Republicans began to balk at following his lead. The sudden panic that struck the financial world in October 1907 speeded the trend considerably. Government policies had no direct bearing on the panic, which began with a run on several important New York trust companies and spread to the Stock Exchange when speculators found themselves unable to borrow money to meet their obligations. In this emergency Roosevelt acted forcefully, sending Secretary of the Treasury George C. Cortelyou to New York and allowing him to deposit large amounts of government cash in New York banks. Roosevelt also informally authorized the acquisition of the Tennessee Coal and Iron Company by U. S. Steel when the bankers told him that the purchase was necessary to prevent a further spread of the panic. But in spite of his efforts, conservatives referred to the financial collapse as "Roosevelt's Panic" and blamed the President for the depression that followed on its heels. Such men argued that dangerous socioeconomic experiments were undermining the confidence of the business community.

Roosevelt, however, turned left after 1907 rather than right. In 1908 he came out for federal income and inheritance taxes, for stricter regulation of interstate corporations, and for reforms designed to help the industrial worker. He denounced "the speculative folly and the flagrant dishonesty" of "malefactors of great wealth," further alienating the conservative, or Old Guard, wing of his party. These politicians felt that economic reform had gone far enough and that political reforms like the direct primary were destroying the basis of their power. They also resented the attacks on their integrity implicit in many of Roosevelt's statements. When the President began criticizing the courts, the last bastion of conservatism, he lost all chance of obtaining further reform legislation. As he put it himself, during his last months in office "the period of stagnation continued to rage with uninterrupted violence."

William Howard Taft

Nevertheless, Roosevelt remained popular and politically powerful; when his term ended, he chose William Howard Taft, his secretary of war, to succeed him and easily obtained his nomination. William Jennings Bryan was again the Democratic nominee. Campaigning on Roosevelt's record, Taft carried the country by well over a million votes, defeating Bryan by 321 to 162 in the Electoral College.

Taft was intelligent, experienced, and public-spirited; he seemed ideally suited to carry out Roosevelt's policies. Born in Cincinnati in 1857, educated at Yale, he had served as an Ohio judge, as solicitor general of the United States under Harrison, and then as a federal circuit court judge before accepting McKinley's assignment to head the Philippine Commission in 1900. His success as civil governor of the Philippines led Roosevelt to make him secretary of war in 1904. He supported the "Square Deal" loyally. This, together with his mentor's ardent endorsement, won him the backing of most progressive Republicans. Yet the Old Guard liked him too; although outgoing, he had none of the Rooseveltian impetuosity and aggressiveness. His antilabor opinions voiced while on the bench also raised his status among conservatives. His genial personality and his obvious desire to avoid conflict appealed to moderates.

However, Taft lacked the physical and mental stamina required of a modern Chief Executive. Although not really lazy, he weighed over 300 pounds and needed to rest this vast bulk more than the job allowed. He liked to eat in leisurely fashion, to idle away mornings on the golf course, to take an afternoon nap. Campaigning bored him, speechmaking seemed a needless chore. The judicial life was his real love; intense partisanship dismayed and confused him. He was too reasonable to control a coalition and too unambitious to impose his will on others. He found extremists irritating, persistent men difficult to resist. He supported many progressive measures, but he never absorbed the progressive spirit.

Taft honestly desired to carry out most of Roosevelt's policies. He enforced the Sherman Act even more vigorously than his predecessor, and continued Roosevelt's policy of adding to the national forest reserves. He pushed for a postal savings system, and approved a measure—the Mann-Elkins Act of 1910—that further strengthened the Interstate Commerce Commission by empowering it to suspend rate increases without waiting for a shipper to complain, and by establishing a Commerce Court to speed the settlement of railroad rate litigation. An eight-hour

Taft was the first Presidential golfer, playing enthusiastically despite his bulk. He ended his career happily as Chief Justice of the Supreme Court. (Culver Pictures.)

day for all persons engaged in work on government contracts, mine-safety legislation, and a number of other reform measures also received his approval. He even summoned Congress into special session specifically to reduce tariff duties—something Roosevelt had not dared to attempt. But Taft had been disturbed by Roosevelt's sweeping use of executive power to achieve reform. "We have got to work out our problems on the basis of law," he insisted. Whereas Roosevelt had excelled at maneuvering around congressional opposition and in finding ways to accomplish his objectives without waiting for Congress to act, Taft adamantly refused to adopt such tactics. His restraint was in many ways admirable, but it sharply reduced his effectiveness.

Moreover, in case after case, Taft's lack of vigor and his political ineptness led to trouble. He had an uncanny ability to aggravate men with views substantially like his own. In the matter of the tariff, he favored downward revision. When the special session met in 1909, the House promptly passed the Payne bill, which was roughly in line with his desires. But Senate protectionists, led by Nelson Aldrich, restored the high rates of the Act of 1897 on most items. A group of "insurgent" senators, led by Robert La Follette of Wisconsin, Jonathan Dolliver of Iowa, and Albert J. Beveridge of Indiana, fought desperately against these changes, producing masses of statistics to show that the proposed schedules on cotton goods, woolens, and other products were unreasonably high. They were fighting the President's battle, but Taft did little to help them. He signed the Payne-Aldrich measure and even called it "the best [tariff] bill that the Republican party ever passed." He had some small justification for this faint praise, since the act did make important reductions in the duties on cotton goods, hides, shoes, and iron ore, but the President's attitude dumbfounded the progressives.

In 1910 Taft got into a similar difficulty with the conservationists. Although he believed in husbanding natural resources carefully, he had disapproved of the way Roosevelt had circumvented Congress in adding to the forest reserves. He demanded, and eventually obtained, specific legislation to accomplish this purpose. Yet he nonetheless roused the wrath of many conservationists. The issue concerned the integrity of his secretary of the interior, Richard A. Ballinger. A less than ardent conservationist, Ballinger returned certain waterpower sites to the public domain that his predecessor in the Roosevelt administration had withdrawn on the legally questionable ground that they were to become ranger stations. Ballinger's action alarmed Chief Forester Gifford Pinchot, the darling of the conservationists, and when Pinchot learned that

Ballinger also intended to validate the shaky claim of some powerful mining interests to a vast tract of coal-rich land in Alaska, he launched an intemperate attack on the secretary. In this Ballinger–Pinchot controversy, Taft felt obliged to support his own man. The coal-lands dispute was complex, and Pinchot's charges were both exaggerated and in poor taste. It was certainly unfair to call Ballinger "the most effective opponent the conservation policies have yet had."

When Pinchot, whose own motives were partly political, persisted in attacking Ballinger, Taft dismissed him, thus bringing down upon himself the wrath of the conservationists. He had really no choice under the circumstances, but a more adept leader would have found some way of avoiding a showdown.

Breakup of the Republican Party

One ominous aspect of the Ballinger–Pinchot affair was the fact that Pinchot was a close friend of Theodore Roosevelt. After Taft's inauguration, Roosevelt had gone off on a hunting expedition to Africa, bearing in his baggage an autographed photograph of his protégé and a touching letter of appreciation, in which the new President said: "I can never forget that the power I now exercise was a voluntary transfer from you to me." For months, as he trudged across Africa, guns blazing, Roosevelt remained almost completely out of touch with affairs in the United States. When he emerged from the wilderness in March 1910, bearing over 3,000 trophies, including 9 lions, 5 elephants, and 13 rhinos, he was quickly caught up in the growing squabble between the progressive members of his party and its titular head. Pinchot met him in Italy, laden with injured innocence and a packet of angry letters from various progressives. His close friend Senator Lodge, essentially a conservative, barraged him with messages, the gist of which was that Taft was lazy and inept and that Roosevelt should prepare to become the "Moses" who would guide the party "out of the wilderness of doubt and discontent" into which Taft had led it.

Roosevelt hoped to steer a middle course, but Pinchot's complaints impressed him. Taft had deliberately decided to strike out on his own, he now concluded. "No man must render such a service as that I rendered Taft and expect the individual . . . not in the end to become uncomfortable and resentful," he wrote Lodge sadly. No immediate break took place, but Taft sensed the former President's coolness and was offended by it. He was egged on by his ambitious wife, who wanted him to stand clear of the Rooseveltian shadow and establish his own reputation.

Probably the resulting rupture was inevitable. The Republican party was dividing into two factions, the progressives and the Old Guard. Forced to choose between them, Taft threw in his lot with the Old Guard. When House progressives revolted against the domination of Speaker Cannon, Taft deprived them of patronage, practically reading them out of the party. Roosevelt, in turn, backed the progressives. Speaking at Osawatomie, Kansas, in August 1910, he came out for a comprehensive program of social legislation, which he called the "New Nationalism." Besides attacking "special privilege" and the "unfair money-getting" practices of "lawbreakers of great wealth," he called for a broad expansion of federal power. "The betterment we seek must be accomplished," he said, "mainly through the National Government."

The final break came in October 1911, when the President ordered an antitrust suit against U. S. Steel. Roosevelt, of course, opposed breaking up large corporations. "The effort at prohibiting all combination has substantially failed," he said in his New Nationalism speech. "The way out lies . . . in completely controlling them." Taft, on the other hand, was prepared "to enforce [the Sherman] law or die in the attempt." What especially enraged Roosevelt, however, was Taft's emphasis in the steel suit on the absorption of the Tennessee Coal and Iron Company by U. S. Steel during the panic of 1907, which Roosevelt had unofficially authorized. The government's antitrust brief made Roosevelt appear to have been either an abettor of monopoly or—far worse—a fool who had been duped by the steel corporation. He began to denounce Taft publicly, and early in 1912 declared himself a candidate for the Republican Presidential nomination.

This dramatic split between the nation's two leading Republicans intensified the progressive—Old Guard conflict within the party. Already the liberal faction had organized (January 1911) a National Progressive Republican League and was pushing Senator La Follette for the Republican nomination. Roosevelt's entry into the race now encouraged the progressives to strike more boldly against the administration. Although some, particularly those from the Middle West, found Roosevelt's position on the Sherman Act unpalatable, in the last analysis the fact that he stood a better chance than La Follette of winning the nomination and carrying the country led most of them to swing to his support.

Roosevelt plunged into the preconvention campaign with typical energy. He was almost uniformly victorious in the states that held Presidential primaries, carrying even Ohio, Taft's home state. However, the President controlled the party machinery and entered the national convention with a small majority of the delegates. Since some of his supporters had been chosen under questionable circumstances, the Roosevelt forces challenged the right of 254 Taft delegates to their seats. Unfortunately for Roosevelt, the Taft-controlled credentials committee, paying little attention to the evidence, gave all but a few of these disputed seats to the President, who won easily on the first ballot.

If Roosevelt had swallowed his resentment and bided his time, Taft would almost certainly have been defeated in the election, and the 1916 Republican nomination would have been Roosevelt's for the asking. But he was understandably outraged by the ruthless manner in which the Taft "steamroller" had overridden his forces. When his leading supporters urged him to organize a third party and when two of them, George W. Perkins, formerly of the House of Morgan, and Frank Munsey, the publisher, offered to finance the campaign, he agreed to make the race. In August, amid scenes of hysterical enthusiasm, the first convention of the Progressive party met at Chicago and nominated him for President. Announcing that he felt "as strong as a bull moose," Roosevelt delivered a stirring "confession of faith," calling for strict regulation of corporations, a tariff commission, national Presidential primaries, minimum-wage and workmen's compensation laws, the elimination of child labor, and many other reforms.

Election of 1912

Meantime, the Democrats were making the most of the opportunity offered by the Republican schism. Had they nominated a conservative or allowed Bryan a fourth chance, they would probably have insured Roosevelt's election. Instead, after battling through 46 ballots at their convention in Baltimore, they nominated Woodrow Wilson, who had achieved a remarkable liberal record as governor of New Jersey.

Although as a political scientist Wilson had sharply criticized the *status quo* and had taken a pragmatic approach to the idea of government regulation of the economy, he had objected strongly to the Bryan brand of politics; in 1896 he voted the Gold Democratic ticket. But by 1912, influenced partly by ambition and partly by the spirit of the times, he had been converted to progressivism. He called his program the "New Freedom." The federal government could best advance the cause of social justice, he argued, by eradicating the special privileges that had enabled the "interests" to flourish. Where Roosevelt seemed to have lost faith in competition as a way of protecting the public against monopolies, Wilson insisted that competition could be restored. The government must break up the great trusts and establish fair rules for doing business, subjecting violators to stiff punishments; thereafter, the classical checks of the free-enterprise system would protect the public against exploitation without destroying individual

The *Life* cartoon above appeared at the time of the 1912 Presidential nominating conventions. Cartoonists had a field day with Roosevelt as a Bull Moose; below, T. R. enters the political zoo, from *Harper's*. (Both: Culver Pictures.)

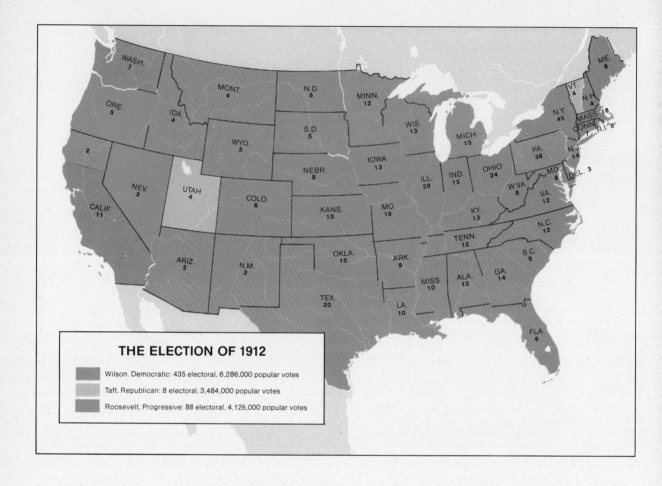

THE ELECTION OF 1912

Wilson. Democratic: 435 electoral, 6,286,000 popular votes

Taft, Republican: 8 electoral, 3,484,000 popular votes

Roosevelt, Progressive: 88 electoral, 4,126,000 popular votes

initiative and opportunity. "If America is not to have free enterprise, then she can have freedom of no sort whatever," he said. Instead of regulating monopoly as Roosevelt proposed, the nation should regulate competition. Although rather vague in explaining how to do this, he won the approval of thousands of voters who found the growing power of great corporations frightening, but who hesitated to make the thoroughgoing commitment to a welfare state that Roosevelt was advocating.

Roosevelt's reasoning was perhaps theoretically sound. Fear of a powerful national government was an inheritance from the 18th century, when political power had been equated with monarchy and tyranny and when America had been sparsely settled and decentralized. In the 20th century, with democratic institutions firmly established and with a highly integrated economy, citizens had less reason to fear political centralization and economic regulation. As Herbert Croly pointed out in *The Promise of American Life* (1909), the time had come to employ Hamiltonian means to achieve Jeffersonian ends. Laissez faire also made less sense than it had in earlier times. Philosophers and scientists had undermined the old view of an orderly society designed by a divine watchmaker and capable of running itself. The complexities of the modern world required a positive approach, a plan, the close application of human intelligence to current social and economic problems.

Yet Wilson's New Freedom, being less drastic and more in line with American experience, had much to recommend it. The danger that selfish individuals would use the power of the state for their own ends had certainly not disappeared, despite the efforts of progressives to make government more responsive to popular opinion. Any considerable increase in national power would increase the danger, and likely create many new difficulties. Furthermore, individual freedom of opportunity surely merited the toleration of a certain amount of inefficiency. To choose between the New Nationalism and the New Freedom, between the dynamic Roosevelt and the idealistic Wilson, was indeed difficult.

While thousands grappled with this problem before going to the polls, partisan politics really determined the outcome of the election. Taft got the hard-core Republican vote but lost the progressive wing of the GOP to Roosevelt. Wilson, on the other hand, had the solid support of both conservative and liberal Democrats. As a result, he won an easy victory in the Electoral College, receiving 435 votes to Roosevelt's 88 and Taft's 8. The popular vote was Wilson, 6,286,000; Roosevelt, 4,126,000; and Taft, 3,484,000. But if partisan politics determined the winner, the election was nonetheless an overwhelming victory for progressivism. The radical temper of the times was shown by the 897,000 votes given Eugene V. Debs, the Socialist candidate. Altogether, professed liberals amassed over 11 million of the 15 million ballots cast. Wilson was a minority President, but he took office with a clear mandate to press forward with further reforms.

Wilson: The New Freedom

No man ever rose more suddenly and spectacularly in American politics than Woodrow Wilson. In the spring of 1910 he was president of Princeton University; he had never held or even run for public office. In the fall of 1912 he was President-elect of the United States. Yet if his rise was meteoric, in a very real sense he had devoted his whole life to preparing for it. Born in Staunton, Virginia, in 1856, son of a Presbyterian minister, Wilson studied political theory avidly as a youth, developing a profound admiration for the British parliamentary system and for such British statesmen as Edmund Burke and William E. Gladstone. While still in college he dreamed of representing his state in the Senate. He studied law solely because he thought it the best avenue to public office, and when he discovered himself temperamentally unsuited for a career at the bar, he took a doctorate at Johns Hopkins in political science.

For years, however, his hopes had seemed doomed to frustration. He taught first at Bryn Mawr, then at Wesleyan, finally at his alma mater, Princeton. He wrote several influential books, including *Congressional Government* and *The State,* and achieved an outstanding success as a teacher and lecturer. In 1902 he was chosen president of Princeton and soon won a place among the nation's leading educators. He revised the curriculum, introducing many new subjects but insisting that students pursue an organized and integrated course of study. He instituted the preceptorial system, which placed the students in close intellectual and social contact with their teachers. He also attracted many outstanding young scholars to the faculty. Eventually, his advanced educational ideas and his overbearing manner of applying them got him in trouble with some of Princeton's alumni and trustees; but though his university career was wrecked, the controversies, in which he appeared to be championing democracy and progress in the face of reactionary opponents, brought him at last to the attention of the politicians. Then, in a great rush, came power and fame.

Wilson was an immediate success as President. Since Roosevelt's last year, Congress had been almost continually at war with the executive branch and with itself. Legislative achievements had been relatively few. Now, although friction persisted, a small avalanche of important new measures received the approval of the lawmakers. In October 1913 came the Underwood Tariff, the first significant reduction of duties since before the Civil War. Food, wool, iron and steel, shoes, agricultural machinery, and other items that could be produced more cheaply in the United States than abroad were placed on the free list, and the rates on most other products were cut substantially, the object being to equalize the cost of foreign and domestic goods in order to make real competition between them possible. To compensate for the expected loss of revenue, the act provided for a graduated tax on personal incomes.°

Two months later the Federal Reserve Act was passed, giving the country a central banking system for the first time since Jackson destroyed the Bank of the United States. This measure divided the nation into 12 banking districts, each under the supervision of a Federal Reserve Bank, which was a sort of bank for bankers. All national banks in each district and those state banks that wished to participate had to invest six per cent of their capital and surplus in the Reserve Bank, which was empowered to exchange (the technical term is rediscount) paper money, called Federal Reserve notes, for the commercial and agricultural paper that member banks took in as security from borrowers. The volume of currency was no longer at the mercy of the supply of gold or any other particular commodity.

The crown and nerve center of the system was a Federal Reserve Board in Washington, which appointed a majority of the directors of the Federal Reserve Banks and had some control over rediscount *rates* (the commission charged by the Reserve Banks for performing the rediscounting function). Thus a true central banking system was created. When inflation threatened, the Reserve Banks could raise the rediscount rate, discouraging borrowing and reducing the amount of money in circulation. In bad times it could lower the rate, making it easier to borrow and injecting new dollars into the economy. Much remained to be learned about the proper management of the money supply, but the nation finally had a flexible yet safe currency.

°The Sixteenth Amendment, ratified in February 1913, authorized the collection of a federal income tax.

In 1914 Congress passed two important laws affecting corporations. One created a Federal Trade Commission to replace Roosevelt's Bureau of Corporations. In addition to investigating interstate corporations and publishing reports, this nonpartisan board could issue "cease and desist" orders against "unfair" trade practices brought to light through its researches. The law did not define the term "unfair," and the commission's rulings could be taken on appeal to the federal courts, but the FTC was nonetheless a powerful instrument for protecting the public against the trusts. The second measure, the Clayton Antitrust Act, made certain specific business practices illegal, including price discrimination that tended to foster monopoly, "tying" agreements—which forbade retailers from handling the products of a firm's competitors—and the creation of interlocking directorates as a means of controlling competing companies. Labor and agricultural organizations were exempted from the antitrust laws, and the use of injunctions in labor disputes was curtailed. Furthermore, the officers of corporations could be held individually responsible when their companies were found guilty of violating the antitrust laws.

While Wilson was not entirely in sympathy with all the terms of these laws, they reflected his desires and could not have been enacted without his hard-driving leadership. The time was ripe for reform. The fact that the Democrats controlled both houses of Congress for the first time since 1890 and were eager to make a good record also helped. But Wilson's imaginative and aggressive use of Presidential power was decisive. He entered office determined, like a British prime minister, to play an active part in the formulation of legislation and the management of Congress. He called the legislators into special session in April 1913, and appeared before them in person to lay out his program, the first President to address Congress since John Adams. Then he followed the course of administration bills closely. He installed a private telephone line between the Capitol and the White House. Administration representatives haunted the cloakrooms and lobbies of both houses. Cooperative congressmen began to receive little notes of praise and encouragement, recalcitrant ones stern demands for support, often written on the President's own portable typewriter. When lobbyists tried to frustrate his plans for tariff reform by bringing pressure to bear on key senators, he made a dramatic appeal to the people. "The public ought to know the extraordinary exertions being made by the lobby in Washington," he told reporters. "Only public opinion can check and destroy it." The voters responded to this appeal so strongly that the Senate stood firm and passed the tariff bill substantially as Wilson desired it.

In short, despite his lack of experience, Wilson proved to be a masterful politician as well as an inspiring leader. He explained his success by saying, only half humorously, that running the government was child's play for anyone who had managed the faculty of a university. Responsible *party* government was his objective; he expected individual Democrats to submit to the will of the party majority, and his idealism never prevented him from awarding the spoils of office to city bosses and conservative congressmen, so long as they supported his program.

Nor did his career as a political theorist make him rigid and doctrinaire. In practice the differences between the New Freedom point of view and that of the New Nationalism tended to disappear. The Underwood Tariff and the Clayton Antitrust Act fitted the philosophy Wilson had expounded during the campaign, but the Federal Trade Commission represented a step toward the kind of regulated economy that Roosevelt advocated, and so did the Federal Reserve system. Wilson drew advice from divergent sources—from the lawyer Louis D. Brandeis, ardent foe of monopoly, and from his mysterious, behind-the-scenes alter ego, Colonel Edward M. House, who was close to many prominent business leaders.

There were, however, limits to Wilson's progressivism, limits imposed partly by his temperament and partly by his philosophy. He disliked all forms of privilege, objecting almost as strenuously to laws granting special favors to farmers and workers as to those benefiting the tycoons.

When a bill was introduced in 1914 placing federal funds at the disposal of rural banks so that they could make low-interest loans to farmers, he refused to support it. "I have a very deep conviction that it is unwise and unjustifiable to extend the credit of the Government to a single class of the community," he said. He considered the provision exempting unions from the antitrust laws equally unsound. Nor would he push for a federal law prohibiting child labor. Such a measure would be unconstitutional, he believed. Wilson also refused to back the constitutional amendment giving the vote to women. Probably he thought it improper for women to mix in politics, but he argued publicly that it was wrong to deprive the states of their control of the suffrage.

Wilson also proved far less unsympathetic to big business than some of his campaign pronouncements had led observers to expect. He appointed men friendly to the corporations to the FTC and conducted no trustbusting crusade. When the business cycle took a turn downward in the fall of 1913, he adopted the Rooseveltian policy of allowing corporation leaders to discuss doubtful practices with Justice Department lawyers, thus arranging informal agreements which protected them against antitrust actions. Delegations of businessmen and bankers were soon trooping through the White House, while the President went out of his way to insist that he had no quarrel with bigness per se.

On balance, by the end of 1914 the Wilsonian record was positive but distinctly limited. The President himself, justly proud of the results of his forceful leadership, believed that the major progressive goals had been achieved; he had no plans for further reform. Many other progressives felt that a great deal more remained to be done.

The Progressives and the Negro

On one important reform issue—the question of Negro rights—Wilson was distinctly reactionary.

Negroes had not, to put it mildly, fared well at the hands of the progressives. In the South the Populist effort to unite white and black farmers led to the imposition of further repressive measures. Segregation became more rigid, white opposition to Negro voting more monolithic. To cite only a few examples, in 1900 the body of a Mississippi black was dug up by order of the state legislature and reburied in a segregated cemetery; in Virginia, in 1902, the daughter of Robert E. Lee was arrested for riding in the Negro section of a railroad car; in Alabama the constitution of 1901 reduced the number of Negro voters to two per cent of the adult Negro males.

Many progressive women, still smarting from the insult to their sex entailed in the Fourteenth and Fifteenth Amendments, and eager to attract southern support for their campaign for the vote, adopted racist arguments. They contrasted the supposed corruption and incompetence of black voters with their own "purity" and intelligence in order to justify their demand for women's suffrage. Southern so-called progressives of both sexes argued that disfranchising blacks would "purify" politics by removing from unscrupulous white politicians the temptation to purchase black votes! The typical southern attitude toward the education of blacks was summed up in the folk proverb: "When you educate a Negro, you spoil a good field hand." As late as 1910, only about 8,000 Negroes in the entire South were attending high schools. Yet despite the almost total suppression of Negro rights, the lynching of Negroes continued on a large scale: between 1900 and 1914 more than 1,100 were murdered by mobs, most, but not all, in the southern states, and in the rare cases where local prosecutors brought the lynchers to trial, juries almost without exception brought in a verdict of not guilty.

Booker T. Washington was shaken by this trend of events, but he could find no way to combat it. The times were passing him by. He appealed to his white southern "friends" to resist Negro disfranchisement but got nowhere. Increasingly, he talked about the virtues of rural life, the evils of big cities, and the uselessness of higher education for his people. By the turn of the century a number of young, well-educated blacks, most of them northerners, were beginning to break away from his leadership.

William E. B. Du Bois was the most prominent of the militants. Du Bois was born in Great Barrington, Massachusetts, in 1868. His father, a restless wanderer of Negro and French Huguenot stock, abandoned the family, and young William grew up on the edge of poverty. Neither accepted nor overtly rejected by the overwhelmingly white community, he devoted himself to his studies, showing such brilliance in the local schools that his future education was assured by scholarships: to Fisk University, then to Harvard, then to the University of Berlin. In 1895 he became the first American black to earn a Ph.D. from Harvard; his dissertation, *The Suppression of the African Slave Trade to the U. S. A., 1638-1870* (1896), is still a standard work on the subject.

But personal success and "acceptance" by whites did not make the proud and sensitive Du Bois complacent. Outraged by white treatment of Negroes and by the tendency of many blacks to accept second-class citizenship, he set out to make American blacks proud of their color— "beauty is black," he said—and of their African origins and culture. American Negroes must organize themselves. They must establish their own businesses, run their own newspapers and colleges, write their own literature, preserve their identity rather than seek to amalgamate themselves into a society that offered them only crumbs and contempt.

Like Washington, Du Bois wanted Negroes to lift themselves up by their own bootstraps, and for a time he cooperated with the head of Tuskegee Institute. But eventually he rejected Washington's limited goals and his accommodating approach to white prejudices. In 1903 in an essay "Of Mr. Booker T. Washington and Others," published in his book *Souls of Black Folk,* he subjected Washington's "attitude of adjustment and submission" to polite but searching criticism. Washington had asked blacks to give up political power, civil rights, and the hope of higher education, not realizing that "voting is necessary to

Vigilante justice in Texas, 1893. A Negro accused of killing a white child was captured and condemned to death without benefit of trial after he was said to have confessed. Before a crowd estimated in the thousands he was burned at the stake, but only after the child's family took their revenge with branding irons. (Library of Congress.)

modern manhood, that . . . discrimination is barbarism, and that black boys need education as well as white boys." Washington "apologizes for injustice," Du Bois charged, "belittles the emasculating effects of caste distinctions, and opposes the higher training and ambitions of our brightest minds." This was totally wrong. "The way for a people to gain their reasonable rights is not by voluntarily throwing them away."

Du Bois was not, however, an uncritical admirer of the ordinary American Negro. He believed that "immorality, crime, and laziness" were common Negro vices. Quite properly he blamed the weaknesses of blacks on the treatment afforded them by whites, but his approach to the solution of racial problems was frankly elitist. "The Negro race," he wrote, "is going to be saved by its exceptional men," what he called the "Talented Tenth" of the black population. As the Negro historian Benjamin Quarles has put it, Du Bois was "uncomfortable in the presence of the rank and file." After vividly describing how white mistreatment had corrupted his people, Du Bois added loftily: "A saving remnant continually survives and persists, continually aspires, continually shows itself in thrift and ability and character."

Whatever his personal prejudices, Du Bois exposed both the weaknesses of Washington's strategy and the callousness of white American attitudes cogently and brilliantly. "Accommodation" was not working. Washington was praised, even lionized by prominent southern whites, but when Theodore Roosevelt invited him to a meal at the White House they exploded with indignation, and Roosevelt, who had no personal prejudice against Negroes, meekly backtracked, never repeating his "mistake."

Not mere impatience but despair led Du Bois and a few like-minded Negroes to meet at Niagara Falls in July 1905 and issue a stirring list of demands: the unrestricted right to vote; an end to every kind of segregation; equality of economic opportunity; the right to higher education for the talented; equal justice in the courts; an end to trade union discrimination. This Niagara Movement did not attract much support among the Negro masses, but it did stir the consciences of some whites, many of them the descendants of abolitionists, who were also becoming disenchanted by the failure of accommodation to provide blacks with real opportunity. In 1909, the centennial of the birth of Abraham Lincoln, a group of these liberals, including Oswald Garrison Villard (grandson of William Lloyd Garrison), the social worker Jane Addams, the philosopher John Dewey, and the novelist William Dean Howells, founded the National Association for the Advancement of Colored People (NAACP). This organization was dedicated to the eradication of racial discrimination. Its leader-

John Henry Adams made this study of William E. B. Du Bois in 1905, the year that Du Bois helped to initiate the Niagara Movement for racial equality. (L. Hughes and M. Meltzer, *A Pictorial History of the Negro in America,* 1956.)

ship was predominantly white in the early years, but Du Bois became a national officer, and editor of its journal, *The Crisis.*

A great turning point had been reached: after 1909 virtually every important leader of the Negroes, black and white alike, rejected the Washington approach. More and more, Negro leaders turned to the study of their past in an effort to stimulate pride in their heritage and to expose the cruelty and injustice of the white treatment of blacks. In 1915, for example, Carter G. Woodson founded the Association for the Study of Negro Life and History, and the next year began editing the *Journal of Negro History,* which became the major organ for the publishing of scholarly studies of the subject.

However, militancy produced few results in the Progressive Era. Whatever his personal views, Roosevelt behaved on the Negro question no differently than earlier Republican Presidents: he courted blacks when he thought it advantageous to do so, turned his back on them when he did not. When he ran for President on the Progressive ticket in 1912, he pursued a "lily-white" policy, hoping to break the Democrats' monopoly in the South. By trusting in "[white] men of justice and of vision," Roosevelt argued in the face of decades of experience to the contrary, "the colored men of the South will ultimately get justice."

The southern-born Wilson was actively antipathetic to Negroes. During the 1912 campaign he appealed to them for support and promised to "assist in advancing the interest of their race" in every possible way. Once elected, he refused even to appoint a privately financed National Race Commission to study the Negro problem. Southerners dominated both his administration and the Congress; as a result, blacks were still further degraded. No less than 35 Negroes in the Atlanta Post Office lost their jobs, while in Washington black employees in many government offices were rigidly segregated, those who objected being summarily discharged. These actions roused such a storm that Wilson backtracked somewhat, but he never abandoned his belief that segregation was in the best interests of both races. "Wilson . . . promised a 'new freedom,'" one Negro newspaperman complained. "On the contrary we are given a stone instead of a loaf of bread." Even Booker T. Washington admitted that his people were more "discouraged and bitter" than at any time in his memory.

Du Bois, who had supported Wilson in 1912, attacked administration policy in *The Crisis*. In November 1914 the militant editor of the Boston *Guardian*, William Monroe Trotter, a classmate of Du Bois at Harvard and a far more caustic critic of the Washington approach, led a delegation to the White House to protest the segregation policy of the government. When Wilson accused him of blackmail, Trotter lost his temper and an ugly confrontation resulted. The mood of black leaders had changed completely.

By this time the Great War had broken out in Europe. Soon its effects would be felt by every American, by the Negroes perhaps more than by any other group. In November 1915, a year almost to the day after Trotter's clash with Wilson, Booker T. Washington died. For the Negro, one era had ended; a new one was beginning.

Supplementary Reading

Two excellent volumes trace the political history of the Progressive Era: G. E. Mowry, *The Era of Theodore Roosevelt*° (1958), and A. S. Link, *Woodrow Wilson and the Progressive Era*° (1954). A number of historians have offered new interpretations of progressivism in recent years. Richard Hofstadter, *The Age of Reform*° (1955), stresses the idea of the status revolution. Gabriel Kolko, *The Triumph of Conservatism*° (1963), sees the period as dominated by the efforts of big business to attain its objectives with the aid of the government. Other interesting studies include R. B. Nye, *Midwestern Progressive Politics* (1951), and R. H. Wiebe, *Businessmen and Reform*° (1962). D. P. Thalen, *The New Citizenship* (1972) is good on the origins of progressivism, although confined to the study of one state, Wisconsin.

The role of muckraking journalism is considered in C. C. Regier, *The Era of the Muckrakers* (1932), Louis Filler, *Crusaders for American Liberalism*° (1939), D. M. Chalmers, *The Social and Political Ideas of the Muckrakers*° (1964), and Peter Lyon, *Success Story: The Life and Times of S. S. McClure* (1963). Arthur and Lila Weinberg (eds.), *The Muckrakers*° (1961), is a convenient collection of writings by the muckrakers. Also useful are Lincoln Steffens, *Autobiography*° (1931), and I. M. Tarbell, *All in the Day's Work* (1939).

State and local progressivism are considered in G. E. Mowry, *The California Progressives*° (1951), R. S. Maxwell, *La Follette and the Rise of Progressives in Wisconsin* (1956), R. E. Noble, *New Jersey Progressivism Before Wilson* (1946), R. M. Abrams, *Conservatism in a Progressive Era* (1964), H. L. Warner, *Progressivism in Ohio* (1964), Sheldon Hackney, *Populism to Progressivism in Alabama* (1969), Z. L. Miller, *Boss Cox's Cincinnati: Urban Politics in the Progressive Era*° (1968), and C. V. Woodward, *Origins of the New South*° (1951). The story of the

°Available in paperback.

fight for reform in San Francisco is told in W. E. Bean, *Boss Ruef's San Francisco*° (1952).

The struggle for women's suffrage is described in A. S. Kraditor, *The Ideas of the Woman Suffrage Movement* (1965), and in Eleanor Flexner, *Century of Struggle* (1959). See also W. L. O'Neill, *Everyone Was Brave: The Rise and Fall of Feminism in America* (1969). Books treating special aspects of progressivism include A. F. Davis, *Spearheads for Reform: The Social Settlements and the Progressive Movement* (1967), Irwin Yellowitz, *Labor and the Progressive Movement in New York State* (1965), J. H. Timberlake, *Prohibition and the Progressive Movement* (1963), Albro Martin, *Enterprise Denied: Origins of the Decline of American Railroads* (1971), and W. L. O'Neill, *Divorce in the Progressive Era* (1967). On the Negro in this period see C. F. Kellogg, *NAACP: A History of the National Association for the Advancement of Colored People* (1970), E. M. Rudwick, *W. E. B. Du Bois: Propagandist of the Negro Protest*° (1960), W. E. B. Du Bois, *The Souls of Black Folk*° (1903), and August Meier, *Negro Thought in America: 1880-1915*° (1963).

Many progressives have written autobiographical accounts of their work. See especially Theodore Roosevelt, *Autobiography* (1913), R. M. La Follette, *Autobiography*° (1913), W. A. White, *Autobiography* (1946), and G. W. Norris, *Fighting Liberal*° (1945).

W. H. Harbaugh, *Power and Responsibility: The Life and Times of Theodore Roosevelt*° (1961), is the soundest scholarly treatment of Roosevelt's career, but H. F. Pringle, *Theodore Roosevelt*° (1931), is still the most entertaining. G. W. Chessman, *Theodore Roosevelt and the Politics of Power*° (1969), is a good brief account, while Chessman's *Governor Theodore Roosevelt: The Albany Apprenticeship* (1965), throws much light on the development of Roosevelt's ideas before 1901. J. M. Blum, *The Republican Roosevelt*° (1954), is a brilliant analysis of his political philosophy and his management of the Presidency. The essays on Roosevelt—and on Wilson—in Richard Hofstadter, *The American Political Tradition*° (1948), also merit close reading. No student should miss sampling Roosevelt's letters. See

E. E. Morison (ed.), *The Letters of Theodore Roosevelt* (1951-54).

For specific events during Roosevelt's Presidency, consult R. J. Cornell, *The Anthracite Coal Strike of 1902* (1957), the essay on the Northern Securities case in J. A. Garraty (ed.), *Quarrels That Have Shaped the Constitution*° (1964), E. R. Richardson, *The Politics of Conservation* (1962), S. P. Hays, *Conservation and the Gospel of Efficiency*° (1959), and J. R. Hollingsworth, *The Whirligig of Politics* (1963).

On Taft see D. F. Anderson, *William Howard Taft: A Conservative's Conception of the Presidency* (1973), and P. E. Coletta, *The Presidency of William Howard Taft* (1973). On the Ballinger-Pinchot controversy, see A. T. Mason, *Bureaucracy Convicts Itself* (1941), and M. N. McGeary, *Gifford Pinchot* (1960). The breakup of the Republican party and the history of the Progressive party are discussed in G. E. Mowry, *Theodore Roosevelt and the Progressive Movement*° (1946), and J. A. Garraty, *Right-Hand Man: The Life of George W. Perkins* (1960).

The standard biography of Wilson, still incomplete, is A. S. Link, *Wilson* (1947-   ). A. C. Walworth, *Woodrow Wilson*° (1958), is a detailed life. Two briefer biographies are J. M. Blum, *Woodrow Wilson and the Politics of Morality*° (1956), and J. A. Garraty, *Woodrow Wilson*° (1956).

Among the many biographies of political leaders in the period are J. M. Blum, *Joe Tumulty and the Wilson Era* (1951), C. G. Bowers, *Beveridge and the Progressive Era* (1932), R. M. Lowitt, *George W. Norris* (1963), B. C. and Fola La Follette, *Robert M. La Follette* (1953), P. C. Jessup, *Elihu Root* (1938), J. A. Garraty, *Henry Cabot Lodge* (1953), A. T. Mason, *Brandeis* (1946), and M. J. Pusey, *Charles Evans Hughes* (1951).

Finally, the student should sample some of the political writings of the progressives themselves. See especially Theodore Roosevelt, *The New Nationalism*° (1910), Woodrow Wilson, *The New Freedom*° (1913), Herbert Croly, *The Promise of American Life*° (1909), Walter Weyl, *The New Democracy*° (1912), and Walter Lippmann, *Drift and Mastery*° (1914).

24

Woodrow Wilson and the Great War

Woodrow Wilson's approach to foreign relations was well intentioned and idealistic, but somewhat confused. He knew that the United States had no wish to injure any foreign state and assumed that all nations would recognize this fact and cooperate. He sincerely desired to help other countries, especially the republics of Latin America, achieve stable democratic governments and improve the living conditions of their people. Imperialism was in his eyes immoral. Yet he also expected to sustain and protect American interests abroad. The maintenance of the Open Door in China and the completion of the Panama

Canal, for example, were as important to him as they had been to Theodore Roosevelt.

Moreover, Wilson's view of nations with traditions different from those of the United States was distressingly shortsighted and provincial. His attitude resembled that of 19th-century Christian missionaries: he wanted to spread the gospel of American democracy, to lift up and enlighten the unfortunate and the ignorant—but in his own way. "I am going to teach the South American republics to elect good men!" he told one British diplomat.

"Missionary Diplomacy"

Wilson set out at once to raise the moral tone of American foreign policy by denouncing dollar diplomacy. Encouraging bankers to lend money to countries like China, he said, implied the possibility of "forcible interference" if the loans were not repaid, a policy "obnoxious to the principles upon which the government of our people rests." The practice of seeking economic concessions in Latin America was "unfair" and "degrading." The United States would deal with Latin American nations "upon terms of equality and honor."

In certain small matters, Wilson succeeded in conducting American diplomacy on this idealistic basis. He withdrew the government's support of the international consortium that was arranging a loan to develop Chinese railroads, and the American bankers pulled out. When the Japanese attempted, in the notorious Twenty-One Demands (1915), to reduce China almost to the status of a Japanese protectorate, he persuaded them to modify their conditions slightly. Congress had passed a law in 1912 exempting American coastal shipping from the payment of tolls on the Panama Canal in spite of a provision in the Hay-Pauncefote Treaty with Great Britain guaranteeing that the canal would be available to the vessels of all nations "on terms of entire equality." Wilson insisted that Congress repeal the law in order to vindicate the national honor. He also permitted Secretary Bryan to negotiate conciliation treaties with some 21 nations. The distinctive feature of these agreements was the provision for a "cooling-off" period of one year, during which signatories agreed, in the event of any dispute, not to engage in hostilities.

Where more vital interests of the United States were concerned, Wilson sometimes failed to live up to his promises. Because of the strategic importance of the Panama Canal, he was unwilling to tolerate "unrest" in the nations of the Caribbean. Within a matter of months he was pursuing the same tactics that circumstances had forced on Roosevelt and Taft. The Bryan–Chamorro Treaty of 1914, which gave the United States an option to build a canal across Nicaragua, made that country virtually an American protectorate and served to maintain in power an unpopular dictator, Adolfo Díaz. When a revolution broke out in the Dominican Republic in 1916, United States marines occupied the country. In Haiti, rocked by eight revolutions in four years, American troops also took over and installed a puppet president. By a treaty of September 1915, Haiti became a United States protectorate.

The most perplexing example of missionary diplomacy occurred in Mexico. The dictator Porfirio Díaz had been exploiting the resources and people of Mexico for the benefit of a small class of wealthy landowners, clerics, and military men for many decades, when, in 1911, a liberal coalition overthrew him and installed Francisco Madero as president. This revolution was no mere squabble between rival bandit cliques. Madero, although a wealthy landowner, was committed to economic reform and to the drafting of a democratic constitution; a highly moralistic man, he had apparently been much influenced by the progressive movement in the United States. Unfortunately, he was both weak-willed and a terrible administrator. Conditions in Mexico deteriorated rapidly, and less than a month before Wilson's inauguration, one of Madero's generals, Victoriano Huerta, treacherously seized power and had his former chief murdered. An unabashed reactionary, Huerta intended to restore things as they had been under Díaz. Since he seemed capable of maintaining the stability that foreign investors desired, most of the powers promptly recognized Huerta's government.

The American ambassador in Mexico City, together with important American financial and business interests in Mexico and in the United States, urged Wilson to do likewise, but he refused. His sympathies were all with the constitutionalists, and the murder of Madero had horrified him. He had a sufficient practical reason for withholding recognition, for the followers of Madero remained in control of a large part of the country, but Wilson chose to act on moral grounds. "I will not recognize a government of butchers," he said firmly. This was an unconventional argument, since nations do not ordinarily consider the means by which a foreign regime has come to power before deciding to establish diplomatic relations.

Wilson then proceeded to bring enormous pressure to bear against Huerta. He dragooned the British into withdrawing recognition, dickered with rebellious Mexican factions, and demanded that Huerta hold free elections as the price of American mediation in the continuing civil war. Huerta would not yield an inch. Indeed, he drew strength from Wilson's effort to oust him, for even his enemies resented American interference in Mexican affairs. Frustration added to Wilson's moral outrage and weakened his judgment. It became a contest of wills between him and the dictator; he subordinated his wish to let the Mexicans solve their own problems to his personal desire to destroy Huerta.

This explosive situation erupted in April 1914, when a small party of American sailors was arrested in the port of Tampico, Mexico. Although a minor Mexican official had been responsible for the arrest and the men had been promptly released by higher authority, the Mexicans refused to supply the apology demanded by the sailors' commander. Wilson fastened upon the affair as an excuse for sending troops into Mexico. Force would be used, he informed Congress, against "General Huerta and those who adhere to him," not against the Mexican people. His only object, he told a reporter, was "to help

the [Mexican] people to secure [their] liberty."

The invasion took place at Veracruz, whence Winfield Scott had launched the assault on Mexico City in 1847. When he learned that a German merchantman laden with munitions was expected at Veracruz, Wilson ordered the city occupied to prevent these weapons from reaching the Huertistas. But instead of meekly surrendering their city, the Mexicans resisted tenaciously, suffering 400 casualties before falling back. This bloodshed caused dismay throughout Latin America and failed to unseat Huerta. The leader of the constitutionalist armies, General Venustiano Carranza, denounced the Americans vociferously.

Fortunately, at this point three South American states, Argentina, Brazil, and Chile, offered to mediate the dispute. Wilson accepted, Huerta also agreed, and the conferees met at Niagara Falls, Ontario, in May. Although no settlement was reached, Huerta, hard pressed by constitutionalist armies, finally abdicated. On August 20, 1914, General Carranza entered Mexico City in triumph.

Carranza's victory allowed Wilson to escape from the consequences of his effort to impose good government on Mexico from the outside,° but the President failed to make the most of his fortune. Carranza proved scarcely more successful than the tyrant Huerta in controlling his turbulent country. Soon one of his own generals, Francisco "Pancho" Villa, rose against him and seized control of Mexico City. At this point Wilson made a monumental blunder. Villa professed to be willing to cooperate with the United States, and Wilson, taking him at his word, gave him his support. However, Villa was little more than an ambitious bandit, a kind of populist but without definite class interests or any objective more so-

°During the occupation of Veracruz, the American forces cleaned up the city, built roads and bridges, improved public services, and made the city, in the words of historian Robert E. Quirk, "the most efficient, most honestly and justly governed city in all of Mexican history." Yet they succeeded only in arousing "the hatred and the scorn of the Mexicans," and when they withdrew, Veracruz quickly reverted to its old ways.

cial than personal power. Carranza, while no social revolutionary, was committed to constitu-
tionalism and had wide support among the
middle class. Fighting back, he drove the Villistas
into the northern provinces.

When Wilson finally realized the extent of
Carranza's influence in Mexico, he reversed himself; in October 1915 he recognized the Carranza
government. Still, his Mexican troubles were not
over, for Villa, seeking to undermine Carranza
by forcing the United States to intervene, began
a series of unprovoked attacks on Americans.
Early in 1916 he stopped a train in northern
Mexico and killed 16 American passengers in
cold blood. Next, he crossed into New Mexico
and burned the town of Columbus, killing 19.
Having learned his lesson, Wilson would have
preferred to bear even this assault in silence, but
public opinion forced him to send American
troops under General John J. Pershing across the
border in pursuit of Villa.

On his own ground, Villa proved impossible
to catch. Cleverly he drew Pershing deeper and
deeper into Mexico, which in turn greatly
alarmed Carranza, who insisted that the Americans withdraw. Several clashes occurred between Pershing's men and Mexican regulars, and
for a brief period in June 1916 war seemed imminent. Wilson now acted bravely and wisely. He
negotiated when it would have been far easier to
fight and, in the end, he was big enough to yield.
Of course the growing threat of involvement in
the European war that was now raging made it
easier to do so. Early in 1917 he recalled Pershing's force to American soil.

Thereafter, the Mexicans proceeded to work
out their own destiny. Missionary diplomacy had
produced mixed, but in the long run essentially
beneficial, results. By opposing Huerta, Wilson
had surrendered to his prejudices, yet he had
also helped the real revolutionaries, although
they opposed his acts. His bungling bred anti-

Troopers of the 10th Cavalry, photographed in Mexico in 1916 during Pershing's pursuit of Villa. Pershing was an advocate of black troops; his nickname, "Black Jack," stemmed from his command of this crack regiment. (Library of
Congress.)

Americanism in Mexico, but by his later restraint in the face of stinging provocations, he permitted the constitutionalists to consolidate their power and preserve their self-respect.

Outbreak of the Great War

On June 28, 1914, in the Austro-Hungarian provincial capital of Sarajevo, Gavrilo Princip, a young student, assassinated the Archduke Franz Ferdinand, heir to the imperial throne. Princip, a member of the Black Hand, a Serbian terrorist organization, was seeking to further the cause of Serbian nationalism. Instead, his rash act precipitated a general European war. Within little more than a month, following a complex series of diplomatic challenges and responses, two great coalitions, the Central Powers (chiefly Germany and Austria-Hungary) and the Allied Powers (chiefly Great Britain, France, and Russia), were locked in a combat that brought one era in world history to a close and inaugurated another.

The outbreak of what contemporaries were soon to call the Great War caught Americans psychologically unprepared; few understood the significance of what had happened. President Wilson promptly issued a proclamation of neutrality and even asked the nation to be "impartial in thought." While no one, including the President, had the superhuman self-control that this request called for, the almost unanimous reaction of Americans, aside from dismay, was that the conflict did not concern them. Of course they were wrong, for this was a world war and Americans were sure to be affected by its outcome. To have remained indifferent would have required an act of self-abnegation without precedent in history.

Yet there were good reasons, aside from a failure to understand the significance of the struggle, why the United States sought to remain neutral. Over a third of its 92 million inhabitants were either foreign-born or the children of immigrants. Sentimental rather than political ties bound these former Europeans to the lands of their ancestors, but most felt strongly, one way or the other, when war broke out. American involvement would create new internal stresses in a society already strained by the task of assimilating so many diverse groups. War was also an affront to the prevailing progressive spirit, which assumed that human beings were reasonable, high-minded, and capable of settling disputes peaceably. Along with the traditional American fear of entanglement in European affairs, these were ample reasons for remaining aloof.

Although most Americans hoped to keep out of the war, nearly everyone was partial to one side or the other. People of German or Austrian descent, about 8 million in number, and the nation's 4.5 million Irish-Americans, motivated chiefly by hatred of the British, sympathized with the Central Powers. The majority of the people, however, influenced by bonds of language and culture, preferred an Allied victory, and when the Germans launched a mighty assault across neutral Belgium in an effort to outflank the French armies, this unprovoked attack on a tiny nation whose neutrality the Germans had previously agreed to respect caused a great deal of anti-German feeling.

As the war progressed, the Allies cleverly exploited American prejudices by such devices as publishing exaggerated tales of German atrocities against Belgian civilians. A supposedly impartial study of these charges by the widely respected James Bryce, author of *The American Commonwealth,* portrayed the Germans as ruthless and cruel barbarians. The Germans also conducted a shrewd and extensive propaganda campaign in the United States, but they labored under severe handicaps and won few converts.

Freedom of the Seas

Propaganda, in fact, did not basically alter American attitudes; far more important were questions rising out of trade and commerce. Naturally, all the warring nations wanted to draw upon American resources. Under international law, neutrals could trade freely with any belligerent. The Americans were prepared to do so, but because the British fleet dominated the North Atlantic, they could not. Although the specific issues differed somewhat, the situation was similar to that which had prevailed during the Napoleonic Wars. Eager to cut off Germany from foreign products, the British declared nearly all commodities, even foodstuffs, to be contraband of war. They rationed imports to neutral nations such as Denmark and the Netherlands so that they could not transship supplies to Germany. They forced neutral merchantmen into Allied ports in order to search them for goods headed for the enemy. Many cargoes were confiscated, often without payment, and American firms that traded with the Central Powers were "blacklisted," which meant that no British subject could deal with them. When these policies caused angry protests in America, the British answered that in a battle for survival they dared not adhere to old-fashioned rules of international law. "If the American shipper grumbles, our reply is that this war is not being conducted for his pleasure or profit," the London *Daily Graphic* explained.

Had the United States insisted that Great Britain abandon these "illegal" practices, as the Germans demanded, no doubt it could have had its way. It is ironic that an embargo, which failed so ignominiously in Jefferson's day, would have been almost instantly effective if applied at any time after 1914, for American supplies were absolutely vital to the Allies. As the British foreign secretary, Sir Edward Grey, later admitted: "The ill-will of the United States meant certain defeat. The object of diplomacy, therefore, was to secure the maximum of blockade that could be enforced without a rupture with the United States."

Although the British tactics frequently exasperated Wilson, he never considered taking such a drastic step. He faced a true dilemma. To allow the British to make the rules meant being unneutral toward the Central Powers. Yet to insist on the old rules, which had never actually been obeyed in wartime, meant being unneutral to-

ward the Allies, for that would have deprived them of much of the value of their naval superiority. *Nothing* the United States might do would be really impartial. Of course Wilson's own sentiments made it doubly difficult for him to object strenuously to British practices. No American admired British institutions and culture more extravagantly than this disciple of Burke and Gladstone, this worshiper of Wordsworth, Dickens, and Scott. "Everything I love most in the world is at stake," he confessed privately to the British ambassador. A German victory "would be fatal to our form of Government and American ideals."

In any case, the immense expansion of American trade with the Allies made an embargo unthinkable. While commerce with the Central Powers fell off to a trickle, that with the Allies soared from $825 million in 1914 to over $3.2 billion in 1916. An attempt to limit this commerce would have raised a storm; to have eliminated it would have caused a catastrophe. Munitionsmakers and other businessmen did not want the United States to enter the war; neutrality suited their purposes admirably, despite British harassments. They did, however, profit from the war and wished to continue to do so.

The Allies soon exhausted their ready cash and had to borrow in order to continue their purchases. Wilson first refused to let American bankers lend them money but soon reversed himself. By early 1917 Britain and France had borrowed well over $2 billion from them. Although these loans violated no principle of international law, they fastened the United States still more closely to the Allies' cause.

During the first months of the Great War, the Germans were not especially concerned about neutral rights or American goods, for they expected to crush the Allied armies quickly. But when their first swift thrust was blunted along the Marne and the war became a bloody stalemate, they began to plan countermeasures aimed at forcing the Allies to permit neutral goods to enter their territories and at cutting off such goods from Great Britain. Unwilling to risk their battleships and cruisers against the much larger British fleet, they resorted to a new weapon, the submarine *(Unterseeboot),* commonly known as the U-boat.

German submarines played a role in World War I not unlike that of American privateers in the Revolution and the War of 1812: they ranged the seas stealthily in search of merchantmen. However, they could not operate under the ordinary rules of war, which required that a raider stop its prey, examine its papers and cargo, and give the crew and passengers time to get off in lifeboats before sending it to the bottom. When surfaced, U-boats were vulnerable to the deck guns that many merchant ships carried; they could even be sunk by ramming, once they had stopped and put out a boarding party. Therefore they commonly launched their torpedoes from below the surface without warning, and the result was often a heavy loss of life on the torpedoed ships.

In February 1915 the Germans declared the waters surrounding the British Isles a zone of war and announced that they would sink, without warning, all enemy merchant ships encountered in the area. Since Allied vessels sometimes flew neutral flags to disguise their identity, neutral ships entering the zone would do so at their own risk. This statement was largely bluff, for the Germans had only a handful of submarines at sea, but they were building more feverishly. Wilson, perhaps too hurriedly considering the importance of the question, warned the Germans that he would hold them to "strict accountability" for any loss of American life or property resulting from violations of "acknowledged [neutral] rights on the high seas." He did not clearly distinguish between losses incurred through the destruction of *American* ships and those resulting from the sinking of other vessels. If he meant to hold the Germans responsible for injuries to Americans on *belligerent* vessels, he was changing the traditional rules of international law as arbitrarily as the Germans were. Secretary of State William Jennings Bryan, who opposed Wilson vigorously on this point, took sound legal ground when he said: "A ship carrying contraband should not rely upon passengers to protect her from attack—it would be like putting women and children in front of an army." Furthermore, Wilson's note

was, in effect, an ultimatum: in the long run, "strict accountability" meant war unless the Germans backed down. Yet Wilson was unprepared to fight; he refused even to ask Congress for increased military appropriations at this time, saying that he did not want to "turn America into a military camp."

Wise or not, Wilson's position accurately reflected the attitude of most Americans. It seemed barbaric to them that defenseless civilians should be killed without warning, and they refused to surrender their "rights" as neutrals to cross the North Atlantic on any ship they wished. The depth of their feeling was quickly demonstrated when, on May 7, 1915, the submarine *U-20* sank the British liner *Lusitania* off the Irish coast. Nearly 1,200 persons, including 128 Americans, lost their lives in this catastrophe.

The torpedoing of the *Lusitania* caused as profound and emotional a reaction in the United States as that following the destruction of the *Maine* in Havana harbor. Wilson, like McKinley in 1898, was shocked, but he kept his head. He demanded that Germany disavow the sinking, indemnify the victims, and promise to stop attacking passenger vessels; but when the Germans quibbled about these points, he responded with further diplomatic correspondence rather than with an ultimatum.

In one sense he acted sensibly. The Germans pointed out that they had published warnings in American newspapers saying they considered the *Lusitania* subject to attack, that the liner was carrying munitions, and that on past voyages it had flown the American flag as a *ruse de guerre.* It would also have been very difficult politically for the German government to have backed down before an American ultimatum, although after dragging the controversy out for nearly a year, it did apologize and agree to pay an indemnity. Finally, after the torpedoing of the French channel steamer *Sussex* in March 1916 had produced another stiff American protest, the Germans at last promised to stop sinking merchantmen without warning. Furthermore, if Wilson had forced a showdown in 1915, he would have alienated a large segment of American opinion. Even his relatively mild notes resulted in the resignation of Secretary of State Bryan,° who believed it unneutral to treat German violations of international law differently than Allied violations, and Bryan reflected the feelings of thousands.

On the other hand, if Wilson had asked for war over the *Lusitania,* a majority of Congress and the country would probably have gone along, and in that event, the dreadful carnage in Europe would have been ended much sooner. This is the reasoning of hindsight, but such a policy would also have been logical, given Wilson's assumptions about the justice of the Allied cause and America's material stake in an Allied victory. However, the President, and most Americans, were not certain enough in their minds in 1915 to act entirely logically. In November 1915, during the long crisis, Wilson at last began to press for increased military and naval expenditures. Nevertheless, he continued to vacillate, dispatching a sharp note of protest against Allied blacklisting of American firms and telling his confidante, Colonel House, that the British were "poor boobs!" His position on preparedness remained so equivocal that his secretary of war, Lindley M. Garrison, resigned in protest.

Election of 1916

Part of Wilson's confusion in 1916 resulted from the political difficulties he faced in his fight for re-election. He had won the Presidency in 1912 only because the Republican party had split in two. Now its segments were rapidly reuniting, for Theodore Roosevelt, the chief defector, had become so incensed by Wilson's refusal to commit the United States to the Allied cause that he was ready to support almost any Republican to guarantee the President's defeat. At the same time, many lesser progressives were complaining about Wilson's unwillingness to work for further domestic reforms. Unless he could find some ad-

°Wilson appointed Robert Lansing, counselor of the State Department, to succeed Bryan.

ditional support, he seemed sure to lose the election.

He attacked this problem by openly wooing the progressives. In January 1916 he appointed Louis D. Brandeis to the Supreme Court. In addition to being an advanced progressive, Brandeis was Jewish, the first American of that religion ever appointed to the Court, and Wilson's action won him many friends among people who favored fair treatment for minority groups. In July he bid for the farm vote by signing the Farm Loan Act to provide low-cost loans based on agricultural credit. Shortly thereafter, he approved the Keating-Owen Child Labor Act barring goods manufactured by the labor of children under 16 from interstate commerce, and a workmen's compensation act for federal employees. He also persuaded Congress to pass the Adamson Act, establishing an eight-hour day for railroad workers, and he modified his position on the tariff by approving the creation of a tariff commission and accepting "antidumping" legislation designed to protect American industry from cutthroat foreign competition after the war. Each of these actions represented a sharp reversal of policy. In 1913 Wilson had considered Brandeis too radical even for a Cabinet post. The new farm, labor, and tariff laws were all examples of the kind of "class legislation" he had refused to countenance in 1913 and 1914. As Arthur S. Link has pointed out, Wilson was putting into effect "almost every important plank of the Progressive platform of 1912." It would be uncharitable to conclude that he was doing so only to win votes; he had been moving in the direction of the New Nationalism for some time. Nevertheless, his actions paid spectacular political dividends when Roosevelt refused a proffered second nomination of the Progressive party and came out for the Republican nominee, Justice Charles Evans Hughes of the Supreme Court. The Progressive party reluctantly endorsed Hughes, who had earlier compiled an excellent record as governor of New York, but many of Roosevelt's 1912 supporters felt he had betrayed them and voted for Wilson in 1916.

Nevertheless, the key issue in the Presidential

A Wilson campaign truck offered voters in New York City a convenient summary of the Democratic platform in 1916. The eight-hour-day plank refers to the President's support of a federal law for railroad workers. (UPI)

election was American policy toward the warring powers. Wilson intended to stress preparedness, which he was at last wholeheartedly supporting. However, during the Democratic convention the delegates responded so enthusiastically whenever orators referred to his success in keeping the country out of the war that he modified his approach. When one spellbinder, for example, pointed out that the President had "wrung from the most militant spirit that ever brooded above a battlefield an acknowledgement of American rights and an agreement to American demands," the convention erupted in a wild demonstration of approval that lasted more than 20 minutes. Thus "He Kept Us Out of War" became the Democratic slogan.

To his credit, Wilson made no promises. "I can't keep the country out of war," he told one member of his Cabinet. "Any little German lieutenant can put us into the war at any time by some calculated outrage." His attitude undoubtedly cost him the votes of extremists on both sides, but it won the backing of thousands of moderates.

The combination of progressivism and the peace issue brought the Democrats on substantially equal terms with the Republicans; thereafter, personal factors probably tipped the balance. Hughes proved a poor campaigner: he was very stiff and a poor speaker; he unintentionally offended a number of important politicians, especially in crucial California, where he inadvertently snubbed the popular progressive governor, Hiram Johnson; and he equivocated on a number of issues. Nevertheless, on election night he appeared to have won, having carried nearly all the

East and Middle West. Late returns gave Wilson California, however, and with it victory by the narrow margin of 277 to 254 in the Electoral College. He led Hughes in the popular vote by 9.1 million to 8.5 million.

The Road to War

Encouraged by his triumph, appalled by the continuing slaughter on the battlefields, fearful that the United States would be dragged into the holocaust, Wilson made one last effort to end the war by negotiation. In 1915 he had sent his friend Colonel Edward M. House on a secret mission to London, Paris, and Berlin to try to mediate among the belligerents. Everywhere House had been received cordially, but he made little progress and his negotiations were disrupted by the *Lusitania* crisis. A second House mission (January–February 1916) had proved equally fruitless, chiefly because each side still hoped for a clear-cut military victory. Now, after another long season of bloodshed, perhaps the powers would listen to reason.

Wilson's own feelings were more genuinely neutral than at any other time during the war, for the Germans had stopped sinking merchantmen without warning and the British had irritated him repeatedly by their arbitrary restrictions on neutral trade. He drafted a note to the belligerents asking them to state the terms on which they would agree to lay down their arms. Neutrals as well as the warring powers were suffering, he reminded them. Unless the fighting ended soon, all would be so ruined that peace would be meaningless. When neither side responded encouragingly, Wilson, on January 22, 1917, delivered a moving, prophetic speech, aimed, as he admitted, at "the *people* of the countries now at war" more than at their governments. Any settlement imposed by a victor, he declared, would breed only hatred and more wars. There must be a "peace without victory," based on the principles that all nations were equal, and that every nationality group should determine its own form of government. He also mentioned, albeit vaguely, disarmament and freedom of the seas, and he suggested the creation of some kind of international organization to preserve world peace. "There must be not a balance of power, but a community of power," he said, and added, "I am speaking for the silent mass of mankind everywhere."

This noble appeal met a tragic fate. The Germans had already decided to unleash their submarines against *all* vessels headed for Allied ports. After February 1 any ship in the war zone would be attacked without warning. Possessed now of more than 100 U-boats, the German military leaders had convinced themselves that they could starve the British into submission and reduce the Allied armies to impotence by cutting off American supplies. The United States would probably declare war, but—the Germans reasoned—they could overwhelm the Allies before the Americans could get to the battlefields in force. "The United States . . . can neither inflict material damage upon us, nor can it be of material benefit to our enemies," Admiral von Holtzendorff boasted. "I guarantee that for its part the U-boat war will lead to victory."

In *Tiger at the Gates* the French playwright Jean Giraudoux makes Ulysses say, while attempting to stave off what he considers an inevitable war with the Trojans: "The privilege of great men is to view catastrophe from a terrace."° Surely this is not always true, but in 1917, after the Germans had made this decision, events moved relentlessly, almost uninfluenced by the actors who presumably controlled the fate of the world:

February 3: U.S.S. *Housatonic* torpedoed. Wilson announces to Congress that he has severed diplomatic relations with Germany. Secretary of State Lansing hands the German ambassador, Count von Bernstorff, his passport. *February 24:* Walter Hines Page, United States ambassador to Great Britain, transmits to the State Department an intercepted German dispatch (the "Zimmermann Telegram") revealing that Ger-

---

° *Le privilège des grands, c'est de voir les catastrophes d'une terrasse.*

In a 1916 drawing by the Dutchman Louis Raemaekers, one of the most effective of the Allied propagandists, Kaiser Wilhelm is flanked by War and Hunger. (L. Raemaekers, *The Great War,* 1916.)

many has proposed a secret alliance with Mexico, Mexico to receive, in the event of war with the United States, "the lost territory in Texas, New Mexico, and Arizona." *February 25:* Cunard liner *Laconia* torpedoed, two American women perish. *February 26:* Wilson asks Congress for authority to arm American merchant ships. *March 1:* Zimmermann Telegram released to the press. *March 4:* President Wilson takes oath of office, beginning his second term. Congress adjourns without passing the Armed Ship bill, the measure having been filibustered to death by antiwar senators. Wilson characterizes the filibusterers, led by Senator Robert M. La Follette, as "a little group of willful men, representing no opinion but their own." *March 9:* Wilson, acting under his executive powers, orders the arming of American merchantmen. *March 12:* Revolutionary provisional government established in Russia. *Algonquin* torpedoed. *March 15:* Czar Nicholas II of Russia abdicates. *March 16: City of Memphis, Illinois, Vigilancia* torpedoed. *March 21:* New York *World,* a leading Democratic newspaper, calls for dec-

laration of war on Germany. Wilson summons Congress to convene in special session on April 2. *March 25:* Wilson calls up the National Guard. *April 2:* Wilson asks Congress to declare war. Germany is guilty of "throwing to the winds all scruples of humanity," he says. America must fight, not to conquer, but for "peace and justice. . . . The world must be made safe for democracy." *April 4, 6:* Congress declares war—the vote, 82-6 in the Senate, 373-50 in the House.

Thus it had to be, once the Germans loosed their submarines, but the bare record conceals Wilson's agonizing search for an honorable alternative. To admit that Germany posed a threat to the United States meant confessing that rabid interventionists had been right all along. To go to war meant, besides sending innocent Americans to their death, unleashing the forces of hatred and intolerance in the United States and allowing "the spirit of ruthless brutality [to] enter into the very fibre of our national life." The President's rigid Presbyterian conscience tortured him relentlessly. He lost sleep, appeared gray and drawn. When someone asked him which side he hoped would win, he answered petulantly, "Neither." "He was resisting," Secretary Lansing recorded, "the irresistible logic of events." In the end, he could satisfy himself only by giving intervention an idealistic purpose. The war had become a threat to humanity. Unless the United States threw its weight into the balance, western civilization itself might be destroyed. Out of the long blood bath must come a new and better world; the war must be fought to end, for all time, war itself. Thus finally, in the name not of vengeance and victory but of justice and humanity, he sent his countrymen into battle.

The Home Front

America's entry into the World War determined its outcome. The Allies were rapidly running out of money and supplies; their troops, decimated by nearly three years in the trenches, were disheartened and rebellious. In February and March 1917 U-boats sent over a million tons of

Allied shipping to the bottom of the Atlantic. The outbreak of the Russian Revolution in March 1917, although at first lifting the spirits of the western democracies, led to the Bolshevik takeover under Lenin. The Russian armies collapsed, and by December 1917 Russia was out of the war and the Germans were moving huge masses of men and equipment from the eastern front to France. Without the aid of the United States, it is likely that the war would have ended in 1918 on terms dictated from Berlin. Instead American men and supplies helped contain the Germans' last drives and then made it possible to push them back to final defeat.

Even so, it was a very close thing, for the United States entered the war little better prepared to fight than it had been in 1898 and never got its full weight into the fray. For this, Wilson was partly to blame. Because of his devotion to peace he had not tried hard enough to ready the country for war.

The conversion of American industry to war production had to be organized and carried out without prearrangement. Much confusion and waste resulted. The hurriedly designed ship-building program proved an almost total fiasco. The gigantic Hog Island yard, which cost $65 million and employed at its peak over 34,000 workers, completed its first vessel only after the Armistice had been signed. The nation's railroads, strained by immensely increased traffic, became progressively less efficient, but only after a monumental tie-up in December and January of 1917–18 did Wilson finally appoint Secretary of the Treasury William G. McAdoo director-general of the railroads, with power to run the roads as a single system. Ambitious airplane, tank, and artillery construction programs developed so slowly that they had no effect on the war. The big guns that backed up American troops in 1918 were made in France and Great Britain. American pilots, such as the great "ace" Captain Eddie Rickenbacker, flew British Sopwiths and De Havillands or French Spads and Nieuports. Theodore Roosevelt's son Quentin was shot down while flying a Spad over Château-Thierry, in July 1918.

Of course the problem of mobilization was complicated. It took Congress six weeks of hot debate merely to decide upon conscription. Only in September 1917, nearly six months after the declaration of war, did the first draftees reach the training camps, and it is hard to see how Wilson could have speeded this process appreciably. He wisely supported the professional soldiers, who insisted that he resist the appeals of politicians who wanted to raise volunteer units, even rejecting, at very considerable political cost, Theodore Roosevelt's offer to raise an entire army division.

Wilson was a forceful and inspiring war leader once he grasped what needed to be done. Waste there was, and inefficiency, but Wilson never lost control of the situation. No one in the country worked harder or devoted himself to the task of mobilizing society so intensely or displayed such unfailing patience in the face of frustration and criticism.

The President also displayed remarkable flexibility in fashioning, by trial and error, his wartime administration. Raising an army was only a small part of the job. The Allies had to be supplied with food and munitions, and immense amounts of money had to be collected. Originally, Wilson placed the whole program in the hands of a Council of National Defense, consisting of six Cabinet officers and a seven-man advisory commission. The council attempted to coordinate the manufacture of munitions and other war goods, but it lacked the authority to do the job properly. After a series of experiments, it created (July 1917) the War Industries Board to oversee all aspects of industrial production and distribution.

However, only after Wilson reorganized the WIB under Bernard M. Baruch in March 1918 did it begin to function effectively. Baruch, a daring Wall Street speculator by trade, performed brilliantly, but it was Wilson's decision to make him practically an economic dictator that enabled Baruch to succeed. The WIB allocated scarce materials, standardized production, fixed prices, and coordinated American and Allied purchasing.

The evaluation of this unprecedented and complicated effort raises some interesting historical questions. The antitrust laws were suspended and producers were encouraged, even compelled, to cooperate with one another. The New Freedom variety of laissez faire had no place in a wartime economy. Wilson accepted the kind of government-industry ententes developed under Theodore Roosevelt which he had denounced in 1912. Prices were set by the WIB at levels that allowed large profits—U. S. Steel, for example, despite very high taxes, cleared over half a billion dollars in two years. Baruch justified these returns with what seemed to him irrefutable logic: "You could be forgiven if you paid too much to get the stuff, but you could never be forgiven if you did not get it, and lost the war." It is at least arguable that producers would have turned out just as much even if compelled to charge somewhat lower prices.

Another important effect of the Wilsonian system was to foster a close relation between business and the military. At the start of the conflict, army procurement was decentralized and inefficient—as many as eight bureaus were purchasing materiel independently. By 1918 the supply system was in a condition approaching chaos. Nevertheless, the army resisted cooperating with civilian agencies, being, as the historian Paul Koistiner puts it, "suspicious of, and hostile toward civilian institutions." Wilson finally compelled the war department to place officers on WIB committees, and when the army discovered that its interests were not injured by the system, the foundation for what was later to be known as the "industrial-military complex" was laid, the close alliance between business and military leaders that was to cause so much controversy after World War II.

In general the history of industrial mobilization was the history of the whole home-front effort in microcosm: prodigies were performed, but the task was so gigantic and unprecedented that a full year passed before an efficient system had been devised, and many unforeseen results occurred.

The problem of mobilizing agricultural re-

sources was solved more quickly, and this was fortunate because in April 1917 the British had on hand only a six-weeks' supply of food. Wilson named Herbert Hoover, a mining engineer who had headed the Belgian Relief Commission earlier in the war, as food administrator. Acting under powers granted by the Lever Act of August 1917, Hoover set the price of wheat at $2.20 a bushel in order to encourage production.° He also established a government corporation to purchase the entire American and Cuban sugar crop, which he then doled out to American and British refiners. Avoiding compulsory rationing, Hoover organized a campaign to persuade consumers to conserve food voluntarily. "Wheatless Mondays" and "Meatless Tuesdays" were the rule, and although no law compelled their observance, the public responded patriotically. Boy Scouts dug up back yards and vacant lots to plant vegetable gardens, chefs devised new recipes to save on scarce items, restaurants added horsemeat, rabbit, and whale steak to their menus. Chicago housewives were so successful in making use of leftovers that the volume of raw garbage in the city declined from 12,862 tons to 8,386 tons per month in a single year. Without subjecting its own citizens to serious inconvenience, the United States increased food exports from 12.3 million tons to 18.6 million tons in one year. Farmers, of course, profited greatly: their real income increased nearly 30 per cent between 1915 and 1918. The increased production, involving as it did the use of much submarginal land, caused grave difficulties during the postwar era, however.

Wilson handled the wartime labor problem in a way that greatly benefited workers. The war created full employment and a remarkable industrial prosperity. With the army siphoning millions of men from the labor market and with immigration reduced to a trickle, wages rose. This produced unprecedented opportunities for disadvantaged groups, especially Negroes. The

---

°Output rose from 619 million bushels in 1917 to 904 million in 1918.

movement of freedmen from the former slave states began with emancipation, but the mass exodus that many northerners had expected did not materialize. Between 1870 and 1890 only about 80,000 came to the North, most of these settling in the cities. Compared with the urban influx from Europe and from northern farms, this was a trivial increase; the proportion of blacks to the total population of New York, for example, fell from over ten per cent in 1800 to under two per cent in 1900.

Around the turn of the century, as the first post-slave generation reached maturity and as southern repression increased, the northward movement quickened—about 200,000 Negroes migrated between 1890 and 1910. After 1914, however, the war boom drew blacks north in a flood, half a million in five years. In this period the Negro population of New York rose from 92,000 to 152,000, of Chicago from 44,000 to 109,000, of Detroit from 5,700 to 41,000.

The wartime emergency roused the public against strikers; some conservatives even demanded that war workers be conscripted just as soldiers were. Although he opposed strikes that impeded the war effort, Wilson set great store in preserving the individual worker's freedom of action. It would be "most unfortunate . . . to relax the laws by which safeguards have been thrown about labor," he said. "We must accomplish the results we desire by organized effort rather than compulsion."

Early in the conflict the government began regulating the wages and hours of workers building army camps and manufacturing uniforms; then, in April 1918, Wilson created a National War Labor Board, headed by former President Taft and Frank P. Walsh, a prominent lawyer, to settle labor disputes. The board considered more than 1,200 cases and prevented many strikes. A War Labor Policies Board, headed by Professor Felix Frankfurter of the Harvard Law School, made an overall study of the labor market and laid down standard wages-and-hours patterns for each major war industry. Since these were determined in consultation with employers and representatives of labor, the WLPB helped speed the

unionization of workers by compelling management, even in antiunion industries like steel, to deal with labor leaders. The administration consciously encouraged the growth of unions and collective bargaining. Union membership rose by 2.3 million during the war; in 1920 the American Federation of Labor could boast a membership of 3.26 million.

Trends in the steel industry reflect the general improvement of the lot of labor in wartime. Wages of unskilled steelworkers had more than doubled by November 1918. Thousands of southern Negroes flocked into the steel towns. Union organizers made inroads in many steel plants, especially after a War Labor Board decision forbidding the companies to interfere with their activities. By the summer of 1918 organized labor was preparing an all-out assault to unionize steel, basing its appeal on the idea that if the world was to be made safe for democracy, there must be "economic democracy [along] with political democracy."

Wilson also managed the task of financing the war effectively. The struggle cost the United States about $33.5 billion, not counting pensions and other postwar expenses. About $7 billion of this was lent to the Allies,* but since this money was largely spent in America, it contributed to the national prosperity. Over two-thirds of the cost of the war was met by borrowing. Five massive Liberty and Victory Loan drives, spurred by advertising, parading, and appeals to patriotism, persuaded the people to open their purses. Industrialists, eager to inculcate a sense of personal involvement in the war effort in their employees, conducted great campaigns in their plants. Some went so far as to threaten "A Bond or Your Job," but more typical was the appeal of the managers of the Gary, Indiana, plant of U. S. Steel, who printed patriotic advertisements in six languages in order to reach their immigrant workers.

In addition to borrowing, the government collected about $10.5 billion in taxes during the

---

*In 1914 Americans owed foreigners about $3.8 billion. By 1919 they *were owed* $12.5 billion by Europeans alone.

REMEMBER!
THE FLAG OF LIBERTY
SUPPORT IT!

BUY
U.S. Government Bonds
3rd. LIBERTY LOAN

The nation's advertising and entertainment industries were mobilized to promote war-bond drives. This poster was aimed at recent immigrants from Europe. (New-York Historical Society.)

war. A steeply graduated income tax took over 75 per cent of the incomes of the wealthiest citizens. A 65 per cent excess-profits tax, yielding over $2 billion in 1918, and a 25 per cent inheritance tax were also enacted. Thus, while many individuals made fortunes out of the war, the cost of the struggle was distributed far more equitably than that of the Civil War. Americans also contributed generously to philanthropic agencies engaged in war work. Most notable, perhaps, was the great 1918 drive of the United War Work Council, an interfaith religious group, which raised over $200 million mainly to finance recreational programs for the troops overseas.

Wilson was pre-eminently a teacher and preacher, a specialist in the transmission of ideas and ideals, and for this reason he excelled at mobilizing public opinion and inspiring men to battle for the better world he hoped would emerge from the war. In April 1917 he created a Committee on Public Information, headed by the journalist George Creel, to marshal the nation behind the war effort. Creel organized an army of speakers and writers to blanket the country with propaganda: they pictured the war as a crusade for freedom and democracy, the Germans as a bestial people bent on world domination.

Creel's committee served a practical function, for thousands of persons—German- and Irish-Americans, for example, and people of socialist and pacifist leanings—did not yet believe the war necessary or just. However, the committee, and more especially a number of unofficial patriotic groups, soon allowed their enthusiasm for the conversion of the hesitant to become outright suppression of dissent. Persons who refused to buy war bonds were often exposed to public contempt, even to assault. Opposition to Germany led to attacks on all things German; people with German names were persecuted without regard for their actual views, school boards outlawed the teaching of the German language, sauerkraut was renamed "liberty cabbage." Opponents of the war of unquestionable patriotism were subjected to ridicule and abuse. For example, the cartoonist Rollin Kirby pictured Senator Robert La Follette receiving an Iron Cross from the German militarists,° and the faculty of his own University of Wisconsin voted to censure La Follette.

Despite his understanding of the danger that the war posed for civil liberties, Wilson failed to keep these superpatriots in check. He approved the Espionage Act of 1917, which imposed fines of up to $10,000 and jail sentences ranging to 20 years on persons guilty of aiding the enemy or obstructing recruiting. This law further authorized the postmaster general to ban from the mails any material which he personally considered treasonable or seditious.

In May 1918, again with Wilson's approval,

°Kirby later expressed his deep regret for having defamed La Follette.

In 1917 the Germania Life Insurance Building in St. Paul was renamed the Guardian Building; since Germania herself could not be disguised, down she came. (National Archives.)

Congress went still further, passing the Sedition Act, which made it a crime even to attempt by persuasion to discourage the sale of war bonds or to "utter, print, write, or publish any disloyal, profane, scurrilous, or abusive language" about the government, the Constitution, or the uniform of the army or navy. Mere criticism became cause for arrest and imprisonment. Socialist periodicals like *The Masses* were suppressed, and Eugene V. Debs was sentenced to ten years for making an antiwar speech. A Hollywood producer, Robert Goldstein, received a ten-year sentence because his movie *The Spirit of '76* contained a scene showing British redcoats attacking women and children.

While legislation to prevent sabotage and control subversives was justifiable, these laws went far beyond what was necessary to protect the national interest. Especially reprehensible was the way some local officials used them to muzzle liberal opinion. Citizens were jailed for suggesting that the draft law was unconstitutional and for criticizing private organizations like the Red Cross and the YMCA. One woman was sent to prison for writing: "I am for the people, and the government is for the profiteers." Conscientious objectors were frequently reviled; labor organizers were attacked by mobs.

The Supreme Court upheld the constitutionality of the Espionage Act in *Schenck v. U. S.* (1919), a case involving a man who had mailed circulars to draftees urging them to refuse to report for induction into the army. Free speech has limits, Justice Oliver Wendell Holmes, Jr., explained. No one has the right to cry *"Fire!"* in a crowded theater. When there is a "clear and present danger" that a particular statement would threaten the national interest, it can be repressed by law. In peacetime Schenck's circulars would be permissible, but not in time of war. This clear-and-present-danger doctrine, however, did not prevent judges and juries from interpreting the Espionage and Sedition acts broadly, and although in many instances their decisions were overturned by higher courts, this usually did not occur until after the war. The wartime hysteria far exceeded anything that happened in Great Britain and France, where the threat to national survival was really acute. In 1916 the French novelist Henri Barbusse published *Le Feu (Under Fire),* a graphic account of the horrors and purposelessness of trench warfare. In one chapter Barbusse described a pilot flying over the trenches on a Sunday, observing French and German soldiers at Mass in the open fields, each worshiping the same God. His message, like that of the German Erich Maria Remarque's *Im Westen nichts Neues (All Quiet on the Western Front),* written *after* the conflict, was unmistakably antiwar. Yet *Le Feu* circulated freely in France, even winning the coveted Prix Goncourt.

With all its failures and successes, the American mobilization experience was part and product of the Progressive Era and of the American industrial revolution. The work of the progressives at both the national and state levels in expanding government power in order to deal with social and economic problems before the war provided precedents and conditioned the people for the all-out effort of 1917–18. This effort, in turn, had a great influence on national policy in later crises, most notably during the New Deal period and in World War II. The concept of social and economic planning and the management of huge business operations by public boards and committees got their first large-scale practical tests. College professors, technicians, and others with complex intellectual skills entered government service en masse. The expansion of federal powers took another giant step forward as the national government for the first time entered actively and continuously in such fields as housing and labor relations.

Many progressives, especially the social workers, saw the war as creating the sense of common purpose that would stimulate the people to act unselfishly to benefit the poor and to eradicate social evils. Patriotism and public service seemed at last united. Secretary of War Newton D. Baker, a prewar urban reformer, expressed this attitude in supporting a federal child labor law: "We cannot afford, when we are losing boys in France to lose children in the United States." Men and women of this sort worked for a dozen causes only remotely concerned with the war effort. The women's suffrage movement was stimulated, as was the campaign against alcohol. Reformers began to talk about health insurance and to press older drives for workmen's compensation laws. A national campaign against prostitution and venereal disease was mounted.°

War-inspired cooperation also brought social benefits to American Negroes to supplement their new economic opportunities. The northern migration worried southern whites and led to some mitigation of conditions. Although there were terrible race riots in a number of northern and southern cities triggered by white resentment of the thousands of migrants who were crowding in to fill war jobs, significant forward steps were taken. The draft law applied to blacks and whites equally, and while it is possible to view this cynically, most Negroes saw it as an important gain, for it implicitly recognized their bravery and patriotism. More important, blacks were accepted for officer training, as Red Cross nurses, and for high posts in government agencies. W. E. B. Du Bois supported the war wholeheartedly. He praised Wilson for making, at last, a strong statement against lynching. He even went along with the fact that black officer candidates were trained in segregated camps. "Let us," he wrote in the *Crisis,* "while the war lasts, forget our special grievances and close ranks shoulder to shoulder with our fellow citizens and the allied nations that are fighting for democracy." Many Negroes condemned Du Bois's accommodationism (which he promptly abandoned

°The effort to wipe out prostitution around military installations was a cause of some misunderstanding with the Allies, who provided licensed facilities for their troops as a matter of course. When the Premier of France graciously offered to supply prostitutes for American units in his country, Secretary of War Baker is said to have remarked: "For God's sake . . . don't show this to the President or he'll stop the war."

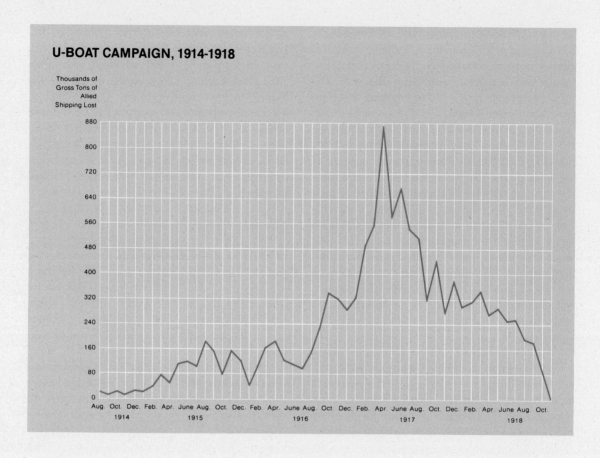

U-BOAT CAMPAIGN, 1914-1918

Thousands of Gross Tons of Allied Shipping Lost

when the war ended), but for the moment the prevailing mood among blacks was one of optimism. "We may expect to see the walls of prejudice gradually crumble"—this was the common attitude in 1917–18.

"Over There"

All activity on the home front, of course, had one ultimate objective: defeating the Central Powers on the battlefield. This it accomplished. The navy performed with special distinction. In April 1917 German submarines sank over 870,000 tons of Allied shipping; after April 1918, monthly losses never reached 300,000 tons. American de-

stroyers helped control the U-boats, but most important was the decision of Admiral William S. Sims, made at the urging of Wilson and accepted by the British only after intense argument, to send merchantmen across the Atlantic only in convoys screened by warships. Checking the U-boats was essential because of the need to transport millions of soldiers to Europe. This feat was carried out without the loss of a single man.

The first units of the American Expeditionary Force (AEF), elements of the regular army commanded by General John J. Pershing, reached Paris on Independence Day 1917 and took up positions on the front near Verdun in October. Not until the spring of 1918, however, did the "doughboys," as they were called, play a significant role in the fighting, except insofar as their mere presence boosted French and British morale. Pershing, as commander of the AEF, insisted upon maintaining his troops as independent units; he would not allow them to be filtered into the Allied armies as reinforcements. This was part of a perhaps unfortunate general policy, reflecting America's isolationism and suspicion of Europeans, of refusing to accept full membership in the Allied coalition. Wilson always referred to the other nations fighting Germany as "associates," not as "allies."

In March 1918 the Germans launched a great spring offensive, their armies strengthened by thousands of veterans from the Russian front. By late May they had reached a point on the Somme River just 12 miles from Amiens, a key British base, and were only 50 miles from Paris itself, on the Marne River near the town of Château-Thierry. Early in June, the AEF fought its first major engagements, driving the Germans back from Château-Thierry and Belleau Wood.

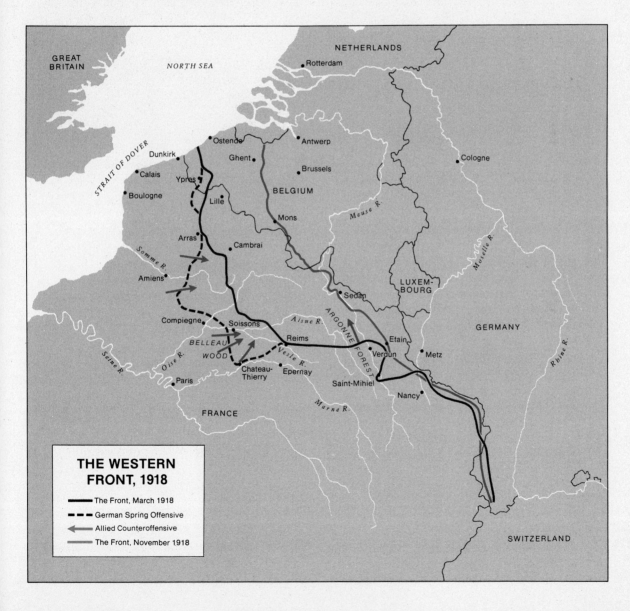

THE WESTERN FRONT, 1918

— The Front, March 1918
--- German Spring Offensive
← Allied Counteroffensive
— The Front, November 1918

A column of American troops, with their walking wounded and their prisoners, was sketched in October 1918 during the Meuse-Argonne offensive by Harvey Dunn, a combat artist attached to the American Expeditionary Force. (Smithsonian Institution.)

In this fighting only about 27,500 Americans saw action, but thereafter the number escalated rapidly. When the Germans advanced again in the direction of the Marne in mid-July, 85,000 Americans were in the lines that withstood their charge; when the Allied armies counterattacked a few days later, 270,000 Americans participated, helping to flatten the German bulge between Reims and Soissons. By late August the American First Army, 500,000 men, was poised before the Saint-Mihiel salient, a deep extension of the German lines southeast of Verdun. On September 12 this army, buttressed by French troops, struck and in two days wiped out the salient.

Then, late in September, began the greatest American engagement of the war. No less than 1.2 million doughboys drove forward west of Verdun into the Argonne Forest. For over a month of indescribable horror they inched ahead through the tangle of the Argonne and the formidable defenses of the Hindenburg Line, while to the west, French and British armies staged similar drives. In this one offensive the AEF suffered 120,000 casualties. Finally, on November 1, they broke the German center and raced ahead toward the vital Sedan-Mézières railroad. On November 11, with Allied armies advancing on all fronts, the Germans signed the Armistice, ending the fighting.°

Preparing for Peace

On November 11, 1918, western civilization stood at a great turning point. The fighting had ended, but the shape of the postwar world re-

°Total American losses in the war amounted to 112,432 dead and 230,074 wounded. More than half of the deaths, however, resulted from disease. Although severe, these casualties were trivial compared with those of the other belligerents. British Commonwealth deaths amounted to 947,000, French to 1.38 million, Russian to 1.7 million, Italian to 460,000. Among the Central Powers, Germany lost 1.8 million men, Austria-Hungary 1.2 million, Turkey 325,000. In addition, about 20 million men were wounded.

mained to be determined. Aside from the loss of life and the destruction of so much wealth and property, the structure of European society had been shaken to its foundations. Confusion reigned. People wanted peace yet burned for revenge. Millions faced starvation, other millions were disillusioned by the seemingly purposeless sacrifices of four years of horrible war. Communism—to some an idealistic promise of human betterment, to others a commitment to rational economic and social planning, and to still others a danger to individual freedom, toleration, and democracy—having conquered Russia threatened to envelop Germany and much of the defunct Austro-Hungarian empire, perhaps even the victorious Allies. How could stability be restored? How could victory be made meaningful?

Woodrow Wilson, who had grasped the true significance of the war while most statesmen still thought that triumph on the battlefield would settle everything automatically, faced the future on November 11 with determination and sober confidence. As early as January 1917, he had realized that victory would be wasted if the winners permitted themselves the luxury of vengeance, that such a policy would disrupt the balance of power and lead to economic and social chaos. American participation in the struggle had not blurred his vision. The victors must build a better society, not punish those they believed had destroyed the old. In a speech to Congress on January 8, 1918, he outlined a plan, known as the Fourteen Points, designed to make the world "fit and safe to live in." The peace treaty should be negotiated in the full view of world opinion, not in secret. It should guarantee that the seas would be free to all nations, in war as in peacetime; it should tear down barriers to international trade, provide for a drastic reduction of armaments, and establish a colonial system that would take proper account of the interests of the native peoples concerned. European boundaries should be redrawn so that no substantial group would have to live under a government not of its own choosing. More specifically, captured Russian territory should be restored, Belgium evacuated, Alsace-Lorraine given back to France, the

heterogeneous nationalities of Austria-Hungary accorded autonomy. Italy's frontiers should be adjusted "along clearly recognizable lines of nationality," the Balkans made free, Turkey divested of its subject peoples, an independent Polish state (with access to the Baltic) created. To oversee the new system, Wilson insisted, "a general association of nations must be formed under specific covenants for the purpose of affording mutual guarantees of political independence and territorial integrity to great and small states alike."

Wilson's Fourteen Points for a fair peace lifted the hopes of well-meaning people everywhere. When the German armies began to crack in the summer of 1918, the plan also helped to undermine the will of the Central Powers to resist, thus hastening the end of the war. After the guns fell silent, however, the vagueness and inconsistencies in the Points became apparent. Complete national self-determination was impossible in polyglot Europe; there were too many regions of mixed population for every group to be satisfied. Self-determination also, like the war itself, fostered the very spirit of nationalism that Wilson's dream of international organization, a league of nations, was designed to de-emphasize. Furthermore, the Allies had made certain territorial commitments to one another in secret treaties that ran counter to the principle of self-determination, and they were unready to give up all claim to Germany's sprawling colonial empire. Freedom of the seas in wartime posed another problem; the British flatly refused to accept the idea. On the other hand, many Americans were alarmed at the thought of abandoning the principle of protective tariffs. In every Allied country millions repudiated the concept of a peace without indemnities; they expected to make the enemy pay for the war, hoping, as David Lloyd George, the British prime minister, put it, to squeeze Germany "until the pips squeak."

Wilson assumed that the practical virtues of his program would compel selfish and shortsighted opponents to fall in line. He had the immense advantage of seeking nothing for his own country and the additional strength of being leader of the one important nation to emerge from the war richer and more powerful than it had been in 1914. Yet this combination of altruism, idealism, and power was his undoing, for it intensified his tendency to be overbearing and undermined his judgment. He had never found it easy to compromise. Once, for example, while at Princeton, he got into an argument over some abstract question with a professor while shooting a game of pool. To avoid acrimony, the professor finally said: "Well, Doctor Wilson, there are two sides to every question." "Yes," Wilson answered, "a right side and a wrong side." Now, believing that the fate of humanity hung on his actions, he became still more unyielding. Always a preacher, he became in his own mind a prophet, almost, one fears, a kind of god.

In the last weeks of the war Wilson proved himself a brilliant diplomat, dangling the Fourteen Points before the German people to encourage them to overthrow the kaiser, Wilhelm II, and sue for an armistice, and then sending Colonel House to Paris to persuade Allied leaders to accept the points as the basis for the peace. When the Allies raised objections, House made certain small concessions, but by hinting that the United States might make a separate peace with Germany, he forced them to agree. Under the Armistice, Germany had to pull back behind the Rhine and surrender its submarines, together with quantities of munitions and other materials, but it received the assurance of the Allies that the Wilsonian principles would prevail at the peace conference.

Wilson next came to a daring decision: he would personally attend the conference, which convened formally on January 12, 1919, at Paris, as a member of the United States Peace Commission. This was a precedent-shattering step, for no previous President had left American territory while in office. Taft, for example, had a summer home on the St. Lawrence River in Canada but never vacationed there during his term, feeling that to do so would be unconstitutional. Wilson probably erred in going to Paris, but not because of the novelty or possible illegality of the act. By

leaving the country, he was turning his back on certain obvious domestic problems, less important than those being settled at Versailles to be sure, but ones that demanded his personal attention far more.

Western farmers felt that they had been discriminated against during the war, since wheat prices had been controlled while southern cotton had been allowed to rise unchecked, skyrocketing from 7 cents a pound in 1914 to 35 cents in 1919. Businessmen had become disaffected because of the administration's drastic tax program; labor, despite its gains, was restive in the face of reconversion to peacetime conditions. Wilson had greatly increased his political difficulties by making a partisan appeal for the election of a Democratic Congress in 1918. Republicans who had, in many instances, supported his war program more loyally than the Democrats, considered the statement a gross affront. The appeal failed, for the Republicans won majorities in both houses; thus Wilson appeared to have been repudiated at home at the very moment that he set forth to represent the nation abroad. Most important of all, Wilson intended to break with the isolationist tradition and bring the United States into a league of nations. Such a revolutionary change required explanation. He should have undertaken a great campaign to convince the people of the wisdom of this step.

Wilson also erred in his choice of the other commissioners. He selected Colonel House, Secretary of State Lansing, General Tasker H. Bliss, and Henry White, a career diplomat. These men were all thoroughly competent, but none except White was a Republican, and he had no stature as a politician. Since the peace treaty would have to be ratified by the Senate, Wilson should have given that body some representation on the commission, and since the Republicans would have a majority in the new Senate, a Republican senator, or someone who had the full confidence of the Republican leadership, should have been appointed. The wily McKinley, it will be remembered, named *three* senators to the American delegation to the peace conference after the Spanish–American War.

The Paris Peace Conference

This blunder did not affect the making of the treaty, however. Wilson arrived in Paris a world hero. He toured England, France, and Italy briefly and was greeted ecstatically almost everywhere. This reception tended to increase his sense of mission and to convince him, in the fashion of a typical progressive, that whatever the European politicians might say about it, "the people" were behind his program.

When the conference settled down to its work, control quickly fell into the hands of the so-called Big Four: Wilson, Lloyd George, Premier Georges Clemenceau of France, and Prime Minister Vittorio Orlando of Italy. Wilson stood out in, but did not dominate, this group. Aside from his dedication, his main advantage in the negotiations was his untiring industry. He alone of the leaders tried to master all the complex details of the task.

The 78-year-old Clemenceau, stooped, white-haired, with a walrus mustache and a powerful jaw, cared only for one thing: French security. He viewed Wilson most cynically, saying that since mankind had been unable to keep God's

Ten Commandments, it was unlikely to do better with Wilson's Fourteen Points. Lloyd George's approach to the peacemaking was pragmatic and almost cavalier. His baby-pink face, framed by a shock of white hair, radiated charm and informality. He sympathized with much that Wilson was trying to accomplish but found the President's frequent sermonettes about "right being more important than might, and justice being more eternal than force" incomprehensible. "If you want to succeed in politics," Lloyd George advised a British statesman, "you must keep your conscience well under control." Orlando, clever, cultured, a believer in international cooperation but inflexible where Italian national interests were concerned, was not the equal of his three colleagues in influence and left the conference in a huff when they failed to meet all his demands.

The conference labored from January to May 1919, and finally brought forth the Versailles Treaty. Many American liberals whose hopes had soared at the thought of a peace based on the Fourteen Points found the document abysmally disappointing. The peace settlement failed to carry out the principle of self-determination completely. It gave Italy a large section of the Austrian Tyrol, although the area contained

Frenchman Edouard Requin drew the Big Four at Versailles. From left, France's Clemenceau, President Wilson, Britain's Lloyd George, and Italy's Orlando. (Musee De La Guerre, Paris.)

200,000 persons who considered themselves Austrians. Other German-speaking groups were incorporated into the new states of Poland and Czechoslovakia. Japan was allowed to take over the Chinese province of Shantung, and one or another of the Allies swallowed up all the German colonies in Africa and the Far East. The victors also forced Germany to accept full responsibility for having caused the war—an act of senseless vindictiveness as well as a gross oversimplification—and to sign a "blank check" agreeing to pay reparations not only for all damage to civilian properties, but also for future pensions and other indirect war costs. The total reparations bill, as finally determined, amounted to $33 billion, a sum far beyond Germany's ability to pay. Thus, instead of attacking imperialism, the treaty attacked *German* imperialism; instead of seeking a new international social order based on liberty and democracy, it created a new great-power entente designed to crush Germany and exclude Bolshevist Russia from the family of nations. It said nothing about freedom of the seas, the reduction of tariffs, or disarmament. To men who had taken Wilson's "peace without victory" speech and the Fourteen Points literally, the Versailles Treaty seemed an abomination.

The complaints of the critics were individually reasonable, but their conclusions were not entirely fair. The new map of Europe left fewer people on "foreign" soil than in any earlier period of history. Although the Allies seized the German colonies, they were required, under the mandate system, to render the League of Nations annual accounts of their stewardship and to prepare the inhabitants for eventual independence. Above all, Wilson made the powers incorporate the League of Nations directly into the treaty.

Wilson expected this League of Nations to make up for all the inadequacies of the Versailles Treaty. Once the League had begun to function, problems like freedom of the seas and disarmament would solve themselves, he argued, and the relaxation of trade barriers would surely follow. The League would arbitrate international disputes, act as a central body for registering treaties, and, in the last analysis, employ sanctions,

military as well as economic, against aggressor nations. Each member promised (Article X) to protect the "territorial integrity" and "political independence" of all other members. No great power could be made to go to war against its will, but—and this Wilson emphasized—all were *morally* obligated to carry out League decisions. Liberal critics of the League were correct in saying that Wilson was seeking to prop up the existing social and economic system, that he was gravely concerned lest communism or even democratic socialism gain the upper hand in central Europe. Any form of class-oriented radicalism appalled him. He hoped, unrealistically as it turned out, to see Europe develop a capitalist-laborer consensus like that which existed in the United States. But by any standard, he had achieved a remarkably moderate peace, one full of hope for the future. Except for the war-guilt clause and the crushing reparations burden imposed on Germany, he could be justly proud of his work.

The Senate and the League of Nations

When Wilson returned from France, he finally directed his attention to the task of winning his countrymen's approval of his handiwork. Probably a large majority of the people favored the League of Nations in principle, although few understood all its implications or were entirely happy with every detail. Wilson had already persuaded the Allies to accept certain changes in the original draft to mollify American opposition. One provided that no nation could be forced to accept a colonial mandate, another that "domestic questions" such as tariffs and the control of immigration did not fall within the competence of the League. The Monroe Doctrine had also been excluded from League control to satisfy American opinion, and a clause was added permitting members to withdraw from the organization after two years' notice.

Many senators, however, found these modifi-

A view of the League of Nations: In London's *Punch* the dove of peace looks askance at Wilson's hefty olive branch, asking, "Isn't this a bit thick?" Below, a New York WORLD cartoon by Rollin Kirby. The intransigent seat-holders are anti-League senators Borah, Lodge, and Hiram Johnson. (*Punch,* March 26, 1919 and Library of Congress.)

cations insufficient. As early as March 1919, 37 Republican senators had signed a Round Robin, devised by Henry Cabot Lodge of Massachusetts, expressing opposition to Wilson's League and demanding that the question of an international organization be put off until "the urgent business of negotiating peace terms with Germany" had been completed. Wilson rejected this suggestion icily. The Allies had exacted major concessions in return for the changes he had already proposed; further alterations were out of the question. "Anyone who opposes me . . . I'll crush!" he told one Democratic senator. "I shall consent to nothing. *The Senate must take its medicine.*" Thus the stage was set for a monumental test of strength between the President and the Republican majority in the Senate.

Partisanship, principle, and prejudice clashed mightily in this contest. A Presidential election loomed ahead. Should the League prove a success, it was politically essential for the Republicans to be able to claim a share of the credit, yet Wilson had refused to allow them to participate in drafting the document. This predisposed all of them to favor changes. Politics aside, genuine alarm at the possible sacrifice of American sovereignty to an international authority led many Republicans to urge modification of the League Covenant, or constitution. Personal dislike of Wilson and his high-handed methods motivated others. On the other hand, the noble purpose of the League made many reluctant to oppose it entirely. The intense desire of the people to have an end to the long war also operated to make GOP leaders hesitate before voting down the Versailles Treaty, and they could not reject the League without rejecting the treaty too.

Wilson could count on the Democratic senators almost to a man, but he had to win over many Republicans to obtain the two-thirds majority necessary for ratification. Republican opinion divided roughly into three segments. At one extreme were some dozen "irreconcilables," led by the shaggy-browed William E. Borah of Idaho, an able, kindly individualist of progressive leanings but uncompromisingly isolationist and almost congenitally predisposed to resist the will of a powerful executive like Wilson. Borah claimed that he would vote against the League even if Jesus Christ returned to earth to argue in its behalf, and most of his followers were equally inflexible. At the other extreme stood another dozen "mild" reservationists who approved the League in principle but who hoped to alter it in minor ways, chiefly for political purposes. In the middle were the "strong" reservationists, men willing to go along with the League only if American sovereignty were fully protected and if it was made perfectly clear that their party had played a major role in fashioning the final document.

The leader of the Republican opposition was Senator Lodge. A haughty, rather cynical, intensely partisan person, Lodge possessed a keen intelligence, a mastery of parliamentary procedures, and, as chairman of the Senate Foreign Relations Committee, a great deal of power. Although not an isolationist, Lodge had little faith in the League. He also had a profound distrust of Democrats, and especially of Wilson, with whom he had clashed repeatedly. Lodge considered Wilson both a hypocrite and a coward; the President's pious idealism left him cold. While perfectly ready to see the country participate actively in world affairs, he insisted that its right to determine its own best interests in every situation be preserved. He had been a senator since 1893 and an admirer of senatorial independence since early manhood; when a Democratic President tried to ram the Versailles Treaty through the upper house, he fought him with every weapon he could muster.

Lodge belonged to the strong reservationist faction. His own proposals, known as the Lodge Reservations, 14 in number to match Wilson's Fourteen Points, spelled out the limits of the United States' obligations to the League and stated in unmistakable terms the right of Congress to decide when to honor these obligations. Some were mere quibbles. One, for example, exempted the Monroe Doctrine from League jurisdiction, although the treaty had already done so. Others, such as the provision that the United States would not endorse Japan's seizure of Chinese territory, were included mainly to embarrass Wilson by pointing up compromises he had made at Versailles. The most important reservation applied to Article X of the League Covenant, committing signatories to protect the political independence and territorial integrity of all member nations, which Wilson had rightly called "the heart of the Covenant." This reservation made Article X inoperable so far as the United States was concerned "unless in any particular case the Congress . . . shall by act or joint resolution so provide."

Lodge performed brilliantly if somewhat unscrupulously in uniting the diverse factions of his own party behind these reservations. He got the irreconcilables to agree to them by conceding their right to vote against the final version in any case, and held the mild reservationists in line by modifying some of his demands and by stressing the importance of party unity. Since the reservations, as distinct from amendments, would not have to win the formal approval of other League members and since Lodge's proposals (whatever his personal motivation) dealt forthrightly with the problem of reconciling traditional concepts of national sovereignty with the new idea of world cooperation, friends of the League could accept them without sacrifice of principle. Wilson, however, refused to agree. "Accept the Treaty with the *Lodge* reservations," the President snorted when a friendly senator warned him that he must accept a compromise. "Never! Never!"

This foolish intransigence seems almost incomprehensible in a man of Wilson's intelligence and political experience. In part his hatred of Lodge accounts for it, in part his faith in his League. But his physical condition in 1919 also played a role. At Paris he had suffered a violent attack of indigestion that was probably a symptom of a minor stroke. Thereafter, many observers noted small changes in his personality, particularly an increased stubbornness and a loss of judgment. In any case, instead of making further concessions, he set out, early in September, on a nationwide speaking tour to rally support for the League. Although some of his speeches were brilliant, they had little effect on senatorial opinion and the effort drained away his last physical reserves. On September 25, after an address in Pueblo, Colorado, he collapsed. The rest of the trip had to be canceled. A few days later, back in Washington, he suffered a severe stroke, which partially paralyzed his left side.

For nearly two months as he slowly recovered, the President was almost totally cut off from affairs of state, leaving his friends leaderless while Lodge maneuvered the reservations through the Senate. Gradually, popular attitudes toward the League shifted. Italian-, Irish-, and German-Americans, angered by what they considered unfair treatment of their native lands in the treaty, clamored for outright rejection. The arguments of the irreconcilables persuaded many other citizens that Wilson had made too sharp a break with America's isolationist past and that the Lodge Reservations were therefore necessary. Other issues connected with the reconver-

sion of society to a peacetime basis increasingly occupied the public mind.

Yet a coalition of Democrats and moderate Republicans could easily have carried the treaty. That no such coalition was organized was largely Wilson's fault. Lodge obtained the simple majority necessary to pass his reservations merely by keeping his own party united. When the time came for the final roll call on November 19, Wilson, bitter and emotionally distraught, ordered the Democrats to vote for rejection. "Better a thousand times to go down fighting than to dip your colours to dishonourable compromise," he explained to his wife. Thus the amended treaty failed, 35 to 55, the irreconcilables and the Democrats voting against it. Lodge then allowed the original draft to come to a vote. Again the result was defeat: 38 to 53. Only one Republican cast his ballot for ratification.

Dismayed but not yet crushed, friends of the League in both parties forced reconsideration of the treaty early in 1920. Neither Lodge nor Wilson, however, would yield an inch. Lodge, who had little confidence in the effectiveness of any league of nations, was under no compulsion to compromise. The fact that Wilson, whose whole being was tied up in the Covenant, would not do so is further evidence of his physical and mental decline. Probably he was incompetent to perform the duties of his office. Almost certainly, had he died or stepped down, the treaty, with reservations, would have been ratified. When the Senate balloted again in March, half the Democrats violated Wilson's orders and voted for the treaty with the Lodge Reservations. The others, mostly southern party regulars, joined with the irreconcilables. Together they mustered 35 votes, 7 more than the one-third that meant defeat.

Wilson still hoped for vindication at the polls in the Presidential election, which he sought to make a "great and solemn referendum" on the League. The election was scarcely a referendum, for while the Democrats, who nominated Governor James M. Cox of Ohio, took a stand for Wilson's Covenant, the Republicans, whose candidate was another Ohioan, Senator Warren G.

Harding, equivocated shamelessly on the issue. To a large extent, the election turned on other matters, largely emotional. Disillusioned by the results of the war, many Americans had had their fill of idealism. They wanted, apparently, to end the long period of moral uplift and reform agitation that had begun under Theodore Roosevelt and get back to what Harding called "normalcy." To the extent that the voters were expressing opinions on Wilson's League, they responded overwhelmingly in the negative. Harding had been a strong reservationist, yet he swept the country, winning over 16.1 million votes to Cox's 9.1 million. In July 1921 Congress formally ended the war with the Central Powers by passing a joint resolution.

That the defeat of the League was a tragedy is undeniable, both for Wilson, whose crusade for a world order based on peace and justice ended in failure, and for the world, which was condemned by the result to endure another still more horrible and costly war. Perhaps this dreadful outcome could not have been avoided. The United States, in 1919-20, was unready to assume the responsibility of preserving peace in other lands. If Wilson had compromised and if Lodge had behaved like a statesman instead of like a politician, America would have joined the League, but it might well have failed to respond when called upon to meet its obligations. As events soon demonstrated, the great League powers themselves acted pusillanimously and even dishonorably when challenged by aggressor nations. Nevertheless, it might have been different had the Senate ratified the Versailles Treaty. America's retreat from international cooperation discouraged supporters of the League in other countries and lessened the dangers that dictators like Mussolini and Hitler had to consider when planning their moves. In the 20-year respite between World War I and World War II, the western democracies might have drawn closer together and become more firm of heart if *all* had been committed to the League. What was lost when the treaty failed in the Senate was not peace, but the *possibility* of peace, a tragic loss indeed.

Supplementary Reading

Wilson's handling of foreign relations is discussed in several volumes by A. S. Link: *Wilson* (1947-   ), *Woodrow Wilson and the Progressive Era*° (1954), and *Wilson the Diplomatist*° (1957), as well as in the Wilson biographies listed in the preceding chapter. See also Harley Notter, *The Origins of the Foreign Policy of Woodrow Wilson* (1937), and N. G. Levin, Jr., *Woodrow Wilson and World Politics: America's Response to War and Revolution* (1968). Latin-American affairs under Wilson are treated in S. F. Bemis, *The Latin American Policy of the United States*° (1943), H. F. Cline, *The United States and Mexico*° (1953), and D. G. Munro, *Intervention and Dollar Diplomacy in the Caribbean* (1964). R. E. Quirk, *An Affair of Honor: Woodrow Wilson and the Occupation of Veracruz*° (1962), is an admirable monograph, and C. C. Clendenen, *The United States and Pancho Villa* (1961), is also interesting.

For American entry into the Great War, see, in addition to the Link volumes mentioned above, E. R. May, *The World War and American Isolation*° (1959), E. H. Buehrig, *Woodrow Wilson and the Balance of Power* (1955), Charles Seymour, *American Diplomacy During the World War* (1934) and *American Neutrality* (1935), all essentially favorable to Wilson. For contrary views, see Walter Millis, *The Road to War* (1935), and C. C. Tansill, *America Goes to War* (1938).

The war on the home front is covered in F. L. Paxson, *American Democracy and the World War* (1936-48), and more briefly in Preston Slosson, *The Great Crusade and After: 1914-28* (1930), and W. E. Leuchtenburg, *The Perils of Prosperity*° (1958). Other useful volumes include B. M. Baruch, *American Industry in War* (1941), M. I. Urofsky, *Big Steel and the Wilson Administration* (1969), Zechariah Chafee, *Free Speech in the United States*° (1941), Donald Johnson, *The Challenge to American Freedoms* (1963), J. R. Mock and Cedric Larson, *Words That Won the War* (1939), David Brody, *Steelworkers in America* (1960), Herbert Stein, *Government Price Policy During the World War* (1939), D. R. Beaver, *Newton D. Baker and the American War Effort* (1966), and S. W. Livermore, *Politics Is Adjourned: Woodrow Wilson and the War Congress*° (1966).

Laurence Stallings, *The Doughboys*° (1963), is a good popular account of the American army in

°Available in paperback.

France, but see also J. J. Pershing, *My Experiences in the World War* (1931), E. E. Morison, *Admiral Sims and the Modern American Navy* (1942), and T. G. Frothingham, *The Naval History of the World War* (1924–26).

On the peace settlement, in addition to the biographies of Wilson, consult A. J. Mayer, *Politics and Diplomacy of Peacemaking* (1967), Paul Birdsall, *Versailles Twenty Years After* (1941), Harold Nicolson, *Peacemaking, 1919°* (1939), T. A. Bailey, *Woodrow Wilson and the Lost Peace°* (1944) and *Woodrow Wilson and the Great Betrayal°* (1945), J. A. Garraty, *Henry Cabot Lodge* (1953), H. C. Lodge, *The Senate and the League of Nations* (1925), Allan Nevins, *Henry White* (1930), J. M. Keynes, *The Economic Consequences of the Peace* (1919), and Robert Lansing, *The Peace Negotiations: A Personal Narrative* (1921). On the election of 1920, see Wesley Bagby, *The Road to Normalcy°* (1962), and R. K. Murray, *The Harding Era* (1969).

25

The Twenties: The Aftermath of the Great War

The Armistice of 1918 ended the fighting, but the Great War had so shaken the world that for a whole generation every major nation lived in its shadow. Americans sought desperately to escape from its influence, tried almost to deny that it had occurred, yet every aspect of their lives in the postwar years reflected its baneful impact. Convinced that they had made a terrible mistake by going to war, a great many people rejected all the values that had led them to do so. Idealism gave way to materialism, naiveté to cynicism, moral purposefulness to irresponsibility, progressivism to reaction, community spirit to rugged individualism, faith to iconoclasm. Yet this reaction, like so many defense mechanisms, was neurotic, based on unreal and conflicting assumptions, and for this reason it was inappropriate.

The nation had put forth an immense effort to win the war, drastically regulating its way of life to increase production and improve social efficiency. Yet when the war ended, all this effort at communal improvement was largely abandoned. The government, in Wilson's words, "took the harness off" at once, blithely assuming that the economy could readjust itself without direction. The army was hastily demobilized, pouring millions of veterans into the job market without plan. Nearly all the controls established by the War Industries Board and other agencies were dropped overnight. Billions of dollars worth of war contracts were suddenly canceled. Despite the obvious benefits that government operation of the railroads had brought, the roads were turned back to private control.°

Business boomed in 1919 as consumers invested wartime savings in the purchase of automobiles, homes, and other goods that had been in short supply during the conflict. Unemployment was only briefly a serious problem as industry expanded to satisfy rising demand. But temporary shortages caused inflation; by 1920 the cost of living stood at more than twice the level of 1913. Inflation, in turn, produced labor trouble. The unions, grown strong during the war, struck for wage increases in order to hold their gains. Work stoppages aggravated shortages, triggering still further inflation and more strikes. Then came one of the most precipitous economic declines in American history. Between July 1920 and March 1922, prices, especially agricultural prices, plummeted, while unemployment soared to 5.75 million in mid-1921. Thus, the unrealistic attitude of the Wilson government toward the complexities of economic readjustment caused much unnecessary strife.

°The Esch-Cummins Transportation Act (1920) did, however, further strengthen the Interstate Commerce Commission's power to set rates and oversee railroad financing. It also authorized the pooling of traffic and the consolidation of some lines in the interest of efficiency.

Radicalism and Xenophobia

Far more important than the economic losses, however, were the social effects of these difficulties. Americans wanted peace, but their wartime tensions did not subside immediately. They continued to need some release for aggressive drives, formerly focused on the Germans, and were unready, as historian John Higham has said, to surrender the "psychic gratifications" the war had provided. They still required, in other words, an enemy. Most persons recognized the services that industrial workers had contributed to the war effort and sympathized with their aspirations for a better way of life, but they found strikes frustrating and drew invidious comparisons between the lot of the unemployed soldier who had risked his life for a dollar a day and that of the striker who had drawn fat wages during the war in perfect safety.

Furthermore, the activities of the radical fringe of the labor movement led millions of Americans to associate unionism and strikes with the new threat of communist world revolution. That threat seemed serious in 1919. Although there were only a handful of communists in the United States—no more than 100,000—Russia's experience indicated to many that a tiny minority of ruthless revolutionaries could take over a nation of millions if conditions were right. The leaders of international communism formed the Third International in March 1919 and announced that world revolution was their aim. In Germany and some other parts of Europe, the danger that they would succeed appeared very real. Communists made themselves the self-appointed champions of the workers; labor unrest attracted them magnetically. When a wave of strikes, sometimes accompanied by violence, broke out in the United States, many persons interpreted them as communist-inspired preludes to revolution. One businessman wrote the attorney general in 1919: "There is hardly a respectable citizen of my acquaintance who does not believe that we are on the verge of armed conflict in this country." Louis Wiley, an experienced New York *Times* reporter, told a friend at this time that anarchists, socialists, and radical labor leaders were "joining together with the object of overthrowing the American Government through a bloody revolution and establishing a Bolshevist republic."

Organized labor in America had seldom been truly radical. The Industrial Workers of the World (IWW), influential in western mining and among migratory workers in the Progressive Era, had advocated violence and the abolition of the wage system but had made little impression in most industries. However, some labor leaders, such as Eugene V. Debs, had been attracted to socialism, and many Americans failed to distinguish between the common ends sought by communists and socialists and the entirely different methods that they proposed to achieve these ends. When a general strike paralyzed Seattle in February 1919, the fact that a pro-communist had helped organize it sent shivers down countless conservative spines. When the radical William Z. Foster began a drive to organize the steel industry for the AFL at about this time, these fears became more intense. In September 1919, 343,000 steelworkers walked off their jobs, and in the same month the Boston police also struck. Violence marked the steel strike and the suspension of police protection in Boston led to looting and fighting, which ended only when Governor Calvin Coolidge (who might have prevented the strike if he had acted earlier) called out the National Guard.

During the same period a handful of anarchists caused a series of alarms by attempting to murder various prominent persons. In April 1919 a servant of Senator Thomas W. Hartwick of Georgia was maimed when an innocent-looking package addressed to the senator exploded while she was unwrapping it. Prompt investigation led to the discovery in a New York post office of 16 similar packages, all containing bombs, addressed to men like John D. Rockefeller and Justice Oliver Wendell Holmes, Jr. On June 2 an explosion shattered the front of the home of Attorney General A. Mitchell Palmer. Anarchism had little in common with communism except a willingness to use violent methods, but many Americans lumped all extremists together and associated them with a monstrous assault on society.

What aroused the public even more was the fact that nearly all the radicals were immigrants, few of them American citizens. Wartime fear of alien saboteurs transformed itself easily into peacetime terror of foreign radicals, and ugly nativist sentiments that had built up during the Progressive Era as a result of mass immigration and rapid social change erupted. Wartime patriotism became "100 per cent Americanism"; instead of Germany, the enemy became the lowly immigrant, usually an Italian or a Jew or a Slav, and usually an industrial worker, too. In this muddled way radicalism, unionism, and questions of racial and national origins combined to make many Americans think their way of life in danger of imminent attack. That few immigrants were radicals, that most workers had no interest in communism, that the extremists themselves were faction-ridden, disorganized, and irresolute did not affect conservative thinking. From all over the country came demands that radicals be ruthlessly suppressed. Thus the "Big Red Scare" was born.

The key figure in the resulting purge was A. Mitchell Palmer, Wilson's attorney general. Palmer had been a typical progressive, a supporter of the League of Nations and of many liberal measures, such as women's suffrage and child labor legislation. When the public clamor against alien radicals began, he tried to resist it. Even after his own home had been bombed, he reminded the country of the traditional American policy "that the oppressed of every clime shall find here a refuge." However, continued pressure from Congress and the press, and his growing conviction that the communists really were a menace, led him to change his mind.

When he did, he joined the "red hunt" with the enthusiasm of the typical convert. Soon he was saying of the radicals: "Out of the sly and crafty eyes of many of them leap cupidity, cruelty, insanity, and crime; from their lopsided faces, sloping brows, and misshapen features may be recognized the unmistakable criminal type."

In August 1919 Palmer established a General Intelligence Division in the Department of Jus-

During the "Big Red Scare" radical cartoonist William Gropper sharply criticized the tactics of Attorney General Palmer. These drawings appeared in *The Liberator* early in 1920. At left, Palmer's agents warn, "Clear the road there, boys—we got a dangerous Red." At right, a suspect faces a loutish, unsympathetic audience. (Both: *The Liberator,* February 1920.)

tice, headed by J. Edgar Hoover, to collect information about clandestine radical activities. In November Justice Department agents swooped down upon the meeting places of an anarchist organization known as the Union of Russian Workers in a dozen cities. More than 650 persons, many of them unconnected with the union, were arrested, but in only 43 cases could evidence be found to justify deportation. Nevertheless, the public reacted so favorably that Palmer, thinking now of winning the 1920 Democratic Presidential nomination, planned an immense roundup of communists. He obtained no less than 3,000 warrants and on January 2, 1920, his agents, reinforced by local police and self-appointed vigilantes, struck simultaneously in 33 cities.

Palmer's biographer, Stanley Coben, has described these "Palmer raids" vividly:

There was a knock on the door, the rush of police. In meeting houses, all were lined up to be searched; those who resisted often suffered brutal treatment. . . . Prisoners were put in overcrowded jails or detention centers where they remained, frequently under the most abominable conditions. . . . Police searched the homes of many of those arrested; books and papers, as well as many people found in these residences, were carried off to headquarters. Policemen also sought those whose names appeared on seized membership lists; they captured many of these suspects in bed or at work, searching their homes, confiscating their possessions, almost always without warrants.

All in all, about 6,000 persons were taken into custody, many of them citizens and therefore not subject to the deportation laws, many others unconnected with any radical cause. Some were held incommunicado for weeks while the authorities made futile efforts to find evidence against them. In a number of cases, individuals who came to visit prisoners were themselves thrown behind bars on the theory that they, too, must be communists. Hundreds of suspects were jammed into filthy "bullpens," beaten, forced to sign "confessions."

The public tolerated these wholesale violations of civil liberties because of the supposed menace of communism. Gradually, however, protests began to be heard, first from lawyers and from liberal magazines like the *Nation* and the *New Republic,* and then from a wider segment of the population. Despite the furor, no revolutionary outbreaks had taken place. Out of 6,000 seized in the Palmer raids, only 556 proved liable to deportation. The widespread ransacking of communists' homes and meeting places produced mountains of inflammatory literature, but only three pistols. The foolish action of the New

York legislature in expelling five socialist assemblymen also had a sobering effect, and the publication of the National Popular Government League's shocking report, *Illegal Practices of the United States Department of Justice* (1920), speeded the shift in public thinking.

Palmer, attempting to maintain the crusade, had announced that the radicals were planning a gigantic terrorist demonstration for May Day, 1920. In New York and other cities thousands of police were placed on round-the-clock duty; federal troops stood by anxiously. But the day passed without even a riot or a rowdy meeting. Suddenly Palmer appeared ridiculous. His Presidential boom collapsed and the Red Scare swiftly subsided.

The ending of the Red Scare unfortunately did not herald the disappearance of xenophobia. It was perhaps inevitable and possibly even wise that some kind of limitation be placed upon the entry of immigrants into the United States after the war. An immense backlog of prospective migrants had piled up during the conflict, and the desperate postwar economic condition of Europe led hundreds of thousands to seek better circumstances in the United States. Immigration rose from 110,000 in 1919, to 430,000 in 1920, and to 805,000 in 1921, with every prospect of continuing upward.

However, instead of setting some general limit on new arrivals, Congress, reflecting a widespread prejudice against eastern and southern Europeans, passed an emergency act establishing a quota system. Each year immigrants equal to three per cent of the number of foreign-born residents of the United States in 1910 might enter the country. Under this law about 350,000 could come in annually, but since each country's quota was based on the number of its nationals in the United States in 1910, only a relative handful of these would be from southern and eastern Europe, because at that time the foreign-born population had still been overwhelmingly of northern- and western-European origin. After further modifications in 1924, Congress established a new system in 1929 that allowed only 150,000 immigrants a year to enter the country. Each national quota was based on the supposed origins of the entire white population of the United States in 1920, not merely upon the foreign-born, a procedure heavily favoring immigrants from Great Britain and northern Europe. The system was complicated and also unscientific, because no one could determine with any real accuracy the "origins" of millions of citizens. It can perhaps best be explained by citing an example:

$$\frac{\text{Italian quota}}{150,000} = \frac{\text{Italian-origin population, 1920}}{\text{White population, 1920}}$$

$$\frac{\text{Italian quota}}{150,000} = \frac{3,800,000}{95,500,000}$$

Italian quota = 6,000 (approximately)

The law actually reduced immigration to far below 150,000 a year, for the favored nations of northern Europe never filled their quotas. Total British immigration between 1931 and 1939, for example, amounted to only 23,000, although the *annual* British quota was over 65,000. Meanwhile, hundreds of thousands of southern and eastern Europeans waited for admission.

The United States had not only closed the gates, it had abandoned the theory of the melting pot. Instead of an open, cosmopolitan society eager to accept, in Emma Lazarus' stirring line, the "huddled masses yearning to breathe free," America now became committed to preserving a homogeneous, "Anglo-Saxon" population.*

Urban–Rural Conflict

The war-born tensions and hostilities of the twenties also found expression in other ways, most of them related to an older rift in American society—the conflict between the urban and the rural way of life. It has often been noted that the

---

*The injustices of the national-origins system were finally eliminated by the Immigration Act of 1965, which allowed 170,000 persons a year to enter the United States, admission being determined on such grounds as skill and the need for political asylum. However, the law also put a limit of 120,000 on Western Hemisphere immigration, which had previously been unrestricted.

census of 1920 revealed that for the first time a majority of Americans (54 million in a total population of 106 million) was living in "urban" rather than "rural" places. These figures are somewhat misleading when applied to the study of social attitudes, for the census classified anyone in a community of 2,500 or more as urban. Of the 54 million "urban" residents in 1920, over 16 million lived in communities of fewer than 25,000 persons, and the evidence suggests strongly that a large majority of these held ideas and values more similar to those of rural citizens than to those of city dwellers. But the truly urban Americans, the one person in four who lived in a city of 100,000 or more and especially the nearly 16.4 million who lived in metropolises of at least half a million, were increasing steadily both in numbers and in influence.

Over 19 million persons moved from farm to city in the 1920's, and the population living in centers of 100,000 or more increased by about a third. To both the scattered millions who still tilled the soil and to the other millions who lived in towns and small cities, the new city-oriented culture seemed sinful, overly materialistic, and unhealthy. But there was no denying its power and compelling fascination. Made even more aware of the appeal of the city by such modern improvements as radio and the automobile, farmers and townspeople coveted the comfort and excitement of city life at the same time that they condemned them.

Out of this ambivalence developed some strange social phenomena, all exacerbated by the backlash of wartime emotions. Rural society, at once attracted and repelled by the city, responded by rigidly proclaiming the superiority of its own ways, as much to protect itself against temptation as to denounce urban life. Change, omnipresent in the postwar world, must be desperately resisted, even at the cost of individualism and freedom. The fact that those who held such views were in the majority, yet conscious that their majority was rapidly disappearing, explains their desperation, thus their intolerance.

One expression of this intolerance of modern urban values was the resurgence of religious fun-

damentalism. Although it was especially prevalent in certain Protestant sects, such as the Baptists and Presbyterians, fundamentalism was primarily an attitude of mind, profoundly conservative, rather than a religious idea. Fundamentalists rejected the theory of evolution, indeed, the whole mass of scientific knowledge about the origins of man and the universe that had been discovered during the 19th century. As we have seen, educated persons had been able to resolve the apparent contradictions between Darwin's theory and religious teachings easily enough, but in rural districts, especially in the southern and border states, this was never the case. Partly, fundamentalism resulted from simple ignorance; where educational standards were low and culture relatively static, old ideas remained unchallenged. Urban sophisticates tended to dismiss the fundamentalists as crude boors and hayseed fanatics, but the persistence of old-fashioned ideas was understandable enough. The power of reason, so obvious in a technologically advanced society, seemed much less obvious to rural people. Even prosperous farmers, in close contact with the capricious, elemental power of nature, tended to have more respect for the force of divine providence than city folk. Beyond this, the majesty and beauty of the King James translation of the Bible, often the only book in rural homes, made it extraordinarily difficult for many persons to abandon their belief in its literal truth.

What made crusaders of the fundamentalists, however, was their resentment of modern urban culture. Although in some cases they did harass liberal ministers, their religious attitudes had little public significance; their efforts to impose their views on public education were another matter. The teaching of evolution must be prohibited, they insisted. Throughout the early twenties they campaigned vigorously for laws banning all mention of Darwin's theory in textbooks and classrooms.

Their greatest asset in this unfortunate crusade was William Jennings Bryan. Age had not improved the "Peerless Leader." Never a profound thinker, after leaving Wilson's Cabinet in 1915 he devoted much time to religious and mor-

In *Baptism in Kansas* (1928) John Steuart Curry viewed sympathetically the sincerity and the depth of feeling that marked the revival of religious fundamentalism in much of rural America during the twenties. Curry was a leader of the rural regionalist painters, seeking, he said, to show the "struggle of man against nature." (Whitney Museum of American Art.)

al issues without applying himself conscientiously to the study of these difficult questions. He went about charging that "they"—meaning the mass of educated Americans—had "taken the Lord away from the schools" and denouncing the expenditure of public money to undermine Christian principles. Bryan toured the country offering $100 to anyone who would admit that he was descended from an ape; his immense popularity in rural areas assured him a wide audience, and no one came forward to take his money.

The fundamentalists won a minor victory in 1925, when Tennessee passed a law forbidding instructors in the state's schools and colleges to teach "any theory that denies the story of the Divine Creation of man as taught in the Bible." The circumstances surrounding the passage of this law reveal that the fundamentalists possessed an influence all out of proportion to their numbers. Although the bill passed both houses by big majorities, few of the legislators really approved of it. They voted "aye" only because they dared not expose themselves to charges that they disbelieved in the Bible. Educators in the state, hoping to obtain larger school appropriations from the legislature, hesitated to protest. Governor Austin Peay, an intelligent and liberal-minded man, feared to veto the bill lest he jeopardize other measures he was backing. "Probably the law will never be applied," he predicted when he signed it. Even Bryan, who used his influence to obtain passage of the measure, urged—unsuccessfully—that it include no penalties.

Upon learning of the passage of this act, the American Civil Liberties Union announced that it would finance a test case challenging its constitutionality if a Tennessee teacher would deliberately violate the statute. Urged on by local friends, John T. Scopes, a young biology teacher in Dayton, reluctantly agreed to do so. He was arrested. A battery of nationally known lawyers came forward to defend him, while the state obtained the services of Bryan himself. The Dayton "Monkey Trial" became an overnight sensation.

Clarence Darrow, chief counsel for the defendant, stated the issue clearly. "Scopes isn't on trial," he said, "civilization is on trial. The prosecution is opening the doors for a reign of bigotry equal to anything in the Middle Ages. No man's belief will be safe if they win." The comic aspects of the trial obscured this issue. Big-city reporters like H. L. Mencken of the Baltimore *Evening Sun* flocked to Dayton to make sport of the fundamentalists. The town took on a carnival air, simple hill folk mingling with cynical urban sophisticates while back-country preachers delivered impromptu sermons in the courthouse square. The judge, John Raulston, was strongly prejudiced against the defendant, even refusing to permit expert testimony on the validity of evolutionary theory. The conviction of Scopes was a foregone conclusion; after the jury rendered its verdict, Judge Raulston fined him $100.

Nevertheless, the trial served to expose both the stupidity and danger of the fundamentalist position. The high point came when Bryan agreed to testify as an expert witness on the Bible. In a sweltering courtroom, both men in shirt sleeves, the lanky, roughhewn Darrow cross-examined the bland, aging champion of fundamentalism, mercilessly exposing his childlike faith and his abysmal ignorance. Bryan admitted to believing literally that the earth had been created in 4004 B.C., that a whale had swallowed Jonah, that Joshua had stopped the sun in its course, and that Eve had been created from Adam's rib.

The Monkey Trial ended in frustration for nearly everyone concerned. Scopes soon moved away from Dayton. Judge Raulston was defeated when he sought re-election to the bench. Bryan departed amid the cheers of his disciples only to die in his sleep a few days later. Moreover, in retrospect the heroes of the Scopes trial—science, tolerance, freedom of thought—seem somewhat less stainless then they did to liberals at the time. The account of evolution in the textbook used by Scopes was far from satisfactory, yet it was advanced as unassailable fact. The book also contained statements that to the modern mind seem at least as bigoted as anything that Bryan said at Dayton. In a section on "the Races of Man," for example, it described Caucasians as "the highest type of all . . . represented by the civilized white inhabitants of Europe and America."

Prohibition: The "Noble Experiment"

The conflict between the countryside and the city, between the past and the future, was fought on many fronts, and in one sector the rural forces achieved a quick victory. This was the prohibition of the manufacture, transporting, and sale of alcoholic beverages by the Eighteenth Amendment, ratified in 1919. Although there were some big-city advocates of prohibition, on no issue did urban and rural views divide more clearly. The Eighteenth Amendment, in the words of historian Andrew Sinclair, marked a triumph of the "Corn Belt over the conveyor belt."

This rural victory was made possible by a peculiar set of circumstances. The temperance movement had been important since the age of Jackson, and by the Progressive Era many reformers were eager to prohibit drinking entirely. More than a quarter of the states were dry by 1914. The war also aided the prohibitionists by increasing the nation's need for food. The Lever

Ben Shahn's *Prohibition Alley* is a richly symbolic summary of the seamier side of the "noble experiment." Under a diagram of the workings of a still, bootleggers stack whisky smuggled in by ship, an operation eyed by Chicago gangster Al Capone. At left is a victim of gang warfare, at right, patrons outside a speakeasy. (Museum of the City of New York.)

Act of 1917 outlawed the use of grain in the manufacture of alcoholic beverages, primarily as a conservation measure. The prevailing dislike of foreigners helped the dry cause still more: beer-drinking was associated with Germans, wine consumption with Italians. To a large degree, the country was dry by 1917, although national prohibition did not become official until January 1920.

This "noble experiment," as Herbert Hoover called it, achieved a number of socially desirable results. Undoubtedly it cut down on the national consumption of alcohol; arrests for drunkenness fell off sharply, as did deaths from alcoholism. Fewer workers squandered their wages on drink. If the drys had been more reasonable—if they had permitted, for example, the use of beer and wine—the experiment might have worked. Instead, by insisting on total abstinence, they drove millions of moderates to direct violation of the law. In such circumstances, strict enforcement became impossible, especially in the cities.

The Prohibition Bureau had only between 1,500 and 3,000 agents to control the illicit liquor trade, and many of these were inefficient and corrupt. In areas where sentiment favored prohibition strongly, liquor remained very difficult to find. Elsewhere, anyone with sufficient money could obtain it easily; application of the Volstead Act (prohibition's enforcement statute) in such regions was never more than sporadic. Smuggling became a major business. Private individuals busied themselves learning how to manufacture "bathtub gin," fraudulent druggists' prescriptions for alcohol were issued freely, and illegal stills and breweries sprang up everywhere. *Bootlegger* became a household word. The saloon disappeared, replaced by the speakeasy, a supposedly secret bar or club, operating usually under the benevolent eye of the local police.

Inevitably most of the liquor traffic fell into the hands of gangsters, of whom Alphonse "Scarface Al" Capone of Chicago was only the most notorious. The gangsters hijacked one another's shipments, fought minor but bloody wars for control of their "territories," invested their profits in countless other businesses, legitimate and illegitimate. Americans had never been a particularly law-abiding people, but in the twenties statistics on crime soared. Gangsters gunned down their enemies in broad daylight and bombed rival distilleries and warehouses without regard for passing innocents. Each year more people died violent deaths in Chicago alone than in the entire British Isles. Capone presided over an army of perhaps a thousand hoodlums and gunmen; the gross income of his enterprises, before he was finally jailed for income tax evasion in 1931, reached $60 million.

Prohibition widened already serious rifts in the social fabric of the country; its repressive spirit, interacting darkly with the lingering hostilities and ambivalent feelings characteristic of the times, pitted city against farm, native against immigrant, race against race. In the South, where the dominant whites had argued that prohibition would improve the morals of the blacks, Negroes actually became the chief bootleggers.

Besides undermining public morality by encouraging hypocrisy and lawbreaking, prohibition had a vicious effect on the politics of the 1920's. It almost destroyed the Democratic party as a national organization; Democratic immigrants in the cities hated it, but southern Democrats sang its praises, often while continuing to drink themselves. The humorist Will Rogers quipped that Mississippi would vote dry "as long as the voters could stagger to the polls." The hypocrisy of prohibition had a particularly deleterious effect on politicians, a class seldom famous for candor. Congressmen catered to the demands of the powerful lobby of the Anti-Saloon League, yet failed to grant adequate funds

to the Prohibition Bureau. Nearly all the prominent leaders, Democrat and Republican, from Wilson and La Follette to Hoover and Franklin D. Roosevelt, equivocated shamelessly on the liquor question. By the end of the decade almost every competent observer recognized that prohibition had failed, but the well-organized and powerful dry forces continued to reject all proposals for modifying it.

The Ku Klux Klan

By far the most horrible example of the social malaise of the 1920's was the spectacular revival of the Ku Klux Klan. Like its predecessor of reconstruction days, the new Klan began as an instrument for Negro repression in the South. In the reactionary postwar period many white southerners set out to undo the gains blacks had made during the war years. Lynchings increased in number; race riots broke out in a dozen cities in the summer and fall of 1919. The new Klan, founded in 1915 by William J. Simmons, an alcoholic former preacher, expanded rapidly in this atmosphere.

Simmons gave his society the kind of trappings and mystery calculated to attract gullible and bigoted persons who yearned to express their frustrations and hostilities without personal risk. Klansmen masked themselves in white robes and hoods, enjoyed a childish mumbo jumbo of magnificent-sounding titles and dogmas (Kleagle, Klaliff, Kludd; kloxology, Kloran) mostly beginning with the letter *K.* They burned crosses, organized mass demonstrations to intimidate black voters, brought pressure on businessmen to fire Negro workers from better-paying jobs. When blacks resisted, the Klan frequently employed more brutal means to achieve its ends.

By 1920, however, it was expanding into new areas and seeking out other victims. From the start it admitted only native-born, white Protestants to membership. The distrust of foreigners, Catholics, and Jews implicit in this regulation burst into the open in a social climate that also spawned religious fundamentalism, immigration restriction, and prohibition. In addition, an agricultural depression sent cotton from 35 cents to 15 cents a pound in 1920, and wheat from $2.16 a bushel to $1.03 between 1919 and 1921, psychologically readying millions of potential Klansmen in the South and Middle West to vent their dissatisfactions in a nativist crusade for "100 per cent Americanism."

In 1920 two unscrupulous publicity agents, Edward Y. Clarke and Mrs. Elizabeth Tyler, got control of the movement and organized a massive membership drive, diverting a major share of the initiation fees into their own pockets. In a little over a year they enrolled 100,000 recruits and by 1923 claimed the astonishing total of 5 million.

The Klan had relatively little appeal in the Northeast or in the largest metropolitan centers in any part of the country, but it found many members in middle-sized cities as well as in the small towns and villages of middle western and western states like Indiana, Ohio, and Oregon. The scapegoats in such regions were immigrants, Jews, and especially Catholics; the rationale, an urge to get back to an older, supposedly finer America and a desperate desire to stamp out all varieties of nonconformity. Klansmen "watched everybody," always themselves safe from observation behind their masks and robes. Posing as guardians of public and private morality, they persecuted gamblers, loose women, violators of the prohibition laws, as well as respectable persons who happened to differ from them on religious questions or who belonged to a "foreign race." They professed to believe that the pope intended to move his headquarters to the United States, that American bishops were stockpiling arms in their cathedrals, that Catholic traitors had already entrenched themselves in many branches of the government. The Klan also conducted crusades against unfriendly politicians

A Ku Klux Klan initiation ceremony, photographed in Kansas in the 1920's. During its peak influence at mid-decade, Klan endorsement was essential to political candidates in many areas of the West and Midwest. Campaigning for re-election in 1924, an Indiana congressman testified, "I was told to join the Klan, or else." (Kansas State Historical Society.)

and in some cases controlled the elections of governors and congressmen as well as countless local officials. Since a considerable percentage of its members were secret libertines and corruptionists, the dark, unconscious drives leading men to join the organization are not hard to imagine.

Fortunately, the very success of the Klan led to its undoing. Factionalism sprang up and rival leaders squabbled over the large sums that had been collected from the membership. The cruel and outrageous behavior of the organization roused both liberals and decent conservatives in every part of the country. And, of course, its victims joined forces against their tormentors. When the powerful leader of the Indiana Klan, a middle-aged reprobate named David C. Stephenson, was convicted of assaulting and causing the death of a young woman, the rank and file abandoned the organization in droves. It remained influential for a number of years, contributing to the defeat of the Catholic Alfred E. Smith in the 1928 Presidential election, but it ceased to be a dynamic force after 1924. By 1930 it had only some 9,000 members.

The Disillusioned

The malaise of postwar society produced dissatisfactions among urban sophisticates too, and among others who looked to the future rather than to the past. To many young people of that generation, the narrowness and prudery of the fundamentalists and the stuffy conservatism of the politicians seemed not merely old-fashioned but ludicrous. The repressiveness of redbaiters and Klansmen made them place an exaggerated importance on their right to express themselves in bizarre ways, the casual attitude of drinkers toward the prohibition laws encouraged them to flout other institutions as well. The new psychology of Sigmund Freud, with its stress on the importance of sex, persuaded many who had never read Freud to adopt what they called "emancipated" standards of behavior which Freud, himself a staid, highly moral man, had neither advocated nor practiced.

This was the "Jazz Age," the era of "flaming youth." Young people danced to syncopated African rhythms, swilled bootleg liquor from pocket flasks, careened about the countryside in automobiles in search of pleasure and forgetfulness, made gods of movie stars and professional athletes. "Younger people," one shrewd observer noted as early as 1922, had only "contempt . . . for their elders." As a result, they were attempting "to create a way of life free from the bondage of an authority that has lost all meaning."

Conservatives bemoaned the breakdown of moral standards, the increasing popularity of divorce, the fragmentation of the family, and the decline of parental authority, and with some reason. Nevertheless, society was not collapsing. Much of the rebelliousness of the times was faddish in nature, soon to peter out.

The twenties also proved disillusioning to feminists, who now paid a price for their single-minded pursuit of the right to vote in the Progressive Era. Superficially, sex-based restrictions and limitations seemed to be breaking down. Women discarded bulky, uncomfortable undergarments and put on short skirts; they could smoke and drink in public places without fear of being considered prostitutes or wantons. The birth-control movement, led by Margaret Sanger, was making progress. The divorce laws had been modified in most states, providing strong guarantees to women when marriages broke up. Moreover, more women were finding jobs in the twenties than ever before; over 10.6 million were working by the end of the decade as contrasted with 8.4 million in 1920. But most of these gains were illusory. More women worked but their jobs were menial or of a kind that men did not seek: domestic service, grade-school teaching, clerical work, selling behind a counter. Where they competed for jobs with men, they usually received much lower wages. Educational opportunities for women expanded, but the colleges began to place more emphasis on preparing them to be wives and mothers, offering courses in home economics and providing, as one Vassar

College administrator (a woman!) put it, "education for women along the lines of their chief interests and responsibilities, motherhood and the home." Relaxing strict standards of sexual morality did not eliminate the double standard.

Part of the difficulty lay in the fact that the prosperity of the postwar years and the general abandonment of many taboos improved the position of women in an absolute sense. This concealed another fact: that the relative position of women remained practically unchanged. But at least equally significant was the confusion resulting from the passage of the Nineteenth Amendment. After its ratification, Carrie Chapman Catt was exultant. "We are no longer petitioners," she announced, "but free and equal citizens." Many activists, assuming the battle won, lost interest in agitating for change and sat back smugly to enjoy the benefits of their new position. Others realized that the fight was not over, but believed that the suffrage amendment had given them the sole weapon needed to achieve whatever women still lacked. In fact, however, the vote reduced rather than strengthened the influence of women, for it soon became apparent that women did not vote as a bloc. The Amendment increased the size of the electorate but did not add to the power of any particular party or interest group. When radical women recognized that this was the case and that, therefore, voting did not automatically bring real equality, they founded the Women's party and began campaigning for an Equal Rights Amendment. Their leader, Alice Paul, a dynamic if somewhat fanatical person, disdained specific goals like ending child labor, disarmament, even liberalized birth control. The party rejected protective social legislation governing the hours and working conditions of women as discriminatory—total equality for women was the one objective.

The Women's party, however, never attracted a wide following. Many more women joined the more moderate League of Women Voters, which attempted to mobilize support for a broad spectrum of reforms, even for some that had no specific connection with the interests of women as such. With feminists also split on generational lines, the younger ones tending to adopt the newer, more liberal attitudes toward sexual relations, the older still bound by Victorian inhibitions, the whole women's movement lost momentum. The battle for the Equal Rights Amendment persisted through the 1930's, but it was lost. By the end of that decade, the women's movement was almost dead.

The excesses of the fundamentalists, the xenophobes, the Klan, the redbaiters, and the prohibitionists also disturbed American intellectuals profoundly. Persons of culture and education found life in the twenties an affront to many deeply held beliefs. More and more they felt

In *The Passion of Sacco and Vanzetti* Ben Shahn included the Lowell Committee (Harvard president Lowell at center), which "confirmed" the trial's fairness, and an approving Judge Thayer (background). (Whitney Museum of American Art.)

alienated from their surroundings, bitter and contemptuous of those who appeared to control the country. Yet their alienation came at the very time that society was growing more dependent upon brains and sophistication; this compounded the confusion and disillusionment characteristic of the period.

Nothing demonstrates this fact so clearly as the Sacco-Vanzetti case. In April 1920 two men in South Braintree, Massachusetts killed a paymaster and a guard in a daring daylight robbery of a shoe factory. Shortly thereafter, Nicola Sacco and Bartolomeo Vanzetti were charged with the crime, and in 1921 they were convicted of murder. Sacco and Vanzetti were anarchists and also Italian immigrants. Their trial was a travesty of justice. The presiding judge, Webster Thayer, conducted the proceedings like a prosecuting attorney; he even referred privately to the defendants as "those anarchist bastards."

The case became a *cause célèbre*. Prominent persons all over the world protested, and for years Sacco and Vanzetti were kept alive by efforts to obtain a new trial. Vanzetti's quiet dignity and courage in the face of death wrung the hearts of millions. "You see me before you, not trembling," he told the court. "I never commit a crime in my life. . . . I am so convinced to be right that if you could execute me two times, and if I could be reborn two other times, I would live again and do what I have done already." When, in August 1927, the two were at last electrocuted, the disillusionment of American intellectuals with current values was profound. Recent historians, impressed by modern ballistic studies of Sacco's gun, now suspect that he, at least, was actually guilty. Nevertheless, the truth and the shame remain: Sacco and Vanzetti paid with their lives for being radicals and aliens, not for any crime.

Literary Trends

The literature of the twenties perfectly reflects the disillusionment of the intellectuals. The prewar period had been an age of hopeful experimentation in the world of letters. Writers, applying the spirit of progressivism to the realism they had inherited from Howells and the naturalists, had been predominantly optimistic. Ezra Pound, for example, talked grandly of an American Renaissance and fashioned a new kind of poetry called Imagism, which, while not appearing to be realistic, abjured all abstract generalizations and concentrated upon concrete word pictures to convey meaning. "Little" magazines and experimental theatrical companies sprang to life by the dozens, each convinced that it would revolutionize its art. New York's Greenwich Village teemed with youthful Bohemians, contemptuous of middle-class values but too fundamentally cheerful to reject the modern world. In Chicago the poet Carl Sandburg, best-known representative of the "Chicago school," denounced the local plutocrats but sang the praises of the city they had made: "Hog Butcher for the World . . . City of the Big Shoulders." Most writers eagerly adopted Freudian psychology without really understanding it. Freud's teachings seemed only to mean that one should cast off the senseless restrictions of Victorian prudery; almost to a man they ignored his essentially dark view of human nature. Theirs was an "innocent rebellion," exuberant—and rather muddle-headed.

As historian Henry F. May has shown, writers, along with most other intellectuals, began to abandon this view about 1912, and World War I completed the destruction of their optimism. Then the antics of the fundamentalists, the cruelty of the redbaiters, and the philistinism of the dull politicos of the day turned them into sharp critics of society. Ezra Pound, for example, dropped his talk of an American Renaissance and wrote instead of a "botched civilization." The soldiers, said he,

> walked eye-deep in hell
> believing in old men's lies, then unbelieving
> came home, home to a lie,
> home to deceits,
> home to old lies and new infamy. . .

Yet out of this negativism came a literary flowering of major importance.

The herald of the new day was Henry Adams,

whose autobiography, *The Education of Henry Adams,* was published posthumously in 1918. Adams' disillusionment long antedated the war, but his description of late-19th-century corruption and materialism and his warning that industrialism was crushing the human spirit beneath the weight of its machines appealed powerfully to those whose pessimism was newborn. Soon hundreds of bright young men and women were referring to themselves with a self-pity almost maudlin as the "lost generation," and either seeking refuge in hedonism or flight to Europe or systematically assaulting American society.

The symbol of the lost generation, in his own mind as well as to his contemporaries and to later critics, was F. Scott Fitzgerald. Born to modest wealth in St. Paul, Minnesota, in 1896, Fitzgerald rose to sudden fame in 1920 when he published *This Side of Paradise,* a somewhat sophomoric but accurate description of the mores and attitudes of modern youth. The novel captured the fears and confusions of the lost generation and also the façade of frenetic gaiety that concealed them; as Alfred Kazin has written, it "sounded all the fashionable lamentations" of the age. In *The Great Gatsby* (1925), a more mature work, Fitzgerald dissected a modern millionaire— coarse, unscrupulous, jaded, in love with another man's wife. Gatsby's tragedy lay in his dedication to this woman, who, Fitzgerald made clear, did not merit his passion. He lived in "the service of a vast, vulgar, meretricious beauty," and in the end, he understood this himself.

The tragedy of *The Great Gatsby* was related to Fitzgerald's own. Like Mark Twain he lusted after the very products of civilization he despised: money, glamour, the sensual satisfactions of the moment. Pleasure-loving and extravagant, he quickly squandered the money earned by *This Side of Paradise.* When *The Great Gatsby* failed to sell as well, he turned to writing potboilers. "I really worked hard as hell last winter," he told the critic Edmund Wilson, "but it was all trash and it nearly broke my heart." Although some of his later work was first class, he descended into the despair of alcoholism, ending his days as a Hollywood scriptwriter.

Many of the younger American writers and artists became expatriates in the twenties, flocking to Rome, Berlin, and especially to Paris, where they could live cheaply and escape what seemed to them the "conspiracy against the individual" prevalent in their own country. The *quartier latin* along the left bank of the Seine was a large-scale Greenwich Village in those days, full of artists and eccentrics of every sort. There the expatriates lived simply and freely, eking out a living as journalists, translators, and editors, perhaps turning an extra dollar from time to time by selling a story or a poem to an American magazine, a painting to a passing tourist.

Ernest Hemingway was the most talented of the expatriates. Born in 1898 in Illinois, Hemingway first worked as a reporter for the Kansas City *Star.* He served in the Italian army during the war, was grievously wounded (in spirit as well as in body), and then, after further newspaper experience, settled in Paris in 1922 to write. His first novel, *The Sun Also Rises* (1926), portrayed the café world of the expatriate and the rootless desperation, amorality, and sense of outrage at life's meaninglessness that obsessed so many in those years. In *A Farewell to Arms* (1929) he drew upon his military experiences to describe the confusion and horror of war.

Hemingway's books were best-sellers and he became a legend in his own time, but his style rather than his ideas explain his towering reputation. Few novelists have been such self-conscious craftsmen or capable of suggesting powerful emotions and action in so few words. Mark Twain and Stephen Crane were his models, Gertrude Stein, a queer, revolutionary genius, his teacher, but his style was his own, direct, simple, taut, sparse:

I went out the door and down the hall to the room where Catherine was to be after the baby came. I sat in a chair there and looked at the room. I had the paper in my coat that I had bought when I went out for lunch and I read it. . . . After a while I stopped reading and turned off the light and watched it get dark outside.　　　　*(A Farewell to Arms)*

This kind of writing, evoking rather than describ-

ing emotion, fascinated readers and inspired hundreds of imitators; it has made a permanent mark on world literature. What Hemingway had to say was of less universal interest. Despite his carefully controlled prose, he was an unabashed, rather muddled romantic, an adolescent emotionally. He wrote about bullfights, hunting, and fishing, violence of all sorts, and while he did so with masterful penetration, these themes placed limits on his work that he never transcended. The critic Kazin has summed him up in a sentence: "He brought a major art to a minor vision of life."

Although neither was the equal of Hemingway or Fitzgerald as an artist, two other writers of the twenties deserve mention: H. L. Mencken and Sinclair Lewis. Each reflected the distaste of intellectuals for the climate of the times. Mencken, a Baltimore newspaperman and founder of one of the great magazines of the era, the *American Mercury*, was a thoroughgoing cynic but never indifferent to those many aspects of American life that roused his contempt. He coined the word "booboisie" to define the complacent, middle-class majority and fired superbly witty broadsides at fundamentalists, prohibitionists, and "Puritans." Politics at once fascinated and repelled him and he assailed the statesmen of his generation with magnificent impartiality:

Ernest Hemingway (above), photographed at Key West, Florida, in 1929, the year that *A Farewell to Arms* was published. Like Hemingway, F. Scott Fitzgerald (right) wrote some of his best work when an expatriate in Paris, including *The Great Gatsby*. (Above: Charles Scribner's Sons; right: Bettmann Archive.)

BRYAN: If the fellow was sincere, then so was P. T. Barnum. . . . He was, in fact, a charlatan, a mountebank, a zany without sense or dignity.

WILSON: The bogus Liberal. . . . A pedagogue thrown up to 1000 diameters by a magic lantern.

HARDING: The numskull, Gamaliel . . . the Marion stonehead. . . . The operations of his medulla oblongata . . . resemble the rattlings of a colossal linotype charged with rubber stamps.

COOLIDGE: A cheap and trashy fellow, deficient in sense and almost devoid of any notion of honor—in brief, a dreadful little cad.

HOOVER: Lord Hoover is no more than a pious old woman, a fat Coolidge. . . . He would have made a good bishop.

While amusing, Mencken's diatribes were not, of course, very profound. In perspective, he appeared more a professional iconoclast than a constructive critic; like both Fitzgerald and Hemingway, he was something of a perennial adolescent. He did, however, consistently support freedom of expression of every sort.

Sinclair Lewis was probably the most popular American novelist of the twenties. Like Fitzgerald, his first major work brought him instant fame and notoriety, and for the same reason. *Main Street* (1920) portrayed the smug ignorance and bigotry of the American small town so accurately that even Lewis' victims recognized themselves; his title became a symbol for provinciality and middle-class meanness. Next he created, in *Babbitt* (1922), an image of the businessman of the twenties, a "hustler," a "booster," blindly orthodox in his political and social opinions, slave to every cliché, gregarious, full of loud self-confidence yet underneath a bumbling, rather timid, decent fellow who would like to be better than he was but dared not. From this point Lewis went on to dissect a variety of American attitudes and occupations: the medical profession in *Arrowsmith* (1925), religion in *Elmer Gantry* (1927), fascism in *It Can't Happen Here* (1935), and many others.

Although his indictment of contemporary society rivaled Mencken's in savagery, Lewis was not a cynic. Superficially as objective as an anthropologist, he remained at heart committed to

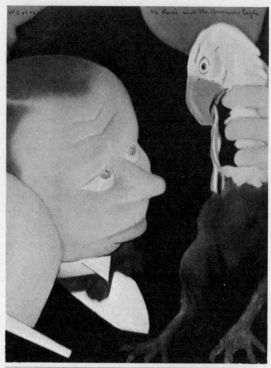

A baleful-looking Sinclair Lewis throttles the American eagle in this caricature by William Cotton that appeared in the magazine *Vanity Fair* in 1931. (© 1931, 1959 Conde Nast Publications, Inc.)

the way of life he was assaulting. His remarkable powers of observation depended upon his identification with the society he described. He was frustrated by the fact that his victims, recognizing themselves in his pages, accepted his criticisms with remarkable good temper and, displaying the very absence of intellectual rigor that he decried, cheerfully sought to reform. At the same time, lacking Mencken's ability to remain aloof, Lewis tended to value his own work in terms of its popular reception. He craved the good opinion and praise of his fellows. When he was awarded the Pulitzer prize for *Arrowsmith,* he petulantly refused it because it had not been offered earlier. He politicked shamelessly for a Nobel prize, which he received in 1930, the first American author to win this honor.

Lewis was pre-eminently a product of the twenties. When times changed, he could no longer portray society with such striking verisimilitude; none of his later novels approached the level of *Main Street* and *Babbitt*. When critics noticed this, Lewis became bewildered, almost disoriented. He died in 1951, a desperately unhappy man.

The New Negro

Even more than for white liberals, the postwar reaction brought bitter despair for many blacks. Aside from the obvious barbarities of the Klan, Negroes suffered from the postwar middle-class hostility to labor (and from the persistent refusal of organized labor to admit black workers to its ranks). The increasing presence of southern Negroes in the great northern cities also caused social conflict.

During the decade the exodus of Negroes from the South continued: over 581,000 left the three southern states of Virginia, South Carolina, and Georgia alone. Some 393,000 Negroes settled in New York, Pennsylvania, and Illinois, most of these in New York City, Philadelphia, and Chicago. The black population of New York City more than doubled between 1920 and 1930.

This influx speeded the development of urban ghettos. In earlier periods Negroes in northern cities had tended to live together, but in many small neighborhoods scattered over large areas. Now the tendency was toward concentration. Harlem, a white, middle-class residential section of New York City as late as 1900–10, had 50,000 blacks in 1914, 73,000 in 1920, and nearly 165,000 in 1930. The restrictions of ghetto life produced a vicious circle of degradation. Population growth and segregation caused a desperate housing shortage; rents in Harlem doubled between 1919 and 1927. Since the average Negro worker was unskilled and ill-paid, tenants were forced to take in boarders. Landlords converted private homes into rooming houses and allowed their properties to fall into disrepair, the process

of decay speeded by the influx of what the Negro sociologist E. Franklin Frazier called "ignorant and unsophisticated peasant people" from the rural South, inexperienced in city living. Such conditions caused disease and crime rates to rise sharply.

Even in small northern cities where they made up only a tiny proportion of the population, Negroes were badly treated. When Robert S. and Helen M. Lynd made their classic sociological analysis of *Middletown* (Muncie, Indiana), they discovered that while black and white children attended the same schools, the churches, the larger movie houses, and other places of public accommodation were segregated. The local YMCA had a gymnasium where high-school basketball was played, but the secretary refused to allow any team with a black player to use it. Even the news in Muncie was segregated, local papers chronicling the affairs of the black community—roughly five per cent of the population—under the heading: "In Colored Circles."

Coming after the rising hopes inspired by wartime gains, the disappointments of the 1920's produced a new militancy among many Negroes. As early as 1919 W. E. B. Du Bois wrote in the *Crisis:* "We are cowards and jackasses if . . . we do not marshal every ounce of our brain and brawn to fight . . . against the forces of hell in our own land." He increased his commitment to black nationalism, organizing a series of Pan African Conferences in an effort—futile as it turned out—to create an international Negro movement.

Du Bois, however, never really made up his mind whether to work for integration or black separatism. Such ambivalence never troubled Marcus Garvey, a West Indian whose Universal Negro Improvement Association attracted hundreds of thousands of followers in the early twenties. Garvey had nothing but contempt for whites, for light-skinned Negroes like Du Bois, and for organizations such as the NAACP that sought to bring whites and blacks together to fight segregation and other forms of prejudice. "Back to Africa" was his slogan; the black man must "work out his salvation in his motherland."

Beginning in the 1930's black artist Jacob Lawrence painted a series of powerful "picture-narratives" dealing with the black experience in America. This painting, of Southern Negroes crowding onto northbound trains during World War I, is the first of a 60-panel narrative that Lawrence titled "The Migration of the Negro." (Phillips Collection.)

(Paradoxically, Garvey's ideas won the enthusiastic support of the Ku Klux Klan and other white racist groups.)

Garvey's message was naive and overly simple, but it served to build racial pride among the masses of poor and unschooled Negroes. He dressed in elaborate braided uniforms, wore a plumed hat, drove about in an expensive limousine. Both God and Christ were black, he insisted. He organized Negro-run businesses of many sorts, including a company that manufactured black dolls for Negro children. He established a corps of Black Cross nurses, and a Black Star Line Steamship Company to transport Negroes back to Africa. Negro leaders like Du Bois detested him, and, in truth, he was something of a charlatan as well as a terrible businessman. In 1923 his steamship line went into bankruptcy. He was convicted of defrauding thousands of his supporters who had invested in its stock and sent to prison. Nevertheless, his message, if not his methods, helped to create the "new" Negro, proud of his color and his heritage and prepared to resist both white mistreatment and white ideas: "Up, you mighty race, you can accomplish what you will!"

The new urban ghettos produced certain compensating advantages for Negroes. One effect, not fully utilized until later, was to increase their political power by enabling them to elect representatives to state legislatures and to Congress, and to exert great influence on the parties in closely contested elections. More immediately, city life stimulated Negro self-confidence; despite their horrors, the ghettos offered economic opportunity, political rights, freedom from the day-to-day debasements of southern life, and above all a black world where black men and women could be themselves. In the ghettos, writers, musicians, and artists found both an audience and the "spiritual emancipation" that unleashed their capacities. Harlem in particular, the largest black city in the world, became a cultural capital, center of the "Harlem Renaissance." Negro newspapers and magazines flourished, along with theatrical companies, libraries, and the like. Du Bois opened the *Crisis* to young Negro writers and artists, and a dozen "little" magazines sprang up. Langston Hughes, one of the best poets of the era, has described the exhilaration of his first arrival in this city within a city, a "magnet" for every black intellectual and artist. "Harlem! I . . . dropped my bags, took a deep breath, and felt happy again."

For Hughes and for thousands of less talented Negroes, the twenties, despite the persistence of prejudice and the sordidness of the ghettos, was a time of hope. Sociologists and psychologists (to whom, incidentally, the ghettos were indispensable social laboratories) were demonstrating that environment rather than heredity was preventing Negro progress. Together with the achievements of creative blacks, which were for the first time being appreciated by white intellectuals, these new discoveries seemed to herald the decline and eventual disappearance of race prejudice. The black man, wrote Alain Locke in *The New Negro* (1925), "lays aside the status of beneficiary and ward for that of a collaborator and participant in American civilization." Alas, as Locke and other black intellectuals were soon to discover, this prediction, like so many others made in the 1920's, did not come to pass.

The Era of "Normalcy"

The men who presided over the government of the United States during this era were Warren G. Harding of Ohio and Calvin Coolidge of Massachusetts. Harding was a newspaperman by trade, publisher of the Marion *Star,* with previous political experience as a legislator and lieutenant governor in his home state and as a United States senator. No President, before or since, looked more like a statesman; few were less suited for running the country. Coolidge, a taciturn New England type with a long record in Massachusetts politics climaxed by his inept but much-admired handling of the Boston police strike while governor, made a less impressive appearance than Harding and did not much excel him as a leader. "Don't hurry to legislate," was one of his slogans. He preferred to follow public opinion and hope for the best. "Mr. Coolidge's genius for inactivity is developed to a very high point," the correspondent Walter Lippmann wrote. "It is a grim, determined, alert inactivity, which keeps Mr. Coolidge occupied constantly."[*]

Harding won the 1920 Republican nomination because the party convention could not decide between General Leonard Wood, who represented the Roosevelt faction, and Frank Lowden, governor of Illinois. His genial nature and lack of strong convictions made him attractive to many of the politicos after eight years of the headstrong Wilson. During the campaign he exasperated sophisticates by his ignorance and imprecision. He coined the famous vulgarism "normalcy" as a substitute for the word "normality," referred, during a speech before a group of actors, to Shakespeare's play "Charles the Fifth," and committed numerous other blunders. "Why does he not get a private secretary who can clothe . . . his 'ideas' in the language customarily used by educated men?" one Boston gentleman demanded of Senator Lodge, who was strongly supporting Harding. Lodge, ordinarily a stickler for linguistic exactitude, replied acidly that he found Harding a paragon by comparison with Wilson, "a man who wrote English very well without ever saying anything." A large majority

---

[*]Coolidge was physically delicate, being plagued by chronic stomach trouble. He required 10 or 11 hours of sleep a day.

of the voters, untroubled by the candidate's lack of erudition, shared Lodge's confidence that he would be a vast improvement over Wilson.

Harding has often been characterized as lazy and incompetent, but he was actually both hard-working and politically shrewd; his true difficulties were indecisiveness and an unwillingness to offend. He turned the most important government departments over to efficient administrators of impeccable reputation: Charles Evans Hughes, the secretary of state, Herbert Hoover in the Commerce Department, Andrew Mellon in the Treasury, and Henry C. Wallace in Agriculture. Harding kept track of what they did but seldom initiated policy in their areas. However, many lesser offices, and a few of major importance, Harding gave to the unsavory "Ohio Gang," headed by Harry M. Daugherty, whom he made attorney general.

The President was too kindly, too well-intentioned, too unambitious to be dishonest. He appointed corruptionists like Daugherty, Secretary of the Interior Albert B. Fall, Director of the Mint "Ed" Scobey, and Charles R. Forbes, head of the new Veterans Bureau, out of a sense of personal obligation or because they were old friends who shared his taste for poker and liquor. Before 1921 he had greatly enjoyed officeholding; he was a good politician, adept at mouthing platitudes, a loyal party man who seldom questioned the decisions of his superiors. In the lonely eminence of the White House, whence, as President Harry Truman later said, the buck cannot be passed, he found only misery. "The White House is a prison," he complained. "I can't get away from the men who dog my footsteps. I am in jail."

In domestic affairs Secretary of the Treasury Mellon, multimillionaire banker and master of the aluminum industry, dominated the Harding administration. Mellon set out to lower the taxes of the rich, reverse the low tariff policies of the Wilson period, return to the laissez-faire philosophy of McKinley, and reduce the national debt by cutting expenses and administrating the government more efficiently. In principle, his program had considerable merit. Wartime tax rates,

designed to check consumer spending as well as to raise the huge sums needed to defeat the Central Powers, were undoubtedly hampering economic expansion in the early twenties. Certain industries which had sprung up in the United States for the first time during the Great War, were suffering from German and Japanese competition now that the fighting had ended. Rigid regulations necessary during a national crisis could well be dispensed with in peacetime. And efficiency and economy in government are always desirable.

Mellon, however, carried his policies to unreasonable extremes. To reduce the national debt he insisted that the Allies repay the money they had borrowed to the last dollar, not seeing that protective tariffs on European products would deprive them of the means of accumulating dollar credits to meet their obligations. Mellon also proposed eliminating inheritance taxes and reducing the tax on high incomes by two-thirds in order to stimulate investment, but he opposed lower rates for taxpayers earning less than $66,000 a year, apparently not realizing that economic expansion required greater mass consumption as well. By freeing the rich from "oppressive" taxation, he argued, they would be able to invest in risky but potentially productive enterprises, the success of which would create jobs for ordinary people. Little wonder that Mellon's admirers called him "the greatest Secretary of the Treasury since Alexander Hamilton."

Although the Republicans had large majorities in both houses of Congress, Mellon's proposals were too drastically reactionary to win unqualified approval. Somewhat halfheartedly, Congress did pass a Budget and Accounting Act (1921), creating a director of the budget to assist the President in preparing a unified budget for the government, and a comptroller general to audit all government accounts. A general budget had long been needed; previously Congress had dealt with the requirements of each department separately, trusting largely to luck that income and expenditures would balance at year's end. The appointment of a comptroller general enabled Congress to check up on how the departments actually used the sums granted them.

Mellon's tax and tariff program, however, ran into stiff opposition from middle-western Republicans and southern Democrats, who combined to form the so-called Farm Bloc. The cause of this alignment was essentially economic. The revival of European agriculture was cutting the demand for American farm produce just when the increased use of fertilizers and machinery was boosting output. As in the era after the Civil War, farmers found themselves burdened with heavy debts while their dollar income dwindled. In the decade after 1919 their share of the national income fell by nearly 50 per cent. The Farm Bloc represented a kind of conservative populism, economic grievances combining with a general prejudice against "Wall Street financiers" and rich industrialists to unite agriculture against "the interests."

Mellon epitomized everything the Farm Bloc disliked. Rejecting his more extreme suggestions, it pushed through the Revenue Act of 1921, which abolished the excess-profits tax and cut the top income tax rate from 73 to 50 per cent, but raised the tax on corporate profits slightly and left inheritance taxes untouched. Three years later Congress cut the maximum income tax to 40 per cent but reduced taxes on lower incomes significantly and raised inheritance levies. The Farm Bloc also overhauled Mellon's tariff proposals, placing heavy duties on agricultural products in 1921 while refusing to increase the rates on most manufactured goods. Although the Fordney–McCumber Tariff of 1922 granted more than adequate protection to the "infant industries" (rayon, china, toys, and chemicals), it held to the Wilsonian principle of moderate protection for most industrial products. Agricultural machinery and certain other items important to farmers remained on the free list.

Mellon nevertheless succeeded in balancing the budget and reducing the national debt. Government expenditures fell from $6.4 billion in 1920 to a low of $2.9 billion in 1927. Throughout the twenties the national debt shrank an average of over $500 million a year. So committed were the Republican leaders to retrenchment that they even resisted the demands of veterans, organized in the politically potent American Legion, for an "adjusted compensation" bonus. Arguing not entirely without reason that they had served for a pittance while war workers had been drawing down high wages, the veterans sought grants equal to a dollar a day for their period in uniform ($1.25 for time overseas). Congress responded sympathetically, but both Harding and Coolidge vetoed bonus bills in the name of economy. Finally, in 1924, a compromise bill granting the veterans paid-up life insurance policies was passed over Coolidge's veto.

The business community heartily approved the policies of Harding and Coolidge, as indeed it should have, since both were uncritical advocates of the business point of view. "We want less government in business and more business in government," Harding pontificated, to which Coolidge added the slogan: "The business of the United States is business." Harding and Coolidge used their executive powers to convert regulatory bodies like the Interstate Commerce Commission and the Federal Reserve Board into pro-business agencies that ceased almost entirely to restrict the activities of the industries they were supposed to be controlling. As one bemused academic observer put it, the Federal Trade Commission seemed, throughout the twenties, to be trying to commit hara-kiri. Senator Norris, an uncompromising progressive, characterized these Harding–Coolidge actions as "the nullification of federal law by a process of boring from within."

The Harding Scandals

At least Mellon and the other pro-business leaders of this period were honest. The "Ohio Gang," however, used its power in the most blatantly corrupt way imaginable. Jesse Smith, a crony of Attorney General Daugherty, was what today would be called an "influence peddler" extraordinary. When his venality was exposed in 1923, he committed suicide. Charles R. Forbes of the Veterans Bureau siphoned millions of dollars appropriated for the construction of hospitals into his own pocket. When he was found out, Forbes fled to Europe and resigned. Later he returned, stood trial, and was sentenced to two years in prison. His assistant, Charles F. Cramer, committed suicide. Daugherty himself was deeply implicated in the fraudulent return of German assets seized by the Alien Property Custodian to their original owners. He escaped imprisonment only by refusing to testify on the ground that he might incriminate himself. Thomas W. Miller, the alien property custodian, was sent to jail for accepting a bribe.

The worst of these scandals involved Secretary of the Interior Albert B. Fall, a former senator. Although Harding had put Fall into the Cabinet chiefly because he liked him, opposition to the appointment had come only from conservationists interested in the national forest reserves; no one considered him morally unfit. However, in 1921, after arranging with the complaisant Secretary of the Navy Edwin Denby for

When the Teapot Dome scandal broke in 1924, a newspaper cartoonist suggested its political repercussions with this drawing, "Assuming definite shape." (Memphis *Commercial Appeal.*)

the transfer to the Interior Department of government oil reserves being held for the future use of the navy, Fall leased these properties to private oil companies. Edward L. Doheny's Pan-American Petroleum Company got the Elk Hills reserve in California, and the Teapot Dome reserve in Wyoming was turned over to Harry F. Sinclair's Mammoth Oil Company. When critics protested, Fall announced that it was necessary to develop the Elk Hills and Teapot Dome properties because adjoining private drillers were draining off the navy's oil. Nevertheless, in 1923 the Senate ordered a full-scale investigation, conducted by Senator Thomas J. Walsh of Montana. It soon came out that Doheny had "lent" Fall $100,000 in hard cash, handed over secretly in a "little black bag." Sinclair had given Fall over $300,000 in cash and negotiable securities. Although the three culprits escaped conviction on the charge of conspiring to defraud the government, Sinclair was sentenced to nine months in jail for contempt of the Senate and for tampering with a jury, while Fall was fined $100,000 and given a year in prison for accepting a bribe. In 1927 the Supreme Court revoked the leases and the two reserves were returned to the government.

The public still knew little of the scandals when, in June 1923, Harding left Washington on a western speaking tour, which included a visit to Alaska. His health was poor, his spirits low, for he had begun to understand how his "Goddamn friends," as he put it, had betrayed him. Returning from Alaska late in July, he came down with what his physician, an incompetent crony whom he had made surgeon general of the United States, diagnosed as ptomaine poisoning resulting from his having eaten a tainted Japanese crab. In fact, the President had suffered a heart attack. After briefly rallying, he died in San Francisco on August 2.

Few Presidents have been more deeply mourned by the people at the moment of their passing. Harding's kindly nature, his very ordinariness, increased his human appeal. "Our hearts are broken; we are sore stricken with the sense of loss," one minister declared. Three million persons viewed the Presidential coffin as it passed across the country. Soon, however, as the scandals came to light, sadness turned to scorn and contempt. The poet E. E. Cummings came closer to catching the final judgment of Harding's contemporaries than has any historian:

> the first president to be loved by his
> bitterest enemies" is dead
> the only man woman or child who wrote
> a simple declarative sentence with seven gram-
> matical
> errors "is dead"
> beautiful Warren Gamaliel Harding
> "is" dead
> he's
> "dead"
> if he wouldn't have eaten them Yapanese Craps
> somebody might hardly never not have been
> unsorry, perhaps

Coolidge Prosperity

Had he lived, Harding might well have been defeated in 1924 because of the scandals. But Vice President Coolidge, unconnected with the troubles and not the type to surround himself with cronies of any kind, seemed the ideal man to clean out the corruptionists. After he replaced Attorney General Daughtery with the eminently respectable Harlan Fiske Stone, dean of the Columbia Law School, the Harding scandals ceased to be a serious political handicap for the Republicans.

Coolidge soon became the darling of the conservatives. His admiration for businessmen and his devotion to laissez faire knew no limit. "The man who builds a factory builds a temple," he said in all seriousness. "The Government can do more to remedy the economic ills of the people by a system of rigid economy in public expenditure than can be accomplished through any other action." Andrew Mellon, whom he continued in office as secretary of the treasury, was his ideal and mentor in economic affairs.

In 1924 Coolidge won the Republican nomi-

nation easily, but the Democrats, badly split, required 103 ballots to choose a candidate. The southern, dry, anti-immigrant, pro-Klan wing had fixed upon William G. McAdoo, Wilson's secretary of the treasury. The eastern, urban, wet element supported Governor Alfred E. Smith of New York, child of the slums, a Catholic, who had compiled a distinguished record in the field of social welfare legislation. After days of futile politicking, the party compromised on John W. Davis, a conservative corporation lawyer closely allied with the Morgan interests. Dismayed by the conservatism of both Coolidge and Davis, the aging Robert M. La Follette, backed by the Farm Bloc, the Socialist party, the American Federation of Labor, and numbers of intellectuals, entered the race as the candidate of a new Progressive party. The progressives adopted a neopopulist platform calling for the nationalization of railroads, the direct election of the President, the protection of labor's right to bargain collectively, and other reforms.

The situation was almost exactly the opposite of 1912, when one conservative had run against two liberals yet been swamped. Coolidge received 15.7 million votes, Davis 8.4 million, La Follette only 4.8 million. In the Electoral College La Follette won only his native Wisconsin, Coolidge defeating Davis by 382 to 136. Conservatism was clearly the dominant mood of the country, not merely of the business classes. A few years later, James M. Beck, one of the nation's most vocal and uncompromising reactionaries, was elected to Congress by a Philadelphia slum district, "a place of endless rows of shabby, featureless houses, inhabited by immigrants and Negroes," by a vote of 60,000 to 2,000.

The glorification of the antedeluvian and inert Coolidge and of the "New Era" over which he presided had its origin in the unprecedented prosperity that the nation enjoyed during his reign. After a brief but sharp slump in 1921 and 1922, business boomed, real wages increased, and unemployment declined. The United States was as rich as all Europe; perhaps 40 per cent of the world's total wealth lay in American hands. Little wonder that thousands came to believe that no one should tamper with the marvelous economic machine that was yielding such bounty.

Prosperity rested on a variety of bases, one of which, it must be admitted, was the friendly, hands-off attitude of the government, which bolstered the confidence of the business community. The Federal Reserve Board consistently kept interest rates low, a further stimulus to economic growth. Pent-up wartime demand helped also to power the boom; the construction business in particular profited from a series of extremely busy years. The continuing mechanization and rationalization of industry provided a more fundamental stimulus to the economy. From heavy road-grading equipment and concrete mixers to devices for making cigars and glass tubes, from pneumatic tools to the dial telephone, machinery was replacing human hands at an ever more rapid rate, a truth demonstrated by the remarkable fact that industrial output almost doubled between 1921 and 1929 without any substantial increase in the industrial labor force. Greater use of power, especially of electricity, also encouraged expansion—by 1929 the United States was producing more electricity than the rest of the world combined. Most important of all, American manufacturing was experiencing an amazing improvement in efficiency. The method of breaking down the complex processes of production into many simple operations and the use of interchangeable parts, turned out by precise machine tools, were 19th-century innovations, but in the 1920's they were adopted on an almost universal scale. The moving assembly line, which carried the product to the worker, first devised by Henry Ford in his automobile plant in the decade before World War I, speeded production and reduced costs. The time-and-motion studies of Frederick W. Taylor, developed early in the century, were applied in hundreds of factories after the war. Taylor's minute analyses of each step and movement in the manufacturing process and his emphasis upon speed and efficiency alarmed some union leaders, but no one could deny the effectiveness of his "scientific shop management" methods.

The growing ability of manufacturers to create new consumer demands also stimulated the economy. Advertising and salesmanship were raised almost to the status of fine arts. Bruce Barton, one of the advertising "geniuses" of the era, wrote a best-selling book, *The Man Nobody Knows* (1925), in which he described Jesus as the "founder of modern business," the man who "picked up twelve men from the bottom ranks . . . and forged them into an organization that conquered the world." Producers concentrated on making their goods more attractive and on changing models frequently to entice buyers into the market. Easy credit, accompanied by an expansion of the practice of selling goods on the installment plan, helped bring expensive items within the reach of the masses. Inventions and technological advances created a host of new or improved products, from radios, automobiles, and electric appliances like vacuum cleaners and refrigerators to gadgets like cigarette lighters and new forms of entertainment like motion pictures, which became, during the twenties, one of the ten largest industries in the country. Materials such as aluminum, synthetic fibers, and plastics gave rise to new industries and led to the development of many more new products.

These factors interacted one with another, serving to increase the effects of each much the way the textile industry in the early 19th century and the railroad industry after the Civil War had been the "multipliers" of earlier eras. Undoubtedly, the automobile had the single most important impact on the nation's economy in the twenties. Although well over a million cars a year were being regularly produced by 1916, the real expansion of the industry came after 1921. Output reached 2.2 million in 1922 and 3.6 million in 1923. It fell below the latter figure only twice during the remainder of the decade. By 1929, 23 million private cars clogged the highways, an average of only slightly less than one per family.

The auto industry also created other industries, such as the manufacture of tires and spark plugs. It consumed immense quantities of rubber, paint, glass, nickel, and, of course, petroleum products. It triggered a gigantic road-build-

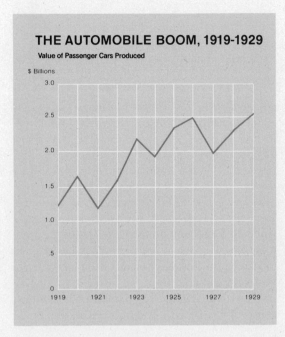

THE AUTOMOBILE BOOM, 1919-1929

Value of Passenger Cars Produced

Henry Ford

The man most directly responsible for the growth of the automobile industry was Henry Ford, a self-taught mechanic from Greenfield, Michigan. Ford was not a great inventor or even one of the true automobile pioneers. He was not even the first to manufacture a good low-priced car, that being the achievement of Ransom E. Olds, producer of the "Merry Oldsmobile." He had two great insights. The first, as he said, was "Get the prices down to the buying power." Through mass production, cars could be made cheaply enough to bring them within reach of the ordinary citizen. In 1908 he designed the famous Model T Ford, a simple, tough box on wheels, powered by a light, durable, easily repaired engine. In a year he proved his point by selling 11,000 Model T's. Thereafter, relentlessly cutting costs and increasing efficiency by installing the assembly-line system, he expanded production at an unbelievable rate. By 1925 he was turning out over 9,000 cars a day, one approximately every ten seconds, and the price of the Model T had been reduced to below $300.

Secondly, Ford grasped the importance of high wages as a means of stimulating output (and incidentally selling more automobiles). The assembly line simplified the laborer's task and increased the pace of work at the same time it made each worker much more productive. Jobs became both boring and fatiguing, absenteeism and labor turnover serious problems. To combat this difficulty, in 1914 Ford established the $5 day, an increase of about $2 over prevailing wages in the industry. At once the rate of turnover in his plant fell 90 per cent, and although critics charged that he recaptured his additional labor costs by speeding up the line, his policy had a revolutionary effect upon American wage rates. Later he raised the minimum to $6 and then to $7 a day.

Ford's profits soared along with sales, and since he owned the entire company, he became a billionaire. Throughout the twenties he cleared an average of about $25,000 *a day*. He also be-

ing program: there were 387,000 miles of paved roads in the United States in 1921, 662,000 in 1929. Hundreds of manufacturers turned out gadgets to decorate, clean, and improve the performance of automobiles; thousands of persons found employment in filling stations, roadside stands, and other businesses catering to the motoring public. The tourist industry profited, and the already growing shift of the population from the cities to the suburbs was much accelerated.

The growth of the automobile industry and of the automobile culture that it fathered continued in the following decades. Eventually certain undesirable, even dangerous results emerged: roadside scenery disfigured by billboards, gas stations, and other enterprises aimed at satisfying the traveler's needs; horrendous traffic jams; soaring accident rates; urban air pollution. All these disadvantages existed and were noticed during the 1920's, but in the springtime of the new industry, they were discounted. The automobile seemed an unalloyed blessing—part toy, part tool, part symbol of American freedom and individualism.

According to his biographer, Allan Nevins, Ford's complex personality included the characteristics of "a wry, cross-grained, brilliant adolescent." Here, on a summer outing, Ford poses as a western badman. (Ford Motor Company.)

moving the lips. Success also made Ford stubborn. The Model T remained essentially unchanged for nearly 20 years and other companies, most notably General Motors, were soon turning out far better vehicles for very little more money. Customers, increasingly affluent and style-conscious, began to shift to Chevrolets and Chryslers. Gradually Ford's share of the market declined. Finally, in 1927, he shut down all operations for 18 months in order to retool for the Model A, his competitors rushing in during this period to fill the vacuum. Although his company continued to make a great deal of money, Ford never regained the dominant position he had held for so long. In truth, the age of the great individualistic tycoon was ending; he was replaced by the business "team" made up of "organization men."

Ford was enormously uninformed, yet—because of his success and the praise the world heaped upon him—he did not hesitate to speak out on subjects far outside his area of competence, from the evils of drink and tobacco to medicine and international affairs. He developed political ambitions, engaged in virulent anti-Semitic propaganda through his newspaper, the Dearborn *Independent,* said he would not give five cents for all the art in the world. While praising his talents as a manufacturer, historians have not dealt kindly with Ford the man, in part, no doubt, because he once said: "History is more or less the bunk."

came an authentic folk hero: his homespun simplicity, his dislike of bankers and sophisticated society, his intense individualism endeared him to millions. He stood as a symbol of the wonders of the American system—he had given the nation a marvelous convenience at a low price, at the same time enriching himself and raising the living standards of his thousands of employees.

Unfortunately, Ford had the defects of his virtues in full measure. He paid high wages but tyrannized over his workers, refusing to deal with any union, employing spies to check up on the private lives of his help and gangsters and bully boys to enforce plant discipline. When he discovered a worker driving any car but a Ford, he had him instantly dismissed. So close was the supervision in the factory that the men devised the "Ford whisper," a means of talking without

Economic Problems

Like Ford, its outstanding success, the American economic system of the twenties also had grave flaws. Certain industries did not share in the good times. The coal business, suffering from the competition of petroleum, entered a period of decline. Textile production lagged, and the industry began to be plagued by falling profit margins and chronic unemployment. In both these businesses, labor troubles multiplied. Moreover, the movement toward consolidation in industry, somewhat checked during the latter part of the Progressive Era, resumed during the twenties. By 1929 the 200 largest corporations controlled nearly half the nation's corporate assets. General Motors, Ford, and Chrysler turned out nearly 90 per cent of all American cars and trucks. Four tobacco companies produced over 90 per cent of the cigarettes. While banking capital doubled, the number of banks declined: 1 per cent of all financial institutions controlled 46 per cent of the nation's banking business and great concerns like Kuhn, Loeb and Company and the House of Morgan extended their already immense influence over the major industries of the country. Even retail merchandising, traditionally the domain of the small shopkeeper, reflected the trend. The A & P food chain expanded from 400 stores in 1912 to 17,500 in 1928. The Woolworth chain of five-and-ten-cent stores flourished.

Consolidation did not necessarily lead to monopoly, for most great manufacturers, aware that bad public relations resulting from the unbridled use of monopolistic power outweighed any immediate economic gain, sought stability and "fair" prices rather than the maximum profit possible at the moment. "Regulated" competition was the order of the day, oligopoly the typical situation. The trade association movement expanded; producers in various industries formed voluntary organizations to exchange information, discuss policies toward government and the public, and "administer" prices. Usually the largest corporation, such as U. S. Steel in the iron and steel business, became the "price leader," its competitors, some themselves giants, following slavishly.

The success of the trade associations depended partly upon the attitude of the federal government, for such organizations might well have been attacked under the antitrust laws. But Harding and Coolidge considered them desirable. Their secretary of commerce, Herbert Hoover, put the facilities of his department at the disposal of these associations. "We are passing from a period of extremely individualistic action into a period of associational activities," Hoover stated. More important, however, were

the good times. With profits high and markets expanding, the most powerful producers could afford to share the bounty with smaller, less efficient competitors. Thus industrial self-restraint and the pro-business attitudes of the Republican administrations account for the lax enforcement of the antitrust laws. The one major action under the Sherman Act during the period, a suit against the National Cash Register Company, resulted only in a $50 fine imposed on one executive of the corporation.

The most important weak spot in the economy was agriculture. In addition to the slump in farm prices caused by overproduction, farmers' expenses mounted steadily in boom times. Besides having to purchase expensive machinery in order to compete, their psychological needs were increasing. Every self-respecting farmer felt he had to own an automobile in the era of the Model T, and conveniences like electricity and good plumbing seemed equally essential. Conditions became steadily worse because per-acre yields rose rapidly, chiefly as a result of the

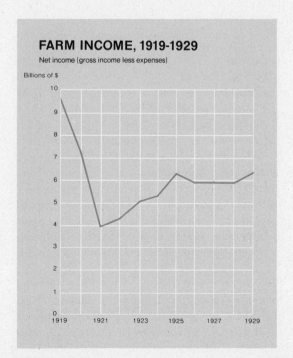

FARM INCOME, 1919-1929

Net income (gross income less expenses)

Billions of $

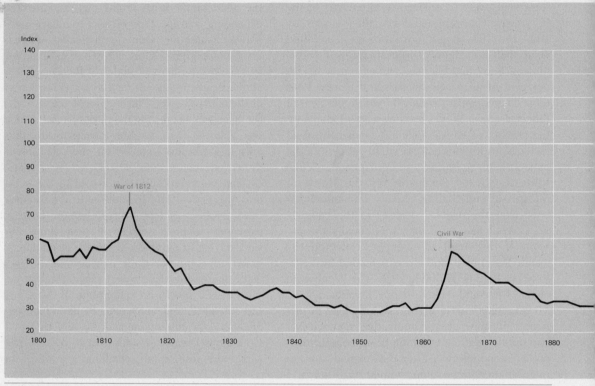

Look at pages 129 or 495 for brief explanation of purpose of chart. The orange part of the line shows the index from 1900 to 1928. Starting with 1913, the information is much more accurate than it was earlier, and reflects prices paid by city wage earners and clerical workers.

increased use of chemical fertilizers. In 1921, 64.5 million acres of wheat land produced about 819 million bushels of wheat. In 1928, 59 million acres yielded 914 million bushels.

Despite the efforts of the Farm Bloc, the government did little to improve the situation. President Harding opposed direct aid to agriculture as a matter of principle. "Every farmer is a captain of industry," he declared. "The elimination of competition among them would be impossible without sacrificing that fine individualism that still keeps the farm the real reservoir from which the nation draws so many of the finest elements of its citizenship." During his administration Congress strengthened the laws regulating railroad rates and grain exchanges and made it easier for farmers to borrow money, but such measures

did nothing to increase agricultural income. Nor did the high tariffs on agricultural produce have much effect. Being forced to sell their surpluses abroad, farmers found that world prices depressed domestic prices despite the tariff wall.

The attitude of Claude R. Wickard, a "master farmer" from Carroll County, Indiana, later secretary of agriculture under Franklin D. Roosevelt, typifies the feelings of American farmers during the twenties:

I was disturbed—genuinely disturbed—by the trend of things, and I think, what was most important of all, my hope began to vanish. I became discouraged with agriculture. We didn't know where we were going.

As early as 1921 George N. Peek, a plow manufacturer from Moline, Illinois, advanced a

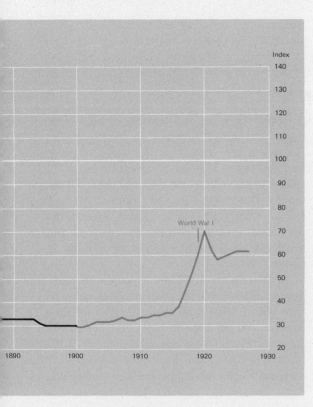

Index
140

130

120

110

100

90

80

World War I   70

60

50

40

30

20

1890   1900   1910   1920   1930

Bloc congressmen took it up and in 1927 the McNary-Haugen bill was passed, only to be vetoed by President Coolidge. Although he raised a number of sound practical objections, Coolidge based his opposition chiefly on constitutional and philosophical grounds. "A healthy economic condition is best maintained through a free play of competition," he insisted, ignoring the fact that the scheme had been devised precisely because competition was proving distinctly unhealthy for American farmers. Congress passed a similar bill again in 1928, but Coolidge again rejected it.

Thus, while most economic indicators reflected an unprecedented prosperity, the boom times rested upon unstable foundations. The problem was mainly one of maldistribution of resources. Productive capacity raced ahead of buying power. Too large a share of the profits went into too few pockets. The 27,000 families with the highest annual incomes in 1929 earned as much money as the 11 million at the bottom of the scale, those with annual incomes of under $1,500, the minimum sum, at that time, required to maintain a family decently. High earnings and low taxes permitted huge sums to pile up in the hands of individuals who could not spend their profits usefully. The money went into further industrial expansion, which aggravated the problem, or into stock market speculation, which led to the "big bull market" and eventually to the Great Depression. While Coolidge reigned, however, few persons realized the danger. Complacency was the order of the day. "The country," Coolidge told Congress in 1928, "can regard the present with satisfaction, and anticipate the future with optimism."

scheme to "make the tariff effective for agriculture." The federal government, Peek suggested in "Equality for Agriculture," should buy up the surplus American production of wheat.° This additional demand would cause domestic prices to rise. Then the government could sell the surpluses abroad at the lower world price, recovering its losses by assessing an "equalization fee" on American farmers.

Peek's plan had flaws, for if the price of staples rose, farmers would tend to increase output, but this problem might have been solved by imposing production controls. It was certainly a most ingenious and promising idea; hundreds of organizations in the farm belt endorsed it. Farm

°He soon extended his plan to cover cotton and other staples.

Election of 1928

The climax of the postwar era in American politics came in 1928, one year before the economy reached its high point. Coolidge—somewhat cryptically, as was his wont—withdrew his name from consideration, and Herbert Hoover, whom he detested, easily won the Republican nomination. Hoover was the intellectual leader, almost the philosopher, of the New Era. He spoke and wrote of "progressive individualism," arguing that American capitalists had learned to curb their selfish instincts and devote themselves to public service and equal opportunity for all. Although stiff and uncommunicative and entirely without experience in elective office, he made an admirable candidate in 1928. His roots in the Middle West and West (Iowa-born, he was raised in Oregon and educated at Stanford University in California) neatly balanced his outstanding reputation among eastern business tycoons. He was very rich, but self-made. His career as a mining engineer had given him a wide knowledge of the world, yet he had become highly critical of Europe, which disarmed the isolationists, who might otherwise have suspected that his long years abroad had made him an effete cosmopolite.

The Democrats, having had their fill of factionalism in 1924, could no longer deny their nomination to Governor Al Smith. Superficially Smith was Hoover's antithesis. Born and raised in New York's Lower East Side slums, affable, witty, determinedly casual of manner, he had been thoroughly schooled in machine politics by Tammany Hall. He was a Catholic, Hoover a Quaker; a wet whereas Hoover supported prohibition vigorously; he dealt easily with men of every race and nationality, while Hoover had little interest in and less knowledge of Negroes and immigrants. However, like Hoover, Smith managed to combine a basic conservatism with his genuine humanitarian concern for the underprivileged. Equally as adept in administration as Hoover, he was also equally uncritical of American capitalism.

Unwilling to challenge the public's complacent view of Coolidge prosperity, the Democrats adopted a conservative platform. Smith appointed John J. Raskob, a wealthy automobile executive, to manage his campaign. Franklin D. Roosevelt, who ran for governor of New York at Smith's urging in 1928, actually charged that Hoover's expansion of the functions of the De-

partment of Commerce had been at least mildly socialistic. This strategy failed miserably. Smith's Catholicism, his brashness, his criticism of prohibition, his machine connections, and his urban background hurt him badly in rural areas, especially in the South. On the other hand, nothing he could do or say was capable of convincing Republican businessmen that he was superior to Hoover. In the election Hoover won a smashing triumph, 444 to 87 in the Electoral College, 21.4 million to 15 million in the popular vote. All the usually Democratic border states, and even North Carolina, Florida, and Texas, went to the Republicans, along with the entire West and Northeast, save for Massachusetts and Rhode Island.

In November 1928 the Democratic party seemed on the verge of extinction. Nothing could have been further from the truth. The religious question and his big-city roots hurt Smith, but the chief reason he lost was the prosperity of the country, and the good times were to be of short duration. Furthermore, Hoover's overwhelming victory concealed a remarkable political realignment that was taking place. The immigrant voters in the major cities, largely Catholic and unimpressed by Coolidge prosperity, had swung heavily to the Democrats. In 1924 the 12 largest cities in the United States had been solidly Republican; in 1928 all of them went Democratic. Even in agricultural states like Iowa, Smith ran far better than Davis had in 1924, for Coolidge's vetoes of the McNary-Haugen bills had caused much resentment. A new coalition of urban workingmen and dissatisfied farmers was in the making. Prosperity, plus Smith's personal disadvantages, held the Republican edifice together in 1928. When the good times ended, it crumbled, suddenly but completely, in one of the greatest political reversals in the nation's history.

Supplementary Reading

The most recent comprehensive survey of the twenties is J. D. Hicks, *Republican Ascendancy*° (1960),

°Available in paperback.

but W. E. Leuchtenburg, *The Perils of Prosperity°* (1958), is equally broad in coverage and more interpretive. A. M. Schlesinger, Jr., *The Age of Roosevelt: The Crisis of the Old Order°* (1957), is rich in detail and sharply anti-Republican in attitude. F. L. Allen, *Only Yesterday°* (1931), is an excellent popular account, a modern classic, oriented especially toward social history. Preston Slosson, *The Great Crusade and After* (1930), is a more comprehensive but less entertaining social history. The economic history of the period is covered in George Soule, *Prosperity Decade°* (1947), but see also J. W. Prothro, *The Dollar Decade* (1954), and Robert Sobel, *The Great Bull Market: Wall Street in the 1920's°* (1968). Other useful volumes include Karl Schriftgiesser, *This Was Normalcy* (1948), and Isabel Leighton (ed.), *The Aspirin Age°* (1949).

The labor history of the postwar decade is discussed in Irving Bernstein, *The Lean Years°* (1960), and Philip Taft, *Organized Labor in the United States* (1964). David Brody, *The Steel Strike of 1919°* (1965), and R. L. Friedheim, *The Seattle General Strike* (1965), are useful special studies. On the Big Red Scare, see R. K. Murray, *Red Scare* (1955), Zechariah Chafee, *Free Speech in the United States°* (1941), and Stanley Coben, *A. Mitchell Palmer* (1963). Nativism and immigration restriction are covered in M. A. Jones, *American Immigration°* (1960), and John Higham, *Strangers in the Land°* (1955). Fundamentalism is treated in N. F. Furniss, *The Fundamentalist Controversy* (1954), the Monkey Trial in Ray Ginger, *Six Days or Forever?°* (1958). The fullest and most thoughtful history of prohibition is Andrew Sinclair, *Prohibition: The Era of Excess°* (1962), but see also Herbert Asbury, *The Great Illusion* (1950), and Charles Merz, *Dry Decade* (1931), a colorful popular account. On the Klan, consult D. M. Chalmers, *Hooded Americanism: The History of the Ku Klux Klan°* (1965), K. T. Jackson, *The Ku Klux Klan in the City°* (1967), and A. S. Rice, *The Ku Klux Klan in American Politics* (1961). W. H. Chafe, *The American Woman: Her Changing Social, Economic, and Political Roles* (1972), is a good scholarly survey. Sacco and Vanzetti are dealt with sympathetically in G. L. Joughin and E. M. Morgan, *The Legacy of Sacco and Vanzetti°* (1948), and in Felix Frankfurter, *The Case of Sacco and Vanzetti°* (1927), but Francis Russell, *Tragedy in Dedham* (1962), casts doubt on their innocence.

The literature of the prewar period is discussed in H. F. May, *The End of American Innocence°* (1959), that of the twenties in Alfred Kazin, *On Native Grounds°* (1942), and F. J. Hoffman, *The Twenties°* (1955). On Fitzgerald, see Arthur Mizener, *The Far Side of Paradise°* (1951); on Hemingway, C. H. Baker, *Hemingway: The Writer as Artist°* (1956); on Mencken, W. R. Manchester, *Disturber of the Peace: The Life of H. L. Mencken°* (1951); on Lewis, Mark Schorer, *Sinclair Lewis°* (1961).

For the history of the Negro in the period, see, besides the sociologist Gunnar Myrdal's classic *An American Dilemma°* (1944), Gilbert Osofsky, *Harlem: The Making of a Ghetto°* (1965), E. M. Rudwick, *W. E. B. Du Bois: Propagandist of the Negro Protest°* (1960), E. D. Cronon, *Black Moses: The Story of Marcus Garvey* (1955), Alain Locke, *The New Negro: An Interpretation°* (1925), J. W. Johnson, *Black Manhattan* (1930), and Nathan Huggins, *Harlem Renaissance* (1971).

The best brief biography of Harding is Andrew Sinclair, *The Available Man°* (1965), the fullest analysis of his Presidency, R. K. Murray, *The Harding Era* (1969). D. R. McCoy, *Calvin Coolidge: The Quiet President* (1967), is the best life of Coolidge, but see also W. A. White, *A Puritan in Babylon°* (1938). Other useful political biographies include B. C. and Fola La Follette, *Robert M. La Follette* (1953), Oscar Handlin, *Al Smith and His America°* (1958), Frank Freidel, *Franklin D. Roosevelt: The Ordeal* (1954), and Arthur Mann, *La Guardia: A Fighter Against His Time°* (1959). David Burner, *The Politics of Provincialism: The Democratic Party in Transition* (1968), discusses the evolution of the Democratic party in the 1920's.

On Henry Ford, see Allan Nevins and F. E. Hill, *Ford* (1954–57), and Keith Sward, *The Legend of Henry Ford°* (1948). J. B. Rae, *The Road and the Car in American Life* (1971), is excellent. Morrell Heald, *The Social Responsibilities of Business* (1970) covers a broader period but is particularly useful for the 1920's. Farm discontent is covered in Theodore Saloutos and J. D. Hicks, *Twentieth Century Populism: Agricultural Discontent in the Middle West°* (1951), Dean Albertson, *Roosevelt's Farmer* (1961), and G. C. Fite, *George N. Peek and the Fight for Farm Parity* (1954). On the election of 1928, see E. A. Moore, *A Catholic Runs for President* (1956).

26

The Great Depression: 1929-1939

In the spring of 1928 prices on the New York Stock Exchange, already at a historic high point, began to surge ahead. As the Presidential campaign gathered momentum, the market increased its pace, stimulated by Hoover's prediction that "the abolition of poverty" lay just around the corner and by Al Smith's efforts to outdo his rival in praising the marvels of the American economic system. "Glamour" stocks skyrocketed—Radio Corporation of America, for example, rose from under 100 to 400 between March and November. A few conservative brokers expressed alarm, warning that most stocks were grossly overpriced, but the majority scoffed at such talk. "Be a bull on America," they urged. "Never sell the United States short."

Through the first half of 1929, despite occasional sharp breaks, the market climbed still higher. A mania for speculation swept the country, thousands of small investors pouring their savings into common stocks. By September 1929 fantastic heights had been reached.

Then the market wavered. For over a month, amid volatile fluctuations, the stock averages moved downward. Most analysts, however, contended that the Exchange was simply "digesting" previous gains. A prominent Harvard economist expressed the prevailing view when he said that stock prices had reached a "permanently high plateau" and would soon resume their advance.

Alas, on October 24 a massive wave of selling sent prices spinning downward. Nearly 13 million shares changed hands, a record. Bankers and politicians rallied to check the decline, as they had during the Panic of 1907. J. P. Morgan, Jr., rivaled the efforts of his father in that earlier crisis, and President Hoover assured the people that "the business of the country . . . is on a sound and prosperous basis." But on Tuesday, October 29, the bottom seemed to drop out of the market. Over 16 million shares were sold, prices plummeting an average of 40 points. The boom was over.

To James N. Rosenberg, a New York attorney and amateur artist who sketched this grim view of the Wall Street financial district, October 29, 1929 ("Black Tuesday") was no less than the Day of Judgment. (Philadelphia Museum of Art.)

Hoover and the Depression

The collapse of the stock market did not cause the depression; stocks rallied late in the year and business activity did not begin to decline significantly until the spring of 1930. The Great Depression was caused basically by the industrialization and urbanization of the United States in the course of a century: too much of the wealth of the nation had fallen into too few hands, with the result that consumers were unable to buy all the goods produced. The trouble came to a head mainly because of the easy-credit policies of the Federal Reserve Board and the Mellon tax struc-

ture, which favored the rich, and its effects were so profound and prolonged because the government (and for that matter the professional economists) did not fully understand what was happening or what to do about it. The chronic problem of underconsumption operated to speed the downward spiral. Unable to rid themselves of mounting inventories, manufacturers closed down plants and laid off workers, thus causing demand to shrink still further. Automobile output fell from 4.5 million units in 1929 to 1.1 million in 1932. When Ford closed his Detroit plants in 1931, some 75,000 men lost their jobs and the decline in auto production affected a host of suppliers and middlemen as well as the workers directly involved.

The financial system soon began to crack under the strain, more than 1,300 banks closing their doors in 1930, 3,700 more in the next two years. Each failure deprived thousands of persons of funds that might otherwise have gone into consumer goods; when the Bank of the United States in New York City became insolvent in December 1930, 400,000 depositors found their savings immobilized. And of course the industrial depression worsened the depression in agriculture, since unemployed workers had literally to tighten their belts, reducing the already inadequate demand for American foodstuffs. Every economic indicator reflected the collapse. New investments declined from $10 billion in 1929 to $1 billion in 1932, and the national income fell from over $80 billion to under $50 billion in the same brief period. Unemployment rose to about 13 million.

President Hoover was an intelligent man, experienced in business matters and with a good layman's grasp of economics. He was also a forceful leader, capable of acting courageously to carry out his policies. Many ultraconservatives, such as Secretary of the Treasury Mellon, insisted that the economy must be allowed to slide unchecked until the cycle had found its bottom. "Let the slump liquidate itself," Mellon urged. "Liquidate labor, liquidate stocks, liquidate the farmers. . . . People will work harder, live a more moral life. Values will be adjusted, and enterprising people will pick up the wrecks from less competent people." Hoover realized that such a policy would cause unbearable hardship for millions, and he determined to try to halt the decline. The government should act vigorously to restore the confidence both of businessmen and the public, since fear and discouragement gravely aggravated the depression.

Hoover's program, evolved gradually between 1929 and 1932, called for cooperative action by businessmen, free from fear of antitrust prosecution, to maintain prices and wages; for tax cuts to increase consumers' spendable income; for public works programs to stimulate production and create jobs for the unemployed; for lower interest rates to make it easier for businesses to borrow in order to expand; for federal loans to banks and industrial corporations threatened with collapse; and for aid to homeowners

unable to meet mortgage payments. The President also proposed measures making it easier for farmers to borrow money, and he suggested that cooperative farm marketing schemes designed to solve the problem of overproduction be supported by the government.

Nor did the wartime savior of Belgium ignore the human misery resulting from the depression. He called for an expansion of state and local relief programs and urged all who could afford it to increase their gifts to charitable institutions. Above all he tried to restore public confidence. The depression was only a minor downturn, he said repeatedly. The economy was basically healthy, prosperity was "just around the corner." In short, Hoover rejected classical economics; indeed, many laissez-faire theorists attacked his handling of the depression. The English economist Lionel Robbins, writing in 1934, criticized Hoover's "grandiose buying organizations" and his efforts to maintain consumer income "at all costs." Numbers of "liberal" economists, on the other hand, praised the Hoover program.

However, while his plans were theoretically sound, they failed to check the economic slide, partly because of curious limitations in his conception of how they should be implemented. He placed far too much reliance on his powers of persuasion and the willingness of citizens to act in the public interest without legal compulsion. He called a series of industrial conferences to urge manufacturers to maintain wages and keep their factories in operation, but the businessmen, under the harsh pressure of economic realities, soon slashed wages and curtailed output sharply. He permitted the Federal Farm Board (created under the Agricultural Marketing Act of 1929) to establish semipublic stabilization corporations with authority to spend millions of dollars supplied by the federal government in an effort to buy up surplus wheat and cotton, but he refused to countenance production controls. As a result, these corporations poured out hundreds of millions of dollars without checking the downward trend of agricultural prices, for farmers increased production faster than the corporations could buy up the excess for disposal abroad.

The anomaly of surplus food and natural resources in a time of want mystified many Americans, a view expressed by cartoonist Daniel Fitzpatrick in 1931. (St. Louis *Post-Dispatch,* January 11, 1931.)

Hoover also resisted all proposals to shift authority from state and local agencies to the federal government, despite the fact—soon obvious—that these lesser governmental bodies lacked the resources to cope with the emergency. For example, by 1932 the federal government, with Hoover's approval, was spending $500 million a year on public works projects, but because of the decline of state and municipal construction, the total public outlay fell nearly $1 billion below what it had been in 1930. More serious was his refusal, on constitutional grounds, to allow federal funds to be used for the relief of individuals. State and municipal agencies and private charities must take care of the needy. Unfortunately the depression was drying up the sources of private charities just as the demands upon these organizations were expanding. State agencies were also swamped at a time when their capacities to tax and borrow were shrinking. By 1932 about one-third of the entire population of Pennsylvania was on relief; in Chicago 700,000 persons—40 per cent of the work force—were unemployed. Only the national government pos-

sessed the power and credit to deal adequately with the crisis. Yet despite his genuine humanitarianism, Hoover would not act. He set up a committee to coordinate local relief activities but insisted on preserving what he called "the principles of individual and local responsibility."

Federal loans to businessmen were constitutional, he believed, because the money could be put to productive use and eventually repaid. When drought destroyed the crops of farmers in the South and Southwest in 1930, Hoover was willing to grant them federal loans to buy seed and even food for their livestock, but he would provide no direct relief for the farmers themselves. In 1932 he approved the creation of the Reconstruction Finance Corporation, which was authorized to lend money to banks, railroads, and insurance companies. The RFC represented an important extension of federal authority, but one thoroughly in line with Hoover's philosophy. Its loans, secured by solid collateral, were commercial transactions, not gifts; the agency did almost nothing for individuals in need of personal relief. The same could be said of the Glass-Steagall Banking Act of 1932, which eased the tight credit situation by permitting Federal Reserve banks to accept a wider variety of commercial paper as security for loans. Although the President's sincerity could not be questioned, the public grew increasingly resentful of his doctrinaire adherence to principle while breadlines lengthened and millions of willing workers searched fruitlessly for jobs.

In addition, Hoover overemphasized the importance of balancing the federal budget. In hard times, he reasoned, everyone ought to live within his means, and the government should set a good example. It is now obvious that this policy was impossible to carry out because the government's income fell precipitously in bad times; by June 1931 the budget was nearly $500 million in the red. The policy was also counterproductive. By reducing its expenditures the government only made the depression worse. Since Hoover understood the value of pumping money into a stagnant economy, he might have been expected to make a virtue of necessity. The difficulty lay in the fact that nearly all "informed" opinion in America and in other nations as well believed that a balanced budget was essential to recovery. The most prestigious economists insisted upon it. So did business leaders, so did labor leaders, so even did most socialists. When Hoover said, "Prosperity cannot be restored by raids on the public Treasury," he was wrong, but it is also wrong to criticize him for failing to understand what no one else understood in the early 1930's.

Hoover can, however, be faulted for allowing his anti-European prejudices to interfere with the implementation of his program. In 1930 Congress passed the Hawley–Smoot Tariff Act, which raised duties on most manufactured products to prohibitive levels. Although over a thousand economists joined in urging Hoover to veto this measure on the grounds that it would encourage inefficiency and stifle world trade, he signed it cheerfully. The new tariff made it impossible for European nations to earn the dollars they needed to continue making payments on their World War I debts to the United States and also helped bring on a financial collapse in Europe in 1931. In that year Hoover wisely proposed a one-year "moratorium" on all international obligations. But the efforts of Great Britain and many other countries to save their own skins by devaluing their currencies in order to encourage foreigners to buy their goods led him to blame them for the depression itself, ignoring the fact that it had started in the United States. He seemed unable to grasp what should have been obvious to a man of his intelligence: that high American tariffs made currency devaluation almost inevitable in Europe and that the curtailment of American investment on the Continent as a result of the depression had dealt a staggering blow to the economies of all the European nations.

No one could have prevented the Great Depression or brought the country back to good times quickly. Much of the contemporary criticism of Hoover and a good deal of that heaped upon him by later historians was unfair. Yet his record as President shows that he was too rigid and doctrinaire, too wedded to a particular the-ory of government to cope effectively with the problems of the day. Since these problems were in a sense insoluble—no one, after all, possessed enough knowledge and intelligence to understand entirely what was wrong or enough authority to enforce the proper corrective measures—flexibility and a willingness to experiment were essential to any program aimed at restoring prosperity. Hoover lacked these qualities. He was also his own worst enemy, being too uncompromising to get on well with the politicians and too aloof to win the public's confidence and affection. He had too much faith in himself and his plans. When he failed to achieve the results he anticipated, he attracted, despite his devotion to duty and his concern for the welfare of the country, not sympathy but scorn.

The Economy Sounds the Depths

During the spring of 1932, as the economy sounded the depths, thousands of Americans were facing starvation. In Philadelphia, during an 11-day period when no relief funds at all were available, hundreds of families existed on stale bread, thin soup, and garbage. In Birmingham, Alabama, landlords in poor districts simply gave up trying to collect rents. "Frequently," one Alabama congressman told a Senate committee, "the landlord prefers to have somebody living there free of charge rather than to have the house . . . burned up for fuel [by scavengers]." In the nation as a whole, only about one quarter of the unemployed were receiving any public aid at all.

In every major city homeless families gathered in ramshackle communities called "Hoover-villes," constructed of packing boxes, rusty sheet metal, and similar refuse on swamps, garbage dumps, and other wasteland. Thousands of hungry tramps roamed the countryside. Yet at the same time, food prices fell so low that farmers were burning corn for fuel. In states like Iowa and Nebraska, farmers organized Farm Holiday movements, refusing to ship their crops to market in protest against 31-cent-a-bushel corn and 38-cent wheat. They blocked roads and rail lines, dumped milk, overturned trucks, and established picket lines to enforce their boycott.

The national mood ranged from apathy to resentment to outright fury. In June and July 1932 unemployed veterans, 20,000 strong, marched on Washington to demand immediate payment of their "adjusted compensation" bonuses. When Congress rejected their appeal, some 2,000 refused to leave, settling down with their families in a jerry-built camp of shacks and tents at Anacostia Flats, a swamp bordering the Potomac. President Hoover, much alarmed, charged incorrectly that the "Bonus Army" was largely composed of criminals and radicals and sent troops into the Flats to disperse it with bayonets, tear gas, and tanks. The task was accomplished amid much confusion, although fortunately no shots were fired. The protest had been aimless and not entirely justified, but the spectacle of the United States government chasing unarmed veterans with tanks appalled the nation.

The unprecedented severity of the depression led some persons to favor radical alterations of the country's economic and political systems. The disparity between the lots of the rich and the poor, always a challenge to democracy, became more striking and engendered much bitterness. "Unless something is done to provide employment," two labor leaders warned Hoover, "disorder . . . is sure to arise. . . . There is a growing demand that the entire business and social structure be changed because of the general dissatisfaction with the present system." The communists gained few converts among the mass of workingmen, but many intellectuals, already alienated by the trends of the twenties, now responded positively to the communists' emphasis on economic planning and the total mobilization of the state to achieve social goals. Even the popular cracker-barrel humorist Will Rogers was impressed by reports of the absence of serious unemployment in Russia. "All roads in our day lead to Moscow," the former muckraker Lincoln Steffens wrote. Communism, John Strachey ar-

gued in his widely read *The Coming Struggle for Power* (1932), offered "the one method by which human civilization can be maintained." Only the disdain of the communists for individual rights and the internecine strife within the Russian party organization kept the communist movement from making more headway in America in the dark days of the early thirties.

As the end of his term approached, President Hoover seemed to grow daily more petulant and pessimistic. The depression, climaxing 12 years of Republican rule, probably insured a Democratic victory in any case, but his attitude as the election neared alienated many voters and turned defeat into rout.

Franklin D. Roosevelt

Confident of victory, the Democrats chose Governor Franklin Delano Roosevelt of New York as their Presidential candidate. Roosevelt owed his nomination chiefly to his success as governor. In 1928, while Hoover was carrying New York against Smith by a wide margin, Roosevelt won election by 25,000 votes. In 1930 he swept the state by a 700,000-vote majority, double the previous record. Under his administration, New York had led the nation in providing relief for the needy and had enacted an impressive program of old-age pensions, unemployment insurance, conservation and public power projects. The governor also had the advantage of the Roosevelt name (he was a distant cousin of the inimitable T.R.), and his sunny, magnetic personality contrasted favorably with that of the glum and colorless Hoover.

Roosevelt was far from being a radical. Although he had made a good record in the Wilson administration while serving as assistant secretary of the navy and had supported the League of Nations vigorously while campaigning for the Vice Presidency in 1920, during the twenties he had not seriously challenged the basic tenets of Coolidge prosperity. For a time he even served as head of the American Construction Council, a

A breadline in New York in 1933. The Great Depression, said an English observer, "outraged and baffled" the nation that took it as "an article of faith . . . that America, somehow, was different from the rest of the world." (UPI.)

trade association. Indeed, his life before 1932 gave very little indication that he understood the aspirations of the masses of the American people or had any deep commitment to social reform.

Born to wealth and social status in Dutchess County, New York, in 1882, pampered in childhood by a doting yet domineering mother, he was educated at the exclusive Groton School and then at Harvard, where he proceeded, as his biographer Frank Freidel has written, "from one extracurricular triumph to another." Ambition as much as the desire to render public service motivated his career in politics; even after an attack of polio in 1921 left him badly crippled in both legs, he refused to abandon his hopes for high office. During the 1920's he had been a hardworking member of the liberal wing of his party,

supporting Smith for President in 1924 and 1928, but he was no extremist and never displayed any difficulty in adjusting his views to the prevailing sentiments of the day.

To some observers he seemed rather a lightweight intellectually. When he ran for the Vice Presidency, the Chicago *Tribune* commented: "If he is Theodore Roosevelt, Elihu Root is Gene Debs, and Bryan is a brewer." Twelve years later many critics judged him too irresolute, too amiable, too eager to please all factions to be a forceful leader. The political analyst Walter Lippmann, in a now-famous observation, called him "a pleasant man who, without any important qualifications for the job, would very much like to be President."

Despite his physical handicap—he could walk

only a few steps, and then only with the aid of steel braces and two canes—Roosevelt was a brilliant campaigner; as Al Smith pointed out during the 1928 contest, "a Governor does not have to be an acrobat." He traveled back and forth across the country, radiating confidence and good humor even when directing his sharpest barbs at the Republicans. Like every great political leader, he took as much from the people as he gave them, understanding the causes of their confusion, sensing their needs. "I have looked into the faces of thousands of Americans," he told a friend. "They have the frightened look of lost children. . . . They are saying: 'We're caught in something we don't understand; perhaps this fellow can help us out.'" Roosevelt soaked up information and ideas from a thousand sources—from professors like Raymond Moley and Felix Frankfurter, from politicians like James A. Farley and John N. Garner, the Vice Presidential candidate, from social workers, businessmen, and lawyers.

To those seeking specific answers to the questions of the day, Roosevelt was seldom very satisfying. On vital matters like farm policy, the tariff, and government spending, he equivocated, contradicted himself, or remained silent. Aided by hindsight, historians have discovered portents of much of his later program in his speeches, but to contemporaries these pronouncements, buried among dozens of conflicting generalities, often passed almost unnoticed. He did say, for example: "If starvation and dire need on the part of any of our citizens make necessary the appropriation of additional funds which would keep the budget out of balance, I shall not hesitate to . . . ask the people to authorize the expenditure of that additional amount," but in the same speech he called for sharp cuts in federal spending and a balanced budget, and he castigated Hoover for presiding over "the greatest spending administration in peace time in our history."

Nevertheless, his basic position was unmistakable. There must be a "New Deal," a "re-appraisal of values." Instead of adhering to old ideas about the scope of federal power, the government should take on any functions necessary to protect the unfortunate and advance the public good. Lacking concrete answers, he advocated a point of view rather then a plan: "The country needs bold, persistent experimentation. It is common sense to take a method and try it. If it fails, admit it frankly and try another. But above all, try something." The effectiveness of this approach was demonstrated in November. Hoover, who had lost only eight states in 1928, won only six, all in the Northeast, in 1932. Roosevelt amassed 22.8 million votes to Hoover's 15.8 million and carried the Electoral College by 472 to 59.

During the interval between the election and Roosevelt's inauguration in March 1933, the Great Depression reached its nadir. The holdover "lame duck" Congress, last of its kind,° proved incapable of effective action. President Hoover, perhaps understandably, hesitated to institute changes without the cooperation of his successor, while Roosevelt, for equally plausible reasons, refused to accept responsibility before assuming power officially. The nation, curiously apathetic in the face of so much suffering, drifted aimlessly, like a sailboat in a flat calm.

Then the banking system disintegrated—no lesser word portrays the extent of the collapse. Starting in the rural West and spreading to major cities like Detroit and Baltimore, a financial panic forced hundreds of banks to close down. All over the country depositors began to line up before the doors of even the soundest institutions, desperate to withdraw their savings. In February, to check the panic, the governor of Michigan declared a "bank holiday," shutting up every bank in the state for eight days. Maryland, Kentucky, California, and a number of other states followed suit; by inauguration day four-fifths of the states had suspended all banking operations. So great was the fear and confusion that the New York Stock Exchange was closed on March 4.

°The Twentieth Amendment (1933) provided for convening new Congresses in January instead of the following December. It also advanced the date of the President's inauguration from March 4 to January 20.

The Hundred Days

Obviously something drastic had to be done. The most conservative business leaders were as ready for government intervention as the most advanced radicals. Partisanship, while not disappearing, was for once subordinated to broad national needs.

Then Roosevelt provided the spark that re-energized the American people. His inaugural address, delivered in a raw mist beneath dark March skies, reassured the country and at the same time stirred it to action: "The only thing we have to fear is fear itself. . . . Our true destiny is not to be ministered unto but to minister to ourselves and to our fellow men. . . . This Nation asks for action, and action now. . . . I assume unhesitatingly the leadership of this great army of our people. . . ." Many such lines punctuated his brief address, which concluded with this stern pledge: "In the event that Congress shall fail . . . I shall not evade the clear course of duty that will then confront me. I shall ask the Congress for the one remaining instrument to meet the crisis—broad Executive power to wage a war against the emergency."

The inaugural captured the heart of the country; almost half a million letters of congratulation poured into the White House. When Roosevelt summoned Congress into special session on March 9, the legislators outdid one another to enact his proposals into law. "I had as soon start a mutiny in the face of a foreign foe as . . . against the program of the President," one representative declared. In the following "Hundred Days" (Congress adjourned on June 16), opposition, in the sense of an organized group committed to resisting the administration, simply did not exist. As a result, an impressive body of new legislation was placed on the statute books. The New Deal was under way.

Roosevelt had the power and the will to act, but no comprehensive plan of action. He and his eager congressional collaborators proceeded in a dozen directions at once, sometimes wisely, sometimes not, often at cross purposes with

themselves and one another. Untangling the national financial mess presented the most immediate problem. On March 5 Roosevelt declared a nationwide bank holiday and placed an embargo on the exportation of gold. Within hours after it convened, Congress passed an emergency banking bill, confirming these measures, outlawing the hoarding of gold, and giving the President broad power over the operations of the Federal Reserve system. A plan for reopening the banks under Treasury Department licenses was devised and soon most of them were functioning again, public confidence in their solvency restored. In April Roosevelt took the country off the gold standard. Before the session ended, Congress had also established the Federal Deposit Insurance Corporation to guarantee bank deposits, forced the separation of investment banking and commercial banking concerns while extending the power of the Federal Reserve Board over both types of institutions, and created the Home Owners Loan Corporation to refinance mortgages and prevent foreclosures. It also passed a Federal Securities Act requiring promoters to make public full financial information about all new stock issues and giving the Federal Trade Commission the right to regulate such transactions.*

After the adjournment of Congress, Roosevelt began buying gold on the open market, hoping thereby to cause a general price rise and increase American world trade. When this policy failed to do much good, Congress, in January 1934, passed the Gold Reserve Act, permitting the President to fix the price of gold by proclamation. Roosevelt promptly set the price at $35 an ounce, about 40 per cent higher than its pre-New Deal level. Roosevelt's monetary policies did not produce any dramatic rise in the price level, but, considering the severity and complexity of the deflation problem, they represented an intelligent and reasonably successful approach.

Problems of unemployment and industrial stagnation also had high priority during the Hun-

---

*In 1934 this task was transferred to the new Securities and Exchange Commission, which also was given broad authority over all the activities of stock exchanges.

dred Days. Congress appropriated $500 million for relief of the needy and created the Civilian Conservation Corps to provide jobs for young men between the ages of 18 and 25 in reforestation and other conservation projects. To stimulate industry, Congress passed one of its most controversial measures, the National Industrial Recovery Act (NIRA). Besides establishing the Public Works Administration, with authority to spend $3.3 billion, this law permitted manufacturers to draw up industrywide codes of fair business practices in order to raise prices and limit production by agreement, without fear of the antitrust laws. The law also gave workers the protection of minimum-wage and maximum-hours regulations, and guaranteed them the right "to organize and bargain collectively through representatives of their own choosing," an immense stimulus to the labor-union movement.

The NIRA was a variant on the idea of the corporate state, a concept that envisaged a system of industrywide organizations of capitalists and workers (supervised by the government) that would resolve conflicts internally, thus avoiding wasteful economic competition and dangerous social clashes. It was similar to Hoover's trade association idea, although Hoover denounced it because of its compulsory aspects, and also to experiments being carried out by the fascist dictator Benito Mussolini in Italy and by the Nazis in Adolf Hitler's Germany. It did not, of course, turn America into a fascist state, but it did herald an increasing concentration of economic power in the hands of interest groups, both industrialists' organizations and labor unions.

The act created a government agency, the National Recovery Administration (NRA), headed by General Hugh Johnson, to supervise the drafting and operation of the business codes. In practice, the codes were drawn up by the largest manufacturers in each industry. Drafting them posed difficult problems, first because each industry insisted on tailoring the agreements to its special needs and second because most manufacturers were unwilling to accept all the provisions of Section 7a of the law dealing with the rights of labor. Although thousands of employers

agreed to the pledge "We Do Our Part" in order to receive the Blue Eagle symbol of NRA, many were more interested in the monopolistic aspects of the act than in boosting wages and encouraging unionization. General Johnson was soon fulminating against "chiselers," and his impetuosity and his violent tongue did much to destroy whatever spirit of cooperation the manufacturers possessed. After Johnson had been a year in office, President Roosevelt forced his resignation.

The effects of NIRA were both more and less than the designers of the system had imagined. It did not end the depression. There was a brief upturn in the spring of 1933, but the expected revival of industry did not take place; in nearly every case the dominant producers in each industry used their power to raise prices and limit production rather than to increase output.

However, the law did achieve important results. Beginning with the cotton textile code, the agreements succeeded in doing away with the centuries-old problem of child labor in industry. They established the principle of federal regulation of wages and hours and led directly to the organization of hundreds of thousands of workers, even in industries like steel and autos where unions had never before been significant. Within a year John L. Lewis' United Mine Workers expanded from 150,000 members to half a million. About 100,000 automobile workers joined unions, as did a comparable number of steelworkers.

Organizers cleverly used the NIRA to persuade workers that the popular President Roosevelt *wanted* them to join unions, which was something of an overstatement. In 1935, after the conservative and craft-oriented AFL had revealed very little enthusiasm for enrolling unskilled workers on an industrywide basis, John L. Lewis, together with officials of the garment trade unions, formed the Committee for Industrial Organization (CIO) and set out to rally workers in each of the mass-production industries into one union without regard for craft lines, a far more effective method of organization. The AFL expelled these unions, however, and in 1938 the CIO became the Congress of Industrial

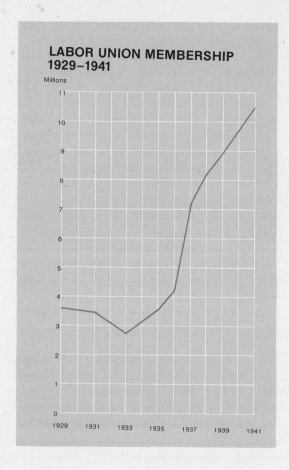

LABOR UNION MEMBERSHIP 1929–1941

their land from cultivation, farmers received "rental" payments from the Agricultural Adjustment Administration (AAA).

Since the 1933 crops were already growing when the law was passed, Secretary of Agriculture Henry A. Wallace, son of Harding's secretary of agriculture and himself an experienced farmer and plant geneticist, decided to pay farmers to destroy their produce in the field. Cotton planters plowed up 10 million acres of growing crops, receiving $100 million in return. Six million baby pigs and 200,000 pregnant sows were slaughtered. Such ruthlessness appalled observers, especially when they thought of the millions of hungry Americans who could have eaten the destroyed food, but no practical alternative existed during that first year of the program. Thereafter, limitation of acreage proved sufficient to raise agricultural prices considerably. A far more serious criticism of the program was its failure to help poor farmers, especially tenants and sharecroppers, many of whom lost their livelihoods completely when owners took land out of production to obtain AAA payments.

But in 1933 even farmers with large holdings were in desperate trouble, and these at least were helped. Acreage restrictions and mortgage relief saved thousands. In addition, the farm program was a remarkable attempt to rationalize the chaotic agricultural economy. As one New Deal official put it, the AAA was "the greatest single experiment in economic planning under capitalist conditions ever attempted by a democracy in times of peace."

Another striking achievement of the Hundred Days was the creation of the Tennessee Valley Authority (TVA). To provide power for factories manufacturing synthetic nitrate explosives during World War I, the government had constructed a hydroelectric plant at Muscle Shoals, Alabama, where the Tennessee River plunges 130 feet in a 40-mile stretch. After 1920 farm groups and public power enthusiasts, led by Senator George W. Norris of Nebraska, had blocked administration plans to turn these facilities over to private capitalists. But their efforts to have the site operated under federal auspices had been defeated by

Organizations. Soon it rivaled the AFL in size and importance.

Roosevelt displayed more concern over the plight of the farmers than over that of any other group in America, for he believed that the nation was becoming overcommitted to industry. The New Deal farm program, incorporated in the Agricultural Adjustment Act of May 1933, combined compulsory restrictions on production with government subsidies of staple commodities like wheat, cotton, tobacco, and pork, paid for by levying processing taxes on middlemen such as flour millers. The object was to lift agricultural prices to "parity" with industrial prices, the ratio in most cases being based on the levels of 1909-14, when farmers had been reasonably prosperous. In return for withdrawing part of

Presidential vetoes. Roosevelt, however, eagerly pressed to have the whole Tennessee Valley area incorporated into a broad experiment in social planning. Besides expanding the hydroelectric plants at Muscle Shoals and developing nitrate manufacturing in order to produce cheap fertilizers, he envisioned a coordinated program of soil conservation, reforestation, and industrialization. Since the Tennessee River flowed through seven states, national control of the project was essential.

Over the objections of private power interests, led by Wendell L. Willkie of the Commonwealth and Southern Corporation, Congress passed the TVA Act in May 1933. This law created a three-man board authorized to build dams, power plants, and transmission lines and sell fertilizers and electricity to individuals and local communities. The board could also undertake flood control, soil conservation, and reforestation projects, and improve the navigation of the river. While the TVA never became the comprehensive regional planning organization some of its sponsors had anticipated, it greatly improved the standard of living of millions of inhabitants of the valley. In addition to producing quantities of electricity and fertilizers and providing a "yardstick" whereby the efficiency, and thus the rates, of private power companies could be tested, it took on other functions, ranging from the eradication of malaria to the development of recreational facilities.

The New Deal Spirit

By the end of the Hundred Days, the country had made up its mind about Roosevelt's New Deal, and despite the many vicissitudes of the next decade, it never really changed it. A large majority was ready to label it a solid success. In the first place, considerable industrial recovery had taken place. More basic was the fact that Roosevelt, recruiting an army of forceful, intelligent officials to staff the new government agencies, had managed to infuse his administration

with a spirit of bustle and optimism. The director of the Presidential Secret Service unit, returning to the White House on inauguration day after escorting Herbert Hoover to the railroad station, found the executive mansion "transformed during my absence into a gay place, full of people who oozed confidence." Within a few weeks Roosevelt's New Dealers had changed the atmosphere of Washington. "They have transformed it," one observer noted, "from a placid leisurely Southern town . . . into a gay, breezy, sophisticated and metropolitan center."

Dozens of persons who lived through those stirring times have left records that reveal the New Deal spirit. "Come at once to Washington," Senator Robert La Follette, Jr., son of "Fighting Bob," telegraphed Donald Richberg, an old Theodore Roosevelt progressive. "Great things are under way." When Richberg arrived, he found his liberal friends "seething with excitement and anticipation." A seasoned newspaperman, looking back on the Hundred Days, wrote: "It was one of the most joyous periods in my life. We came alive, we were eager." And Justice Harlan Fiske Stone of the Supreme Court recorded: "Never was there such a change in the transfer of government."

Although Roosevelt was anything but an intellectual, his openness to suggestion made him eager to draw upon the ideas and energies of experts of all sorts. New Deal agencies soon teemed with college professors and young lawyers without previous political experience. Largely because of the influence of Eleanor Roosevelt, the administration also employed unprecedented numbers of women in positions of real importance, not merely Secretary of Labor Frances Perkins, the first woman ever appointed to a Cabinet post, but dozens of others. (According to the historian William H. Chafe, "Washington seemed like a perpetual convention of social workers as women . . . [took] on government assignments.") The President also encouraged women to be more active in the Democratic party. The Women's Division, headed by Mary Dewson, a close friend of both the Roosevelts, became a major force in the party, winning a larger influence for women in conventions and campaigns, and a larger share of "the spoils" that came with victory. Between 1932 and 1938, the number of women postmasters increased by 50 per cent.

Roosevelt himself seemed to have been "transfigured," as one reporter said, "from a man of charm and buoyancy to one of dynamic aggressiveness." During the first days of the New Deal, the financial expert Norman H. Davis, who had known Roosevelt since the time of their joint service under Woodrow Wilson, encountered a mutual friend on the White House steps. "That fellow in there is not the fellow we used to know," he said. "There's been a miracle here."

The New Deal lacked any consistent ideological base. Although the so-called Brain Trust (a group of college professors headed by Raymond Moley, a Columbia political scientist, and including Columbia economists Rexford G. Tugwell and Adolf A. Berle, Jr., Felix Frankfurter of the Harvard Law School, and a number of others) attracted a great deal of attention, theorists never impressed Roosevelt very much. His New Deal drew upon the old populist tradition as seen in its antipathy to bankers and its willingness to adopt schemes for inflating the currency; upon the New Nationalism of Theodore Roosevelt in such matters as its dislike of competition and its de-emphasis of the antitrust laws; and upon the ideas of social workers trained in the Progressive Era. Techniques developed by the Wilsonians also found a place in the system: Louis D. Brandeis had considerable influence on Roosevelt's financial reforms, and New Deal labor policy grew directly out of the experience of the War Labor Board of 1917-18.

Within the administrative maze that Roosevelt created, rival bureaucrats battled to enforce their views. The "spenders," led by Tugwell of the Brain Trust, clashed with those favoring strict economy, who gathered around Lewis Douglas, director of the budget. Blithely disregarding logically irreconcilable differences, Roosevelt mediated between the factions, deciding this time in favor of one group, next in favor of the other. Washington became a battleground

for dozens of special-interest groups: the Farm Bureau Federation, the big unions, the trade associations, the silver miners, and so on. William E. Leuchtenburg has described New Deal policy as "interest-group democracy," another historian, Ellis W. Hawley, as "counterorganization" policy, aimed at creating "monopoly power" among groups previously unorganized, such as farmers and industrial workers. While, as Leuchtenburg says, the system was greatly superior to that of Roosevelt's predecessors, who had allowed one interest group, big business, to predominate, it slighted the unorganized majority. The NRA aimed frankly at raising the prices paid by consumers of manufactured goods; the AAA processing tax came ultimately from the pocketbooks of ordinary citizens. Yet the public assumed that Roosevelt's ultimate objective was to improve the lot of all classes of society and that he was laboring diligently and imaginatively in pursuit of this goal.

The Unemployed

Although at least 9 million persons were still without work, the Democrats confounded the political experts, including their own, by increasing their already large majorities in both houses of Congress in the 1934 elections. All the evidence indicates that even most of the jobless continued to support the administration. Their loyalty can best be explained by Roosevelt's unemployment policies.

In May 1933 Congress had established the Federal Emergency Relief Administration and given it $500 million to be dispensed through state relief organizations. Roosevelt appointed Harry L. Hopkins, an eccentric but brilliant and dedicated social worker, to direct FERA. However, Hopkins insisted that the unemployed needed jobs, not merely handouts. In November he persuaded Roosevelt to create a Civil Works Administration and within a month put over 4 million persons to work building and repairing roads and public buildings, teaching, decorating

YEARS OF DUST

RESETTLEMENT ADMINISTRATION
Rescues Victims
Restores Land to Proper Use

Ben Shahn did this lithograph in 1937 for the government's Resettlement Administration, an agency established to aid victims of "Dust Bowl" conditions. (Museum of Modern Art.)

of Roosevelt's determination to attack the unemployment problem on a broad front.

After the midterm elections, Roosevelt committed himself wholeheartedly to the Hopkins approach. Returning "unemployables" to the care of state and local agencies (where their fate was often miserable), the federal government assumed the task of making work for many of the rest. In May 1935 Roosevelt put Hopkins in charge of a new agency, the Works Progress Administration (WPA). By the time this agency was disbanded in 1943 it had spent $11 billion and found employment for 8.5 million persons. Besides carrying out an extensive public works program, the WPA developed the Federal Theatre Project, which put thousands of actors, directors, and stagehands to work; the Federal Writers' Project, which turned out valuable guidebooks, collected local lore, and published about a thousand books and pamphlets; and the Federal Art Project, which made work for needy painters and sculptors. In addition, the National Youth Administration created part-time jobs for over 2 million high school and college students and an even larger number of other youths who could not technically be classified as unemployed, but who needed financial help.

Nevertheless, WPA did not reach all the un-

the walls of post offices with murals, and utilizing their special skills in dozens of other ways. The cost of this program frightened Roosevelt—Hopkins spent about $1 billion in less than five months—and he soon abolished the CWA, but an extensive public works program was continued throughout 1934 under FERA. Despite charges by critics that many of the projects were mere "boondoggles," thousands of roads, bridges, schools, and other valuable structures were built or refurbished, and the morale of several million otherwise jobless workers was immeasurably raised. Even those who did not benefit directly took the program as an indication

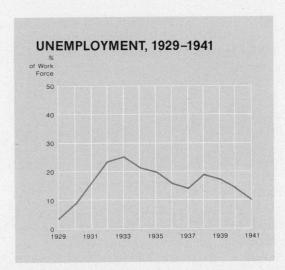

UNEMPLOYMENT, 1929–1941

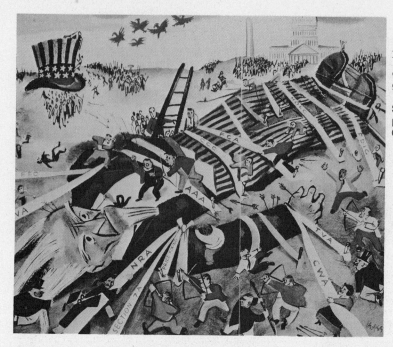

The proliferation of federal agencies during the New Deal inspired a legion of satirists. In this example, from *Vanity Fair*, Uncle Sam becomes Swift's Gulliver besieged by the Lilliputian brain-trusters. (© 1935, 1963 Conde-Nast Publications, Inc.)

employed; like so many New Deal programs, it did not go far enough, chiefly because Roosevelt could not escape from his fear of unbalancing the federal budget too drastically. Halfway measures did not provide the massive stimulus the economy needed. The President also hesitated to pay adequate wages to WPA workers and to undertake projects that might compete with private enterprises for fear of offending business. Yet his caution did him no good politically; the very interests he sought to placate were becoming increasingly hostile to the New Deal.

The Extremists

Roosevelt's moderation also roused extremists, both on the left and on the right. Of these, the most formidable was Louisiana's Senator Huey Long, the "Kingfish." Raised on a farm in northern Louisiana, Long was progressively a traveling salesman, a lawyer, state railroad commissioner, governor, and, after 1930, United States senator.

By 1933 he ruled Louisiana with the absolutism of an oriental monarch.

Long was a controversial figure in his own day and so he has remained. In many ways he was a typical southern conservative, and he was certainly a demagogue. Yet the plight of all poor people concerned him deeply and—more important—he tried to do something about it. His record in Louisiana is a mixture of egotism, sordid politicking, and genuine efforts to improve the lot of the poor, black as well as white. He did not question segregation or white supremacy, nor did he suggest that Louisiana blacks should be allowed to vote. He used the word *nigger* with total unself-consciousness, even when addressing northern Negro leaders. But he treated Negro-baiters with scathing contempt. When Hiram W. Evans, Imperial Wizard of the Ku Klux Klan, announced his intention to campaign against him in Louisiana, Long told reporters: "Quote me as saying that that Imperial bastard will never set foot in Louisiana, and that when I call him a sonofabitch I am not using profanity, but am referring to the circumstances of his birth."

As a reformer, Long stood in the populist tradition; he hated bankers and "the interests." He believed that all poor people, regardless of color, should have a chance to earn a decent living and get an education. His arguments were simplistic, patronizing, possibly insincere, but effective. "Don't say I'm working for niggers," he told a northern Negro journalist. "I'm for the poor man—all poor men. Black and white, they all gotta have a chance. . . . 'Every Man a King'— that's my slogan."

Raffish, totally unrestrained, yet extremely shrewd—a fellow southern politician called him "the smartest lunatic I ever saw"—Long had supported the New Deal at the start, but partly because he thought Roosevelt too conservative and partly because of his own ambition, he soon broke with the administration. Although Roosevelt was himself more hostile to the big financiers than to any other group, Long denounced him as a stooge of Wall Street. By 1935 he was heading a national "Share-Our-Wealth" movement with a membership of over 4.6 million. His program called for the confiscation of all family fortunes of more than $5 million and a tax of 100 per cent on incomes of over $1 million a year. The money thus collected would provide every family with a "homestead" (including a car and other necessities as well as a house) and an annual income of $2,000–$3,000, plus old-age pensions, educa-

At left, Senator Huey Long explains his "Share-Our-Wealth" plan to an Iowa audience in April of 1935. That same month, Father Charles Coughlin (above), the "Radio Priest," was photographed in Detroit as he promoted his National Union for Social Justice. (Both: UPI.)

tional benefits, and veterans' pensions. In addition, Long proposed that the hours of labor be limited to make more jobs, and that a farm price-support program be established. As the 1936 election approached, he was planning to organize a third party to split the liberal vote. He assumed that the Republicans would win the election and so botch the job of fighting the depression that he could himself sweep the country in 1940.

Less powerful than Long but more widely influential was Father Charles E. Coughlin, the "Radio Priest." A big, genial Irishman of Canadian birth, Coughlin began his public career in 1926, broadcasting a weekly religious message over station WJR in Detroit. His mellifluous voice and orotund rhetoric soon won him a huge national audience, and the depression gave him a secular cause. In 1933 he had been an eager New Dealer, but his dislike of New Deal financial policies—he believed that inflating the currency drastically would end the depression—and his need for ever more sensational ideas to hold his public from week to week led him to turn against the New Deal by 1935. Soon he was calling Roosevelt a "great betrayer and liar." Although his National Union for Social Justice was especially appealing to Catholics, it attracted people of every faith, especially in the lower-middle-class districts of the big cities. Some of his more sensational radio talks caused more than a million persons to send him messages of congratulation; contributions amounting to perhaps $500,000 a year flooded into his headquarters. Coughlin attacked bankers, New Deal planners, Roosevelt's farm program, and the alleged sympathy of the administration for communism. His program resembled fascism more than any leftist philosophy, but he posed a serious threat, especially in combination with Long, to the continuation of Democratic rule.

Another rapidly growing movement alarmed the Democrats in 1934–35: Dr. Francis E. Townsend's campaign for "Old-Age Revolving Pensions." Townsend, a retired California physician, differed from Long and Coughlin in that he was colorless and low-keyed, the opposite of a demagogue, but like them he had an oversimplified

and thus appealing "solution" to the nation's troubles. He was shocked by the pitiful state of thousands of elderly persons, whose job prospects were even dimmer than those of the mass of the unemployed. "We owe a decent living to the older people," he insisted. He advocated paying every person 60 and over a pension of $200 a month, the only conditions being that the pensioners must give up all gainful employment and spend the entire sum within 30 days. Their purchases, he argued, would stimulate production tremendously, thus creating new jobs and revitalizing the economy. A stiff transactions tax, collected whenever any commodity changed hands, would pay for the program.

Economists quickly pointed out that with about 10 million persons eligible for the Townsend pensions, the cost would amount to $24 billion a year, roughly half the national income; but among the elderly the scheme proved extremely popular. Local Townsend Clubs, their proceedings conducted in the spirit of revivalist camp meetings, flourished everywhere, and the *Townsend National Weekly* soon reached a circulation of over 200,000. Although the Townsendites were anything but radical in point of view, their plan, like Long's Share-Our-Wealth scheme, would have revolutionized the distribution of wealth in the country. On the one hand, they reflected a reactionary spirit like that of religious fundamentalists, on the other, the emergence of a new force in American society. With medical advances rapidly lengthening the average life span, the percentage of old people in the population was rising steadily. The physical demands placed on workers by the pace of modern industry and the breakdown of close family ties in an increasingly mobile society were causing many of these citizens to be cast adrift to live out their last years poor, sick, idle, and alone. Dr. Townsend's simple-minded program focused the attention of the country on a new problem—one it has not yet entirely resolved.

With the possible exception of Long, the extremists had little understanding of practical affairs. (It might almost be said that Townsend knew what to do with money but not how to get

fered horribly from the depression, they gained from New Deal efforts to counteract its effects both some relief and a measure of hope.

Among other important social changes, the TVA and the New Deal rural electrification program made farm life literally more civilized. Urban public housing, while never undertaken on a massive scale, helped rehabilitate some of the nation's worst slums. Government public power projects, such as the giant Bonneville and Grand Coulee dams in the Pacific Northwest, were only the most spectacular parts of a broad New Deal program to develop the natural resources of the country. The NIRA and later labor legislation forced businessmen to re-examine their role in American life and to become far more socially conscious than they had ever been before. The WPA art and theater programs widened the horizons of millions. All in all, the spirit of the New Deal heightened the people's sense of community, revitalized national energies, and stimulated the imagination and creative instincts of countless citizens.

How much of the credit for these achievements belongs personally to Franklin D. Roosevelt is debatable. He had very little to do with many of the details and even with some of the broad principles behind the New Deal. His knowledge of economics was skimpy, his understanding of many social problems superficial, his political philosophy distressingly vague.

Nevertheless, every aspect of the New Deal bears the brand of his remarkable personality. His political genius constructed the coalition that made the program possible, his fundamental humanitarianism made it a reform movement of truly major significance. Although considered by many a terrible administrator because he encouraged rivalry among his subordinates, established countless special agencies often with overlapping responsibilities, failed to discharge many incompetents, and frequently put off making difficult

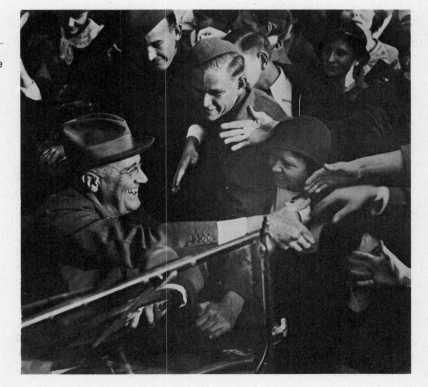

Well-wishers greet the President at Warm Springs, Georgia, in 1933. The Roosevelt "magic," unfeigned and inexhaustible, amazed his associates. "I have never had contact with a man who was loved as he is," reported Secretary of the Interior Harold L. Ickes. (UPI.)

decisions, he was actually one of the most effective Chief Executives in the nation's history. His seemingly haphazard practice of dividing authority among competing administrators unleashed the energies and sparked the imaginations of his aides, giving the ponderous federal bureaucracy a remarkable flexibility and *élan.*

Like Wilson he was almost a prime minister, taking charge of the administration forces in Congress, drafting bills, buttonholing legislators, deluging the lawmakers with special messages. Like Jackson he maximized his role as leader of all the people. No earlier President used the newspapers so effectively in calling attention to his activities. His informal, biweekly press conferences proved a matchless means of keeping the public in touch with developments and himself in tune with popular thinking. He made the radio an instrument for communicating with the masses in the most direct way imaginable: his "fireside chats" convinced millions that he was personally interested in their lives and welfare, as indeed he was. At a time when the increasing size and complexity of the federal government made it impossible for any one person to direct the nation's destiny, Roosevelt managed the minor miracle of personifying that government to 130 million people. "There was a real dialogue between Franklin and the people," Eleanor Roosevelt said after his death, and she did not exaggerate. Under Hoover, a single clerk was able to handle the routine mail that flowed into the office of the President from ordinary citizens. Under Roosevelt, the task required a staff of 50.

While the New Deal was still evolving, contemporaries recognized Roosevelt's right to a place beside Washington, Jefferson, and Lincoln among the great Presidents. The years have not altered their judgment. Yet as his second term drew toward its close, some of his most important work still lay in the future.

Supplementary Reading

The Great Depression and the New Deal are covered briefly but comprehensively in J. D. Hicks, *Re-* *publican Ascendancy°* (1960), and W. E. Leuchtenburg, *Franklin Roosevelt and the New Deal°* (1963). The first three volumes of A. M. Schlesinger, Jr.'s still incomplete *The Age of Roosevelt°* (1957-60) treat the period to 1936 in vivid fashion. L. V. Chandler, *America's Greatest Depression°* (1970), is also important. Both Dixon Wecter, *The Age of the Great Depression* (1948), and F. L. Allen, *Since Yesterday°* (1940), are important for social history, while Broadus Mitchell, *Depression Decade°* (1947), is a good economic history of the period.

For the stock market crash, consult Robert Sobel, *The Great Bull Market: Wall Street in the 1920's°* (1968), which is highly analytical; John Brooks, *Once in Golconda: A True Drama of Wall Street* (1969), a more lively account; and J. K. Galbraith, *The Great Crash°* (1955). The Hoover administration is discussed in H. G. Warren, *Herbert Hoover and the Great Depression°* (1959), in A. U. Romasco, *The Poverty of Abundance* (1965), in R. L. Wilbur and A. M. Hyde, *The Hoover Policies* (1937), and in Herbert Hoover's *Memoirs: The Great Depression* (1951-52). Roger Daniels, *The Bonus March: An Episode of the Great Depression* (1971), is fascinating and insightful. Robert Bendiner, *Just Around the Corner°* (1968), is full of interesting details. Irving Bernstein, *The Lean Years°* (1960) contains an excellent account of the early years of the depression but is too critical of Hoover.

Franklin D. Roosevelt's early career is treated exhaustively in Frank Freidel, *Franklin D. Roosevelt* (1952-73), but see also Bernard Bellush, *Franklin D. Roosevelt as Governor of New York* (1955). Of the many biographies of Roosevelt, see especially J. M. Burns, *Roosevelt: The Lion and the Fox°* (1956), R. G. Tugwell, *The Democratic Roosevelt°* (1957), and John Gunther, *Roosevelt in Retrospect°* (1950). Daniel Fusfeld, *The Economic Thought of Franklin D. Roosevelt and the Origins of the New Deal* (1958) is also important. Richard Hofstadter has interesting essays on Hoover and Roosevelt in *The American Political Tradition°* (1948). On Eleanor Roosevelt, see J. P. Lash, *Eleanor and Franklin* (1971). J. T. Patterson, *Congressional Conservatism and the New Deal°* (1967), is a solid study of congressional politics.

Useful special studies of the New Deal include J. M. Blum, *From the Diaries of Henry Morgenthau, Jr.* (1959-64), Gilbert Fite, *George N. Peek and the*

°Available in paperback.

Fight for Farm Parity (1954), R. S. Kirkendall, *Social Scientists and Farm Politics in the Age of Roosevelt* (1966), D. E. Conrad, *The Forgotten Farmers: The Story of Sharecroppers in the New Deal* (1965), S. F. Charles, *Minister of Relief: Harry Hopkins and the Depression* (1963), E. E. Witte, *The Development of the Social Security Act°* (1962), Roy Lubove, *The Struggle for Social Security* (1968), E. W. Hawley, *The New Deal and the Problem of Monopoly°* (1966), J. D. Matthews, *The Federal Theatre* (1967), Irving Bernstein, *The New Deal Collective Bargaining Policy* (1950) and *Turbulent Years* (1970), and two books by Sidney Fine, *The Automobile Under the Blue Eagle* (1963) and *Sit Down: The General Motors Strike of 1936–1937* (1969). On constitutional questions, see P. L. Murphy, *The Constitution in Crisis Times* (1972).

For the activities of the "radical fringe" consult D. R. McCoy, *Angry Voices: Left-of-Center Politics in the New Deal Era* (1958), and D. H. Bennett, *Demagogues in the Depression: American Radicalism and the Union Party* (1969). On Huey Long, see T. H. Williams, *Huey Long: A Biography* (1969). On blacks during the 1930's, see Raymond Wolters, *Negroes and the Great Depression°* (1970); on women, W. H. Chafe, *The American Woman* (1972).

Of the many published memoirs and diaries of New Deal figures, the following are outstanding: Raymond Moley, *After Seven Years* (1939), Frances Perkins, *The Roosevelt I Knew°* (1946), Eleanor Roosevelt, *This I Remember°* (1949), H. L. Ickes, *The Secret Diary of Harold L. Ickes* (1953–54), Marriner Eccles, *Beckoning Frontiers* (1951), and D. E. Lilienthal, *Journals: The TVA Years: 1939–1945* (1964).

27

Isolationism and War: 1921–1945

Presidents Harding, Coolidge, and Hoover did not handle foreign relations very differently from the way they managed domestic affairs. Harding left policy formulation to his secretary of state, Charles Evans Hughes, and deferred to senatorial prejudice against executive domination in the area. Coolidge adopted a similar course. Hoover understood his diplomatic problems clearly and constructed intelligent plans for dealing with them, but he would not take legitimate risks.

In trying to direct the nation's foreign relations, all three faced the obstacle of a resurgent isolationism. The same forces of war-bred hatred, postwar disillusionment, and fear of communist subversion that produced the Red Scare at home also led Americans to turn their backs on the rest of the world. The bloodiness and apparent senselessness of the long conflict combined with an awareness of the fact that war was the ultimate weapon for settling international controversies convinced millions that the only way to be sure it would not happen again was to "steer clear" of "entanglements." That these famous words had been used by Washington and Jefferson in vastly different contexts did not deter isolationists from attributing to them the same authority they gave to Scripture.

Americans were so suspicious of internationalism in the early twenties that the Harding administration treated the League of Nations with what the diplomatic historian Richard W. Leopold calls "studied hostility." In 1922 the career diplomat Joseph C. Grew, later ambassador to Japan, was stationed in Switzerland. One day, while waiting for a friend outside the League of Nations headquarters in Geneva, he ran into a reporter from the Chicago *Tribune.* Poor Grew felt obliged to explain at length why he was standing in so incriminating a place and to plead with the reporter not to publicize his "indiscretion." For a time, the State Department refused even to answer letters from the League Secretariat in Geneva.

Peace Without a Sword

The Presidents of the twenties did not cease to concern themselves with foreign affairs, but they backed away from responsibility for maintaining world peace and for disabusing the public of its naive belief that foreign affairs did not affect American interests. Too often the Presidents allowed domestic questions to control American relations with the rest of the world. Their interest in disarmament flowed chiefly from their desire to cut taxes. Philippine policy was determined more by the domestic conflict between American sugar growers and American refiners

than by international considerations or the needs of the Filipinos. Tariffs were adjusted to satisfy American manufacturers without regard for their effects on the world political situation.

The first important diplomatic event of the period revealed a great deal about American foreign policy after World War I. In November 1921 delegates representing the United States, Great Britain, Japan, France, Italy, China, and three other nations gathered at Washington to discuss disarmament and the problems of the Far East. By the following February this Washington Armament Conference had drafted three major treaties and a number of lesser agreements. The Four-Power Treaty, signed by the United States, Great Britain, Japan, and France, committed these nations to respect one another's interests in the islands of the Pacific and to confer in the event that any other country launched an attack in this area. The Five-Power Treaty, in which Italy joined these four, committed the signatories to stop building battleships for ten years and to reduce their fleets of capital ships to a fixed ratio, with Great Britain and the United States limited to 525,000 tons, Japan to 315,000 tons, and France and Italy to 175,000 tons. All the conferees signed the Nine-Power Treaty, agreeing to respect China's independence and maintain the Open Door. In a separate pact they permitted China to raise its tariffs on imports.

On the surface the Washington Conference seemed a remarkable achievement, and, indeed, its effects were certainly salutary. For the first time in history, the major powers accepted certain limitations on their right to arm themselves. The Open Door, never before more than a pious expression of American hopes, received the formal endorsement of all nations with far eastern interests except Russia. Japan committed itself to restricting its ambitions in the Pacific area. By taking the lead in drafting the agreements, America regained some of the moral influence it had lost by not joining the League of Nations.

However, these gains masked grave weaknesses both in the treaties themselves and in underlying American attitudes toward world affairs. The treaties were uniformly toothless. The sign-

President-elect and Mrs. Hoover aboard the battleship *Maryland,* 1928. The Washington Armament Conference's halting of battleship construction began the aircraft carrier's rise to capital-ship status. (Underwood and Underwood.)

ers of the Four-Power pact agreed only to consult in case of aggression in the Pacific; they made no promises to help one another or to restrict their freedom of action. As President Harding assured the Senate: "There [was] no commitment to armed force, no alliance, no written or moral obligation to join in defense." The naval disarmament treaty said nothing about the number of other warships that the powers might build, about the far more important question of land and air forces, or about the underlying industrial and financial structures that really controlled the ability of the nations to make war.°

°A second disarmament conference, held at London in 1930, attempted to place limits on smaller warships, but no agreement could be reached.

Nor did any of the imperialist powers that signed the Nine-Power Treaty intend to surrender their special privileges in China.

The United States remained fundamentally irresponsible; Congress failed to provide enough money to maintain the navy even at the limit set by the Five-Power pact. Many Americans were also fundamentally anti-Japanese, as seen in the refusal of Congress to grant *any* immigration quota to Japan under the National Origins Act of 1924, although the formula applied to other nations would have allowed only 100 Japanese a year to enter the country. While stressing the fact that they had won overall naval equality with Great Britain, American diplomats failed to make clear that the 5–5–3 ratio permitted the Japanese to dominate the western Pacific. This ratio left the Philippine Islands undefendable and exposed Hawaii to possible attack. They boasted of having "forced" the powers to "recognize" the Open Door principle in China but remained as unwilling as ever to fight to keep the door open when a more determined nation slammed it shut.

The Americans of the twenties wanted peace, but would neither surrender their prejudices and dislikes nor build the defenses necessary to make it safe to indulge these passions. Nor would they contribute significantly to the building of stable institutions and prosperous economic conditions in other parts of the world. Peace societies flourished: the Carnegie Endowment for International Peace, designed "to hasten the abolition of war, the foulest blot upon our civilization"; the Woodrow Wilson Foundation, aimed at helping "the liberal forces of mankind throughout the world . . . who intend to promote peace by the means of justice"; and many others. In 1923 Edward W. Bok, retired editor of the *Ladies' Home Journal,* offered a prize of $100,000 for the best workable plan for preserving international peace and was flooded with suggestions. But too many lovers of peace were like Senator William E. Borah of Idaho—sincerely opposed to war yet committed to isolationism with equal fervor. When Franklin D. Roosevelt drafted a peace plan for the Bok contest while recovering from his attack of infantile paralysis,° he felt constrained to include in the preamble this statement:

We seek not to become involved as a nation in the purely regional affairs of groups of other nations, nor to give to the representatives of other peoples the right to compel us to enter upon undertakings calling for a leading up to the use of armed force without our full and free consent, given through our constitutional procedure.

So great was the opposition to international cooperation that the United States refused even to accept membership on the World Court, although this tribunal could settle disputes only when all the nations involved agreed. Probably a

°Roosevelt did not submit the plan because his wife Eleanor was named one of the judges.

majority of the American people favored joining the Court, but its advocates were never able to bring enough pressure on Senate isolationists to prevent them from blocking ratification of the necessary treaty. Too many peace lovers believed that their goal could be attained simply by pointing out the moral and practical disadvantages of war. In their opinion, any attempt to discourage aggressors by building up one's own strength seemed more likely to cause trouble than prevent it.

The culmination of this illusory faith in preventing war by criticizing it came with the signing of the Kellogg–Briand Pact in 1928. This treaty was born in the fertile brain of French Foreign Minister Aristide Briand. France, concerned over its future security, was eager to collect allies against possible attack by a resurgent Germany. In 1927 Briand proposed to Secretary of State Frank B. Kellogg that their countries agree never to go to war with each other. Kellogg found the idea as repugnant as any conventional alliance, but American isolationists as well as pacifists found the suggestion fascinating. They plagued Kellogg with demands that he negotiate such a treaty.

To extricate himself from this situation, Kellogg cleverly suggested that the pact be broadened to include *all* nations. Briand was furious. Like Kellogg, he saw how meaningless such a treaty would be, especially when hedged, as Kellogg insisted, with a proviso that "every nation is free at all times . . . to defend its territory from attack and it alone is competent to decide when circumstances require war in self-defense." Nevertheless, Briand also found public pressures irresistible. In August 1928, at Paris, diplomats from 15 nations bestowed upon one another an "international kiss," condemning "recourse to war for the solution of international controversies" and renouncing war "as an instrument of national policy." Seldom has so unrealistic a promise been made by so many intelligent men. Most Americans, however, considered the Kellogg–Briand Pact a milestone in the history of civilization: the Senate, habitually so suspicious of international commitments, ratified it 85 to 1.

The Good Neighbor Policy

Isolationism did not, however, deter the government from seeking to advance American economic interests abroad. The Open Door concept remained predominant; the State Department worked to obtain opportunities for businessmen and investors in underdeveloped countries, hoping both to stimulate the American economy and to bring stability to "backward" nations in the interests of world peace. Although this policy sometimes roused local resentments because of the tendency of the United States to cooperate with conservative forces abroad, it did result in a further retreat from active interventionism.

The pattern is well illustrated by events in Latin America. "Yankeephobia" had long been a chronic condition south of the Rio Grande. The continued presence of marines in Central America fed this bad feeling, as did the failure of the United States to enter the League of Nations, which all but four of the Latin American nations had joined. Basic, of course, was the immense wealth and power of the "Colossus of the North" and the feeling of Latin Americans that the wielders of this strength had little respect for the needs and values of their southern neighbors. However, the evident desire of the United States to limit its international involvements had a gradually mollifying effect on Latin American opinion.

In dealing with this area of the world, Harding and Coolidge performed neither better nor worse than Wilson, while Hoover advanced significantly toward a wiser and more humane position. American interference in Central America declined steadily. In the face of continued radicalism and instability in Mexico, which caused Americans with interests in land and oil rights to suffer heavy losses, President Coolidge acted with forbearance. His appointment of Dwight W. Morrow, a patient, sympathetic, and thoughtful lawyer, as ambassador to Mexico in 1927 resulted in a gradual improvement in Mexican–American relations. The Mexicans were able to complete their social and economic revolution in the twenties without significant interference from the United States.

Under Herbert Hoover, the United States began at last to treat Latin American nations as equals. Hoover reversed Wilson's policy of trying to teach them "to elect good men." The Clark Memorandum (1930), written by Undersecretary of State J. Reuben Clark, disassociated the right of intervention in Latin America from the Roosevelt Corollary. The corollary had been an improper extension of the Monroe Doctrine, Clark declared. The right of the United States to intervene depended rather upon "the doctrine of self-preservation." The distinction seemed slight to Latin Americans, but the underlying reasoning was important. Obviously any nation capable of doing so will intervene in the affairs of another when its own existence is at stake. But the long-established "right" of the United States under the Monroe Doctrine to keep *other* nations out of Latin America as a matter of principle did not give it a similarly broad authority to intervene there itself.

Hoover's policies were taken over and advanced by Franklin Roosevelt. At the Montevideo Pan-American Conference (December 1933) his secretary of state, Cordell Hull, voted in the affirmative on a resolution that "no state has the right to intervene in the internal or external affairs of another," a statement scarcely more meaningful than the Kellogg–Briand denunciation of war, but gratifying to sensitive Latin Americans. By 1934 all the marines had been withdrawn from Nicaragua, the Dominican Republic, and Haiti. Roosevelt also, in 1934, renounced the right to intervene in Cuban affairs, thus abrogating the Platt Amendment to the Cuban constitution.

Beyond doubt the "Good Neighbor Policy" of Hoover and Roosevelt* helped to convince many Latin Americans that the United States had no aggressive intentions south of the Rio Grande. Unfortunately, however, the United States did

---

*Hoover invented this term, but it was typical of the relative political effectiveness of the two Presidents that Roosevelt got most of the credit.

little to try to improve social and economic conditions in the region, so that the underlying jealousy and resentment of "rich Uncle Sam" did not disappear. Although isolationism paid some unearned dividends when applied to a part of the world that posed no possible threat to the United States, the essential blindness of the policy meant the loss of many opportunities to advance the national interest by *helping* other countries.

The Fascist Challenge

The futility and danger of isolationism were glaringly exposed in September 1931, when the Japanese invaded Chinese Manchuria. China had been torn by revolution since 1911; by the twenties the nationalists, led by Chiang Kai-shek, had adopted a policy of driving all "foreign devils" from their country. The western powers, including the United States, offered little resistance to the loss of special privileges in China, but when Chiang attempted to exert full control over Manchuria, which both Japan and Russia considered vital to their interests, he ran into trouble. In 1920 he tried to deprive the Russians of their control of the Chinese Eastern Railway. Russia promptly sent in troops and forced Chiang to back down. Efforts to invoke the new Kellogg–Briand Pact in the conflict demonstrated the ineffectiveness of this agreement, for the Russians insisted they were acting in self-defense and no other power was ready to challenge them. Japan's attack was a far more serious affair, for the Japanese were not satisfied merely to protect rights already held. They speedily overran all Manchuria and converted it into a puppet state called Manchukuo. This clearly violated both the Kellogg–Briand and Nine-Power pacts.

Unable to contain the invaders, China had appealed both to the League of Nations and to the United States for help. Neither would intervene. When the League asked the United States if it would cooperate in any police action—it is far from certain that it would have moved decisively against Japan even if cooperation had been forthcoming—President Hoover refused to consider either economic or military reprisals. When pressed to enforce the Nine-Power and Kellogg–Briand treaties, he replied that these were "solely moral instruments."

Thus Japan was allowed to keep a large and valuable territory that it had seized by force. The League sent a commission to investigate, and Secretary of State Henry L. Stimson, unable to persuade Hoover to take a stronger hand, announced (the Stimson Doctrine) that the United States would never recognize the legality of seizures made in violation of American treaty rights. Unbacked by either force or the support of Great Britain and France, the doctrine served only to irritate the Japanese. In January 1932 they attacked Shanghai, the bloody battle marked by the indiscriminate bombing of residential districts. When the League at last officially condemned their aggressions, they withdrew from the organization, sure that the powers would not back admonitions with action, and extended their control of northern China. The lesson of Manchuria, of course, was not lost upon Adolf Hitler, who became chancellor of Germany on January 30, 1933.

It is easy, in surveying the diplomatic events of 1920–39, to condemn the western democracies for their unwillingness to stand up for principles, their refusal to resist when Germany, Italy, and Japan embarked on the aggressions that led to World War II and cost the world millions of lives and billions of dollars. The democracies failed, until almost too late, to realize that a new ideology, totalitarianism, had arisen in Europe and that unless they resisted it forcefully, it would destroy them.

It is also possible to place some of the blame for the troubles of that era on these same powers: they controlled much of the world's resources and were far more interested in holding on to what they had than in helping other nations to improve the lives of their citizens or in righting international wrongs.

Nevertheless, the new totalitarian states were clearly the aggressors. Their system, involving subordination of the individual to the state and the concentration of political power in the hands of a dictator, was made possible by the industrial revolution, which produced tightly integrated national economies and the instruments of power and communication needed to control closely the actions of masses of people. The social and economic dislocations that followed World War I created the desperate conditions that led millions of Europeans to adopt totalitarian ideas. The doctrine first assumed importance in 1922 in Italy, when Benito Mussolini seized power. Over the next few years Mussolini abolished universal suffrage, crushed every dissenter who dared speak out against him, and established a kind of dictatorial socialism which he called fascism *(fascismo)*, the term referring to the Roman *fasces*, a symbol of governmental authority consisting of a bundle of rods bound around an ax. Mussolini blamed all the ills plaguing the Italian people on foreign sources, a convenient way to avoid the responsibilities that should have accompanied power. Since state control of every aspect of social and economic life characterized his regime, his movement was essentially a violent kind of nationalism, epitomized in the person of the leader *(Il Duce)*.

Mussolini was an absurd poseur and mountebank whose power in world affairs remained relatively slight. Western leaders could perhaps be excused for failing to take him seriously. But the German fascist dictator Hitler presented a threat that the democracies ignored at their peril. Besides ruthlessly persecuting innocent Jews, whom he blamed for all Germany's troubles, Hitler denounced democracy and established a monolithic police state that crushed every form of dissent, every humane value. He announced plainly that he intended to extend his control over all German-speaking peoples. He dismissed the international agreements made by his predecessors with contempt. Germany possessed a potential for war far greater than Italy's, yet to Hitler's cruelest and most flagrantly aggressive actions, the western nations responded only by making concession after concession, in the vain hope of pacifying him.

In a way the democracies failed to resist to-talitarianism because of their very virtues: their faith in man's essential goodness, their willingness to see the other side of complicated questions, their horror of war. Any history of the period that treats the leading figures and their followers as fools or cowards grossly distorts the truth. Nevertheless, an unbiased account must conclude that the western diplomats failed to control events, that they and the citizens of their respective lands should have acted more courageously than they did. This statement applies as fully to the Americans as to the Europeans.

They did not stand together firmly against the aggressors in part because they disagreed among themselves. Particularly divisive was the controversy over war debts—those of Germany to the Allies and those of the Allies to the United States. The United States had lent more than $10 billion to its comrades in arms for munitions and other supplies. Since most of this money had been spent in the United States, it might well have been considered part of America's contribution to the war effort. The public, however, demanded full repayment—with interest. "These were loans, not contributions," the "greatest Secretary of the Treasury since Alexander Hamilton" firmly declared. Even when the Foreign Debt Commission scaled the interest rate down from 5 per cent to about 2 per cent, the total, to be repaid over a period of 62 years, amounted to over $22 billion.

Repayment of such a colossal sum was almost impossible. In the first place, the money had not been put to productive use. Dollars lent to build factories or roads might be expected to earn profits for the borrower, but those devoted to the purchase of shells actually destroyed wealth. Furthermore, the American protective tariff reduced the ability of the Allies to earn the dollars needed to pay the debts.

The Allies tried to load their obligations to the United States, along with all the other costs of the war, upon the backs of the Germans, demanding reparations amounting to $33 billion. If this sum were collected, they declared, they could rebuild their economies and obtain the international exchange needed to pay their debts

A German magazine's bitter 1922 comment on the issue of war reparations. American loans intended to restore the German economy go instead, in the form of reparations, to fatten a militaristic Frenchman. (*Simplicissimus*, June 28, 1922.)

hopes of avoiding their international obligations; the Americans because they refused to recognize the connection between the tariff and the debt question; the Allies because they made little effort to pay even a reasonable proportion of their debts.

In 1924 an international agreement, known as the Dawes Plan, attempted to solve the problem by granting Germany a $200 million loan designed to stabilize its currency. Under this arrangement, Germany agreed to pay about $250 million a year in reparations. In 1929 the Young Plan scaled down the reparations bill to a more reasonable $8 billion. In practice, Allied payments to the United States amounted roughly to the sums actually collected from Germany. Since the money Germany paid during the twenties came largely from private American loans, the United States would have served itself and the rest of the world far better if it had written off the war debts at the start. In any case, when the Great Depression struck, Americans stopped lending money to Germany, Germany defaulted on its reparations payments, and the Allies soon gave up all pretense of meeting their obligations to the United States.

In 1931 President Hoover arranged a one-year moratorium on all international obligations, and when this period of grace expired, the whole question of reparations and debts expired with it—the last token debt payments were made in 1933. All that remained was a heritage of mistrust and hostility, shared by all concerned. In 1934 Congress passed the Johnson Debt Default Act, banning further loans to nations that had not paid their war debts.

Besides putting an end to the debt question, the worldwide depression affected international relations in another way. Faced with declining production and shrinking foreign markets, most of the powers abandoned the gold standard, devaluing their currencies in hopes of increasing their exports. These efforts failed, partly because the nations also raised their tariffs, but mainly because when *everyone* went off the gold standard, the device was self-defeating. Abandoning gold also hampered international commerce,

to the United States. But as John Maynard Keynes had predicted in his *Economic Consequences of the Peace* (1919), Germany could not pay such huge reparations. When Germany defaulted, so did the Allies.

Everyone was bitterly resentful: the Germans because they felt they were being bled white; the Americans, as Senator Hiram Johnson of California put it, because the wily Europeans were treating the United States as "an international sucker"; the Allies because (as the French said) *"l'oncle Shylock"* was demanding his pound of flesh with interest. "If nations were only business firms," Clemenceau wrote Calvin Coolidge in 1926, "bank notes would determine the fate of the world. . . . Come see the endless lists of dead in our villages." Everyone also shared the blame: the Germans because they resorted to a wild inflation that reduced the mark to less than one-*trillionth* of its prewar value, at least in part in since an inconvertible currency was useless outside the nation issuing it. Any country with a favorable balance of trade soon accumulated large amounts of paper money it could not put to productive use.

President Roosevelt took the United States off the gold standard in April 1933. The next month a World Economic Conference met in London. Delegates from 64 nations sought ways to increase world trade, perhaps by a general reduction of tariffs and the stabilization of currencies. After flirting with the idea of currency stabilization, Roosevelt threw a bombshell into the conference by announcing that the United States would not return to the gold standard. Like most world leaders, Roosevelt placed revival of America's own limping economy ahead of general world recovery; his decision further increased international ill-feeling. The London Conference collapsed amid much anti-American recrimination. In every country, narrow-minded nationalists increased their strength. The German financier Hjalmar Schacht announced smugly that Roosevelt was adopting the maxim of the great *Führer*, Adolf Hitler: "Take your economic fate in your own hands."

American Isolationism

Against this background of depression and international tension, vital changes in American foreign policy took place. Unable to persuade the country that positive action against aggressors was necessary, internationalists like Secretary of State Stimson had begun, in 1931, to work for a *discretionary* arms embargo law, to be applied by the President in time of war against whichever side had broken the peace. As early as December 1931, while Japan was overrunning Manchuria, a resolution was introduced in Congress prohibiting the sale of arms to any nation violating the Kellogg–Briand Pact. By early 1933 Stimson had obtained Hoover's backing for an embargo bill, as well as the support of President-elect Roosevelt. The munitions interests managed to

delay this bill; then the isolationists pounced upon it, and in the resulting debate it was amended to make the embargo apply impartially to *all* belligerents. While Roosevelt somewhat inexplicably accepted this change, the internationalists in Congress did not, and when they withdrew their support the measure died.

The amendment would have completely reversed the impact of any embargo. Instead of providing an effective, if essentially negative, weapon for influencing international affairs, a blanket embargo would only intensify America's ostrichlike isolationism. Stimson's original idea would have permitted arms shipments to China but not to Japan, which might have discouraged the Japanese from attacking. As amended, the embargo would have automatically applied to both sides, thus removing the United States as an influence in the conflict.

The attitude of the munitions-makers, who opposed both forms of the embargo, led to a series of studies of the industry. The most important of these was a Senate investigation (1934–36) headed by the isolationist Gerald P. Nye of North Dakota. Nye, a progressive of the La Follette type, was convinced that "the interests" had conspired to drag America into World War I; his investigation was more an inquisition than an honest effort to discover what the bankers and munitions-makers had been doing between 1914 and 1918. His assistants, ferreting into subpoenaed records, uncovered some sensational facts about the lobbying activities and profits of various concerns. The Du Pont company's earnings, for example, had soared from $5 million in 1914 to $82 million in 1916. When one senator suggested to Irénée Du Pont that he was displaying a somewhat different attitude toward war than most citizens, Du Pont replied coolly: "Yes; perhaps. You were not in the game, or you might have a different viewpoint." Munitions-makers had profited far more from neutrality than from participation in the war, but Nye, abetted by the press, exaggerated the significance of his findings. Millions of Americans became convinced that the House of Morgan and the "merchants of death" had tricked the country into war and that the "mistake" of 1917 must never be repeated.

While the Nye committee labored, Walter Millis published *The Road to War: America, 1914-1917* (1935). In this best-seller, Millis advanced the thesis that British propaganda, the heavy purchases of American supplies by the Allies, and Wilson's differing reactions to violations of neutral rights by Germany and Great Britain had drawn the United States into a war it could and should have steered clear of. Thousands found Millis' logic convincing. International lawyers, most notably Charles Warren, a former assistant attorney general, were also beginning to argue at this time that modern warfare had made freedom of the seas for neutrals meaningless. The United States could stay out of future wars, Warren claimed, only by abandoning the seas, clamping an embargo on arms shipments, closing American ports to belligerent vessels, and placing quotas based on prewar sales upon the exportation of all contraband. "Under modern conditions there is no reason why the United States Government should run the risk of becoming involved in a war simply to preserve and protect . . . [the] excessive profits to be made out of war trading by some of its citizens," Warren wrote.

These developments led, in 1935, to what historian Robert A. Divine has called "the triumph of isolation." The danger of a general war mounted steadily, as Germany, Italy, and Japan repeatedly resorted to force to achieve their expansionist aims. In March 1935 Hitler instituted universal military training and began to raise an army of half a million. In May Mussolini massed troops in Italian Somaliland, using a trivial border clash as the pretext for threatening the primitive kingdom of Ethiopia. Each aggression only drove the United States deeper into its shell; Congress responded by passing the Neutrality Act of 1935, which forbade the sale of munitions to *all* belligerents whenever the President should proclaim that a state of war existed. Americans who took passage on belligerent ships after such a proclamation had been issued would do so at their own risk. Roosevelt, reverting to his position at the time of his inauguration, fought hard

for a discretionary embargo, but he dared not risk rousing the ire of the isolationists by vetoing the bill.

In October 1935 Italy invaded Ethiopia, and Roosevelt invoked the new neutrality law. Secretary of State Hull asked American exporters to support a "moral embargo" on the sale of oil and other products not covered by the act, but his plea was ignored. Oil shipments to Italy tripled between October and January. Italy quickly overran and annexed Ethiopia. In February 1936 Congress passed a second neutrality act forbidding all loans to belligerents.

Then, in the summer of 1936, civil war broke out in Spain. The rebels, led by the reactionary General Francisco Franco and strongly backed by Italy and Germany, sought to overthrow the somewhat leftist Spanish Republic. Here, clearly, was a clash between democracy and the new fascism, and the neutrality laws did not apply to civil wars. Roosevelt, however, now became more fearful of involvement than some of the isolationists. (Senator Nye, for example, favored selling arms to the legitimate Spanish government.) The President evidently believed that American interference might cause the conflict in Spain to escalate into a global war, and he was also wary of antagonizing the pro-Franco element in the United States. At his urging, Congress passed another neutrality act broadening the arms embargo to cover civil wars.

Now isolationism reached its peak. A Gallup public-opinion poll revealed in March 1937 that 94 per cent of the people thought that American policy should be directed at keeping out of all foreign wars rather than trying to prevent the wars from breaking out. In April Congress passed still another neutrality law, which continued the embargo on munitions and loans, *forbade* Americans to travel on belligerent ships, and gave the President discretionary authority to place the sale of other goods to belligerents on a cash-and-carry basis. In theory, this would preserve the nation's profitable foreign trade without the risk of war, but in fact it played directly into the hands of the aggressors. While German planes and cannon were turning the tide in Spain, the

University of Chicago undergraduates were photographed as they prepared to march in support of a nationwide antiwar demonstration in April 1937. During the spring of that year American isolationism reached its height. (Wide World.)

United States was denying the hard-pressed Spanish loyalists even a case of cartridges. The blindness of this policy appalled those who recognized the fascist danger. "With every surrender the prospects of a European war grow darker," Claude G. Bowers, the American ambassador to Spain, warned. The New York *Herald Tribune* pointed out that the neutrality legislation was literally reactionary—designed to keep the United States out of the war of 1914-18, not the new conflict looming on the horizon. President Roosevelt, partly because of his own vacillation, seemed to have lost control over the formulation of American foreign policy. The American people, like wild creatures before a forest fire, were rushing in blind panic from the conflagration.

The Road to Pearl Harbor

Yet there were limits beyond which Americans would not go merely to avoid the possibility of war. In July 1937 the Japanese again attacked China. Peiping fell and the invaders pressed ahead on a broad front. Roosevelt felt that by invoking the neutrality law he would be helping the well-armed Japanese. Taking advantage of the fact that neither side had formally declared war, he pursued a waiting policy, allowing the shipment of arms and supplies to both sides. In the last half of 1937 Chinese munitions purchases exceeded $7 million; those of Japan were less than $2 million. The President tried to go still further. Speaking at Chicago in October, he proposed a "quarantine" of nations—he mentioned none by name—who were "creating a state of international anarchy and instability *from which there is no escape through mere isolation or neutrality.*" However, this roused a windy burst of isolationist rhetoric, which forced him to abandon the idea of a quarantine. "It's a terrible thing," he said, "to look over your shoulder when you are trying to lead—and to find no one there."

Roosevelt came only gradually to the conclusion that resisting aggression was more important than keeping out of war, and when he did, the need to keep the country united led him at times to be less than candid in his public statements. Hitler's annexation of Austria in March 1938 caused him deep concern. Then in September Hitler demanded that Czechoslovakia cede the German-speaking Sudetenland region to the Reich. British Prime Minister Neville Chamberlain and French Premier Edouard Daladier, in a fateful conference with Hitler at Munich, yielded to Hitler's threats and promises, and persuaded the Czechs to surrender the Sudetenland. Roosevelt, although he found this example of appeasement disturbing, did not speak out. But when the Nazis seized the rest of Czechoslovakia in March 1939, no one could any longer question the aggressive purposes of Hitler's National Socialist (Nazi) movement. In a memorable address to Congress, Roosevelt said: "Acts of aggression against sister nations . . . automatically undermine all of us." He called for "methods short of war" to demonstrate America's determination to defend its institutions. "God-fearing democracies," he added, "cannot safely be indifferent to international lawlessness anywhere."

When the insatiable Hitler began to threaten Poland in the spring of 1939, demanding the free city of Danzig and the Polish Corridor separating East Prussia from the rest of Germany, and when Mussolini invaded Albania, Roosevelt sent both dictators urgent appeals to keep the peace, but he was no longer an appeaser. He urged Congress to repeal the 1937 Neutrality Act so that the United States could sell arms to Britain and France in the event of war.

Congress refused. "Captain," Vice President Garner told Roosevelt after counting noses in the Senate, "you haven't got the votes," and the President, perhaps unwisely, accepted this judgment and did not press the issue. In August 1939 Germany and Russia signed a "nonaggression" pact, prelude to their joint assault on Poland. On September 1 Hitler's troops invaded Poland, at last provoking Great Britain and France to declare war. Roosevelt immediately summoned Congress into special session and again asked for repeal of the arms embargo. In November, in a vote that followed party lines closely, the Democratic majority pushed through a new neutrality law permitting the sale of arms and other contraband on a cash-and-carry basis. Short-term loans were also authorized, but American vessels were forbidden to carry any products to the belligerents. Since the Allies controlled the seas, cash-and-carry gave them a tremendous advantage.

The German attack on Poland effected a basic change in American thinking. Keeping out of the war remained an almost universal hope, but preventing a Nazi victory became the ultimate, if not always conscious, wish of most citizens. In Roosevelt's case the wish was clearly conscious, although he dared not express it candidly because of continued isolationist strength in Congress and the country. He moved slowly, responding to rather than directing the course of events. But his course was perfectly consistent.

Time quickly proved that cash-and-carry was not enough to stop the Nazis. Poland fell in less than a month; then, after a winter lull that cynics called the "phony war," Hitler loosed his armored divisions against the western powers. Between April 9 and June 22 he taught the world the awful meaning of *Blitzkrieg*—lightning war. Denmark, Norway, the Netherlands, Belgium, and France were successively battered into submission. The British army, pinned against the sea at Dunkirk, saved itself from annihilation only by fleeing across the English Channel. After the French submitted to his harsh terms on June 22, Hitler controlled nearly all of western Europe.

Roosevelt responded to these disasters in a number of ways. In the fall of 1939, reacting to warnings from Albert Einstein and other scientists that the Germans were seeking to develop an atomic bomb, he committed federal funds to a top-secret atomic energy program. Even while the British and French were falling back, he sold them, without legal authority, surplus government arms. When Italy entered the war against France while that nation was reeling before Hitler's panzer divisions, the President cast aside all pretense of impartiality and characterized the invasion as a stab in the back. He also froze the American assets of the conquered nations to keep them out of German hands. During the first five months of 1940 he asked Congress to appropriate over $4 billion for national defense. To strengthen national unity he named Henry L. Stimson secretary of war,[*] and another Republican, Frank Knox, secretary of the navy. The United States, in short, had abandoned neutrality for nonbelligerency.

After the fall of France, Hitler attempted to bomb and starve the British into submission. The great air battles over England during the summer of 1940 ended in a decisive defeat for the Nazis, but the Royal Navy, which had only about 100 destroyers, could not control German submarine attacks on shipping. In this desperate hour, Prime Minister Winston Churchill, who had replaced Chamberlain in May 1940, asked Roosevelt for 50 old American destroyers to fill the gap. The navy had 240 destroyers in commission and more than 50 others on the way. But a direct loan or sale of these vessels would have violated both international and American laws. Any attempt to obtain new legislation would have meant long delay if not defeat. Roosevelt, therefore, arranged to "trade" the destroyers for six British naval bases in the Caribbean. In addition, Great Britain leased bases in Bermuda and Newfoundland to the United States and Churchill also promised that even if the Germans invaded

Great Britain, the British fleet would never be scuttled or surrendered.

This destroyers-for-bases deal was one of Roosevelt's most masterful achievements, both as a statesman and as a politician. It helped save Great Britain, and also circumvented isolationist prejudices, because the President could present it as a shrewd bargain that bolstered America's defenses. A string of island bastions along the Atlantic frontier was surely more valuable to the country than 50 World War I destroyers.

Lines were hardening, all over the world. In September, despite bitter isolationist resistance, Congress enacted the first peacetime draft in American history. Some 1.2 million draftees were summoned for one year of service and 800,000 reservists were called to active duty. That same month, Japan signed a mutual-assistance pact with Germany and Italy directed primarily against the United States. This Rome–Berlin–Tokyo axis fused the conflicts in Europe and Asia, turning the struggle between fascism and democracy into a global war.

In the midst of these events the 1940 Presidential election took place. Why Roosevelt decided to run for a third term is a much-debated question. Partisanship had something to do with it, for no other Democrat seemed so likely to carry the country. Nor would the President have been human had he not been tempted to hold on to power, especially in such critical times. His conviction that no one else could keep a rein on the isolationists was probably decisive. In any case, he used his authority as party chief to control the Democratic convention and was overwhelmingly renominated. Vice President Garner, who had become disenchanted with Roosevelt and the New Deal, did not seek a third term; at Roosevelt's dictation, the party chose Secretary of Agriculture Henry A. Wallace for the second spot on the ticket.

The two leading Republican candidates were Senator Robert A. Taft of Ohio, son of the former President, and District Attorney Thomas E. Dewey of New York, who had won fame as a "racket buster" and political reformer. But Taft was too conservative and lacking in political

[*]Stimson had held this post from 1911 to 1913 in the Taft Cabinet!

glamour, while Dewey, barely 38, seemed too young and inexperienced. Instead, the Republicans nominated the darkest of dark horses, Wendell L. Willkie of Indiana, the utility magnate who had led the fight against the TVA in 1933.

Despite his political inexperience and Wall Street connections, Willkie made an appealing candidate. He was an energetic, charming, open-hearted man capable of inspiring deep loyalties. His roughhewn, rural manner (one Democrat called him "a simple, barefoot Wall Street lawyer") won him wide support in farm districts. He had difficulty, however, finding issues on which to oppose Roosevelt. Good times were at last returning. The New Deal reforms were both too popular and too much in line with his own thinking to invite attack. He believed as strongly as the President that America could no longer ignore the Nazi threat.

In the end Willkie focused his campaign on Roosevelt's conduct of foreign relations. A preponderance of the Democrats favored all-out aid to Britain, while most Republicans still wished to avoid foreign "entanglements." But the crisis was causing many persons to shift sides. Among interventionists, organizations like the Committee to Defend America by Aiding the Allies, headed by Republican William Allen White, and the small but influential Century Group contained important men of both parties. On the other side, the America First Committee, led by Robert E. Wood of Sears Roebuck, included Democrats as well as Republicans in its ranks. Unwilling to take an isolationist position, Willkie argued that Roosevelt intended to make the United States a direct participant in the war. "If you re-elect him," he told one audience, "you may expect war in April, 1941," to which Roosevelt retorted, disingenuously since he knew he was not a free agent in the situation, "I have said this before, but I shall say it again and again and again: Your boys are not going to be sent into any foreign wars." In November Roosevelt carried the country handily, although by a smaller majority than in 1932 or 1936. The popular vote was 27 million to 22 million, the electoral count 449 to 82.

While the election by no means ended the debate over foreign policy, it indicated the direction in which the nation was moving and encouraged Roosevelt to act more boldly against the Axis powers. When Churchill informed him that the cash-and-carry system would no longer suffice because Great Britain was rapidly exhausting its financial resources, he decided at once to provide the British with whatever they needed. Instead of proposing to lend them money, a step sure to rouse memories of the vexatious war debt controversies of the twenties, he devised the "lend-lease" program, one of his most ingenious and imaginative creations.

First he spoke directly to the people in a "fireside chat," stressing the evil intentions of the Nazis and the dangers that their triumph would create for America. Aiding Britain should be looked at simply as part of the general defense effort. "As planes and ships and guns and shells are produced," he said, American defense experts would decide "how much shall be sent abroad and how much shall remain at home." When this talk provoked a favorable public response, Roosevelt went to Congress in January 1941 with a plan calling for the expenditure of $7 billion for war materials that the President could sell, lend, lease, exchange, or transfer to any country whose defense he deemed vital to that of the United States. After two months of debate, Congress gave him what he had asked for.

Although the wording of the Lend-Lease Act obscured its immediate purpose, the saving of Great Britain, the President was frank in explaining his plan to the public. He did not minimize the risks involved nor repeat his campaign promise not to send American boys into "foreign" wars. Yet his mastery of practical politics was never more in evidence. To counter Irish-American prejudices against the English, he pointed out that the Irish Republic would surely fall under Nazi domination if Hitler won the war. He also coupled his demand for heavy military expenditures with his enunciation of the idealistic "Four Freedoms"—freedom of speech, freedom of religion, freedom from want, and freedom from fear—for which, he said, the war was being fought.

A cartoon of August 1941 reflects the growing shift away from isolationism. Montana Senator Burton K. Wheeler and the famous aviator Charles A. Lindbergh join an America Firster in "Appeasing a Polecat." (Franklin D. Roosevelt Library.)

After the enactment of lend-lease, aid short of war was no longer seriously debated. The American navy rapidly expanded its operations in the North Atlantic, shadowing German submarines and radioing their locations to Allied warships and planes. In April 1941 United States forces occupied Greenland; in May the President declared a state of unlimited national emergency. When Hitler invaded the Soviet Union in June, Roosevelt moved slowly, for anti-Russian feeling in the United States was intense,° but it was obviously to the nation's advantage to help anyone who was resisting Hitler's armies. In November $1 billion in lend-lease aid was put at the disposal of the Russians.

°During the 1930's Russia took a far firmer stand against the fascists than any other power, but after joining Hitler in swallowing up Poland, it also attacked and defeated Finland during the winter of 1939–40 and annexed the Baltic states. These cynical acts practically destroyed the small communist movement in the United States and caused much indignation in liberal as well as conservative circles.

Meanwhile, Iceland was occupied in July 1941, and the draft law was extended in August—by the margin of a single vote in the House of Representatives. In September the German submarine *U-652* attacked the destroyer *Greer* in the North Atlantic. The *Greer* had provoked the attack by tracking the *U-652* and flashing its position to a British plane, which had dropped depth charges in the area. However, Roosevelt (no action has provided more ammunition for his critics) announced that the *Greer* had been innocently "carrying mail to Iceland." He used the incident as an excuse to order the navy to "shoot on sight" any German craft in the waters south and west of Iceland and to convoy merchant vessels as far as that island. After the sinking of the destroyer *Reuben James* on October 30, Congress voted to allow the arming of American merchantmen and to permit them to carry cargoes to Allied ports.

By December 1941 the United States was actually at war, but it is hard to see how a formal declaration could have come about or how American soldiers could have been committed to the fray had it not been for Japan. Japanese-American relations had worsened steadily after Japan resumed its war against China in 1937. As they extended their control over ever larger areas of Chiang Kai-shek's domain, the invaders systematically froze out American and other foreign business interests, declaring that the Open Door policy was obsolete. Roosevelt, already shocked by Japan's cold-blooded expansionism, retaliated by lending money to Chiang's government and by asking American manufacturers not to sell airplanes to Japan. In July 1940, with Japanese troops threatening French Indochina, Congress placed exports of aviation gasoline and certain types of scrap iron to Japan under a licensing system; in September all sales of scrap were banned and loans to China increased. After the creation of the Rome–Berlin–Tokyo axis in September 1940, Roosevelt extended the embargo to include machine tools and several other items, but the Japanese, determined to create what they euphemistically called a Greater East Asia Co-Prosperity Sphere, pushed ahead relentlessly despite these economic pressures.

Neither the United States nor Japan wished to fight with the other. In the spring of 1941 Secretary of State Cordell Hull began a long series of talks in Washington with the Japanese ambassador, Kichisaburo Nomura, in an effort to resolve their differences. Hull's approach, while morally sound, showed little appreciation of the political and military situation in the Far East. He demanded that Japan withdraw from China and pledge not to attack the Dutch and French colonies in southeast Asia, ripe for the plucking after Hitler's victories in Europe. The Japanese had no moral right to their conquests, but how Hull expected to get them to give them up without either making concessions or going to war is not clear. He refused to recognize that the old balance of power that had enabled the United States to attain its modest objectives in the Far East without the use of force had ceased to exist.

Japan might well have accepted a limited victory in the area in return for the removal of American trade restrictions, but Hull, confident of his moral position, insisted upon total withdrawal. He seemed bent on converting the Japanese to pacifism by exhortation. Even the moderates in Japan rejected this solution to the problem. When Hitler invaded the Soviet Union, thus removing the threat of Russian intervention in the Far East, Japan decided to occupy Indochina even at the risk of war with America. Roosevelt retaliated (July 1941) by freezing Japanese assets in the United States and clamping a total embargo on oil.

Now the war party in Japan assumed control. Nomura was instructed to tell Hull that his country would refrain from further expansion if the United States and Great Britain would cut off all aid to China and lift the economic blockade. Japan also promised to pull out of Indochina once "a just peace" had been established with China. When the United States rejected these demands and repeated (November 26) its insistence that Japan "withdraw all military, naval, air, and police forces" from China and Indochina, the Japanese prepared to assault the Dutch East Indies, British Malaya, and also the Philippines. To immobilize the United States Pacific Fleet, they planned a surprise aerial raid on the great Hawaiian naval base at Pearl Harbor.

An American cryptanalyst, Colonel William F. Friedman, had "cracked" the Japanese diplomatic code and the government therefore knew that war was imminent. As early as November 27 Hull warned an American general: "Those fellows mean to fight and you will have to watch out." The code-breakers had also made it possible to keep close tabs on the movements of Japanese navy units. But in the hectic rush of events both the military and civilian authorities failed to make effective use of the information collected. They expected the blow to fall somewhere in southeast Asia, possibly in the Philippines.

The garrison at Pearl Harbor was alerted against "a surprise aggressive move in any direction," but the commanders there, Admiral Husband E. Kimmel and General Walter C. Short, believed an attack impossible and took precautions only against Japanese sabotage. Thus when

The American battleships at Pearl Harbor were sitting ducks for Japanese bombers on December 7. A picture taken three days later shows (from left) the damaged *Maryland* inboard of the capsized *Oklahoma*; the *West Virginia*, hit by six torpedoes, awash next to the *Tennessee*; and the shattered *Arizona*, on which 1,100 seamen died. (Navy Department, National Archives.)

planes from Japanese aircraft carriers swooped down upon Pearl Harbor on the morning of December 7, they found easy targets. In less than two hours they reduced the Pacific Fleet to a flaming ruin: two battleships destroyed, six others heavily battered, nearly a dozen lesser vessels put out of action. More than 150 planes were wrecked, over 2,300 servicemen killed and 1,100 wounded.

Never had American arms suffered a more devastating or shameful defeat, and seldom has an event roused so much controversy or produced such intensive historical study. The official blame was placed chiefly on Admiral Kimmel and General Short, but while they might well have been more alert, it is clear that responsibil-

ity for the disaster was widespread. Military and civilian officials in Washington failed to pass on all that they knew to Hawaii or even to each other. Moreover, the crucial intelligence that the code-breakers provided, easy to isolate in retrospect, was mixed in with huge masses of other information and thus extremely difficult to evaluate at the moment. Perhaps, instead of seeking to find a scapegoat, we should admit that the Japanese attack, while immoral, was both daring and brilliantly executed.

In any case, the next day Congress declared war on Japan. Formal war with Germany and Italy was still not inevitable, for isolationists were far more ready to resist the "yellow peril" in the Orient than to fight in Europe. The Axis powers, however, honored their treaty obligations to Japan and on December 11 declared war on the United States. America was now fully engaged in the great conflict.

Mobilizing the Home Front

Entry into the war put immense strains on the American economy and produced immense results. About 15 million men and women entered the armed services; they, and in part the millions more in Allied uniforms, had to be fed, clothed, housed, and supplied with equipment ranging from typewriters and paper clips to rifles and grenades, tanks and airplanes, and (eventually) atomic bombs. As in every national crisis, Congress granted wide emergency powers to the President. It also, in this instance, refrained from excessive meddling in administrative problems and in military strategy. However, although the Democrats retained control of both houses throughout the war, their margins were relatively narrow. A coalition of conservatives in both parties frequently prevented the President from having his way and exercised close control over all government spending.

Roosevelt was an imaginative and inspiring war leader but not a very good administrator. Any honest account of the war on the home front must reveal glaring examples of confusion, inefficiency, and pointless bickering. The squabbling and waste characteristic of the early New Deal period made relatively little difference—what mattered then was raising the nation's spirits and keeping men occupied; efficiency was less than essential, however desirable. In wartime, however, the nation's fate, perhaps that of the whole free world, depended on the volume of weapons and supplies delivered to the battle fronts.

Yet the confusion attending economic mobilization can easily be overstressed. Nearly all Roosevelt's basic decisions were wise and humane: to pay a large part of the cost of the war by collecting taxes rather than by borrowing and to base

taxation on the individual citizen's ability to pay; to ration scarce raw materials and consumer goods; to regulate prices and wages. If these decisions were not always translated into action with perfect effectiveness, they always operated in the direction of efficiency and the public good. Furthermore, what happened in Washington, while important, had less to do with war production than what happened in the factories and in the fields. Roosevelt's greatest accomplishment was his inspiring of businessmen, workers, and farmers with a sense of national purpose. In this respect his function exactly duplicated his earlier role in fighting the depression, and he performed it with even greater success.

A sense of the tremendous economic expansion caused by the demands of war can most easily be captured by reference to official statistics of production. The gross national product of the United States in 1939 was valued at $91.3 billion. In 1945, after allowing for changes in the price level, it was $166.6 billion. More specifically, manufacturing output nearly doubled, agricultural output rose 22 per cent. In 1939 the United States turned out fewer than 6,000 airplanes, in 1944 more than 96,000. Shipyards produced 237,000 tons of vessels in 1939, 10 million tons in 1943. The index of iron and steel production leaped from 87 in 1938 to 258 in 1944, of rubber goods from 113 to 238 in the same years. Raw materials were produced in equal profusion. Petroleum output rose from 1.2 billion barrels in 1939 to 1.7 billion in 1945, iron ore from 28 million tons in 1938 to 105 million in 1942, copper from 562,000 tons in 1938 to over 1 million in 1942, aluminum from 286 million pounds in 1938 to 1 billion in 1942 and 1.8 billion in 1943.

Wartime experience proved how shrewd had been the insights of the Keynesian economists, how vital the role of government spending in sparking economic growth. About 8 million persons were unemployed in June 1940. After Pearl Harbor, unemployment declined swiftly and by 1945 the *civilian* work force had increased by nearly 7 million more. Millions of women flocked into the new defense industries, a trend memorialized in the popular song, "Rosie the Riveter."

The women welders photographed in 1943 by Margaret Bourke-White of *Life,* work on an aircraft carrier. (Life, © 1943 Time, Inc.)

The task of mobilization had begun well before December 1941. At that time, 1.6 million men were already under arms. Economic mobilization got under way in August 1939, when the President created a War Resources Board to plan for possible conversion of industry to war production. This board became the Office of Production Management (January 1941) under William S. Knudsen, president of General Motors. As early as June 1940 scientific research planning was put under the control of a National Defense Research Committee (later the Office of Scientific Research and Development) headed by Dr. Vannevar Bush of the Carnegie Institution. In April 1941 Roosevelt set up an Office of Price Administration (OPA), headed by the economist Leon Henderson, in an attempt to check profiteering and control consumer prices, and in August a Supplies Priorities and Allocation Board, directed by Donald M. Nelson of Sears Roebuck,

to coordinate the requests for scarce materials of American and Allied military purchasers with those of industry.

With the exception of scientific planning, these prewar efforts worked poorly, mainly because the President refused to centralize authority and to accept the need for fundamental changes in the structure of the economy. The separation of responsibility for dispensing materials from the control of the prices paid for materials, for example, practically hamstrung both Nelson's and Henderson's organizations. Throughout this period, and for months after Pearl Harbor, these civilian boards had to battle constantly with the military over everything from the allocation of scarce raw materials to the technical specifications of weapons. Roosevelt refused to settle these conflicts as only he could have.

Yet long before the formal outbreak of hostilities the concept of economic planning and control had been firmly established, and by early 1943 the nation's economic machinery had been converted to a wartime footing and was functioning smoothly. Supreme Court Justice James F. Byrnes, a former senator from South Carolina, resigned from the Court to become a sort of "economic czar." His Office of War Mobilization had complete control over the issuance of priorities and also over prices. Strict regulation of rents, food prices, and wages had been put into effect, and items in short supply were being rationed to consumers. While wages and prices had soared during 1942, after April 1943 they leveled off. Thereafter the cost of living scarcely changed at all until controls were lifted after the war.

Expanded industrial production together with the military draft produced a labor shortage which greatly increased the bargaining power of workers. On the other hand, the national emergency required placing some limitation on the workers' right to exercise this power. As early as March 1941 Roosevelt appointed a National Defense Mediation Board to assist labor and management in avoiding work stoppages. After Pearl Harbor he created a National War Labor Board to arbitrate disputes and "stabilize" wage rates and banned all changes in wages without NWLB approval. In the "Little Steel" case (July 1942), the NWLB laid down the principle that wage increases should not normally exceed 15 per cent of the rates of January 1941, a figure roughly in line with the increase in the cost of living since that date.

Prosperity and stiffer government controls added significantly to the strength of organized labor. The last bastions of industrial resistance to collective bargaining crumbled, and as workers began to see the material benefits of union membership at every turn, they flocked into the organizations. Strikes declined sharply at first: 23 million man-hours had been lost in 1941 because of strikes; only 4.18 million were lost in 1942. However, some crippling work stoppages did occur. In May 1943 the government was forced to seize the coal mines when John L. Lewis' United Mine Workers walked out of the pits. This strike led

Congress to pass, over Roosevelt's veto, the Smith-Connally War Labor Disputes Act (June 1943), which gave the President the power to take over any war plant threatened by a strike. The act also declared strikes against seized plants illegal and imposed stiff penalties on violators. Although strikes continued to occur—the man-hour loss zoomed to 38 million in 1945—when Roosevelt asked for a labor draft law, Congress refused to go along.

Generally speaking, however, labor-management relations during the war were harmonious, and wages and prices remained in fair balance. Overtime work fattened pay checks and a new stress in labor contracts on fringe benefits such as paid vacations, premium pay for night work, and various forms of employer-subsidized health insurance added to the prosperity of labor.

The war effort had almost no adverse effect on the standard of living of the average citizen, a vivid demonstration of the productivity of the American economy. The manufacture of automobiles ceased and pleasure driving became next to impossible because of gasoline rationing, but most ordinary civilian activities went on much as they had before Pearl Harbor. Because of the need to conserve cloth, cuffs disappeared from men's trousers, and the vest passed out of style. Plastics replaced metals in toys, containers, and various other items. Although many items such as meat, sugar, and shoes were rationed, they were doled out in amounts adequate for the needs of most persons. Americans had both guns *and* butter; belt-tightening of the type experienced by the other belligerents was unheard of.

The federal government spent twice as much money between 1941 and 1945 as in its entire previous history. This unprecedented expense made heavy borrowing necessary. The national debt, which stood at less than $49 billion in 1941, increased by more than that amount *each year* between 1942 and 1945 and totaled nearly $260 billion when the war ended. Roosevelt, however, insisted that as much of the cost as possible be paid for at the time: over 40 per cent of the total was met by taxation, a far larger proportion than in any earlier war. This policy helped to check inflation by siphoning off money that would otherwise have competed for scarce consumer goods. Heavy excise taxes on amusements and luxuries further discouraged spending, as did the government's war-bond campaigns, which persuaded patriotic citizens to lend part of their income to Uncle Sam. The tax program also helped to maintain public morale. High taxes on incomes (up to 94 per cent), on corporation profits (up to 40 per cent), and on excess profits (95 per cent), together with a limit of $25,000 a year after taxes on salaries, convinced the people that no one was profiting inordinately from the war effort.

Furthermore, the income tax, which had never before touched the mass of white-collar and industrial workers, was extended downward to cover nearly everyone. To collect efficiently the relatively small sums paid by most persons, Congress adopted the payroll-deduction system proposed by Beardsley Ruml, chairman of the Federal Reserve Bank of New York, whereby employers withheld the taxes of wage earners and salaried personnel and paid them directly to the government.

The steeply graduated tax system combined with a general increase in the income of workers and farmers effected a substantial shift in the distribution of wealth in the United States. The poor got richer, while the rich, if not actually poorer, collected a smaller proportion of the national income. The wealthiest 1 per cent of the population had received 13.4 per cent of the national income in 1935 and 11.5 per cent as late as 1941. In 1944 this group received only 6.7 per cent.

Enormous social effects stemmed from this shift, but World War II altered the patterns of American life in so many ways that it would be wrong to ascribe the transformations to any single source. Never was the population more fluid. The millions who put on uniforms found themselves transported first to training camps in every section of the country and then to battlefields scattered from Europe and Africa to the far reaches of the Pacific. Burgeoning new defense plants drew other millions to places like Hanford, Washington, and Oak Ridge, Tennessee,

where great atomic energy installations were constructed, and to the aircraft factories of California and other states. As in earlier periods the trend was from east to west, from south to north, and from countryside to the cities. The population of California increased by more than 50 per cent in the forties, that of other far-western states almost as much. New England, the South (except for Florida and Texas), and the plains states either grew more slowly than the national average or in some cases, such as Mississippi, Arkansas, and North Dakota, declined in population.

The war also affected blacks in many ways. Several factors operated to improve their lot. One was the reaction of Americans to Hitler's senseless murder of millions of Jews, an outgrowth of his doctrine of Aryan superiority, which compelled many Americans to re-examine their own views about race. If the nation expected Negroes to risk their lives for the common good, how could it continue to treat them as second-class citizens? Black leaders did not hesitate to point out the inconsistency between fighting for democracy abroad while ignoring it at home. "We want democracy in Alabama," the NAACP announced, and this argument, too, had some effect on white thinking.

Negroes in the armed forces were treated somewhat better than in World War I. Although segregation in the military continued, blacks were enlisted for the first time in the air force and the marines, and permitted to hold more responsible positions in the army and navy. The army commissioned its first Negro general. Some 600 Negro pilots won their wings. Altogether about a million served, about half of these overseas, and the extensive and honorable performance of many of these Negro units could not be ignored by the white majority.

Economic realities operated even more importantly to the Negro's advantage. More blacks had been unemployed in proportion to their numbers than any other group; now the manpower shortage brought employment for all. The CIO industrial unions continued to enroll blacks by the thousands.

War-related gains, however, failed to satisfy

most Negro leaders. The NAACP, which increased its membership from 50,000 in 1940 to almost 405,000 in 1946, adopted a more militant stand than in World War I. Discrimination in defense plants seemed far less tolerable than it had in 1917–18. Even before Pearl Harbor, A. Philip Randolph, president of the Brotherhood of Sleeping Car Porters, organized a massive march of blacks on Washington to demand equal opportunity for black workers. To prevent this march from taking place at a time of national crisis, President Roosevelt agreed to issue an order prohibiting discrimination in plants with defense contracts, and he set up a Fair Employment Practices Committee to see that the order was carried out. Executive Order 8802 was not perfectly enforced, but it opened up better jobs to black workers and led many employers to change their hiring practices.

Prejudice and the mistreatment of Negroes did not cease. Race riots erupted in many cities, black soldiers were often provided with inferior recreational facilities and otherwise discriminated against in and around army camps. Negro blood plasma was kept separate from white, even though the two "varieties" were indistinguishable and the process of storing plasma had been devised by a Negro, Dr. Charles Drew. Blacks, therefore, became increasingly embittered. Roy Wilkins, head of the NAACP, put it this way as early as 1942: "No Negro leader with a constituency can face his members today and ask full support for the war in the light of the atmosphere the government has created." Many black newspaper editors were so critical of the administration that conservatives began to demand that they be indicted for sedition.

Roosevelt would have none of this, but the militants annoyed him; he felt that they should hold their demands in abeyance until the war had been won. He apparently failed to realize the depth of black anger, and in this he was no different from the majority of whites. A revolution was in the making, yet in 1942 a poll revealed that six out of ten whites still believed that black Americans were "satisfied" with their place in society.

Although World War II affected the American people far more drastically than World War I, it produced much less intolerance and fewer examples of the repression of individual freedom of opinion. Perhaps this reflected the soberer, less emotional reaction of the nation to this war than to the war of 1914–18. The people seemed able to distinguish between the Nazis and Americans of German descent in a way that had escaped their fathers. The fact that nearly all German-Americans were vigorously anti-Nazi helps explain this, but the underlying public attitude was even more important. Americans went to war in 1941 without illusions and without enthusiasm, determined to win but expecting only to preserve what they had. They therefore found it easier to tolerate dissent, to view the dangers they faced realistically, and to concentrate on the real foreign enemy without venting their feelings on domestic scapegoats. The nation's 100,000 conscientious objectors met with little hostility. The only flagrant example of intolerance was the deportation of the West Coast Japanese to internment camps in the interior of the country. About 110,000 Americans of Japanese ancestry were rounded up, simply because of a totally unjustified fear that they might be disloyal. The Supreme Court, generally vigilant in the protection of civil liberties, upheld this action in the case of *Korematsu v. U. S.* (1944), but in *Ex parte Endo,* it forbade the internment of Japanese-American *citizens,* that is, of the *Nisei,* the Japanese who had been born in the United States.

Other social changes that occurred during the war included a sharp increase in marriage and birthrates, a response both to prosperity and to the natural desire of young men going off to risk death in distant lands to establish roots before departing. The population of the United States had increased by only 3 million during the depression decade of the thirties; during the next five years it rose by 6.5 million. However, large numbers of hasty marriages followed by long periods of separation also produced a great acceleration of the national divorce rate, from about 170 per thousand marriages in 1941 to 310 per thousand in 1945.

The War in Europe

Within days after Pearl Harbor, Prime Minister Churchill and his military chiefs were meeting in Washington with Roosevelt and his advisers to plan the strategy of the Grand Coalition against the Axis. In every quarter of the globe, disaster threatened. The Japanese were gobbling up the Far East for their Greater East Asia Co-Prosperity Sphere. The Philippines, Guam, Wake, Hong Kong, Malaya, Burma, the Dutch Indies, the Solomon Islands, and northern New Guinea were all in Japanese hands by April 1942. In Russia, Hitler's armies, checked outside Leningrad and Moscow, were preparing a massive attack in the south, directed at Stalingrad, on the Volga River. German divisions in Africa, under General Erwin Rommel, were beginning a drive toward the Suez Canal. U-boats were taking a heavy toll in the North Atlantic. British and American leaders believed that eventually they could muster enough force to smash their enemies, but whether or not the troops already in action could hold out until this force arrived was an open question.

The decision of the strategists was to concentrate first against the Germans. Japan's conquests were in remote and, from the Allied point of view, relatively unimportant regions. On the other hand, if Russia surrendered or if Rommel cut the Suez life line, Hitler might well be able to invade Great Britain, thus making his position in Europe impregnable by depriving the United States of a base for any counterattack. But how to strike at Hitler? American leaders wanted to aim directly at establishing a second front in France, and the harried Russians backed them up. The British, however, felt that this would require more power than the Allies could presently command and advocated instead air bombardment of German industry combined with small-scale, peripheral attacks by land forces to harass the enemy while armies and supplies were being massed. Later events proved the soundness of the British position, for when the invasion of France did come against a greatly weakened

Germany in 1944, the difficulties were still enormous. A major landing in 1942 would almost certainly have been repulsed.

During the summer of 1942 Allied planes began to hit at German cities. In a rising crescendo throughout 1943 and 1944, British and American bombers pulverized the centers of Nazi might. While air attacks did not destroy the German armies' capacity to fight, they hampered war production, tangled communications, and brought the war home to the German people in awesome fashion. Humanitarians deplored the heavy loss of life among the civilian population, but the response of the realists was that Hitler had begun indiscriminate bombing, and Allied survival depended upon smashing the German war machine.

In November 1942 an Allied army commanded by General Dwight D. Eisenhower struck at French North Africa. After the fall of France, the Nazis had set up a puppet regime in those parts of France not occupied by their troops, headed by the octogenarian French World War I hero Marshal Henri-Philippe Pétain, with headquarters at Vichy. This collaborationist Vichy government controlled French North Africa. But the local commandant, Admiral Jean Darlan, promptly switched sides when Eisenhower's forces landed. After a brief show of resistance, the French surrendered. The Allies were willing to do business with Darlan despite his record as a collaborationist. This angered General Charles de Gaulle, who had organized a government-in-exile immediately after the collapse of France and who considered himself the true representative of the French people. Many liberals in the United States agreed with de Gaulle and denounced the "deal" with Darlan. Darlan was assassinated in December, and eventually the Free French obtained control of North Africa, but the Allied attitude had much to do with de Gaulle's postwar suspicion of both Britain and the United States.

In 1942, however, the arrangement with Darlan paid large dividends. Eisenhower was able to press forward quickly against the Germans. In February 1943 at Kasserine Pass in the desert

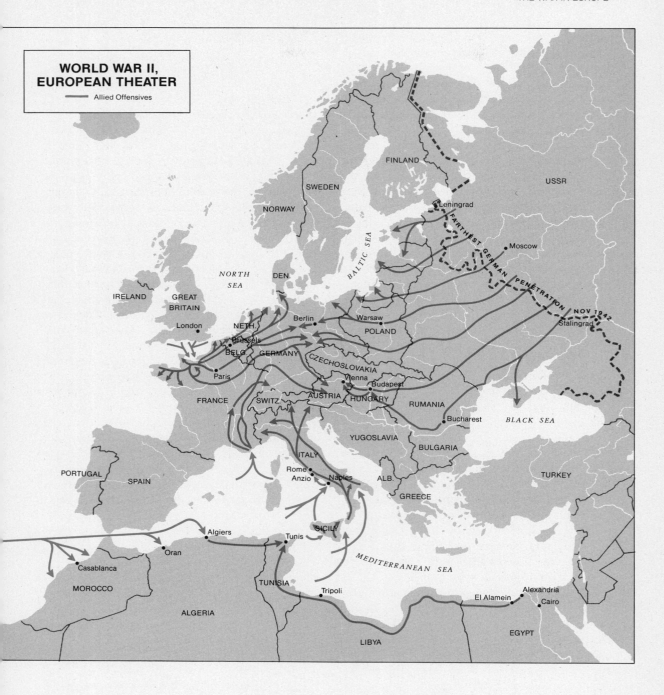

WORLD WAR II,
EUROPEAN THEATER
———— Allied Offensives

south of Tunis, American tanks met Rommel's *Afrika Korps.* This battle ended in a stand-off, but with British troops closing in from their Egyptian bases to the east, the Germans were soon trapped and crushed. In May, after Rommel had been recalled to Germany, his army surrendered.

In July 1943, while air attacks on Germany continued and the Russians slowly pushed the Germans back from the gates of Stalingrad, the Allies invaded Sicily from Africa. Then in September they advanced to the Italian mainland. Mussolini had already fallen from power (eight months later he was caught and killed by Italian partisans) and his successor, Marshal Pietro Badoglio, surrendered. However, the Germans seized control and threw up an almost impregnable defense across the rugged Italian peninsula. The Anglo-American army inched forward, paying heavily for every advance. Monte Cassino, halfway between Naples and Rome, did not fall until May 1944, the capital itself until June; months of bitter fighting still remained before the country was cleared of Germans. The Italian campaign was an Allied disappointment, although it did further weaken the enemy.

By the time the Allies had taken Rome, the mighty army needed to invade France had been collected in England under Eisenhower's command. On D-Day, June 6, supported by a great armada and thousands of planes and paratroops, the assault forces stormed ashore at five points along the coast of Normandy. Against fierce but ill-coordinated German resistance, they established a solid beachhead: within a few weeks a million Allied troops were on French soil. Thereafter, victory was certain, although nearly a year of hard fighting still lay ahead. In August the American Third Army under General George S. Patton, an eccentric, ruthless, but brilliant field commander, erupted southward into Brittany and then veered east toward Paris. Another Allied army invaded France from the Mediterranean in mid-August and drove rapidly north. Free French troops were given the honor of liberating Paris on August 25, Belgium was cleared by British and Canadian units a few days later,

and by mid-September the Allies were fighting on the edge of Germany itself.

The front now stretched from the Netherlands along the borders of Belgium, Luxembourg, and France all the way to Switzerland. If the Allies had mounted a massive assault at any one point, as the British commander, Field Marshal Bernard Montgomery, urged, the struggle might have been brought to a quick conclusion. Although the two armies were roughly equal in size, the Allies had complete control of the air and 20 times as many tanks as the foe. The pressure of the advancing Russians on the eastern front made it very difficult for the Germans to reinforce their troops in the west. General Siegfried Westphal, chief of staff to the German commander in the west, later claimed that the Allies could have broken through at almost any point at this time. But General Eisenhower believed a concentrated attack too risky. His supply and communications problems were fantastically complex and the defenses of Hitler's Siegfried Line, in some regions three miles deep, presented a formidable obstacle. He prepared instead for a general advance.

While he was regrouping, however, the Germans, on December 16, launched a counterattack, planned by Hitler himself, against the Allied center in the Ardennes Forest. The Germans hoped to break through to the Belgian port of Antwerp, thus splitting the Allied armies in two. The plan was foolhardy, but therefore unexpected, and it almost succeeded. On December 20 the Germans surrounded the key communications center of Bastogne. When a party under a flag of truce demanded its surrender, the American commander, General Anthony C. McAuliffe, replied "Nuts!" The Germans expressed puzzlement over the meaning of this cryptic colloquialism, so one of McAuliffe's aides added: "If you don't understand what 'Nuts!' means, in plain English it is the same as 'Go to hell!'"

The Germans pressed ahead without capturing Bastogne, extending their salient about 50 miles into Belgium, but once the element of surprise had been overcome, their hopes of breaking through to the sea were destroyed. Eisen-

Bill Mauldin's long-suffering Willie and Joe (above) discover their enemies will stop at nothing: ''Them rats! Them dirty cold-blooded, sore-headed, stinkin' Huns! Them atrocity-committin' skunks!'' Below, GI's counterattack during the Battle of the Bulge. (Bill Mauldin, *Up Front,* 1945, and Signal Corps.)

hower concentrated first on preventing them from broadening the break in his lines and then on blunting the point of their advance. On Christmas Day the drive was stopped a few miles from the Meuse River near Dinant. By late January 1945 the old line had been re-established. This "Battle of the Bulge" cost the United States 77,000 casualties and delayed Eisenhower's planned offensive, but it also destroyed the Germans' last reserves.

Quickly the Allies then pressed forward to the Rhine, winning a bridgehead on the right bank of the river across from Remagen on March 7. Thereafter, some German city fell almost daily. With the Russians racing westward against crumbling resistance, the end could not be long delayed. In April American and Russian forces made contact at the Elbe River. A few days later, with Russian shells reducing his capital to rubble, Hitler, by then insane, took his own life in his luxurious Berlin air raid shelter. On May 8 Germany officially surrendered.

The War in the Pacific

Defeating Germany first had not meant abandoning the Pacific region entirely to the Japanese; while armies were being trained and materiel accumulated for the attack on Hitler, much of the already available American strength was diverted to the task of maintaining vital communications in the Far East and checking further Japanese expansion. The navy's aircraft carriers had escaped destruction at Pearl Harbor, a stroke of immense good fortune, since the airplane had revolutionized naval warfare. Commanders discovered that because of their greater range and more concentrated fire power, carrier-based planes were far more effective against warships than the heaviest naval artillery. Battleships made excellent gun platforms from which to pound shore installations and support land operations, but against other vessels aircraft were of prime importance.

This truth was demonstrated in May 1942 in

the Battle of the Coral Sea. Repeated success had made the Japanese overconfident. Having captured an empire in a few months without the loss of any warship larger than a destroyer, they believed the war already won and suffered from what one of their admirals who knew better called the "victory disease." This led them to overextend themselves.

The Coral Sea lies northeast of Australia and south of New Guinea and the Solomon Islands. Domination of these waters would cut Australia off from Hawaii, and thus from American aid. Admiral Isoroku Yamamoto, believing that he could range freely over all the waters west of Pearl Harbor, had dispatched a large fleet of transports, screened by many warships, to attack Port Moresby, on the southern New Guinea coast. On May 7–8 planes from the American

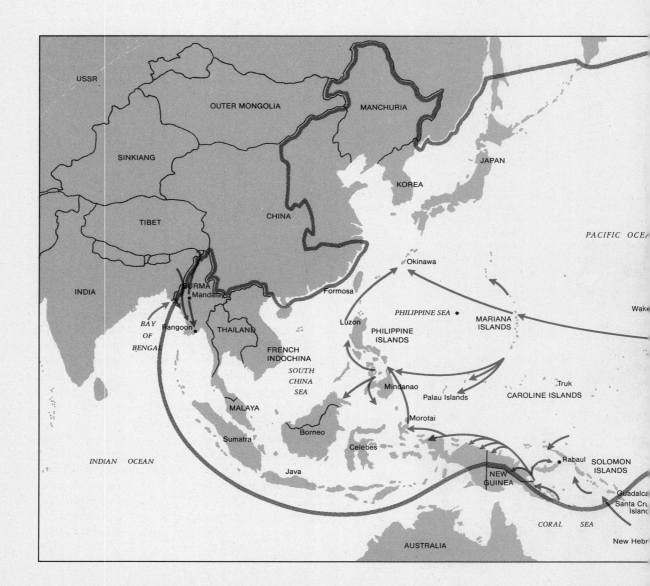

carriers *Lexington* and *Yorktown* struck the convoy's screen, sinking a small carrier and damaging a large one. Superficially, the battle seemed a victory for the Japanese, for their planes mortally wounded the *Lexington* and destroyed two other ships, but the troop transports had been forced to turn back—Port Moresby was saved. Although large numbers of cruisers and destroyers took part in the action, none came within sight or gun range of an enemy ship. All the destruction was wrought by carrier aircraft.

Encouraged by this Coral Sea "victory," Yamamoto decided to force the American fleet into a showdown battle by assaulting Midway Island, west of Hawaii. His armada never reached the island. Between June 4 and 7 control of the Central Pacific was decided, entirely by air power. American dive bombers sent four large carriers to the bottom. About 300 Japanese planes were destroyed. The United States lost only the *Yorktown* and a destroyer, retaining the bulk of its planes. The powerful fleet of Japanese battleships played no role in the action and when deprived of air cover had to withdraw ignominiously. Thereafter, the initiative in the Pacific war shifted to the Americans.

Victory, however, came slowly and at painful cost. American land forces were under the command of Douglas MacArthur, a brilliant but egocentric general whose judgment was sometimes distorted by his intense concern for his own reputation. Son of General Arthur MacArthur, who had played a major role in the original conquest of the Philippines, MacArthur had been in command of American troops in the islands when the Japanese struck in December 1941. After his heroic but hopeless defense of Manila and the Bataan peninsula, President Roosevelt had him evacuated by PT boat to escape capture. Thereafter, MacArthur was obsessed with the idea of personally leading the American army back to the islands, although many strategists believed they should be by-passed in the drive on the Japanese homeland.

In the end he convinced the Joint Chiefs of Staff, who determined strategy. The Americans organized two separate drives, one from New Guinea toward the Philippines under MacArthur, the other through the Central Pacific toward Tokyo, under Admiral Chester W. Nimitz. Before commencing this two-pronged advance, the Americans had to eject the Japanese from the Solomon Islands in order to protect Australia against a flank attack. Beginning in August 1942, a series of land–sea–air battles raged around Guadalcanal Island in this archipelago. Once

WORLD WAR II, PACIFIC THEATER

← Allied Offensives, 1942-1945

▨ Extent of Japanese Control, Aug. 1942

ALEUTIAN ISLANDS

Midway

HAWAIIAN ISLANDS

Pearl Harbor

PACIFIC OCEAN

MARSHALL ISLANDS

GILBERT ISLANDS

Samoa Islands

Islands

again, American air power was decisive, although the bravery and skill of the ground forces that actually won the island must not be underemphasized. American pilots, better trained and with tougher planes, had a relatively easier task. They inflicted losses five to six times heavier on the enemy than they sustained themselves. Japanese air power disintegrated progressively during the long battle, and this in turn helped the fleet take a heavy toll of the Japanese navy. By February of 1943 Guadalcanal had been secured.

In the autumn of 1943 the American drives toward Japan and the Philippines got under way at last. In the Central Pacific campaign the Guadalcanal action was repeated on a smaller but equally bloody scale from Tarawa in the Gilbert Islands to Kwajalein and Eniwetok in the Marshalls, islets theretofore unknown to history. The Japanese soldiers fought like the Spartans at Thermopylae for every foot of ground. They had to be blasted and burned from tunnels and concrete pillboxes with hand grenades, flame throwers, and dynamite. They almost never surrendered. But Admiral Nimitz's forces were in every case victorious. By mid-summer of 1944 this arm of the American advance had taken Saipan and Guam in the Marianas, bringing land-based bombers within range of Tokyo.

Meanwhile, MacArthur was leapfrogging along the New Guinea coast toward the Philippines, and in October 1944 he made good his promise to return to the islands, landing on Leyte, south of Luzon. Two great naval clashes in Philippine waters, the Battle of the Philippine Sea (June 1944) and the Battle for Leyte Gulf (October 1944), completed the destruction of Japan's sea power and reduced its air force to a band of fanatical suicide pilots called *kamikazes,* who tried to crash bomb-laden planes against American warships and airstrips. The *kamikazes* caused much damage but could not turn the tide. In February 1945 MacArthur liberated Manila.

The end was now inevitable. B-29 Superfortress bombers from the Marianas were raining high explosives and fire bombs on the Japanese homeland. The islands of Iwo Jima and Okinawa, only a few hundred miles from Tokyo, fell to the Americans in March and June 1945. But such was the blind courage of the Japanese soldiers that military experts were predicting another year of fighting and a million additional American casualties before the main islands could be subdued.

At this point came the most controversial decision of the entire war, perhaps of all history, and it was made by a newcomer on the world scene. In November 1944 Roosevelt had been elected to a fourth term, easily defeating Thomas E. Dewey. But instead of renominating Henry A. Wallace for Vice President, the Democrats had picked Senator Harry S Truman of Missouri, who had done an excellent job as head of a special Senate committee investigating military spending. The conservative Democratic politicos had considered Wallace too radical and too unstable, whereas Truman, although possessed of a good liberal record, was a regular party man well liked by the hierarchy. In April 1945, however, Roosevelt died of a cerebral hemorrhage. Thus it was Truman, a man painfully conscious of his inferiority to his great predecessor but equally aware of the power and responsibility of his office, who had to decide what to do when, in July 1945, American scientists placed in his hands a new and awful weapon, the atomic bomb.

After Roosevelt had responded to Albert Einstein's warning in 1939, government-sponsored atomic research had proceeded rapidly, especially after the establishment of the so-called Manhattan Project in May 1943. The manufacture of the artificial element plutonium at Hanford, Washington, and uranium 235 at Oak Ridge, Tennessee, went on side by side with the design and construction of a transportable atomic bomb at Los Alamos, New Mexico, under the direction of the physicist J. Robert Oppenheimer. Almost $2 billion was spent before a successful bomb was exploded at Alamogordo, in the New Mexican desert, on July 16.

Should a bomb with the destructive force of 20,000 tons of TNT be employed against Japan? By striking a major city, its dreadful power could be demonstrated convincingly, yet doing so would bring death to tens of thousands of Japa-

In this sequence a blazing Japanese *kamikaze* rams the flight deck of the carrier *Essex* off the Philippines in November 1944. In the Okinawa campaign in 1945 *kamikaze* attacks killed over 4,000 U.S. seamen. (Both: Navy Department, National Archives.)

nese civilians. Many of the scientists who had made the bomb now somewhat inconsistently argued against its use. To Truman, there really seemed no choice. Every past experience indicated that the Japanese army intended to fight to the last man,° but the bomb might cause a revolution in Japan, might lead the emperor to inter-

°In recapturing Guam, for example, the Americans killed 17,238 Japanese but took only 438 prisoners.

vene, might even persuade the military fanatics to give up. Weighing American lives against Japanese, and also influenced by a desire to end the Pacific war before Russia could intervene effectively and thus claim a role in the peacemaking, the President chose to go ahead. On August 6 the Superfortress *Enola Gay* dropped an atom bomb on Hiroshima, killing about 75,000 persons and injuring nearly 100,000 more out of a population of 344,000. Over 96 per cent of the buildings in the city were destroyed or damaged. Three days later, while the stunned Japanese still hesitated, a second bomb hit Nagasaki. This second drop was far less defensible morally, but it had the desired result. On August 15 Japan surrendered.

Thus ended the greatest war in history. Its cost had been beyond calculation; no accurate count could be made even of the dead, although the total came to somewhere in the neighborhood of 20 million. As in World War I, American casualties—291,000 battle deaths and 671,000 wounded—were relatively smaller than those of the other major belligerents. About 7.5 million Russians died in battle, 3.5 million Germans, 1.2 million Japanese, and 2.2 million Chinese; Britain and France, despite much smaller populations, suffered losses almost as large as America's. But far more than in World War I, American power, human and material, had made victory possible.

No one could account the war a benefit to mankind, but in the late summer of 1945 the future looked bright. Fascism was dead. Successful wartime diplomatic dealings between Roosevelt, Churchill, and Joseph Stalin, the Soviet dictator, encouraged many to hope that the communists were ready to abandon their implacable opposition to the capitalist way of life and cooperate in rebuilding Europe. In America isolationism had almost disappeared; the message of Wendell Willkie's best-selling *One World,* written after a globe-circling tour made by the 1940 Republican Presidential candidate at the behest of President Roosevelt in 1942, appeared to have been absorbed by the great majority of the people. Out of the death and destruction had also come technological advances that seemed to herald a better world as well as a peaceful one. Above all, there was the power of the atom. The force that seared Hiroshima and Nagasaki could be harnessed to serve peaceful needs, the scientists promised, with results that might free humanity forever from poverty and toil. Great strides in transportation and communication lay ahead, products of wartime research in electronics, airplane design, and rocketry. The development of penicillin and other antibiotics, which had greatly reduced the death rate among troops,

would perhaps banish all infectious disease.

The period of reconstruction would be prolonged, but with all the great powers adhering to the new United Nations charter, drafted at San Francisco in June 1945, international cooperation could be counted upon to ease the burdens of the victims of war and help the poor and underdeveloped parts of the world toward economic and political independence. Above all, although in some respects a less powerful organization than the defunct League of Nations, the UN would stand guard over the peace of the world. Such at least was the hope of millions in the victorious summer of 1945.

Supplementary Reading

There are good summaries of diplomatic developments in Selig Adler, *The Uncertain Giant: American Foreign Policy Between the Wars* (1965), and F. R. Dulles, *America's Rise to World Power°* (1955); see also J. D. Hicks, *Republican Ascendancy°* (1960), and W. E. Leuchtenburg, *Franklin Roosevelt and the New Deal°* (1963). J. C. Vinson, *The Parchment Peace* (1955), is the standard account of the Washington Armament Conference. R. H. Ferrell, *Peace in Their Time* (1952), is excellent on the Kellogg-Briand Pact. Other important works on the diplomacy of the twenties include A. W. Griswold, *The Far Eastern Policy of the United States°* (1938), J. H. Wilson, *American Business and Foreign Policy* (1971), E. E. Morison, *Turmoil and Tradition: A Study of the Life and Times of Henry L. Stimson°* (1960), and R. N. Current, *Secretary Stimson* (1954). R. H. Ferrell, *American Diplomacy and the Great Depression* (1957), and Alexander De Conde, *Herbert Hoover's Latin American Policy* (1951), are also useful.

On isolationism and the events leading to Pearl Harbor, see R. A. Divine, *The Reluctant Belligerent°* (1965), brief but comprehensive, and *The Illusion of Neutrality°* (1962), two volumes by W. L. Langer and S. E. Gleason, *The Challenge to Isolation°* (1952) and *The Undeclared War* (1953), Selig Adler, *The Isolationist Impulse°* (1957), Manfred Jonas, *Isolationism in America°* (1966), Dorothy Borg, *The*

°Available in paperback.

United States and the Far Eastern Crisis (1964), T. R. Fehrenbach, *F.D.R.'s Undeclared War* (1967), W. S. Cole, *Senator Gerald P. Nye and American Foreign Relations* (1962) and *America First* (1953), Herbert Feis, *The Road to Pearl Harbor°* (1962), Roberta Wohlstetter, *Pearl Harbor: Warning and Decision°* (1962), and J. W. Pratt, *Cordell Hull* (1964). C. C. Tansill, *Back Door to War* (1952), C. A. Beard, *American Foreign Policy in the Making* (1946) and *President Roosevelt and the Coming of the War* (1948), are interesting interpretations by isolationists, while L. C. Gardner, *Economic Aspects of New Deal Diplomacy°* (1971) is a recent, rather critical scholarly analysis.

The home front is discussed in Richard Polenberg, *War and Society* (1972). Special aspects of the subject are covered in Bruce Catton, *War Lords of Washington* (1948), Eliot Janeway, *The Struggle for Survival* (1951), David Novik *et al., Wartime Production Controls* (1949), Joel Seidman, *American Labor from Defense to Reconversion* (1953), D. M. Nelson, *Arsenal of Democracy* (1946), W. W. Wilcox, *The Farmer in the Second World War* (1947), R. E. Paul, *Taxation for Prosperity* (1947), Roland Young, *Congressional Politics in the Second World War* (1956), and J. P. Baxter, *Scientists Against Time°* (1946). Social trends are covered in Jack Goodman (ed.), *While You Were Gone* (1946). On the treatment of conscientious objectors, see P. E. Jacob and M. Q. Sibley, *Conscription of Conscience* (1952); on the relocation of the Japanese, see Roger Daniels, *Concentration Camps USA: Japanese Americans and World War II°* (1971). The effect of the war on Negroes is discussed in Ulysses Lee, *The Employment of Negro Troops* (1966), and Herbert Garfinkel, *When Negroes March* (1959).

A. R. Buchanan, *The United States in World War II°* (1964), provides an excellent overall survey of the military side of the conflict. The role of the army is covered exhaustively in the Department of the Army's multivolume *The United States Army in World War II* (1947-　) by various authors; that of the navy, in similar fashion, in S. E. Morison, *History of United States Naval Operations in World War II* (1947-62), which Morison has condensed in *The Two-Ocean War* (1963). For the air force, see W. F. Craven *et al., The Army Air Forces in World War II* (1948-58).

28

Foreign Affairs: 1942–1964

On Christmas Eve 1943 Franklin D. Roosevelt reported to the nation on his first meeting with Soviet Premier Joseph Stalin at Teheran, Iran. "I 'got along fine' with Marshal Stalin," he said, "and I believe that we are going to get along very well with him and the Russian people—very well indeed." A little over a year later, describing to Congress his second meeting with Stalin, at Yalta in the Crimea, the President stressed again the good feeling that existed between the two nations and their leaders. "We argued freely and frankly across the table," he explained. "But at the end, on every point, unanimous agreement was reached. I may say we achieved a unity of thought and a way of getting along together." Privately he characterized Stalin as "a very interesting man" whose rough exterior clothed an "old-fashioned elegant European manner." He referred to him almost affectionately as "that old buzzard," and on one occasion even called him "Uncle Joe" to his face. At Yalta Stalin gave Roosevelt a portrait photograph, with a long Cyrillic inscription in his small, tightly written hand.

By April 1945, however, Roosevelt was writing to Stalin of his "astonishment," "anxiety," and "bitter resentment" over the Soviet Union's "discouraging lack of application" of the agreements made at Yalta. A few days after dictating these words Roosevelt was dead. Before the end of the month, his successor, President Harry S Truman, was complaining that "our agreements with the Soviet Union had so far been a one-way street" and telling Foreign Minister Vyacheslav M. Molotov with characteristic bluntness that Stalin must learn to keep his promises. "I have never been talked to like that in my life," said Molotov. "Carry out your agreements," Truman retorted, "and you won't get talked to like that!" Thus ended the brief period of amity born of the struggle against Hitler.

Wartime Diplomacy

During the course of World War II every instrument of mass persuasion in the country was directed at convincing the people that the Russians were fighting America's battle as well as their own. Even before Pearl Harbor, former Ambassador Joseph E. Davies wrote in his best-selling *Mission to Moscow* (1941): "Russia is in the thick of this fight. . . . Hundreds of thousands of Russian men, women, and Soviet leaders . . . are now very gallantly fighting and dying for a cause which is vital to our security." According to Davies, the communist leaders were "a group of able, strong men" with "honest convictions and integrity of purposes" who were "devoted to the

cause of peace for both ideological and practical reasons." Communism was based "on the same principle of the 'brotherhood of man' which Jesus preached." Stalin possessed great dignity and charm, combined with much wisdom and strength of character, Davies said. "His brown eye is exceedingly kind and gentle. A child would like to sit in his lap and a dog would sidle up to him."

During the war men as different in point of view as General Douglas MacArthur and Vice President Henry A. Wallace took strongly pro-Soviet positions, and American newspapers and magazines published many laudatory articles about Russia. *Life* reported that Russians "think like Americans," and described the Russian secret police (the NKVD) as "similar to the FBI." In 1943 *Time* named Stalin its "Man of the Year." A number of motion pictures also contributed to revising the attitude of the average American toward the USSR. *Song of Russia* described the heroic defense the Soviet people were throwing up against the Nazi hordes; *Mission to Moscow*, a whitewash of the dreadful Moscow treason trials of the thirties based on Ambassador Davies' book, portrayed Stalin as a wise, grandfatherly type, puffing comfortably on an old pipe. In *One World* (1943), Wendell Willkie wrote glowingly of the Russian people, their "effective society," and their simple, warm-hearted leader. When he suggested jokingly to Stalin that if he continued to make progress in improving the education of his people he might educate himself out of a job, the dictator "threw his head back and laughed and laughed," Willkie recorded. "Mr. Willkie, you know I grew up a Georgian peasant. I am unschooled in pretty talk. All I can say is I like you very much."

These views of the character of Joseph Stalin were naive, to say the least, but the identity of interest of the United States and the Soviet Union was very real during the war. Russian military leaders conferred regularly with their British and American counterparts and fulfilled their obligations scrupulously. As early as October 1943 Foreign Minister Molotov committed his country to joining in the war against Japan as soon as the

Above: The close wartime cooperation between Roosevelt and Churchill is captured in this 1943 cartoon, from a London magazine. Right is a Persian print, done at the 1943 Teheran Conference, which depicts Churchill, Stalin, and Roosevelt tying up the Axis. (Courier Magazine, 1943 and Franklin D. Roosevelt Library.)

Germans were defeated, a promise confirmed the following month by Stalin at his meeting with Churchill and Roosevelt at Teheran.

The Soviets also repeatedly expressed a willingness to cooperate with the Allies in dealing with postwar problems. Russia was one of the 26 signers of the Declaration of the United Nations (January 1942), in which the Allies promised to eschew territorial aggrandizement after the war, respect the right of all peoples to determine their own form of government, work for freer trade and international economic cooperation, and force the disarmament of the aggressor nations.* In May 1943 Russia dissolved the Comintern, its official agency for the promulgation of world

revolution. That October, during a conference in Moscow with Secretary of State Cordell Hull and British Foreign Minister Anthony Eden, Molotov joined in setting up a European Advisory Commission to divide Germany into occupation zones after the war. At the Teheran Conference Stalin willingly discussed plans for a new league of nations. When Roosevelt described the kind of world organization he envisaged, the Russian dictator offered a number of constructive suggestions.

Between August and October 1944, Allied representatives met at Dumbarton Oaks, outside Washington. The chief Russian delegate, Andrei A. Gromyko, adamantly opposed all suggestions for limiting the use of the veto by the great powers on the future UN Security Council, but he did not take a deliberately obstructionist posi-

---

*These were the principles first laid down in the so-called Atlantic Charter, drafted by Roosevelt and Churchill at a dramatic meeting on the U.S.S. *Augusta* off Newfoundland in August 1941.

tion. At the Yalta Conference in 1944 Stalin joined in the call for a conference to be held in April 1945 at San Francisco to draft a charter for the United Nations, incidentally modifying the Russian position on the veto slightly by agreeing that no power might veto Security Council *discussion* of a controversy in which it had a stake.

Although the powers argued at length over the form of that charter at the 50-nation San Francisco Conference, they conducted the debates in an atmosphere of optimism and international amity. Each UN member received a seat in the General Assembly, a body designed for discussion rather than action. The locus of authority in the new organization resided in the Security Council, "the castle of the great powers." This consisted of five permanent members (the United States, Russia, Great Britain, France, and China) and six others elected for two-year terms. The Council was charged with the responsibility for maintaining world peace. It could apply diplomatic, economic, or military sanctions against any nation threatening that peace, but any great power could block UN action whenever it wished to do so. The United States insisted upon

this veto power as strongly as the Soviet Union. In effect the charter paid lip service to the Wilsonian ideal of a powerful international police force, but to assure Senate ratification it incorporated the limitations that Senator Lodge had proposed in his 1919 reservations. For example, the big-power veto represented Lodge's reservation to Article X of the League Covenant, which would have relieved the United States from the obligation of enforcing collective security without the approval of Congress.

The UN charter also provided for a Secretariat to handle routine administration, headed by a secretary general who was in addition the chief executive officer of the entire organization; a Trusteeship Council to supervise dependent areas much in the fashion of the mandate system of the League; and an International Court of Justice. An Economic and Social Council was created to supervise a host of agencies related to the UN such as the International Labor Organization; the International Bank for Reconstruction and Development; the International Monetary Fund; the World Health Organization; and the United Nations Educational, Scientific, and Cul-

Oscar Berger made this sketch during the UN Conference in San Francisco at a cocktail party given by Russian Foreign Minister Vyacheslav Molotov (right). Among the others are Michigan Senator Arthur H. Vandenberg, a one-time isolationist (2nd from left); Texas' Tom Connally, chairman of the Senate Foreign Relations Committee (3rd from left); and Secretary of State Edward R. Stettinius, Jr. (3rd from right). (Oscar Berger, New York *Times*.)

tural Organization (UNESCO), which was assigned the task of "promoting collaboration among the nations through education, science, and culture." Although Russia displayed less enthusiasm for the UN than most of the powers, it went along with the others.

Developing Conflicts

Yet long before the war in Europe ended, the Allied powers had clashed over important policy matters. Since later world tensions developed from decisions made at this time, an understanding of these disagreements is essential for evaluating whole decades of history. Unfortunately, complete understanding is not yet possible, which explains why the subject remains controversial. Much depends upon one's opinion of the Soviet system: if Russian communism is a threat to democracy and humane values the world over, or even if the Soviet government under Stalin was bent on world domination, events of the so-called Cold War fall readily into one pattern of interpretation. If Russia is seen as a nation that, having bravely and at enormous cost endured an unprovoked assault by the Nazis, was determined to protect itself against the possibility of another invasion, these events are best explained differently. In other words, the conflicts have had roots in ideological differences and in national rivalries. If the former are stressed, compromise solutions are harder to justify than if the latter are considered more important. The problem is made more difficult by the fact that relatively little is known of the motivations and inner workings of Soviet policy.

The Russians naturally resented the British-American delay in opening up a second front, for they were fighting for survival against the full power of the German armies and knew that any invasion, even an unsuccessful one, would relieve some of the pressure. Roosevelt and Churchill would not move until they were ready, and the Russians had to accept their decision. On the other hand, the Russians never concealed their determination to protect themselves against future attacks by extending their western frontier after the war. In December 1941 Stalin had demanded that Great Britain recognize his right to a large section of eastern Poland. He warned the Allies repeatedly that he would not tolerate any anti-Soviet government along Russia's western frontier. Most Allied leaders, including Roosevelt, admitted privately during the war that the Soviet Union would annex territory and possess preponderant power in eastern Europe after the defeat of Germany, but they never said this publicly. Somehow, they believed free governments could be created in countries like Poland and Bulgaria that the Russians would trust enough to leave to their own devices. "The Poles," said Winston Churchill early in 1945, "will have their future in their own hands, with the single limitation that they must honestly follow . . . a policy friendly to Russia. This is surely reasonable."

But however reasonable, Churchill's statement was impractical. The Polish question was a terribly difficult one. The war, after all, had been triggered by the German attack on Poland; the British particularly felt a moral obligation to restore that nation to its prewar independence. During the war a Polish government-in-exile was set up in London, and its leaders were determined, especially after the murder of some 5,000 Polish officers in 1943 at Katyn, in Russia, presumably by the Soviet secret police, to make no concessions to Soviet territorial demands. More generally, public opinion in Poland (and indeed in all the states along Russia's western frontier) was bitterly anti-Soviet. Yet Russia's legitimate interests (to say nothing of its power in the area) could not be ignored. Stalin apparently could not understand why his allies were so concerned about the fate of a small country so remote from their strategic spheres; that they professed to be concerned seemed to him an indication that they had some secret, devious purpose. He could see no difference (and "revisionist" American historians agree with him) between the Soviet Union dominating Poland and maintaining a government there that did not reflect the wishes of a majority of the Polish people, and the United

States dominating many Latin American nations and supporting unpopular regimes within them. Roosevelt, however, was worried about the domestic political effects of Russian control of Poland. Voters of eastern European extraction would be furious if the communists took over their homelands. Yet instead of explaining the realities of the situation to the country, he tried to sidestep the problem; apparently he hoped that if a confrontation were postponed, the problem would go away. He repeatedly called for a government in Poland that would be both representative of the popular will and friendly to Russia—an impossibility.

At the Yalta Conference, Roosevelt and Churchill agreed to Soviet annexation of large sections of eastern Poland. In return, Stalin agreed, almost certainly without intending to keep his promise, to allow free elections in the reconstituted Polish republic. The elections were never held, and Poland was run by a pro-Russian puppet regime. Thus, the West "lost" Poland. How it might have "won" the country when it was already occupied by Russian armies has never been explained, but if Roosevelt had been more candid with the American public, its reaction might have been less angry.

Alarmed by rapid Russian advances into central Europe in the closing days of the war, which he saw as a drastic disruption of the balance of power, Churchill urged Truman to order General Eisenhower to press forward as far as possible against the rapidly crumbling German armies in order to limit the area of Russian control. Had his advice been taken, Allied troops could probably have occupied most of Czechoslovakia and Germany as far east as Berlin. However, when Eisenhower pointed out the military disadvantage of such a headlong advance, Truman refused to overrule him.

After the surrender of Germany, Truman, Stalin, and Churchill met at Potsdam,° outside Berlin. They agreed to try the Nazi leaders as war criminals, made plans for exacting repara-

°Clement R. Attlee replaced Churchill during the conference after his Labour party won the British elections.

tions from Germany, and confirmed the division of the country into four zones to be occupied separately by American, Russian, British, and French forces. Berlin itself, deep in the Soviet zone, had also been split into four sectors. Stalin rejected all arguments that he loosen his hold on eastern Europe, and Truman (who received news of the successful testing of the atom bomb while at Potsdam) took a much tougher stance in the negotiations. On both sides, suspicions were mounting, positions hardening.

At this point the United States stood, as Cassius said of Caesar, "bestride the narrow world like a Colossus." Besides its army, navy, and air force and its immense industrial potential, alone among the nations it possessed the atomic bomb. When Stalin's actions made it clear that he intended to control all eastern Europe and to exert an important influence elsewhere in the world, most Americans first reacted somewhat in the manner of a mastiff being worried by a yapping terrier: their resentment was tempered by amazement. They refused to believe that the Russians could honestly suspect their motives, and they viewed Stalin's obvious determination to control the nations along Russia's western border with horror. They were slow to grasp the fundamental change that the war had produced in international politics. America might be the strongest country in the world, but all the western European nations, victors and vanquished alike, had been reduced to the status of second-class powers. Russia, however, had regained the influence it had held under the czars and lost as a result of World War I and its communist revolution.

American and Russian attitudes stood in sharp confrontation when the control of atomic energy came up for discussion in the UN. Everyone realized the threat to human survival posed by the atomic bomb. As early as November 1945, the United States suggested allowing the UN to supervise all nuclear energy production, and the General Assembly promptly created an Atomic Energy Commission to study the question. In June 1946 Commissioner Bernard Baruch offered a plan under which atomic weapons would be outlawed. UN inspectors would have the authority to operate without restriction anywhere in the world to make sure that no country was making bombs clandestinely. When such a supranational system had been established, the United States would destroy its stockpile of bombs.

Most Americans thought the Baruch plan exceedingly magnanimous and some considered it positively foolhardy, but the Soviets rejected it. Displaying an almost paranoid fear of any invasion of their sovereign independence, they would neither permit UN inspectors in Russia nor surrender their veto power over Security Council actions dealing with atomic energy. At the same time they demanded that the United States destroy its bombs at once. Unwilling to trust the Russians not to produce bombs secretly under these conditions, the United States refused to agree. The result was a stalemate and increased international tension.

The Containment Policy

Postwar cooperation had failed. In a series of actions the Soviets were probing outward in every direction, seeking to expand their power and influence. By the end of 1945, besides dominating most of eastern Europe, they controlled Outer Mongolia, parts of Manchuria, and northern Korea. They had annexed the Kurile Islands and regained from Japan the southern half of Sakhalin Island.* They were also fomenting trouble in Iran, where they hoped to take over the northern province of Azerbaijan and win important oil concessions, and soon they began to exert heavy pressure on Turkey and Greece in order to obtain access to the eastern Mediterranean.

The United States reacted to Russia's moves first by direct diplomatic appeals and threats and then by strenuous objections in the UN, where American influence was great. But by early 1946

*Roosevelt and Churchill had agreed to these Russian moves in the Far East as part of the Yalta settlement.

a new policy was emerging. Many minds contributed to its development, but the key ideas were provided by George F. Kennan, a scholarly Foreign Service officer. Kennan had been stationed for five years in Russia and had studied Soviet history carefully. He now argued that the Soviet leaders were prisoners of their own ideology. They saw the world as divided into socialist and capitalist camps and based their policies on the assumption that irreconcilable differences existed between them. Nothing the United States might do, however conciliatory, would reduce Russian hostility. Therefore, the nation should accept this hostility as a fact of life and either resist Russian aggression firmly wherever it appeared, or wait for time to bring about some change in Soviet policy.

Kennan's second alternative seemed both irresponsible and dangerous, whereas "getting tough with Russia" would find wide popular support; according to polls, a substantial majority considered current American policy "too soft." At the same time, however, the public remained reluctant to bear the expense of maintaining a powerful military force and providing aid to nations threatened by the Soviets. During 1946 the Truman administration increasingly adopted a tougher line, but the decisive shift came early in 1947 as a result of a crisis in Greece. Local Greek communists, waging a guerrilla war against the monarchy, were receiving aid from the Russian-dominated "satellite" nations of Yugoslavia, Bulgaria, and Albania. Great Britain was assisting the monarchists. For more than a year an inconclusive civil war had been wracking the country. However, Britain, its economy shaken by World War II, could not long afford this drain on its resources. In February 1947 the British informed President Truman that they would have to cut off further aid to Greece.

Russia's "Iron Curtain" (a phrase popularized by Winston Churchill) seemed about to ring down on still another nation. The Greek government was conservative, even reactionary, but it was threatened by outside forces. On March 12 President Truman went before a joint session of Congress and enunciated what became known as the Truman Doctrine. If Greece or Turkey fell to the communists, he said, all the Middle East might be lost. This, in turn, might shake the morale of anti-communist elements throughout western Europe. To prevent this "unspeakable tragedy," he asked Congress for $400 million in military and economic aid for Greece and Turkey. "It must be the policy of the United States to support free peoples who are resisting attempted subjugation by armed minorities or by outside pressures," he said. By justifying his request for so much money on these ideological grounds, Truman obtained his objective. Congress appropriated the necessary funds by margins approaching three to one in both houses. But once official sanction was given to the communism-versus-democracy approach to foreign relations, policy became more rigid, compromise more difficult, even when Soviet attitudes began to change.

Of course this problem was not apparent in 1947 when the communist threat loomed extremely large. At that moment in history, even a number of western European nations stood in danger of falling into the communist orbit. Neither the Red Army nor Soviet subversion had anything to do with this. The war had shattered their economies. The Continent, as Winston Churchill said, had become "a rubble-heap, a charnel house, a breeding-ground of pestilence and hate," and these conditions fostered the growth of communism. For ideological as well as humanitarian reasons the United States felt obliged to protect this vital area and provide the means of restoring its prosperity and social health.

But how to do so without appearing to be as imperialistic and expansionist as the Russians? George F. Kennan provided an answer in an anonymous article in the July 1947 issue of *Foreign Affairs*, "The Sources of Soviet Conduct." This article gave public expression to the argument Kennan had previously advanced in his diplomatic reports. A policy of "long-term, patient but firm and vigilant containment" based on the "application of counter-force" was the best means of dealing with Soviet pressures. The Cold

War might be "a duel of infinite duration," Kennan admitted, but it could be won if, without bluster, America maintained its own strength and convinced the communists that it would resist aggression firmly in any quarter of the globe.

But Kennan disagreed with the *psychology* of the Truman Doctrine, which seemed to him essentially defensive as well as open to criticism by anti-imperialists. He proposed, therefore, along with containment, a broad aid program, free of "ideological overtones," to be offered even to Russia, provided the Soviets would contribute some of their own resources to the cause of European economic recovery. The European nations themselves should work out the details, America providing only money, materials, and technical advice.

George C. Marshall, army chief of staff during World War II and now secretary of state, formally suggested this aid program, which became known as the Marshall Plan on June 5, 1947. The objective, he said, was to restore "the confidence of the European people in the economic future of their own countries." America intended to attack no nation or political system, only "hunger, poverty, desperation, and chaos," the real enemies of freedom and democracy. It would be "neither fitting nor efficacious" for the United States to impose such a plan on any country. "This is the business of the Europeans. . . . The program should be a joint one, agreed to by a number, if not all European nations."

The Marshall Plan and the policy of containment succeeded brilliantly. Led by Great Britain and France, the European powers seized avidly on Marshall's suggestion. Although the Soviet Union refused to participate, within six weeks 16 nations were setting up a Committee for European Economic Cooperation, which soon submitted plans calling for up to $22.4 billion in American aid. After protracted debate, much influenced by a communist coup in Czechoslovakia in February 1948, which drew still another country behind the Iron Curtain, Congress appropriated over $13 billion for the program. Results exceeded the expectations even of the optimists. By 1951 western Europe was booming and

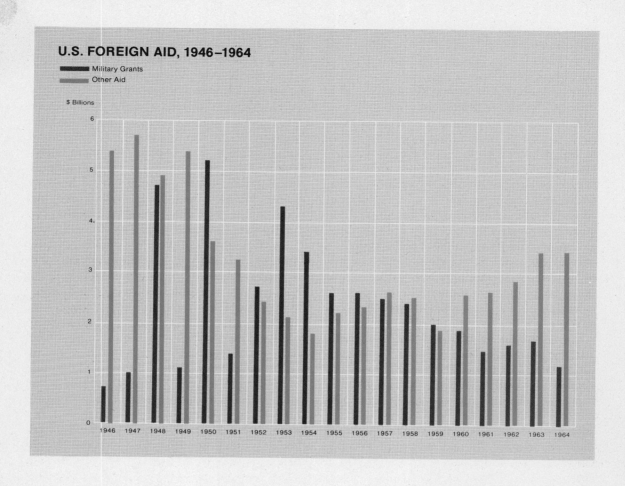

U.S. FOREIGN AID, 1946–1964

■ Military Grants
▨ Other Aid

$ Billions

Communist parties in all the democracies were shrinking. Whether the policy-makers realized it or not, containment and the Marshall Plan were America's response to the power vacuum created in Europe by the debilitating effects of the war, comparable to the Soviet Union's response. Just as Russia extended its influence over the eastern half of the Continent, the United States extended its influence in the west. But with this vital difference: in the east "influence" meant (and still means) almost total domination, in the west it meant what the dictionaries say it means— "power independent of force or authority."

Economic aid laid the basis for a broader European political cooperation. In March 1948,

Great Britain, France, Belgium, the Netherlands, and Luxembourg signed an alliance aimed at social and cultural collaboration as well as economic. The western nations soon abandoned their understandable but self-defeating policy of crushing Germany economically. They instituted currency reforms in their zones and announced plans for creating a single West German Republic, with a large degree of autonomy.

These decisions caused the Russians to close off Allied surface access to Berlin in June 1948. For a time it seemed that the Allies must either fight their way into the city or abandon it to the communists. Unwilling to adopt either of these alternatives, Truman decided to fly supplies through the air corridors leading to the capital from Frankfurt, Hanover, and Hamburg. This "Berlin Airlift" put the Russians in an uncomfortable position; if they were really determined to keep supplies from West Berlin, they would have to begin the fighting. They were unprepared to do so. C-47 and C-54 transports shuttled back and forth in weather fair and foul, carrying the food, fuel, and other goods necessary to maintain more than 2 million West Berliners. Berlin was saved, and in May 1949 the Russians gave up the blockade. The success of the Berlin Airlift boosted European morale, solidly vindicated the containment policy, and—incidentally—greatly increased President Truman's popularity in the United States.

Containment, however, also required the development of a powerful military force. In May 1948 Republican Senator Arthur H. Vandenberg of Michigan, a prewar leader of the isolationists who had been converted to internationalism largely by President Roosevelt's solicitous consideration of his views, introduced a resolution stating the "determination" of the United States "to exercise the right of individual *or collective* self-defense . . . should any armed attack occur affecting its national security." The Senate approved this resolution by a vote of 64 to 4, further proof that isolationism was no longer an effective force in American politics. Negotiations began promptly with the western powers, and in April 1949 the North Atlantic Treaty was signed in Washington. The United States, Great Britain, France, Italy, Belgium, the Netherlands, Luxembourg, Denmark, Norway, Portugal, Iceland, and Canada° agreed "that an armed attack against one or more of them in Europe or North America shall be considered an attack against them all," and that in the event of such an attack each would take "individually and in concert with the other Parties, such action as it deems necessary, including the use of armed force." No more entangling alliance could be imagined, yet the Senate ratified this treaty by a vote of 82 to 13.

°In 1952 Greece and Turkey also joined the alliance, and in 1954 West Germany was admitted.

Under this pact the North Atlantic Treaty Organization (NATO) was established. Further alarmed by the news, released in September 1949, that the Russians had produced an atomic bomb, Congress appropriated $1.5 billion to arm NATO, and in 1951 General Eisenhower was recalled to active duty and placed in command of all NATO forces. This international army never approached the Soviet armies in size, but along with the nuclear power of the United States it persuaded the Russians to restrain themselves in Europe. Restraint, of course, did not mean passivity; every effort at containment evoked a Russian response. The Marshall Plan led to the seizure of Czechoslovakia, the build-up of Germany to the Berlin blockade, the creation of NATO to the multilateral military alliance known as the Warsaw Pact. Whatever the origins of the contest, both sides contributed by their actions and their continuing suspicions to the heightening of Cold War tensions.

Containing Communism in Asia

Containment worked well in Europe at least in the short run; in the Far East, where the United States lacked powerful and determined allies, it was both more expensive and less effective. V-J Day found the Far East a shambles. Much of Japan was a smoking ruin. In China social chaos was complicated by a disorganized political situation, the nationalists under Chiang Kai-shek dominating the south, the communists under Mao Tse-tung controlling the northern countryside, and Japanese troops still holding most of the northern cities. Faced with tremendous problems in this whole region, President Truman acted decisively and effectively with regard to Japan, unsurely and with unfortunate results where China was concerned.

Even before the Japanese surrendered, Truman had decided not to allow the Soviet Union any significant role in the occupation of Japan. A four-power Allied Control Council was established, but American troops, commanded by General MacArthur, ran the country. MacArthur displayed exactly the proper combination of imperiousness, tact, and intelligence needed to accomplish his purposes, and the Japanese, revealing the same remarkable adaptability that had made possible their swift "westernization" in the latter half of the 19th century, placidly accepted a new political and social system that involved de-emphasizing the importance of the emperor, universal suffrage and parliamentary government, the encouragement of labor unions, and the break-up of both large estates and big industrial combines. Japan lost its far-flung island empire as well as all claim to Korea and the Chinese mainland. Efforts to restrict economic development, however, were soon abandoned, partly because of the high cost of the occupation to the United States but mainly in order to build up the country as a Far Eastern bastion against communism. In 1951 a peace treaty formally ended the occupation, although American troops remained in Japan under an agreement with the new government. Japan emerged from the occupation economically strong, politically stable, and firmly allied with the United States.

The difficulties in China were probably insurmountable. No one, not even Marshal Stalin, appreciated the latent power of the Chinese communists. When the war ended, the United States tried to install Chiang in control of all China, allowing the Japanese to hold key north Chinese sectors until Chiang could take them over and even sending 50,000 marines into the region, a step which infuriated Mao Tse-tung. At the same time, however, Truman made a sustained effort to bring Chiang's nationalists and Mao's communists together, for he realized that no strong Chinese government could exist without the support of both groups. He sent General Marshall to try to arrange a settlement. Marshall managed to bring Chiang and Mao together twice during the first half of 1946, but neither would make significant concessions. Mao was convinced—rightly as time soon proved—that he could win all China by force, while Chiang, presiding over a corrupt,

incredibly incompetent regime almost totally out of contact with the Chinese masses, grossly exaggerated his own strength. The kindly and hardworking Marshall finally gave up in disgust, having been "frustrated time and again," as he explained, "by extremist elements of both sides." In January 1947 Truman recalled him and named him secretary of state. Soon thereafter a full-scale civil war erupted in China.

This war resulted in the total defeat of the nationalists; by the end of 1949 Mao ruled all China, and Chiang's shattered armies had fled to sanctuary on the island of Formosa, now called Taiwan. The "loss" of China to communism deeply divided the American people. Critics claimed that Truman had not backed the nationalists strongly enough and that he had stupidly underestimated both Mao's power and his dedication to the cause of world revolution. Despite a superficial plausibility, neither of these charges made much sense. Nothing short of massive American military aid, including the commitment of American troops, could have prevented the communist victory. This American opinion would not have supported. Furthermore, American intervention in the civil war would unquestionably have alienated the Chinese people, who were fed up with foreign meddling in their affairs. That *any* action could have prevented the loss of China is unlikely, given the unpopularity of Chiang's government and the ruthless zeal of the Chinese communists. Probably the United States gave the nationalists too much aid rather than too little. A hands-off policy might have tempered Mao's resentment. Such a policy was also impracticable, considering the hostility of Americans to communism in the midst of the Cold War.

The attacks of his American critics roused Truman's combativeness and led him into serious miscalculations elsewhere in the Orient. After the war, the province of Korea was taken from Japan and divided along the 38th parallel, the Russians controlling the northern half of the country, the Americans the southern. In December 1945 the occupying powers agreed in principle to set up a unified and independent Korean republic at some future date, but in the highly charged atmosphere of the postwar years, they could not agree as to how this should be done. By September 1948 there were two "independent" governments in Korea, the Democratic People's Republic, backed by the Soviet Union, and the Republic of Korea, backed by the United States and the UN. Both the major powers withdrew their troops from the peninsula, but the Russians left behind a well-armed local force, whereas the Republic of Korea's army was weak and ill-trained.

American military strategists had decided as early as 1947 that Korea was not worth defending. Truman accepted this decision without facing its implications: by leaving Korea weak he was tempting the communists to take it over, despite the fact that it was nominally under the protection of the UN. In January 1950, defining the "defensive perimeter" of the United States in the Far East, Dean Acheson, who had succeeded Marshall as secretary of state, deliberately excluded Korea, saying that it was up to the local populace, backed by the UN, to protect the country against attack. Although Congress appropriated large sums for Korean economic rehabilitation, it did little for the Korean army. Thus, when North Korean armored divisions struck suddenly across the 38th parallel in June 1950, they quickly routed the defenders.

At this point, Truman exhibited his finest qualities: decisiveness and courage. Recalling the dire results that had followed when earlier acts of aggression—beginning with the Japanese assault on Manchuria—had been allowed to pass unchecked, he decided to defend South Korea. With the backing of the UN Security Council,* he sent American planes into battle. Ground troops soon followed.

Nominally, the Korean War was a struggle between the invaders and the United Nations. General MacArthur, placed in command, flew

the blue UN flag over his headquarters and no less than 16 nations supplied troops for his army. However, more than 90 per cent of the forces employed were American. At first the North Koreans pushed them back rapidly, but by the beginning of September a front was stabilized around the port of Pusan, at the southern tip of Korea. Then General MacArthur executed a brilliant amphibious flanking maneuver, striking at

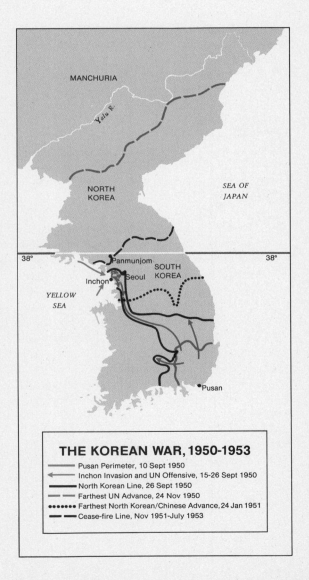

THE KOREAN WAR, 1950-1953

——— Pusan Perimeter, 10 Sept 1950
⟵ Inchon Invasion and UN Offensive, 15-26 Sept 1950
——— North Korean Line, 26 Sept 1950
— — Farthest UN Advance, 24 Nov 1950
•••••• Farthest North Korean/Chinese Advance, 24 Jan 1951
— — Cease-fire Line, Nov 1951-July 1953

*Russia, which could have vetoed this action, was at the moment boycotting the Security Council because the UN had refused to give the Mao Tse-tung regime China's seat on that body.

the west coast city of Inchon, about 50 miles south of the 38th parallel. Outflanked, the North Koreans fled northward, losing thousands of men and much equipment. By October the battle front had moved *north* of the old boundary.

Truman, with UN approval, now permitted MacArthur to drive toward the Yalu River, boundary between North Korea and Communist China. It was a momentous and unfortunate decision, an example of how power, once unleashed, so often gets out of hand. As the UN army advanced, ominous rumblings came from north of the Yalu, Foreign Minister Chou En-lai warning the world that the Chinese would not "supinely tolerate seeing their neighbors being savagely invaded by imperialists." Chinese "volunteers" began to turn up among the captives taken by UN units. Much alarmed, Truman flew to Wake Island, in the Pacific, to confer with MacArthur, but the general assured the President that the Chinese would not dare to intervene. If they did, he added, his army would crush them easily; the war would be over by Christmas.

Seldom has a general miscalculated so badly. On November 26, 33 Chinese divisions smashed suddenly through the center of MacArthur's line. Overnight a triumphant advance became a disorganized retreat. Amid incredible hardships, across broken country in subzero weather, the UN troops fled southward, suffering heavy casualties. MacArthur now spoke of the "bottomless well of Chinese manpower" and justified his earlier confidence by claiming, not without reason, that he was fighting "an entirely new war."

The UN army finally rallied south of the 38th parallel and even managed to battle its way back across that line in the eastern sector. By the spring of 1951 the front had been stabilized. MacArthur then urged that he be permitted to bomb Chinese installations north of the Yalu. He also suggested a naval blockade of the coast of China and the use of Chinese nationalist troops in Korea. When Truman rejected these proposals on the ground that they would lead to a third world war, MacArthur, who tended to ignore the larger political aspects of the conflict, attempted to rouse Congress and the public against the President by issuing public statements criticizing administration policy. Truman first ordered him to be silent, and when the general persisted, he removed him from command.

This unpopular but necessary step (a fundamental principle of democracy, civilian control over the military, was at stake) brought down a storm of abuse on the President. At first the Korean "police action" had been popular in the United States, but as the months passed and the casualties mounted, many citizens became disillusioned and angry. The war had brought into the open a basic political (or better, psychological) disadvantage of the containment policy: its object was not victory but balance; it involved apparently unending tension without the satisfying release of an action completed. To Americans accustomed to triumph and fond of oversimplifying complex questions, containment seemed, as its costs in blood and dollars mounted, a monumentally frustrating policy. MacArthur's simple if dangerous strategy offered at least the hope of victory; all the President seemed to offer was a further loss of American lives and money. MacArthur returned home to launch what he called a "crusade" to rally opinion to his cause.

Fortunately, the fundamental correctness of both Truman's policy and his decision to remove MacArthur eventually became apparent to the public. As he reminded the country, an all-out war with Communist China, besides costing thousands of lives, would alarm America's allies and weaken the nation while Russia watched from the sidelines unscathed. Military men backed the President almost unanimously, the highly respected General Omar N. Bradley, chairman of the Joint Chiefs of Staff, declaring that a showdown with the Chinese "would involve us in the wrong war, at the wrong place, at the wrong time and with the wrong enemy." In June 1951 the communists agreed to negotiate an armistice in Korea, and although the talks dragged on, with interruptions, for two years while thousands more died along the static battle front, both MacArthur and talk of bombing China subsided.

Photographer David Douglas Duncan was with the 1st Marine Division in Korea when it was virtually isolated by the sudden Red Chinese offensive in November 1950. Conducting in frigid weather what the military historian S. L. A. Marshall called "the greatest fighting withdrawal of modern history," the marines broke out to safety. (© David Douglas Duncan, *Life*.)

The Communist Issue at Home: McCarthyism

The frustrating Korean War highlighted the paradox that at the very pinnacle of its power, America's influence in world affairs was declining. Its monopoly of nuclear weapons had been broken. China had passed into the communist orbit. Elsewhere in Asia and throughout Africa, new nations, formerly colonial possessions of the western powers, were adopting a "neutralist" position in the Cold War similar in purpose and method to the policy adopted by the United States after the Revolution, when it had steered a middle course in the struggle between Britain and France. Despite all the billions poured into arma-

ments and foreign aid, the safety, even the survival of the country seemed far from assured.

Internal as well as external dangers appeared to threaten the nation. Alarming examples of communist espionage in Canada, Great Britain, and in America itself convinced many citizens that clever conspirators were everywhere at work undermining American security. In 1947, responding to these fears, Truman established a Loyalty Review Board to check up on government employees. Investigators found no significant trace of subversion, but apprehension remained in many hearts.

In 1948 Whittaker Chambers, an editor of *Time* who had formerly been a communist, charged that Alger Hiss, president of the Carnegie Endowment for International Peace and a former State Department official, had been a communist in the thirties. Hiss denied the charge and sued Chambers for libel. Chambers then produced microfilms purporting to show that Hiss had spied for Russia by making copies of classified documents for dispatch to Moscow. Hiss could not be indicted for espionage because of the statute of limitations; instead he was charged with perjury. His first trial resulted in a hung jury, his second, ending in January 1950, in conviction and a five-year jail term.

Although many thought Chambers a pathological liar and Hiss the innocent victim of anti-communist hysteria, the case fed the fears of those who believed in the existence of a powerful communist underground in the United States. The disclosure in February 1950 that a respected British scientist, Dr. Klaus Fuchs, had betrayed atomic secrets to the Russians heightened these fears, as did the arrest and conviction of his American associate, Harry Gold, and two other American traitors, Julius and Ethel Rosenberg, on the same charge.

Beyond doubt, information gathered by spies had aided Russian development of nuclear weapons. This fact encouraged some Republicans to make political capital of the communists-in-government issue. On February 9, 1950, an obscure senator, Joseph R. McCarthy of Wisconsin, casually introduced this theme in a speech before the Women's Republican Club of Wheeling, West Virginia. "The reason we find ourselves in a position of impotency," he stated, "is not because our only powerful potential enemy has sent men to invade our shores, but rather because of the traitorous actions of those who have been treated so well by this nation." The State Department, he added, was "infested" with communists. "I have here in my hand a list of 205°—a list of names that were known to the Secretary of State as being members of the Communist Party and who nevertheless are *still working and shaping . . . policy.*"

McCarthy had no shred of evidence to back up these statements, and a Senate committee headed by the conservative Democrat Millard Tydings of Maryland soon exposed his mendacity. But thousands of persons were too eager to believe him to listen to reason. Within a few weeks of the Wheeling speech, he had become the most talked-of man in Congress. Inhibited neither by scruples nor logic, he lashed out in every direction, attacking international experts like Professor Owen Lattimore of Johns Hopkins and professional diplomats such as John S. Service and John Carter Vincent, who had pointed out the deficiencies of the Chiang Kai-shek regime during the Chinese civil war. When McCarthy's victims indignantly denied his charges, he distracted the public by striking out with still more sensational accusations directed at other innocents. Even General Marshall, a man of the highest character and patriotism, was subject to McCarthy's abuse. The general, he said, was "steeped in falsehood," part of a "conspiracy so immense and an infamy so black as to dwarf any previous venture in the history of man." The "big lie" was McCarthy's most effective weapon: the enormity of his charges and the status of his targets convinced thousands that there must be *some* truth to what he was saying.

Although McCarthy was at least potentially a fascist, he probably had no specific plan for seizing power. He was too disorganized, too muddleheaded to be a leader of any kind. Nevertheless, by the fall of 1950 he had become a major force, the word *McCarthyism* a part of the lexicon of politics.

In the 1950 election McCarthy "invaded" Maryland and contributed mightily to the defeat of Senator Tydings; two years later William Benton of Connecticut, who had introduced a resolution calling for McCarthy's expulsion from the Senate, also failed of re-election when McCarthy campaigned against him. Thereafter, many congressmen who detested him dared not incur his wrath, and large numbers of Republicans found the temptation to take advantage of his voter-

---

°McCarthy was speaking from rough notes and no one made an accurate record of his words. The exact number mentioned has long been in dispute. On other occasions, he said there were 57 and 81 "card-carrying communists" in the State Department.

appeal irresistible. Even the Republican Senate leader, Robert A. Taft of Ohio, son of the former President and generally a man of the highest integrity, condoned McCarthy's methods.

The frustrations attending the Korean War added to McCarthy's effectiveness. Naturally, he championed the cause of General MacArthur. In the 1952 Presidential campaign the Wisconsin senator led a merciless assault on Truman's handling of the conflict. The Republicans nominated General Eisenhower for President, the Democrats the articulate and witty Governor Adlai E. Stevenson of Illinois. Eisenhower's tremendous popularity probably assured his election in any case, but McCarthyism and the Korean War issue added to his strength. Many Democrats considered McCarthy a hero, others voted Republican because they thought the senator would restrain himself once his own party was in power. General Eisenhower aided his cause immeasurably by promising to go to Korea himself if elected to try to bring the long conflict to an end. The result was a Republican landslide: Eisenhower received almost 34 million votes to Stevenson's 27 million, and in the Electoral College his margin was 442 to 89.

After the election, President-elect Eisenhower kept his pledge to go to Korea. His trip produced no immediate results, but the truce talks, suspended before the election, were resumed. In July 1953, perhaps influenced by an American hint that it might use small "tactical" atomic bombs in Korea, the communists agreed to an armistice. Korea remained divided, its poverty-stricken people far worse off than when the fighting began. The United States had suffered over 135,000 casualties, including 33,000 dead. Yet aggression had been confronted and fought to a standstill. Containment had proved extremely expensive, but it had worked.

John Foster Dulles

Troubled and uncertain, the American people were counting upon Eisenhower to find a way to employ the nation's immense strength constructively. The new President had no intention of abandoning internationalism, but he shared the general feeling that a drastic change of tactics in foreign affairs was needed. Lacking political training and uninterested in the small details of complex operations, he counted upon Congress and his secretary of state to solve the practical problems.

Given this attitude, his choice of John Foster Dulles as secretary of state seemed inspired. Like Eisenhower, Dulles believed in change within the framework of internationalism. "What we need to do," he said, "is to recapture the kind of crusading spirit of the early days of the Republic." He saw himself as a man of high moral principle. "There is no way to solve the great perplexing international problems except by bringing to bear on them the force of Christianity," he insisted. His experience in diplomacy dated back to 1907, when he had served as secretary to the Chinese delegation at the Second Hague Conference.° Later he had a small place among the army of experts advising Wilson at Versailles. More recently he had been an adviser to the American delegation to the San Francisco Conference and a representative of the United States in the UN General Assembly. Since 1948 he had been recognized as one of the Republican party's chief foreign policy experts, by no one more unquestioningly than himself. "With my understanding of the intricate relationships between the peoples of the world and your sensitiveness to the political considerations involved, we will make the most successful team in history," he told Eisenhower.

As secretary, Dulles combined strong moral convictions with amazing energy. His objectives were magnificent, his strategy grandiose. Instead of waiting for the communists to attack and then "containing" them, the United States should warn the enemy that "massive retaliation," directed at Moscow or Peking would be the fate of

---

°The delegation was headed by Dulles' grandfather John W. Foster, who had been secretary of state under Benjamin Harrison.

The Washington Post's Herblock was a sharp critic of the Eisenhower administration. In a comment on John Foster Dulles' "brinkmanship" diplomacy, Dulles assures Uncle Sam, "Don't be afraid—I can always pull you back." (Herbert Block, *Herblock's Special For Today,* 1958.)

all aggressors. With the communists held in check by this threat, positive measures aimed at "liberating" eastern Europe and "unleashing" Chiang Kai-shek against the Chinese mainland would follow. Dulles placed great faith in grand alliances in the image of NATO, forging the Southeast Asia Treaty Organization (SEATO) and the Central Treaty Organization (CENTO) in the Middle East, but he believed that if America's allies lacked the courage to follow its lead, the nation would have to undertake an "agonizing reappraisal" of its commitments to them.

In short, Dulles envisioned a policy broader, more idealistic, and more aggressive than Truman's. Not the least of its virtues, he claimed, was that it would save money; by concentrating on nuclear deterrents and avoiding "brushfire" wars in remote regions, the cost of defense could be dramatically reduced.

Despite his determination, energy, and high ideals, Dulles failed to make the United States a

more effective force in world affairs. Massive retaliation made little sense when Russia possessed nuclear weapons as powerful as those of the United States. In November 1952 America had won the race to make a hydrogen bomb, but the Russians duplicated this feat the following August. Thereafter, the only threat behind massive retaliation was the threat of human extinction.

Most of Dulles' other schemes were equally unrealistic. "Unleashing" Chiang Kai-shek would have been like matching a Pekingese against a tiger. "Liberating" Russia's European satellites would of necessity have involved a third world war. "You can count on us," Dulles told the peoples of eastern Europe in a radio address in January 1953. But when East German workers rioted in June of that year and when the Hungarians revolted in 1956, no help was forthcoming from America. Although Dulles certainly did not err in refusing to prevent the Russians from crushing these rebellions, his earlier statements had roused hopes behind the Iron Curtain that now were shattered.

Furthermore, Dulles' saber-rattling tactics were badly timed. While he was planning to avert future Koreas, the Soviet Union was shifting its approach. Stalin died in March 1953, and after a period of internal conflict within the Kremlin, Nikita Khrushchev emerged as the new master of Russia. Khrushchev cleverly set out to obtain communist objectives by indirection rather than by arms. He appealed to the antiwestern prejudices of the underdeveloped countries just emerging from under the yoke of colonialism, offering them economic aid and pointing to Russian achievements in science and technology, such as the launching of the first earth satellite (1957), as proof that communism would soon "bury" the capitalist system without troubling to destroy it by force. The Soviet Union was the friend of all peace-loving nations, the dictator insisted.

Of course Khrushchev was a master hypocrite, but he was a realist, too. While Dulles, product of a system that made a virtue of compromise and tolerance, insisted that the world must choose sides between American good and

Russian evil, Khrushchev, trained to believe in the incompatibility of communism and capitalism, began to talk of "peaceful coexistence." The battle of words had relatively little impact on events or on world opinion, but what effect it did have generally favored the Russians.

Dulles also failed to win the confidence of America's allies and even of his own department. His sanctimonious manner and generous estimation of his own talents irritated western diplomats; some came to the conclusion that in spite of his stress on morality, his word could not be counted upon. His truckling to Senator McCarthy, who continued his pursuit of imaginary communists in the State Department even when his own party was in control, gravely weakened the morale of career Foreign Service officers. He spent so much time traveling about the world that he neglected the proper administration of general State Department affairs.

The "New Look" in Asia

While the final truce talks were taking place in Korea, new trouble was erupting far to the south in French Indochina. Since December 1946 nationalist rebels led by the communist Ho Chi Minh had been harassing the French in Vietnam, one of three puppet kingdoms (the others were Laos and Cambodia) fashioned by France in Indochina after the defeat of the Japanese. When Communist China began supplying arms to the rebels, who were known as the Vietminh, Truman, applying the containment policy, countered with economic and military assistance to the French. After Eisenhower succeeded to the Presidency, he continued and expanded this assistance.

Early in 1954 the situation became critical when Ho Chi Minh trapped a French army in the remote stronghold of Dien Bien Phu. Faced with the loss of 20,000 soldiers, France asked the United States to commit its air force to the battle. The logic of massive retaliation dictated a strike not at Dien Bien Phu but at Peking, yet Eisenhower, after long deliberation, decided against doing anything. In May the garrison at Dien Bien Phu surrendered, and in July, while Dulles watched from the sidelines, France, Great Britain, Russia, and China signed an agreement at Geneva dividing Vietnam along the 17th parallel. France withdrew from the whole area. The northern sector became the Democratic Republic of Vietnam controlled by Ho Chi Minh; the southern remained in the hands of the emperor, Bao Dai. In 1955 Bao Dai was overthrown by Ngo Dinh Diem, who established an authoritarian but pro-western republic. The United States recognized Diem at once and supplied him liberally with aid.

Dulles responded to the diplomatic setback in Vietnam by establishing the Southeast Asia Treaty Organization (September 1954), but only three Asian nations—the Philippine Republic, Thailand, and Pakistan—joined this alliance.* At the same time, the unleashed Chiang Kai-shek was engaging in a meaningless artillery duel with the Chinese communists from the tiny, nationalist-held islands of Quemoy and Matsu, which lay in the shadow of the mainland. Eisenhower's decision to allow Chiang to take the offensive against Communist China was responsible for this fracas, but when it was suggested that the United States join in the fight, the President refused, on the ground, sensible but inconsistent with Dulles' rhetoric, that intervention might set off an atomic war. Thereafter, the administration devoted much energy to restraining the weak but ambitious Chiang. The United States would not protect the offshore islands, Dulles announced, but it would defend Taiwan at all costs.

Dulles and the Allies: Suez

In Europe the Eisenhower and Dulles policies differed little from those of Truman, but when

*The other signatories were Great Britain, France, the United States, Australia, and New Zealand.

Eisenhower announced his plan to rely more heavily upon nuclear deterrents, the Europeans drew back in alarm, believing that in any atomic showdown the Continent was sure to be destroyed. In this atmosphere Khrushchev's talk of peaceful coexistence also found many receptive ears, especially in France.

The President therefore yielded to European pressures for a diplomatic "summit" conference with the Russians. In July 1955 Eisenhower, Prime Minister Anthony Eden of Great Britain, and French Premier Edgar Faure met at Geneva with Khrushchev and his then co-leader, Nikolai Bulganin, to discuss disarmament and the reunification of West and East Germany. The meeting produced no specific agreements, but with the Russians beaming cheerfully for the cameramen and talking of peaceful coexistence and with Eisenhower pouring martinis and projecting his famous charm, observers noted a softening of tensions which was promptly dubbed "the spirit of Geneva."

Actually, Geneva represented only a brief thaw in the Cold War; within a year the world teetered once again on the brink of a major conflict. This time trouble erupted in the Middle East. American policy in that region, aside from the ubiquitous question of restraining Russian expansion, was influenced by the huge oil resources of Iran, Iraq, Kuwait, and Saudi Arabia—about 60 per cent of the world's known reserves—and by the conflict between the new Jewish state of Israel and its Arab neighbors. Although he tried to woo the Arabs, President Truman had consistently placed support for Israel before other considerations in the Middle East. As early as 1945, he had urged the admission of large numbers of Jewish refugees into British-controlled Palestine, and when Israel formally declared its independence after the withdrawal of the British in 1948, he recognized it even more promptly than Theodore Roosevelt had recognized Panama in 1903.

Alarmed by the creation of Israel, the surrounding Arab nations tried to smash the country by force, but although badly outnumbered, the Israelis were better organized and better armed than their enemies and drove them off with relative ease. With them departed nearly a million Palestinian Arabs, creating a desperate refugee problem in nearby countries. Truman's support of Israel and the millions of dollars contributed to the new state by American Jews greatly increased Arab resentment of the United States.

Dulles and Eisenhower, worried by the growing influence of Russia in the Arab nations, tried to redress the balance by de-emphasizing American support of Israel. In 1952 a revolution in Egypt had overthrown the dissolute King Farouk. Colonel Gamal Abdel Nasser emerged as the strong man of Egypt and began to make his country the leader of the Arab states. Dulles promptly offered Nasser economic aid and tried to entice him into a broad Middle East security pact. Nasser, however, stayed clear of any commitment to the West. No one has accurately untangled his mental processes, but his main object was probably the destruction of Israel, partly because he genuinely hated the Jews and partly because the Israeli question had the same impact on Arab emotions that the "bloody shirt" had on Republicans after the Civil War. Dulles would not sell Egypt arms; the communists would. For this reason, while he accepted American economic assistance, Nasser drifted steadily toward the communist orbit.

In July 1956, when Dulles finally realized the futility of helping Nasser, he dramatically withdrew his offer of American financial support for the giant Aswan Dam project, the key element in an Egyptian irrigation program designed to expand agricultural production. Nasser responded a week later by nationalizing the Suez Canal. This action galvanized the British and French. Influenced by Dulles' argument that Egypt could be made an ally by cajolery, the British had acceded in 1954 to Nasser's demand that they evacuate their military base at Suez. Now what they considered Dulles' bad faith had left their traditional "life line" to the Orient at Nasser's mercy. In conjunction with the French, and without consulting the United States, the British decided to take the canal back by force. The Israelis, concerned by Nasser's mounting military strength and by repeated Arab hit-and-run raids along their borders, also decided to attack Egypt.

Events then moved swiftly. The Israelis crushed the Egyptian army in the Sinai Peninsula in a matter of days. France and Britain occupied Port Said, at the northern end of the canal. Nasser blocked the canal by sinking ships in the channel. In the UN both Russia and the United States introduced resolutions calling for a cease-fire. Both were vetoed by Britain and France. Then Khrushchev thundered a warning from Moscow that he might send "volunteers" to Egypt and launch atomic missiles against France and Great Britain if they did not withdraw. In Washington President Eisenhower also demanded that the invaders pull out of Egypt. In London angry crowds demonstrated against their own government. On November 6, only nine days after the first Israeli troops attacked Egypt, British Prime Minister Eden, haggard and shaken, announced a cease-fire. Israel also withdrew its troops. The crisis subsided as rapidly as it had arisen.

The United States had adhered to its principles, thus winning a measure of respect in the Arab countries, but at great cost. Its major allies had been humiliated. Their ill-timed attack had enabled Russia to recover much of the prestige lost as a result of its brutal suppression of a Hungarian revolt which had broken out only a week before the Suez fiasco. Although no American action justified the Anglo-French assault, Eden and French Premier Guy Mollet could argue with considerable plausibility that Dulles' futile attempt to win Arab friendship without abandoning Israel had placed them in a dilemma and that the secretary had behaved dishonorably or at least disingenuously in handling the Egyptian problem.

Fortunately, the bad feeling within the western alliance soon passed away. When Russia seemed likely to profit from its "defense" of Egypt in the crisis, the United States adopted a more determined stance with the full support of its allies. In January 1957 the President announced the "Eisenhower Doctrine," declaring that the United States was "prepared to use armed force" anywhere in the Middle East

against "aggression from any country controlled by international communism."

The doctrine represented, of course, a restatement of the policy of containment. No sudden shift in the Middle Eastern balance of power resulted. Capitalizing on the Suez crisis, Nasser entered into a political union with Syria, creating the United Arab Republic. But his efforts to expand elsewhere in the area failed, in part because of the jealousies of other Arab leaders and in part because the United States and Britain responded to the requests of Lebanon and Jordan and sent troops into those countries when pro-Nasser elements threatened them in 1958.

The national mood in 1958 was one of sober, restrained determination; hopes of pushing back Russia with clever stratagems and moral fervor were fading. America's first successful earth satellite, launched in January 1958, brought cold comfort. It was so much smaller than the Russian "Sputniks" that many feared the Soviet Union had obtained an insurmountable lead in rocketry, which everyone acknowledged to be vital for national defense. At last the public was beginning to realize that no quick or cheap triumph over communism could be achieved.

The failure of Dulles' policies coincided with his physical decline. In 1957 he underwent surgery for an abdominal cancer. He returned courageously to his duties, but in April 1959 he had to resign. The next month he was dead. Christian A. Herter, a former congressman and governor of Massachusetts, became the new secretary of state, but in the remaining months of the Eisenhower era the President took over personally much of the task of conducting foreign relations.

Actually, although he allowed Dulles to occupy center stage, Eisenhower never abdicated his responsibilities in the foreign policy area. The key to his policy was restraint; he exercised commendable caution in every crisis. Like U. S. Grant, whom he resembled in so many ways, he was a soldier who hated war. From Korea through the crises over Indochina, Hungary, and Suez, he held back from risky new commitments. His behavior, like his temperament, contrasted sharply with that of the aggressive, oratorically perfervid Dulles. The difference between the rhetoric of American foreign policy under Eisenhower and its underlying philosophy was, of course, confusing, and brought down upon the administration much unnecessary criticism.

The U-2 Affair

Amid the tension that followed the Suez crisis, the belief persisted in many quarters that the "spirit of Geneva" could be revived if only a new summit meeting could be arranged. World opinion was increasingly insistent that the great powers stop making and testing nuclear weapons, because every test explosion was contaminating the atmosphere with radioactive debris that threatened the future of all life on earth. Unresolved controversies, especially the argument over divided Germany, might erupt at any moment into a globe-shattering war.

Neither the United States nor the Soviet Union dared ignore these dangers; each, therefore, adopted a more accommodating attitude. In the summer of 1959 Vice President Richard M. Nixon visited the Soviet Union and his opposite number, Vice Premier Anastas I. Mikoyan, toured the United States. Although Nixon's visit was marred by a heated argument with Khrushchev, conducted before a gaping crowd in the kitchen of a model American home that had been set up at a Moscow fair, the results of these exchanges raised hopes that a summit conference would prove profitable. In September 1959 Khrushchev himself came to America. His cross-country tour had its full share of comic contretemps—when denied permission to visit Disneyland because authorities feared they could not protect him properly on the grounds, the heavy-handed Khrushchev accused the United States, only half humorously, of concealing rocket launching pads there. But the general effect of his visit was salutary. In talks with Eisenhower at the end of his stay, he and the President agreed to the summoning of a new four-power summit conference.

This meeting was scheduled for May 16, 1960, at Paris. It never took place. On May 1, high over Sverdlovsk, an industrial center deep in the Soviet Union, an American U-2 reconnaissance plane was shot down by antiaircraft fire. In announcing the event, the Russians merely stated that an American plane had been downed over their territory. Assuming that the pilot had died in the crash, officials in Washington foolishly claimed that a Turkish-based American weather plane had strayed accidentally across the frontier.

Khrushchev then sprang his trap. The Americans lied, he said. The pilot of the plane, Francis Gary Powers, was alive, and he had confessed to being a spy. His cameras contained aerial photographs of military installations more than a thousand miles inside the Soviet Union. Eisenhower could still have avoided personal responsibility for Powers' flight; despite his show of righteous indignation, Khrushchev seemed willing to allow him to do so. But—perhaps goaded by criticisms that he habitually delegated too much authority to subordinates—the President assumed full responsibility. Such missions were "distasteful but vital," he said.

The statement left Khrushchev no choice but to demand an apology. Making full use of the impact of the U-2 affair on world opinion, he came to Paris in a rage, accusing the United States of "piratical" and "cowardly" acts of aggression and threatening to launch atomic missiles against American bases if such overflights were not stopped at once. Khrushchev's intemperance (and perhaps his own chagrin, for he must have realized that he had blundered) infuriated the usually amiable Eisenhower. He refused to apologize, although he did shortly announce that the U-2 flights would be stopped. The summit conference collapsed.

Latin American Problems

Meanwhile events in Latin America compounded Eisenhower's difficulties. During World

War II the United States, needing Latin American raw materials, had supplied its southern neighbors liberally with economic aid. In the period following victory an era of amity and prosperity seemed assured. A great hemispheric mutual-defense pact was signed at Rio de Janeiro in September 1947, and the following year the Organization of American States (OAS) came into being. The United States appeared to have committed itself to a policy of true cooperation with Latin America. In the OAS, decisions were reached by a two-thirds vote; the United States had neither a veto nor any special position.

But the United States tended to neglect Latin America during the Cold War years. Economic problems plagued the region, and in most nations reactionary governments did little to improve the lot of their peoples. Radical Latin Americans accused the United States of supporting cliques of wealthy tyrants, while conservatives tended to use the United States as a scapegoat, blaming lack of sufficient American economic aid for the desperate plight of the local masses. Neither charge was entirely fair, but under Truman the United States did appear to be more concerned with suppressing communism in Latin America than with improving economic conditions.

Eisenhower appeared eager to redress the balance. He sent his brother Dr. Milton Eisenhower on a South American tour, and when Dr. Eisenhower recommended stepped-up economic assistance, the President concurred heartily. Nevertheless, he continued to give resistance to communism first priority. In 1954 the pro-red government of Jacobo Arbenz Guzmán in Guatemala began to import munitions from behind the Iron Curtain. The United States, much alarmed, promptly dispatched arms to the neighboring state of Honduras. Within a month, an army led by an exiled Guatemalan officer marched into the country from Honduras and overthrew Arbenz. Elsewhere in Latin America, Eisenhower, like Truman before him, continued to support unpopular conservative regimes, often kept in power only by the bayonets of the local military, simply because the alternative seemed communist revolution and social chaos.

The depth of Latin American resentment of the United States became clear in the spring of 1958, when Vice President Nixon arrived at Montevideo, Uruguay, to open an eight-nation good-will tour. Everywhere he was met with hostility. In Lima, Peru, he was mobbed; in Caracas, Venezuela, radical students kicked his shiny Cadillac and pelted him with eggs and stones. He had to abandon the remainder of his trip. For the first time, the American people gained some inkling of Latin American opinion and of the social and economic troubles behind this opinion.

There was no easy solution to Latin American problems. This sad truth was made clear by the course of events in Cuba. During the late fifties a revolutionary movement headed by Dr. Fidel Castro gradually undermined the government of Fulgencio Batista, one of the most noxious of the Latin American dictators. In January 1959 Batista finally fled from Cuba, and Castro assumed power. Eisenhower recognized Castro at once, but the Cuban quickly demonstrated his fundamental anti-Americanism. He attacked the United States in interminable and highly colored speeches, seized American property in Cuba without adequate compensation, set up a communist-type government, entered into close relations with the Soviet Union, suppressed civil liberties, and drove many of his original supporters into exile. After he negotiated a trade agreement with Russia in February 1960, which enabled the Russians to obtain Cuban sugar at bargain rates, the United States retaliated by prohibiting the importation of Cuban sugar into America. Further Cuban trade agreements followed with other communist countries, and Khrushchev announced that if the United States intervened in Cuba, he would defend the country with atomic weapons. "The Monroe Doctrine has outlived its time," Khrushchev warned. The worst aspect of the situation was that Castro's movement—called *Fidelismo*—was making inroads in many Latin American countries. Finally, shortly before the end of his second term, Eisenhower broke off diplomatic relations with Cuba.

The new President, Democrat John F. Kennedy, had criticized Eisenhower's Latin Ameri-

In Herblock's cartoon, Russia's Khrushchev poses as James Monroe to announce "Another historic first!" to an aide, Anastas Mikoyan, and a Red Army general. (Herbert Block, *Straight Herblock,* 1964.)

can policy as being unimaginative; his own policy, while certainly not unimaginative, was initially almost a disaster. Recognizing that American economic aid could accomplish little unless accompanied by internal reforms, he organized the Alliance for Progress, which committed the Latin American nations to undertake land reform and economic development projects with the assistance of the United States. He also reversed the Truman–Eisenhower policy of backing reactionary regimes merely because they were anti-communist. In dealing with Cuba, however, Kennedy blundered badly. Anti-Castro exiles were eager to invade their homeland, reasoning that the Cuban masses would rise up against Castro as soon as "democratic" forces provided a standard they could rally to. Already the Central Intelligence Agency was training a group of some 2,000 of these men in Central

America. The President, unwilling to use American troops and planes to drive Castro from Cuba, as might conceivably have been justified on the ground of the national interest, provided the guns and ships that enabled these exiles to attack.

They struck on April 17, 1961, landing at the Bay of Pigs, on Cuba's southern coast. The local populace, however, failed to flock to their lines, and the invaders were soon pinned down and forced to surrender. Since America's involvement could not be disguised, the affair exposed the country to all the criticisms that a straightforward assault would have produced without accomplishing the overthrow of Castro. Still worse, it made the new President appear indecisive as well as unprincipled.

Kennedy's mismanagement of the Bay of Pigs affair encouraged the communists to adopt a more aggressive stance in the Cold War. Castro soon openly admitted that he was a Marxist and further tightened his connections with the Soviet Union. In June Kennedy met with Khrushchev in Vienna. Their conference, marked, like the Eisenhower-Khrushchev meeting at Geneva, by much posing before the cameras and other superficial indications of good-will, evidently failed to convince the Russian that the President would resist pressure with real determination. As soon as Khrushchev returned to Moscow, he threatened to turn over control of the West's access routes to West Berlin to his East German puppet. Since the western powers did not recognize East Germany, this would have precipitated another serious crisis. In August, alarmed by the continuing flow of dissident East Germans into the western sector of Berlin, Khrushchev suddenly closed the border between East and West Berlin and erected an ugly wall of concrete blocks and barbed wire across the city. When Kennedy did not order the wall destroyed by American forces in Berlin, the Russian leader found further reason to believe he could pursue aggressive tactics with impunity. Resuming the testing of nuclear weapons, he exploded a series of gigantic hydrogen bombs, one with a power 3,000 times that of the bomb which devastated Hiroshima.

When the Russians resumed nuclear testing, Kennedy ordered American tests as well. He also ordered an intensification of the American space program,* and called upon Congress for a large increase in the military budget. At the same time, he pressed forward along more constructive lines, pushing the Alliance for Progress, visiting Latin America in an effort to counteract the bad impression resulting from the Bay of Pigs incident, establishing an Agency for International Development to administer American economic aid throughout the world, and creating the Peace Corps, an organization that attempted to mobilize American idealism and technical skills to help underdeveloped nations. Peace Corps volunteers committed themselves to work for two years for a pittance as teachers and technicians in Africa, Asia, and South America. They were supervised by local authorities, and every effort was made to avoid the impression that they were acting to serve any direct American interest.

None of these examples of constructiveness and firmness had much effect on the Russians. Indeed, in 1962 Khrushchev devised the boldest and most reckless challenge of the Cold War, one that brought the world to the verge of nuclear disaster. During the summer months he began moving Russian military equipment and thousands of Soviet technicians into Cuba. Soon American intelligence reports revealed that, in addition to planes and conventional weapons, guided missiles were being imported and launching pads constructed on Cuban soil. Kennedy ordered U-2 reconnaissance planes to photograph these sites and by mid-October he had proof that intermediate-range missile sites capable of delivering hydrogen warheads to points as widely dispersed as Quebec, Minneapolis, Denver, and Lima, Peru, were rapidly being completed.

The President now faced a dreadful decision.

*Russian superiority in this area was gradually reduced. In April 1961 the "cosmonaut" Yuri Gagarin orbited the earth; in August another Russian circled the globe 17 times. The first American to orbit the earth, John Glenn, did not make his voyage until February 1962, but by 1965 the United States had kept a two-man Gemini craft in orbit two weeks, effecting a rendezvous between it and a second Gemini.

To blast these sites before they became operational might result in a third world war. Yet to delay would be to expose the United States to tremendous danger and would certainly increase the Russians' ability to obtain their objectives elsewhere in the world by threats. In a meeting with Soviet Foreign Minister Andrei Gromyko, Kennedy, without revealing what he knew, asked for an explanation of Russian activity in Cuba. In a flat lie, Gromyko told him that only "defensive" (antiaircraft) missiles were being installed. This duplicity strengthened Kennedy's conviction that he must take strong action at once. On October 22 he went before the nation on television. Characterizing the Russian build-up as "a deliberately provocative and unjustified change in the status quo," he ordered the navy to stop and search all vessels headed for Cuba and to turn back any containing "offensive" weapons. He called upon Khrushchev to dismantle the missile bases and remove from the island all weapons capable of striking the United States. Any Cuban-based nuclear attack would result, he warned, in "a full retaliatory response upon the Soviet Union." This was the Dulles concept of massive retaliation, but with the significant difference that Kennedy advanced it with every indication that he meant what he said.

For several days, while the whole world held its breath, work on the missile bases continued. Then Khrushchev backed down. He withdrew the missiles and cut back his military establishment in Cuba to modest proportions. Kennedy then lifted the blockade.

The President's firmness in the missile crisis repaired the damage done his reputation by the Bay of Pigs affair. It also led to a lessening of Soviet–American tensions. At last, it seemed, the Russians were beginning to realize what an all-out nuclear war would mean. Khrushchev agreed to the installation of a "hot line" telephone between the White House and the Kremlin so that in any future crisis leaders of the two nations could be in instant communication. In July 1963 all the powers except France and China signed a treaty banning the testing of nuclear weapons in the atmosphere, a small but significant step toward disarmament. Peaceful coexistence seemed more and more inevitable. Even the fall from power of Khrushchev in 1964 did not lead to an increase in Soviet pressure on the West. Russia, the United States, and all the major nations were finally recognizing that no power could shape the earth in its own exclusive image, that the planet's teeming, diverse billions must live together in mutual tolerance if they would live at all.

Supplementary Reading

For a recent, thoughtful, and well-balanced treatment of wartime diplomacy see J. L. Gaddis, *The United States and the Origins of the Cold War* (1972). Other important books on the subject include W. H. McNeill, *America, Britain and Russia: Their Cooperation and Conflict* (1953), W. L. Neumann, *After Victory: Churchill, Roosevelt, Stalin and the Making of the Peace*° (1967), Gar Alperovitz, *Atomic Diplomacy*° (1965), Gaddis Smith, *American Diplomacy During the Second World War*° (1965), Herbert Feis, *Churchill, Roosevelt, Stalin*° (1957) and *Between War and Peace: The Potsdam Conference*° (1960), R. E. Sherwood, *Roosevelt and Hopkins*° (1948), and Winston Churchill, *The Second World War*° (1948–53).

A good summary of the Cold War is J. M. Spanier, *American Foreign Policy Since World War II*° (1962), but see also L. J. Halle, *The Cold War as History* (1967), and J. A. Lukacs, *A History of the Cold War*° (1960). More critical of American policy are Gabriel Kolko, *The Politics of War*° (1968), Walter La Feber, *America, Russia and the Cold War*° (1968), and D. F. Fleming, *The Cold War and Its Origins* (1961). H. S Truman's *Memoirs*° (1955–56) contain much useful information, as does D. D. Eisenhower's *Mandate for Change*° (1963). Among many analyses and evaluations of American foreign policy, the following are important: W. W. Rostow, *The United States in the World Arena*° (1960), Norman Graebner, *New Isolationism* (1956), H. A. Kissinger, *Nuclear Weapons and Foreign Policy*° (1957), G. F. Kennan, *Realities of American Foreign Policy*° (1954) and *Russia and the West under Lenin and Stalin*° (1961).

On the Truman Doctrine, see J. M. Jones, *The Fifteen Weeks*° (1955); on the Marshall Plan, see H. B. Price, *The Marshall Plan and its Meaning* (1955). R. E. Osgood, *NATO: The Entangling Alliance* (1962), is excellent. For the rebuilding of West Germany, consult Harold Zink, *The United States in Germany* (1957), and Eugene Davidson, *The Death and Life of Germany* (1959).

American relations with China are covered in Herbert Feis, *The China Tangle*° (1953), Tang Tsou, *America's Failure in China*° (1963), and A. D. Barnett, *Communist China and Asia: Challenge to American Policy*° (1960); for Japan, see E. O. Reischauer, *The United States and Japan*° (1957). On the Korean War, consult David Rees, *Korea: The Limited War* (1964), and J. W. Spanier, *The Truman-MacArthur Controversy and the Korean War*° (1959).

McCarthyism and the Hiss case are covered in Earl Latham, *The Communist Conspiracy in Washington* (1966), Alan Barth, *The Loyalty of Free Men* (1951), Alistair Cooke, *A Generation on Trial: USA v. Alger Hiss*° (1950), Whittaker Chambers, *Witness*° (1952), J. W. Caughey, *In Clear and Present Danger* (1958), and R. H. Rovere, *Senator Joe McCarthy*° (1959).

John Foster Dulles' views are discussed in Richard Goold-Adams, *The Time of Power: A Reappraisal of John Foster Dulles* (1962), Roscoe Drummond and Gaston Coblenz, *Duel at the Brink* (1960), J. R. Beal, *John Foster Dulles* (1959), and in Dulles' own *War or Peace* (1950). For developments in the Far East, see R. H. Fifield, *The Diplomacy of Southeast Asia* (1958); for the Middle East, see J. C. Campbell, *Defense of the Middle East*° (1960), and Herman Finer, *Dulles over Suez* (1964), which is extremely critical of the secretary. The diplomacy of the Eisenhower era is also discussed in R. J. Donovan, *Eisenhower: The Inside Story* (1956), Marquis Childs, *Eisenhower: Captive Hero* (1958), E. J. Hughes, *The Ordeal of Power*° (1963), J. E. Smith, *The Defense of Berlin* (1963) and *The United States and Cuba*° (1960).

On the Kennedy period, see A. M. Schlesinger, Jr., *A Thousand Days*° (1965), T. C. Sorensen, *Kennedy*° (1965), H. B. Johnson, *The Bay of Pigs* (1964), and Elie Abel, *The Missile Crisis* (1966).

°Available in paperback.

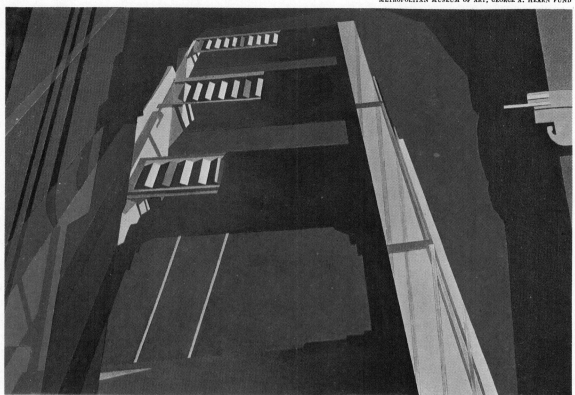

Portfolio 6

20th-Century American Painting

American painting in the 20th century has been called everything from "psychological balderdash" to "anti-art." But by the seventies it seemed more likely that history would judge the best American painting of this century, as represented in the nation's 700 galleries, 500 museums, and 200 corporate art collections, to be a fitting, modern expression of Aristotle's classic definition: "In part art completes what nature cannot elaborate; and in part it imitates nature." The startling modernity of some of these canvases is, as one American painter has suggested, a reflection of 20th-century man's "fresh relationship to the courses of the sun and to the living swing of the earth."

Revolutionary times have called forth a procession of stylistic revolutions, yet transcending the diversity is a much older American quality, the pioneer's love of adventure and space. Charles Sheeler would not, for example, add *Bridge* to the title of his 1955 painting *Golden Gate* (above). "Then it would be limited to be the connecting link between two dots on the map," Sheeler said. "It is an opening, . . . a gateway, a beckoning into the new."

THE ASHCAN SCHOOL

"Apostles of Ugliness," "The Revolutionary Blackgang," screamed the academicians. "To hell with artistic values," replied Robert Henri, teacher and leader of a group of eight pioneers determined to paint whatever they saw around them and not merely what others considered "proper" subjects. Today much of the painting of the ashcan school seems like the pleasant effulgence of French impressionism set in New York rather than in Paris. But in 1908, when The Eight (as the school was then called) held an independent showing in defiance of the National Academy of Design, their work "stabbed" the public right "in the optic nerve." An appreciative critic pointed out that the ashcan painters had offended by calling attention to what no one wanted to see—"our crude, vibrating, nervous, uncertain civilization."

As Everett Shinn, one of the original eight, later wrote, in the early 1900's "art in America . . . was merely an adjunct of plush and cut glass. . . . Its heart pumped only anemia." By daring, as John Sloan advocated, to paint the city in all its "drab, shabby, happy, sad, and human moods," these artists rescued American painting from being largely parlor ornamentation and an object of conspicuous consumption. Art should depict the life (in Aristotelian terms, the nature) of its times, pleasant or grim, they said. Secondly, and of equal importance, the ashcan artists adopted a highly personal approach toward painting. "Art . . . is an individual thing, the question of one man facing certain facts and telling his relations to them," Robert Henri never tired of reminding his students. For more than half a century Henri's dictum has been the watchword of American painters—as it has been the watchword of great artists in every age.

Upper left: William Glackens painted *The Green Car* in 1910 using the bright palette and feathery strokes of the French impressionists to depict New York City in winter.

Far left: John Sloan's *The Lafayette,* 1928. Believing cameras "mentally blind," Sloan thought painting should portray "the things that a blind man knows about the world."

Left: Because of subject matter, Everett Shinn's warmly colored pastel, *The Laundress,* was called "vulgar" by critics who objected to artists painting the life of the poor.

Above: "Brutal" George Bellows' 1917 lithograph of his famous *Stag at Sharkey's* is an example of the kind of realism that made the ashcan school an object of outrage.

Arthur Dove, *Ferry Boat Wreck*, 1931.

Max Weber, *Chinese Restaurant*, 1915.

PIONEERS OF MODERNISM

Between 1880 and about 1920 such European artists as Cézanne, Matisse, Kandinsky, and Picasso led a series of artistic revolutions and laid the foundations for modern art. They abandoned the rendering of three-dimensional space by means of linear perspective in favor of new visual orientations: cubism, which dissected, selected, and reassembled forms in terms of shifting planes and geometric shapes; abstraction, which cast aside the representations of visual reality in favor of the artist's personal conceptions of beauty, shape, and design; and expressionism, which concentrated on portraying the feeling a subject inspired rather than on its outward appearance. In the realm of color the Fauves, or "Wild Beasts," used unmixed pigments to record the artist's (and reject the camera's) vision.

Followers of no one school, American painters adapted all these innovations to their own individual and generally expressionistic purposes. Arthur Dove's *Ferry Boat Wreck,* for instance, combines realistic and abstract elements to express a sense of tragedy which goes beyond the single incident. The ocean is recognizable; the ferry is not, but its demise is clearly suggested by the semiabstract, loglike shapes in the foreground. Max Weber's *Chinese Restaurant* borrows the cubist technique of shattering and reassembling shapes to create the artist's own personal fantasy. In explaining his use of cubism, Weber wrote, "On entering a Chinese restaurant from the darkness of the night outside, a maze and blaze of light seemed to split into fragments the interior and its contents. . . . The light so piercing and so luminous, the color so liquid and the life and movement so enchanting! To express this, a kaleidoscopic means had to be chosen." Charles Burchfield's specter-ridden watercolor, *Church Bells Ringing . . . ,* however, owes its effect more to Burchfield's exploration of "a completely personal mood" than to any other influence. John Marin was another pioneer of American modernism whose style was largely of his own devising. Using brilliant colors and simplified shapes in cityscapes and seascapes, such as *Sun Spots,* Marin painted nature's "warring, pushing, pulling" forces which, he said, made "the whole human critter expand nigh to the bustin' point."

Charles Burchfield, *Church Bells Ringing . . . ,* 1917.

John Marin, *Sun Spots,* 1920.

Strongly influenced by the European futurists' fascination with industrial landscapes, Joseph Stella painted *Coal Pile* (top) in 1908 after a trip to Pittsburgh.

Above: To explain how *South of Scranton* (1931) developed into a surrealist fantasy, Peter Blume wrote, "As I tried to weld my impressions into the picture they lost all their logical connections. I moved Scranton into Charleston, and Bethlehem into Scranton, as people do in a dream. The German sailors appeared to lose the purpose of exercising and became . . . like birds soaring through space."

At right is Edward Hopper's *Early Sunday Morning* (1930). Hopper's aim was to paint "the most exact transcription" of his "most intimate impressions."

VISIONS OF REALITY

In "The Man with the Blue Guitar" Wallace Stevens wrote, "They said, 'You have a blue guitar,/ You do not play things as they are.'/ The man replied, 'Things as they are/ Are changed upon the blue guitar.'" The artist's imagination is his blue guitar. The individualism that Henri encouraged, combined with the moderns' technical innovations, enormously widened the imaginative scope of 20th-century American painting. These canvases by Joseph Stella, Edward Hopper, and Peter Blume represent dramatically varied interpretations of typical American landscapes. Stella, an Italian immigrant, was thrilled to find that in America "Steel and electricity had created a new world. . . . A new polyphony was ringing all around with the scintillating, highly-colored lights. . . . A new architecture was created, a new perspective." This insight permeated industrial landscapes such as *Coal Pile* and his many renderings of the Brooklyn Bridge in which he sought to "exalt the joyful, daring endeavor of the American civilization." Edward Hopper responded very differently. Like Stella, he filled his canvases with light, but of a cruel and penetrating kind. In paintings such as *Early Sunday Morning* he used it to describe the "fear and anxiety" which he felt America's urban civilization inspired. Where Stella was dazzled by modern America and Hopper probed its loneliness, Blume translated its diversity into surrealist fantasies. *South of Scranton* recreates a trip through Pennsylvania steel and mining towns to Charleston, South Carolina, where the artist watched sailors doing calisthenics on the deck of a visiting German cruiser.

AMERICA, AMERICA

In painting as in life, every innovation produces a complex variety of reactions. By the mid-1920's many painters felt that the "modern" artist had become too dependent upon European techniques and had lost his grip on reality—specifically, American reality. Generally speaking, these painters divided into two groups, rural and urban regionalists.

The rural regionalists set out to portray the virtues of America's farmlands. Their most vocal representative, Thomas Hart Benton, proclaimed in 1932, "no American art can come to those who do not live an American life, who do not have an American psychology, and who cannot find in America justification for their lives." Benton denounced the whole modern movement as "dirt."

Urban regionalists, largely centered in New York, were not so much concerned about painting "American" as they were about catching the many-sided and often vulgar life of America's most dynamic, polyglot metropolis. "Well-bred people are no fun to paint," Reginald Marsh said. The urban regionalists had no single artistic credo. Rather they sought, as the ashcan painters had before them, to let the city and all its complexities be their guide. "It offers itself," as Marsh put it.

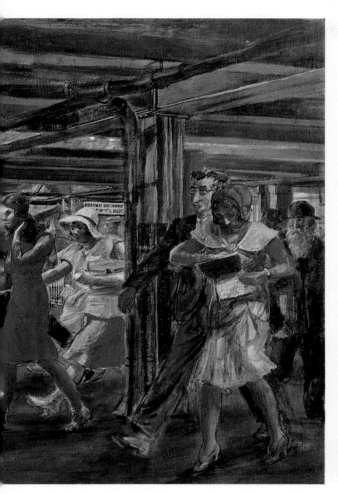 

Regionalists paintings show a broad range of interests, from Reginald Marsh's 1930 canvas *Subway, 14th Street* (above left) with its concentration on New York's energy, through Louis Bouché's quiet ferryboat scene, *Ten Cents a Ride* (above right), done in 1942, to Grant Wood's 1933 pencil sketches (below) for *Dinner for Threshers*, with their loving description of rural life.

THE SOCIAL REALISTS

On February 14, 1936, the first Artists' Congress ever held in America opened with a speech by the social historian Lewis Mumford. It was a grim era. The Great Depression gripped the United States, fascism was riding high in Germany and Italy, and there were portents of another world war. ''The time has come,'' Mumford said, ''. . . to be ready to protect, and guard, and if necessary, fight for the human heritage which we, as artists, embody.'' A number of American painters, now known as the social realists, were already using their work as just such a weapon. Their painting was social in its direct concern for American problems and, by appealing to emotions, dramatically realistic in technique.

The distinction of the social realists is largely attributable to three artists whose skill matched their concern for their fellow men—Philip Evergood, Ben Shahn, and Jack Levine. Shahn expressed their credo when he said, ''I hate injustice. I guess that's about the only thing I really do hate . . . and I hope to go on hating it all my life.'' The social realists were also angered by the lack of commitment on the part of their ''modern'' colleagues. ''Is all our pity and anger to be reduced to a few tastefully arranged straight lines or petulant squirts from a tube held over a canvas?'' Shahn asked. Their anger was tempered by an awareness that mankind could never be wholly condemned. ''On one hand we see gluttony and self-aggrandizement,'' Evergood pointed out, ''and on the other self-abnegation, sacrifice, generosity, and heroism, in different members of the same human race.''

"You distort for editorial reasons," is Jack Levine's succinct artistic canon. In *The Feast of Pure Reason* (above), painted in 1937, Levine used distortion and a startling, unnatural light to explore the faces of the three cronies. In *Willis Avenue Bridge* (1940) on the opposite page, Ben Shahn stunted and shriveled the old ladies to make them at once grotesque and pathetic, while Philip Evergood's *American Tragedy* (left), painted to commemorate a bloody labor clash in Chicago in 1937, is a compilation of dramatic distortion.

THE FEDERAL ART PROJECT

The year 1933 inaugurated a New Deal in art as well as in politics. The Roosevelt administration decided that artists, along with the other millions of unemployed, were a national resource and deserved federal assistance. The largest such effort was the Federal Art Project, begun in 1935 as a division of the Works Progress Administration. A truly gargantuan undertaking, the project employed over 5,000 persons in mural and easel painting, sculpture, crafts, photography, art instruction, the planning and creation of new museums, and other related ventures.

In statistical terms alone the project achieved immense results. It placed over a million pieces of art in the nation's galleries and museums, commissioned hundreds of murals for post offices, schools, and other public buildings, and started scores of new museums in rural areas.

Although project director Holger Cahill insisted that "We shall not tell painters what to paint or how to paint it," he believed that much of modern painting had become too obscure, and consequently he encouraged what he called "imaginative realism." At its best, imaginative realism combined the strengths of regional and social realist painting with an imaginative flair for interpreting American culture; at its worst, it degenerated into chauvinistic illustration.

In 1939 Congress terminated the Federal Art Project amid accusations that it had been a frivolous expense. Today it is clear that the contribution of the project to American culture was large, if difficult to pinpoint. Millions of Americans had their artistic horizons broadened. For the artists it provided not only a shelter in the storm—"a moment of peace," as one artist expressed it—but also the exhilarating experience of helping their country in a time of crisis.

In 1964 Ben Shahn, recalling his days with the project, said, "I felt in complete harmony with the times. I don't think I've ever felt that way before or since." Finally, the project produced for the public a number of 20th-century classics at bargain rates. For example, in 1965 a WPA mural, discovered in a New York City radio station, was valued by appraisers at between $60,000 and $100,000. It was the work of Stuart Davis, who was paid $24.50 a week in 1939 for the ten weeks it took him to paint it.

Jacob Lawrence, *Blind Beggars,* 1938.

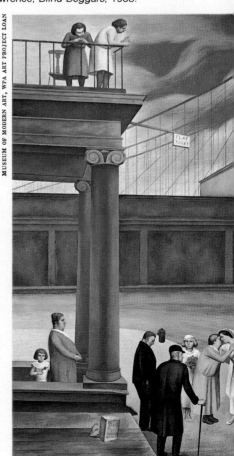

L. Guglielmi, *Wedding in South Street,* 1936.

In 1937 John Steuart Curry did two murals, *Comedy* and *Tragedy,* for a Westport, Connecticut, school. *Comedy* (above) has in its cast many of the comic-strip characters of the thirties, including Mutt and Jeff, Popeye and Olive Oyl, and Mickey Mouse. Below Charlie Chaplin (with roller skates and cane) are Amos and Andy of radio fame, dancers Vernon and Irene Castle, Will Rogers (in the cowboy hat) and, on either side of the curtain, Curry and his wife, Kathleen.

P6-XIII

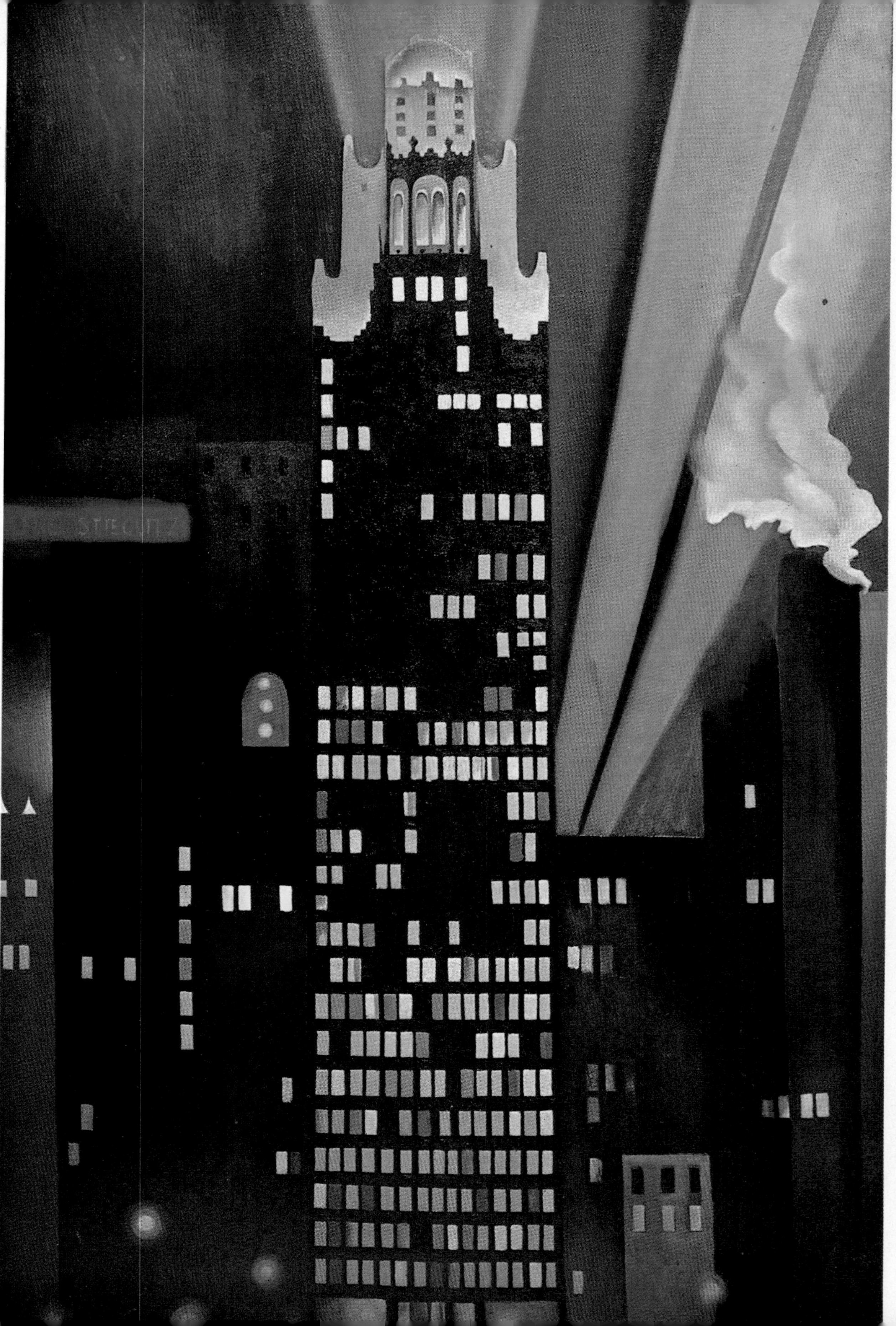

ALFRED STIEGLITZ COLLECTION, FISK UNIVERSITY

THE PRECISIONISTS

While the regionalists, the social realists, and the imaginative realists were rejecting the more daring visual perspectives of modern art, another group of painters in the twenties and thirties embraced them as a means of portraying the shape and feel of a machine-created civilization. Although the precisionists (sometimes called the "immaculates") were not a school and had no one artistic credo, they did share a common attitude toward reality. Unconcerned about the state of society, they painted, like the later "hard edge" artists, with the cool detachment of a scientific observer. This effect of emotional distance was achieved by a precision of style that has given them their name. "I favor the picture which arrives at its destination without the evidence of a trying journey rather than the one which shows the marks of battle. An efficient army buries its dead," Charles Sheeler once said. Another precisionist, Charles Demuth, who put perspective to often-dramatic uses, commented that he had drawn out his inspiration "with a teaspoon, but I never spilled a drop."

The immaculate surfaces and the careful geometric arrangement of forms give precisionist paintings their apparent impersonality, yet from this meticulousness emerges a pervasive, if understated, feeling of awe and excitement at the order, beauty, and power of industrial America. "Our factories," Sheeler said, "are our substitute for religious experience." The paintings of Stuart Davis illustrate another and far more lighthearted dimension of the precisionists' work. In brilliantly colored, collage-like canvases Davis combined ideas, symbols, and objects to express the jazzy tempo of 20th-century America. The components of his vision, which Davis called EYDEAS, included "the brilliant colors on gasoline stations, chain store fronts, and taxicabs . . . fast travel by train, auto, and airplane, which brought new and multiple perspectives; electric signs; the landscape and boats of Gloucester, Massachusetts; five-and-ten-cent-store kitchen utensils, movies and radio; Earl Hines's piano."

In Georgia O'Keeffe's *American Radiator Building* (left), telescopic clarity dramatizes the size and power of the skyscraper. The receding perspective in Charles Demuth's *I Saw the Figure 5 in Gold* (1928) was inspired by his friend William Carlos Williams' poem "The Great Figure": "Among the rain / and lights / I saw the figure 5 / in gold / on a red / firetruck / moving / tense / unheeded / to gong clangs / siren howls / and wheels rumbling / through the dark city." *House and Street* (1931) by Stuart Davis revels in its childlike perspective.

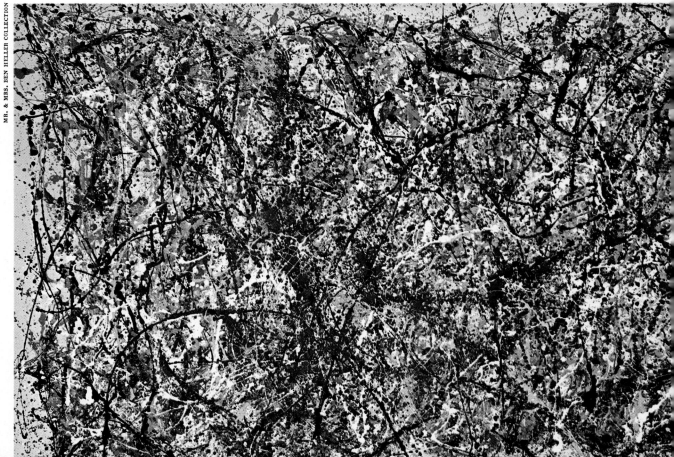

Above: Hans Hofmann, *Fantasia,* 1943.

Left: Arshile Gorky, *Agony,* 1947.

Below: Jackson Pollock, *One,* 1950.

ABSTRACT EXPRESSIONISM

In 1946 the public got its first view of abstract expressionism; two decades later the shock waves were still reverberating. Neither abstraction nor expressionism were new to 20th-century painting, but combining them was not only new but revolutionary. Almost overnight New York replaced Paris as the world capital of avantgarde art. The abstract expressionists abandoned linear perspective, avoided all objects except those that symbolized the primary forces of life, and worked seemingly without plan or precision. But what they left out was far less shocking than what they often literally threw in— great splashes of color, tangles of paint, rude shapes in dramatic opposition, which combined to express powerful emotions devoid of specific allusion.

Conservatives cried "fraud," but these pioneering artists insisted that only revolutionary painting could express revolutionary times. In 1950 Jackson Pollock said, "The modern painter cannot express this age, the airplane, the atom bomb, the radio, in the old forms of the renaissance or any other past culture." A year later Robert Motherwell added, "The need is for felt experience—intense, immoderate, direct, subtle, unified, warm, vivid, rhythmic." Hans Hofmann, the movement's foremost teacher and theoretician, explained that abstract expressionism sought to "present" the inner and often subconscious world of the artist's mind rather than to "represent" the outer world of known objects. Thus Arshile Gorky's *Agony* is not a representation of a man in pain, but a presentation of pain itself. Pollock's *One* and Mark Rothko's *Number 10* carry this introspective bent to another conclusion. Neither painting is "of" anything; each is its own subject.

In order to tap the resources of the subconscious, the abstract expressionists painted as freely and as intuitively as their materials permitted. Pollock, the creator of "action painting," put his huge canvases on the floor, where he felt "nearer, more a part of the painting, since this way I can walk around it, work from the four sides, and literally be in the painting." Abstract expressionists held that spontaneity turned art into exploration, "an unknown adventure into an unknown space."

Robert Motherwell, *Elegy to the Spanish Republic,* 1954.

Adolph Gottlieb, *Blast I,* 1957.

Mark Rothko, *Number 10,* 1950.

Willem de Kooning, *Woman VIII*, 1961.

Theodoros Stamos, *High Snow-Low Sun, II*, 1957.

THE FIGURE

"Today, the figure is the hardest thing in the world to do. If it doesn't turn into some sort of cornball realism, it becomes anecdotal." These words of artist Larry Rivers express a dilemma which has both plagued and stimulated figurative painters since the postwar move toward abstract expressionism. Paintings, the new figurative artists argue, need to have real subjects, but they insist that their works must speak a far more general language than what realistic portraiture or photographic realism allow.

Of the three artists represented here, Andrew Wyeth is the most realistically oriented, yet he says, "I honestly consider myself an abstractionist," and is concerned lest his superbly crafted paintings become "overfed and the objects over-expressed." He wants his subjects to transcend their individuality and become symbols of man's precious mortality.

Richard Diebenkorn, who left abstract expressionism because he came to distrust his desire "to explode the picture," considers figurative painting "a fantastic clutter of possibilities filled with booby traps and corn fields"—that is, the trite and the sentimental. As one critic has said, his canvases provide "the actual forms: figure, landscape, indication of action. . . . Now the viewer must project self into the mood, character, inner contemplation of human space within."

Larry Rivers, perhaps the most enigmatic of the three, says, "I can't put down on canvas what I can't see. I think of a picture as a smorgasbord of the recognizable." He is so deeply distrustful of "cornball realism" that he insists, "I can't express pity, hatred, joy, anxiety; I have to work on it until the expression or the look is something that you can't give a name to."

The figurative works reproduced here are attempts to go beyond the limits of realistic portraiture and, as Andrew Wyeth has advocated, show ''Americans what America is like.'' Wyeth detests ''the sweetness'' of much current figurative painting and hopes that his studies of small-town, rural Americans, such as *Albert's Son* (above), painted in Maine in 1959, will reveal the ''real American personality.'' Richard Diebenkorn's *July* (upper left), painted in California in 1957, welds figure, landscape, and symbol together to create an American ''rough-hewn, frontier quality.'' Larry Rivers' featureless *The Next to Last Confederate Soldier* (1959), left, uses a similar juxtaposition to satirize the romanticized myth of the Civil War.

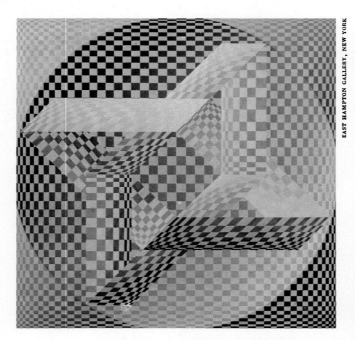

Benjamin Cunningham, *Equivocation,* 1964.

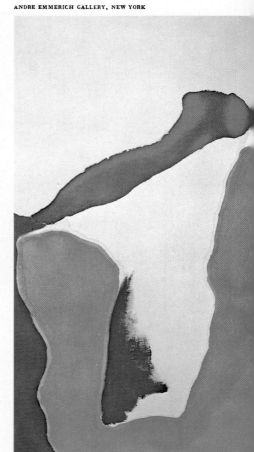

Helen Frankenthaler, *Good Luck Orange,* 1969.

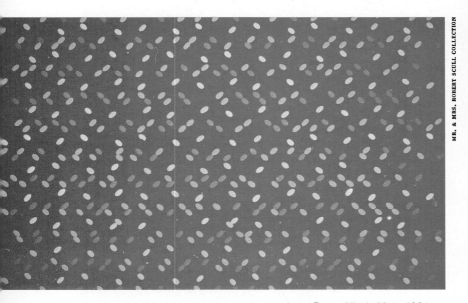

Larry Poon, *Nixe's Mate,* 1964.

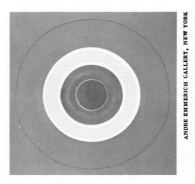

Kenneth Noland, *Noon, Afloat,* 1962.

M. KNOEDLER & CO. INC.

Barnett Newman, *Who's Afraid of Red, Yellow, and Blue III,* 1966–67.

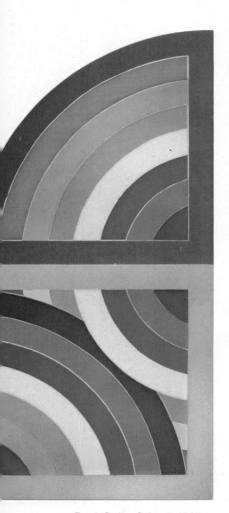

Frank Stella, *Sabra II,* 1967.

NEW VISIONS OF VISION

In the sixties American painters continued to explore new modes of perception. Defining their work, as one did, as the "programming of information permitting a confrontation with visual situations," these artists abandoned what they called the "easel-weasel" in order to probe the process of vision itself.

Using the science of modern optics, "op" artists—in such works as Larry Poon's *Nixe's Mate* or Ben Cunningham's *Equivocation*—investigated how the eye and the psyche respond to highly calculated arrangements of line, shape, color, density, and mass. While such paintings create remarkable visual effects in which stationary dots appear to move and flat surfaces to have infinite depth, the meaning of "op," according to its proponents, lies primarily not in such illusions but in the intellectual and emotional experiences it generates.

Insisting that paintings are not "space boxes" for creating an illusory "window on the world," artists such as Kenneth Noland and Frank Stella explore the potential of canvases shaped and designed in geometrical color patterns. Helen Frankenthaler employs non-geometric shapes and "expressionistic" colors to probe the psyche. Whatever the method, such painters find their work enormously challenging. As Barnett Newman, who spent a lifetime experimenting with monumental works (*Who's Afraid of Red, Yellow, and Blue III,* above, is 8 feet by 18 feet), put it: "I always want to do something I can't do. . . . Risk is the high road to glory."

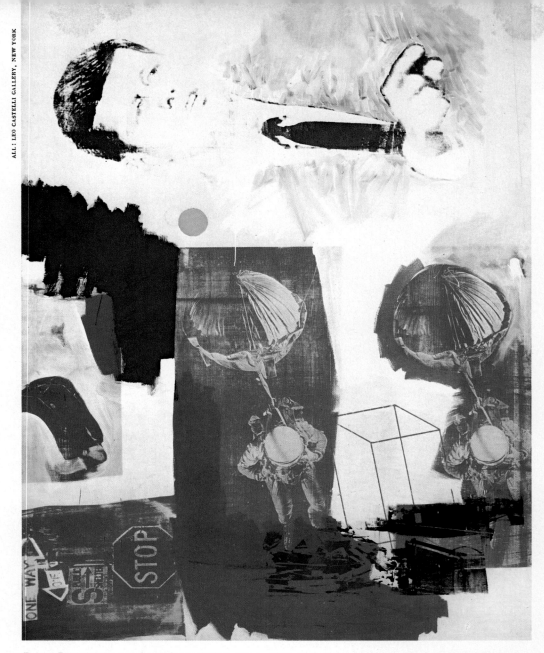

Robert Rauschenberg painted *Quote* (1964), above, after years of experimenting with collages and "combines" to find a medium that would "affect a sense of non-selectivity." Andy Warhol's *Marilyn Monroe* (1967), below, is a detail from one of his many multiple-imaged renderings of the actress. Roy Lichtenstein's *Varoom* (1967), opposite, employs magnification to gain the texture of newsprint.

THE PROCESSED IDIOM

While some American painters were exploring the potential of new kinds of visual confrontation, others chose to confront the nation with itself. By transferring (sometimes directly) to the canvas the multiple images of a consumer-oriented, advertising-hounded, mass-media society, "pop" artists, the painters of the popular and commercial image, presented a satirical reflection of contemporary America. As one pop artist said, "When the remains of our civilization are dug up in a thousand years, it will be our washing machines more than the contents of our museums that will define our culture." Pop's cataloguing of American banalities made it heir to the tradition of social realism begun by the ashcan artists.

Although the techniques of pop painters differ, they share an urge to present images that go to the heart of contemporary experience by ingeniously displaying "processed idioms to express the quality of a way of life that is increasingly processed." For example, Andy Warhol's multi-imaged *Marilyn Monroe* employs a grotesque frame-by-frame mimicry of the movie idiom itself to produce a visual mime of the tortured and tragic career of a cinematic sex goddess. Roy Lichtenstein's *Varoom* holds up a mirror to the tragicomic American admiration for the comic-strip world of action and romance.

On the other hand, the work of Robert Rauschenberg goes beyond the exhibiting of a microcosm of mass culture. Its processed idioms create a new kind of American landscape. By combining silk-screen reproductions of photographs with rich swatches of color, Rauschenberg attempts to retain the high tensions of abstract expressionism within a landscape "peopled" by "real" images drawn from the mass media. Painted a year after President Kennedy's assassination, but without deliberately exploiting the emotionalism of that event, Rauschenberg's *Quote* (opposite) creates an impression of the dynamic excitement and dramatic turbulence of the Kennedy years and their traumatic climax.

It is impossible to predict what directions American painting will take in the future. One thing does seem likely, however: American painters will continue the 20th-century tradition of employing their art to explore both the inner and the outer landscapes of American civilization.

29

The Postwar Scene: 1945–1964

While foreign affairs dominated American political history after World War II, domestic events and conditions occupied the lion's share of the time and attention of most citizens. In one sense, the era was one of consolidation rather than of innovation. The social and economic changes wrought by the New Deal were confirmed; no major New Deal reform was done away with or even significantly reduced in scope. But the postwar decades were also a time of enormous development and change. American society evolved steadily and at an increasing pace, until by the mid-sixties it was an open

801
HARRY S TRUMAN

question whether it was evolving or passing through a revolution.

The Political Climate

Superficially, the Democrats controlled the national government during most of the period. Only one Republican, Dwight D. Eisenhower, was elected President and he more in spite of being a Republican than because of it. In only two of the ten Congresses of these years did the GOP command majorities. Yet the Democrats seldom *really* dominated politics. In Congress particularly, southern Democrats tended to side with Republicans on key issues, forming a loose conservative coalition capable of thwarting legislation although not itself able to overturn institutions or laws.

The times apparently favored moderation. The country seemed ever more homogeneous, prosperity fostered complacency, and the rapidity of social change and the danger of nuclear annihilation frightened millions of Americans into adopting a cautious, conservative attitude that militated against drastic policies. The repeated glorification of democratic principles, especially the idea of majority rule, seemed at times to have made the United States a nation of what the sociologist David Riesman called "other directed" persons more concerned with conforming to established mores than with realizing themselves fully as individuals. From the failure of Henry A. Wallace's Progressive party to poll more than 1.2 million votes in 1948 to the overwhelming defeat of the Republican reactionary Barry Goldwater in 1964, the public rejected extremism, both of the left and of the right.

Within the federal government, the great expansion of the size and authority of the executive branch that had taken place as a result of the Great Depression and World War II continued. Between 1933 and 1964 the number of its civilian employees rose from less than half a million to 1.5 million. An ever-more-complex society placed a premium on centralized regulation and

rapid decision. Congress—its internal divisions aside—seemed to lack both the expertise and the efficiency to run the nation. It could and did resist many Presidential initiatives, but when it sought to act positively it tended to delegate responsibility to the White House. That successive Cold War crises with their threat of instant nuclear annihilation had practically extinguished the constitutional power of Congress to declare war was widely noted, but the growth of Presidential authority was occurring also in the domestic arena. The absence of workable majorities in Congress obscured this trend; the Presidents certainly felt themselves hampered by congressional resistance to many of their policies. Nevertheless, Presidential power continued to expand.

Until the mid-1960's, however, the political system seemed stalled at dead center. The least partisan branch of the government, the Supreme Court, emerged as the most powerful instrument for change, not only in its decisions involving the rights of Negroes, but also in those requiring the redistricting of state legislatures, the great effect of which has scarcely begun to be felt.

Harry S Truman

None of the Presidents of the period ranks with Lincoln or Franklin D. Roosevelt, nor was any a Buchanan, a Grant, or a Harding. Harry S Truman was the most controversial. He was born in Missouri in 1884. After service with a World War I artillery unit, he opened a men's clothing store in Kansas City but failed in the postwar depression. Then he became a minor cog in the Missouri political machine of boss Tom Pendergast. In 1934 he was elected to the United States Senate, where he proved to be a loyal but obscure New Dealer. During World War II his "watchdog" committee on defense spending worked with admirable devotion and efficiency, saving the government immense sums. The 1944 Vice Presidential nomination marked for him the height of achievement; he seems never to have seriously considered the possibility that fate would place him in the White House itself.

When Roosevelt died in April 1945, Truman confessed frankly that he felt as though "the moon, the stars, and all the planets" had suddenly fallen upon him. Acutely conscious of his limitations, yet determined to live up to his new responsibilities, he sought to carry on in the Roosevelt tradition, and also to win a place in history in his own right. Curiously, he was both humble and cocky, idealistic and cold-bloodedly political. He had an immense fund of information about American history, but like most amateurs he lacked historical judgment and was prone to interpret past events in whatever manner best suited his current convenience. He read books but distrusted ideas, adopted liberal objectives only to pursue them sometimes by rash, even repressive, means.

Truman was his own worst enemy. Too often he insulted opponents instead of convincing or conciliating them. Complications tended to confuse him, in which case he dug in his heels or struck out blindly, usually with unfortunate results. Much of his energy was funneled into heated controversies with politicians and reporters; even a music critic who disparaged Truman's daughter Margaret's talents as a singer incurred the Presidential wrath. Although he appointed a number of first-rate men to high office, especially in the field of foreign affairs, many of his advisers were men much like himself in background and training, some of them, alas, without his honesty and dedication to the public service.

Truman bungled the task of converting the economy back to peacetime conditions, angering both labor and capital by his efforts to control their activities, but failing to prevent a sharp rise in the cost of living. In rooting out "security risks" in the federal bureaucracy, he paid insufficient attention to fair judicial procedures and thus caused the discharge and disgrace of a number of innocent persons without uncovering more than a handful of real subversives. Yet he tried to dismiss the accusations against Alger Hiss as a "red herring" designed by the Republicans to discredit his administration.

Nevertheless, Truman was a strong and in many ways a successful Chief Executive. Like Jackson, Wilson, and the two Roosevelts, he effectively epitomized the national will and projected a sense of dedication and purposefulness in his management of national affairs. His greatest triumph came in the 1948 election. The international frustrations and domestic economic problems of the postwar period had enabled the Republicans to win the 1946 congressional elections handily, and the trend over the next two years seemed even more in their favor. The 1948 Republican candidate, Governor Thomas E. Dewey of New York, ran confidently, even complacently, sure that he would carry the country with ease.

Truman's position seemed hopeless because he had alienated both southern conservatives and northern liberals. The former were particularly distressed because the President had established a Committee on Civil Rights in 1946, which had recommended antilynching and antipoll tax legislation and the creation of a permanent Fair Employment Practices Commission. The southerners founded the States' Rights ("Dixiecrat") party and nominated J. Strom Thurmond of South Carolina for President. Among the liberals, a faction led by former Vice President Henry A. Wallace, which believed Truman's containment policy a threat to world peace, favored greater cooperation with the Soviet Union. This group organized a new Progressive party and nominated Wallace. With two minor candidates sure to cut into the Democratic vote, the President's chances seemed minuscule. Public opinion polls showed Dewey far ahead.

Truman, however, launched an aggressive "whistle-stop" campaign, making hundreds of informal but hard-hitting speeches. He excoriated the "do-nothing" Republican Congress, which had rejected his Fair Deal program and had passed a labor relations act that the unions considered reactionary, and he warned labor, farmers, and consumers that a Republican victory would undermine all the gains of the New Deal years.

Millions were moved by his arguments and by

In 1948 the strongly Republican Chicago *Daily Tribune* guessed disastrously wrong in headlining its post-election editions before all the returns were in. For Truman, it was the perfect climax to his hard-won victory. (UPI.)

his courageous one-man fight against great odds. The success of the Berlin airlift during the Presidential campaign also helped him considerably. The Progressive party fell increasingly into the hands of communist sympathizers, driving away many liberals who might otherwise have supported Wallace. Dewey's smug, lackluster campaign failed to attract independents. The President, therefore, was able to reinvigorate the New Deal coalition, and he won an amazing upset victory on Election Day. He collected 24.1 million votes to Dewey's 21.9 million, the two minor candidates being held to about 2.3 million. In the Electoral College his margin was a thumping 303 to 189.

Dwight D. Eisenhower

This lesson was not lost on the Republicans. In 1952 they passed over the twice-defeated Dewey and their most prominent leader, Senator Robert A. Taft of Ohio, an outspoken conservative, and nominated General Dwight D. Eisenhower for the Presidency. Eisenhower's enormous popularity did not grow merely out of his achievements in World War II. Although a West Pointer (class of 1915), he struck most persons as anything but warlike. After Truman, his genial tolerance and evident desire to avoid controversy proved widely appealing. His reluctance to enter the political arena reminded the country of Washington, while his relative ignorance of current political issues was no more a handicap to his campaign than the similar ignorance of Jackson and Grant in their times. He defeated Adlai Stevenson decisively on Election Day.

In office, Eisenhower was the antithesis of Truman. His prejudices were all against expanding the role of the national government in social and economic affairs. He spoke scornfully of "creeping socialism," called for more local control of governmental affairs, and promised to reduce federal spending in order to balance the budget and cut taxes. In addition, he believed that under Roosevelt and Truman the Presidency had lost much of its essential dignity. By battling with congressmen and pressure groups over the details of legislation, his immediate predecessors had sacrificed part of their status as chief representative of the American people. Instead, he proposed to concentrate on broad questions of policy, leaving to functionaries the task of translating policy into action. Besides allowing John Foster Dulles to manage the details of foreign affairs, he granted his other advisers a remarkable degree of authority in their respective departments.

Eisenhower rarely found time for the newspapers and disliked reading long reports, preferring that any problem requiring his attention be summarized in a few paragraphs before being submitted to him. "If a proposition can't be stated in one page, it isn't worth saying," he claimed. He named former governor of New Hampshire Sherman Adams as his personal assistant and gave him almost unlimited control over the Presidential appointments calendar. Adams, in effect, determined whom the President saw and what he read; thus he came perilously close to determining his decisions as well.

The President almost never attempted personally to dragoon reluctant congressmen into supporting administration measures. "You do not *lead* by hitting people over the head," he was fond of saying. The conservative and McCarthyite elements in the Republican party repeatedly subjected him to abuse and harassment, but while he fumed in private, in public he bore their attacks patiently. When he nominated the career diplomat Charles E. Bohlen as ambassador to Russia, for example, the Republican right wing raised a storm, for Bohlen had been Roosevelt's adviser and interpreter at the now-notorious Yalta Conference. After Bohlen told the Senate Foreign Relations Committee that he did not consider Yalta "a sellout and a betrayal" of American interests, men like McCarthy denounced him as "worse than a security risk." The nomination was finally confirmed, largely because Senator Taft, after making a personal study of FBI records, gave him a clean bill of health. Nevertheless, when Taft then irrationally demanded that there be "no more Bohlens," Eisenhower meekly agreed to avoid "controversial" appointments in the future.

However, Eisenhower was neither a reactionary nor a fool. His administration made no effort to repeal existing social and economic legislation. Some economists believed that Eisenhower reacted too slowly in dealing with the several business recessions of his two terms and that he showed insufficient concern for speeding the rate of national economic growth, but he generally adopted a Rooseveltian, almost a Keynesian approach to these problems. In his memoir *Mandate for Change* (1963) he wrote of resorting to "preventative action to arrest the downturn [of 1954] before it might become severe" and of being ready to use "any and all weapons in the federal arsenal, including changes in monetary and credit policy, modification of the tax structure, and a speed-up in the construction of . . . public works" to accomplish this end.

The President also approved the extension of social security to an additional 10 million persons, created a new Department of Health, Education, and Welfare, and, in 1955, came out for federal support of school and highway construction. But his somewhat doctrinaire belief in decentralization and private enterprise reduced the effectiveness of his social welfare measures. His administration compiled a poor record in the area of conservation, for example, because of its tendency to turn control of natural resources

With his wife at his side and flashing his famous grin, Eisenhower prepares to make his acceptance speech to the delegates at the 1952 Republican National Convention who nominated him on the first ballot. (UPI.)

over to state and private interests. When Dr. Jonas Salk's polio vaccine was introduced in 1955, Secretary of Health, Education, and Welfare Oveta Culp Hobby opposed its free distribution by the government as leading to socialized medicine "by the back door."

In general, political experience made Eisenhower less doctrinaire. His "conservatism" became first "dynamic conservatism" and then "progressive moderation." He summarized his new attitude by saying that he was liberal in dealing with individuals but conservative "when talking about . . . the individual's pocketbook," which led his Democratic rival, Adlai Stevenson,

to retort: "I assume what [this] means is that you will strongly recommend the building of a great many new schools to accommodate the needs of our children, but not provide the money."

Americans loved Eisenhower because he epitomized what they wished the world was like. This helps explain why, although devoted to the goal of permanently liberalizing the Republican party, he never succeeded in forging an effective political coalition. The Republicans lost control of Congress as early as 1954 and did not regain it, even in 1956, when Eisenhower again defeated Stevenson decisively, although he had undergone a heart attack and a serious abdominal operation in the interval. It also explains why he could not transfer his popularity to a successor. In the 1960 election Vice President Richard M. Nixon ran with his full support but was narrowly defeated by Senator John F. Kennedy of Massachusetts.

John F. Kennedy

The new President was only 43, the youngest since Theodore Roosevelt and the youngest ever elected in his own right. He was born in Massachusetts in 1917, son of Joseph P. Kennedy, a wealthy financier and promoter, later ambassador to Great Britain under Franklin Roosevelt. After being graduated from Harvard, young Kennedy saw duty in the Pacific as a PT-boat commander in World War II and was severely injured in action. In 1946 he was elected to Congress.

Few men seemed so clearly destined for political success. Besides wealth, intelligence, good looks, and charm, he had the advantage of his war record and his Irish-Catholic ancestry, the latter a particularly valuable asset in Massachusetts. After three terms in the House, he moved on to the Senate in 1952 by defeating Henry Cabot Lodge, Jr., whose grandfather, Wilson's inveterate foe, had beaten Kennedy's grandfather for the Senate in 1916. However, Kennedy's religion seemed to limit his political future. No Catholic had ever been elected President, and the defeat of Alfred E. Smith in 1928 had convinced most students of politics that none ever would be elected.

Nevertheless, Kennedy struck out boldly for the White House. As early as 1956 he made a strong bid for the Democratic Vice Presidential nomination. Four years later, after victories in the Wisconsin and West Virginia primaries had established him as an effective campaigner in non-Catholic regions, he was nominated for President by the Democratic convention.

During the campaign against Nixon, Kennedy stressed his youth and "vigor" (a favorite word), promising an imaginative, forward-looking ad-

ministration. Nixon ran on the Eisenhower record, which he promised to extend in liberal directions. A series of television debates between the candidates, observed by some 70 million viewers, helped Kennedy greatly by enabling him to demonstrate his warmth, maturity, and mastery of the issues. Whereas Nixon appeared to lecture the huge unseen audience like an ill-at-ease schoolmaster, Kennedy seemed relaxed, thoughtful, and confident of his powers. Although both candidates laudably avoided it, the religious issue was important. His Catholicism helped Kennedy in eastern urban areas, but injured him in many farm districts and throughout the West. Kennedy's margin of victory, 303 to 219 in the Electoral College, was paper thin in the popular vote, 34,227,000 to 34,109,000.

Kennedy made a striking and popular President. He created an impression of originality and imaginativeness combined with moderation. He appointed two important Republicans to his Cabinet, but he also named Arthur J. Goldberg, a liberal Jewish lawyer, as secretary of labor and flouted convention by making his younger brother Robert F. Kennedy attorney general. (When critics objected to this appointment, the President responded with a quip, saying that "he had always thought it was a good thing for a young attorney to get some government experience before going out into private practice.")

Notable among Kennedy's characteristics was the respect he paid to culture and learning. Although his personal taste was not especially refined (one critic compared it to that of Ian Fleming's hero, James Bond), he recognized a responsibility to honor high intellectual and artistic achievement. He had also a genuinely inquiring mind. Unlike Eisenhower, he waded eagerly through long, tedious reports. He kept up with dozens of magazines and newspapers and consumed books of all sorts voraciously. He invited leading scientists, artists, writers, and musicians to the White House, along with a variety of other intellectuals. As Jefferson had sought to teach Americans to value the individual man regardless of status, Kennedy seemed intent on teaching the country to respect and understand its most tal-

President Kennedy offers congratulations to the virtuoso cellist Pablo Casals after his performance at a White House concert. At right is the First Lady. (Cecil Stoughton, White House Photo.)

ented minds. This policy enabled him to recruit a record number of intellectuals for government service.

He also seemed bent on being a strong President. He could act decisively upon occasion, as witnessed by his behavior in the Cuban missile crisis. In 1962, to cite another example, he brought the weight of his entire administration, even of the FBI, to bear upon the great steel corporations when they attempted to raise prices after having made what he considered a tacit promise not to do so in return for government help in persuading the steelworkers to forgo sub-

stantial wage increases. Faced with such a massive display of Presidential disapproval, including the threat of an antitrust suit, the steelmen backed down. Kennedy also lavished much energy upon Congress, showering the legislators with special messages and keeping himself closely informed about their doings, even to the extent of assigning to one of his aides the unenviable task of wading through the entire *Congressional Record* every day.

But the President was no Wilson or Franklin Roosevelt when it came to bending Congress to his will. Perhaps he was too reasonable, too amiable, too diffident and conciliatory in his approach. The same coalition of Republicans and conservative southern Democrats that had plagued Truman resisted his plans for federal aid to education, for a new civil rights law, for medical care for the aged, even for reducing taxes without cutting federal expenditures in order to stimulate economic growth.

The President reacted mildly, almost ruefully, when partisan foes blocked proposals that in his view were both reasonable and moderate. He seemed to doubt, at times, that the cumbersome structure of the federal government could actually be made to work. Even to some of his warmest supporters, he sometimes appeared strangely paralyzed, unwilling either to exert strong pressure on congressmen or to appeal over their heads to their constituents. According to public opinion polls, the President was as popular as Eisenhower, but although unfettered by the ideological inhibitions that had kept Eisenhower from being a forceful leader, he seemed no more able than his predecessor to achieve his objectives. Some pundits began to talk of a permanent "deadlock of democracy," in which party discipline had crumbled and positive legislative action had become next to impossible.

On the other hand, Kennedy's very mildness and the reasonableness of his objectives might in time have broken the stalemate. In the fall of 1963 most observers believed he would easily win re-election. On November 22, however, while visiting Dallas, Texas, he was shot in the head by an assassin, Lee Harvey Oswald, and died almost instantly. This awful and senseless murder shocked the whole world and precipitated an extraordinary series of events. Oswald had fired upon the President with a rifle from the window of a distant warehouse. No one actually saw him pull the trigger. He was apprehended largely because, in his demented state, he killed a policeman later in the day in another part of the city. He denied his guilt, but a mass of evidence connected him with the crime. Yet before he could be brought to trial, he was himself murdered by one Jack Ruby, the owner of a small Dallas night club, while being transferred, in the full view of television cameras, from one place of detention to another.

This amazing incident, together with the fact that Oswald had defected to Russia in 1959 and then returned to the United States, convinced many people that some nefarious conspiracy lay at the root of the tragedy. Oswald, the argument ran, was a pawn, his murder designed to keep him from exposing the masterminds who had engineered the assassination. No shred of evidence supported this theory, but even an investigation by a special commission headed by Chief Justice Earl Warren failed to allay the suspicions of some persons.

Lyndon B. Johnson

Kennedy's death made Lyndon B. Johnson President. A 55-year-old Texan, the first southerner to reach the White House since Woodrow Wilson, Johnson could draw upon a bottomless supply of political experience, having served in Congress almost continuously since 1937. A good New Deal liberal, he was also a practical man, a shrewd bargainer, a legislator who preferred to move with contemporary currents rather than to flail fruitlessly against them in search of perfection. Like General St. Pé in Jean Anouilh's play *The Waltz of the Toreadors,* he believed that the relentless pursuit of an ideal would cause more harm than good, to the pursuer and to innocent bystanders alike.* Johnson had little patience with intellectuals and their theories, little of Kennedy's eloquence and urbanity and precision. He was a backslapper—or rather a lapel-grabber—who accomplished his purposes behind the scenes in Capitol cloakrooms, not on the rostrum or before the television cameras.

However, again like General St. Pé, Johnson was an idealist at heart, a compromiser where

---

*The general says that the ideal is like a life buoy toward which all good swimmers head but never reach. "Fanatics who try a faster stroke to reach it at all costs, deluge everybody else and always finish up by drowning, generally dragging God knows how many poor devils under with them."

President Johnson and Vice-President Elect Hubert Humphrey celebrate their 1964 election victory in Texas style, complete with Western clothes and a barbeque. (UPI.)

means were concerned but seldom of ultimate values. Early in his career he had voted against a federal antilynching bill and opposed bills outlawing state poll taxes and measures establishing a federal Fair Employment Practices Commission, but he was never a Negro-baiter, and after he became important in national affairs he consistently championed racial equality. During the Eisenhower era he refused to make party advantage the chief object of his policy; as Senate majority leader he cooperated with the adminis-

tration better than most Republicans, placing political responsibility above partisan ambition.

Upon taking office, Johnson benefited from the sympathy of the world and from the shame felt by many of those who had opposed Kennedy's proposals for political or selfish reasons. Measures that had long been buried in committee suddenly moved through Congress and became law, most notably the tax reform bill and the new civil rights legislation. But Johnson could claim much personal credit for these accomplishments. No 20th-century President excelled him at untangling executive-legislative conflicts. His prestige in Congress, where he had long been a major figure, enabled him to convert many whom Kennedy had failed to budge. His energy, his persuasiveness, his earthy, often scatological humor, won him a series of victories on Capitol Hill. By a combination of bullying and the reconciliation of conflicting interests, he achieved what he called a "national consensus" without slipping into a series of meaningless compromises.

Johnson eagerly sought re-election in his own right in 1964. Although, despite his colorful personality, he was not a good campaigner (his speaking style was stiff and unctuous), he fulfilled this ambition in unparalleled fashion. His championing of civil rights won him the almost unanimous support of Negroes; his economy drive attracted the well-to-do and the business interests; his "war on poverty" held the allegiance of labor and other elements traditionally Democratic. His southern antecedents counterbalanced his liberalism on the race question in the eyes of all but the most bigoted white southerners. The Republicans played into his hands by nominating an archconservative isolationist, Senator Barry M. Goldwater, who also proved to be an inept campaigner.

In November Johnson won a sweeping victory, collecting over 61 per cent of the popular vote and carrying all the country except Goldwater's home state of Arizona and five states in the Deep South.

Other National Leaders

A number of other postwar political figures demand brief consideration. During the Truman years Robert A. Taft was the outstanding leader of the opposition. "Mr. Republican," as his partisans fondly called him, was a man of keen intelligence and the finest character. An old-fashioned conservative, he believed in equality of opportunity and individual liberty, but not in government support of the unsuccessful. While backing public housing, federal aid to education, and civil rights legislation, he objected in principle to government control over private enterprise. He seldom allowed political expediency to influence his behavior. He denounced the trials of Nazi leaders after World War II because he thought they were based on vengeance rather than law. If the victors had simply locked the Nazis up in order to make sure they caused no more trouble, as had been done with Napoleon after Waterloo, he would not have objected, but "to use the *forms* of justice to carry out a predetermined policy" was in his opinion a travesty of justice. When critics called him pro-Nazi for expressing these sentiments he reacted with almost regal indifference.

Taft was totally unpretentious and straightforward. Despite a heavy schedule, he wrote all his own speeches. He lacked only the common touch to become a great leader. He hated the ballyhoo and mindless, false friendliness of the campaign trail and could not conceal his discomfiture from the voters. When reporters, immediately after the war, asked him what people could do about the soaring price of meat, Taft responded coldly: "Eat less."

Taft's blind spot was foreign policy. Almost alone among the major statesmen of his generation, he never outgrew his prewar isolationism. He opposed the Truman Doctrine, the Marshall Plan, and the maintenance of an American army in Europe. He saw no danger to the United States in Soviet expansionism. "Keep America solvent and sensible," he said in 1947, "and she has nothing to fear from any foreign country." On the other hand, he believed the Democrats guilty of a "sympathetic acceptance of communism," which accounts for the major blot on his record, his willingness to tolerate the outrageous methods of Senator McCarthy.

As early as 1940, Taft was a prominent candidate for the Republican Presidential nomination, but, chiefly because of his colorlessness, he never attained it. After losing out to Eisenhower in 1952, he loyally supported the general. They became, in Eisenhower's words, "right good friends," and Taft was of inestimable help to the

President until he died of cancer in July 1953.

During the Eisenhower era the outstanding Democratic leader was Adlai E. Stevenson. Stevenson emerged suddenly upon the national scene in 1952, when Truman decided that the 52-year-old governor of Illinois, whose grandfather had been Vice President under Cleveland, was Presidential timber. He had resisted Truman's suggestion that he run but was nominated nonetheless in one of the few genuine "drafts" in the history of American political conventions. Lucid, witty, urbane, his speeches captivated intellectuals, who found Eisenhower's garbled syntax and cliché-ridden phraseology disconcerting. Stevenson's common sense and genuine humility won him the sympathy of millions, and led large numbers of intelligent and well-educated young persons to become active in the Democratic party at a time when it was much in need of new blood.

In retrospect, it is clear that Stevenson had not the remotest chance of defeating the popular Eisenhower. Disillusionment with the Korean War and a general feeling that the Democrats had been too long in power were added handicaps. His foes turned his strongest assets against him, denouncing his humor as frivolity, characterizing his appreciation of the complexities of life as self-doubt, and tagging his intellectual followers as "eggheads," an appellation that effectively caricatured the balding, slope-shouldered, endomorphic candidate. "The eggheads are for Stevenson," one Republican pointed out, "but how many eggheads are there?" There were far too few to carry the country, as the election revealed.

For the next eight years, Stevenson functioned as a critic of the Eisenhower administration, calling the President to task for failing to denounce McCarthyism and shrewdly exposing the inconsistencies of his "middle-of-the-road" philosophy. In 1956 he ran for President again, only to be still more convincingly rejected by the voters. In truth, he made a less appealing candidate. He sought the office more eagerly and campaigned with somewhat less regard for his principles. In 1960 his undeclared but very real effort to win a third nomination led some observers to accuse him of hypocrisy. The victorious Kennedy, although obviously annoyed by Stevenson's tactics and less than enchanted by his equivocal attitude on many issues, named Stevenson ambassador to the UN, where his eloquence served the nation and his own reputation admirably until his death in July 1965.

In sharp contrast to Stevenson stood Republican Richard M. Nixon. One of the first to believe the worst of Alger Hiss, he had skyrocketed to national prominence by exploiting the public fear of communist subversion. "Traitors in the high councils of our government," he charged in 1950 without advancing a shred of proof, "have made sure that the deck is stacked on the Soviet side of the diplomatic tables." In 1947 he had been an obscure young congressman from California; in 1950 he won a seat in the Senate; two years later Eisenhower chose him as his running mate.

Whether Nixon actually believed what he said at this period of his career is not easily discovered; with his "instinct for omnidirectional placation," he seemed wedded to the theory that statesmen should slavishly represent their constituents' opinions rather than hold to their own views. Frequently, he appeared to count noses before deciding what he thought.° He projected an image of almost frantic earnestness, yet he pursued a flexible course more suggestive of calculation than sincerity. Reporters generally had a low opinion of Nixon and independent voters seldom found him attractive. He was always a sharply controversial character, distrusted by liberals even when he supported liberal measures. Following his loss to Kennedy in 1960, he sought to rebuild his fences by running for governor of California in 1962. His defeat, which he blamed on the newspapers, seemed to end his career.

Another prominent figure of the Eisenhower years was Senator Joseph R. McCarthy. His rise

---

°During the 1960 Presidential campaign John F. Kennedy said to a friend: "Nixon doesn't know who he is, and so each time he makes a speech he has to decide which Nixon he is, and that will be very exhausting."

we have already noted; his fall came when the public finally tired of his endless unproved charges and deliberately obstructive tactics. McCarthy moderated his attacks on the State Department not a jot when it came under the control of his own party. In 1953 its overseas information program received his special attention. He denounced "Voice of America" broadcasters for quoting the works of "controversial" authors and sent Roy M. Cohn, youthful special counsel of his Committee on Governmental Operations, on a mission to Europe to ferret out subversives in the United States Information Service.

Then, early in 1954, McCarthy turned his guns on the army. After a series of charges and countercharges, he accused army officials of trying to blackmail his committee and announced a broad investigation. The resulting Army–McCarthy Hearings, televised before the country, proved the senator's undoing. For weeks his dark scowl, his blind combativeness and disregard for every human value stood exposed for millions to see. When the hearings ended in June 1954 after some million words of testimony, his spell had been broken. The Senate moved at last to censure him in December of 1954, and this reproof completed the destruction of his influence. Although he continued to issue statements and wild charges,* the country no longer listened. In 1957 he died, victim of cirrhosis of the liver.

Regulating the Economy

In the years since 1945, every administration has accepted the necessity of employing federal authority to stabilize the economy and speed national development—the Great Depression taught this lesson to Democrats and Republicans alike. Nevertheless, regulating the economy remained a source of political controversy, for the

*During the censure debate, McCarthy announced that "the Communist party has now extended its tentacles to the United States Senate."

rejection of laissez faire did not mean that all citizens would thereafter always agree as to what should be done.

When World War II ended, nearly everyone wanted to demobilize the armed forces, remove wartime controls, resume production of civilian goods, and reduce taxes. Yet everyone also hoped to avoid a postwar depression, prevent any sudden economic dislocation, check inflation, and make sure that goods in short supply were fairly distributed. Neither the politicians nor the public were able to choose between these conflicting objectives. No group seemed willing to limit its own demands in the general interest. Labor wanted price controls retained but wage controls lifted; businessmen wished to raise prices but keep the lid on wages. Farmers wanted subsidies but opposed price controls and the extention of social security benefits to agricultural workers. As a result, confusion sometimes approaching chaos marked the immediate postwar period.

In this admittedly difficult situation, President Truman could not decide whether the threat of inflation or of unemployment and depression was the greater danger. Unlike Roosevelt in 1933, who had been equally in doubt as to how to proceed, Truman could not hold either the confidence of the people or the support of Congress.

This resulted partly from his asking for too much and demanding it too vociferously, and partly from the obviousness of his own uncertainty. On the one hand, he proposed a comprehensive program of new legislation including a federal public housing scheme, aid to education, medical insurance, civil rights guarantees, a higher minimum wage, broader social security coverage, new conservation and public power projects patterned after TVA, increased aid to agriculture, and the retention of many anti-inflationary controls. However desirable individually, so many new ventures proposed at a time when millions hoped to relax after the tensions of the war were sure to arouse strong resistance.

On the other hand, Truman ended rationing and other controls and in November 1945 signed a bill cutting taxes by some $6 billion. He speeded the sale of government war plants and surplus goods to private interests. Whenever opposition to his plans developed, he vacillated between compromise and inflexibility.

Yet the country weathered the reconversion period with remarkable ease. The pent-up demand for housing, automobiles, clothing, washing machines, and countless other products, backed by the war-enforced savings of millions, kept factories operating at capacity. The GI Bill of Rights, passed in 1944, which provided demobilized veterans with loans to start new businesses and subsidies to continue their education or acquire new skills, prevented unemployment from becoming a serious problem. However, the absence of uniform price and wage policies caused much resentment and frustration, and late in 1946 all price and wage controls, except those on rents, were abandoned.

A period of rapid inflation followed. Food prices rose over 25 per cent between 1945 and 1947. Labor had already won large wage increases. These contributed to the rise of prices, which led to demands for still higher wages. Postwar strikes—nearly 5,000 in 1946 alone—delayed the satisfaction of consumer demands. Employers found it easier to raise prices than to engage in lengthy struggles with powerful unions. Between 1946 and 1948 three distinct "rounds" of wage and price increases took place.

Truman's handling of economic problems and of the Cold War disturbed many former New Dealers. In 1947 a group of them founded Americans for Democratic Action (ADA) and sought an alternative candidate for the 1948 election. Most of them, however, considered Wallace too pro-Soviet and in the end, the ADA supported Truman. His victory gave this group considerable influence over what Truman called his "Fair Deal" program. The ADA stood for a middle-of-the road approach, well-described in Arthur M. Schlesinger, Jr.'s *The Vital Center* (1949). These liberals of the center stressed both individualism and social welfare, government regulation of the economy and the encouragement of private enterprise. They rejected the remnants of New Deal scarcity economics;

"Of course, the steering wheel costs $750, but we knock off fifty bucks for ex-soldiers . . . ." Bill Mauldin's Willie and Joe frequently found it difficult to adjust to the harsh realities of civilian life. (Bill Mauldin, *Back Home,* 1947.)

growth was the key to abundance for all, technology the key to growth. They talked of a "National Prosperity Budget," the government setting the goals and laying down and enforcing the basic rules of the game, the private sector providing the energy to achieve the desired results. The poor could be helped without taking anything away from the rich. The way to check inflation, for example, was not by freezing prices, profits, or wages, but by expanding production.

The results of this economic strategy during Truman's second term were not very large. Congress approved a federal housing program and measures increasing the minimum wage and social security benefits, but these were mere extensions of New Deal legislation. Hopes for more basic policy changes foundered on the Korean War, which strengthened anti-communist conservatives and triggered another inflationary outburst that discredited the National Prosperity budgeteers.

The Korean inflation—over eight per cent in 1951—helps explain the almost obsessive concern of the Eisenhower administration for "preserving the value of the dollar," and its great but largely futile attempt to reduce government spending and balance the federal budget. Since defense and foreign aid outlays accounted for well over half the government's expenditures and since Eisenhower was committed to maintaining these programs, he could not reverse the trend. The national debt—$260 billion when Eisenhower took office—increased steadily to $286 billion in 1960. Yet in part because of the President's efforts, the consumer price index rose only one per cent a year during his administration.

The trend of the Eisenhower years alarmed many of the "growth-minded" economists. Although the gross national product jumped from less than $350 billion in 1952 to over $502 billion in 1960, America's economy was expanding at a much slower *rate* than those of Russia and the industrial nations of western Europe. Three recessions occurred between 1953 and 1961, each marked by sharp increases in unemployment. During the decline of 1958 over 5.2 million were out of work, in January 1961 over 5.3 million.

Each upward surge of prices added to the cost of government, making it more difficult to reduce taxes and balance the budget, and stimulated labor to press for new wage increases, which handicapped American producers trying to compete in foreign markets. During each recession the Eisenhower administration reacted in what by the fifties had become the orthodox manner, cutting taxes, easing credit, and expanding public works programs. There could be no better proof that the principles of the Employment Act of 1946 had become gospel, that the welfare-state idea had been accepted by both parties. The administration's obsession with budget balancing, however, led critics to charge that these measures were not employed vigorously enough.

President Kennedy had fewer inhibitions than his predecessor about federal spending. He was also deeply concerned about the lagging growth rate of the economy and the increasingly large percentage of the population that remained unemployed even in good times. He concentrated his efforts on projects aimed at social reform that would incidentally stimulate the economy: medical care for the aged, low-cost public housing, school construction, broader social security benefits, and an increase of the minimum wage. Like Eisenhower, he was worried about the danger of inflation. Hoping to balance the budget, he rejected suggestions that taxes be cut. However, conservatives in Congress blocked most of his proposals. No noticeable improvement in the rate of economic growth occurred. Finally, in January 1963, he yielded to the pressure of some of his advisers, most notably economist Walter Heller, and came out for a large reduction in taxes.

Any considerable increase in federal spending, Heller argued, would either require higher taxes that would drain money out of the private sector of the economy and thus tend to be self-defeating, or spark a new inflationary explosion. But if taxes were lowered, the public would have more money to spend on consumer goods and corporations could invest in new facilities for producing these goods. Federal expenditures would not need to be cut because the increase in economic activity would raise private and corporate incomes so much that tax revenues would rise despite the fact that the tax rate had been lowered.

Although the prospect of lower taxes was tempting, Kennedy's call for reductions of $13.5 billion, combined with some redistribution of the tax burden and other reforms, ran into strong opposition. Both Republicans and many conservative Democrats thought the reasoning behind the scheme too complex and theoretical to be practicable. After Kennedy's assassination, however, President Johnson persuaded Congress to take the risk. Early in 1964 an $11.5 billion tax-cut bill was passed. By the end of the year the rate of economic growth had quickened markedly. The gross national product soared to $628 billion—an increase of $39 billion over 1963.

Industrial Labor

The postwar decades were good ones, by and large, for American workers. Wartime gains were consolidated and expanded. The civilian labor force grew from 53.8 million in 1945 to 71.6 million in 1963. The average weekly earnings of workers in manufacturing industries rose from about $44 to $97 in the same years, and when allowances are made for the inflation of the period, the increase still amounted to about 50 per cent.

As the labor force grew its influence increased. Labor leaders tended to support the Democrats, for they remembered gratefully the Wagner Act and other help given them by the Roosevelt administration during the titanic labor-management struggles of the 1930's. In 1943 the CIO had created a Political Action Committee to mobilize the labor vote. Labor's political importance was highlighted at the Democratic National Convention of 1944, when Roosevelt, debating the question of a replacement for Vice President Henry Wallace, allegedly instructed his lieutenants to "clear it with Sidney," referring to Sidney Hillman of the Amalgamated Clothing Workers, a power in the PAC. The backing of Hillman and other union leaders had much to do with the choice of Harry Truman by the convention.

Partly because the graduated income tax reduced the real value of every rise in wages, unions continued to stress "fringe benefits" such as pensions and health insurance when bargaining with employers. By 1962 about 90 per cent of all industrial workers were enjoying the protection of life insurance and hospitalization schemes at least partially financed by their employers. Nearly 65 per cent were covered by insurance against the loss of pay resulting from illness; nearly 70 per cent were participating in pension plans. Paid vacations had become almost universal. Unions also expanded their efforts to improve the lives of members. Union-financed housing, vacation resorts, and educational programs became more common. The growth of pension

funds, which placed billions of dollars in their hands for investment, even made some union officials powers in the financial world.

The trend of the times also produced new problems for labor. Inflation constantly gnawed away at hard-won wage increases. The same expansion and integration of the economy that strengthened labor's bargaining power roused the public against its chief weapon, the strike, for a tie-up in a single vital field, such as steel or automobiles, quickly affected millions of innocent bystanders, leading to government intervention and threats of restrictive legislation.

Workers also faced new difficulties resulting from the very industrial advances that had elevated their living standards and working conditions. Rises in productivity grew out of the use of more complicated processes and automatic machinery. Manufacturers needed more technicians, engineers, and other specially trained hands, but far fewer unskilled laborers. In coal mining, for example, new machines replaced thousands of pick-and-shovel miners; between 1947 and 1962 employment in the industry dropped from over 400,000 to 123,000. But in the new electronics industry, dependent upon highly skilled operatives, employment soared to 788,000 by 1961.

From the perspective of the present, the history of labor-management relations after 1945 appears relatively untroubled. The labor disturbances of 1946, which led President Truman to seize the coal mines, threaten to draft railroad workers, and ask Congress for other special powers to prevent national tie-ups, subsided quickly after wage and price controls were lifted. The number of workers involved in strikes declined from 4.6 million in 1946 to 2.1 million in 1947, and the figure seldom exceeded 2.4 million after that date, despite the growth of the labor force.

However, when the Republicans won control of Congress in 1946, postwar disturbances were still very much in the air. In June 1947 Congress passed the Taft-Hartley Act, over the veto of President Truman. This measure outlawed the closed shop, a provision written into many labor contracts requiring new workers to join the union before they could be employed. The act also declared illegal certain "unfair labor practices" such as strikes called over jurisdictional disputes between unions, secondary boycotts, and union contributions to political campaigns. It compelled unions to register and file financial reports with the secretary of labor, and, unlike the Wagner Act, it allowed employers to present their side in labor disputes, provided they used no "threat of reprisal or force or promise of benefit" in so doing. Most important of all, the act authorized the President to seek court injunctions preventing strikes that endangered the national interest. These injunctions would hold for 80 days—a "cooling off" period during which a Presidential fact-finding board could investigate and make recommendations.° This procedure was employed no less than 17 times by Presidents Truman and Eisenhower.

The Taft–Hartley Act—which they called a "slave labor law" greatly alarmed labor leaders. Union members resented especially the provision of the act that made union officers state under oath that they were not communists, a gratuitously insulting and largely ineffective requirement. The law made the task of unionizing unorganized industries more difficult, but it did not hamper existing unions seriously. Although it outlawed the closed shop, it permitted union-shop contracts, which forced new workers to join the union *after* accepting employment. The provision requiring unions to file financial statements and others aimed at protecting individual members against union officials had only salutary effects. Neither the unions nor the conditions of labor declined after the law was passed.

Indeed, by rousing labor's fears, the Taft–Hartley Act tended to unify the labor movement and turn its energies and financial resources toward political action. Unions became a major source of campaign funds, most often for the Democrats. Truman's re-election in 1948 was one result of this development. The unions also expanded at this time. From a low point of 2.8

million in 1937, the AFL grew steadily until in 1950 it had 7.1 million members. The CIO, after its original spectacular gains, leveled off by 1950 at about 5 million. As early as 1942, John L. Lewis, leading founder of the CIO, was claiming that the "accouplement" of the AFL and the CIO would benefit workers, the government, and the public at large, but jurisdictional conflicts, as well as philosophical differences and personal jealousies, kept the two organizations apart.

Common dislike of the Taft–Hartley Act, however, together with the development of industrial unions within the AFL gradually drew them together. In 1953, after George Meany of the plumbers' union succeeded William Green as president of the AFL, and Walter P. Reuther of the automobile workers was elected president of the CIO, new merger negotiations began. Studies proving that the attempts of both organizations to invade the other's domain had been almost totally unsuccessful led to the signing of a "no-raiding" agreement, and in December 1955, a formal merger took place that recognized the need for both craft and industrial unions. Meany became president of the new AFL–CIO, which boasted over 16 million members.

Senate investigations conducted in the fifties by Estes Kefauver of Tennessee and John McClellan of Arkansas exposed scandals of crime and labor racketeering, darkening the public's image of organized labor—somewhat unfairly, since most union officials were honest and dedicated men. As unions grew larger, however, they became less responsive to rank-and-file opinion; that more restraints should be imposed on the power of labor leaders became steadily more apparent. The Landrum–Griffin Act of 1959 sought to correct these ills. In effect, it made unions quasi-public organizations, requiring that their officials be chosen by secret ballot and that disciplinary actions taken by unions against individual members be conducted fairly and in public. Control over the management of the financial resources of unions was also tightened, and the law further strengthened some of the restraints imposed by the Taft–Hartley Act on union tactics vis-à-vis employers.

°If the dispute were still unsettled, the President was to recommend "appropriate action" to Congress.

Cartoonist John Berryman of the Washington *Evening Star* drew President Truman in a classic doomed pose fighting the passage of the Taft-Hartley Labor Act. (Washington *Evening Star.*)

It is revealing that in recent years the sharpest criticisms of organized labor have come from the left rather than from the right. During the New Deal period labor was in the position of an underdog seeking to improve its position in society by arguing for democracy and social justice. Its very success, and the general postwar prosperity, gradually changed the attitudes and social philosophy of many union leaders and also of large numbers of the rank and file. Big labor organizations were often undemocratic, ordinary members having little to say about who represented them or what policies these representatives adopted. In 1956 the sociologist C. Wright Mills classified union officials among the "power elite"; their views, he argued, were not very different from those of corporation executives. As for ordinary workers (in and out of unions) they also tended to become more conservative—to be more concerned with preserving their gains against the ravages of inflation and taxation than with the interests of the larger society. Heavy government expenditures for public housing, welfare, and education ran into increasing opposition in labor circles, although most union leaders continued to support the Democratic party.

The Farm Problem

One of the most notable and uninterrupted trends in the history of the United States has been the movement of the population from rural areas to the cities. In the middle of the 18th century over 90 per cent of the American people earned their living in agriculture and related activities like fishing and lumbering. In the middle of the 20th century nearly 90 per cent did not. By the late 1960's there were fewer than 3 million farms in the entire country, over half of these so small as to yield crops worth less than $2,000 a year. Between 1950 and 1959 alone,

An enormous hanger in Ottumwa, Iowa, serves as temporary storage for a giant pile of surplus corn in the early 1950s. (Wide World.)

farm employment fell from 9.9 million to 7.4 million, although the population of the United States increased by over 25 million in that decade. By 1972 only 4.2 per cent of the population was living on farms.

Despite this decline in numbers, agricultural production expanded enormously after World War II, mainly because a veritable technological revolution swept across the farm country. Besides using more machines, farmers stepped up their consumption of fertilizers by half during the 1950's alone. At the same time, new chemicals reduced the ravages of weeds, insect pests, and plant diseases. Better feeds made for meatier cattle and hogs; new antibiotics checked animal diseases. The vaunted efficiency of American manufacturing enabled industrial workers to increase their man-hour output from an index of 100 in

1947 to 135.7 in 1960, but in the same period agricultural output per man-hour jumped from 100 to 195.8 and during the next decade it continued to soar.

Efficiency and expansion, however, did not bring prosperity to most farmers. Conditions roughly resembled those after the Civil War and after World War I; once again, overproduction and declining foreign markets caught the agriculturalist in a price squeeze. His relative share of the national income declined sharply. This situation made the farm problem an important political issue after 1945.

No significant group suggested abandoning the New Deal policy of subsidizing agriculture. The controversy concerned how much aid and what kind, not the idea of aid itself. The New Deal system of maintaining the price of staple crops like wheat and cotton at or near "parity" with the prices paid by farmers for manufactured goods, while reasonable in theory, left much to be desired in practice. For one thing, declining farm income did not mean cheaper food for consumers; prices in groceries and butcher shops kept pace with those of other goods, for the cost of distributing and processing food rose rapidly. By boosting food prices still higher, the support program aggravated the problem of the rising cost of living. Second, acreage controls proved an ineffective means of curtailing production. When farmers withdrew land from cultivation, they plowed more fertilizer into their remaining acres and continued to increase output. Also, Henry Wallace's ever-normal-granary concept resulted in the piling up of huge reserves in government elevators and warehouses at great expense to the public. Finally, the system had never been helpful to small farmers, nor had it aided those who raised perishable commodities. Many critics argued that the program was accelerating the trend toward large-scale agriculture, thus stimulating the movement of people from farm to city.

Despite the flaws in the New Deal system, it had won over many traditionally Republican farmers to the Democrats. As late as 1948, thousands of rural voters supported Truman largely because he convinced them that a return to Republican rule would mean scrapping the price-support program.° In formulating his own farm policy, Truman was influenced by his secretary of agriculture, Charles F. Brannan, a former administrator of New Deal agricultural programs. In 1949 Brannan, enthusiastically supported by those in the administration who saw economic growth as the solution to every difficulty, drafted a new approach to the problem. While continuing to support the prices of storable crops, the government, he suggested, should guarantee fixed minimum incomes to farmers raising perish-

able crops. These products could then seek their own levels in the marketplace. Consumers would therefore benefit, but not at the expense of farmers.

This scheme ran into a wall of resistance. Big farmers objected to its $26,000 upper limit on guaranteed income, but even smaller operators disapproved of extending social security and minimum wage legislation to farm workers, which Brannan also advocated. Conservatives charged that the Brannan plan was socialistic, but their real objection was to the method to be used in paying for the program. Since the price-support system was financed by processing taxes, consumers paid the bills. Under Brannan's proposal, payments would be made directly from the federal treasury, which would mean that the income tax payer would contribute most of the money. In any case, Congress rejected the plan along with most of President Truman's other suggestions and continued to support many items, including butter, wool, sugar, and tobacco as well as cotton and cereal grains, at 90 per cent of parity.

The Korean War eased the situation for farmers temporarily, but after it ended, surplus crops began to pile up alarmingly. Soon the government was even storing grain in the holds of idle merchant ships. In June 1952 there were $1.4 billion worth of crops in storage; by June 1956 this figure had risen to $8.3 billion. Yet food prices had gone up relentlessly during the period.

The Eisenhower administration tried to deal with this problem by adopting a system of flexible price supports, dropping the levels to as little as 75 per cent of parity, and by setting up in 1956 a "soil bank" plan, under which farmers were paid to divert land from commercial production to various conservation purposes. By 1960 some 28.7 million acres had been placed in the soil bank. However, the basic difficulties—high food prices, expensive support programs, and chronic poverty for tens of thousands of small farmers—remained. In 1965 the net income of all American farmers was less than $15.2 billion, $2.5 billion of this represented by federal grants.

°The 80th Congress had failed to pass a bill providing for adequate crop-storage facilities. Truman made devastating use of this fact while campaigning in states like Iowa, which he carried, and Kansas, which he lost by a narrow margin.

The Politics of Civil Rights

As we have seen, the World War II record of the federal government on civil rights was mixed. Except for the Japanese in California, there was no hysterical pursuit of imaginary spies and subversives. A beginning was made at increasing opportunities for Negroes in the armed forces, and because of the labor shortage, black workers improved their economic position considerably. After the war, the ideological conflict with the communists provided an additional reason for concern about racial intolerance. In Asia and Africa particularly, news of the mistreatment of Negroes or other signs of color prejudice in the United States always damaged the nation's reputation.

Nevertheless, civil rights became the most controversial political and social problem in the United States after 1945, for two quite separate reasons. Fear of communist subversion led to repressions, culminating in the excesses of McCarthyism, that alarmed liberals without quieting the fears of conservatives. And the rising aspirations of American Negroes, highlighted by their awareness that as the centennial of the Emancipation Proclamation approached they were still second-class citizens, produced an increasing militancy among members of the race that shook the political structure of the country.

As early as 1940, in the Smith Act, Congress made it illegal to advocate or teach the overthrow of the government by force, or even to be a member of an organization with this objective. A dead letter during the era of Soviet-American cooperation, this law was used in the Truman era to jail the leaders of the American Communist party. The Supreme Court upheld its constitutionality in *Dennis et al. v. U. S.* (1951), in effect modifying the "clear and present danger" test established in the Schenck case of 1919. In 1950 Congress passed the McCarran Internal Security Act, restricting the civil rights of communists still further. Besides making it unlawful "to combine, conspire or agree with any other person to per-

form any act that would substantially contribute to the establishment . . . of a totalitarian dictatorship," this measure required every "Communist-front organization" to register with the attorney general. Members of front organizations were barred from defense work and from traveling abroad, while aliens who had ever been members of any "totalitarian party" were denied admission to the United States. This foolish provision prevented many anti-communists behind the Iron Curtain from fleeing to America; even a person who had belonged to a communist youth organization was kept out by its terms.

Although his own loyalty program was not always administered with sufficient regard for individual rights, President Truman vetoed the McCarran Act, saying that it would "put the Government into the business of thought control." However, Congress overrode the veto by a voice vote. Truman also tried harder than any previous President to improve the lot of the Negro. As we have seen, he created a Committee on Civil Rights, and he pressed for the desegregation of the armed forces. But his efforts to obtain federal antipoll tax and antilynching legislation were filibustered to death in the Senate, and Congress also refused his request for a permanent Fair Employment Practices Commission.

Under Eisenhower, while the McCarthy hysteria reached its peak and declined, the government compiled a spotty record on civil rights. The search for subversive federal employees continued. Although only a handful were charged with disloyalty, nearly 7,000 were declared "security risks" and fired. The refusal to grant security clearance to J. Robert Oppenheimer, one of the fathers of the atomic bomb, on the ground that he had associated with certain communists and communist sympathizers, was the most ill-advised instance of the administration's catering to anti-communist extremists, for it was based on the supposition that Oppenheimer could be denied access to his own discoveries.

As for the Negro, Eisenhower completed the formal integration of the armed forces and appointed a Civil Rights Commission, but he was temperamentally incapable of making a frontal assault on the racial problem. All in all, civil libertarians had little to cheer about as the nation passed mid-century.

At this point, the Supreme Court interjected itself into the civil rights controversy in dramatic fashion. Under pressure of litigation sponsored by the National Association for the Advancement of Colored People, the Court had been gradually undermining the "separate but equal" principle laid down in *Plessy v. Ferguson* (1896). Attention focused on the segregated public schools of the South. First the Court insisted that in graduate education segregated facilities be truly equal. In 1938 it ordered a Negro admitted to the University of Missouri law school because no Negro law school existed in the state. This decision gradually forced some southern states to admit Negroes to advanced programs. "You can't build a cyclotron for one student," the president of the University of Oklahoma confessed when the Court, in 1948, ordered Oklahoma to provide equal facilities for a petitioning Negro. Two years later, when Texas actually attempted to fit out a separate law school for a single Negro applicant, the Court ruled that truly equal education could not be provided under such circumstances.

Then, in 1953, President Eisenhower appointed California's Governor Earl Warren as chief justice. Warren was a Republican moderate, a man of great dignity, good sense, and courage. Convinced that the Court must take the offensive in the cause of civil rights, he succeeded in welding his associates into a unit on the question. In 1954 an NAACP-sponsored case, *Brown v. Board of Education of Topeka,* came up for decision. In this case, Thurgood Marshall, leader of the NAACP campaign, directly challenged the "separate but equal" doctrine even at the elementary school level, submitting a mass of sociological evidence to show that the mere fact of segregation made equal education impossible and did serious psychological damage to both Negro children and white. Speaking for a unanimous Court, Warren accepted Marshall's reasoning and specifically reversed the Plessy decision. "In the field of public education, the doctrine of

'separate but equal' has no place," Warren declared. "Separate educational facilities are inherently unequal." Recognizing the problems posed by this edict, the Court, in 1955, ordered the states to proceed "with all deliberate speed" in integrating their schools.

The Warren Court also handed down a series of rulings protecting the civil rights of radicals and persons accused of disloyalty. In *Yates v. U.S.* (1957) it modified the Dennis decision by holding that mere advocacy of revolution was not a crime, and in other cases it ruled that the State Department could not refuse passports to communists arbitrarily. The powers of congressional and state legislative investigators to compel witnesses to testify were also subjected to reasonable restraints by the Court in this period.

Such actions led conservatives to denounce the Court, but the justices held their ground. In 1962 and 1964 they moved in still another direction, requiring that both state legislative and federal congressional districts be apportioned strictly in terms of population, in accordance with the principle of "one man, one vote." In nearly all the states rural areas were heavily overrepresented, chiefly because as the trend of population toward the cities proceeded, legislators had refused to reapportion election districts. Since this resulted in the votes of some citizens having less weight than others, the Court held that their right to equal protection of the law was being violated. It applied this rule even to the upper houses of state legislatures, some of which, in imitation of the United States Senate, were organized on a purely geographical basis. In *Lucas v. Colorado* (1964) the justices rejected this "federal analogy" even when the voters, in a referendum, had specifically approved the system. "A citizen's constitutional rights can hardly be infringed simply because a majority of the people choose to do so," they declared.

In the long run, these reapportionment decisions might become the most significant in the Court's history; the most immediately important, however, was the school desegregation case. Despite the Brown decision, few districts in the 17 southern and border states seriously tried to integrate their schools. Within two months after the ruling, White Citizens Councils dedicated to all-out opposition were springing up all over the South. Some southern employers took reprisals against Negro jobholders who tried to enroll their children in white schools and some landlords evicted their tenants. When the school board of Clinton, Tennessee, integrated the local high school in September 1956, a mob roused by a northern fanatic rioted in protest, shouting "Kill the niggers!" and destroying Negro property. The school was kept open with the help of the National Guard, but the next year segregationists blew up the building with dynamite. In Virginia the governor announced a plan for "massive resistance" to integration that even denied state aid to local school systems willing to desegregate on an experimental basis. When the University of Alabama admitted a single black girl in 1956, riots broke out and university officials forced her to withdraw and then expelled her when she complained more forcefully than they deemed proper.

President Eisenhower hoped to avoid federal involvement in these conflicts. Personally, he thought real equality for Negroes could not be obtained by government edict. "I am convinced that the Supreme Court decision *set back* progress in the South *at least fifteen years*," he remarked to one of his advisers. "The fellow who tries to tell me you can do these things by *force* is just plain *nuts*." But in 1957 events compelled him to act. That September the school board of Little Rock, Arkansas, opened Central High School to a handful of carefully picked black children. However, the governor of the state, Orval M. Faubus, called out the National Guard to prevent them from attending. Egged on by the governor, unruly crowds taunted the children and their parents. Eisenhower could not ignore this direct flouting of federal authority. He dispatched a thousand paratroopers to Little Rock and summoned 10,000 National Guardsmen to federal duty. The black children then began to attend classes, but it was necessary to maintain a token force of soldiers at Central High for the entire school year to protect them.

Such extremist resistance strengthened the determination both of Negroes and of many northern whites to make the South comply with the desegregation decision. Besides pressing a variety of cases in the federal courts, leaders of the movement sought to bring internal pressure on the southern states by conducting a drive to win political power for southern blacks, long systematically excluded from the polls. In September 1957 Congress established a Civil Rights Commission with broad investigatory powers and a new Civil Rights Division in the Department of Justice. This law also authorized the attorney general to obtain injunctions to stop southern registrars and election officials from interfering with Negroes seeking to register and vote.

President Kennedy's original approach to the civil rights problem was to make full use of existing laws rather than to seek new legislation. Under the vigorous direction of his brother Robert, the Justice Department acted to force the desegregation of interstate transportation facilities in the South, to compel southern election officials to obey civil rights legislation, and to override resistance to school integration. In 1962, when Mississippi authorities, led by Governor Ross Barnett himself, blocked the admission of a Negro student, James H. Meredith, to the University of Mississippi, President Kennedy called the Mississippi National Guard to federal duty and, despite bloody riots, made the university accept the student.

But progress remained painfully slow. The new aggressiveness of blacks caused alarm in some quarters in the North and there was ominous talk of a "white backlash." Nevertheless, the belief that all citizens should be guaranteed the basic civil rights was growing steadily stronger. In 1961 the Twenty-third Amendment to the Constitution was ratified, giving residents of the District of Columbia the suffrage in Presidential elections. Three years later the Twenty-fourth Amendment outlawed state poll taxes in federal elections, a device traditionally employed to keep poor Negroes from voting in the South. After Kennedy's assassination, the Civil Rights Act of 1964 outlawed discrimination in all places of

School desegregation comes to Arkansas, 1957. Acting on President Eisenhower's orders, 101st Airborne Division paratroopers escort black students (there were nine in all) into Central High School in Little Rock. (Burt Glinn, Magnum.)

public accommodation, such as hotels, restaurants, and theaters. It also empowered the attorney general to bring suits on behalf of individuals to speed school desegregation and strengthened his hand still further in the campaign to register Negro voters. Racial discrimination by both employers and unions was also declared illegal, and federal agencies were authorized to withhold funds from state-administered programs that failed to treat blacks and whites equally.

The Supreme Court promptly upheld the constitutionality of this law and the southern reaction, while anything but enthusiastic, was much less violent than many observers had feared. By the end of 1964 the public accommodations section was being enforced in such key southern cities as Jackson, Natchez, Baton Rouge, Montgomery, and Savannah. But at the end of the 1963–64 school year, only half the black children in the border states and barely one per cent of the 2.84 million in the states of the old Confederacy were attending white schools. Local customs died hard. In many communities, for example, traveling blacks mixed with whites in restaurants and bus terminals, but local Negroes kept to themselves, partly out of fear, partly for lack of money, partly through choice. Fear also kept many from appearing before the new federal registrars. "Too many Negroes are not desegregated mentally yet," one Nashville clergyman explained.

The Negro struggle for equality influenced and was paralleled by that of Mexican Americans, principally in the southwestern states. The fortunes of *la raza*, as the Spanish-speaking community in the Southwest called itself, were affected by the same forces that affected blacks. During both World Wars the labor shortage led to improvement of their lot; during bad times, especially during the Great Depression, they were the first to suffer—indeed, about half a million were either deported or "persuaded" to return to Mexico during the 1930's. In general, Mexican Americans were underpaid, badly housed, and subject to all sorts of discrimination. At the same time their labor was badly needed in many areas. Both during World War II and again between 1948 and 1965 federal legislation encouraged the importation of *braceros* (temporary farm workers) from Mexico, and many other Mexicans entered the country illegally. The latter were known as *mojados,* or "wetbacks," because they often slipped across the border by swimming the Rio Grande.

Spanish-speaking residents of the Southwest had been traditionally apolitical and submissive—they tended to accept their fate with resignation, to mind their own business, not to "make trouble." But in the early 1960's a new spirit of resistance arose. Leaders of the new movement called themselves *Chicanos,* possibly a shortened form of the word *Mexicano,* a Mexican. The Chicanos demanded better schools for their children and easier access to higher education. They urged their fellows to take pride in their traditions and culture, to demand their legal and human rights, to organize themselves politically. As with the blacks, many of the Chicano leaders were college students. But as was also the case with the blacks, the dominant middle-class majority adjusted itself to Chicano demands grudgingly and very slowly. Much remained to be done before true racial equality could be achieved in the United States.

Supplementary Reading

Postwar domestic politics is treated briefly in E. F. Goldman, *The Crucial Decade—And After°* (1961), Walter Johnson, *1600 Pennsylvania Avenue°* (1960), Herbert Agar, *The Price of Power°* (1957), and G. E. Mowry, *The Urban Nation°* (1965). For more detail, consult Congressional Quarterly Service (ed.), *Con-*

°Available in paperback.

gress and the Nation: 1945-1964 (1965), an indispensable reference work. Interpretive works useful for understanding the period include Samuel Lubell, *The Future of American Politics°* (1952) and *Revolt of the Moderates* (1956), A. M. Schlesinger, Jr., *The Vital Center°* (1949), R. E. Neustadt, *Presidential Power°* (1960), J. M. Burns, *The Deadlock of Democracy°* (1963), Daniel Bell, *The End of Ideology°* (1959), C. Wright Mills, *The Power Elite°* (1962), and R. H. Rovere, *The American Establishment°* (1962).

Biographical material on postwar political leaders is voluminous but seldom satisfactory from the scholarly point of view. On Truman, see H. S Truman, *Memoirs°* (1955-56) and *Mr. Citizen°* (1960), and A. L. Hamby, *Beyond the New Deal: Harry S Truman and American Liberalism* (1973). Eisenhower's own view of his two terms can be found in D. D. Eisenhower, *Mandate for Change°* (1963) and *Waging Peace* (1965). Of the biographies, R. J. Donovan, *Eisenhower: The Inside Story* (1956), and M. J. Pusey, *Eisenhower: The President* (1956), are favorable, while Marquis Childs, *Eisenhower: Captive Hero* (1958), is critical. See also Dean Albertson (ed.), *Eisenhower as President°* (1963). Sherman Adams, *Firsthand Report°* (1961), is a pro-Eisenhower memoir, E. J. Hughes, *The Ordeal of Power°* (1963), an anti-Eisenhower one. For Kennedy, consult J. M. Burns, *John Kennedy: A Political Profile°* (1960), which covers his pre-Presidential career, Theodore Sorenson, *Kennedy°* (1965), and A. M. Schlesinger, Jr., *A Thousand Days°* (1965). The best biography of Johnson is Rowland Evans and Robert Novak, *Lyndon B. Johnson: The Exercise of Power°* (1966). Jack Bell, *The Johnson Treatment* (1965), is a good account of Johnson's political philosophy and method of operations. See also Tom Wicker, *JFK and LBJ* (1968), and E. F. Goldman, *The Tragedy of Lyndon Johnson* (1969). The Presidential elections of 1960 and 1964 are described in two books by T. H. White, each called *The Making of the President°* (1961, 1965).

On the lesser figures, see J. T. Patterson, *Mr. Republican: A Biography of Robert A. Taft* (1972), K. S. Davis, *A Prophet in His Own Country* (1957), on Adlai Stevenson, R. M. Nixon, *Six Crises°* (1962), and R. H. Rovere, *Senator Joe McCarthy°* (1959).

Economic trends are considered in A. A. Berle, *The 20th Century Capitalist Revolution°* (1954) and *Power Without Property°* (1959), J. K. Galbraith, *American Capitalism°* (1952) and *The Affluent Soci-*

ety° (1958), H. G. Vatter, *The U. S. Economy in the 1950's* (1963), Walter Heller, *New Dimensions of Political Economy°* (1966), S. E. Harris, *Economics of the Kennedy Years°* (1964), The Editors of *Fortune, America in the Sixties: The Economy and the Society°* (1960), and Walter Adams and H. M. Gray, *Monopoly in America* (1955).

On labor, consult Philip Taft, *Organized Labor in American History* (1964), Joel Seidman, *American Labor from Defense to Reconversion* (1953), H. A. Millis and E. C. Brown, *From the Wagner Act to Taft-Hartley* (1950), B. J. Widick, *Labor Today* (1964), E. L. Dayton, *Walter Reuther* (1958), W. M. Leiserson, *American Trade Union Democracy* (1959), and P. A. Brinker, *The Taft-Hartley Act After Ten Years* (1958). On agriculture, see A. J. Matusow,

Farm Policies & Politics in the Truman Years° (1970), M. R. Benedict and O. C. Stine, *The Agricultural Commodity Programs* (1956), and Lauren Soth, *Farm Trouble in an Age of Plenty* (1957).

The civil liberties issue is discussed in Alan Barth, *The Loyalty of Free Men* (1951), Robert Griffith, *The Politics of Fear* (1970), and C. P. Curtis, *The Oppenheimer Case* (1955). On Negro rights, see B. M. Ziegler, *Desegregation and the Supreme Court°* (1958), Anthony Lewis *et al.*, *Portrait of a Decade* (1964), J. A. Garraty (ed.), *Quarrels That Have Shaped the Constitution°* (1964), and W. C. Berman, *The Politics of Civil Rights in the Truman Administration* (1970). On Mexican-Americans, see M. S. Meier and Feliciano Rivera, *The Chicanos°* (1972).

30

Modern American Society

On March 4, 1929, Herbert Hoover, fresh from his overwhelming victory over Alfred E. Smith, delivered his inaugural address as President of the United States. The country was riding a wave of prosperity; everywhere pundits spoke of a new era of unlimited social and economic achievement. "In no nation are the institutions of progress more advanced," Hoover said. "In a large view we have reached a higher degree of comfort and security than ever existed before in the world. . . . I have no fears for the future." This prediction proved monumentally incorrect;

within a year the nation was mired in the Great Depression.

On January 20, 1965, after a still more one-sided electoral triumph, Lyndon B. Johnson took the Presidential oath. The United States was even more prosperous than in 1929. Like Hoover, President Johnson extolled the virtues and achievements of the United States. "We have become a nation; prosperous, great and mighty," he said. But his view of the future, while hopeful, was far less complacent than Hoover's had been. "We have no promise from God that our greatness will endure," he warned. And he spoke of "this fragile existence," reminding the people that they lived "in a world where change and growth seem to tower beyond the control, and even the judgment, of men." The difference in mood between these two speeches tells us much about modern America.

American Society in Flux

The postwar years saw enormous social changes in addition to those especially affecting minorities. The population expanded rapidly and also became even more mobile than in earlier generations. During the depressed thirties the population had increased by only 9 million. In the fifties it rose by more than 28 million, in the sixties by another 24 million, reaching a total of 203 million in 1970.

Population experts also observed some startling internal shifts within the country. The historic westward movement by no means ended with the closing of the frontier in the 1890's. One obvious indication of this was the admission of Hawaii and Alaska to the Union in 1959; between 1940 and 1970 the population of Alaska more than tripled, that of Hawaii grew by over 50 per cent. More significant was the enormous growth of California and the Southwest. California added over 5 million to its numbers between 1950 and 1960 and in 1963 passed New York to

A picture taken in Los Angeles in 1953 showing moving-in day in a Los Angeles suburban housing development is testimony to southern California's huge population gains. (J. R. Eyerman, *Life*, © Time Inc.)

become the most populous state in the Union. Nevada and Arizona were expanding at an even greater rate.

Close study of the Southwest and especially of California throws much light on many of the changes taking place in the United States. The climate of the area was particularly attractive to older people, and the enormous growth reflected the prosperity of the times, which enabled pensioners and other retired persons to settle there.° On the other hand, the area attracted millions of young workers, for it became the center of the aircraft and electronics industries and of the federal government's atomic energy and space pro-

---

°Florida experienced a similar boom; its population more than doubled between 1950 and 1965. The growth of the subtropical sections of the country was much stimulated by the perfection of cheap, mass-produced air conditioners.

grams. Such industries displayed the best side of modern capitalism: high wages, comfortable working conditions, complex, highly efficient machinery, and the marriage of scientific technology and commercial utility.

These modern industries employed increasing numbers of women, for much of the work demanded manual dexterity rather than strength. This reflected another national trend. In 1940 male workers outnumbered female by nearly three to one, in 1966 by under two to one. Yet being gainfully employed did not seem to discourage women from marrying and having children: in 1940 about 15 per cent of American women in their early thirties were unmarried, in 1965 only 5 per cent.

Geographical mobility was greatly stimulated by improvements in transportation and communication. Although air travel had developed rapidly in the thirties and had profited enormously from wartime technical advances in military aircraft, it really came of age when the first jetliner—the Boeing 707, built in Seattle, Washington—went into service in 1958. Almost immediately, jets came to dominate long-distance travel, while railroad passenger service and transatlantic liners steadily declined in importance. Meanwhile, developments in rocketry stimulated by competition to "beat the Russians in space" produced as by-products significant improvements in communication. By the early sixties the National Aeronautics and Space Agency (NASA) had launched a number of satellites capable of transmitting television pictures back to earth and collecting masses of meteorological data and the American Telephone and Telegraph Company had a private commercial satellite in orbit that could relay television programs between America and Europe. When American astronauts landed on the moon in July 1969, they

Astronaut Edwin Aldrin on the moon, July 1969. Reflected in his helmet visor are flight commander Neil Armstrong, who took this picture, and part of their spacecraft. Television enabled some 600 million people to witness the historic event. (NASA.)

were able to transmit live television pictures of their activities and of the earth itself to millions of viewers all over the world.

The era saw also a marked broadening of the American middle class and a greater emphasis on leisure, entertainment, and cultural activities. In 1947 only 5.7 million American families had annual incomes equivalent to over $7,500 in 1959 dollars, but by the latter year 12.3 million families had such incomes. As they prospered, middle-class Americans became both more culturally homogeneous and broader-gauged in their interests.

The percentage of immigrants in the population declined steadily; by the mid-sixties over 95 per cent of all Americans were native-born. This trend made for social and cultural uniformity. So did the rising incomes of industrial workers and the changing character of their labor. Blue-collar workers invaded the middle class by the tens of thousands; they populated suburbs previously reserved for junior executives, shopkeepers, and the like; they shed their work clothes for business suits; they took up golf and adopted values and attitudes commensurate with their new status. A study of one Philadelphia suburb in the late fifties revealed that about half of some 12,500 single-family homes were occupied by production workers and other persons who in a previous generation would have been classified as members of the proletariat.

Many social scientists found in this expansion of the middle class another explanation of the tendency of the country to glorify the conformist. They attributed to it the blurring of party lines in politics, the national obsession with "moderation" and "consensus," the complacency of so many Americans, their tendency, for example, to be at once more interested in churchgoing and less concerned with the philosophic aspects of religion than their forebears. One prominent divine complained of "the drive toward a shallow and implicitly compulsory common creed," a "religion-in-general, superficial and syncretistic, destructive of the profounder elements of faith." But no one could deny that the new middle class had more creature comforts (automo-biles, household appliances—even swimming pools), more leisure, and wider cultural interests (as witnessed by a phenomenal increase in the sale of books, recorded classical music, and art reproductions) than any earlier generation. What *Fortune* magazine dubbed the "fun market" absorbed $41 billion of consumer income in 1959.

More debatable was the impact of the expansion of the middle class on national standards of taste, but these, too, seemed on the rise. Sales of tickets to concerts zoomed, people took the best modern architecture to their hearts, increased their consumption of vintage wines and exotic foods. Businessmen made increasing use of works of art, traditional and modern, in their advertisements. The concept of the avant-garde as a revolt of creative minds against the philistinism of the middle class was rapidly crumbling, as witnessed by the quick acceptance of "pop" art and "action" painting, of "beatnik" literature, of "the theater of the absurd," and of the most difficult atonal music. Many critics found cause for alarm in this new popular enthusiasm for culture, arguing that the nation's really high culture was being engulfed by "status seekers" aping upper-class standards in their frenetic rush to conform. But in the long run the result would surely be a general improvement of taste.

Literature and Art

In the world of books and periodical literature, 20th-century Americans continued and expanded trends begun in the 19th. There were fewer newspapers, but they had larger circulations. Magazine sales soared. The success of tabloid newspapers like the New York *Daily News* and of magazines like *Reader's Digest*, founded in 1922, showed how the hectic pace of modern civilization was discouraging people from reading long articles. Illustrations occupied more and more space in newspapers, magazines—and textbooks. The public's desire for up-to-the-minute news and commentary found satisfaction in weeklies like *Time* (1923), *Newsweek* (1933), and the picture magazine *Life* (1936).

The most important new development in book publishing was the sudden flourishing of the paperback. In 1939 a new company, Pocket Books, began to publish respectable modern fiction and many of the classics in paper covers. After World War II, others began to experiment with cheap paper reprints of popular works of nonfiction. Sales reached enormous proportions; by 1965 about 25,000 titles were in print and sales were approaching 1 million copies *a day*.

Cheapness and portability only partly explained the popularity of paperbacks. Readers could purchase them in thousands of drugstores, bus terminals, and supermarkets, as well as in the bookstores. Teachers, delighted to find out-of-print volumes easily available, assigned hundreds of them in their classes. There was also a psychological factor at work: the paperback became fashionable. Persons who rarely bought hardcover books cheerfully purchased by the tens of thousands weighty volumes of literary criticism, translations of the works of obscure foreign novelists, specialized historical monographs, and difficult philosophical treatises. A considerable "feedback" stimulated the hardcover book market. Year after year, the sales of books increased, despite all the talk about how television and other diversions were undermining the public's interest in reading. This flourishing of the book business heartened everyone concerned with improving American civilization and provided a powerful answer to those who claimed that Americans lacked intellectual interests.

It is difficult to generalize about the effect of modern conditions on American writers and artists. The expansion of the book market, for example, brought prosperity to many novelists, but not always to the best, and it remained hard for unknown writers of fiction to earn a decent living. At the same time, the temptations involved in book club contracts and movie rights undoubtedly diverted some authors from making the best use of their talents. The enthusiasm of an ever broader segment of the public for modern paintings and the quick acceptance of every new style placed a premium on innovation and broke down the traditional isolation of the artist, bringing within his ken the advertiser and the public relations expert. Under such circumstances, it remained an open question whether modern civilization was helping or hindering the full development of its most creative individuals.

In the thirties the Great Depression and the rise of fascism in Europe had stirred the social consciences of many writers and restored their faith in the positive values of their heritage. Shaken by the economic collapse, some writers found Soviet communism attractive and wrote "proletarian" novels. Most of these were dull and of little artistic merit. More interesting were the works of men like John Dos Passos, James T. Farrell, and John Steinbeck, who, while critical of many aspects of American life, avoided the party line. Dos Passos had been a minor figure during the twenties. Born into a well-to-do family of Portuguese descent, he was educated at Harvard, drove an ambulance during the Great War, and wrote an antiwar novel, *Three Soldiers* (1921), and a number of other books, but it was his trilogy *U.S.A.* (1930–36) that established his reputation. This massive work, rich in detail and intricately constructed, advanced a fundamentally anticapitalist and deeply pessimistic point of view. It portrayed American society between 1900 and 1930 in the broadest perspective, interweaving the stories of five major characters and a galaxy of lesser figures. Throughout the narrative, Dos Passos scattered graphic capsule sketches of famous men of the era, ranging from Andrew Carnegie and William Jennings Bryan to the movie idol Rudolph Valentino and the architect Frank Lloyd Wright. He also included "newsreel" sections recounting the actual events of the period and "camera eye" sections in which he revealed his personal reactions to the passing parade.

Dos Passos' method was relentless, cold, methodical—utterly realistic. He displayed immense craftsmanship, but no human sympathy for his characters or their world. His style was impressionistic yet concrete, experimental yet tightly controlled, his book a true epic, a monument to the despair and anger of liberals confronted with the Great Depression. However, *U.S.A.* seemed to exhaust his creativity. After World War II broke out, he rapidly abandoned his radical views and by the fifties had located himself far to the right, a caustic critic of the welfare state.

James T. Farrell was less talented than Dos Passos, a clumsy novelist in the naturalist tradition established by Theodore Dreiser around the turn of the century. He, too, wrote a trilogy in the thirties, the saga of *Studs Lonigan* (1932–35), which described the squalid life of Chicago's Irish slums. Farrell's realism was overly literal, but full of the man's anger and conviction, and therefore powerful. Unlike Dos Passos, Farrell held to his radical views in later, more prosperous times.

The novel that best portrayed the desperate plight of the millions impoverished by the depression was John Steinbeck's *The Grapes of Wrath* (1939), which described the fate of the Joads, an Oklahoma family driven by drought and bad times to abandon their land and become migratory laborers in California. Steinbeck captured the patient bewilderment of the downtrodden, the callous brutality bred of fear that characterized their exploiters, and the furious resentments of the radicals of the thirties. He depicted the parching blackness of the Oklahoma dust bowl, the grandeur of California, the backbreaking toil of the migrant fruit pickers, and the ultimate indignation of a people repeatedly degraded. "In the eyes of the hungry there is a growing wrath. In the souls of the people the grapes of wrath are filling and growing heavy, growing heavy for the vintage." Like so many other writers of the thirties, Steinbeck was an angry man. "There is a crime here that goes beyond denunciation," he wrote. But he had a compassion that Dos Passos and Farrell lacked, and this quality raised *The Grapes of Wrath* to the level of great tragedy. In other works, such as *Tortilla Flat* (1935) and *The Long Valley* (1938), he described the life of California cannery workers and ranchers with moving warmth, yet without becoming overly sentimental.

Although too much wrapped up in himself to produce the kind of systematic analysis of America achieved by Dos Passos or the humane studies of Steinbeck, Thomas Wolfe also stands as a major interpreter of his times. Wolfe was born in Asheville, North Carolina, in 1900 and was educated at the state university and at Harvard. A passionate, intensely troubled young man of vast but undisciplined talents, he sought to describe in a series of novels the kaleidoscopic character of American life, the limitless variety of the nation. "I will know this country when I am through as I know the palm of my hand, and I will put it on paper and make it true and beautiful," he boasted. During the last ten years of his short life (he died in 1938), he wrote four major novels: *Look Homeward Angel* (1929), *Of Time and the River* (1935), and two published posthumously, *The Web and the Rock* (1939) and *You Can't Go Home Again* (1940). All were autobiographical and to some extent repetitious, for Wolfe was an unabashed egoist. Nevertheless, he was a superb interpreter of contemporary society. He crammed his pages with unforgettable vignettes—a train hurtling across the Jersey meadows in the dark, a young girl clutching her skirts on a windswept corner, a group of derelicts huddled for shelter in a public toilet on a frigid night. And no writer caught more clearly the frantic pace and confusion of the great cities, the despair of the depression, the divided nature of man, his fears, his hopes, his undirected, uncontrollable energy.

Probably the finest talent among modern American novelists was William Faulkner. Although born in 1897, within a year of both Fitzgerald and Hemingway, like Wolfe he attained literary maturity only in the thirties. After service in the Canadian air force in World War I, he returned to his native Mississippi, working at a series of odd jobs and publishing relatively inconsequential poetry and fiction. Suddenly, between 1929 and 1932, he burst into prominence with four major novels—*The Sound and the Fury, As I Lay Dying, Sanctuary,* and *Light in August.*

Faulkner created a local world, Yoknapatawpha County, and peopled it with some of the

"I am completely partisan," Steinbeck (left) wrote. "Every effort I can bring to bear is . . . at the call of the common working-people." Accepting the Nobel literature prize, Faulkner (above) spoke of a life-long attempt "to create out of the materials of the human spirit something which did not exist before." (Steinbeck: Erich Hartmann, Magnum. Faulkner: Bern Keating, Black Star.)

most remarkable characters in American fiction—the Sartoris family, typical of the old southern aristocracy worn down at the heels, the Snopes clan, shrewd, unscrupulous, boorish representatives of the new day, and many others. He pictured vividly the South's poverty and its pride, its dreadful racial problem, the guilt and obscure passions plaguing white and black alike. He also dealt effectively with the clash of urban and rural values. But Faulkner was more by far than a local colorist. No contemporary excelled him as a commentator on the multiple dilemmas of modern life. His characters are possessed, driven to pursue high ideals yet weighted down with their awareness of their inadequacies and sinfulness. They are imprisoned in their surroundings however they may strive to escape them.

Although capable of genuine humor, full of the joy of life, Faulkner was essentially a pessimist. His weakness as a writer, aside from a sometimes exasperating obscurity and verbosity, resulted from his somewhat confused view of himself and of the world he described. Much of his work was passion frozen into words without

discernible meaning; his characters continually experienced emotions too intense to be bearable, often too profound and too subtle for the natures he had given them. Nevertheless, his great stature was beyond question, and unlike so many other novelists of the period he maintained a high level in his later years, with works like *The Hamlet* (1940), *Intruder in the Dust* (1948), *A Fable* (1954), and *The Reivers* (1962). He was awarded the 1949 Nobel prize for literature and two Pulitzer prizes, one in 1955 and one in 1963.

For a time after World War II, the nation seemed on the verge of a literary outburst comparable to that which followed World War I. A number of excellent novels based on the military experiences of young writers appeared, the most notable being Norman Mailer's *The Naked and the Dead* (1948), and James Jones's *From Here to Eternity* (1951). However, the new renaissance did not develop. It is, of course, impossible to estimate the eventual reputation of contemporary authors with assurance, but the majority of the most talented seemed lacking in conviction and obsessed more with themselves than with their surroundings. The generation of the twenties saw itself as "lost," that of the forties and fifties as alienated, or "beat." It preferred to bewail its fate rather than to rebel against it; it demanded admiration while deliberately insulting, even assaulting, its audience. A founder of the "beatnik school," Jack Kerouac, reveled in the chaotic description of violence, perversion, and madness, ignoring the writer's obligation to be a craftsman. At the other extreme, J. D. Salinger, perhaps the most popular postwar writer and the particular favorite of college students (*The Catcher in the Rye* sold nearly 2 million copies in hardcover and paperback editions), was an impeccable stylist, witty, contemptuous of all pretense; but he also wrote about people entirely wrapped up in themselves.

In *Catch-22*, which replaced *Catcher in the Rye* in the hearts of college students, Joseph Heller produced a war novel at once farcical and an indignant denunciation of the stupidity and waste of warfare. Saul Bellow's *Adventures of Augie March* portrayed the confusion and sordidness of modern urban society without descending to mere sensationalism. Bellow exposed human weaknesses, but did not condemn humanity or lose sight of the positive values of modern existence. It was heartening also that talented Negro writers, such as Ralph Ellison and James Baldwin, and Jewish authors, such as Bellow and Bernard Malamud, were able, without ignoring their heritages or neglecting the social issues that most directly concerned their peoples, to transcend parochial concerns of interest chiefly to Negroes and Jews and write books that were enjoyed by a general audience.

American painting, historically an appendage of European, achieved independence explosively after World War II. By the twenties some American painters had begun to absorb the new cubist abstractionism first introduced in the Armory Show in 1913, although they tended to maintain a closer contact with objective forms than the European cubist masters. The geometric flowers of Georgia O'Keeffe, Joseph Stella's brilliant studies of the Brooklyn Bridge, the poster-like work of Stuart Davis, and John Marin's wild glimpses of Maine landscapes stand among the finest achievements of the decade. Cubist influences could also be seen in Charles Sheeler's starkly oversimplified studies of buildings and machinery. During the Great Depression, while such painters continued to flourish, others turned to a kind of regionalism, more conservative in technique, as illustrated by the work of Thomas Hart Benton, John Steuart Curry, and Grant Wood. Social critics roused by depression problems, such as William Gropper, Jack Levine, and Ben Shahn, spiritual descendants of the ashcan school, also did important work, and there was a new appreciation of American folk artists, both those of earlier periods and of modern primitives like John Kane and that amazing septuagenarian, "Grandma" Moses.

But in the forties and fifties, with the development of the abstract expressionism ("action" painting) of the "New York school," Americans placed themselves for the first time in the vanguard of the modern movement in art. Led by Jackson Pollock (1912–56), who composed huge abstract designs by laying his canvas on the floor of his studio and squeezing paint on it directly from the tube in a wild tangle of color, these men were utterly subjective in their approach to art. "The source of my painting is the Unconscious," Pollock explained. "I am not much aware of what is taking place; it is only after that I see what I have done." He tried to produce not the representation of a landscape, but, as the critic Harold Rosenberg put it, "an inner landscape that is part of himself."

Untutored critics found the abstract expressionists crude, chaotic, devoid of interest. The swirling, dripping chaos of the followers of Pollock, the vaguely defined planes of color favored by Mark Rothko and his disciples, and the sharp spacial confrontations composed by painters like Franz Kline, Robert Motherwell, and Adolph Gottlieb required too much verbal explanation to communicate their meaning to the average observer. On the other hand, viewed in its social context, abstract expressionism reflected, like so much of modern literature, the estrangement of the artist from the world of the atomic bomb and the computer, a revolt against contemporary mass culture, with its unthinking acceptance of novelty for its own sake.

The experimental spirit released by the abstract expressionists led on to "op" art, which employed the physical impact of pure complementary colors to produce dynamic optical effects. Even within the rigid limitations of severely formal designs composed of concentric circles, stripes, squares, and rectangles, such paintings appeared constantly in motion, almost alive. "Op" was devoid of social connotations, but another variant, "pop" art, playfully but often with acid incisiveness, satirized many aspects of American culture: its vapidity, its crudeness, its violence. Painters like Andy Warhol created huge portraits of mundane objects such as soup cans and packing cases. "Op" and "pop" art grew out of the mechanized aspects of life; these painters made use of modern technology in their work, enhancing the shock of vibrating complementary colors with new fluorescent paints. Pop artists imitated newspaper-photograph techniques by fashioning their images of sharply defined dots of color; both borrowed from contemporary commercial art, employing spray guns, stencils, and masking tape to produce flat, "hard-edge" effects. The line between "op" and "pop" was frequently crossed, as, for example, in Robert Indiana's *Love,* which was reproduced and imitated on posters, Christmas cards, book jackets, buttons, rings, and on a postage stamp.

Color and shape as ends in themselves, stark and on a heroic scale, typified the new styles. Color-field painters covered vast planes with flat, sometimes subtly shaded hues. Frank Stella, one of the most universally admired of the younger artists, composed complicated bands and curves of color on enormous, eccentrically shaped canvases. To an unprecedented degree, the artist's hand, the combination of patience and skill that had characterized traditional art, was removed from painting.

The pace of change in artistic fashion was dizzying and exciting. Although some believed it put too high a premium on mere novelty, it gave to both artists and art lovers a sense of participating in events of historic importance. Successful artists, like the most popular writers, film directors, and other creative people, became national personalities, a few of them enormously rich. For these, each new work was exposed to the glare of publicity and subject to minute critical analysis, sometimes with unfortunate results. Too much attention, like too much money, could be distracting, even corrupting, especially for young artists, who needed time and obscurity to develop their talents.

Robert Indiana's versions of *Love* (this is a 1966 oil) include an aluminum sculpture. (Dayton's Gallery 12.)

Two Dilemmas

The ambiguous impact of modern society on artists was only one example of the uncertainties afflicting the American people. Two dilemmas seemed to confront them. First of all, progress was often self-defeating. Reforms and innovations instituted with the highest of motives often made things worse rather than better. Illustrations of this dilemma, large and small, are so numerous as to defy summary. A powerful chemical, DDT, developed to kill insects that were spreading disease and destroying valuable food crops, proved to have lethal effects on birds, fish, and perhaps indirectly on human beings. Goods manufactured to make life fuller and happier (automobiles, detergents, electric power) produced waste products that disfigured the land and polluted air and water. Cities built to bring culture and comfort to millions became pestholes of poverty and depravity.

Moreover, change was occurring so fast that experience (the recollection of how things had been) tended to become less useful, and sometimes even counterproductive as a guide for dealing with current problems. Foreign policies designed to prevent wars, devised on the basis of knowledge of the causes of past wars, led, because the circumstances were different, to new wars. Parents who sought to transmit to their children the accumulated wisdom of their years found their advice rejected and often with good reason, since that "wisdom" had little application to the problems their children had to face.

The second dilemma was that modern industrial society put an enormous premium on social cooperation, but at the same time undermined the individual citizen's sense of being essential to the proper functioning of society. The economy was as complicated as a fine watch; a breakdown in any sector had ramifications that spread swiftly to other sectors. Yet specialization had progressed so far that individual workers had little sense of the importance of their personal contributions and thus felt little responsibility for the smooth functioning of the whole. Effective democratic government required that all voters be knowledgeable and concerned, but few could feel that their individual voices had any effect on elections or public policies. The exhaust fumes of millions of automobiles were poisoning the air, but it was difficult to expect the single motorist to inconvenience himself by leaving his car in the garage when his restraint would have no measurable effect on the total pollution.°

People tried to deal with this dilemma by joining groups, but the groups became so large that members felt as incapable of influencing

°Shortly after writing these lines, I received a letter from my teen-age daughter: "It is frustrating because one person just can't feel that she's doing anything. I can use soap instead of detergents and no paper bags, but what good do I feel I'm doing when there are people next door having a party with plastic spoons and paper plates?"

them as they did of the larger society. Furthermore, the groups were so numerous and had so many conflicting objectives that instead of making citizens more socially minded they often made them more self-centered. The organization—union, club, party, pressure group—was a potent force in society, but few organizations were really concerned with the common interest, although logic required that the common interest be regarded if individuals or groups were to achieve their special interests.

These dilemmas produced a paradox. The United States was the most powerful nation in the world, its people the best educated, richest, and probably the most energetic. American society was technologically advanced and dynamic, American traditional values idealistic, humane, democratic. Yet the nation seemed incapable of mobilizing its resources intelligently to confront the most obvious challenges, citizens of achieving personal happiness or identification with their fellows, the society of living up to its most universally accepted ideals. President Johnson recognized this problem when he talked of establishing a "consensus" and of building a Great Society, but no real consensus emerged, and American society remained fragmented, its members divided against themselves and often within themselves.

Mixed Blessings

The vexing character of modern conditions could be seen in every aspect of life. The economy, after decades of rapid growth, speeded ahead even faster. The gross national product exceeded one trillion dollars in 1970. But inflation became increasingly serious. Prices rose faster than wages, so that workers were under constant pressure to demand raises, which only served to drive prices still higher. The effect was socially devastating; it became impossible to expect workers to see inflation as a social problem and to restrain their personal demands. They put their individual interests before those of the whole and were

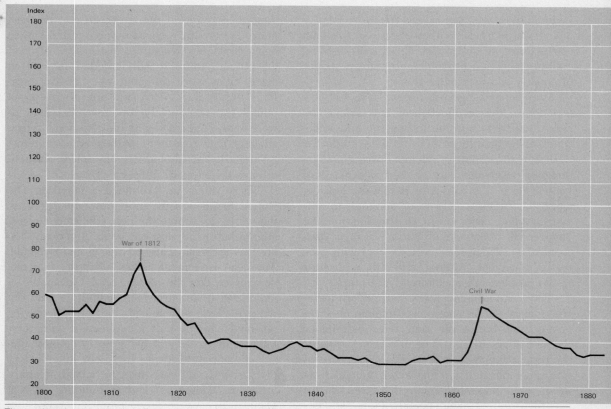

The explanation of the basis of this chart appears on pages 129 and 495. Recalling that the base line of 100 is the 1957–1959 average, the never-ending inflation that started right after World War II is

prepared to disrupt the economy whatever the social cost. Even public employees—teachers, garbage collectors, policemen, and firemen—traditionally committed to a no-strike policy because they worked for the whole community, succumbed to this selfish, if understandable, way of looking at life.

Economic expansion resulted in large measure from technological advances, but these, too, proved to be mixed blessings. As we have seen, World War II needs stimulated the development of plastics like nylon, of synthetic rubber, and of radar, television, and other electronic devices. After the war, such products really came into their own. Plastics invaded field after field—automobile parts, building materials, adhesives, shoe "leather," packaging materials. Television sets, produced only experimentally before the war, swept the country after 1946.

In 1951 scientists began to manufacture electricity from controlled nuclear energy; in 1954 the first atomic-powered ship, the submarine *Nautilus,* was launched. Although the peaceful use of atomic energy remained small compared to other sources of power, its implications were immense. Equally significant was the perfection of the electronic computer, which revolutionized the collection and storage of records, solved mathematical problems beyond the scope of the most brilliant human minds, and speeded up the work of bank tellers, librarians, billing clerks, statisticians—and income-tax collectors. Computers also lay at the heart of industrial automation, for they could control the integration and adjustment of the most complex machinery. In automobile factories they made it possible to machine entire engine blocks automatically. In steel mills molten metal could be poured into molds,

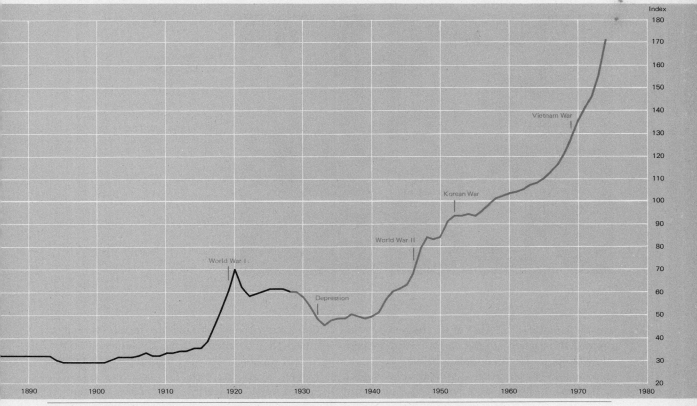

Index

shown in startling detail. The contrast with all early periods, looking at the orange part of the graphed line, is particularly striking.

cooled, rolled, and cut into slabs without the intervention of a human hand, the computers locating defects and adjusting the machinery to correct them far more accurately than the most skilled steelworker, and in a matter of seconds. Taken in conjunction with a new oxygen smelting process some six or eight times faster than the open-hearth method, computer-controlled continuous casting promised to have an impact on steel-making as great as that of the Bessemer process in the 1870's.

But the material benefits of technology had counterbalancing effects. The consumption of petroleum necessary to produce power soared, and soon began to outstrip supplies, threatening shortages that would disrupt the entire economy. Moreover, the burning of this fuel released unmeasurable tons of smoke and other polluting gases into the atmosphere, endangering the

health of millions and, some alarmists warned, threatening to alter the climate of the world drastically, even to make the globe incapable of supporting life. The vast outpouring of flimsy plastic products and the increased use of paper, metal foil, and other "disposable" packaging materials seemed about to bury the country beneath mountains of trash. The commercial use of nuclear energy also caused problems. Scientists insisted that the danger from radiation was nonexistent, but the possibility of accidents could not be eliminated entirely, and the safe disposal of radioactive wastes grew steadily more difficult.

Even an apparently ideal form of scientific advance, the use of commercial fertilizers to boost food output, had unfortunate side effects: phosphates washed from farmlands into streams sometimes upset the ecological balance and turned the streams into malodorous death traps

An all-too-common scene in recent years is this frantic attempt by Audubon Society volunteers to save oil-soaked waterfowl that had been stranded on the beach after huge quantities of oil were spilled from two tankers in a collision in San Francisco Bay. (UPI.)

for all aquatic life. Above all, technology increased the capacity of the earth to support people—temporarily. As population increased, production and consumption increased, speeding the pollution of the air and water supplies. And where would the process end? When viewed from a world perspective, it was obvious that the population explosion must be checked, or it would check itself by pestilence, war, starvation, or some combination of these scourges. Yet how to check it?

Technology also influenced American culture, and again the results were mixed. Around 1900 the motion picture made its appearance. The first films, such as the eight-minute epic *The Great Train Robbery* (1903), were brief, crude, and unpretentious, but they succeeded instantaneously. By 1908 the nation had between 8,000 and 10,000 nickelodeons, as the primitive exhibition halls were called, usually seating fewer than 100 persons each. However, the length and complexity of movies expanded rapidly, especially after David W. Griffith released his 12-reel *Birth of a Nation* in 1915, and by the mid-twenties the industry, centered in Hollywood, was the fourth largest in the nation in capital investment. Immense movie "palaces," each seating several

thousand persons, sprang up in all the major cities. They counted their yearly audiences in the tens of millions. With the introduction of talking movies, beginning with *The Jazz Singer* (1927), and of color films a few years later, the motion picture reached technological maturity. Costs and profits mounted to enormous heights: by the thirties million-dollar productions were common; by the fifties films grossing over $10 million were not unusual and average weekly attendance figures ran in the neighborhood of 55 million.

In the years before and after World War II, most movies were tasteless, gaudy, mindless trash, aimed at titillating the senses and catering to the prejudices of the multitude. Sex, crime, war, romantic adventure, broad comedy, and luxurious living were their main themes, endlessly repeated in predictable patterns. Most popular actors were handsome, talentless sticks, type-cast over and over again as heroes, villains, comedians; yet they attracted armies of adoring fans and received thousands of dollars a week for their services. Critics charged that the movies were destroying the legitimate stage (which indeed underwent a sharp decline in the 20th century), corrupting the morals of youth, glorifying the materialistic aspects of life, and blackening the image of America abroad with their distorted images of American civilization.

Nevertheless, the motion picture made positive contributions to American culture. Beginning with the work of Griffith, film-makers created an entirely new theatrical art, using close-ups to portray character and heighten tension, broad panoramic shots to transcend the limits of the stage. They employed special lighting effects, the fade-out, and other techniques impossible in the live theater with remarkable results. Movies also enabled dozens of established actors to reach wider audiences and developed many first-rate new ones. In Charlie Chaplin, whose characterization of the sad little tramp, with his cane, tight frock coat, and baggy trousers became famous all over the world, the new form found perhaps the supreme comic artist of all time. The animated cartoon, perfected by Walt Disney, was a lesser, but still significant achievement, giving endless delight to millions of children.

As the medium matured, it produced many works of the highest artistic quality. It was an art in tune with modern technology; at its best it offered a breadth and power of impact superior to anything on the traditional stage. By its nature, the motion picture was international in scope. After World War II the finest films of every nation could be seen, either with dubbed-in dialogue or with translated subtitles, in every major city: by the sixties New York City had at least two dozen houses specializing in foreign productions. The motion picture, although made possible by technology, was a medium of astonishing variety and versatility. Millions still flocked to the great, empty spectacles, to the inane comedies and brutal "horse operas," and to the sordid and sexy potboilers, but films of subtle dramatic power, often dealing with serious social problems, also attracted large audiences, especially among intellectuals and students.

Even more pervasive was the impact of radio. Wireless transmission of sound was first developed in the late 19th century by many individual scientists in Europe and the United States, but an American, Lee De Forest, working in the decade

Man against machine: Charlie Chaplin duels a folding Murphy bed in the film *One A.M. The Great Dictator* (1940), one of Chaplin's most famous satires, flailed Hitler with deadly aim. (Museum of Modern Art.)

before World War I, devised the key improvements that made long-distance broadcasting possible. During the war, radio was put to important military uses and was strictly controlled, but although the European nations maintained their government monopolies, in the United States the air waves were thrown open to everyone in 1919. Radio remained briefly the domain of hobbyists, thousands of "hams" chatting back and forth in indiscriminate fashion. Even under these conditions, the manufacture of radio equipment quickly became a big business. In 1920 the first commercial station (KDKA in Pittsburgh) began broadcasting. It succeeded at once, and by the end of 1922 over 500 stations were in operation. Radio became a giant industry almost overnight.

It took little time for broadcasters to discover the power of the new medium. When one pioneer interrupted a music program to ask listeners to phone in requests, the station received 3,000 calls in an hour. The immediacy of radio explained its tremendous impact. As a means of communicating the latest news, it had no peer; beginning with the broadcast of the 1924 Presidential nominating conventions, all major public events were covered "live."

Franklin Roosevelt was the first political leader to master the use of radio as an instrument of mass persuasion. During World War II listeners heard the rantings of Hitler and Winston Churchill's deathless periods as they were actually delivered, and kept up with every aspect of the global war through the reports of dozens of on-the-spot correspondents and commentators. But the most convincing example of radio's power was provided accidentally in 1938, when Orson Welles presented a dramatization of H. G. Wells' novel *The War of the Worlds,* which described an invasion of the earth by Martians. Welles imitated radio techniques of news coverage so effectively that thousands of set owners, tuning in while the program was under way, believed an invasion was really taking place and fled their homes in panic.

Advertisers seized upon radio at once, for it was as useful a device for selling soap and automobiles as for transmitting news. Advertising had mixed effects on broadcasting. The huge sums paid by businesses for air time made possible elaborate entertainments performed by the finest actors and musicians, and without cost to listeners, but advertisers hungered for mass markets and generally insisted on programs of little intellectual content, aimed at the lowest tastes and utterly uncontroversial. "Soap operas"—turgid, sentimental serial stories of domestic life—so dominated daytime programming in the 1930's that an investigator reported listening to 15 in a single day on one network and counting 35 others that he could have heard on other national hook-ups. Programs good and bad alike were constantly interrupted by irritating pronouncements extolling the supposed virtues of one product or another.

In 1927 Congress undertook to regulate the industry, limiting the number of stations and parceling out wavelengths to prevent interference. Further legislation in 1934 established the Federal Communications Commission with power to revoke the licenses of stations failing to operate in the public interest, but the FCC placed no effective controls either on programming or on advertising practices. The general level remained lamentably inferior to that of government-owned European systems.

After World War II television, which combined the immediacy of radio with the visual impact of the motion picture, quickly replaced radio as a major means of entertainment and communication. Throughout the 1950's the public bought sets at the rate of 6 or 7 million annually, and by 1961 there were 55 million in operation, receiving the transmissions of 530 stations.

Television displayed most of radio's strengths and weaknesses in exaggerated form. It became indispensable to the political system, both in its coverage of public events and as a vehicle for political advertising. Television's handling of the events following President Kennedy's assassination, of national conventions and inaugurations, and other news developments made history come alive for tens of millions. It brought sports events before the viewer vividly, attracting enormous audiences and thus producing so much money in advertising charges° that the economics of professional sports was revolutionized. Team franchises were bought and sold for millions and star players commanded salaries in the hundreds of thousands.

Some excellent drama was presented on television, along with many filmed documentaries dealing with contemporary issues. By capturing so much of the mass audience, the medium indirectly improved the level of radio broadcasting. Much more radio time was devoted to high-quality discussion programs and to classical music, especially after the introduction of static-free frequency modulation (FM) transmission.

On the other hand, the entertainment offered on television was generally abominable. Uninspired and vulgar plays, routine variety shows, reruns of third-rate movies, giveaway programs, and quiz programs apparently designed to reveal the ignorance of the average citizen consumed the lion's share of TV time. Most sets had poor acoustical qualities, making them very inferior instruments for listening to good music. Educational programs were too often relegated to inconvenient periods, and there were not enough of them. Yet children found television especially fascinating, remaining transfixed before the TV screen when—their elders said—they should have been out of doors or curled up with a book.

Another defect of television's virtues was its capacity for influencing the opinions and feelings of viewers. The insistent and strident claims of advertisers punctuated every program with monotonous regularity. Politicians discovered that no other device or method approached television as a means of reaching large numbers of voters with an illusion of intimacy. But since television time was extremely expensive, only candidates who possessed or had access to huge sums could afford to use the medium, obviously a dangerous state of affairs in a democracy. In addition, television put a premium on appearances, real and contrived. The sudden tendency of movie actors to seek political office (Governor Ronald Reagan

°A single minute of advertising during the 1974 Superbowl football championship cost $210,000.

and Senator George Murphy of California being pioneer examples) was undoubtedly a by-product of the use of television in politics.

Poverty Amid Plenty

In spite of the nation's prosperity and the vitality of its society, a major problem was the persistence of poverty. During the New Deal, Franklin Roosevelt had shocked the country by claiming that one-third of the nation was "ill-housed, ill-clad, ill-nourished." Actually, Roosevelt had underestimated the extent of American poverty. If it is fair to assume that a family of four with an annual income of less than $4,500 in current dollars is poor, then two-thirds of the population fell into that category in 1937. Nor did the New Deal produce any dramatic change in this situation; it was World War II that caused the really significant reduction of American poverty. Nevertheless, 37 per cent of the population still fell below the level of income necessary for a decent existence in 1947. During the prosperous postwar years this percentage shrank still further. In 1960, however, between one-fifth and one-fourth of all American families (perhaps 40 million persons) were still living below the poverty line. During the sixties, more rapid progress in the "war" on poverty was made, yet over 27 million people remained in that category in 1970.

That so many could be poor in an "affluent" society was deplorable, but not difficult to explain. In any community a certain number of persons cannot support themselves because of physical incapacity, low intelligence, or psychological difficulties. There were also in the United States whole regions, the best-known being the Appalachian area, which had been by-passed by economic development and no longer provided their inhabitants with adequate economic opportunities.

In addition, certain less obvious influences were at work. Poverty is naturally more prevalent among the old and the young than among those in the prime of life: in the postwar decades these two groups were growing more rapidly than any other. Social security payments amounted to far less than an elderly person needed to maintain himself decently, and some of the poorest workers, such as agricultural laborers, were not covered by the system to begin with. Unemployment was about twice as prevalent among youths in their late teens as in the nation as a whole. With the movement of the middle class to the suburbs, poverty became, in the words of Michael Harrington, whose book *The Other America* (1962) did much to call attention to the problem, "less visible" to those well-meaning citizens whose energies had to be mobilized if it was to be eradicated. Furthermore, the poor were becoming alienated from society, less hopeful, more resigned to their fate. In earlier times most of the poor were recent immigrants, believers in the American dream of rags-to-riches, strivers who accepted their low status as temporary. The modern poor, many studies indicated, tended to lack motivation; they felt trapped by their condition and gave up. In the slums, sociologist Christopher Jencks has written, "young people are not seizing the opportunities. . . . Too many are dropping out of school before graduation (more than half in many slums)."

Poverty exacted a heavy price, both from its victims and from society. Statistics indicated the relationship between low income and bad health. Only about 4 per cent of persons from families with over $10,000 a year (the median for the nation) were chronically ill, whereas 8 per cent of those in the $2–4,000 bracket and 16.5 per cent of those with less than $2,000 were so afflicted. Mental illness also varied inversely with

Bar, with Pusher and Addict, painted in 1968 by 18-year-old Dorrence Howell, is an interpretation of Harlem, New York's black ghetto, as viewed by one of its residents. Howell was enrolled in a commercial art workshop that was established in Harlem in 1964 under the auspices of the federal government's anti-poverty program. (Dorrence Howell and Haryou-Act.)

income, as did alcoholism, drug addiction and crime. Thus, aside from the cost of direct relief, the well-to-do majority suffered in a variety of ways because of the poor, to say nothing of the general waste of human potential involved.

The major federal effort to eradicate poverty was the Economic Opportunity Act of 1964, which set up a mélange of programs, including a Job Corps similar to the New Deal Civilian Conservation Corps, a community action program to finance local efforts, an educational program for small children (Project Head Start), and a system for training the unskilled unemployed and for lending money to small businessmen in poor areas. Steadily increasing sums were spent under this act, with mixed results: much of the money was wasted, some even stolen, but many poor people benefited. Medicare and increases in social security payments also helped many of the aged poor.

Race Relations

Poverty was intimately related to the vexing problem of race relations. In 1960 a quarter of the poor were nonwhite, although nonwhites comprised only 11 per cent of the population. The average Negro earned only slightly more than half of what the average white earned; twice as large a percentage were unemployed. Half of New York City's million Negroes lived below the minimum subsistence level. Between 1960 and 1968, 17 million white Americans escaped from poverty as officially defined; only 3 million blacks did so. Yet, obviously, the racial problem was not solely an economic one. Deep-seated prejudices blighted the lives of even those Negroes who were relatively well off.

During the fifties and sixties the pent-up resentments of blacks against this prejudice burst forth in a grass-roots drive for civil rights. The legal assault on school desegregation had been carefully planned by the NAACP, but the hopes roused by *Brown v. Board of Education of To-*

peka inspired a few Negroes to act spontaneously against the system and when they did, thousands of others rushed to join them. This phenomenon first occurred in the tightly segregated city of Montgomery, Alabama. On the evening of December 1, 1955, Mrs. Rosa Parks boarded a Montgomery bus on her way home from work. She dutifully took a seat toward the rear as law and custom required, but after white workers and shoppers had filled the forward section of the bus the driver ordered her to give up her place. She refused, having suddenly made up her mind, she later recalled, "never to move again."

Mrs. Parks was arrested. The Negroes of Montgomery, led by a young Baptist clergyman, Martin Luther King, Jr., promptly organized a boycott of the buses. For a full year they refused to ride and finally, after a Supreme Court ruling in their favor, Montgomery desegregated its public transportation system. This success encouraged blacks elsewhere in the South to band together against the caste system. It also made King, who preached civil disobedience as the best way to destroy segregation, a national figure. His organization, the Southern Christian Leadership Conference, moved into the forefront of the civil rights movement, and in 1964 his work won him the Nobel peace prize.

Other new organizations also joined in the struggle, most notably the Congress of Racial Equality (CORE) and the Student Nonviolent Coordinating Committee (SNCC). However, the most significant developments resulted from the actions of ordinary individuals, chiefly students. In February 1960 four black students in Greensboro, North Carolina, sat down at a segregated lunch counter in a local five-and-ten and refused to leave when they were denied service. Their "sit-in," a tiny defiance in itself, sparked a national movement. CORE rushed field workers to Greensboro, students in dozens of other southern towns and cities copied their example, until, by late 1961, over 70,000 persons had participated in sit-ins and over a hundred lunch counters had been desegregated.

In May 1961 another group of Negro and white foes of segregation organized a "freedom ride" to test the effectiveness of federal regulations prohibiting discrimination in interstate transportation. Boarding buses in Washington, they traveled across the South, heading for New Orleans. In Alabama they ran into trouble: at Anniston racists set fire to their bus, in Birmingham they were assaulted by a mob. Quickly other groups of freedom riders descended on the South, many deliberately seeking arrest in order to test local segregation ordinances in the courts. Repeatedly, these actions resulted in the breaking down of legal racial barriers.

The civil rights crusade soon spread to the North. Negroes, often joined by sympathetic whites, boycotted stores that refused to hire members of their race and picketed construction

In Selma, Alabama, in 1965 Dr. Martin Luther King, Jr., knelt on the sidewalk with his followers to offer a prayer. They had been arrested and were on their way to jail after committing an act of civil disobedience. (UPI.)

sites where black workers were not employed. In New York City some militants organized "rent strikes" to call attention to the noxious condition of Harlem tenements and school boycotts to protest against the de facto segregation that existed in predominantly black neighborhoods. The nationwide impact of the "Freedom Now" crusade was highlighted in August 1963 when 200,000 persons participated in an impressive "March on Washington" to demand racial equality. The orderly nature of the immense throng that gathered before the Lincoln Memorial and the evident sincerity of all concerned had a considerable impact upon public opinion.

The passage of the Civil Rights Act of 1964 seemed like a major step forward, but the forces resisting change remained formidable. In the spring of 1965 peaceful demonstrators in Selma, Alabama, were brutally assaulted by state policemen wielding clubs and tossing canisters of tear gas into their ranks. Liberal opinion was shocked as never before; thousands descended upon Selma from all over the nation to demonstrate their sympathy and support for American blacks. Congress passed still another civil rights act, giving the federal government power to send officials into the South to register black voters. Another law, passed in 1968, took important steps in the direction of outlawing discrimination in the sale and rental of housing, and imposed stiff criminal penalties on persons found guilty of interfering with anyone's civil rights.

Yet in spite of and to an extent because of civil rights legislation, racial conflict remained America's most serious domestic problem. As in so many other aspects of modern life, progress itself caused new difficulties to arise. Official recognition of past injustices made Negroes more insistent that all discrimination be ended, and the very process of righting past wrongs gave them the strength to carry on their fight more vigorously.

Black militancy, building steadily during the war and postwar years, had long been ignored by the white majority, but in the middle sixties it burst forth so powerfully that the most smug and obtuse white citizens had to accept its existence.

From the early black supporters of African colonization schemes through the late-19th-century efforts of men like Bishop Henry Turner and the 20th-century movement of Marcus Garvey, Negroes proud of their race and culture and contemptuous of white prejudices had urged their fellows to reject "American" society and all it stood for. In the 1950's and 1960's, however, black nationalism became a far more potent force than ever before. The followers of Elijah Muhammad, leader of the Black Muslim movement, disliked the dominant white majority so intensely that they favored racial separation, demanding that a part of the United States be set aside for the exclusive use of Negroes. The Muslims rejected Christianity as "a white man's religion." They urged their followers to be industrious, thrifty, and abstemious, but they also urged them to view all whites with suspicion and hatred. "This white government has ruled us and given us plenty hell, but the time has arrived that you taste a little of your own hell," Elijah Muhammad said. "There are many of my poor black ignorant brothers . . . preaching the ignorant and lying stuff that you should love your enemy. What fool can love his enemy?"

Out of the Black Muslim movement came one of the most remarkable Americans of the 20th century, Malcolm X. Born Malcolm Little in 1925, son of a Baptist minister who was an organizer for Marcus Garvey's Universal Negro Improvement Association, he grew up in poverty in Michigan. At 15 he moved to Boston, then to New York's Harlem. For several years he lived on the edge of the underworld, taking and selling narcotics, working in the numbers racket, acting as a procurer for prostitutes. Soon he was carrying a gun. He became, as he later explained, "a true hustler—uneducated, unskilled at anything honorable . . . exploiting any prey that presented itself." At the age of 21 he was convicted of stealing a watch and sentenced to ten years in jail.

While in prison Malcolm was converted to the Black Muslim faith. He cast off his dissolute ways, and after being paroled in 1952, he rose rapidly in the Muslim hierarchy. A brilliant

Calling for black separatism, Malcolm X told an interviewer in 1964, "The Negro (must) develop his character and his culture in accord with his own nature." (Bert Shavita, Pix.)

speaker and organizer, he preached the standard Muslim combination of idealism and hate. "Let us rid ourselves of immoral habits and God will be with us to protect and guide us," he told a Harlem audience in 1960. But he also said: "For the white man to ask the black man if he hates him is just like the rapist asking the *raped,* or the wolf asking the *sheep,* 'Do you hate me?'"

Gradually, however, Malcolm became disillusioned with Elijah Muhammad, especially after the 67-year-old Muslim leader was accused by two of his former secretaries of fathering their four illegitimate children. The militant black comedian, Dick Gregory, among others, told Malcolm that Muhammad was unworthy of his support and urged him to break with the Black Muslims. A trip through the Arab world served further to broaden his horizons, and in 1964 he left the Muslims and founded his own Organization of Afro-American Unity. While continuing to stress black self-help and the militant defense of black rights, he now saw the crusade as part of a larger struggle for all human rights. "What we do . . . helps all people everywhere who are fighting against oppression," he said. In February 1965, however, Malcolm was assassinated by Black Muslim gunmen. His posthumously published *Autobiography,* which tells his story vividly, has already become a classic.

Soon after the death of Malcolm X, Negro militants found a slogan: "Black Power." The term was given national currency by Stokely Carmichael, chairman of SNCC, in 1966. The time for white involvement in the fight for Negro rights has ended, Carmichael announced. "If we are to proceed toward true liberation, we must set ourselves off from white people." Since whites "cannot relate to the black experience," the movement "should be black-staffed, black-controlled, and black-financed." Black Power caught on swiftly among militant Negroes, but deeply troubled white liberals because of its "refusal to discriminate between degrees of inequity" among whites and because the liberals feared that it would needlessly antagonize white conservatives. Since Negroes made up only slightly more than ten per cent of the population, liberals argued that any attempt to obtain racial justice through the use of naked power was sure to fail.

Meanwhile, black anger erupted in a series of destructive urban riots. The most important of these occurred in Watts, the black ghetto of Los Angeles, in August 1965. A trivial incident—policemen halted a Negro motorist who seemed to be drunk and attempted to give him a sobriety test—brought thousands of protesting blacks into the streets. The neighborhood almost literally exploded, and for six days Watts was swept by fire, looting, and bloody fighting between local residents and 15,000 National Guardsmen, called up to assist the police. Order was restored only after 34 persons had been killed, over 850 wounded, 3,100 arrested. Property damage in Watts was

staggering, amounting to nearly $200 million.

The following summer saw similar outbursts in New York, Chicago, and other cities. In 1967, still more riots broke out, the most serious in Newark, where 25 were killed, and Detroit, where the death toll came to 43 and where looting and arson assumed monstrous proportions.

Then, in April 1968, the revered Negro leader, Martin Luther King, apostle of nonviolence, was murdered in Memphis, Tennessee, by a white man, James Earl Ray.° Blacks in more than 100 cities swiftly unleashed their anger in paroxysms of burning and looting. The whole nation was shocked and profoundly depressed: the Negroes' anger was understandable even to those who would not condone their actions, and the death of King appeared to destroy the hope that his doctrine of pacific appeal to reason and right could solve the racial problem.

Public fear and puzzlement led to many investigations of the causes of these riots, the most important being that of the commission headed by Governor Otto Kerner of Illinois, which President Johnson appointed after the murder of Dr. King. The conclusions of most of these studies were complex but fairly clear. Race riots had a long history in the United States, but the outbursts of the 1960's were without precedent. Earlier troubles usually began with attacks by whites, which naturally led to black counterattacks. Riots of the Watts type were begun by blacks, and the fighting was mostly between blacks and law enforcement officers trying to control them; white citizens tended to avoid the centers of trouble, and blacks seldom ranged outside their own neighborhoods.

The rioters, in general, were expressing frustration and despair; their resentment was directed more at the social system than at individuals. As the Kerner commission put it, the basic cause was an attitude of mind, the "white racism" that deprived blacks of access to good jobs, crowded them into terrible slums, and, especially

---

°Ray fled to England, but he was eventually apprehended, extradited, convicted, and sentenced to 99 years in prison.

for the young, eroded all hope of escape from such misery. Ghettos bred crime and depravity—as slums always have—but the passive, complacent refusal of the white majority adequately to invest its wealth and energy in helping ghetto residents, or even truly to admit that the black poor deserved help, made the modern Negro slum unbearable. While the ghettos expanded, the white middle classes in the great cities tended more and more to "flee" to the suburbs or to call upon the police "to maintain law and order," a euphemism for cracking down mercilessly on every form of deviant black behavior no matter how obvious the connection between that behavior and the slum environment.

The victims of this racism employed violence not so much to force change as to obtain release; it was a way of destroying what they could not stomach. Thus the concentration of the riots in the ghettos themselves, the smashing, Samson-like, of the source of degradation even when this meant self-destruction. When fires broke out in black districts, the very firemen who tried to extinguish them were often showered with bottles and bricks, even shot at, while above the roar of the flames and the hiss of steam rose the apocalyptic chant: *"Burn, baby, burn!"*

The most frightening aspect of all these developments was their tendency to polarize society still more sharply on racial lines. Advocates of Black Power became more determined than ever to separate themselves from white influence. They exasperated white supporters of school desegregation by demanding schools of their own. Extremists formed the Black Panther party, and collected weapons to resist the police. "Shoot, don't loot," the radical H. Rap Brown advised all who would listen. The Panthers demanded public compensation for injustices done to Negroes in the past, pointing out that after World War II, West Germany had made such payments to Jews to make up for Hitler's persecutions, and in 1968, they nominated Eldridge Cleaver, a convict on parole, for President. Although Cleaver was an articulate and intelligent man, whose autobiographical *Soul on Ice,* written while in prison, had attracted much praise,

his nomination for the Presidency widened the racial breach still further.

On the other hand, both black violence and black separatism hardened the resistance of many whites against further efforts to aid Negroes. Middle-class city residents often resented what seemed the "favoritism" of the federal government and of many state and local administrations, which sought to provide blacks with new economic opportunities and social benefits. Efforts to desegregate ghetto schools, involving the transportation of black children, and white ones too, out of their local neighborhoods, was a particularly bitter cause of conflict. Such persons, already subjected to the pressures caused by inflation, specialization, and rapid change that were undermining social solidarity, and worried by the sharp rise in urban crime rates and in welfare costs, found black radicalism infuriating. In the face of the greatest national effort in history to aid Negroes, the Negroes (they said) were displaying not merely ingratitude but contempt.

In recent years Chicanos and Indians have responded to discrimination in much the same manner as have Negroes. One Chicano nationalist group, the *Alianza* (alliance) led by Reies López Tijerina, sought to organize a secessionist movement in New Mexico, an act which brought it into confrontation with the army and which ended with Tijerina in prison. Another, the Crusade for Justice headed by Rodolfo "Corky" Gonzales, a professional boxer, poet, and experienced politician, focused on achieving social reforms and setting up political action groups. Its slogan, *Venceremos,* was Spanish for Martin Luther King's pledge: We shall overcome. But the Chicano leader with the widest influence was César Chávez, who concentrated on what superficially was a more limited goal—organizing migrant farm workers into unions.

Chávez, who was born in 1927, grew up in migrant camps in California; he had no schooling beyond the seventh grade. After serving in the navy during World War II he went to work for the Community Service Organization, a group seeking to raise the political consciousness of the poor and develop self-help programs among them. Chávez rose to be general director of the CSO by 1958, but in 1962 he resigned because he felt it was not devoting enough attention to the plight of migrant workers. He then founded the National Farm Workers' Association, later known as the United Farm Workers' Organizing Committee. In 1965 the grape-pickers in his union in Delano, California, struck for higher wages and union recognition. Chávez, seeing the strike as an opportunity to attack the very structure of the migrant labor system, turned it into a countrywide crusade. Avoiding violence, he enlisted the support of church leaders; he organized sit-ins, a march on the state capital, eventually a national consumer boycott of grapes. By 1970 most of the growers had capitulated and signed contracts with the union. Chávez then moved on to unionize migrant workers in other areas. He demonstrated convincingly that supposedly indifferent migrant workers could be

unionized and that the militant demands of minorities for equal treatment did not necessarily lead to separatism and class or racial antagonism.

Yet it was impossible to predict what the future would bring. Racial controversies were as heated as ever. Even the long-suffering American Indians were up in arms—literally so in the case of those who occupied the town of Wounded Knee, South Dakota, site of one of the most disgraceful Indian massacres of the 19th century, and held it at gunpoint for weeks. On the other hand, by the early 1970's mistreated minorities had achieved gains that would have seemed inconceivable a generation earlier. President Johnson had placed a black on the Supreme Court (Thurgood Marshall, tactician of the legal fight for school desegregation), and another in his Cabinet (Robert Weaver, Secretary of Housing and Urban Development). The first Negro since Reconstruction (Edward W. Brooke of Massa-

In 1973 César Chávez was still determinedly walking a picket line outside the regional headquarters of a national grocery chain. His United Farm Workers Union affiliation with the AFL-CIO had not prevented the Teamster's Union from becoming a serious rival in organizing farm workers. (UPI.)

chusetts) had been elected to the U. S. Senate. A number of important cities, including Atlanta, Georgia, in the Deep South, had elected black mayors. Hundreds of thousands of black children were attending schools with whites in the southern states. By 1968, more than 3.1 million adult southern blacks (62 per cent of the black voting-age population) were registered to vote. Above all, American ethnic groups had achieved real self-awareness. They continued to differ among themselves in style and tactics, as all persons do. Some still sought accommodation; others favored confrontation; others outright revolution. But the attitude of mind that ran from the lonely Denmark Vesey, to Frederick Douglass, to W. E. B. Du Bois had become the black consensus. The old complacency was dead. Ethnic minorities had become a formidable force in society and they were determined to exercise that force like other groups.

Women's Liberation

Concern for improving the position of blacks in society encouraged American women—as it had frequently in earlier times—to speak out more forcefully for their own rights as well. During the immediate postwar period the women's movement had gone through a period of relative quiescence. However, pressures were mounting steadily even during the years of "Eisenhower complacency," for social and economic conditions were changing. When the war ended, many women who had taken jobs because of the manpower shortage did not meekly return to the home. Some young wives worked to help pay for their veteran-husbands' war-interrupted educations, others to counterbalance the onslaughts of inflation, still others (some married, some not) simply because they had enjoyed the money and independence that jobs made possible. Between 1940 and 1960 the number of women workers doubled, and in the next decade it increased still more rapidly.

The rise was particularly swift among married women even after the immediate effects of the war period had passed. The difficulties faced by anyone trying to hold down a job while performing the traditional household duties acted both to increase the resentment of these workers and to persuade their husbands that some shift in male and female family responsibilities was justified. Moreover, married or single, more numerous or not, women workers still faced job discrimination of many kinds. In nearly every occupation they were paid less than men for exactly the same work. Many types of interesting jobs that they were capable of holding were either closed to them entirely, or doled out on the basis of some illogical and often unwritten quota system, and in challenging occupations where they could find employment they were rarely given a chance to rise to positions of leadership.

Of course many women objected to this state of affairs even in the 1950's, but in the 1960's their protest suddenly erupted into an organized and vociferous demand for change. One of the earliest leaders of this new women's liberation movement was Betty Friedan, whose book, *The Feminine Mystique* (1963), sold over a million copies. Friedan argued that society was stifling women's potential by a pervasive and not-very-subtle form of brainwashing designed to convince them of the virtues of domesticity. Advertisers, popular magazines, and other opinion-shaping forces were thus warping and even obliterating the capacity of women to use their intelligence and talents creatively. In 1966 Friedan founded the National Organization for Women (NOW), which called for equal employment opportunities and equal pay for women, for publicly supported child day-care centers, and other reforms.

Soon, however, NOW seemed almost a right-wing organization as more radical groups demanded the total "liberation" of the sex. Dissatisfaction with women's job opportunities interacted with the revived civil rights movement and the general social malaise of the times to encourage activism and extremism. Reformers like Kate Millet, author of *Sexual Politics,* and Germaine

Greer, author of *The Female Eunuch,* books that rivaled *The Feminine Mystique* in popularity, denounced every form of "male chauvinism." Some of the radicals advocated doing away with marriage as a legal institution and raising children in communal centers; others turned their hatred of the system against the whole male sex, and extolled the benefits of homosexuality for women.

Militants attacked all aspects of the standard image of the female sex. Avoiding the error of the Progressive Era reformers who had fought for the vote by stressing differences between the sexes (the supposed "purity" and high moral character of women), they insisted upon total equality. Clichés like "the fair sex" and "the weaker sex" made them see red. They took courses in self-defense in order to be able to protect themselves against muggers, rapists, and casual mashers. They denounced the use of masculine words like "chairman" (favoring "chairperson") and of such terms as "mankind" and "men" to designate people in general,° and they substituted the term "Ms." for both "Miss" and "Mrs." on the ground that the language drew no such distinction between unmarried and married men. They fought for legalized abortion, insisting that every woman has the right to control her own body.

By no means every American woman accepted the arguments of even the moderate feminists like Betty Friedan, but few escaped being affected by the women's movement, directly or indirectly. It was too soon to tell how extensive the changes would be. The presence of women in new roles—as television commentators and airline pilots, on police forces, even as professional jockeys—did not necessarily prove that a large-scale shift in employment patterns had taken place. But even the most unregenerate male chauvinist seemed to recognize that the bal-

Every inch the competitor, as here at Wimbledon in the world's most prestigious tennis matches, Ms. Billie Jean Moffitt King is an outstanding example of today's woman as successful athlete, with her active promotion of professional tennis as a sport and as a business. (Wide World.)

ance of power and influence between the sexes had been altered. The Civil Rights Act of 1964 had outlawed job discrimination based on sex, and both government agencies and the courts were steadily increasing the pressure on employers to conform to its terms. An equal rights amendment to the Constitution passed both houses of Congress in 1972, although as late as 1974 it had not yet been ratified by the necessary three-fourths of the states. Surely the new women's liberation movement was, if not the culmination at least a continuation, of a trend that had been going on for many decades, in America and throughout the world.

°The difficulty here was that this form of discrimination was built into the very structure of the language. Efforts to avoid the use of masculine words in general references led to such awkwardnesses as "his/her" and "(s)he". Even the word "woman" derives from the Anglo-Saxon *wif-mann,* wife of a man.

Education: Youth in Revolt

Young people were in the forefront in both the fight for the rights of blacks and in the women's liberation movement. Clearly, in a time of uncertainty and discontent, full of conflict and dilemmas, youth was affected more strongly than the older generation, and reacted more forcefully. No established institution escaped its criticisms, even the vaunted American educational system, which, it discovered, poorly suited its needs. This was still another paradox of modern life, for the American educational system was probably the best (it was certainly the most comprehensive) in the world. By 1974 three of every four American youths were completing high school, and the annual number earning college and university degrees had passed 1 million. Yet dissatisfaction reigned.

After World War I, under the impact of Freudian psychology, the emphasis in elementary education shifted from using the schools as instruments of social change, as John Dewey had recommended, to using them to promote the emotional development of the students. "Child-centered" educators played down academic achievement in favor of "adjustment." The training they offered probably stimulated the students' imaginations and may possibly have improved their psychological well-being, but observers soon noted that poor work habits, fuzzy thinking, and plain ignorance inevitably resulted. The "educationists" insisted that they were not abandoning traditional academic subjects, yet they surely de-emphasized them. "We've built a sort of halo around reading, writing, and arithmetic," one school principal explained. To say that "every student must know the multiplication tables before graduation," he added, "attaches more importance to those tables than I'm willing to accord them."

The demands of society for rigorous intellectual achievement made this distortion of progressive education increasingly less satisfactory in the modern world. After World War II, critics began a concerted assault on the system. The leader of the attack was James B. Conant, former president of Harvard. His book *The American High School Today* (1959) sold nearly half a million copies and his later studies of teacher education and the special problems of urban schools attracted wide attention. Conant flayed the schools for their failure to teach English grammar and composition effectively, for neglecting foreign languages, and for ignoring the needs of both the brightest and the slowest of their students. He insisted that teachers' colleges should place subject matter above educational methodology in their curricula.

The success of the Russians in launching their first "Sputnik" in 1957 greatly increased the influence of critics like Conant. To match this achievement, the United States needed thousands of engineers and scientists, but the schools were not turning out enough graduates prepared to study science and engineering at the college level. Suddenly the schools were under enormous pressure, for with more and more young people desiring to go to college, the colleges were raising their admission standards. As a result, the "traditionalists" gained the initiative, academic subjects a revived prestige. The National Defense Education Act of 1958 supplied a powerful stimulus by allocating funds for upgrading work in the sciences, foreign languages, and other subjects, and for expanding guidance services and experimenting with television and other new teaching devices.

However, other developments, most notably concern for improving the training of the children of disadvantaged minority groups (Mexican-Americans, Puerto Ricans, and Indians, as well as blacks), pulled the system in a different direction. Many of these children lived in horrible slums, often in broken homes. They lacked the incentives and training that most white middle-class children received in the family. Many of them did poorly in school, partly because they were poorly motivated, partly because the system was poorly adapted to their needs. The Elementary and Secondary Education Act of 1965, America's first general federal-aid-to-education law, concentrated large sums on upgrading the training of students in urban slums and in impoverished rural areas in an effort to deal with this problem. But catering to the requirements of such children threatened to undermine the standards being set for other children. Especially in the great cities, where the blacks and other minorities were becoming steadily more numerous, many schools failed to serve adequately either the disadvantaged or those fairly well off. Added to the strains imposed by racial conflicts, the effect was to create the most serious crisis American public education had ever faced.

The post-Sputnik stress on academic achievement also profoundly affected higher education. "Prestige" institutions like Harvard, Yale, Columbia, Stanford, Swarthmore, and a dozen other colleges, inundated by floods of first-rate applicants, became training centers for the nation's intellectual elite. The federal and state governments, together with private philanthropic institutions such as the Carnegie Corporation and the Ford Foundation, poured millions into dormitory and classroom construction, teacher education, and scholarship funds. At the graduate level, the federal government's research and development program, administered by the National Science Foundation, established in 1950, provided billions of dollars for laboratories, equipment, professors' salaries, and student scholarships.

Directly or indirectly, such infusions affected every department of the great universities. Expansion created a shortage of professors, leading to higher professorial salaries. Competition for talent developed on an international scale. In Great Britain, for example, alarmists warned of a "brain drain" caused by the migration of top-flight British professors to American institutions.

At the same time, population growth and the demands of society for specialized intellectual skills were causing American colleges to burst at the seams. In 1870 only 1.7 per cent of those in the 17–21 year age group were in college, in 1970 about 40 per cent. To bridge the gap between high school and college, the two-year junior college proliferated. Almost unknown before 1920, there were 600-odd junior colleges by the late sixties. They were the most rapidly grow-

ing educational institutions in the country, their enrollment leaping from about 300,000 in 1955 to over 840,000 in 1965, and to 1.7 million in 1970!

For a time after the war, the expansion of higher education took place with remarkable smoothness. Thousands of veterans took advantage of the G.I. bill to earn college degrees, and more thousands of young men and women whose parents had not gone to college seized the new opportunity eagerly. During the 1950's the general mood among students was complacency. But in the 1960's the mood changed. For one thing, a college degree was ceasing to seem like a privilege or opportunity and was becoming a necessity. Few interesting or remunerative careers were open to those who did not have one; thus many students began to look upon higher education as a chore, still another academic hurdle to be surmounted, a restriction on freedom of choice more than the gateway to a freer, more fruitful existence.

Moreover, many of the universities, each with its tens of thousands of students, were in danger of becoming soulless educational factories. Especially for undergraduates (who needed it most), the close contact between professor and student tended to disappear in these institutions. Student dissatisfaction increased rapidly under such conditions and often led to protests, riots, and other troubles. The first great outburst of unrest convulsed the University of California at Berkeley in the fall of 1964. Angry students staged sit-down strikes in university buildings, organized a "filthy speech" campaign, and generally disorganized the institution over a period of weeks. Hundreds were arrested; the state legislature threatened reprisals; the faculty became involved in the controversy; and the crisis led eventually to the resignation of the president of the University of California, Clark Kerr.

In the late 1960's the situation was exacerbated by the war in Vietnam. Many students considered the war immoral and objected to university involvement in war-related research projects. Since college students were deferred from the draft, large numbers of young men without much interest in a college education enrolled merely to avoid military service. These tended to find the experience meaningless.

Still more significant in altering the student mood was the frustration that so many of them felt with the colleges and with the larger society. Rapid change was making numerous traditional aspects of college life outmoded, yet like all institutions the colleges adapted only slowly to new conditions. The so-called now generation swiftly lost patience with the glacial pace of campus adjustment. Regulations that students had formerly merely grumbled about now evoked determined, even violent opposition. Dissidents denounced parietal rules that restricted their personal lives, such as prohibitions on the use of alcohol and the banning of members of the opposite sex from dormitories. They complained that required courses inhibited their intellectual development. They demanded a share in the government of their institutions, long the private preserve of administrators and professors.

Beyond their specific dissatisfactions, they developed an almost total refusal to endure anything they considered wrong. The knotty social problems which made their elders gravitate toward moderation led these students to become intransigent absolutists. The line between right and wrong became for radicals as sharply defined as the edge of a ruler. Racial prejudice was evil: it must be totally eradicated. War in a nuclear age was insane: armies must be disbanded. Poverty amid plenty was an abomination: eliminate poverty *now*. To the counsel that evil can only be eliminated gradually, that misguided persons must be persuaded to mend their ways, that compromise was the path to true progress, they responded with scorn. Extremists among them, observing the weaknesses of American civilization, adopted a nihilistic position—the only way to deal with a "rotten" society was to destroy it; reform was impossible; constructive compromise corrupting.

Critics found the radical students infantile, old-fashioned, and authoritarian: infantile because they could not tolerate frustration or delay, old-fashioned because their absolutist ideas had

been exploded by several generations of philosophers and scientists, authoritarian because they rejected majority rule, and would not tolerate views in disagreement with their own. The radicals were seldom very numerous in any college, but they were tightly knit (in organizations such as the Students for a Democratic Society) and totally committed. On campus after campus in the late sixties, they roused large numbers of their less extreme fellows to take part in sit-ins and other disruptive tactics. Frequently, faculties and administrators played into their hands, being so offended by their methods and manners that they refused to recognize the legitimacy of some of their demands. At Columbia, in 1968, SDS and black students—the latter sharply disassociating themselves from the former—occupied university buildings and refused to leave unless a series of "non-negotiable" demands (including such matters as the university's involvement in secret military research and its relations with minority groups living in the Columbia neighborhood) were granted. When, after long delays, President Grayson Kirk called in the police to clear the buildings, a riot broke out in which dozens of bystanders were clubbed and beaten. General student revulsion against the use of the police led to the resignation of Kirk and to many university reforms. A similar incident convulsed Harvard in 1969; indeed literally hundreds of colleges were shaken by riots and lesser disturbances. In May 1970 Ohio National Guardsmen, called in to control demonstrators at Kent State University, caused a national crisis by firing into the crowd, killing four students, three of them innocent bystanders. Only days later, Mississippi state police shot down two black students at Jackson State.

The turmoil seemed endless. Extremist groups were torn by factionalism and found it increasingly difficult to mobilize mass campus support, but—it was the bane of modern society—the ability of small groups to disrupt did not diminish.

One heartening aspect of the situation was the great increase of black students in the colleges and their generally responsible, if radical, way of handling themselves. Almost without ex-

Prelude to violence: Behind a tear gas barrage, National Guardsmen march across the campus of Ohio's Kent State University in May 1970. Soon after this picture was taken, they opened fire, killing four students. (UPI.)

ception, the colleges tried to increase the number of blacks enrolled, even when it meant allocating large percentages of their scholarship funds and lowering academic requirements to compensate for the poor preparation many of these students had received in the schools. Between 1964 and 1972 Negro enrollments increased by 211 per cent, and the proportion of black students to the total college enrollment (9 per cent) was approaching the black proportion of the total population (11 per cent).

Black college students tended to keep to themselves, and they wanted more control over all aspects of their education than did the typical white. They called for the creation of Black Studies programs, taught and administered by blacks, and often under student control.

Achievement of these goals was difficult, both because of the shortage of Negro teachers and because professors—even some Negro professors—considered student control of appointments and curricula unwise and in violation of the principles of academic freedom. Nevertheless, the general academic response to black demands was accommodating; "confrontations" occurred frequently but were usually resolved by negotiation. Unlike white radical students, the blacks tended to confine their demands to matters directly related to local conditions. Generalization is difficult, but probably the majority of academics drew a distinction between black radicals, whose actions they found understandable even when they could not in conscience approve of them, and white radicals, most of whom they thought self-indulgent, overly pampered, or emotionally disturbed.

In the early 1970's the rapid expansion of the colleges and universities leveled off and the turmoil within them subsided. Demographic factors and reduced economic opportunities accounted for the former trend, but the latter had more complicated causes, of which a loss of confidence, characteristic of the whole society, was probably the most important. That graduates found jobs harder to get was a sobering influence, as was the students' growing awareness that protest and disruption had not significantly altered their situation. Peace descended upon the American campuses but the mood of frustration and discontent persisted.

The Sexual Revolution

Young people also made the most striking contribution to the revolution that took place in the late 1960's in public attitudes toward sexual relationships. The changes came with startling swiftness. Almost overnight (it seemed in retrospect) conventional ideas about premarital sex, about contraception and abortion, about homosexuality, about pornography, and a host of related matters were openly challenged. Probably the behavior of the majority of Americans did not alter radically, but the majority's beliefs and practices were no longer automatically acknowledged to be the only valid ones. It became possible for individuals to espouse different values and to behave differently with at least relative impunity. Actions that in one decade would have led to social ostracism or even to imprisonment were in the next decade accepted almost as a matter of course.

The causes of this revolution were complex and interrelated; one change led to others. The development of more efficient methods of birth control and the discovery of antibiotics that provided simple cures for venereal disease removed the two principal practical arguments against sex outside marriage; with these barriers down, many found their moral attitudes changing. Almost concurrently, the studies of Alfred C. Kinsey, *Sexual Behavior in the Human Male* (1948), and *Sexual Behavior in the Human Female* (1953), based on thousands of confidential interviews with persons from nearly every walk of life, revealed that large numbers of Americans did not practice what they preached in matters concerning sex. Premarital sex, marital infidelity, homosexuality, and various forms of perversion were, Kinsey's figures showed, far more common than most persons had suspected, among women as well as among men. Once it became possible to look at sex in purely physical and emotional terms and to accept the idea that one's own urges might not be as uncommon as one had been led to believe, it became much more difficult to object to any sexual activity practiced in private by consenting adults. Homosexuals, for example, began openly to admit their feelings and to demand that the heterosexual society cease to harass and discriminate against them.

A sharp increase in divorces both reflected and contributed to the sexual revolution. The increase did not mark a basic change; the reader will perhaps recall that the divorce rate was rising as early as the 1880's. But between 1969 and 1972 the annual number of divorces granted jumped from 639,000 to 837,000. The revolution was by no means the only cause for this rise. The broadening of the legal grounds for divorces and a great reduction in their cost (some states even permitted "do-it-yourself" divorces, performed without the services of lawyers) were also important, as were social and geographical mobility, changing religious attitudes, and the new concern for women's rights. Nevertheless, the relaxation of sexual taboos was of vital significance.

Sexual freedom also contributed to the revival of the women's rights movement of the 1960's. For one thing, freedom involved a more drastic revolution for women than for men. Effective methods of contraception, for example, obviously affected women more directly than men. The new attitudes also heightened many women's consciousness of the way the old sexual standards and patterns of family living had restricted their whole existence. Actually, the two revolutions re-enforced each other in innumerable ways. Concern both for job equality and for sexual freedom fed the demand for day-care centers for children. An advocate of legalized abortion could be motivated by the belief that women should be as free not to have children as to have them, or by concern for sexual rights as such. Was a militant who denounced "male chauvinist pigs" a feminist or a lesbian?

That the sexual revolution in its many aspects served useful functions was unarguable. Reducing irrational fears and inhibitions was liberating for many persons of both sexes, and tended to help young people form permanent associations on the basis of deeper feelings than their sexual drives. Women surely profited from the new freedom, just as a greater sharing of family duties by husbands and fathers opened men's lives to many new satisfactions. The sexual revolution undoubtedly contributed to the steep decline of the birthrate that set in at the end of the 1960's. In 1972 there were two per cent more women of childbearing age in the country than in 1971, but nine per cent fewer babies were born. With the nation increasingly concerned about overcrowding, this trend (which resulted in a population-growth rate slightly below zero) was hailed by demographers as sure to relieve many pressing social problems.

But like most rapid changes, the revolution also produced new problems and some of its results were at best ambiguous. Equality could mean the loss of special advantages for women as well as the shuffling off of restrictions. The proposed equal rights amendment to the Constitution, critics claimed, would sweep away a mass of protective legislation governing the position of women in industry. Especially for young people, sexual freedom could be very unsettling; sometimes it generated social pressures that propelled them into relationships they were not yet prepared to handle, with grave psychological results. Easy *cures* did not eliminate venereal disease; on the contrary the relaxation of sexual taboos produced what public health officials called a veritable epidemic of gonorrhea and a frightening increase in the incidence of syphilis. Equally perplexing was the rise in the number of illegitimate births.

Exercising the right to advocate and practice previously forbidden activities involved subjecting those who found these offensive—still a large proportion of the population—to embarrassment and even to acute emotional distress. Matters as different as pornography and abortion seemed ethically wrong to many people; their legalization thus exacerbated already serious social conflicts. Clearly, however, the revolution was not about to end, the direction of change not to be reversed.

Supplementary Reading

There are a great many interesting volumes that attempt to describe and explain various aspects of modern American society. It is difficult to evaluate or even to categorize these books—time must pass before we can know which are the most insightful. For the present, each reader must test these works against his own experience and knowledge in determining their worth. Among those dealing most comprehensively with American life, Max Lerner, *America as a Civilization*° (1957), is probably the most ambitious. W. M. O'Neill, *Coming Apart: An Informal History of the 1960's* (1971), deals broadly with that decade. Others include F. L. Allen, *The Big Change*° (1952), R. E. Spiller and Eric Larrabee (eds.), *American Perspectives* (1961), Bernard Rosenberg and D. M. White (eds.), *Mass Culture*° (1957), Philip Olson (ed.), *America as a Mass Society* (1963), Jacques Barzun, *God's Country and Mine*° (1954), David Riesman, *Individualism Reconsidered*° (1954), and J. W. Gardner, *The Recovery of Confidence* (1970).

Books attempting to analyze economic trends include Peter Drucker, *The New Society*° (1950), J. K.

°Available in paperback.

Galbraith, *The Affluent Society°* (1958) and *The New Industrial State°* (1967), the Editors of *Fortune, America in the Sixties: The Economy and the Society°* (1960), T. C. Cochran, *The American Business System°* (1957), A. A. Berle, *Power Without Property°* (1959), and Leonard Silk, *Nixonomics* (1972).

Students of the contemporary American character should begin with David Riesman *et al., The Lonely Crowd°* (1950), and continue with two works by C. Wright Mills, *White Collar°* (1951) and *The Power Elite°* (1956). Other interesting volumes include W. H. Whyte, Jr., *The Organization Man°* (1956), Paul Goodman, *Growing Up Absurd°* (1960), Kenneth Kenniston, *The Uncommitted* (1965), and C. A. Reich, *The Greening of America°* (1970).

Population trends are described in C. and I. B. Taeuber, *The Changing Population of the United States* (1958), the movement to the suburbs in R. C. Wood, *Suburbia°* (1959). For critical analyses of modern American novelists, consult Alfred Kazin, *On Native Grounds°* (1942) and *Contemporaries°* (1962), Malcolm Cowley, *The Literary Situation°* (1954), Robert Bone, *The Negro Novel in America* (1965), and Edmund Wilson, *The Shock of Recognition°* (1955). Modern American art is discussed in J. I. Baur, *Revolution and Tradition in Modern American Art* (1951), O. W. Larkin, *Art and Life in America* (1949), Samuel Hunter, *Modern American Painting and Sculpture°* (1959), and Barbara Rose, *American Art Since 1900°* (1967).

Educational trends are discussed in Richard Hofstadter and C. D. Hardy, *The Development and Scope of Higher Education in the United States* (1952), Jacques Barzun, *The House of Intellect°* (1959), R. N. Sanford (ed.), *The American College* (1962), R. O. Bower (ed.), *The New Professors* (1960), Martin Mayer, *The Schools°* (1961), A. E. Bestor, *The Restoration of Learning* (1955), J. B. Conant, *The American High School Today°* (1959) and *Slums and Suburbs°* (1964), and Robert Coles, *Children of Crisis°* (1967). On militancy among college students, see S. M. Lipset and P. G. Altbach (eds.), *Students in Revolt* (1969), and Roger Kahn, *The Battle of Morningside Heights* (1970).

On mass tastes, see, in addition to many of the volumes mentioned above, Russell Lynes, *The Tastemakers°* (1954), Gilbert Seldes, *The Great Audience* (1950) and *The Public Arts°* (1957). Lewis Jacobs, *The Rise of the American Film°* (1939), Hortense Powdermaker, *Hollywood°* (1950), Nathan Leites and Martha Wolfenstein, *Movies* (1950), Llewellyn White, *The American Radio* (1947), G. A. Steiner, *The People Look at Television* (1963), F. L. Mott, *American Journalism* (1962), and B. A. Weisberger, *The American Newspaperman* (1961), treat the changing communications and amusement industries.

On contemporary poverty and urban problems, see Michael Harrington, *The Other America°* (1962), J. C. Donovan, *The Politics of Poverty°* (1967), Oscar Lewis, *La Vida: A Puerto Rican Family in the Culture of Poverty°* (1966), Mitchell Gordon, *Sick Cities: Psychology and Pathology of American Urban Life°* (1963), R. C. Weaver, *The Urban Complex°* (1964), and Jane Jacobs, *The Death and Life of Great American Cities°* (1962).

Students of contemporary race relations should begin with a number of brilliant, highly personal books by black Americans. James Baldwin, *The Fire Next Time°* (1963), first called the new black anger to white attention, but see also M. L. King, Jr., *Stride Toward Freedom°* (1958), Malcolm X, *Autobiography°* (1966), Stokely Carmichael and C. V. Hamilton, *Black Power: The Politics of Liberation in America°* (1967), and Eldridge Cleaver, *Soul on Ice°* (1967). Other important books on race relations include C. E. Silberman, *Crisis in Black and White°* (1964), K. B. Clark, *Youth in the Ghetto* (1964), L. E. Lomax, *The Negro Revolt°* (1963), and August Meier and Elliott Rudwick, *CORE: A Study in the Civil Rights Movement* (1973). The *Report°* of the National Advisory (Kerner) Commission on Civil Disorders (1968) is full of interesting material. M. S. Meier and Feliciano Rivera, *The Chicanos°* (1972), provides a sympathetic discussion of the problems and aspirations of Mexican-Americans, but see also Joan London and Henry Anderson, *So Shall Ye Reap: The Story of Cesar Chávez & the Farm Workers' Movement* (1970), and Peter Matthiessen, *Sal Si Puedes: Cesar Chávez and the New American Revolution* (1969).

The literature on the new women's movement is voluminous and difficult to evaluate. In addition to W. H. Chafe, *The American Woman* (1972), see Betty Friedan, *The Feminine Mystique°* (1963).

31

Vietnam and Its Aftermath

Historians, drawing upon masses of evidence and applying to this data the analytical tools of their profession, tend to describe the past in terms of a more or less inevitable progression from cause to effect; they confidently "explain" what happened and why it happened. When they try to deal with very recent events, however, their confidence begins to evaporate, their "explanations" become much more tentative and circumspect. This is so because the meaning of events—that is, their significance—is difficult to discern when they are taking place, or rather, when so many are occurring that no one can be aware of more than a fraction of them or recognize the interrelations between one and another.

Having said this much, we must nevertheless attempt to make sense (or at least *a* sense) out of our recent history. That the most pervasive influence has been America's war in Vietnam few would deny. This is an excellent illustration of the difficulty of understanding contemporary events, since no one in the country realized how important Vietnam would be when the American involvement there began. Yet it is now clear that nearly all the contemporary problems of the United States were at least in part outgrowths of the Vietnam adventure, and that its effects upon the nation are still unfolding.

The War in Vietnam

When Vietnam was divided after the defeat of the French in 1954 and the United States began supplying aid to Bao Dai's anti-communist regime, a handful of American military "advisers" were sent in to train a South Vietnamese army. After Bao Dai was deposed, American aid and "advice" were increased, but President Ngo Dinh Diem was unable to establish a stable government. Rebel forces, called Vietcong, soon controlled large sections of the country; in 1956 Diem refused to permit the Vietnam-wide elections called for by the international settlement of 1954, which he felt he could not win. Gradually, the Vietcong, drawing supplies from North Vietnam and indirectly from China and the Soviet Union, increased in strength. As they did, more American money and more military advisers were sent to bolster Diem's regime.

President Kennedy continued this policy and by the end of 1961 there were 3,200 American military men in the country. Kennedy insisted that the South Vietnamese themselves must win what he called "their war," but he also stressed the strategic importance of the country; by the time of his assassination, the American military

presence had risen to over 16,000. No combat troops were involved, however, and only 120 Americans had so far been killed.

At first President Johnson did not change Kennedy's tactics significantly. But in August 1964, after claiming that North Vietnamese gunboats had fired on American destroyers in the Gulf of Tonkin, he demanded, and in an air of crisis obtained, an authorization from Congress to "repel any armed attack against the forces of the United States and to prevent further aggression." With this blank check and buttressed by his sweeping defeat of Goldwater in the 1964 Presidential election, Johnson began to send *combat* troops to South Vietnam and to unleash air attacks against targets in both South and North Vietnam. His "escalation" of the American commitment occurred piecemeal and apparently without plan. By the end of 1964, 184,000 Americans were in the field; a year later, 385,000; after another year, 485,000; and by the middle of 1968, the number exceeded 538,000. Each increase was met by corresponding increases from the other side. Russia and China stepped up their aid, and thousands of North Vietnamese regulars filtered across the 17th parallel to join the Vietcong insurgents. The United States was engaged in a full-scale war, yet war was never declared: Johnson based his decisions on the highly controversial Gulf of Tonkin resolution.

From the beginning, the war bitterly divided the American people. Defenders of the President's policy emphasized the nation's moral responsibility to resist aggression, its supposed treaty obligations under the SEATO pact, and what President Eisenhower had called the "domino" theory (based on an analogy with the western powers' failure to resist Hitler before 1939), which hypothesized that if the communists were allowed to "take over" one country, they would soon take its neighbors, then *their* neighbors, and so on until the whole world had been conquered. They insisted that the United States was not an aggressor in Vietnam, stressing Johnson's oft-expressed willingness to negotiate a general withdrawal of "foreign" forces from the country,

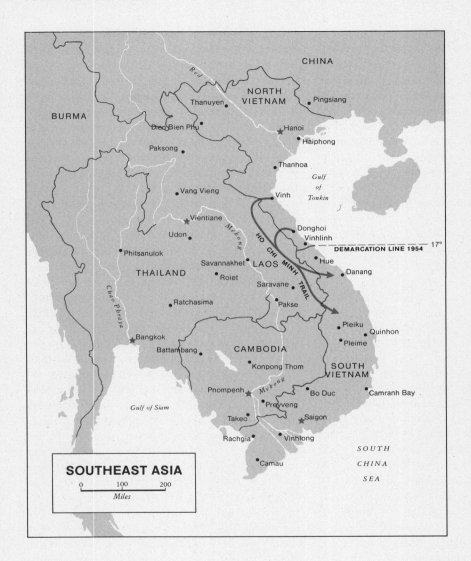

SOUTHEAST ASIA

0   100   200
Miles

which the communists repeatedly rejected.

Johnson's critics, popularly called "doves,"° argued that the struggle between the South Vietnamese government and the Vietcong was a civil war in which Americans should not meddle. They stressed the repressive, reactionary charac-

°Supporters of the war were dubbed "hawks," but some of these also disapproved of the Johnson policy. Extremists wanted to extend ground action into North Vietnam, use nuclear weapons if necessary, and convert the conflict into a general war against China, perhaps even against Russia.

ter of the Diem government and of those that followed it after Diem was assassinated in 1963 as proof that the war was not a contest between democracy and communism. They objected to the massive aerial bombings (more explosives were dropped on Vietnam between 1964 and 1968 than on Germany and Japan combined in World War II), to the use of napalm and of other chemical weapons such as the defoliants that were sprayed on forests and crops, which wreaked havoc among noncombatants, and to the direct killing of civilians by American troops. They discounted the domino theory, pointing both to the growing communist split into Chinese and Russian camps, and to the traditional hostility of all Vietnamese to the Chinese, which they claimed made Chinese expansion into Southeast Asia unlikely. And they deplored both the heavy loss of American life—over 40,000 dead by 1970—and also the enormous cost in money, which came to exceed $20 billion a year. Besides being a major cause of the inflation of the 1960's, the war was diverting public funds from domestic programs aimed at solving the problems of poverty and race relations, at reducing pollution, at improving education and urban life.

Although President Johnson sometimes acted deviously, there is little reason to doubt that he and his advisers sincerely believed they were fighting in defense of freedom and democracy. There were, in short, moral arguments on both sides of the issue. What became increasingly clear as time passed and the costs mounted, was that an American military victory was impossible. Yet American military leaders were extraordinarily slow to grasp this fact. Repeatedly they advised the President that one more escalation (so many more soldiers, so many more air raids) would break the enemy's will to resist. Like the proverbial donkey plodding after the carrot on the stick, Johnson repeatedly followed their advice. And for a long time, as the polls demonstrated, a majority of the American people believed he was correct. All the forces of patriotism and pride, along with the hard-won "lessons" of 1931–39 and their stubborn refusal to admit that a mistake had been made, held them to this course.

Election of 1968

Gradually, however, the doves increased in number. Students, for idealistic reasons and because they resented being drafted to fight in Vietnam; businessmen, alarmed by the effects of the war on the economy; and others for different reasons became increasingly dissatisfied with the President's policy. But as late as the fall of 1967 outspoken opposition to the war, in Congress and elsewhere, remained small. Then, in November 1967, Senator Eugene McCarthy of Minnesota, a low-keyed, rather introspective man, never a leading figure in the Upper House, announced that he was a candidate for the 1968 Democratic Presidential nomination against Johnson, making opposition to the war his issue.

McCarthy had no real organization and few of the traditional political skills, nor did he seriously think he could be nominated. But he felt that someone must step forward to put the war issue before the voters. He prepared to campaign in the primaries. Suddenly, early in 1968, immediately on the heels of the latest announcement by the American military that the communists were about to crack, North Vietnam and Vietcong forces launched a general offensive against South Vietnamese cities to correspond with their Lunar New Year (Tet). Striking everywhere at once, they managed to hold parts of Saigon, the capital, and other cities for days.

This Tet offensive was eventually thrown back, but it thoroughly discredited the American military. When General William C. Westmoreland described the Tet offensive as a communist defeat and asked for an additional 206,000 troops to follow up his "victory," American public opinion rebelled. McCarthy, who was campaigning in New Hampshire, at once became a formidable figure. Thousands of students and other volunteers flocked to the state to ring doorbells and distribute leaflets in his behalf. When he polled 42 per cent of the vote in the Democratic primary and seemed sure to win the Wisconsin primary, President Johnson, acknowledging that he could no longer "unify" the country, withdrew as a candidate for re-election.

The political situation was monumentally confused. Before the New Hampshire primary, former Attorney General Robert F. Kennedy, brother of the slain President, had refused either to seek the Democratic nomination or support McCarthy, although he was opposed to the Johnson policy in Vietnam. After McCarthy's strong

Graphic proof of the effectiveness of defoliation: at top, an unsprayed mangrove forest, and at bottom, a mangrove forest that had been sprayed with herbicides in 1965 as it looked in 1970. (Wide World.)

The London *Observer* suggested that President Johnson was playing with fire in Asia: "All I'm trying to do is to limit our conflict to this small area." (Abu Abraham, *The Observer.*)

showing, Kennedy reversed himself and entered the race. Had he done so earlier, McCarthy might have withdrawn in his favor, for Kennedy had powerful political and popular support, but after New Hampshire, McCarthy quite naturally decided to remain in the contest. Vice President Hubert Humphrey, backed by Johnson, also announced his candidacy, although not until it was too late for him to run in the primaries.

Kennedy carried the primaries in Indiana and Nebraska, but McCarthy defeated him in Oregon. In the climactic contest in California, Kennedy won by a small margin. However, immediately after his victory speech in a Los Angeles hotel, he was assassinated by Sirhan Sirhan, a young Arab nationalist who had been incensed by Kennedy's support of Israel. In effect, Kennedy's death assured the nomination of Humphrey; most of the professional politicians distrusted McCarthy, who was indeed rather diffident and aloof for a politician, unwilling or unable to organize an effective campaign despite his articulateness, intelligence, and evident sincerity.

The contest for the Republican nomination was far less dramatic, although its outcome, the nomination of Richard M. Nixon, would have been hard to predict a few years earlier. After his defeat in the California gubernatorial election of 1962, Nixon appeared to have lost all chance of achieving his Presidential ambitions. He moved to New York City and joined a prominent law firm. However, he remained active in Republican affairs, making countless speeches and attending political meetings all over the country. In 1967 Governor George Romney of Michigan seemed the likely Republican nominee, but he failed to develop extensive support. Although Governor Nelson Rockefeller of New York was also widely mentioned, conservative Republicans would not forgive his refusal to help Goldwater in 1964, and he decided not to enter the race. Nixon announced his candidacy in February 1968, and after Romney withdrew in the midst of the New Hampshire contest, he swept the Republican primaries. Rockefeller belatedly declared himself a candidate, but by the time of the Republican National Convention in August, Nix-

on had a large majority of the delegates in his pocket and won an easy first-ballot victory.

He then astounded the country and dismayed liberals by choosing Governor Spiro T. Agnew of Maryland as his running mate. Aside from the fact that he had little national reputation ("Spiro who?" jokesters asked) Agnew had taken a tough, almost brutal stand on such matters as racial disturbances, urban crime, and other social problems. Nixon chose him primarily to attract southern votes. Placating the South seemed necessary because Governor George C. Wallace of Alabama was making a determined bid to win enough electoral votes for his American Independent party to prevent either major party from obtaining a majority. Wallace was flagrantly anti-Negro and sure to attract wide southern and conservative support. His meetings drew large crowds and he was frequently cheered to the rafters when he denounced federal "meddling," the "coddling" of criminals, and the forced desegregation of schools. Wallace ridiculed intellectuals, planners, and any form of professional ability or mental distinction. Nixon's choice of Agnew seemed an effort to appeal to the very groups that Wallace was attracting—bigots, lower-middle-class white city dwellers, suburbanites, and the residents of small towns. This Republican strategy gravely disturbed liberals, and heightened the tension surrounding the Democratic convention, which met in Chicago in late August.

Humphrey–Johnson delegates controlled the convention. The Vice President had a solid liberal record on domestic issues, but he had supported Johnson's Vietnam policy with equal solidity. Those who could not stomach the Nixon–Agnew ticket but who opposed the war faced a difficult choice. Hordes of radicals and young activists descended upon Chicago to put pressure on the delegates to repudiate the Johnson Vietnam policy. In the tense and bitter atmosphere that resulted, the party hierarchy overreacted. Mayor Richard J. Daley, an old-fashioned political boss, ringed the convention with barricades and policemen to protect it from disruption, a policy that was reasonable in purpose but which he carried out with foolish bravado and display. Inside the building, administration forces easily nominated Humphrey and passed a war plank satisfactory to Johnson. Outside, the police, provoked by the abusive language and violent behavior of radical demonstrators, tore into the crowds of protestors, brutally beating dozens of them while millions watched on television in fascinated horror.

At first these dreadful developments seemed to benefit Nixon. The violence at Chicago strengthened the convictions of many persons that the tougher treatment of criminals and dissenters that he and Agnew were calling for was necessary, and those who were offended by the actions of the police tended to blame Humphrey. Nixon campaigned at a deliberate, dignified

pace, making relatively few public appearances and relying heavily on carefully arranged television interviews and taped commercials prepared by an advertising agency. He stressed moderation, firm enforcement of the law, and his desire "to bring us together." Agnew, in a series of blunt, coarse speeches—critics, remembering Nixon's own political style in the era of Joseph McCarthy, called Agnew "Nixon's Nixon"—assaulted Humphrey, the Democrats, and left-wing dissident groups.

Humphrey's campaign was badly organized, the candidate subject to merciless heckling from antiwar audiences. But he endured this ordeal without losing his temper, and he displayed boundless, almost frantic (some said mindless) energy. He seemed far behind in the early stages,

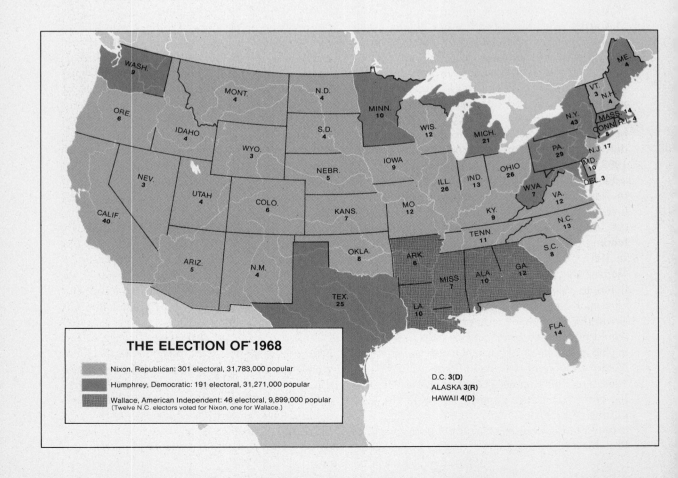

THE ELECTION OF 1968

Nixon, Republican: 301 electoral, 31,783,000 popular

Humphrey, Democratic: 191 electoral, 31,271,000 popular

Wallace, American Independent: 46 electoral, 9,899,000 popular
(Twelve N.C. electors voted for Nixon, one for Wallace.)

D.C. **3(D)**
ALASKA **3(R)**
HAWAII **4(D)**

but gradually gained ground. Shortly before Election Day, President Johnson helped him greatly by suspending air attacks on North Vietnam, and in the long run the Republican strategy helped him too. Black voters and the urban poor had no practical choice but to vote Democratic. As a result, the popular vote was close. Nixon received slightly less than 31.8 million votes, Humphrey nearly 31.3 million. Nixon's Electoral College margin was, however, substantial—301 to 191. The remaining 46 went to Wallace, whose 9.9 million votes came to 13.5 per cent of the total. Despite Nixon's triumph, the Democrats retained control of both houses of Congress.

Nixon as President

When he took office in January 1969, Nixon projected an image of calm and deliberate statesmanship; he introduced no startling changes, demanded no important new legislation. The major economic problem facing him, inflation, was primarily a result of the heavy military expenditures and "easy money" policies of the Johnson administration. Nixon cut federal spending and balanced the 1969 budget, while the Federal Reserve Board forced up interest rates in order to slow the expansion of the money supply. The aim of this strategy was to reduce the rate of economic growth without causing heavy unemployment or precipitating a recession (the word *depression* had apparently passed out of the vocabulary of economists). Even its supporters admitted that this policy would check inflation only slowly, and when prices continued to go up, there was mounting uneasiness and a continuation of labor's demands for wage increases. The problem was complicated by mounting deficits in the United States' balance of trade with foreign nations, product of an overvaluation of the dollar, which encouraged Americans to buy foreign goods.

In 1970 Congress passed a law giving the President power to control prices and wages.

Nixon had opposed this legislation but in the summer of 1971 he decided to use it. First he announced a 90-day price and wage freeze (Phase I) and placed a ten per cent surcharge on imports. Then he set up a Pay Board and a Price Commission with authority to limit wage and price increases when the freeze ended (Phase II).

Candidate Nixon at a press conference in 1968. Previously unskilled at press relations, Nixon tried to establish rapport with reporters during that campaign. (UPI.)

These controls did not check inflation completely—and they angered union leaders, who felt that labor was being shortchanged—but they did slow the upward spiral. An 8.5 per cent devaluation of the dollar in December 1971 helped the economy by making American products more competitive in foreign markets.

In handling other domestic issues, the President was less firm, sometimes appearing confused and ambivalent. In matters concerning poverty and race, for example, he advocated a bold plan for shifting the burden of welfare payments to the federal government and equalizing such payments in all the states. He even came out for a "minimum income" for poor families, which alarmed his conservative supporters. But he and his attorney general, John N. Mitchell, were so openly resistant to further federal efforts to force school desegregation upon reluctant local districts as to dismay southern moderates and northern liberals. And in his eagerness to add what he called "strict constructionists" to the Supreme Court, which he believed had swung too far to the left in such areas as race relations and the rights of persons accused of committing crimes, Nixon allowed himself to be drawn into two foolish confrontations with the Senate.

When Chief Justice Earl Warren retired from the Court in June 1969, Nixon named a respected conservative, Warren E. Burger, as the new chief justice, which caused no difficulties. But when he sought to fill the seat of Justice Abe Fortas, who had resigned under fire after it was learned that he had accepted fees from questionable sources while on the bench, he blundered. He first selected Judge Clement F. Haynesworth, Jr., of South Carolina, whom the Senate rejected because of his having failed to disqualify himself when cases involving corporations in which he had invested came before his court. His second nominee, Judge G. Harrold Carswell of Florida, was turned down because of his alleged racist attitudes and because of his generally mediocre record. In the face of a mass of evidence, Nixon refused to believe that these nominations were rejected for the reasons stated; he declared that "no southern conservative" could run the "lib-

eral" Senate gauntlet successfully, and to prevent the Senate from proving him wrong he nominated Harry A. Blackmun of Minnesota. Blackmun won the unanimous approval of the Senate, but Nixon's analysis was as incorrect as his political tactics were ineffective, and his prestige suffered accordingly.

Whatever his difficulties on the domestic front, Nixon considered the solution of the Vietnam problem his chief task. When the war in Southeast Asia first burst upon American consciousness in 1954, he had favored military intervention in keeping with the containment policy, but he went along with Eisenhower's decision merely to send in aid and advisers. As controversy over American policy developed, Nixon generally supported the actions of Presidents Kennedy and Johnson. During the 1968 campaign, he played down the Vietnam issue on the ground that he did not want to risk upsetting negotiations between the United States and North Vietnam, which had been going on in Paris, albeit without significant results, since May 1968. Basically he suggested nothing very different from what Johnson was doing, although he insisted he would end the war on "honorable" terms if elected.

In office, Nixon strove to make good on this promise. When the Paris negotiations, now expanded to include representatives of South Vietnam and the Vietcong, continued to show no progress, he offered a plan for a phased withdrawal of all non-South Vietnamese troops and for an internationally supervised election in South Vietnam. The North Vietnamese rejected this scheme, insisting that the United States withdraw all its forces unconditionally.

Their intransigence left the President in a difficult position. Probably the majority of Americans considered his proposal eminently fair, but with equal certainty a majority was unwilling to increase the scale of the fighting to compel the communists to accept it, and as the war dragged on, costs in men and money rising, the desire to extricate American troops from the conflict became more intense. However, large numbers would not face up to the consequences of gratifying this desire: ending the war on the communists' terms. Nixon could not compel the foe to negotiate meaningfully, yet every passing day added to the strength of antiwar sentiment, which, as it expressed itself in ever more emphatic terms, in turn led to deeper divisions in the country.

The President responded to this dilemma by trying to build up the South Vietnamese army so that American troops could withdraw without allowing the communists to overrun South Vietnam. The trouble with this strategy (called Vietnamization) was that the United States had been employing it without success for 15 years. For complicated reasons—the incompetence, corruption, and reactionary character of the South Vietnamese government probably being the most important—South Vietnamese troops had seldom displayed much enthusiasm for the kind of tough jungle fighting at which the North Vietnamese and the Vietcong excelled. Nevertheless, efforts at Vietnamization were stepped up, and in June 1969, Nixon announced that he would soon reduce the number of American soldiers in Vietnam by 25,000. In September he promised that an additional 35,000 men would be withdrawn by mid-December.

These steps did not quiet the protesters. On October 15 a nationwide antiwar demonstration, Vietnam Moratorium Day, organized by students, produced an unprecedented outpouring all over the country. This massive display produced one of Vice President Agnew's most notorious blasts of adjectival invective: he said that the moratorium was an example of "national masochism," led by "an effete corps of impudent snobs who characterize themselves as intellectuals."°

A month later, a second Moratorium Day brought a crowd estimated at 250,000 to Washington to march past the White House. The President was unmoved. He could not be influ-

enced by protests, he insisted, and indeed, during one of the Washington demonstrations he passed the time watching a football game on television. Then, on November 3, he defended his policy in a televised speech. He stressed the sincerity of his peace efforts, the unreasonableness of the communists, the responsibility of the United States to protect the South Vietnamese people from communist reprisals and to honor its international commitments. He also announced that he planned to remove all American ground forces from Vietnam, although he did not specify the details of the withdrawal. The next day, reporting a flood of telegrams and calls supporting his position, he declared that a "silent majority" of the American people approved his course.

For a season, events appeared to vindicate Nixon's position. A gradual reduction of military activity in Vietnam had lowered American casualties to what those who did not find the war morally unbearable considered "tolerable" levels. Troop withdrawals continued in an orderly fashion, 150,000 by the spring of 1970. A new lottery system for drafting men for military duty eliminated some of the inequities in the selective service law. These developments reduced the level of protest. But the war continued. Early in 1970 reports that in 1968 an American unit had massacred civilians, including dozens of women and children, in a Vietnamese hamlet known as Mylai 4, revived the controversy about the purposes of the war and its corrosive effects on those who were fighting it. The American people, it seemed, were being torn apart by the war: one from another according to each one's interpretation of events, many within themselves as they tried to balance the war's hopeless horrors against their pride, their detestation of communism, and their unwillingness to turn their backs on their elected leader.

Nixon's most bitter enemy could find no reason to think he wished the war to go on. Its human, economic, and social costs could only vex his days and threaten his future reputation. When he reduced the level of the fighting, the communists merely waited for further reductions. When he raised it, many of his own people

°A few days later he called upon the country to "separate" radical students from society "with no more regret than we should feel over discarding rotten apples from a barrel," which at least had a quality of terseness that most of Agnew's pronouncements lacked.

denounced him. If he pulled out of Vietnam entirely, other Americans would be outraged.

Perhaps his error lay in his unwillingness to admit his own uncertainty, something the greatest Presidents—one thinks immediately of Lincoln and Franklin Roosevelt—were never afraid to do. Facing a dilemma, he tried to convince the whole world that he was firmly in control of events, with the result that at times he seemed more like a high school valedictorian declaiming sententiously about the meaning of life than the mature statesman he so desperately wished to be. Thus he heightened the tensions he sought to relax—in America, in Vietnam, elsewhere too.

Late in April 1970 Nixon confidently announced that Vietnamization was proceeding more rapidly than he had hoped, that communist power was weakening, that within a year another 150,000 American soldiers would be extracted from Vietnam. Then a week later he announced that military intelligence had indicated that the enemy was consolidating its "sanctuaries" in neutral Cambodia and that he was therefore dispatching thousands of American troops to destroy these bases.° In other words he was escalating (dread word) the war; indeed, he even resumed the bombing of targets in North Vietnam.

To foes of the war, Nixon's decision seemed so appallingly unwise that a few of them began to fear that he had become mentally unbalanced. The contradictions between his confident statements about Vietnamization and his alarmist description of powerful enemy forces poised like a dagger 30-odd miles from Saigon did not seem the product of a reasoning mind. His failure to consult congressional leaders or many of his personal advisers before drastically altering his policy, the critics claimed, was both unconstitutional and irresponsible. His insensitive response to the avalanche of criticism that descended upon him from the universities, from Congress, and from other quarters further disturbed observers.

Students took the lead in opposing the inva-

°American planes had been bombing Cambodia for some time, but this fact was not known to the public (or to Congress) until 1973.

sion of Cambodia. The coincidental killing of the Kent State demonstrators by National Guardsmen (which the President reacted to with one of his homilies about violence begetting violence) added to their indignation. A wave of student strikes closed down hundreds of colleges, including many that had seen no previous unrest, as moderate students by the tens of thousands joined with the radicals.

Nixon Triumphant

The almost universal condemnation of the invasion and of the way it had been planned and announced to the country shook Nixon hard. He backtracked, pulling American ground troops out of Cambodia quickly. But he did not change his Vietnam policy, and, in fact, Cambodia apparently hardened his determination. As American ground troops were withdrawn, he stepped up air attacks and the balance of forces remained in uneasy equilibrium through 1971.

Then, late in March 1972, the North Vietnamese mounted a series of assaults all over South Vietnam. Again the President responded by still heavier bombing, and he ordered the approaches to Haiphong and other northern ports sown with mines to cut off the communists' supplies. Meanwhile, he had devised a bold and (even his critics admitted it) an ingenious diplomatic offensive. He sent his principal foreign policy adviser, Henry Kissinger, to China and the USSR to arrange summit meetings with the heads of the two major communist nations. In February 1972 Nixon flew to Peking to consult with Premier Chou En-lai and other Chinese leaders. Full formal recognition of China did not follow, but the two nations agreed to develop contacts at many levels. Although the specific results appeared small, the visit, ending more than twenty years of adamantine American refusal to accept the results of Mao's revolution, marked a dramatic reversal of policy; as such it was widely hailed both in the United States and throughout the world.

The famous meeting of February, 1972, in Peking: from the left, Chinese Premier Chou En-lai; an interpreter; Communist Party Chairman Mao Tse-tung; President Nixon; and Dr. Henry A. Kissinger, then Nixon's foreign policy adviser and later Secretary of State. (UPI.)

Nixon's trip to Moscow in May 1972 produced equally striking results. A treaty limiting strategic missiles was the main concrete gain, but that the meetings took place at all after the mining of Haiphong was of enormous significance. Clearly, both China and the USSR were willing to work for improved relations with the United States *before* America withdrew from Vietnam. This fact, plus the failure of their offensive to overwhelm South Vietnam, led the North Vietnamese to make some diplomatic concessions in the interest of getting the United States out of the war. Kissinger began negotiating seriously with their representatives in Paris in the summer of 1972, and by October the draft of a settlement calling for a cease-fire in place, the return of American prisoners of war, and the withdrawal of all U. S. forces from Vietnam had been hammered out. Shortly before the presidential election Kissinger announced that peace was "at hand."

A few days later President Nixon was reelected, defeating the Democratic candidate, Senator George McGovern of South Dakota, in a landslide—521 electoral votes to 17. McGovern carried only Massachusetts and the District of Columbia, and Nixon obtained 61 per cent of the popular vote. McGovern's campaign had been hampered by divisions within the Democratic party and by the discovery, shortly after the nominating convention, that his running mate, Senator Thomas Eagleton of Missouri, had in the past undergone shock treatments following serious psychological difficulties. After some hesitation, which left many voters with the impression that he was indecisive, McGovern forced Eagleton to withdraw. Sargent Shriver, former head of the Peace Corps, took Eagleton's place on the ticket, but the affair hurt McGovern badly. Nevertheless, Nixon's triumph was so convincing that he interpreted it as a positive indication that the people approved of everything he stood for.

Suddenly Nixon loomed as one of the most powerful and successful Presidents in American history. His bold attack on the inflation problem, his tough-minded handling of the foreign trade question, even his harsh Vietnamese policy suggested decisiveness and self-confidence, qualities he had often seemed to lack. His willingness, despite his long history as a militant "cold warrior," to negotiate with the communist nations in order to arrive at a détente that would lessen world tensions indicated a new flexibility and reasonableness. His landslide victory appeared to demonstrate that a large majority of the voters approved his way of tackling the major problems of the times.

His first reaction was to try to extract more

favorable terms from the Vietnamese communists. Announcing that they were not bargaining in good faith over the remaining details of the peace treaty, he resumed the bombing of North Vietnam in December 1972, this time sending the mighty B-52s directly over Hanoi and other cities. The destructiveness of these attacks was large but their effectiveness as a means of forcing concessions from the North Vietnamese was at best debatable. They also led for the first time to the loss of large numbers of the huge strategic bombers. Nevertheless, both sides had much to gain from ending the war and in January 1973 a settlement was finally reached. The North Vietnamese retained control of large sections of the South, but they agreed to release the American prisoners of war within 60 days. When this was accomplished, the last American troops were pulled out of Vietnam. Nearly 46,000 American soldiers had died in the long war, and over 300,000 more had been wounded. The cost in dollars had reached a staggering 109 billion.

Yet whatever the price, the war was over for the United States, and Nixon took credit for having ended it. He immediately turned his major attention to the domestic scene, determined, he made clear, to change the direction in which the nation had been moving for decades. He sought on the one hand to strengthen the power of the Presidency vis-à-vis Congress, and on the other to decentralize administration by encouraging state and local management of government programs. He announced that he intended to reduce the interference of the federal government in the affairs of individuals and to encourage people to be more self-reliant. He denounced what he called "permissiveness." Overconcern for the interests of blacks and other minorities must end. Criminals should be dealt with "without pity." No person or group should be coddled by the state. These aims brought Nixon into direct conflict with liberal congressmen of both parties, with the leaders of minority groups, and with persons concerned about the increasing power of the executive.

The conflict came to a head over the President's anti-inflation policy. After his second inauguration he ended Phase II price and wage controls and substituted Phase III, which called for voluntary "restraints" (except in the areas of food, health care, and construction). But this did not work. Prices soared; it was the most rapid inflation since the Korean War. In an effort to check the rise he set a rigid limit on federal expenditures; to keep within the limit, he cut back or eliminated a large number of social welfare programs, most especially the Office of Economic Opportunity; and he also sharply reduced federal grants in support of science and education. He even impounded (refused to spend) funds already appropriated by Congress for such purposes. Impoundment created a furor on Capitol Hill, but when Congress, despite the fact that the Democrats were in the majority in both houses, failed to override presidential vetoes of bills challenging his policy, it appeared that Nixon was in total command of the situation. His White House staff, headed by H. R. Haldeman (known as "the Prussian") and John Ehrlichman, dominated the Washington bureaucracy like princes of the blood or oriental viziers and treated congressmen as though dealing with lackeys or eunuchs. When asked to account for their actions they took refuge behind the shield of "executive privilege," the doctrine, never before applied so broadly, that discussions and communications within the executive branch were totally confidential and thus immune from congressional scrutiny. Critics began to grumble about a new "imperial presidency." But no one seemed capable of checking Nixon at any point.

Nixon: Decline And Fall

Then, on March 19, 1973, James McCord, a former FBI agent accused of burglary, wrote a letter to the judge presiding at his trial. This act precipitated a series of disclosures that disrupted the Nixon administration. McCord had been employed during the 1972 campaign as a security officer of the Committee to Re-elect the President (CREEP). About 1:00 A.M. on June 17,

1972, he and four other men had broken into Democratic headquarters at the Watergate, an apartment house and office building complex in Washington. The burglars had been caught rifling the party files and installing electronic eavesdropping devices. Two other Republican campaign officials were also implicated. Their arrest naturally aroused suspicions that the Republican party was behind the break-in, but Nixon denied responsibility for their actions. "I can say categorically," he announced on June 22, "that no one on the White House staff, no one in this Administration presently employed, was involved in this very bizarre incident." Most persons evidently took the President at his word and the affair did not materially affect the election. When brought to trial early in 1973, most of the defendants pleaded guilty.

McCord, who did not, was convicted by the jury. Before Judge John J. Sirica imposed sentences on the culprits, however, McCord wrote his letter. In it he stated that high Republican officials had known about the burglary in advance and had persuaded most of the defendants to keep their connection secret, and that perjury had been committed during the trial.

The truth of McCord's charges swiftly became apparent. Both the head of CREEP, Jeb Stuart Magruder, and President Nixon's lawyer, John W. Dean, III, admitted their involvement, Dean claiming, in testimony before a special Senate Watergate investigation committee headed by Sam Ervin, Jr., of North Carolina, that Nixon had participated in efforts to cover up the affair. Among the disclosures that emerged over the following months were these:

That the acting director of the FBI, L. Patrick Gray, had destroyed documents related to the case.

That large sums of money had been paid the burglars at the instigation of the White House to insure their silence.

That agents of the Nixon administration had burglarized the office of a psychiatrist, seeking evidence against one of his patients, Daniel Ellsberg, who had been charged with leaking classified documents relating to the Vietnam War.

(This disclosure led to the immediate dismissal of the charges against Ellsberg by the presiding judge.)

That the Central Intelligence Agency had (perhaps unwittingly) supplied equipment used in this burglary.

That CREEP officials had attempted to disrupt the campaigns of leading Democratic candidates during the 1972 primaries in a number of illegal ways.

That a number of corporations had made large (and illegal) secret contributions to the Nixon re-election campaign.

That E. Howard Hunt, one of the Watergate criminals, had earlier forged State Department documents in an effort to make it appear that President Kennedy had been implicated in the assassination of President Ngo Dinh Diem of South Vietnam.

That the Nixon administration had placed wiretaps on the telephones of some of its own officials as well as on those of newspapermen critical of its policies without first obtaining authorization from the courts.

These revelations led to the resignations of most of Nixon's closest advisers, including H. R. Haldeman, John Ehrlichman, John Dean, and Attorney General Richard Kleindienst. They also, of course, raised the question of the President's personal connection with the scandals. This he steadfastly denied. He insisted that he would investigate the Watergate affair thoroughly and see that the guilty were punished. But he refused to allow investigators access to White House documents, again on grounds of executive privilege, which he continued to assert in very broad terms. When it came out during hearings held by the Ervin committee that the President had systematically made secret tape recordings of White House conversations and telephone calls—a disclosure that naturally caused a sensation—he took the same position, although it seemed obvious that these tapes would settle the question of his involvement once and for all.

One result of the scandals and of Nixon's attitude was a precipitous decline in his standing in public opinion polls. Calls for his resignation, even for impeachment, began to be heard. Yielding to pressure, he finally agreed to the appointment of an "independent" special prosecutor to investigate the affair and he promised the appointee, Professor Archibald Cox of the Harvard Law School, full cooperation. Cox, however, swiftly aroused the President's ire by demanding White House records, including the tapes, and also by digging into a number of other questions, such as the relationship between the administration and the giant International Telephone and Telegraph Company, which, it was charged, had offered to pay $400,000 toward the expenses of the 1972 Republican convention in return for favorable treatment of an antitrust case. When Nixon refused to turn over the tapes, Cox obtained a subpoena from Judge Sirica ordering him to do so. The administration appealed, lost in the appellate court, but while the case was headed for the Supreme Court, Nixon ordered the current attorney general, Elliot Richardson, to dismiss Cox. Both Richardson, who had promised the Senate during his confirmation hearings that the special prosecutor would have a free hand, and his chief assistant, William Ruckelshaus, resigned rather than do so, but the solicitor general, third-ranking officer of the Justice Department, carried out Nixon's order.

These events, which occurred on Saturday, October 20, were promptly dubbed the "Saturday Night Massacre." They caused an outburst of public indignation. Congress was bombarded by thousands of letters and telegrams demanding the President's impeachment. The House Judiciary Committee, headed by Peter W. Rodino, Jr., of New Jersey, began an investigation to see if enough evidence for impeachment existed. Once again, Nixon backed down. He agreed to turn over the tapes to Judge Sirica with the understanding that relevant materials would be presented to the grand jury investigating the Watergate affair, but that nothing would be revealed to the public. He then named a new special prosecutor, Leon Jaworski, and promised him access to whatever White House documents he needed. However, it soon came out that some of the tapes were missing and that an important section of

another had been erased—deliberately, according to a panel of technical experts appointed by Sirica.

The nation had never before experienced such a series of morale-shattering crises. While the seemingly infinite complications of Watergate were emerging during 1973, a number of unrelated disasters struck. First, pushed by a shortage of grains resulting from massive Russian purchases authorized by the administration as part of its "détente" with the Soviet Union, food prices soared to unprecedented heights, wheat from $1.45 a bushel to over $5. Nixon imposed another price freeze, which led to shortages, and when the freeze was lifted, prices resumed their steep ascent. Then Vice President Agnew (defender of law and order, foe of permissiveness) was accused of having accepted bribes while county executive of Baltimore and governor of Maryland, and of income tax fraud. After vehemently denying all the charges for two months, Agnew (to escape a jail term) admitted in October that he had been guilty of tax evasion and resigned as Vice President. (He was fined $10,000 and placed on three years' probation, and the Justice Department published a 40,000-word summary of his wrongdoings.)

Under the new Twenty-fifth Amendment, President Nixon nominated Gerald R. Ford of Michigan as Vice President and he was confirmed by Congress. Ford, a graduate of the University of Michigan and the Yale Law School, had served continuously in Congress since 1949, as minority leader since 1964. His positions on public issues were close to Nixon's; he was an internationalist in foreign affairs, a Vietnam hawk, and both conservative and a convinced Republican partisan on domestic issues. Most observers considered him unimaginative and certainly not brilliant, but he was hard-working and (particularly important considering the circumstances of his nomination) honest. Despite his partisan record he was liked and respected by nearly all congressional Democrats. He differed from Nixon both in personality—he was far more gregarious and open—and in his conception of legislative-executive relations. During his confirmation hearings he assured his former colleagues that he believed Congress and the President should work together as partners; he took a dim view of Nixon's impoundment of appropriated funds.

Not long after the Agnew fiasco, Nixon, responding to charges that he had paid almost no income taxes during his presidency, published his 1969-72 returns. These showed that he had indeed paid very little—only about $1,600 in two years during which his income had exceeded half a million dollars. Nixon claimed that his tax return had been perfectly legal—he had taken huge deductions for the gift of some of his Vice Presidential papers to the National Archives—but both the legality and the propriety of his action were widely questioned. Combined with charges that millions of dollars of public funds had been spent on improvements for his private residences in California and Florida, the tax issue further eroded his public support, so much so that he felt obliged, during a televised press conference, to assure the audience: "I am not a crook."

Still another disaster followed as a result of the new war that broke out in October 1973 between Israel and the Arab states. The fighting, while bloody, was brief and inconclusive; a truce was soon arranged under the auspices of the United States and the Soviet Union. But the Arabs, in an effort to force the western nations to compel Israel to withdraw from lands held since the "six-day" war of 1967, cut off oil shipments to the United States, Japan, and most of western Europe. This act produced a worldwide energy crisis. It suddenly became obvious—conservationists had been warning of the danger for years—that the profligate use of petroleum and other sources of power must be curtailed. Yet the American economy was so dependent upon cheap energy that cutbacks threatened to disrupt it completely. Soaring prices of fuel oil and gasoline worsened the already serious inflation problem. The automobile industry, after two record-breaking years, slumped. Almost overnight, big, heavy cars, voracious consumers of gasoline, became a drug on the market. Unemployment in the industry rose, and threatened to spread as automobile suppliers, the tourist industry, and other ancillary businesses were affected. A hundred different questions were raised about how to adjust to the shortage, and for each there seemed to be a hundred possible answers, none, alas, self-evidently correct.

The immediate shortage resulting from the Arab boycott was ended by the patient diplomacy of Henry Kissinger, whom Nixon had made secretary of state at the beginning of his second administration. After weeks of negotiating in the spring of 1974, first with Egypt and Israel, then with Syria and Israel, he obtained a tentative agreement which involved the withdrawal of Israel from some of the territory it had occupied in the 1967 war. Convinced of American good will, the Arab nations lifted the boycott. Oil prices, however, remained extremely high, and the trend of all prices soared at a rate of over ten per cent a year. This "double digit" inflation, which afflicted nearly all the countries of the world, added considerably to President Nixon's woes.

Meanwhile, special prosecutor Jaworski continued his investigation of the Watergate scandals, and the House Judiciary Committee pursued its study of the impeachment question. In March 1974 a grand jury indicted Haldeman, Ehrlichman, former Attorney General John Mitchell, who had been head of CREEP at the time of the break-in, and four other White House aides for conspiring to block the Watergate investigation. The jurors also named Nixon an "unindicted co-conspirator," Jaworski having informed them that their power to indict a president was constitutionally questionable. Judge Sirica thereupon turned over the jury's evidence against Nixon to the Judiciary Committee. Next, both the Internal Revenue Service and a joint congressional committee, after separately auditing the President's income-tax returns, announced that most of his deductions had been unjustified. The IRS assessed him nearly half a million dollars in taxes and interest, which he agreed to pay.

In an effort to check mounting criticism, Nixon, late in April, released edited transcripts of the tapes he had turned over to the court the previous November. If he had expected this material to convince the public that he had been ignorant of the attempt to conceal the administration's connection with the Watergate cover-up, he was sadly mistaken. In addition to much incriminating evidence, the transcripts provided a fascinating and to most persons shocking view of how he conducted himself in private. His repeated use of vulgar language, so out of keeping with his public image, offended millions. "Expletive deleted" became overnight a catchword. His apparent ignorance of many simple legal principles, the general impression of confusion and indecisiveness, and the absence of concern for the public interest that the tapes revealed led even some of his strongest supporters to join in the demand that he resign. When the Judiciary Committee obtained the actual tapes, it also became clear that the White House transcripts were in crucial respects inaccurate and that much material prejudicial to the President's case had been suppressed.

Yet impeaching a president seemed so drastic an action that many people felt more direct proof of Nixon's involvement in the cover-up was necessary before this step was taken. And Nixon insisted that all the relevant information was contained in these tapes; he adamantly refused to turn over others, to either the special prosecutor or the Judiciary Committee. However, with the defendants in the Watergate case demanding access to tapes which they claimed would prove their innocence, Jaworski was compelled either to get them or to risk having the charges dismissed on the ground that the government was withholding evidence. He therefore subpoenaed 64 additional tapes. Nixon, through his lawyer, James St. Clair, refused to obey. Swiftly, the case of *U.S. v. Richard M. Nixon* went to the Supreme Court.

In the summer of 1974—after so many months of alarms and crises—the ordeal of Watergate reached its climax. The Judiciary Committee had unsuccessfully subpoenaed over 100 of Nixon's tapes. Since the courts had no jurisdiction in an impeachment proceeding, the commit-

tee, following months of study of the available evidence behind closed doors, decided to go ahead without the materials Nixon had refused it, and to conduct its deliberations in open session. While millions watched on television, these 38 relatively obscure congressmen, representing a broad spectrum of the national life, debated the charges, revealing in the process both the thoroughness of their investigation and their soul-searching efforts to render an impartial judgment. Three articles of impeachment were then adopted, accusing the President of obstructing justice, misusing the powers of his office, and failing to obey the committee's subpoenas. Except in the case of this last article, substantial numbers of the Republicans on the committee joined with the Democrats in voting "aye," a clear indication that a large majority of the full House would vote to impeach.

On the eve of these public debates, the Supreme Court had ruled unanimously that the President must turn over the 64 subpoenaed tapes to the special prosecutor. Executive privilege had its place, the Court stated, but no person, not even a president, could "withhold evidence that is demonstrably relevant in a criminal trial." For reasons that soon became obvious, Nixon seriously considered defying the Court. Only when convinced that to do so would make his impeachment and conviction certain—and would also compel his lawyer, St. Clair, to withdraw from the case—did he agree to comply.

But he would not resign. He conceded that the House would impeach him, but he was counting on his ability to hold the support of at least 34 senators (one-third plus one of the whole Senate) and thus escape conviction. Events, however, were passing beyond his control. The 64 subpoenaed tapes had to be transcribed and analyzed; after the Supreme Court decision, Judge Sirica pointedly reminded St. Clair of his personal responsibility to prepare this material promptly. Incredibly, up to this time St. Clair had not listened to the tapes; Nixon had assured him that they contained no relevant evidence but had refused to allow him to judge the correctness of this statement for himself. Now St. Clair *had* to listen, and when he did, Nixon's fate was sealed. Three recorded conversations between the President and H. R. Haldeman on June 23, 1972 (less than a week after the break-in and only one day after Nixon had assured the nation that no one in the White House had been involved in the affair) proved conclusively that Nixon had tried to obstruct justice by engaging the CIA in an effort to persuade the FBI not to follow up leads in the case on the spurious ground that national security was involved. The President's defenders had insisted not so much that he was innocent as that solid proof of his guilt had not been demonstrated. Where, in the popular metaphor of the moment, was the "smoking gun"? That weapon had now been found and it bore, unmistakably, the fingerprints of Richard M. Nixon.

Exactly what happened in the White House after St. Clair listened to the Nixon-Haldeman conversations is not yet known, but the President's chief advisers pressed him to release the material at once and also to admit that he had erred in holding it back. This he did on August 5; that in so doing he specifically admitted that he had withheld information from his lawyer suggests that St. Clair, whose professional reputation was at stake, had played a major role. These new revelations shattered the remnants of the President's congressional support. When they read the new transcripts, all the Republican members of the Judiciary Committee who had voted against the impeachment articles reversed themselves; they had accepted the President's assurances that all the evidence was in and had gone on record before millions of eyes in his defense. Understandably, they felt betrayed. Republican congressional leaders informed Nixon categorically that no more than a handful of the senators would vote to acquit him.

And so, on August 8, Nixon announced his resignation. "Dear Mr. Secretary," his terse official letter to the secretary of state ran, "I hereby resign the Office of President of the United States. Sincerely, Richard Nixon." The resignation took effect at noon on August 9, when Gerald Ford was sworn in as president.

On August 9, 1974, Gerald Ford was sworn in as the 38th President of the United States. Warren Burger, Chief Justice of the Supreme Court, administered the oath of office. A week or so later Ford nominated Nelson Rockefeller, former governor of New York, as his vice-presidential choice. (Wide World.)

The meaning of "Watergate" became immediately the subject of much speculation and shall no doubt so remain for many years. Whether Nixon's crude efforts to dominate Congress, crush or inhibit dissent, and subvert the electoral process would have permanently altered the American political system if they had succeeded is probably unanswerable, although the orderly way in which these efforts were checked suggests that the system would have survived in any case. Whether the long trend toward ever-increasing presidential authority was ended and reversed by Nixon's disgrace, the future will reveal.

Nixon's own drama is and must remain one of the most fascinating and enigmatic episodes in all our history, but despite his fall from the heights because of personal flaws, his was not a tragedy in the Greek sense. Even when he finally yielded power he seemed without either remorse or real awareness of his transgressions. Although he enjoyed the pomp and circumstance attendant upon his high office and trumpeted his achievements to all the world, he was also devoid of the classic hero's pride. Did he really intend to smash all opposition and rule like a tyrant, or was he driven by lack of confidence in himself? His stubborn aggressiveness and his overblown view of executive privilege may have reflected a need for constant reassurance that he *was* a mighty leader, that the nation accepted his right to exercise authority. One element in his downfall, preserved for posterity in videotapes of his television appearances, was that he did not look like the victim of the machinations of over-zealous supporters even when he was assuring the country of his innocence most vehemently. Perhaps at some profound level he did not want to be believed. And why, the immorality of his clandestine tapes aside, did he allow them to run on while he discussed the embarrassments attending Watergate with his closest advisers?

This explanation of Richard Nixon may or may not be correct. But it is at least a comforting one. It makes him appear less menacing. Americans can then deplore the injuries he inflicted upon their society and still feel for him a certain compassion.

A Search for Meaning

As long as Americans have been conscious of their existence as a nation, their historians have tried to find some special significance in the course of national development and to understand the unique qualities that distinguish Americans from other peoples. Nearly all have concluded that the country's democratic institutions were of special importance in shaping both American civilization and the national character. In the Age of Jackson, George Bancroft saw American history as the working out of a divine plan. "A favoring Providence, calling our institutions into being, has conducted the country to its present happiness and glory," he wrote in 1834. In essence, God's plan called for "the diffusion of intelligence among the masses" and the triumph of democracy.

Thousands of Americans still accept this analysis, but over the years many historians have subjected Bancroft's faith to sharp re-examination. In the 1890's Frederick Jackson Turner attempted to explain American history in terms of the frontier, which, he said, had branded the whole country with particular characteristics. While he believed that the frontier had been a democratizing influence, Turner also stressed the internal conflicts in the American experience. In the next generation, Charles A. Beard expanded upon this aspect of the Turnerian interpretation, arguing that the history of democracy in the United States was the sum of a series of clashes between rival social and economic interests: the Constitution between owners of land and owners of government securities, the Civil War between southern agriculture and northern industry, and so on.

Still later, the historian David M. Potter found the unique quality of American life in the material abundance which the rich continent bestowed upon the people. Out of this abundance, he wrote, has come a relatively classless, mobile, democratic society, America's sense of mission, a fundamental optimism. Other modern historians emphasized the absence of basic conflicts among Americans. Historians like Turner and Beard, they reasoned, had unintentionally exaggerated the conflicts, either in order to make their narratives more dramatic or because they were misled by the rhetoric of politicians, the enthusiasms of reformers, or the ravings of fanatics. What was most significant about the United States, these writers claimed, was the remarkable degree of "consensus" that had always existed among its people, the sameness of their chief assumptions and objectives, which made the democratic system work. On the other hand, "New Left" historians, pointing to the mistreatment of blacks and other minorities and to the extremes of wealth and poverty that have existed in the United States, insisted that America had always been riven by conflicts and that its government had never been truly democratic.

In one sense, none of the later historians escaped entirely from George Bancroft's naive assumption that he was telling the story of God's American Israel. For Americans had always assumed, and not entirely without reason, that their society represented man's best hope, if not necessarily the Creator's. The pride of the Puritans in their wilderness Zion, the Jeffersonians' fondness for contrasting American democracy with European tyranny, what Tocqueville called the "garrulous patriotism" of the Jacksonians, even the paranoid rantings of the latter-day isolationists all reflected this underlying faith. Historians, immersed in the records of this belief, have inevitably been affected by it. Their doubts have risen from what the theologian Reinhold Niebuhr called "the irony of American history": the people of the United States have been beguiled by their real achievements and the relative superiority of their institutions into assuming that they are better than they are.

Recent history, however, has shaken, if it has not shattered, their illusions. Ironically, the possession of great wealth and power has made Americans aware of their human weaknesses, of what President Johnson referred to as their "fragile existence" in his 1965 inaugural. The struggle against Marxian materialism has exposed the preoccupation of Americans with the things of this world; the by-products of technological advance have been the humbling of Americans' pride in their individualism and self-reliance and the undermining of their belief in inevitable, unending progress.

What effect this awareness will have on the American character (and on American actions) remains for time to reveal, and prediction is not the task of the historian. However, one may fairly ask two questions about the future of the United States, actually of all nations. First: *Has modern technology outstripped human intelligence?* This is not the question, often asked by writers of science fiction, of thinking machines dominating their human creators. But does modern society require more brains than its members collectively possess? We rightly seek to improve each individual's education, and many talents are presently undeveloped, but is there enough *potential* intelligence to satisfy the demands of society for technicians, professionals, and other trained minds? Can we, moreover, learn to control both technology and our desire to enjoy its fruits? Can we strike a happy medium between the advantages and ease that result from industrialization and its inhuman, destructive results? Can we achieve a decent sufficiency of material goods without demanding more than the delicate balance of nature can indefinitely supply? Can we have efficient means of transportation without pollution and congestion, enough power to lighten our labors without exhausting our sources of power? In short, can we, as a people, be energetic and ambitious, but not greedy?

Second: *Has our social development outstripped our emotional development?* We must live at peace or face annihilation. All nations, the United States as much as any other, need to reexamine their basically parochial, highly emotional commitment to nationalism, to learn that pride in one's heritage does not entail hostility or contempt for others. One of the paradoxes of modern life is that to effect change through constructive action is difficult, to do so by destructive behavior easy. This explains much of the violence in the world today. (Martin Luther King and a host of other Americans failed to eliminate race prejudice, but a sordid drifter, shooting King down from ambush, could cause a dozen cities to burn.) Human beings must find new ways to express their individuality in a world of enormous, ego-stifling institutions, to gain some sense of personal achievement through socially constructive activity. Is the human organism temperamentally capable of such adjustments?

No one can currently answer these questions. Nevertheless, we may surely hope that with their growing maturity, their awareness of their own limitations as a political entity, the American people will grapple with them realistically yet with all their customary imagination and energy.

Supplementary Reading

On political developments, not only for the details of legislation but also for useful summaries of many aspects of recent history, see Congressional Quarterly Service, *Congress and the Nation: 1965-1968* (1969). On the election of 1968, T. H. White's *The Making of the President, 1968°* (1969) is lively and entertaining, while Joe McGinniss, *The Selling of the President, 1968* (1969) is a fascinating account of the Republican advertising and television campaign. We have as yet no adequate biography of Nixon, but his own *Six Crises°* (1962) offers some insights into his character and view of political life, and Garry Wills, *Nixon Agonistes°* (1970) is a thoughtful, though unfriendly analysis. See also, Rowland Evans, Jr., and R. D. Novak, *Nixon in the White House* (1971).

°Available in paperback.

White's *The Making of the President, 1972°* (1973) is less satisfactory than his earlier volumes. The literature on the war in Vietnam is, of course, already enormous. The following are only a few of the most important studies: B. B. Fall, *Viet-Nam Witness* (1966), A. M. Schlesinger, Jr., *Bitter Heritage: Vietnam and American Democracy°* (1967), Robert Shaplen, *The Lost Revolution°* (1965), and R. N. Goodwin, *Triumph or Tragedy: Reflections on Vietnam°* (1966), Frances Fitzgerald, *Fire in the Lake°* (1972). David Halberstam, *The Best and the Brightest°* (1972), contains a mass of detail on the evolution of American policy, based on extensive interviews.

A convenient summary of the almost infinite complexities of the Watergate affair is *New York Times,* ed., *The End of a Presidency°* (1974), but see also the account of the Washington reporters who first "broke" the story, Carl Bernstein and Robert Woodward, *All the President's Men* (1974), and *The White House Transcripts°* (1974), the Nixon-edited versions of the famous tapes.

The Declaration of Independence

When in the Course of human events, it becomes necessary for one people to dissolve the political bands which have connected them with another, and to assume among the Powers of the earth, the separate and equal station to which the Laws of Nature and of Nature's God entitle them, a decent respect to the opinions of mankind requires that they should declare the causes which impel them to the separation.

We hold these truths to be self-evident, that all men are created equal, that they are endowed by their Creator with certain unalienable Rights, that among these are Life, Liberty and the pursuit of Happiness. That to secure these rights, Governments are instituted among Men, deriving their just powers from the consent of the governed, That whenever any Form of Government becomes destructive of these ends, it is the Right of the People to alter or to abolish it, and to institute new Government, laying its foundation on such principles and organizing its powers in such form, as to them shall seem most likely to effect their Safety and Happiness. Prudence, indeed, will dictate that Governments long established should not be changed for light and transient causes; and accordingly all experience hath shown, that mankind are more disposed to suffer, while evils are sufferable, than to right themselves by abolishing the forms to which they are accustomed. But when a long train of abuses and usurpations, pursuing invariably the same Object evinces a design to reduce them under absolute Despotism, it is their right, it is their duty, to throw off such Government, and to provide new Guards for their future security.—Such has been the patient sufferance of these Colonies; and such is now the necessity which constrains them to alter their former Systems of Government. The history of the present King of Great Britain is a history of repeated injuries and usurpations, all having in direct object the establishment of an absolute Tyranny over these States. To prove this, let Facts be submitted to a candid world.

He has refused his Assent to Laws, the most wholesome and necessary for the public good.

He has forbidden his Governors to pass Laws of immediate and pressing importance, unless suspended in their operation till his Assent should be obtained; and when so suspended, he has utterly neglected to attend to them.

He has refused to pass other Laws for the accommodation of large districts of people, unless those people would relinquish the right of Representation in the Legislature, a right inestimable to them and formidable to tyrants only.

He has called together legislative bodies at places unusual, uncomfortable, and distant from the depository of their Public Records, for the sole purpose of fatiguing them into compliance with his measures.

He has dissolved Representative Houses repeatedly, for opposing with manly firmness his invasions on the rights of the people.

He has refused for a long time, after such dissolutions, to cause others to be elected; whereby the Legislative Powers, incapable of Annihilation, have returned to the People at large for their exercise; the State remaining in the mean time exposed to all the dangers of invasion from without, and convulsions within.

He has endeavoured to prevent the population of these States; for that purpose obstructing the Laws of Naturalization of Foreigners; refusing to pass others to encourage their migration hither, and raising the conditions of new Appropriations of Lands.

He has obstructed the Administration of Justice, by refusing his Assent to Laws for establishing Judiciary Powers.

He has made Judges dependent on his Will alone, for the tenure of their offices, and the amount and payment of their salaries.

He has erected a multitude of New Offices, and

sent hither swarms of Officers to harass our People, and eat out their substance.

He has kept among us, in times of peace, Standing Armies without the Consent of our legislature.

He has affected to render the Military independent of and superior to the Civil Power.

He has combined with others to subject us to a jurisdiction foreign to our constitution, and unacknowledged by our laws; giving his Assent to their acts of pretended legislation:

For quartering large bodies of armed troops among us:

For protecting them, by a mock Trial, from Punishment for any Murders which they should commit on the Inhabitants of these States:

For cutting off our Trade with all parts of the world:

For imposing taxes on us without our Consent:

For depriving us in many cases, of the benefits of Trial by Jury:

For transporting us beyond Seas to be tried for pretended offences:

For abolishing the free System of English Laws in a neighbouring Province, establishing therein an Arbitrary government, and enlarging its Boundaries so as to render it at once an example and fit instrument for introducing the same absolute rule into these Colonies:

For taking away our Charters, abolishing our most valuable Laws, and altering fundamentally the Forms of our Governments:

For suspending our own Legislature, and declaring themselves invested with Power to legislate for us in all cases whatsoever.

He has abdicated Government here, by declaring us out of his Protection and waging War against us.

He has plundered our seas, ravaged our Coasts, burnt our towns, and destroyed the lives of our people.

He is at this time transporting large armies of foreign mercenaries to compleat the works of death, desolation and tyranny, already begun with circumstances of Cruelty & perfidy scarcely paralleled in the most barbarous ages, and totally unworthy the Head of a civilized nation.

He has constrained our fellow Citizens taken Captive on the high Seas to bear Arms against their Country, to become the executioners of their friends and Brethren, or to fall themselves by their Hands.

He has excited domestic insurrections amongst us, and has endeavoured to bring on the inhabitants of our frontiers, the merciless Indian Savages, whose known rule of warfare, is an undistinguished destruction of all ages, sexes and conditions.

In every stage of these Oppressions We have Petitioned for Redress in the most humble terms: Our repeated Petitions have been answered only by repeated injury. A Prince, whose character is thus marked by every act which may define a Tyrant, is unfit to be the ruler of a free People.

Nor have We been wanting in attention to our British brethren. We have warned them from time to time of attempts by their legislature to extend an unwarrantable jurisdiction over us. We have reminded them of the circumstances of our emigration and settlement here. We have appealed to their native justice and magnanimity, and we have conjured them by the ties of our common kindred to disavow these usurpations, which, would inevitably interrupt our connections and correspondence. They too have been deaf to the voice of justice and of consanguinity. We must, therefore, acquiesce in the necessity, which denounces our Separation, and hold them, as we hold the rest of mankind, Enemies in War, in Peace Friends.

We, therefore, the Representatives of the united States of America, in General Congress, Assembled, appealing to the Supreme Judge of the world for the rectitude of our intentions, do, in the Name, and by Authority of the good People of these Colonies, solemnly publish and declare, That these United Colonies are, and of Right ought to be Free and Independent States; that they are Absolved from all Allegiance to the British Crown, and that all political connection between them and the State of Great Britain, is and ought to be totally dissolved; and that as Free and Independent States, they have full Power to levy War, conclude Peace, contract Alliances, establish Commerce, and to do all other Acts and Things which Independent States may of right do. And for the support of this Declaration, with a firm reliance on the Protection of Divine Providence, we mutually pledge to each other our Lives, our Fortunes and our sacred Honor.

The Constitution of the United States

We the people of the United States, in Order to form a more perfect Union, establish Justice, insure domestic Tranquility, provide for the common defence, promote the general Welfare, and secure the Blessings of Liberty to ourselves and our Posterity, do ordain and establish this CONSTITUTION for the United States of America.

ARTICLE I

Section 1. All legislative Powers herein granted shall be vested in a Congress of the United States, which shall consist of a Senate and House of Representatives.

Section 2. The House of Representatives shall be composed of Members chosen every second Year by the People of the several States, and the Electors in each State shall have the Qualifications requisite for Electors of the most numerous Branch of the State Legislature.

No Person shall be a Representative who shall not have attained to the Age of twenty-five Years, and been seven Years a Citizen of the United States, and who shall not, when elected, be an Inhabitant of that State in which he shall be chosen.

Representatives and direct Taxes shall be apportioned among the several States which may be included within this Union, according to their respective Numbers, which shall be determined by adding to the whole Number of free Persons, including those bound to Service for a Term of Years, and excluding Indians not taxed, three fifths of all other Persons. The actual Enumeration shall be made within three Years after the first Meeting of the Congress of the United States, and within every subsequent Term of ten Years, in such Manner as they shall by Law direct. The Number of Representatives shall not exceed one for every thirty Thousand, but each State shall have at Least one Representative; and until such enumeration shall be made, the State of New Hampshire shall be entitled to chuse three, Massachusetts eight, Rhode-Island and Providence Plantations one, Connecticut five, New-York six, New Jersey four, Pennsylvania eight, Delaware one, Maryland six, Virginia ten, North Carolina five, South Carolina five, and Georgia three.

When vacancies happen in the Representation from any State, the Executive Authority thereof shall issue Writs of Election to fill such Vacancies.

The House of Representatives shall chuse their Speaker and other Officers; and shall have the sole Power of Impeachment.

Section 3. The Senate of the United States shall be composed of two Senators from each State, chosen by the Legislature thereof, for six Years; and each Senator shall have one Vote.

Immediately after they shall be assembled in Consequence of the first Election, they shall be divided as equally as may be into three Classes. The Seats of the Senators of the first Class shall be vacated at the Expiration of the second Year, of the second Class at the Expiration of the fourth Year, and of the third Class at the Expiration of the sixth Year, so that one-third may be chosen every second Year; and if Vacancies happen by Resignation, or otherwise, during the Recess of the Legislature of any State, the Executive thereof may make temporary Appointments until the next Meeting of the Legislature, which shall then fill such Vacancies.

No Person shall be a Senator who shall not have attained to the Age of thirty Years, and been nine Years a Citizen of the United States, and who shall not, when elected, be an Inhabitant of that State in which he shall be chosen.

The Vice President of the United States shall be President of the Senate, but shall have no vote, unless they be equally divided.

The Senate shall chuse their other Officers, and also a President pro tempore, in the absence of the Vice President, or when he shall exercise the Office of the President of the United States.

The Senate shall have the sole Power to try all Impeachments. When sitting for that purpose, they shall be on Oath or Affirmation. When the President of the United States is tried, the Chief Justice shall preside: And no person shall be convicted without the Concurrence of two thirds of the Members present.

Judgment in Cases of Impeachment shall not extend further than to removal from Office, and disqualification to hold and enjoy any Office of honor, Trust, or Profit under the United States: but the Party convicted shall nevertheless be liable and subject to Indictment, Trial, Judgment, and Punishment, according to Law.

Section 4. The Times, Places and Manner of holding Elections for Senators and Representatives, shall be prescribed in each state by the Legislature thereof; but the Congress may at any time by Law make or alter such Regulations, except as to the Places of Chusing Senators.

The Congress shall assemble at least once in every Year, and such Meeting shall be on the first Monday in December, unless they shall by Law appoint a different Day.

Section 5. Each House shall be the Judge of the Elections, Returns and Qualifications of its own Members, and a Majority of each shall constitute a Quorum to do Business; but a smaller number may adjourn from day to day, and may be authorized to compel the Attendance of absent Members, in such Manner, and under such Penalties, as each House may provide.

Each House may determine the Rules of its Proceedings, punish its Members for disorderly Behavior, and, with the Concurrence of two thirds, expel a Member.

Each House shall keep a Journal of its Proceedings, and from time to time publish the same, excepting such Parts as may in their Judgment require Secrecy; and the Yeas and Nays of the Members of either House on any question shall, at the Desire of one fifth of those Present, be entered on the Journal.

Neither House, during the Session of Congress, shall, without the Consent of the other, adjourn for more than three days, nor to any other Place than that in which the two Houses shall be sitting.

Section 6. The Senators and Representatives shall receive a Compensation for their Services, to be ascertained by Law, and paid out of the Treasury of the United States. They shall in all Cases, except Treason, Felony, and Breach of the Peace, be privileged from Arrest during their Attendance at the Session of their respective Houses, and in going to and returning from the same; and for any Speech or Debate in either House, they shall not be questioned in any other Place.

No Senator or Representative shall, during the Time for which he was elected, be appointed to any civil Office under the Authority of the United States, which shall have been created, or the Emoluments whereof shall have been increased, during such time; and no Person holding any Office under the United States shall be a Member of either House during his continuance in Office.

Section 7. All Bills for raising Revenue shall originate in the House of Representatives; but the Senate may propose or concur with Amendments as on other bills.

Every Bill which shall have passed the House of Representatives and the Senate, shall, before it become a Law, be presented to the President of the United States; If he approve he shall sign it, but if not he shall return it, with his Objections, to that House in which it shall have originated, who shall enter the Objections at large on their Journal, and proceed to reconsider it. If after such Reconsideration two thirds of that House shall agree to pass the bill, it shall be sent, together with the objections, to the other House, by which it shall likewise be reconsidered, and if approved by two thirds of that House, it shall become a Law. But in all such Cases the Votes of both Houses shall be determined by Yeas and Nays, and the Names of the Persons voting for and against the Bill shall be entered on the Journal of each House respectively. If any Bill shall not be returned by the President within ten Days (Sundays excepted) after it shall have been presented to him, the Same shall be a Law, in like Manner as if he had signed it, unless the Congress by their Adjournment prevent its Return, in which Case it shall not be a Law.

Every Order, Resolution, or Vote to which the Concurrence of the Senate and House of Representatives may be necessary (except on a question of Adjournment) shall be presented to the President of the United States; and before the Same shall take Effect, shall be approved by him, or being disapproved by him, shall be repassed by two thirds of the Senate and House of Representatives, according to the Rules and Limitations prescribed in the Case of a Bill.

Section 8. The Congress shall have Power To lay and collect Taxes, Duties, Imposts and Excises, to pay the Debts and provide for the common Defence and general Welfare of the United States; but all Duties, Imposts and Excises shall be uniform throughout the United States;

To borrow money on the credit of the United States;

To regulate Commerce with foreign Nations, and among the several States, and with the Indian Tribes;

To establish an uniform Rule of Naturalization, and uniform Laws on the subject of Bankruptcies throughout the United States;

To coin Money, regulate the Value thereof, and of foreign Coin, and fix the Standard of Weights and Measures;

To provide for the Punishment of counterfeiting the Securities and current Coin of the United States;

To establish Post Offices and post Roads;

To promote the Progress of Science and useful Arts, by securing for limited Times to Authors and Inventors the exclusive Right to their respective Writings and Discoveries;

To constitute Tribunals inferior to the Supreme Court;

To define and punish Piracies and Felonies committed on the high Seas, and Offences against the Law of Nations;

To declare War, grant Letters of Marque and Reprisal, and make Rules concerning Captures on Land and Water;

To raise and support Armies, but no Appropriation of Money to that Use shall be for a longer Term than two Years;

To provide and maintain a Navy;

To make Rules for the Government and Regulation of the land and naval forces;

To provide for calling forth the Militia to execute the Laws of the Union, suppress Insurrections and repel Invasions;

To provide for organizing, arming, and disciplining the Militia, and for governing such Part of them as may be employed in the Service of the United States, reserving to the States respectively, the Appointment of the Officers, and the Authority of training the Militia according to the discipline prescribed by Congress;

To exercise exclusive Legislation in all Cases whatsoever, over such District (not exceeding ten Miles square) as may, by Cession of particular States, and the acceptance of Congress, become the Seat of Government of the United States, and to exercise like Authority over all Places purchased by the Consent of the Legislature of the State in which the Same shall be, for the Erection of Forts, Magazines, Arsenals, dockYards, and other needful Buildings;—And

To make all Laws which shall be necessary and proper for carrying into Execution the foregoing Powers, and all other Powers vested by this Constitution in the Government of the United States, or in any Department or Officer thereof.

Section 9. The Migration or Importation of such Persons as any of the States now existing shall think proper to admit, shall not be prohibited by the Congress prior to the Year one thousand eight hundred and eight, but a tax or duty may be imposed on such Importation, not exceeding ten dollars for each Person.

The privilege of the Writ of Habeas Corpus shall not be suspended, unless when in Cases of Rebellion or Invasion the public Safety may require it.

No Bill of Attainder or ex post facto Law shall be passed.

No capitation, or other direct, Tax shall be laid unless in Proportion to the Census or Enumeration herein before directed to be taken.

No Tax or Duty shall be laid on Articles exported from any State.

No Preference shall be given by any Regulation of Revenue to the Ports of one State over those of another: nor shall Vessels bound to, or from, one State, be obliged to enter, clear, or pay Duties in another.

No Money shall be drawn from the Treasury, but in Consequence of Appropriations made by Law; and a regular Statement and Account of the Receipts and Expenditures of all public Money shall be published from time to time.

No Title of Nobility shall be granted by the United States: And no Person holding any Office of Profit or Trust under them, shall, without the Consent of the Congress, accept of any present, Emolument, Office, or Title, of any kind whatever, from any King, Prince, or foreign State.

Section 10. No State shall enter into any Treaty, Alliance, or Confederation; grant Letters of Marque and Reprisal; coin Money; emit Bills of Credit; make any Thing but gold and silver Coin a Tender in Payment of Debts; pass any Bill of Attainder, ex post facto Law, or Law impairing the Obligation of Contracts, or grant any Title of Nobility.

No State shall, without the Consent of the Congress, lay any Imposts or Duties on Imports or Exports, except what may be absolutely necessary for executing its inspection Laws: and the net Produce of all Duties and Imposts, laid by any State on Imports or Exports, shall be for the Use of the Treasury of the United States; and all such Laws shall be subject to the Revision and Control of the Congress.

No State shall, without the Consent of Congress,

lay any duty of Tonnage, keep Troops, or Ships of War in time of Peace, enter into any Agreement or Compact with another State, or with a foreign Power, or engage in War, unless actually invaded, or in such imminent Danger as will not admit of delay.

ARTICLE II

Section 1. The executive Power shall be vested in a President of the United States of America. He shall hold his Office during the Term of four years, and, together with the Vice-President, chosen for the same Term, be elected, as follows:

Each State shall appoint, in such Manner as the Legislature thereof may direct, a Number of Electors, equal to the whole Number of Senators and Representatives to which the State may be entitled in the Congress; but no Senator or Representative, or Person holding an Office of Trust or Profit under the United States, shall be appointed an Elector.

The Electors shall meet in their respective States, and vote by Ballot for two persons, of whom one at least shall not be an Inhabitant of the same State with themselves. And they shall make a List of all the Persons voted for, and of the Number of Votes for each; which List they shall sign and certify, and transmit sealed to the Seat of the Government of the United States, directed to the President of the Senate. The President of the Senate shall, in the Presence of the Senate and House of Representatives, open all the Certificates, and the Votes shall then be counted. The Person having the greatest Number of Votes shall be the President, if such Number be a Majority of the whole Number of Electors appointed; and if there be more than one who have such Majority, and have an equal Number of Votes, then the House of Representatives shall immediately chuse by Ballot one of them for President; and if no Person have a Majority, then from the five highest on the List the said House shall in like Manner chuse the President. But in chusing the President, the Votes shall be taken by States, the Representation from each State having one Vote; a quorum for this Purpose shall consist of a Member or Members from two-thirds of the States, and a Majority of all the States shall be necessary to a Choice. In every Case, after the Choice of the President, the Person having the greatest Number of Votes of the Electors shall be the Vice President. But if there should remain two or more who have equal votes, the Senate shall chuse from them by Ballot the Vice-President.

The Congress may determine the Time of chusing the Electors, and the Day on which they shall give their Votes; which Day shall be the same throughout the United States.

No person except a natural-born Citizen, or a Citizen of the United States, at the time of the Adoption of this Constitution, shall be eligible to the Office of President; neither shall any Person be eligible to that Office who shall not have attained to the Age of thirty-five years, and been fourteen Years a Resident within the United States.

In Case of the Removal of the President from Office, or of his Death, Resignation, or Inability to discharge the Powers and Duties of the said Office, the same shall devolve on the Vice President, and the Congress may by Law provide for the Case of Removal, Death, Resignation, or Inability, both of the President and Vice President, declaring what Officer shall then act as President, and such Officer shall act accordingly, until the disability be removed, or a President shall be elected.

The President shall, at stated Times, receive for his Services a Compensation, which shall neither be increased nor diminished during the Period for which he shall have been elected, and he shall not receive within that Period any other Emolument from the United States, or any of them.

Before he enter on the execution of his Office, he shall take the following Oath or Affirmation:—"I do solemnly swear (or affirm) that I will faithfully execute the Office of President of the United States, and will, to the best of my Ability, preserve, protect, and defend the Constitution of the United States."

Section 2. The President shall be Commander in Chief of the Army and Navy of the United States, and of the Militia of the several States, when called into the actual Service of the United States; he may require the Opinion, in writing, of the principal Officer in each of the executive Departments, upon any subject relating to the Duties of their respective Offices, and he shall have Power to Grant Reprieves and Pardons for Offences against the United States, except in Cases of Impeachment.

He shall have Power, by and with the Advice and Consent of the Senate, to make Treaties, provided two thirds of the Senators present concur; and he shall nominate, and by and with the Advice and Consent of the Senate, shall appoint Ambassadors, other public Ministers and Consuls, Judges of the supreme Court, and all other Officers of the United States, whose Appointments are not herein otherwise provided for, and which shall be established by Law: but the Congress may by Law vest the Appointment of such inferior

Officers, as they think proper, in the President alone, in the Courts of Law, or in the Heads of Departments.

The President shall have Power to fill up all Vacancies that may happen during the Recess of the Senate, by granting Commissions which shall expire at the End of their next Session.

Section 3. He shall from time to time give to the Congress Information of the State of the Union, and recommend to their Consideration such Measures as he shall judge necessary and expedient; he may, on extraordinary occasions, convene both Houses, or either of them, and in Case of Disagreement between them, with respect to the Time of Adjournment, he may adjourn them to such Time as he shall think proper; he shall receive Ambassadors and other public Ministers; he shall take Care that the Laws be faithfully executed, and shall Commission all the Officers of the United States.

Section 4. The President, Vice President and all civil Officers of the United States, shall be removed from Office on Impeachment for, and Conviction of, Treason, Bribery, or other high Crimes and Misdemeanors.

ARTICLE III

Section 1. The judicial Power of the United States, shall be vested in one supreme Court, and in such inferior Courts as the Congress may from time to time ordain and establish. The Judges, both of the supreme and inferior Courts, shall hold their Offices during good Behaviour, and shall, at stated Times, receive for their Services, a Compensation, which shall not be diminished during their Continuance in Office.

Section 2. The judicial Power shall extend to all Cases, in Law and Equity, arising under this Constitution, the Laws of the United States, and treaties made, or which shall be made, under their Authority;—to all Cases affecting ambassadors, other public ministers and consuls;—to all cases of admiralty and maritime Jurisdiction;—to Controversies to which the United States shall be a Party;—to Controversies between two or more States;—between a State and Citizens of another State;—between Citizens of different States,—between Citizens of the same State claiming Lands under Grants of different States, and between a State, or the Citizens thereof, and foreign States, Citizens or Subjects.

In all Cases affecting Ambassadors, other public Ministers and Consuls, and those in which a State shall be Party, the supreme Court shall have original Jurisdiction. In all the other Cases before mentioned, the supreme Court shall have appellate Jurisdiction, both as to Law and Fact, with such Exceptions, and under such Regulations as the Congress shall make.

The trial of all Crimes, except in Cases of Impeachment, shall be by Jury; and such Trial shall be held in the State where the said Crimes shall have been committed; but when not committed within any State, the Trial shall be at such Place or Places as the Congress may by Law have directed.

Section 3. Treason against the United States, shall consist only in levying War against them, or in adhering to their Enemies, giving them Aid and Comfort. No Person shall be convicted of Treason unless on the Testimony of two Witnesses to the same overt Act, or on Confession in open Court.

The Congress shall have power to declare the Punishment of Treason, but no Attainder of Treason shall work Corruption of Blood, or Forfeiture except during the Life of the Person attainted.

ARTICLE IV

Section 1. Full Faith and Credit shall be given in each State to the public Acts, Records, and judicial Proceedings of every other State. And the Congress may by general Laws prescribe the Manner in which such Acts, Records and Proceedings shall be proved, and the Effect thereof.

Section 2. The Citizens of each State shall be entitled to all Privileges and Immunities of Citizens in the several States.

A Person charged in any State with Treason, Felony, or other Crime, who shall flee from Justice, and be found in another State, shall on demand of the executive Authority of the State from which he fled, be delivered up, to be removed to the State having Jurisdiction of the crime.

No Person held to Service or Labour in one State, under the Laws thereof, escaping into another, shall, in Consequence of any Law or Regulation therein, be discharged from such Service or Labour, but shall be delivered up on Claim of the Party to whom such Service or Labour may be due.

Section 3. New States may be admitted by the Congress into this Union; but no new State shall be formed or erected within the Jurisdiction of any other State; nor any State be formed by the Junction of two or more States, or parts of States, without the Consent of the Legislatures of the States concerned as well as of the Congress.

The Congress shall have Power to dispose of and make all needful Rules and Regulations respecting the

Territory or other Property belonging to the United States; and nothing in this Constitution shall be so construed as to Prejudice any Claims of the United States, or of any particular State.

Section 4. The United States shall guarantee to every State in this Union a Republican Form of Government, and shall protect each of them against Invasion; and on Application of the Legislature, or the Executive (when the Legislature cannot be convened) against domestic Violence.

ARTICLE V

The Congress, whenever two-thirds of both Houses shall deem it necessary, shall propose Amendments to this Constitution, or, on the Application of the Legislatures of two-thirds of the several States, shall call a Convention for proposing Amendments, which, in either Case, shall be valid to all Intents and Purposes, as part of this Constitution, when ratified by the Legislatures of three-fourths of the several States, or by Conventions in three-fourths thereof, as the one or the other Mode of Ratification may be proposed by the Congress; Provided that no Amendment which may be made prior to the Year One thousand eight hundred and eight shall in any Manner affect the first and fourth Clauses in the Ninth Section of the first Article; and that no State, without its Consent, shall be deprived of its equal Suffrage in the Senate.

ARTICLE VI

All Debts contracted and Engagements entered into, before the Adoption of this Constitution, shall be as valid against the United States under this Constitution, as under the Confederation.

This Constitution, and the Laws of the United States which shall be made in Pursuance thereof; and all Treaties made, or which shall be made, under the Authority of the United States, shall be the supreme Law of the Land; and the Judges in every State shall be bound thereby, any Thing in the Constitution or Laws of any State to the Contrary notwithstanding.

The Senators and Representatives before mentioned, and the Members of the several State Legislatures, and all executive and judicial Officers, both of the United States and of the several States, shall be bound by Oath or Affirmation to support this Constitution; but no religious Test shall ever be required as a qualification to any Office or public Trust under the United States.

ARTICLE VII

The Ratification of the Conventions of nine States shall be sufficient for the Establishment of this Constitution between the States so ratifying the same.

Done in Convention by the Unanimous Consent of the States present the Seventeenth Day of September in the Year of our Lord one thousand seven hundred and Eighty seven, and of the Independence of the United States of America the Twelfth. In Witness whereof We have hereunto subscribed our Names.

Articles in Addition to, and Amendment of, the Constitution of the United States of America, Proposed by Congress, and Ratified by the Legislatures of the Several States, Pursuant to the Fifth Article of the Original Constitution.

AMENDMENT I [1791]

Congress shall make no law respecting an establishment of religion, or prohibiting the free exercise thereof; or abridging the freedom of speech, or of the press; or the right of the people peaceably to assemble, and to petition the Government for a redress of grievances.

AMENDMENT II [1791]

A well regulated Militia, being necessary to the security of a free State, the right of the people to keep and bear Arms shall not be infringed.

AMENDMENT III [1791]

No Soldier shall, in time of peace, be quartered in any house, without the consent of the Owner, nor in time of war, but in a manner to be prescribed by law.

AMENDMENT IV [1791]

The right of the people to be secure in their persons, houses, papers, and effects, against unreasonable searches and seizures, shall not be violated, and no Warrants shall issue, but upon probable cause, supported by Oath or affirmation, and particularly describing the place to be searched, and the persons or things to be seized.

AMENDMENT V [1791]

No person shall be held to answer for a capital or otherwise infamous crime, unless on a presentment or indictment of a Grand Jury, except in cases arising in the land or naval forces, or in the Militia, when in actual service in time of War or public danger; nor shall any person be subject for the same offence to be twice put in jeopardy of life or limb; nor shall be compelled in any criminal case to be a witness against himself, nor be deprived of life, liberty, or property, without due process of law; nor shall private property be taken for public use, without just compensation.

AMENDMENT VI [1791]

In all criminal prosecutions, the accused shall enjoy the right to a speedy and public trial, by an impartial jury of the State and district wherein the crime shall have been committed, which district shall have been previously ascertained by law, and to be informed of the nature and cause of the accusation; to be confronted with the witnesses against him; to have compulsory process for obtaining witnesses in his favor, and to have the Assistance of Counsel for his defence.

AMENDMENT VII [1791]

In suits at common law, where the value in controversy shall exceed twenty dollars, the right of trial by jury shall be preserved, and no fact tried by a jury, shall be otherwise reexamined in any Court of the United States, than according to the rules of the common law.

AMENDMENT VIII [1791]

Excessive bail shall not be required, nor excessive fines imposed, nor cruel and unusual punishments inflicted.

AMENDMENT IX [1791]

The enumeration in the Constitution, of certain rights, shall not be construed to deny or disparage others retained by the people.

AMENDMENT X [1791]

The powers not delegated to the United States by the Constitution, nor prohibited by it to the States, are reserved to the States respectively, or to the people.

AMENDMENT XI [1798]

The Judicial power of the United States shall not be construed to extend to any suit in law or equity, commenced or prosecuted against one of the United States by Citizens of another State, or by Citizens or Subjects of any Foreign State.

AMENDMENT XII [1804]

The Electors shall meet in their respective States and vote by ballot for President and Vice-President, one of whom, at least, shall not be an inhabitant of the same State with themselves; they shall name in their ballots the person voted for as President, and in distinct ballots the person voted for as Vice-President, and they shall make distinct lists of all persons voted for as President, and of all persons voted for as Vice-President, and of the number of votes for each, which lists they shall sign and certify, and transmit sealed to the seat of the government of the United States, directed to the President of the Senate;—The President of the Senate shall, in the presence of the Senate and House of Representatives, open all the certificates and the votes shall then be counted;—The person having the greatest number of votes for President, shall be the President, if such number be a majority of the whole number of Electors appointed; and if no person have such majority, then from the persons having the highest numbers not exceeding three on the list of those voted for as President, the House of Representatives shall choose immediately, by ballot, the President. But in choosing the President, the votes shall be taken by states, the representation from each state having one vote; a quorum for this purpose shall consist of a member or members from two-thirds of the states, and a majority of all the states shall be necessary to a choice. And if the House of Representatives shall not choose a President whenever the right of choice shall devolve upon them, before the fourth day of March next following, then the Vice-President shall act as President, as in the case of the death or other constitutional disability of the President.—The person having the greatest number of votes as Vice-President, shall be the Vice-President, if such number be a majority of the whole number of Electors appointed, and if no person have a majority, then from the two highest numbers on the list, the Senate shall choose the Vice-President; a quorum for the purpose shall consist of two-thirds of the whole number of Senators, and a majority of the whole number shall be necessary to a choice. But no person constitutionally ineligible to the office of President shall be eligible to that of Vice-President of the United States.

AMENDMENT XIII [1865]

Section 1. Neither slavery nor involuntary servitude, except as a punishment for crime whereof the party shall have been duly convicted, shall exist within the United States, or any place subject to their jurisdiction.

Section 2. Congress shall have power to enforce this article by appropriate legislation.

AMENDMENT XIV [1868]

Section 1. All persons born or naturalized in the

United States, and subject to the jurisdiction thereof, are citizens of the United States and of the State wherein they reside. No State shall make or enforce any law which shall abridge the privileges or immunities of citizens of the United States; nor shall any State deprive any person of life, liberty, or property, without due process of law; nor deny to any person within its jurisdiction the equal protection of the laws.

Section 2. Representatives shall be apportioned among the several States according to their respective numbers, counting the whole number of persons in each State, excluding Indians not taxed. But when the right to vote at any election for the choice of electors for President and Vice-President of the United States, Representatives in Congress, the Executive and Judicial officers of a State, or the members of the Legislature thereof, is denied to any of the male inhabitants of such State, being twenty-one years of age, and citizens of the United States, or in any way abridged, except for participation in rebellion, or other crime, the basis of representation therein shall be reduced in the proportion which the number of such male citizens shall bear to the whole number of male citizens twenty-one years of age in such State.

Section 3. No person shall be a Senator or Representative in Congress, or elector of President and Vice-President, or hold any office, civil or military, under the United States, or under any State, who, having previously taken an oath, as a member of Congress, or as an officer of the United States, or as a member of any State legislature, or as an executive or judicial officer of any State, to support the Constitution of the United States, shall have engaged in insurrection or rebellion against the same, or given aid or comfort to the enemies thereof. But Congress may by a vote of two-thirds of each House, remove such disability.

Section 4. The validity of the public debt of the United States, authorized by law, including debts incurred for payment of pensions and bounties for services in suppressing insurrection or rebellion, shall not be questioned. But neither the United States nor any State shall assume or pay any debt or obligation incurred in aid of insurrection or rebellion against the United States, or any claim for the loss or emancipation of any slave; but all such debts, obligations, and claims shall be held illegal and void.

Section 5. The Congress shall have the power to enforce, by appropriate legislation, the provisions of this article.

AMENDMENT XV [1870]

Section 1. The right of citizens of the United States to vote shall not be denied or abridged by the United States or by any State on account of race, color, or previous condition of servitude—

Section 2. The Congress shall have power to enforce this article by appropriate legislation.

AMENDMENT XVI [1913]

The Congress shall have power to lay and collect taxes on incomes, from whatever source derived, without apportionment among the several States, and without regard to any census or enumeration.

AMENDMENT XVII [1913]

The Senate of the United States shall be composed of two Senators from each State, elected by the people thereof, for six years; and each Senator shall have one vote. The electors in each State shall have the qualifications requisite for electors of the most numerous branch of the State legislatures.

When vacancies happen in the representation of any State in the Senate, the executive authority of such State shall issue writs of election to fill such vacancies: *Provided,* That the legislature of any State may empower the executive thereof to make temporary appointments until the people fill the vacancies by election as the legislature may direct.

This amendment shall not be so construed as to affect the election or term of any Senator chosen before it becomes valid as part of the Constitution.

AMENDMENT XVIII [1919]

Section 1. After one year from the ratification of this article the manufacture, sale, or transportation of intoxicating liquors within, the importation thereof into, or the exportation thereof from the United States and all territory subject to the jurisdiction thereof for beverage purposes is hereby prohibited.

Section 2. The Congress and the several States shall have concurrent power to enforce this article by appropriate legislation.

Section 3. This article shall be inoperative unless it shall have been ratified as an amendment to the Constitution by the legislatures of the several States, as provided in the Constitution, within seven years from the date of the submission hereof to the States by the Congress.

AMENDMENT XIX [1920]

The right of citizens of the United States to vote shall not be denied or abridged by the United States or by any State on account of sex.

Congress shall have power to enforce this article by appropriate legislation.

AMENDMENT XX [1933]

Section 1. The terms of the President and Vice-President shall end at noon on the 20th day of January, and the terms of Senators and Representatives at noon on the 3d day of January, of the years in which such terms would have ended if this article had not been ratified; and the terms of their successors shall then begin.

Section 2. The Congress shall assemble at least once in every year, and such meeting shall begin at noon on the 3d day of January, unless they shall by law appoint a different day.

Section 3. If, at the time fixed for the beginning of the term of the President, the President elect shall have died, the Vice-President elect shall become President. If a President shall not have been chosen before the time fixed for the beginning of his term, or if the President elect shall have failed to qualify, then the Vice-President elect shall act as President until a President shall have qualified; and the Congress may by law provide for the case wherein neither a President elect nor a Vice-President elect shall have qualified, declaring who shall then act as President, or the manner in which one who is to act shall be selected, and such person shall act accordingly until a President or Vice-President shall have qualified.

Section 4. The Congress may by law provide for the case of the death of any of the persons from whom the House of Representatives may choose a President whenever the right of choice shall have devolved upon them, and for the case of the death of any of the persons from whom the Senate may choose a Vice-President whenever the right of choice shall have devolved upon them.

Section 5. Sections 1 and 2 shall take effect on the 15th day of October following the ratification of this article.

Section 6. This article shall be inoperative unless it shall have been ratified as an amendment to the Constitution by the legislatures of three-fourths of the several States within seven years from the date of its submission.

AMENDMENT XXI [1933]

Section 1. The eighteenth article of amendment to the Constitution of the United States is hereby repealed.

Section 2. The transportation or importation into any State, Territory, or possession of the United States for delivery or use therein of intoxicating liquors, in violation of the laws thereof, is hereby prohibited.

Section 3. This article shall be inoperative unless it shall have been ratified as an amendment to the Constitution by conventions in the several States, as provided in the Constitution, within seven years from the date of the submission hereof to the States by the Congress.

AMENDMENT XXII [1951]

No person shall be elected to the office of the President more than twice, and no person who has held the office of President, or acted as President, for more than two years of a term to which some other person was elected President shall be elected to the office of the President more than once.

But this Article shall not apply to any person holding the office of President when this Article was proposed by the Congress, and shall not prevent any person who may be holding the office of President, or acting as President, during the term within which this Article becomes operative from holding the office of President or acting as President during the remainder of such term.

AMENDMENT XXIII [1961]

Section 1. The District constituting the seat of Government of the United States shall appoint in such manner as the Congress may direct:

A number of electors of President and Vice President equal to the whole number of Senators and Representatives in Congress to which the District would be entitled if it were a State, but in no event more than the least populous State; they shall be in addition to those appointed by the States, but they shall be considered, for the purposes of the election of President and Vice President, to be electors appointed by a State; and they shall meet in the District and perform such duties as provided by the twelfth article of amendment.

Section 2. The Congress shall have power to enforce this article by appropriate legislation.

AMENDMENT XXIV [1964]

Section 1. The right of citizens of the United States to vote in any primary or other election for President or Vice President, for electors for President or Vice President, or for Senator or Representative in Congress, shall not be denied or abridged by the

United States or any State by reason of failure to pay any poll tax or other tax.

Section 2. The Congress shall have the power to enforce this article by appropriate legislation.

AMENDMENT XXV [1967]

Section 1. In case of the removal of the President from office or his death or resignation, the Vice President shall become President.

Section 2. Whenever there is a vacancy in the office of the Vice President, the President shall nominate a Vice President who shall take the office upon confirmation by a majority vote of both houses of Congress.

Section 3. Whenever the President transmits to the President pro tempore of the Senate and the Speaker of the House of Representatives his written declaration that he is unable to discharge the powers and duties of his office, and until he transmits to them a written declaration to the contrary, such powers and duties shall be discharged by the Vice President as Acting President.

Section 4. Whenever the Vice President and a majority of either the principal officers of the executive departments, or of such other body as Congress may by law provide, transmit to the President pro tempore of the Senate and the Speaker of the House of Representatives their written declaration that the President is unable to discharge the powers and duties of his office, the Vice President shall immediately assume the powers and duties of the office as Acting President.

Thereafter, when the President transmits to the President pro tempore of the Senate and the Speaker of the House of Representatives his written declaration that no inability exists, he shall resume the powers and duties of his office unless the Vice President and a majority of either the principal officers of the executive departments, or of such other body as Congress may by law provide, transmit within four days to the President pro tempore of the Senate and the Speaker of the House of Representatives their written declaration that the President is unable to discharge the powers and duties of his office. Thereupon Congress shall decide the issue, assembling within 48 hours for that purpose if not in session. If the Congress, within 21 days after receipt of the latter written declaration, or, if Congress is not in session, within 21 days after Congress is required to assemble, determines by two-thirds vote of both houses that the President is unable to discharge the powers and duties of his office, the Vice President shall continue to discharge the same as Acting President; otherwise, the President shall resume the powers and duties of his office.

AMENDMENT XXVI [1971]

Section 1. The right of citizens of the United States, who are 18 years of age or older, to vote shall not be denied or abridged by the United States or any state on account of age.

Section 2. The Congress shall have the power to enforce this article by appropriate legislation.

Presidential Elections, 1789–1972

Year	Candidates	Party	Popular Vote	Electoral Vote
1789	**George Washington**			69
	John Adams			34
	Others			35
1792	**George Washington**			132
	John Adams			77
	George Clinton			50
	Others			5
1796	**John Adams**	Federalist		71
	Thomas Jefferson	Democratic-Republican		68
	Thomas Pinckney	Federalist		59
	Aaron Burr	Democratic-Republican		30
	Others			48

Year	Candidates	Party	Popular Vote	Electoral Vote
1800	**Thomas Jefferson**	Democratic-Republican		73
	Aaron Burr	Democratic-Republican		73
	John Adams	Federalist		65
	Charles C. Pinckney	Federalist		64
1804	**Thomas Jefferson**	Democratic-Republican		162
	Charles C. Pinckney	Federalist		14
1808	**James Madison**	Democratic-Republican		122
	Charles C. Pinckney	Federalist		47
	George Clinton	Independent-Republican		6
1812	**James Madison**	Democratic-Republican		128
	DeWitt Clinton	Federalist		89
1816	**James Monroe**	Democratic-Republican		183
	Rufus King	Federalist		34
1820	**James Monroe**	Democratic-Republican		231
	John Quincy Adams	Independent-Republican		1
1824	**John Quincy Adams**	Democratic-Republican	108,740 (30.5%)	84
	Andrew Jackson	Democratic-Republican	153,544 (43.1%)	99
	Henry Clay	Democratic-Republican	47,136 (13.2%)	37
	William H. Crawford	Democratic-Republican	46,618 (13.1%)	41
1828	**Andrew Jackson**	Democratic	647,231 (56.0%)	178
	John Quincy Adams	National Republican	509,097 (44.0%)	83
1832	**Andrew Jackson**	Democratic	687,502 (55.0%)	219
	Henry Clay	National Republican	530,189 (42.4%)	49
	William Wirt	Anti-Masonic ⎫	33,108 (2.6%)	7
	John Floyd	National Republican ⎭		11
1836	**Martin Van Buren**	Democratic	761,549 (50.9%)	170
	William H. Harrison	Whig	549,567 (36.7%)	73
	Hugh L. White	Whig	145,396 (9.7%)	26
	Daniel Webster	Whig	41,287 (2.7%)	14
1840	**William H. Harrison** (**John Tyler**, 1841)	Whig	1,275,017 (53.1%)	234
	Martin Van Buren	Democratic	1,128,702 (46.9%)	60
1844	**James K. Polk**	Democratic	1,337,243 (49.6%)	170
	Henry Clay	Whig	1,299,068 (48.1%)	105
	James G. Birney	Liberty	62,300 (2.3%)	
1848	**Zachary Taylor** (**Millard Fillmore,** 1850)	Whig	1,360,101 (47.4%)	163
	Lewis Cass	Democratic	1,220,544 (42.5%)	127
	Martin Van Buren	Free Soil	291,263 (10.1%)	
1852	**Franklin Pierce**	Democratic	1,601,474 (50.9%)	254
	Winfield Scott	Whig	1,386,578 (44.1%)	42
1856	**James Buchanan**	Democratic	1,838,169 (45.4%)	174
	John C. Frémont	Republican	1,335,264 (33.0%)	114
	Millard Fillmore	American	874,534 (21.6%)	8

Year	Candidates	Party	Popular Vote	Electoral Vote
1860	**Abraham Lincoln**	Republican	1,865,593 (39.8%)	180
	Stephen A. Douglas	Democratic	1,382,713 (29.5%)	12
	John C. Breckinridge	Democratic	848,356 (18.1%)	72
	John Bell	Constitutional Union	592,906 (12.6%)	39
1864	**Abraham Lincoln**	Republican	2,206,938 (55.0%)	212
	(**Andrew Johnson**, 1865)			
	George B. McClellan	Democratic	1,803,787 (45.0%)	21
1868	**Ulysses S. Grant**	Republican	3,013,421 (52.7%)	214
	Horatio Seymour	Democratic	2,706,829 (47.3%)	80
1872	**Ulysses S. Grant**	Republican	3,596,745 (55.6%)	286
	Horace Greeley	Democratic	2,843,446 (43.9%)	66
1876	**Rutherford B. Hayes**	Republican	4,036,572 (48.0%)	185
	Samuel J. Tilden	Democratic	4,284,020 (51.0%)	184
1880	**James A. Garfield**	Republican	4,449,053 (48.3%)	214
	(**Chester A. Arthur**, 1881)			
	Winfield S. Hancock	Democratic	4,442,035 (48.2%)	155
	James B. Weaver	Greenback-Labor	308,578 (3.4%)	
1884	**Grover Cleveland**	Democratic	4,874,986 (48.5%)	219
	James G. Blaine	Republican	4,851,981 (48.2%)	182
	Benjamin F. Butler	Greenback-Labor	175,370 (1.8%)	
1888	**Benjamin Harrison**	Republican	5,444,337 (47.8%)	233
	Grover Cleveland	Democratic	5,540,050 (48.6%)	168
1892	**Grover Cleveland**	Democratic	5,554,414 (46.0%)	277
	Benjamin Harrison	Republican	5,190,802 (43.0%)	145
	James B. Weaver	People's	1,027,329 (8.5%)	22
1896	**William McKinley**	Republican	7,035,638 (50.8%)	271
	William J. Bryan	Democratic; Populist	6,467,946 (46.7%)	176
1900	**William McKinley**	Republican	7,219,530 (51.7%)	292
	(**Theodore Roosevelt**, 1901)			
	William J. Bryan	Democratic; Populist	6,356,734 (45.5%)	155
1904	**Theodore Roosevelt**	Republican	7,628,834 (56.4%)	336
	Alton B. Parker	Democratic	5,084,401 (37.6%)	140
	Eugene V. Debs	Socialist	402,460 (3.0%)	
1908	**William H. Taft**	Republican	7,679,006 (51.6%)	321
	William J. Bryan	Democratic	6,409,106 (43.1%)	162
	Eugene V. Debs	Socialist	420,820 (2.8%)	
1912	**Woodrow Wilson**	Democratic	6,286,820 (41.8%)	435
	Theodore Roosevelt	Progressive	4,126,020 (27.4%)	88
	William H. Taft	Republican	3,483,922 (23.2%)	8
	Eugene V. Debs	Socialist	897,011 (6.0%)	
1916	**Woodrow Wilson**	Democratic	9,129,606 (49.3%)	277
	Charles E. Hughes	Republican	8,538,221 (46.1%)	254
1920	**Warren G. Harding**	Republican	16,152,200 (61.0%)	404
	(**Calvin Coolidge**, 1923)			
	James M. Cox	Democratic	9,147,353 (34.6%)	127
	Eugene V. Debs	Socialist	919,799 (3.5%)	

Year	Candidates	Party	Popular Vote	Electoral Vote
1924	**Calvin Coolidge**	Republican	15,725,016 (54.1%)	382
	John W. Davis	Democratic	8,385,586 (28.8%)	136
	Robert M. La Follette	Progressive	4,822,856 (16.6%)	13
1928	**Herbert C. Hoover**	Republican	21,392,190 (58.2%)	444
	Alfred E. Smith	Democratic	15,016,443 (40.8%)	87
1932	**Franklin D. Roosevelt**	Democratic	22,809,638 (57.3%)	472
	Herbert C. Hoover	Republican	15,758,901 (39.6%)	59
	Norman Thomas	Socialist	881,951 (2.2%)	
1936	**Franklin D. Roosevelt**	Democratic	27,751,612 (60.7%)	523
	Alfred M. Landon	Republican	16,681,913 (36.4%)	8
	William Lemke	Union	891,858 (1.9%)	
1940	**Franklin D. Roosevelt**	Democratic	27,243,466 (54.7%)	449
	Wendell L. Wilkie	Republican	22,304,755 (44.8%)	82
1944	**Franklin D. Roosevelt** **(Harry S Truman**, 1945)	Democratic	25,602,505 (52.8%)	432
	Thomas E. Dewey	Republican	22,006,278 (44.5%)	99
1948	**Harry S Truman**	Democratic	24,105,812 (49.5%)	303
	Thomas E. Dewey	Republican	21,970,065 (45.1%)	189
	J. Strom Thurmond	States' Rights	1,169,063 (2.4%)	39
	Henry A. Wallace	Progressive	1,157,172 (2.4%)	
1952	**Dwight D. Eisenhower**	Republican	33,936,234 (55.2%)	442
	Adlai E. Stevenson	Democratic	27,314,992 (44.5%)	89
1956	**Dwight D. Eisenhower**	Republican	35,590,472 (57.4%)	457
	Adlai E. Stevenson	Democratic	26,022,752 (42.0%)	73
1960	**John F. Kennedy** **(Lyndon B. Johnson**, 1963)	Democratic	34,227,096 (49.9%)	303
	Richard M. Nixon	Republican	34,108,546 (49.6%)	219
1964	**Lyndon B. Johnson**	Democratic	43,126,233 (61.1%)	486
	Barry M. Goldwater	Republican	27,174,989 (38.5%)	52
1968	**Richard M. Nixon**	Republican	31,783,783 (43.4%)	301
	Hubert H. Humphrey	Democratic	31,271,839 (42.7%)	191
	George C. Wallace	Amer. Independent	9,899,557 (13.5%)	46
1972	**Richard M. Nixon**	Republican	45,767,218 (60.6%)	520
	George S. McGovern	Democratic	28,357,668 (37.5%)	17
1974	**Gerald R. Ford**	Republican	Appointed on August 9, 1974 as President after the resignation of Richard M. Nixon. No election was held.	

Because only the leading candidates are listed, popular vote percentages do not always total 100. The elections of 1800 and 1824, in which no candidate received an electoral-vote majority, were decided in the House of Representatives.

Vice President

John Adams	1789-97
Thomas Jefferson	1797-1801
Aaron Burr	1801-05
George Clinton	1805-13
Elbridge Gerry	1813-17
Daniel D. Tompkins	1817-25
John C. Calhoun	1825-33
Martin Van Buren	1833-37
Richard M. Johnson	1837-41
John Tyler	1841
George M. Dallas	1845-49
Millard Fillmore	1849-50
William R. King	1853-57
John C. Breckinridge	1857-61
Hannibal Hamlin	1861-65
Andrew Johnson	1865
Schuyler Colfax	1869-73
Henry Wilson	1873-77
William A. Wheeler	1877-81
Chester A. Arthur	1881
Thomas A. Hendricks	1885-89
Levi P. Morton	1889-93
Adlai E. Stevenson	1893-97
Garret A. Hobart	1897-1901
Theodore Roosevelt	1901
Charles W. Fairbanks	1905-09
James S. Sherman	1909-13
Thomas R. Marshall	1913-21
Calvin Coolidge	1921-23
Charles G. Dawes	1925-29
Charles Curtis	1929-33
John Nance Garner	1933-41
Henry A. Wallace	1941-45
Harry S Truman	1945
Alben W. Barkley	1949-53
Richard M. Nixon	1953-61
Lyndon B. Johnson	1961-63
Hubert H. Humphrey	1965-69
Spiro T. Agnew	1969-73
Gerald R. Ford	1973-74
Nelson Rockefeller	1974-

Secretary of State (1789-   )

Thomas Jefferson	1789
Edmund Randolph	1794
Timothy Pickering	1795
John Marshall	1800
James Madison	1801
Robert Smith	1809
James Monroe	1811
John Q. Adams	1817
Henry Clay	1825
Martin Van Buren	1829
Edward Livingston	1831
Louis McLane	1833
John Forsyth	1834
Daniel Webster	1841
Hugh S. Legaré	1843
Abel P. Upshur	1843
John C. Calhoun	1844
James Buchanan	1845
John M. Clayton	1849
Daniel Webster	1850
Edward Everett	1852
William L. Marcy	1853
Lewis Cass	1857
Jeremiah S. Black	1860
William H. Seward	1861
E.B. Washburne	1869
Hamilton Fish	1869
William M. Evarts	1877
James G. Blaine	1881
F.T. Frelinghuysen	1881
Thomas F. Bayard	1885
James G. Blaine	1889
John W. Foster	1892
Walter Q. Gresham	1893
Richard Olney	1895
John Sherman	1897
William R. Day	1897
John Hay	1898
Elihu Root	1905
Robert Bacon	1909
Philander C. Knox	1909
William J. Bryan	1913
Robert Lansing	1915
Bainbridge Colby	1920
Charles E. Hughes	1921
Frank B. Kellogg	1925
Henry L. Stimson	1929
Cordell Hull	1933
E.R. Stettinius, Jr.	1944
James F. Byrnes	1945
George C. Marshall	1947
Dean Acheson	1949
John Foster Dulles	1953
Christian A. Herter	1959
Dean Rusk	1961
William P. Rogers	1969
Henry A. Kissinger	1973

Secretary of the Treasury (1789-   )

Alexander Hamilton	1789
Oliver Wolcott	1795
Samuel Dexter	1801
Albert Gallatin	1801
G.W. Campbell	1814
A.J. Dallas	1814
William H. Crawford	1816
Richard Rush	1825
Samuel D. Ingham	1829
Louis McLane	1831
William J. Duane	1833
Roger B. Taney	1833
Levi Woodbury	1834
Thomas Ewing	1841
Walter Forward	1841
John C. Spencer	1843
George M. Bibb	1844
Robert J. Walker	1845
William M. Meredith	1849
Thomas Corwin	1850
James Guthrie	1853
Howell Cobb	1857
Philip F. Thomas	1860
John A. Dix	1861
Salmon P. Chase	1861
Wm. P. Fessenden	1864
Hugh McCulloch	1865
George S. Boutwell	1869
William A. Richardson	1873
Benjamin H. Bristow	1874
Lot M. Morrill	1876
John Sherman	1877
William Windom	1881
Charles J. Folger	1881
Walter Q. Gresham	1884
Hugh McCulloch	1884
Daniel Manning	1885
Charles S. Fairchild	1887
William Windom	1889
Charles Foster	1891
John G. Carlisle	1893
Lyman J. Gage	1897
Leslie M. Shaw	1902
George B. Cortelyou	1907
Franklin MacVeagh	1909
William G. McAdoo	1913
Carter Glass	1919
David F. Houston	1919
Andrew W. Mellon	1921
Ogden L. Mills	1932
William H. Woodin	1933
Henry Morgenthau, Jr.	1934
Fred M. Vinson	1945
John W. Snyder	1946
George M. Humphrey	1953
Robert B. Anderson	1957
C. Douglas Dillon	1961
Henry H. Fowler	1965
David M. Kennedy	1969
John B. Connally	1970
George P. Shultz	1972
William E. Simon	1974

Secretary of War (1789-1947)

Henry Knox	1789
Timothy Pickering	1795
James McHenry	1796
John Marshall	1800
Samuel Dexter	1800
Roger Griswold	1801
Henry Dearborn	1801
William Eustis	1809
John Armstrong	1813
James Monroe	1814
William H. Crawford	1815
Isaac Shelby	1817
George Graham	1817
John C. Calhoun	1817
James Barbour	1825
Peter B. Porter	1828
John H. Eaton	1829
Lewis Cass	1831
Benjamin F. Butler	1837
Joel R. Poinsett	1837
John Bell	1841
John McLean	1841
John C. Spencer	1841
James M. Porter	1843
William Wilkins	1844
William L. Marcy	1845
George W. Crawford	1849
Charles M. Conrad	1850
Jefferson Davis	1853
John B. Floyd	1857
Joseph Holt	1861
Simon Cameron	1861
Edwin M. Stanton	1862
Ulysses S. Grant	1867
Lorenzo Thomas	1868
John M. Schofield	1868
John A. Rawlins	1869
William T. Sherman	1869
William W. Belknap	1869
Alphonso Taft	1876
James D. Cameron	1876
George W. McCrary	1877
Alexander Ramsey	1879
Robert T. Lincoln	1881
William C. Endicott	1885
Redfield Proctor	1889
Stephen B. Elkins	1891
Daniel S. Lamont	1893
Russell A. Alger	1897
Elihu Root	1899
William H. Taft	1904
Luke E. Wright	1908
J.M. Dickinson	1909
Henry L. Stimson	1911
L.M. Garrison	1913
Newton D. Baker	1916
John W. Weeks	1921
Dwight F. Davis	1925
James W. Good	1929
Patrick J. Hurley	1929
George H. Dern	1933
H.A. Woodring	1936
Henry L. Stimson	1940
Robert P. Patterson	1945
Kenneth C. Royall	1947

Secretary of the Navy (1798-1947)

Benjamin Stoddert	1798
Robert Smith	1801
Paul Hamilton	1809

William Jones	1813	John McLean	1823	Roger B. Taney	1831	Caleb B. Smith	1861
B.W. Crowninshield	1814	William T. Barry	1829	Benjamin F. Butler	1833	John P. Usher	1863
Smith Thompson	1818	Amos Kendall	1835	Felix Grundy	1838	James Harlan	1865
S.L. Southard	1823	John M. Niles	1840	Henry D. Gilpin	1840	O.H. Browning	1866
John Branch	1829	Francis Granger	1841	John J. Crittenden	1841	Jacob D. Cox	1869
Levi Woodbury	1831	Charles A. Wickliffe	1841	Hugh S. Legaré	1841	Columbus Delano	1870
Mahlon Dickerson	1834	Cave Johnson	1845	John Nelson	1843	Zachariah Chandler	1875
James K. Paulding	1838	Jacob Collamer	1849	John Y. Mason	1845	Carl Schurz	1877
George E. Badger	1841	Nathan K. Hall	1850	Nathan Clifford	1846	Samuel J. Kirkwood	1881
Abel P. Upshur	1841	Samuel D. Hubbard	1852	Isaac Toucey	1848	Henry M. Teller	1881
David Henshaw	1843	James Campbell	1853	Reverdy Johnson	1849	L.Q.C. Lamar	1885
Thomas W. Gilmer	1844	Aaron V. Brown	1857	John J. Crittenden	1850	William F. Vilas	1888
John Y. Mason	1844	Joseph Holt	1859	Caleb Cushing	1853	John W. Noble	1889
George Bancroft	1845	Horatio King	1861	Jeremiah S. Black	1857	Hoke Smith	1893
John Y. Mason	1846	Montgomery Blair	1861	Edwin M. Stanton	1860	David R. Francis	1896
William B. Preston	1849	William Dennison	1864	Edward Bates	1861	Cornelius N. Bliss	1897
William A. Graham	1850	Alexander W. Randall	1866	Titian J. Coffey	1863	E.A. Hitchcock	1899
John P. Kennedy	1852	John A.J. Creswell	1869	James Speed	1864	James R. Garfield	1907
James C. Dobbin	1853	James W. Marshall	1874	Henry Stanbery	1866	R.A. Ballinger	1909
Isaac Toucey	1857	Marshall Jewell	1874	William M. Evarts	1868	Walter L. Fisher	1911
Gideon Welles	1861	James N. Tyner	1876	Ebenezer R. Hoar	1869	Franklin K. Lane	1913
Adolph E. Borie	1869	David M. Key	1877	Amos T. Ackerman	1870	John B. Payne	1920
George M. Robeson	1869	Horace Maynard	1880	George H. Williams	1871	Albert B. Fall	1921
R.W. Thompson	1877	Thomas L. James	1881	Edward Pierrepont	1875	Hubert Work	1923
Nathan Goff, Jr.	1881	Timothy O. Howe	1881	Alphonso Taft	1876	Roy O. West	1928
William H. Hunt	1881	Walter Q. Gresham	1883	Charles Devens	1877	Ray L. Wilbur	1929
William E. Chandler	1881	Frank Hatton	1884	Wayne MacVeagh	1881	Harold L. Ickes	1933
William C. Whitney	1885	William F. Vilas	1885	Benjamin H. Brewster	1881	Julius A. Krug	1946
Benjamin F. Tracy	1889	Don M. Dickinson	1888	A.H. Garland	1885	Oscar L. Chapman	1949
Hilary A. Herbert	1893	John Wanamaker	1889	William H.H. Miller	1889	Douglas McKay	1953
John D. Long	1897	Wilson S. Bissel	1893	Richard Olney	1893	Fred A. Seaton	1956
William H. Moody	1902	William L. Wilson	1895	Judson Harmon	1895	Stewart L. Udall	1961
Paul Morton	1904	James A. Gary	1897	Joseph McKenna	1897	Walter J. Hickel	1969
Charles J. Bonaparte	1905	Charles E. Smith	1898	John W. Griggs	1897	Rogers C.B. Morton	1971
Victor H. Metcalf	1907	Henry C. Payne	1902	Philander C. Knox	1901		
T.H. Newberry	1908	Robert J. Wynne	1904	William H. Moody	1904	**Secretary of Agriculture**	
George von L. Meyer	1909	George B. Cortelyou	1905	Charles J. Bonaparte	1907	**(1889-)**	
Josephus Daniels	1913	George von L. Meyer	1907	G.W. Wickersham	1909		
Edwin Denby	1921	F.H. Hitchcock	1909	J.C. McReynolds	1913	Norman J. Colman	1889
Curtis D. Wilbur	1924	Albert S. Burleson	1913	Thomas W. Gregory	1914	Jeremiah M. Rusk	1889
Charles F. Adams	1929	Will H. Hays	1921	A. Mitchell Palmer	1919	J. Sterling Morton	1893
Claude A. Swanson	1933	Hubert Work	1922	H.M. Daugherty	1921	James Wilson	1897
Charles Edison	1940	Harry S. New	1923	Harlan F. Stone	1924	David F. Houston	1913
Frank Knox	1940	Walter F. Brown	1929	John G. Sargent	1925	Edward T. Meredith	1920
James V. Forrestal	1945	James A. Farley	1933	William D. Mitchell	1929	Henry C. Wallace	1921
		Frank C. Walker	1940	H.S. Cummings	1933	Howard M. Gore	1924
		Robert E. Hannegan	1945	Frank Murphy	1939	William M. Jardine	1925
Secretary of Defense		J.M. Donaldson	1947	Robert H. Jackson	1940	Arthur M. Hyde	1929
(1947-)		A.E. Summerfield	1953	Francis Biddle	1941	Henry A. Wallace	1933
		J. Edward Day	1961	Tom C. Clark	1945	Claude R. Wickard	1940
James V. Forrestal	1947	John A. Gronouski	1963	J.H. McGrath	1949	Clinton P. Anderson	1945
Louis A. Johnson	1949	Lawrence F. O'Brien	1965	J.P. McGranery	1952	Charles F. Brannan	1948
George C. Marshall	1950	W. Marvin Watson	1968	H. Brownell, Jr.	1953	Ezra Taft Benson	1953
Robert A. Lovett	1951	Winton M. Blount	1969	William P. Rogers	1957	Orville L. Freeman	1961
Charles E. Wilson	1953			Robert F. Kennedy	1961	Clifford M. Hardin	1969
Neil H. McElroy	1957			Nicholas Katzenbach	1964	Earl L. Butz	1971
Thomas S. Gates, Jr.	1959	**Attorney General**		Ramsey Clark	1967		
Robert S. McNamara	1961	**(1789-)**		John N. Mitchell	1969	**Secretary of Commerce**	
Clark M. Clifford	1968			Richard G. Kleindienst	1972	**and Labor**	
Melvin R. Laird	1969	Edmund Randolph	1789	Elliot L. Richardson	1973	**(1903-1913)**	
Elliot L. Richardson	1973	William Bradford	1794	William Saxbe	1974		
James R. Schlesinger	1973	Charles Lee	1795			George B. Cortelyou	1903
		Theophilus Parsons	1801			Victor H. Metcalf	1904
		Levi Lincoln	1801	**Secretary of the Interior**		Oscar S. Straus	1906
Postmaster General		Robert Smith	1805	**(1849-)**		Charles Nagel	1909
(1789-)		John Breckinridge	1805				
		Caesar A. Rodney	1807	Thomas Ewing	1849	**Secretary of Commerce**	
Samuel Osgood	1789	William Pinkney	1811	T.M.T. McKennan	1850	**(1913-)**	
Timothy Pickering	1791	Richard Rush	1814	Alexander H.H. Stuart	1850		
Joseph Habersham	1795	William Wirt	1817	Robert McClelland	1853	William C. Redfield	1913
Gideon Granger	1801	John M. Berrien	1829	Jacob Thompson	1857	Joshua W. Alexander	1919
Return J. Meigs, Jr.	1814						

Herbert Hoover	1921	William N. Doak	1930
William F. Whiting	1928	Frances Perkins	1933
Robert P. Lamont	1929	L.B. Schwellenbach	1945
Roy D. Chapin	1932	Maurice J. Tobin	1948
Daniel C. Roper	1933	Martin P. Durkin	1953
Harry L. Hopkins	1939	James P. Mitchell	1953
Jesse Jones	1940	Arthur J. Goldberg	1961
Henry A. Wallace	1945	W. Willard Wirtz	1962
W.A. Harriman	1946	George P. Shultz	1969
Charles Sawyer	1948	James D. Hodgson	1970
Sinclair Weeks	1953	Peter J. Brennan	1973
Lewis L. Strauss	1958		
F.H. Mueller	1959		
Luther Hodges	1961		
John T. Connor	1965		
A.B. Trowbridge	1967		
C.R. Smith	1968		
Maurice H. Stans	1969		
Peter G. Peterson	1972		
Frederick B. Dent	1973		

**Secretary of Health,
Education, and Welfare
(1953–)**

Oveta Culp Hobby	1953
Marion B. Folsom	1955
Arthur S. Flemming	1958
Abraham A. Ribicoff	1961
Anthony J. Celebrezze	1962
John W. Gardner	1965
Wilbur J. Cohen	1968
Robert H. Finch	1969
Elliot L. Richardson	1970
Caspar W. Weinberger	1973

**Secretary of Labor
(1913–)**

William B. Wilson	1913
James J. Davis	1921

**Secretary of Housing and
Urban Development
(1966–)**

Robert C. Weaver	1966
George W. Romney	1969
James T. Lynn	1973

**Secretary of Transportation
(1967–)**

Alan S. Boyd	1967
John A. Volpe	1969
Claude S. Brinegar	1973

Territorial Expansion

Louisiana Purchase	1803
Florida	1819
Texas	1845
Oregon	1846
Mexican Cession	1848
Gadsden Purchase	1853
Alaska	1867
Hawaii	1898
The Philippines	1898–1946
Puerto Rico	1899
Guam	1899
Amer. Samoa	1900

Canal Zone	1904
U.S. Virgin Islands	1917
Pacific Islands Trust Terr.	1947

Population, 1790–1970

1790	3,929,214
1800	5,308,483
1810	7,239,881
1820	9,638,453
1830	12,866,020
1840	17,069,453
1850	23,191,876
1860	31,443,321
1870	39,818,449
1880	50,155,783
1890	62,947,714
1900	75,994,575
1910	91,972,266
1920	105,710,620
1930	122,775,046
1940	131,669,275
1950	151,325,798
1960	179,323,175
1970	204,765,770

Index

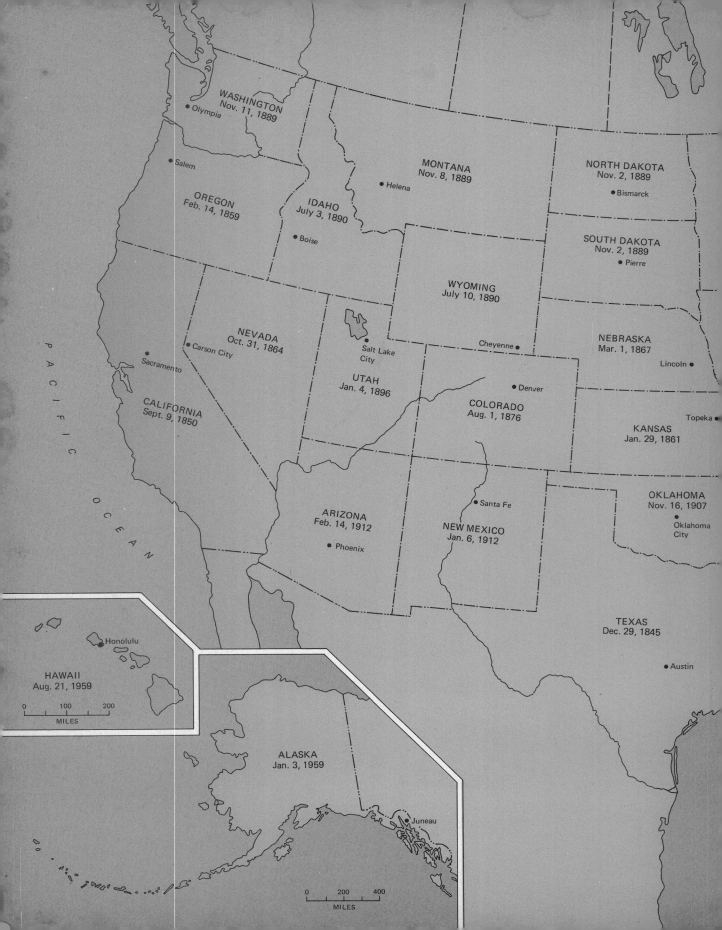